GILTE LEGENDE

VOLUME 3

EARLY ENGLISH TEXT SOCIETY

O.S. 339

2012

OXFORD
UNIVERSITY PRESS

Great Clarendon Street, Oxford OX2 6DP

Oxford University Press is a department of the University of Oxford.
It furthers the University's objective of excellence in research, scholarship,
and education by publishing worldwide in

Oxford New York

Auckland Cape Town Dar es Salaam Hong Kong Karachi
Kuala Lumpur Madrid Melbourne Mexico City Nairobi
New Delhi Shanghai Taipei Toronto

With offices in

Argentina Austria Brazil Chile Czech Republic France Greece
Guatemala Hungary Italy Japan Poland Portugal Singapore
South Korea Switzerland Thailand Turkey Ukraine Vietnam

Oxford is a registered trade mark of Oxford University Press
in the UK and in certain other countries

Published in the United States
by Oxford University Press Inc., New York

First published 2012

British Library Cataloguing in Publication Data
Data available

Library of Congress Cataloging in Publication Data
Data applied for

ISBN 978-0-19-966817-5

1 3 5 7 9 10 8 6 4 2

Typeset by Anne Joshua, Oxford
Printed in Great Britain
on acid-free paper by
T.J. International Ltd., Padstow, Cornwall

PREFACE AND ACKNOWLEDGEMENTS

This edition had its origin in 1961 when Eric Dobson suggested that my thesis for the Oxford degree of B.Litt. should consist of a study of the *Gilte Legende* with a critical edition of selections. Having been elected to a teaching post I did not complete the thesis, but it became the basis for an edition published as *Three Lives from the Gilte Legende* in 1978 in the series Middle English Texts. Work thereafter proceeded slowly, owing to the demands of teaching, college offices, and various diversions. In 1976 Vida Russell, then of the University of Adelaide, volunteered to join the project, and our collaboration has continued ever since, resulting in the meantime in an edition of four lives from the *Légende dorée* and the EETS volume *Supplementary Lives in Some Manuscripts of Gilte Legende*. She has modestly insisted that for the present work she should be described as my assistant rather than collaborator, but her contribution has been far greater than that suggests; she is almost entirely responsible for the two lives which are given with full collation, *Paul* and *All Saints*, and for the chapters on *Alban, Malchus, Adam*, and *Five Wiles of Pharaoh*, as well as contributing substantially to almost all other aspects of the edition. My debt to her is therefore enormous, and it is certain that the edition would never have been finished without her.

During much of the long period of its gestation we have been geographically remote, Vida in Australia and myself in England. The resultant difficulties were in due course greatly eased by the invention of electronic mail. Our work has also benefitted during this time from the publication of important works, notably the completion of the *Middle English Dictionary* and the publication of G. P. Maggioni's edition of the Latin text and Brenda Dunn-Lardeau's of the French. Over the years there have been a number of translations of *Legenda Aurea* into various languages; of these the most helpful for sorting out the more difficult passages of the Latin have been those of J. B. Roze, Richard Benz, and W. G. Ryan, and the selections by Christopher Stace; more recently Alain Boureau's French translation and a parallel Italian translation coordinated by Francesco Stella in Maggioni's revised edition of 2007 have appeared, both of which publications also contain valuable notes. These, which would have been even more valuable at an earlier stage, came out in time to solve a number of outstanding problems.

I wish also to record my gratitude to many other scholars who have generously given their time and expertise at various stages over the many years the edition has taken, most particularly Alexandra Barratt, Richard Beadle, Lucy Davey, Ian Doyle, Graham Edwards, Manfred Görlach, the late Jeremy Griffiths, Paul B. Harvey Jr, Martin Kauffmann, Margaret Lewis, Linne Mooney, Malcolm Parkes, Oliver Pickering, Jayne Ringrose, Kathleen Scott, Simon Tugwell, and Claire Waters. To the Libraries acknowledged with thanks in volume I must now be added the Archive of Westminster Abbey and the Lichfield Record Office.

I also gratefully acknowledge support and guidance from the late Pamela Gradon, formerly Editorial Secretary of the EETS, and from John Burrow, former Director, and above all Helen Spencer, the current Editorial Secretary, whose care and patience in dealing with a variety of problems along the way have been exemplary. Lastly I wish to express my thanks to Bonnie Blackburn, copy-editor, for much constructive advice, and the printer, Anne Joshua, for her skill and accuracy in handling a long and complicated edition in a variety of manifestations over many years.

R.H.

CONTENTS

LIST OF ILLUSTRATIONS

SIGLA OF MANUSCRIPTS

A1	London, British Library, Add. MS 11565
A2	London, British Library, Add. MS 35298
B	Oxford, Bodleian Library, MS Bodley 596
Ca	Cambridge, University Library, MS Gg.6.26
Cb	Cambridge, University Library, MS Ff.6.33
D	Oxford, Bodleian Library, MS Douce 372
Db	Paris, Bibliothèque nationale de France, MS fr. 242
Do	Oxford, Bodleian Library, MS Douce 15
Du	Durham, University Library, MS Cosin V.ii.14
E	London, British Library, MS Egerton 876
F	Cambridge, Fitzwilliam Museum, MS McClean 129
Fb	Paris, Bibliothèque nationale de France, MS fr. 416
G	Gloucester, Cathedral Library, MS 12
H1	London, British Library, MS Harley 630
H2	London, British Library, MS Harley 4775
Ha	London, British Library, MS Harley 1197
Hb	London, British Library, MS Harley 2388
Hc	London, British Library, MS Harley 1704
K	Cambridge, Corpus Christi College, MS 142
L	London, Lambeth Palace Library, MS 72
La	London, Lambeth Palace Library, MS 306
M	Tokyo, Professor Toshiyuki Takamiya Collection, MS 45/23 and Bloomington, Indiana, Lilly Library, Poole MS 98/58
P1	Paris, Bibliothèque nationale de France, MS fr. 241
P2	Paris, Bibliothèque nationale de France, MS fr. 244–5
Re	Vatican City, Biblioteca Apostolica Vaticana, MS Reg. lat. 485
S	Rennes, Bibliothèque municipale, MS 266
S2	Stonyhurst College Archives, MS 43
T1	Dublin, Trinity College, MS 319
T2	Cambridge, Trinity College, MS O. 9. 1
Wh	London, British Library, Add. MS 39574 (Wheatley MS)
Wm	London, Westminster Abbey Archives, WAM 33329
Ya	New Haven, Yale University, Beinecke Library, MS Marston 243
Z	London, British Library, MS Egerton 645

ABBREVIATIONS

AASS	*Acta Sanctorum*, 64 vols. (Antwerp, 1643–1940)
Archiv	*Archiv für das Studium der neueren Sprachen und Literaturen*
Batallier	Printed edition of *Légende dorée* by Jean Batallier, ed. Dunn-Lardeau (see below)
Benz	Richard Benz, *Die Legenda Aurea des Jacobus de Voragine aus dem lateinische übersetzt* (Jena, 1917; 9th edn., Heidelberg, 1979)
BHL	*Bibliotheca Hagiographica Latina Antiquae et Mediae Aetatis* (Brussels, 1898–1901)
BL	British Library, London
BN	Bibliothèque nationale de France, Paris
Boureau	Jacques de Voragine, *La Légende dorée*, ed. Alain Boureau (Paris, 2004)
Butler	Pierce Butler, *Legenda Aurea—Légende Dorée—Golden Legend* (Baltimore, 1899)
Capgrave	*Ye Solace of Pilgrimes*, ed. C. A. Mills (London, 1911)
CCSL	Corpus Christianorum Series Latina
Day	*The Wheatley Manuscript*, ed. Mabel Day, EETS OS 155 (London, 1921)
Dunn-Lardeau	Jacques de Voragine, *La Légende Dorée: Édition critique, dans la révision de 1476 par Jean Batallier, d'après la traduction de Jean de Vignay (1333–1348) de la* Legenda Aurea *(c. 1261–1266)*, publiée par Brenda Dunn-Lardeau (Paris, 1997)
EETS OS	Early English Text Society, Original Series
EHR	*English Historical Review*
Ekwall	Ekwall, Eilert, *The Concise Oxford Dictionary of English Place-names* (4th edn., Oxford, 1960)
EStn	*Englische Studien*
GiL	*Gilte Legende*
Görlach (1972)	Manfred Görlach, *The South English Legendary, Gilte Legende and Golden Legend* (Braunschweig, 1972) (revised and included in next item)
Görlach (1998)	Görlach, Manfred, *Studies in Middle English Saints' Legends* (Anglistische Forschungen, 257; Heidelberg, 1998)
Graesse	T. Graesse, *Jacobi a Voragine Legenda Aurea vulgo Historia Lombardica dicta ad optimorum librorum fidem*

	recensuit (1st edn., Dresden, 1846; 2nd edn., Leipzig, 1850; 3rd edn., Breslau,1890; *reproductio phototypica*, Osnabruck, 1969).
Greimas	A. J. Greimas, *Dictionnaire de l'ancien français jusqu'au milieu du XIVe siècle* (Paris, 1968)
Horstmann, *Barlaam*	Carl Horstmann, *Barlaam and Josaphat, eine Prosaversion aus MS Egerton 876 fol. 301* (Sagan, 1877)
IMEP	*Index of Middle English Prose*
IMEV	Carleton Brown and Rossell Hope Robbins, *The Index of Middle English Verse* (New York, 1943)
IPMEP	R. E. Lewis, N. F. Blake, and A. S. G. Edwards, *Index of Printed Middle English Prose* (New York and London, 1985)
JEBS	*Journal of the Early Book Society*
JTS	*Journal of Theological Studies*
Knowles	Christine Knowles, 'Jean de Vignay, un traducteur français du XIVe siècle', *Romania*, 75 (1954), 353–83
Kurvinen, Thesis	*The Life of St Catherine of Alexandria in Middle English Prose*, ed. Auvo Kurvinen (D.Phil. thesis, Oxford University, 1960)
LALME	A. McIntosh, M. L. Samuels, and M. Benskin, *A Linguistic Atlas of Late Mediaeval English*, 4 vols. (Aberdeen, 1986)
Lewis & Short	Charlton T. Lewis and Charles Short, *Latin Dictionary* (Oxford, 1879)
LgA	*Legenda Aurea*
LgD	*Légende dorée*
MÆ	*Medium Ævum*
Maggioni	*Iacopo da Varazze: Legenda Aurea, edizione critica*, ed. Giovanni Paolo Maggioni, 2 vols. (2nd edn., Florence, 1999)
Maggioni (2007)	*Iacopo da Varazze: Legenda Aurea, con le miniature dal codice Ambrosiano C 240 inf., con traduzione italiana coordinata da Francesco Stella*, ed. Giovanni Paolo Maggioni, 2 vols. (Florence, 2007)
ME	Middle English
MED	*The Middle English Dictionary*, ed. H. Kurath, S. M. Kuhn, et al. (Ann Arbor, 1952–2001)
MET	Middle English Texts
M.G.H.	*Monumenta Germaniae Historica*
MLGB	*Medieval Libraries of Great Britain: A List of Surviving Books*, ed. N. R. Ker (Royal Society Guides and Handbooks, 3; 2nd edn., London, 1964)

MMBL	N. R. Ker and A. J. Piper, *Medieval Manuscripts in British Libraries*, 5 vols. (Oxford, 1969–2002)
NJBC	*The New Jerome Biblical Commentary*, ed. Raymond E. Brown, Joseph A. Fitzmyer, and Roland E. Murphy (2nd edn., London, 1990)
NM	*Neuphilologische Mitteilungen*
NS	New Series
ODCC	F. L. Cross and E. A. Livingstone, *The Oxford Dictionary of the Christian Church* (3rd edn., Oxford, 1997)
ODS	David Hugh Farmer, *The Oxford Dictionary of Saints* (3rd edn., Oxford, 1992)
OED	*The Oxford English Dictionary*, ed. J. A. H. Murray et al. (13 vols., Oxford, reissued 1933)
OT	Old Testament
PL	*Patrologia Latina*, ed. J. P. Migne, 221 vols. (Paris, 1844–65)
RES	*Review of English Studies*
Roze	*La Légende dorée de Jacques de Voragine nouvellement traduite en français*, trans. J.-B. M. Roze (Paris, 1902; reissued 1967 without original Introduction)
RS	Rolls Series (London, 1858–1911)
Ryan	*Jacobus de Voragine, The Golden Legend, Readings in the Saints*, trans. William Granger Ryan, 2 vols. (Princeton, 1993)
SC	*A Summary Catalogue of Western Manuscripts in the Bodleian Library at Oxford* (Oxford, 1895–1953)
Stace	*Jacobus de Voragine, the Golden Legend: Selections*, trans. Christopher Stace (Harmondsworth, 1998)
Supplementary Lives	*Supplementary Lives in Some Manuscripts of the Gilte Legende*, ed. R. Hamer and V. Russell, EETS 315 (2000)
s.w.	The 'synfulle wrecche', the English translator
Three Lives	*Three Lives from the Gilte Legende*, ed. Richard Hamer, MET 9 (Heidelberg, 1978)
trs.	transposed
VMalc	*Vita Malchi Monachi Captivi*
Waters	Claire M. Waters, *Virgins and Scholars: A Fifteenth-Century Compilation of the Lives of John the Baptist, John the Evangelist, Jerome and Katherine of Alexandria* (Turnhout, 2008)

INTRODUCTION

1. *GILTE LEGENDE* AND ITS SOURCES

The *Gilte Legende*, the first attempt at a complete version in English of Jacobus de Voragine's *Legenda Aurea*, is for the most part a close translation of Jean de Vignay's *Légende Dorée*, itself a close translation of the Latin. The English translator also made use of a copy of LgA for purposes of correction.

Jacobus de Voragine completed the original version of *Legendae Sanctorum*, which soon acquired the alternative name *Legenda Aurea*, in about 1265. It is a compilation of up to 178 chapters consisting of accounts of saints' lives and the church festivals in the order of the ecclesiastical calendar, derived with modifications from various works, principally Jean de Mailly, *Abbreviatio in gestis et miraculis sanctorum*, and Bartholomew of Trent, *Liber Epilogorum in gesta sanctorum*, and also Eusebius, *Historia Ecclesiastica*, Cassiodorus, *Historia Tripartita*, Petrus Comestor, *Historia Scholastica*, and a host of other works, used both directly and at second hand.[1]

Until recently the only 'modern' edition of *Legenda Aurea* available was that of T. Graesse (1845, etc.), based on Ebert's edition printed in 1472. In 1991 G. P. Maggioni published a study of its composition and development, showing how Voragine continued to modify it after its initial compilation (which he calls LA1) more or less up to his death in 1298,[2] following this with an edition representing the latest state (LA2), using early manuscripts originating within the geographical and chronological span of Voragine's career, and giving as a secondary apparatus the variants from a manuscript representing LA1.[3] Ebert's edition and the manuscript used by Vignay for his French translation belonged to an intermediate type, as did the early

[1] For a comprehensive list of sources acknowledged by Voragine see Maggioni, *Legenda Aurea* (1999), i, pp. xxxvii–lxvi; also in Maggioni, *Legenda Aurea* (2007), i, pp. xxxvii–lxxi. The extent of his use of the Dominican Lectionary has yet to be established (see Parkes, 'Compilation'). For recent studies of his use of sources see Geith, 'Jacques de Voragine — auteur indépendant ou compilateur?'; Fleith, 'De Assumptione'; and Boyle, 'Dominican Lectionaries'.

[2] Maggioni, *Ricerche*.

[3] Maggioni, *Legenda Aurea, edizione critica* (1998; rev. edn. 1999; new edn. with further revision, commentary, and parallel Italian translation, 2007).

manuscript (Paris, BN n. a. lat. 1800, dated 1281) used by Alain Boureau for his translation.[4]

The enormous popularity of the *Legenda Aurea* can be judged from the survival today of nearly a thousand manuscripts and many early printed editions,[5] and it was translated into almost every European language, more than once in some cases. The most successful French translation, if not necessarily the best, was that made by Jean de Vignay in Paris between 1333 and 1346; more than thirty manuscript copies of this survive. A group of additional lives, Jean Golein's *Festes Nouvelles*, is found at the end of ten of them, and a further three manuscripts contain a reorganized version with further additions. The earliest printed French text, probably from Bruges, was of this third type; but the main French printed tradition derives from a version of Vignay's work edited and substantially corrected from the Latin by the Dominican Jean Batallier and printed by Barthelémy Buyer in Lyon in 1476, the *Festes Nouvelles* being given in a separate volume. Brenda Dunn-Lardeau's edition (1997) of the first of these two volumes, the *Légende Dorée* itself, is the only modern edition of the whole of Vignay's version.[6]

The *Gilte Legende*, according to a colophon to MS D, was 'drawen out of Frensshe into Englisshe the yere of oure Lorde a M^{l}.CCCC and xxxviij bi a synfulle wrecche whos name I beseche Ihesu Criste bi his meritis of his passionne and of alle these holie seintis afore written that hit mai be written in the boke of everlastinge life'. The 'Frensshe' concerned was Vignay's original version, and may have contained the *Festes Nouvelles* (see below, p. 42); the exemplar used belonged to a branch of the stemma which shares various errors accumulated during the course of transmission, as has been shown by collation from all identified manuscripts of the chapters on *Nicholas*, *George*, *Bartholomew*, and *All Saints*.[7] In particular a few correspondences in *All Saints* make it possible to refine this to a subsection of this branch consisting of some six manuscripts, including Paris, BN fr. 244–5 (P2); Rennes, Bibliothèque municipale, MS 266 (S); London, BL Egerton 645 (Z); and three others which also contain the *Festes*

[4] Boureau, *Jacques de Voragine: La Légende dorée*.

[5] Fleith, *Studien zur Überlieferungsgeschichte*; Seybolt, 'Fifteenth-Century Editions of the *Legenda Aurea*'.

[6] *Jacques de Voragine: La Légende dorée*, ed. Dunn-Lardeau; on Vignay, see Knowles, 'Jean de Vignay, un traducteur français du XIVe siècle'.

[7] Hamer and Russell, 'Four Chapters from the Légende dorée'. The LgD line numbers cited are to this edition.

Nouvelles. Thus at 155 *All Saints* GiL has 98 *a* from *vng* for *septiesme* (LgD 89), 182 *is* from *est* for *en* (LgD 164), and five omissions at 43, 102, 121, 145, and 154 (LgD 39, 92–4, 111, 130, and 138–9), and although it is recognized that certain types of error, including eyeskip omissions, can be independently replicated, these seven agreements are cumulatively sufficient to place the exemplar used by the *synfulle wrecche* (hereafter s.w.) within this group. To establish the text in the present edition, therefore, reference has been made to MSS P2, S, and occasionally Z. Readings from Paris, BN fr. 241 (P1), which most closely represents the text as composed by Vignay, are also given in relevant cases in the notes.

Of the 178 chapters in the fullest version of LgA, one (St Syro of Genoa) is found only in a few thirteenth-century manuscripts from Lombardy, and is not in Vignay's or Batallier's LgD or in GiL. GiL differs from LgD mainly in the addition of 66 *Malchus*, 79 *Alban*, and 177–9 *Conception of the Virgin, Adam and Eve*, and the *Five Wiles of Pharaoh*, omission of *Resurrection*, *The Virgin of Antioch*, and *Stephen pope*, conflation of the two chapters on John the Baptist with other material as 80 *John the Baptist*, substitution of an expanded version of 165 *Catherine*, accidental duplication of *Cecilia* as 124 and 162, and the transfer of 176 *Advent* from the beginning to near the end. The changes give a total of 179 chapters. These new and modified chapters are discussed below. While the translation is generally close, in a few places GiL either follows LgD loosely or substitutes or adds material from another source, notably in the lives of 77 *Marina* and 133 *Matthew* 1–17 and 92–131. Three of the GiL manuscripts, A1, A2, and L, contain additional chapters, and these have been edited for EETS as *Supplementary Lives*. For his *Golden Legend* Caxton made use as one of his sources of a manuscript close to A2, which contained some but not all of the A2 additions (ibid., pp. xvii–xviii). GiL also omits the 'etymologies' with which most lives in LgA and LgD begin.

2. THE MANUSCRIPTS

There are eight known surviving copies of *Gilte Legende* of varying completeness, two small fragments of a ninth, one damaged leaf of a tenth, and an incomplete contents list of an eleventh; a further thirteen manuscripts contain one or more of its chapters.

E London, British Library, MS Egerton 876

Mid-fifteenth century, parchment, 323 leaves (of which ff. 1 and 321–3 are later paper additions) measuring 375 × 230 mm, written space 255 × 165 mm, in double columns of 45 or 46 lines, with illuminated capitals and borders, paragraph marks alternately in gold and in blue filigree on a red background, and red chapter headings. The paper flyleaf f. 1 is preceded by another added at the same time and numbered i, and at each end of the manuscript three new protective paper flyleaves were added during conservation in 2010–11. E contains only *Gilte Legende*, and is incomplete at beginning and end. Inside the back cover is a note stating that there are '328 folios' with a further note about errors in the first foliation, which was supplied in arabic numerals in the eighteenth century after the losses described below. Secundo folio *Andrewe*.

Collation: 41 quires of 8, as follows: 1^8 (wants 1 and 7–8 after f. 6), 2^8 (wants 1 before f. 7), $3–5^8$, 6^8 (wants 4–8 after f. 56), 7^8 (wants 8 after f. 63), 8^8, 9^8 (wants 7–8 after f. 85), $10–28^8$, 29^8 (wants 4–5 after f. 240), $30–1^8$, 32^8 (wants 5 after f. 264), $33–9^8$, 40^8 (wants 2–5 after f. 315), 41^8 (wants 2–3 after f. 319 and 5–8 after f. 320), a total of 25 missing leaves. There are catchwords on all surviving final versos of quires except f. 318.

The manuscript is in two hands, hand A from f. 1 to f. 194rb (vol. 1 frontispiece), Hand B from f. 194rb to end (vol. 2 frontispiece).

Inside the cover is a coat of arms and motto 'Tria Juncta in Uno', below which 'Ingenuas suspicit artes', the motto of Charles Long, Baron Farnborough, 1760–1838, a donation from whom made possible the purchase of much of the Egerton collection for the British Museum. On the flyleaf numbered i are a coded signature consisting of two six-letter names, 'Joseph Dixon Sept. 13th 1765', 'Purchased of Sten. Bohn 26 Sept. 1840' (? for the bookseller John Bohn), and at foot of page, apparently in the same hand as the preceding, 'See MS Add 11,565 for another copy of this work.' On the flyleaf, f. 1, are a contents list in an eighteenth-century hand in four columns on recto and verso, numbered according to the earlier foliation and completed on the first two columns of the verso, the last two columns containing a 'glossary' of fifty-seven words, including 'Cuss—Kiss', 'Eyr—Egg', 'Guerdon—Reward', 'Hit—it', 'Ho—Who', 'Mesell—Leper', 'Not—Nought', 'Orison—Prayer', 'Tourbe—Multitude'. At the end of the fourth column, 'N.B. Read with this Legend a Book callid Reflections upon y[e] Devotions of y[e] Roman Church, printed at London for Rich. Royston An. Dom. 1674'.

In a note in his copy (now MS Douce 372, see D below), Francis Douce describes a manuscript in the possession of Richard Heber, which appears to be this manuscript. If so, it was lot 1680, sold in Part XI, day 10 of his sale in February 1836, described in the catalogue as 'slightly imperfect'. It fetched £9.12.–.

Descriptions: Kurvinen, Thesis, 32–3; Butler, 62–4.

A1 London, British Library, Additional MS 11565

Late fifteenth century, parchment, i +214 + i leaves measuring 425 × 310 mm, written space 305 × 205 mm, in double columns of 56 lines, with red headings, gold initials, and blue paragraph marks. Additional flyleaves were supplied when it was rebound in 1969.

Collation: After one or more missing quires, 1^{8} (wants 4 after f. 3), 2–4^{8}, 5^{8} (wants 3 and 4 after f. 33), 6^{8} (wants 8 after f. 44), 7^{8}, quire 8 missing after f. 52, 9^{8} (wants 3 after f. 54), 10^{8} (wants 3 after f. 61), 11–12^{8}, 13^{8} (wants 3 after f. 84 and 8 after f. 88), 14^{8}, quire 15 missing after f. 96, 16^{8}, 17^{8+1}, $18^{8?}$ missing but one damaged folio now reinserted back to front as f. 114, 19–22^{8}, 23^{8} missing after f. 146, 24^{8} (wants 4 and 5 after f. 149), 25^{8}, 26^{8} (wants 8 after f. 167), 27^{8} (wants 7 after f. 173), 28–32^{8}, with one quire missing at the end if the text ended with 166 *Saturnine* as in H1, or four or five if complete as in E, D, etc. Space left on f. 113 after the end of a chapter may indicate that it was originally the end of a volume, but loss of most of the following quire makes it impossible to determine. The missing f. 114, having been identified in fragmentary condition as f. 1 of BL MS Lansdowne 350, was restored to its place in this manuscript, but inserted back to front. On the earlier flyleaf is a note: 'The Legenda Aurea beginning at f. 34 is imperfect wanting leaves after ff. 44, 52, 61, 84, 88, 96, 113, 146, 167, 173 and at the end. Edward Scott 3 Febr. 1899.' To this has been added, 'and the half-leaf at f. 114 has been inserted from Lansd. MS 350'. The manuscript had been foliated before the Lansdowne fragment was reinserted, and this was then numbered 114 and all subsequent foliation altered. There is no contents list either for the manuscript as a whole or for GiL.

The two items in the manuscript are in one hand, and small marginal corrections may be by the same scribe. See Plate 1 in *Supplementary Lives*. They are:

1. ff. 1^{r}–33^{v}, *Speculum vite Domini nostri Ihesu Christi* translated by Nicholas Love, incomplete at the beginning and end.

2. ff. 34^{r}–214^{v}, *Gilte Legende*, beginning *Here begynnyth the life of seyntes and this boke is called yn Latyn Legenda Sanctorum*, incomplete at the end, breaking off in 'Catherine', which is item 165 out of 179 of the original GiL. Early foliation was supplied independently for each of the items, and that for GiL from *j* to *CCxxj* reveals that forty leaves have been lost as well as an unknown number at the end. The surviving Additional Lives are on ff. 53^{r}–61^{v}, and were originally preceded by a further six to eight (see *Supplementary Lives*, pp. xiv–xvi).

Inside the front cover is a bookplate of George Courtenay, and on the earlier flyleaf 'Purchased of J. Cooper 18 Aug. 1839'. On f. 170^{v} are marginal scribblings: 'Tho: Elger IOHN ELGER 1680 IOHN ELGER INR'.

Descriptions: Kurvinen, Thesis, 4–6b; Görlach (1998), 84–5; Butler, 64–70; Nicholas Love, *The Mirror of the Blessed Life of Jesus Christ*, ed. Sargent, intro. p.113; it is recorded in *IMEP* Handlist V, 36–8.

A2 London, British Library, Additional MS 35298

Late fifteenth century, parchment, iii + 173 + i leaves in two hands, Hand A on ff. 2^{r}–9^{v}, Hand B on ff. 10^{r}–end, measuring 420 × 300 mm, written space 315 × 240 mm, in double columns of 67–73 lines for Hand A and 70–83 for Hand B, with red headings, gold initials, alternate red and blue paragraph marks, and a full border on f. 2^{r}. Original foliation j to Clxxiij starts on the present f. 2. For Hand A see Frontispiece to this volume and for Hand B see *Supplementary Lives*, Plate 2.

Collation: ii + 1–8^{8}, 9^{7} (ending in f. 72va, leaving the rest of the page blank), 10–21^{8}, 22^{8} (wanting 7, 8) + ii. The flyleaves are of paper; the outer ones supplied when the manuscript was rebound in 1972.

A2 contains:

1. ff. 2^{r}–168^{v} *Gilte Legende.*

2. ff. 168^{v}–174^{v} *Certein tretys that declarith whate the churche betokenyth and dyvers oþer maters*, incomplete at the end. A table of contents in Hand B on both sides of f. 1 gives subject headings for this item as well as naming the GiL chapters, recording foliation rather than chapter numbers.

A table of contents in a third hand is supplied on the last of the preliminary flyleaves, now f. 1. Additional lives and other material added to GiL are described in *Supplementary Lives*, pp. xiii–xxi.

A2 was formerly Ashburnham Appendix 91. A note on the flyleaf reads: 'Quaritch Ashburnham Sale Lot 1 1899'. Previous owners include Wm. Browne, Thomas North knight, and Wm. Herbert 1776, named on f. 1^r and identified by Kurvinen as respectively the poet (*c.*1590–*c.*1643, (?) the translator of Plutarch (1535–1604), and the bibliographer (1718–1795).

Pasted inside the front cover are the arms of Elias Ashmole with his motto 'EX VNO OMNIA', and above them 'LEGENDA SANCTORUM IN ENGLISH M.S.' To the left is the armorial bookplate of the Duke of Sussex with the motto 'SI DEUS PRO NOBIS QUIS CONTRA NOS'. This plate is numbered E b^{VI} 8, with I in top right corner. To the right are the arms of the 2nd Earl of Shelburne (subsequently the 1st Marquis of Lansdowne), with the motto VIRTUTE NON VERBIS. At bottom: 'From the Library of the Earl of Ashburnham Appendix No. LXXXXI May 1897 200.' On the verso of the first of the earlier flyleaves, 'Rf 1435 VI. E b 8 Pickering A. 91 Th. 58 2 4/7. The arms on the cover are those of Elias Ashmole.' On the recto of the next flyleaf at top in pencil: 'Conclude this was wrote before the institution of the Order of the Garter as no mention is made thereof in the life of S. George, as in Caxton's first edition of Legenda Aurea 1483.' On recto of the next, 'Purchas^d of Quaritch (Ashburnham Sale lot 1) 1899.'

Descriptions: Kurvinen, Thesis, 9–10; Butler, 149–54, rather loosely described together with L.

D Oxford, Bodleian Library, MS Douce 372 (SC 21947)

Between 1438 and 1460, parchment except ff. 164–9 of paper, now 170 leaves numbered 1–40, 40*, 41–169, measuring 400 × 280 mm, written space 310 × 210 mm, in double columns of 47 lines, with red headings, gold initials on a coloured background, and paragraph marks alternately of gold and of blue on a red background. D contains only *Gilte Legende*. It is badly mutilated, with many lost leaves, damaged margins, and excised initials. In a skilful reconstruction Kurvinen showed that it originally had 33 quires of eight leaves, of which 100 are now lost, and the order of the survivors should be: 33–4, 1–26, 28–9, 27, 30, 31–2, 41–4, 40*, 45–105, 35–40, 106–63.[8]

[8] Kurvinen, Thesis, 25–9; she also recorded: 'Twenty-eight original signatures are preserved either wholly or in part on ff. 33, 35–37, 40*, 47, 48, 54, 64–66, 70, 76, 82–84, 89, 90, 94, 95, 101, 102, 115, 116, 120, 121 and 126. Twelve catchwords are preserved on the reverse of ff. 45, 53, 80, 88, 99, 119, 124, 128, 134, 153, 155 and 157.'

Collation as reconstructed by Kurvinen, with foliation given as open numbers and bracketed numbers showing numbers of lost leaves:

a (8) b (8) c (2) 33 (2) 34 (2) d 1–8 e 9–16 f 17–24 g 25–6 (1) 28–9 (1) 27 30 h (1) 31 (4) 32 (1) i (2) 41–4 (2) k (8) l 40* (6) 45 m 46–53 n (2) 54–7 (2) o 58 (1) 59–62 (1) 63 p (1) 64–9 (1) q (1) 70–4 (2) r 75–8 (2) 79–80 s 81–8 t (1) 89–90 (2) 91–2 (1) v 93 (1) 94–9 x 100–2 (2) 103–5 y (1) 35–40 106 z 107–10 (1) 111–13 & 114–16 (2) 117–19 aa 120 (2) 121–2 (1) 123–4 bb 125 (2) 126–7 (2) 128 cc 129–33 (2) 134 dd (1) 135–40 (1) ee 141–3 (2) 144–6 ff (1) 147–53 gg 154 (6) 157 hh 156 (6) 157 ii 158 (1) 159–62 (1) 163

The text is written in four hands as follows: Hand A 33–4, 1–3ra; B 3rb–32, 40*, 41–105; C 35–40, 106; D 107–63 (plate of Hand A f. 32^{r} in Watson, *Catalogue . . . Oxford Libraries*, ii, pl. 380; and plates of Hand A f. 2^{r}, Hand B f. 104^{v}, Hand C f. 106^{r}, Hand D f. 110^{r}, and the colophons on f. 163^{v} in Hamer, 'Spellings of Ricardus Franciscus', 63–73).

On f. 163^{v} are two colophons, of which the first begins: *And also here endith the lives of Seintis that is called in latynne Legenda Aurea. And in Englissh the gilte legende. the which is drawen out of Frensshe into Englisshe the yere of oure Lorde a M^{l}.CCCC and xxxviij bi a synfulle wrecche . . .* The second, partly illegible, reads: *[B]e hit remembryd that Iohn Burton, citizen and mercer of london, past oute of this lyfe the xx day of Nouember the yere of oure lorde Mill'.CCCC.lx and the yere of kynge Herry the sixte after the conquest xxxix. And the said Iohn Burton bequethe to dame Kateryne Burton his douȝter a boke callyd Legenda Sanctorum. the seyde Kateryne to haue hit and to occupye to hir owne vse and at hir owne liberte durynge hur lyfe and after hur decesse to remayne to the prioresse and the couent of Halywelle for euermore. they to pray for the saide Iohn Burton and Iohanne his wife and alle crystene savles. And who that lettithe the execucion . . . .s bequest be the lawe standeth . . . .* Writing of the manuscript can therefore be dated between 1438 and 1460.

Inside the front cover is pasted a slip describing a copy of this text as follows: '32423 [?]. Legenda Sanctorum in Englysshe — A large folio manuscript on vellum, the initials lightly illuminated. From Mr Herbert's collection 5l. 5s.' However, this does not relate to this manuscript, but was probably A2, previously owned by William Herbert (see above). Among various notes by Francis Douce on the following flyleaf is the following: 'Another copy, but likewise damaged and imperfect, was in Mr. J. Towneley's library and sold at his auction for £12. Query if this copy of Mr Towneley's Ms was not that mentioned in the extract from some bookseller's catalogue which I have pasted in the inside of the cover, and whether it is not now in Mr Heber's possession. Mr Heber's copy begins mutilated with the life of S Andrew, has lost several leaves in various places, and ends, mutilated, in the Storie of Cain.' . . . 'It is a large folio written in the middle of the 15th century and has some illuminated borders.' Of the surviving manuscripts, this description can be applied only to E.

D's first known owner, John Burton, is recorded in some detail in Stow's *Survey of London*, including details of his and his wife Agnes's benefaction to the church of St Michael Bassishaw and his burial there with his wife, now called Genet, and some details of his will of 1459, in which he left 500 l. each to his wife and his son John; his daughter Catherine is referred to as a nun of Holywell. Whether Agnes and Genet were different wives or the result of misspelling is unclear, and indeed how either of them might relate to the Iohanne referred to in D. A further implied benefaction to the church at Wadworth in Yorkshire, about 4 miles from Doncaster, suggests that he may have originated from there. He is mentioned in some considerable detail in the records of the Mercers' Company, for which see Jefferson, *Medieval Account Books*.

Descriptions: Kurvinen, Thesis, 25–9; *IMEP* IV, 91–3; *MLGB*, 121; Butler, 56–62; Pächt and Alexander, *Illuminated Manuscripts in the Bodleian Library*, iii, no. 901; Watson, *Catalogue of Dated and Datable Manuscripts . . . in Oxford Libraries*, i, no. 481.

G Gloucester Cathedral, MS 12

Mid fifteenth century, paper, 214 leaves measuring now 255 × 200 mm (the top of the pages having been cropped, removing all or part of the original headings), written space 210 × 140 mm, with 35–41 lines to the page, gold initials on backgrounds of red and blue, and alternating red and blue paragraph marks. The binding is of the late seventeenth century. Secundo folio *Achaia*.

Collation: $1–14^{12}$ (15 missing), $16–18^{12}$, 19^{12} (wants 11, 12 after f. 214 (ff. 211–13, 205–10, 214). Quires signed a–o, q–t.

G was identified by Görlach (1972), 15, as the first half of a *Gilte Legende*; it ends with 93 *James the Greater*, the last few words of which have been inserted in a later hand at the foot of the page. Otherwise the text is in one hand. Spaces were originally left for the rubricated incipits of the chapters, but from f. 75 these have been filled in later, perhaps by the same hand writing more formally; for plate see vol. 1, facing p. xiv. The last few leaves are wrongly bound and should be in the order 204, 211–13, 205–10, 214. A quire (12 leaves) is missing after f. 168, which ends in 78 *Gervase and Prothase*, and f. 169 begins in 79 *Alban*.

Ker suggested that the missing quire may have contained extra lives, pointing out that A2 has lives of Edward, Winifred, and Erkenwald at this point; but calculation of the ratios of page lengths in E and G shows that the missing part of Alban would have filled about ten leaves of G, and the missing end of Gervase would have filled the other two.

A note on f. 1 records ownership by 'Henricus Fowler Rector de Minchinhampton in Com Gloucester', and it is number 14 in the list of gifts of his son (Dr Fowler of Gloucester, d. 1685) on p. 25 of the Benefactors' Book of Gloucester Cathedral.

Description: *MMBL* 2. 945.

H1 London, British Library, MS Harley 630

Mid fifteenth century, parchment, 1* + 367 leaves, measuring 280 × 205 mm, written space 210 × 160 mm, in double columns of 39 lines, with a few initials and borders touched with gold and others in blue on a red background, and alternate red and blue paragraph marks. A total of eight leaves is lost at the beginning and elsewhere. H1 contains only *Gilte Legende* and ends after 166 *Saturnine* with the words: *Here endeth the Boke of the life of Seintes called in Latyn legenda aurea compiled and drawen into englissh bi worthi clerkes and doctours of Diuinite suengly after þe tenure of þe Latin.* Secundo folio *yong men sailing*.

For Plate see vol. 2, facing p. viii.

Collation 1^{8} (wanting 1 and 3–6), $2–10^{8}$, 11^{8} (wanting 4, 5 after f. 78), 12^{8}, 13^{6}, $14–20^{8}$, 21^{9} (with f. 163 as an insertion after 3), $22–47^{8}$, 48^{8} (wanting 8 after f. 367)

The text ends on f. 365rb, and is followed on ff. 365^{v}–366vb by a contents table with chapter numbers, followed on ff. 366vb to 367^{v} by another in a different fifteenth-century hand giving foliation (which was also supplied throughout the manuscript in this hand), ending with 161 *Elizabeth of Hungary* and thus omitting the final chapter 166 *Saturnine*.

At f. 164[ra] four lines up the scribe omitted from 79.651–2 *atte one stroke* to 79.726 *we that*, and this has been supplied in the hand of Stephen Dodesham on an inserted leaf, f. 163, which was not included in the earlier foliation. (see Doyle, 'Stephen Dodesham of Witham and Sheen', 104).

Apart from that insertion, although the writing varies considerably, the text seems to be the work of one scribe, though this is not certain. For example, there seems to be a change after f. 95vb, which ends with *Reprouethe Austin in the persone of God in þe persone of God*, below which catchwords *of God seyng* resemble the rather different writing on f. 96ra, with the repetition at the end of the column possibly designed to fill a space resulting from miscalculation of the point at which another scribe was taking over. But careful study of the forms of letters favours a single scribe. On the other hand, numerous corrections both within the text and in the margins are in a variety of hands. Some of these corrections are to readings found in the GD branch of the stemma (see p. 29 below), suggesting that the manuscript was subject to multiple use at a centre where a copy from that branch was also kept.

Six Latin verses in LgA on the three Marys are omitted from LgD and GiL (see note to 123.56) but are on a fragment pasted into H1 as f. 1*, where they are rubbed and hard to read. They are followed by a couplet in a different hand:

Congeries lapidum variis constructa rapinis
Aut ruet aut raptor alter habebit eam

A similar couplet is recorded as a forecast of the fate of the Palazzo Marino in Milan:

Congeries lapidum, multis constructa rapinis,
aut uret, aut ruet, aut alter raptor rapiet.

(reported on various websites, e.g. <www.storiadimilano.it>).
A third version appeared as a lampoon on Wolsey's foundation of Cardinal College:

Non stabit illa domus, aliis fundata rapinis,
Aut ruet, aut alter raptor habebit eam.

(Cassan, *Lives of the Bishops of Winchester*, 436).

A third entry, again in a different hand, consists of the single verse *Omnia sunt hominum pendentia reum filo*. A similar verse is quoted by

William Fleetwood, recorder of London, in Harvard Law Library MS 15 f. 104^{v}: *Omnia sunt hominem reum pendentia filo et subito casu que Valuere rumit.* He adds: *An auncyente wryter of our Lawe did vse the Sence of these olde verses for this purpose*; see Lancashire, 'Law and Modern English Lexicons'. The *auncyente wryter* has not been identified, but the ultimate source is Ovid, *Ex Ponto* 4.3.35–6 (*Omnia sunt hominum tenui pendentia filo / et subito casu, quae valuere, ruunt*).

All the hands on this fragment appear to be mid- to late fifteenth-century.

At the top of H1 f. 233^{v} is written *Bis septem triginta tribus bis octo maria // Virgo mater vidua vixit in orbe patria*, and also *Edwardo Goldisburgh constat liber.* For discussion of the identity of Edward Goldisburgh, see Tracy, 'British Library MS Harley 630', 43–7.

Descriptions: Kurvinen, Thesis, 43–4; Butler, 54–6; see also Tracy, 'British Library MS Harley 630', 36–58.

H2 London, British Library, MS Harley 4775

Mid-fifteenth century, parchment, 264 leaves measuring 455 × 325 mm, written space 320 × 215 mm, in double columns of 48 lines, with illuminated capitals, red or blue paragraph marks, and red chapter headings.

Collation: 1–2^{8}, (3^{8} wanting), 4–11^{8}, 12^{8} (–4 after f. 83), 13–18^{8}, 19^{8} (wanting 2–7 after f. 136), 20^{8}, 21 (missing 1 after f. 145), 22–32^{8}, 33^{8} (wanting 5 after f. 244), 33–34^{8}, 35^{8} (wanting 8 after f. 262), after which four more folios are needed to complete the final item. The losses of 22 folios took place after an early, perhaps sixteenth-century, foliation (which repeated 99) was supplied. Secundo folio: *THe Commemoracioun.*

H2 contains only *Gilte Legende* and is incomplete at the end, finishing during the last item, 179 *Five Wiles of Pharaoh*. It begins on f. 1^{r} with an introductory paragraph beginning *Here biginnyth the meroure and the liuynge of holie martires* (see vol. 1, p. 3), followed by a table of contents ending on f. 2^{v}. GiL begins on f. 3^{r}: *This book is compiled of the lyues of the seyntes. Callid in latyn Legenda Aurea. First bygynnyth the lyff of Saynt Andrewe.*

The manuscript was written by Ricardus Franciscus, for whom see Jefferson, 'Two Fifteenth-Century Manuscripts'; Scott, 'A Mid-Fifteenth-Century Illuminating Shop', n. 3; Nall, 'Ricardus Franciscus Writes for William Worcester'. The best published illustrations of his hand (from other manuscripts) are in Scott, *Later Gothic*

Manuscripts, ii, ills. 437–44; for a brief account of Ricardus see her vol. 1, pp. 318–19.

Descriptions: Kurvinen, Thesis, 48–9; Butler, 50–4.

L London, Lambeth Palace Library, MS 72

Mid fifteenth century, parchment, ii + 421 + i (first and last flyleaves are paper, otherwise parchment), measuring 330 × 225 mm, written space 225 × 160 mm, in double columns of 42 lines, with blue initials on a red background, alternate red and blue paragraph marks, and red chapter headings. From f. 459 the spaces left for the large capitals and paragraph marks have not been filled in. The text was written throughout by one hand (see *Supplementary Lives*, plate facing p. xxii), which was also responsible for Corpus Christi College Cambridge MS 142 (K in this edition, see below).

Collation: (1–5^8 lost after first foliation), 6–57^8, 58^5 (1 and 2 transposed after first foliation). Because of the loss of the first five quires, the first foliation runs from 41 to 462, but 48 and 303 were omitted and 170 repeated. An attempt to rectify the error at 48 by changing 49 to 48 and adding 49 on f. 50 was not pursued. A second foliator, working after the losses, gave the skeleton of a new foliation starting at 1 on the first surviving leaf, thereafter giving the correct figure on the first recto of each quire, but not noticing the transposition of ff. 458 and 459. For the present study the foliation beginning with 41 has been adopted, despite its errors.

L was at Lambeth Palace by 1633, and must therefore have been acquired either by Archbishop Bancroft or Archbishop Abbot.[9] Among a number of marginal scribbles appear on f. 136^r 'James Clarke', on f. 207^r 'ffr Clarke' five times, smudged as though to erase, on f. 233^r 'Fr Clarke', several 'FC' monograms, and 'James Francis Clarke'; there are further 'FC' monograms on ff. 274^r and 287^r, on f. 298 is a shield containing various unclear monograms, and on f. 461^v is a large FC monogram with 'Francis Clarke' faintly above it. Numerous scribbles on f. 462^v give no certain names. On ff. 263^v and 264^r have been written what appear to be two drafts for part of a document, beginning 'By me William James of this Parresh . . .'. On f. 252 appears the verse:

Hope well and haue well
So it may fall

[9] Ker, 'Archbishop Sancroft's Rearrangement'.

But hope not to myche
and at last lose all

Before the losses L consisted of a text of *Gilte Legende* omitting chapters 96–8, 106–9, 111, 114–15, 118–21, 125–7, 130–2, 134–41, 143–5, 147, 150, 153, 157, and containing a group of lives not in the main corpus of GiL (the Additional Lives), a St Barbara, and an alternative version of St Jerome on ff. 202^{r}–285^{v} (for details see *Supplementary Lives*, pp. xiv–xvi). It also contains on ff. 437^{v}–461^{v} *The Three Kings of Cologne*. L now begins in chapter 23 *Agnes*. A table of contents on f. 462^{r-v} in a hand probably of the early sixteenth century includes the missing first twenty-two chapters.

Archbishop Sancroft reinstated Lambeth Palace Library after its return from Cambridge, whither it had been removed during the Civil War, and many of the manuscripts, including L, were rebound under his care. 'Sancroft's bindings are all just the same, a lightish calf, plain except for a double fillet all round the edges and two double fillets vertically down each cover a bit out of the spine; also . . . Sancroft's arms as Archbishop in gilt on each cover.'[10]

For a possible origin at or related to Syon Abbey, see Görlach (1998), 80–1 and Keiser, 'Patronage and Piety'.

Descriptions: James, *A Descriptive Catalogue . . . Lambeth Palace*, 116–17; Kurvinen, Thesis, 73–4; Görlach, *Studies in Middle English Saints' Legends*, 85. For contents, see *IMEP* Handlist XIII, 3–13. The above description supersedes and in part corrects those in *Three Lives* and *Supplementary Lives*.

Short Descriptions of Manuscripts Containing One or More Chapters of GiL (or Parts thereof)

T1 Dublin, Trinity College, MS 319

Parchment, mid- to late fifteenth century, 96 leaves (numbered 1–95 with 81 repeated) measuring 215 × 150 mm, written space 195 × 125 mm, of 25–35 lines to the page, with red titles, initials, and paragraph marks. It has suffered various sorts of damage, and leaves are lost at the beginning and end and after f. 24. The survivors are wrongly bound, and Kurvinen has shown that the order should be: 7–14, 5–6, 1–4, 15–40, 43–50, 41, 51–6, 42, 57–95. T1 contains nineteen lives, consisting of eighteen GiL lives and a *Dorothy*, for which see

[10] Ker, 'Archbishop Sancroft's Rearrangement', 7.

Plate 1. Trinity College Dublin, MS 319, f. 28v
Reproduced by permission of the Board of Trinity College Dublin

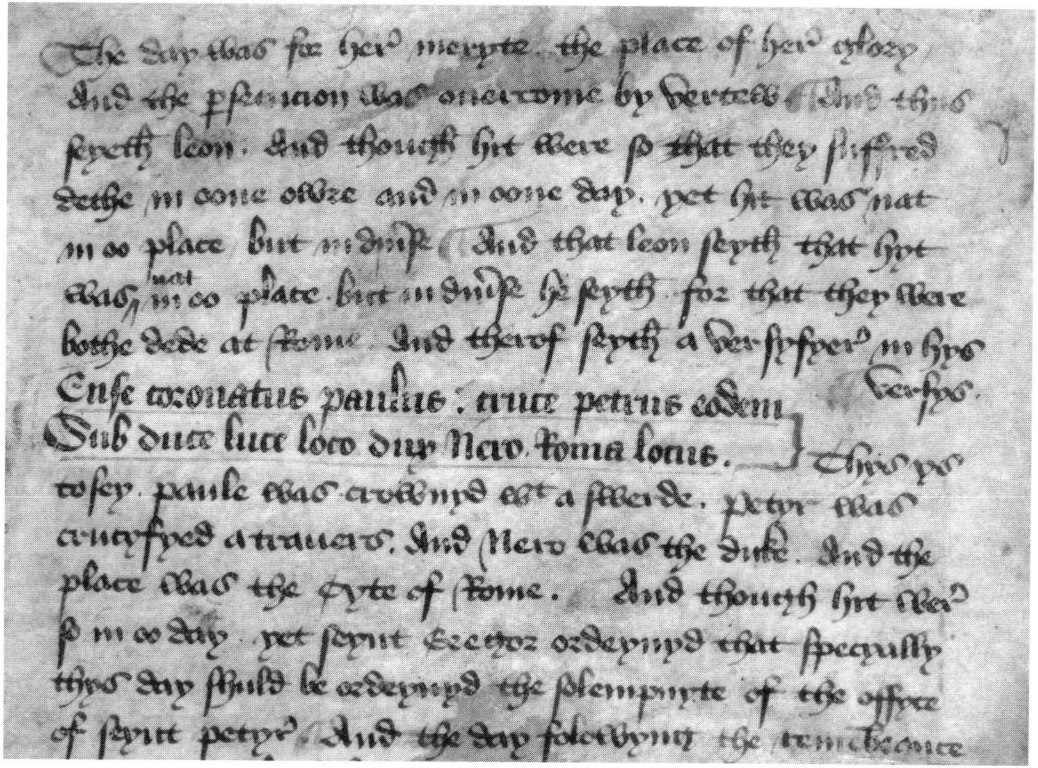

Supplementary Lives, pp. xvi and 241–9. Variation in the size and neatness of the writing would support Kurvinen's view that T1 is in several hands, but the shapes of the letters seem fundamentally the same throughout. See plate 1, p. 15. On f. 87^r are four lines of verse, IMEV 3569.

The manuscript came to Trinity College from the library of Archbishop Ussher.

Description: Kurvinen, Thesis, 121–2.

T2 Cambridge, Trinity College, MS O.9.1

Parchment, before 1477, 225 + vi leaves, in various hands, measuring 300 × 215 mm, written space 215 × 155 mm, of 30–7 lines to a page.

Among other items T2 contains five chapters from GiL, 165 *Catherine* ff. 9–24, 93 *James the Greater* ff. 24^v–29^v, 36 *Purification of VM* ff. 30–5, 49 *Annunciation* ff. 35–39^v, 112 *Assumption of VM* 39^v–48^v and 1–8^v; f. 48^v ends at 112.560 *worde* followed by: *Turne to þe first of this boke after þe Calander and ye shall fynde þe remmenant of the Assumpcioun*, resuming on f. 1 with *Hit is tyme*.

The manuscript is in several hands, one of which wrote the *Catherine*, another the other GiL chapters. The introductory heading of *Catherine* gives it as *Capitulo lxiiij.*^{to}, suggesting that it was copied from a complete GiL, in which its chapter number would have been 164, the preliminary *C* for hundred having here been omitted

Apart from one or two later insertions, the manuscripts in the O series, including this one, were presented to Trinity College by Roger Gale in 1738. An indenture dated 26 December 1477 on one of the closing flyleaves records the lease of lands by the Guild of the Assumption in St Margaret's, Westminster, to James Fytt, citizen and tailor of London.

Description: James, *The Western Manuscripts in the Library of Trinity College*, iii 439–41; Kurvinen, Thesis, 125; *IMEP* Handlist XI, 136–8.

K Cambridge, Corpus Christi College, MS 142

Parchment, mid- to late fifteenth century, 126 + ii leaves measuring 330 × 225 mm, written space 285 × 200 mm, in double columns of 40 lines, with gold initials on a coloured background and red paragraph marks and chapter headings. Names of two early owners are recorded, on f. 126^v: 'Thys ys betrys beuerleys book', and on the last flyleaf:

'Thys booke ys Wylliam Bodleys and Elizabethe hys wyffe.' K contains eight religious pieces, all in the hand of one scribe, who also wrote L; they include on ff. 1–85 *The myrrour of þe blessid liif of oure lord ihesu criste*, by Nicholas Love (also in A1, but there incomplete), and on ff. 93^{r}–107^{v} three GiL items, 2 *Nicholas*, 165 *Catherine*, and 87 *Margaret*.

Descriptions: James, *A Descriptive Catalogue . . . Corpus Christi College Cambridge*, i. 327–9; Kurvinen, Thesis, 70–2; *IMEP* Handlist XX, 11–17. Images of the entire manuscript are available on the website 'Parker on the Web', <http://parkerweb.stanford.edu/parker>, including description and bibliography.

Du Durham University Library, MS Cosin V.ii.14

Lydgate, Sege of Thebes, etc., in one hand, mid-fifteenth century, includes as item 6 on ff. 106^{r}–111^{v} 90 *Mary Magdalen* lacking the last quarter. This life is edited by Zupitza, 'Das Leben der heiligen Maria Magdalena', from this copy, misstated to be in Durham Cathedral Library.

Descriptions: Rud, *Catalogi Veteres*, 155–6; a draft description by A. J. Piper and A. I. Doyle is currently available on the Durham University Library website.

La London, Lambeth Palace Library, MS 306

Contains 154 *Eustace* on ff. 127–131^{v}. The manuscript consists of 'an amalgam of separate units . . . which came from different sources and yet were early on bound together' (Boffey and Thompson, 'Anthologies and Miscellanies', 290–1). In *IMEP* Handlist XIII it is described as 'a composite commonplace book . . . assembled and transcribed piecemeal by several different hands in s. xv^{2} and s. xvi^{1}, and later supplemented by memoranda in the hand of the antiquary John Stow'.

Descriptions: James and Jenkins, *A Descriptive Catalogue*, 421–6; *Three Fifteenth-Century Chronicles*, ed. Gairdner, pp. i–xv; *IMEP* Handlist XIII, 18–24, where Eustace is item [20] on p. 21.

M Tokyo, Professor Toshiyuki Takamiya Collection, MS 45–23 and Bloomington, Indiana, Lilly Library, MS Poole 98–13

Parchment, two consecutive leaves containing part of 11 *Silvester*, mid-fifteenth century, 350 × 210 mm, written space 252 × 159 mm, in double columns of 40 lines. The running title gives it as *þe xi chapter*, so it was part of a complete GiL.

Christopher de Hamel, 'Phillipps Fragments in Tokyo', 42, traces the progress of these leaves from the Sotheby's sale of 26 June 1919, where as lot 678 they were unsold, having apparently been among the fragments which made up Phillipps MS 19117. For the Poole fragment see Faye and Bond, *Supplement to the Census of Medieval Manuscripts*, 183, no. 84.

P*

A damaged leaf containing parts of a contents list of a lost manuscript, pasted into the binding of **Paris, BN nouv. acq. lat. 3175**; described by W. Sauer, Review of Görlach, *The South English legendary*, in *Anglia*, 93 (1975), 247–50; see *Supplementary Lives*, pp. xvii–xviii.

Lichfield fragment

In January 2010 Thorlac Turville-Petre discovered in the William Salt Library, Stafford, a copy of 'an old illuminated fly parchment leaf in a small folio black covered book of Wills, Causes and Presentations ranging from 1603–1665 and upwards belonging to the Bishop's Registry at Lichfield', which he recognized as a passage from GiL. The copy is on ff. 163^{v}–165^{r} of a volume of transcripts made by W. L[ong] in 1849 (reference number S. MS 229/1), and consists of GiL 66.211 to 68.33, comprising the end of *Malchus*, the whole of *Gordian*, and the beginning of *Nereus and Achilleus*. Long seems to have reproduced the lines of the original precisely as they were on the manuscript, giving forty-seven lines to the page. The leaf must have been reversed, since the later part of the text is given first. It was copied from the first volume of the Black Book of Lichfield, now kept in the Lichfield Record Office (reference number B/C/10iv), at the end of the contents list of which is the statement, dated 1855: 'The Fly Parchment leaves contain Translations from the works of St Jerome, some evidently from his "History of the Fathers of the Desert".' This is correct only to the extent that GiL *Malchus* was a translation of Jerome's *Vita Malchi monachi captivi*; also there is now only one parchment flyleaf, and it is not the one Long copied, though it is from GiL. It is in very bad condition, distorted, heavily cropped and otherwise cut, and apparently having suffered some burning, and it is therefore largely illegible. Despite this, it has been skilfully mounted. It runs from 73.23 to 74.99 (*Primus and Felician* and *Barnabas*) but it is reversed, like the leaf copied by Long. Of the latter there is no sign, though in view of the plural used in the note in the contents list it was presumably also in this volume. It seems probable that the surviving leaf was already in bad condition in 1849, which could explain why Long did not copy it; he makes no reference to it.

The manuscript to which the surviving leaf belonged was of the mid-fifteenth century, in two columns of forty-seven lines, written space about 255 × 145 mm, with rubric chapter heads and some other use of red. Comparison of the text of the transcript and what is legible in the flyleaf with all other surviving manuscripts of GiL suggests that its closest relatives were DH2, with which it shares more than twenty trivial variants in the transcript alone, too many for coincidence, against agreeing EGH1 readings, such as additions of *it* after 66.271 *tell*, *aweie* after 67.8 *stole*, *agene* after 68.15 *saide*. Among more significant cases of correct readings shared with EGH1 are 66.254 *sore anhungrid* against *so sore and hungrid* DH2, 68.6 *to her gretly virginite* against *hir gret virginite* DH2, inclusion of 68.20–2 *virginite . . . but*, which DH2 omit; but it shares the incorrect DH2 reading 66.263 *man* for *woman* EH1G; and at 73.25 it omits *was nygh*, found in EH1G and H2 (D not running). The limited evidence obtainable from the small amount of text is enough to indicate that the manuscript to which the fragment belonged was neither the exemplar for D nor copied from it or from H2.

The following manuscripts contain 178 *Adam and Eve* and/or 179 *Five Wiles of Pharaoh*, in some cases incompletely (see pp. 42–6 below).

Ca Cambridge, University Library, MS Gg.6.26, ff. 104^{r}–105^{r} (Five Wiles)

Cb Cambridge, University Library, MS Ff.6.33, ff. 67^{v}–88^{r} (Five Wiles)

Do Oxford, Bodleian Library, MS Douce 15 (SC 21589), ff. 8^{v}–141^{r} (both)

Ha London, British Library, MS Harley 1197, ff. 75^{r}–76^{v} (Five Wiles)

Hb London, British Library, MS Harley 2388, ff. 7^{v}–20^{r} (both)

Hc London, British Library, MS Harley 1704, ff. 18–26^{v} (Adam)

Wh London, British Library, Additional MS 39574 (Wheatley), ff. 60^{r}–88^{r} (Adam)

Ya New Haven, Yale, Beinecke Library, MS Marston 243, ff. 106^{r-v} and 2^{r}–3^{v} (Five Wiles)

Wh is described in *The Wheatley Manuscript*, ed. Day, pp. vii–ix, and in an improved version in *Three Alliterative Saints' Hymns*, ed. Kennedy, pp. xxii–xxviii. For Cb, see *Deonise Hid Diuinite*, ed. Hodgson, pp. xiv–xv. For Ya, see Shailor, *Catalogue of Medieval and Renaissance Manuscripts*, 461–4.

There are also copies of Adam and Eve in late sixteenth-/early seventeenth-century Bodleian Library MSS Ashmole 244 and 802, in the hand of Simon Forman (see *IMEP* IX, 12 and 31, and *IPMEP* 25).

Lost or unidentified

The Duchess of Buckingham, d. 1480, bequeathed 'to my doughter Richmond a boke of English of Legenda sanctorum' and three other books. This daughter(-in-law) was Margaret Beaufort, mother of the future Henry VII. It seems likely this was a copy of GiL.[11]

3. MANUSCRIPT CONTENTS

The chapter numbers are those of the present edition, and represent the original condition of GiL. Chapters which have been lost from a manuscript are indicated by an asterisk, and chapters which are partly missing, through loss rather than omission, by an asterisk before the foliation. A blank indicates that the chapter was never present. The contents of the minor manuscripts are given after the tables.

[11] Recorded by Routh, *Lady Margaret: A Memoir of Lady Margaret Beaufort*, ch. 2.

Volume 1

	E	H1	G	D	H2	A1	A2	L
1. St Andrew	*1^{r}–4^{r}	*1^{r-v}	1^{r}–4^{v}	*	3^{r}–5^{v}	34^{r}–36^{r}	2^{r}–3^{r}	*
2. St Nicholas	*4^{r}–6^{v}	*2^{r}–4^{r}	4^{v}–8^{r}	*	5^{v}–8^{r}	36^{r}–38^{r}	3^{r}–4^{r}	*
3. St Lucy	*	4^{r}–5^{r}	8^{r}–9^{r}	*	8^{r}–9^{r}	38^{r}–39^{r}	4^{r-v}	*
4. St Thomas, apostle	*7^{r-v}	5^{r}–8^{r}	9^{r}–11^{v}	*	9^{r}–11^{r}	39^{r}–40^{v}	4^{v}–5^{r}	*
5. Nativity	7^{v}–10^{v}	8^{r}–11^{v}	12^{r}–15^{r}	*	11^{r}–13^{v}	40^{v}–42^{r}	5^{r}–6^{v}	*
6. St Anastasia	10^{v}–11^{v}	11^{v}–12^{v}	15^{r-v}	*	13^{v}–14^{v}	42^{r-v}	6^{v}	*
7. St Stephen	11^{v}–13^{v}	12^{v}–15^{r}	16^{r}–18^{v}	*	14^{v}–16^{r}	42^{v}–44^{r}	6^{v}–7^{v}	*
8. St John, evangelist	13^{v}–15^{v}	15^{r}–18^{r}	18^{v}–21^{r}	*	*16^{r-v}	*44^{r-v}	7^{v}–8^{r}	*
9. Innocents	15^{v}–17^{r}	18^{r}–19^{v}	21^{r}–22^{v}	*	*	*45^{r-v}	8^{r}–9^{r}	*
10. St Thomas of Canterbury	17^{r}–18^{v}	19^{v}–21^{r}	22^{v}–24^{r}	*	*		9^{r-v}	*
11. St Silvester	18^{v}–22^{v}	21^{r}–25^{v}	24^{r}–28^{r}	*33^{r-v}	*	62^{r}–64^{v}	9^{v}–11^{r}	*
12. Circumcision	22^{v}–23^{v}	25^{v}–26^{v}	28^{v}–29^{v}	*	*	64^{v}–65^{r}	11^{r}	*
13. Epiphany	23^{v}–25^{v}	26^{v}–29^{v}	29^{v}–31^{v}	*34^{r}	*17^{r}–18^{r}	65^{r}–66^{v}	11^{r}–12^{r}	*
14. St Paul, hermit	25^{v}–26^{v}	29^{v}–30^{v}	31^{v}–32^{r}	34^{r-v}	18^{r-v}	66^{v}–67^{r}	12^{r}	*
15. St Remy	26^{v}–27^{r}	30^{v}–31^{v}	32^{v}–33^{r}	*34^{v}	18^{v}–19^{r}	67^{r-v}	12^{r-v}	*
16. St Hilary	27^{r}–28^{r}	31^{v}–32^{r}	33^{r}–34^{r}	*	19^{r-v}	67^{v}–68^{r}	12^{v}–13^{r}	*
17. St Macarius	28^{r-v}	32^{r}–33^{r}	34^{r-v}	*	19^{v}–20^{r}	68^{r-v}	13^{r}	*
18. St Felix of Nola	28^{v}–29^{r}	33^{r-v}	35^{r-v}	*	20^{r-v}	68^{v}–69^{r}	13^{r-v}	*
19. St Marcellus, pope	29^{r}	33^{v}–34^{r}	35^{v}	*	20^{v}	69^{r}	13^{v}	*
20. St Anthony	29^{r}–30^{v}	34^{r}–36^{r}	35^{v}–37^{r}	*1^{r}–2^{r}	20^{v}–22^{r}	69^{r}–70^{r}	13^{v}–14^{r}	*
21. St Fabian	30^{v}–31^{r}	36^{r}	37^{r-v}	2^{r}	22^{r}	70^{r}	14^{r}	*
22. St Sebastian	31^{r}–33^{r}	36^{r}–38^{v}	37^{v}–39^{v}	2^{r}–3^{v}	22^{r}–23^{v}	70^{r}–71^{v}	14^{r-v}	*
23. St Agnes	33^{r}–34^{v}	38^{v}–40^{v}	39^{v}–41^{v}	3^{v}–4^{v}	23^{v}–25^{r}	71^{v}–72^{v}	14^{v}–15^{v}	*41^{r}–42^{v}
24. St Vincent	34^{v}–36^{r}	40^{v}–42^{r}	41^{v}–43^{r}	5^{r}–6^{r}	25^{r}–26^{r}	72^{v}–73^{v}	15^{v}–16^{r}	42^{v}–44^{r}
25. St Basil	36^{r}–38^{r}	42^{r}–45^{r}	43^{r}–45^{v}	6^{r}–7^{v}	26^{r}–27^{v}	73^{v}–75^{r}	16^{r}–17^{r}	44^{r}–46^{v}
26. St John almoner	38^{r}–41^{r}	45^{r}–48^{v}	45^{v}–49^{r}	7^{v}–10^{r}	27^{v}–30^{r}	75^{r}–77^{r}	17^{r}–18^{r}	46^{v}–50^{v}
27. Conversion of Paul	41^{r}–42^{r}	48^{v}–50^{r}	49^{r}–50^{r}	10^{r-v}	30^{r-v}	77^{r-v}	18^{r}	50^{v}–51^{v}
28. St Paula	42^{r}–44^{r}	50^{r}–52^{v}	50^{r}–52^{v}	10^{v}–12^{r}	30^{v}–32^{r}	77^{v}–79^{r}	18^{r}–19^{r}	51^{v}–54^{r}
29. St Julian, hospitaller	44^{r}–46^{v}	52^{v}–55^{v}	52^{v}–55^{v}	12^{r}–14	32^{r}–34^{r}	79^{r}–80^{v}	19^{r}–20^{r}	54^{r}–56^{v}
30. Septuagesima	46^{v}–47^{v}	55^{v}–57^{r}	55^{v}–56^{v}	14^{r-v}	34^{r-v}	80^{v}–81^{r}	20^{r}	56^{v}–57^{v}
31. Sexagesima	47^{v}–48^{r}	57^{r-v}	56^{v}–57^{r}	14^{v}–15^{r}	34^{v}–35^{r}	81^{r-v}	20^{r-v}	57^{v}–58^{r}
32. Quinquagesima	48^{r-v}	57^{v}–58^{r}	57^{r}–58^{r}	15^{r-v}	35^{r-v}	81^{v}	20^{v}	58^{r}–59^{r}
33. Lent	48^{v}–49^{v}	58^{r}–59^{r}	58^{r}–59^{r}	15^{v}–16^{r}	35^{v}–36^{r}	81^{v}–82^{r}	20^{v}–21^{r}	59^{r-v}
34. Ember Days	49^{v}–50^{r}	59^{r}–60^{r}	59^{r-v}	16^{r-v}	36^{r-v}	82^{r-v}	21^{r}	59^{v}–60^{v}
35. St Ignatius	50^{r}–51^{r}	60^{r}–61^{v}	60^{r}–61^{v}	16^{v}–17^{v}	36^{v}–37^{v}	82^{v}–83^{v}	21^{r-v}	60^{v}–61^{v}
36. Purification of the Virgin	51^{r}–54^{v}	61^{v}–66^{r}	61^{v}–66^{r}	17^{v}–20^{v}	37^{v}–40^{v}	*83^{v}–84^{v}	21^{v}–22^{v}	61^{v}–65^{v}
37. St Blaise	54^{v}–56^{r}	66^{r}–67^{v}	66^{r}–68^{r}	20^{v}–21^{v}	40^{v}–41^{r}	*85^{r-v}	22^{v}–23^{r}	65^{v}–67^{r}
38. St Agatha	*56^{r-v}	67^{v}–69^{v}	68^{r}–70^{r}	21^{v}–22^{v}	41^{r}–42^{v}	85^{v}–86^{v}	23^{r-v}	67^{r}–69^{r}
39. St Vedast	*	69^{v}–70^{r}	70^{r-v}	22^{v}–23^{r}	42^{v}	86^{v}	23^{v}–24^{r}	69^{r}
40. St Amand	*	70^{r-v}	70^{v}–71^{r}	23^{r-v}	42^{v}–43^{r}	86^{v}–87^{r}	24^{r}	69^{r-v}
41. St Valentine	*	70^{v}–71^{r}	71^{r-v}	23^{v}	43^{r}	87^{r-v}	24^{r}	69^{v}–70^{r}
42. St Juliana	*	71^{r-v}	71^{v}–72^{v}	23^{v}–24^{r}	43^{r-v}	87^{v}	24^{r-v}	70^{r-v}

Volume 1 (*cont.*)

	E	H1	G	D	H2	A1	A2	L
43. Chair of St Peter	*	71^{v}–73^{r}, 74^{r}–75^{r}	72^{v}–75^{r}	24^{r}–25^{v}	43^{v}–45^{r}	*87^{v}–88^{v}	24^{v}–25^{r}	70^{v}–72^{v}
44. St Matthias, apostle	*57^{r}–58^{v}	73^{r}–74^{r}, 75^{r}–76^{v}	75^{r}–76^{v}	*25^{v}–26^{v}	45^{r}–46^{v}	*89^{r-v}	25^{r}–26^{r}	72^{v}–75^{r}
45. St Gregory	*58^{v}–63^{v}	*76^{v}–82^{r}	77^{v}–85^{r}	*28^{r}–29^{v}, 27^{r-v}, 30^{r}	46^{v}–51^{v}	89^{v}–93^{r}	26^{r}–28^{r}	75^{r}–81^{r}
46. St Longinus	*	82^{r-v}	85^{r-v}	30^{r-v}	51^{v}	93^{r-v}	28^{r}	81^{r-v}
47. St Benedict	*64^{r}–68^{r}	82^{v}–87^{v}	85^{v}–90^{v}	30^{v}–31^{v}	51^{v}–54^{v}	93^{v}–96^{r}	28^{r}–29^{v}	81^{v}–85^{v}
48. St Patrick	68^{r}–69^{r}	87^{v}–89^{r}	90^{v}–92^{r}	*	54^{v}–55^{v}	96^{r-v}	29^{v}–30^{r}	85^{v}–87^{r}
49. Annunciation	69^{r}–72^{r}	89^{r}–92^{v}	92^{r}–94^{v}	*32^{r}	55^{v}–57^{v}	*96^{v}	30^{r}–31^{r}	87^{r}–90^{r}
50. Passion	72^{r}–77^{r}	92^{v}–99^{r}	94^{v}–102^{r}	32^{r-v}, 41^{r}	57^{v}–61^{v}	*	31^{r}–33^{r}	90^{r}–96^{r}
51. St Secundus	77^{r}–78^{r}	99^{r}–100^{r}	102^{r}–103^{r}	41^{r-v}	61^{v}–62^{r}	*	33^{r}	96^{r}–97^{r}
52. St Mary of Egypt	78^{r}–79^{v}	100^{r}–101^{v}	103^{v}–105^{r}	41^{v}–42^{v}	62^{r}–63^{r}	*	33^{r-v}	97^{r}–98^{r}
53. St Ambrose	79^{v}–83^{v}	101^{v}–106^{r}	105^{r}–110^{v}	*42^{v}–44^{v}	63^{r}–66^{r}	*97^{r}–98^{r}	33^{v}–35^{r}	98^{r}–102^{r}
54. St George	83^{v}–85^{v}	106^{r}–109^{r}	110^{v}–113^{v}	*	66^{r}–68^{r}	98^{r}–99^{v}	35^{r}–36^{r}	102^{v}–105^{r}
55. St Mark	*85^{v}–86^{v}	109^{r}–112^{v}	113^{v}–118^{r}	*	68^{r}–70^{r}	99^{v}–101^{v}	36^{r}–37^{r}	105^{r}–107^{v}
56. St Marcellinus, pope	86^{v}–87^{r}	112^{v}–113^{r}	118^{r}	*	70^{r-v}	101^{v}	37^{r}	107^{v}–108^{r}
57. St Vitalis	87^{r}	113^{r}	118^{v}	*	70^{v}	101^{v}–102^{r}	37^{r}	108^{r-v}
58. St Peter, martyr	87^{r}–92^{r}	113^{r}–119^{r}	119^{r}–125^{v}	*	70^{v}–74^{v}	102^{r}–105^{r}	37^{r}–38^{v}	108^{v}–113^{v}
59. St Philip, apostle	92^{r-v}	119^{r-v}	125^{v}–126^{v}	*	74^{v}	105^{r}	38^{v}	113^{v}–114^{r}
60. St James the Less	92^{v}–96^{r}	119^{v}–124^{r}	126^{v}–132^{r}	*40^{r-v}	74^{v}–77^{v}	105^{r}–107^{v}	38^{v}–40^{r}	114^{r}–118^{r}
61. Finding of the Cross	96^{r}–99^{v}	124^{r}–128^{r}	132^{r}–137^{r}	*	77^{v}–80^{v}	107^{v}–109^{v}	40^{r}–41^{r}	118^{r}–121^{v}
62. St John before the Latin gate	99^{v}–100^{r}	128^{r}–129^{r}	137^{r}–138^{r}	*	80^{v}	109^{v}–110^{r}	41^{r-v}	121^{v}–122^{r}
63. Litanies	100^{r}–101^{v}	129^{r}–131^{r}	138^{r}–140^{v}	*	80^{v}–82^{r}	110^{r}–111^{r}	41^{v}–42^{r}	122^{r}–123^{v}
64. Ascension	101^{v}–105^{r}	131^{r}–135^{v}	140^{v}–146^{r}	*45^{r}–47^{r}	*82^{r}–84^{r}	111^{r}–113^{v}	42^{r}–43^{v}	123^{v}–127^{v}
65. Pentecost	105^{r}–110^{r}	135^{v}–141^{v}	146^{r}–153^{v}	47^{r}–51^{r}	84^{r}–88^{r}	*	43^{v}–45^{r}	127^{v}–132^{v}
66. St Malchus	110^{r}–113^{r}	141^{v}–145^{r}	153^{v}–157^{v}	51^{r}–53^{r}	88^{r}–90^{r}	*		132^{v}–135^{v}
67. St Gordian	113^{r}	145^{r-v}	158^{r}	53^{r}	90^{r}	*	45^{r}	135^{v}–136^{r}
68. Sts Nereus and Achilleus	113^{r}–114^{r}	145^{v}–146^{r}	158^{r}–159^{r}	53^{r-v}	90^{r}–91^{r}	*114^{v}	45^{r-v}	136^{r-v}
69. St Pancras	114^{r-v}	146^{r}–7^{r}	159^{r-v}	*	91^{r}	*114^{v-r}	45^{v}	136^{v}–137^{r}
70. St Urban	114^{v}–115^{r}	147^{r-v}	159^{v}–160^{v}	*	91^{r-v}	*114^{r}	45^{v}	137^{r-v}
71. St Petronilla	115^{r}	147^{v}–148^{r}	160^{v}–161^{r}	*	91^{v}	*114^{r}	45^{v}	137^{v}
72. St Peter, deacon	115^{r-v}	148^{r-v}	161^{r-v}	*	91^{v}–92^{r}	*	45^{v}–46^{r}	137^{v}–138^{r}
73. Sts Primus and Felicianus	115^{v}–116^{r}	148^{v}–149^{r}	161^{v}–162^{r}	*	92^{r-v}	*	46^{r}	138^{r-v}
74. St Barnabas, apostle	116^{r}–117^{v}	149^{r}–150^{v}	162^{v}–164^{v}	*54^{r-v}	92^{v}–93^{v}	*	46^{r-v}	138^{v}–140^{r}
75. Sts Vitus and Modestus	117^{v}–118^{r}	150^{v}–151^{v}	164^{v}–165^{v}	54^{v}–55^{r}	93^{v}–94^{r}	*	46^{v}–47^{r}	140^{r}–141^{r}
76. Sts Quiricus and Julitta	118^{r-v}	151^{v}–152^{r}	165^{v}–166^{r}	55^{r-v}	94^{r-v}	*115^{r}	47^{r}	141^{r}
77. St Marina	118^{v}–119^{v}	152^{r}–153^{r}	166^{v}–167^{v}	55^{v}–56^{r}	94^{v}–95^{r}	115^{r-v}	47^{r-v}	141^{r}–142^{r}
78. Sts Gervase and Protase	119^{v}–120^{v}	153^{r}–154^{v}	*167^{v}–168^{v}	56^{r}–57^{r}	95^{r}–96^{r}	115^{v}–116^{r}	47^{v}	142^{r}–143^{r}

Volume 1 (*cont.*)

	E	H1	G	D	H2	A1	A2	L
79. St Alban	120^{v}–132^{r}	154^{v}–168^{v}	*169^{r}–174^{r}	*57^{r}–62^{v}	96^{r}–104^{v}	116^{r}–123^{r}	57^{r}–61^{v}	143^{r}–155^{r}
80. St John the Baptist	132^{r}–135^{r}	168^{v}–172^{r}	174^{v}–178^{v}	*62^{v}	104^{v}–107^{r}	123^{r}–125^{r}	61^{v}–62^{v}	155^{r}–158^{r}
81. Sts John and Paul	135^{r}–136^{v}	172^{r}–173^{v}	178^{v}–180^{v}	*63^{r}–64^{r}	107^{r}–108^{r}	125^{r}–126^{r}	62^{v}–63^{v}	158^{r}–159^{v}
82. St Leo, pope	136^{v}–137^{r}	173^{v}–174^{v}	180^{v}–181^{r}	64^{r-v}	108^{r-v}	126^{r-v}	47^{v}–48^{r}	159^{v}–160^{r}
83. St Peter, apostle	137^{r}–141^{v}	174^{v}–180^{r}	181^{v}–188^{r}	64^{v}–68^{r}	108^{v}–112^{v}	126^{v}–129^{v}	63^{v}–65^{r}	160^{r}–165^{r}
84. St Paul, apostle	141^{v}–147^{r}	180^{r}–186^{v}	188^{r}–195^{r}	*68^{r}–70^{r}	112^{v}–116^{v}	129^{v}–132^{v}	66^{v}–68^{v}	165^{r}–170^{v}
85. Seven Brothers	147^{r-v}	186^{v}–187^{r}	195^{v}–196^{r}	70^{r-v}	116^{v}	132^{v}–133^{r}	68^{v}	170^{v}–170^{*r}
86. St Theodora	147^{v}–149^{r}	187^{r}–189^{r}	196^{r}–198^{r}	70^{v}–71^{v}	116^{v}–117^{v}	133^{r-v}	68^{v}–69^{v}	170^{*r}–171^{v}
87. St Margaret of Antioch	149^{r}–150^{r}	189^{r}–190^{v}	198^{r}–199^{v}	71^{v}–72^{v}	117^{v}–118^{v}	133^{v}–134^{v}	69^{v}	171^{v}–172^{v}
88. St Alexis	150^{r}–151^{v}	190^{v}–192^{v}	199^{v}–201^{v}	72^{v}–73^{v}	118^{v}–120^{r}	134^{v}–135^{v}	69^{v}–70^{v}	172^{v}–174^{r}
89. St Praxedes	151^{v}	192^{v}	201^{v}	73^{v}	120^{r}	135^{v}	70^{v}	174^{r}
90. St Mary Magdalen	151^{v}–156^{r}	192^{v}–197^{v}	201^{v}–204^{v}, 211^{r}–213^{r}	*73^{v}–74^{v}	120^{r}–123^{r}	135^{v}–138^{r}	70^{v}–72^{r}	174^{r}–178^{v}
91. St Apollinaris	156^{r}–157^{r}	197^{v}–199^{r}	213^{r-v}, 205^{r-v}	*75^{r}	123^{r-v}	138^{r-v}	72^{r-v}	178^{v}–179^{v}
92. St Christina	157^{r}–158^{r}	199^{r}–200^{r}	205^{v}–207^{r}	75^{r}–76^{r}	123^{v}–124^{v}	138^{v}–139^{r}	84^{r-v}	179^{v}–180^{v}
93. St James the Greater	158^{r}–161^{v}	200^{r}–204^{v}	207^{r}–210^{v}, 214^{r-v}	76^{r}–78^{v}	124^{v}–127^{r}	139^{r}–141^{v}	84^{v}–86^{v}	180^{v}–184^{r}

Volume 2

	E	H1	D	H2	A1	A2	L
94. St Christopher	161^{v}–163^{v}	204^{v}–207^{r}	*78^{v}	127^{r}–128^{v}	141^{v}–142^{v}	86^{v}–87^{v}	184^{r}–186^{v}
95. Seven Sleepers of Ephesus	163^{v}–165^{r}	207^{r}–209^{v}	*79^{r}	128^{v}–130^{r}	142^{v}–143^{v}	87^{v}–88^{v}	186^{v}–188^{r}
96. Sts Nazarius and Celsus	165^{r}–166^{v}	209^{v}–211^{r}	79^{r}–80^{r}	130^{r}–131^{r}	143^{v}–144^{v}	88^{v}–89^{r}	
97. St Felix, pope	166^{v}	211^{r}	80^{r}	131^{r}	144^{v}	89^{r}	
98. Sts Simplicius and Faustinus	166^{v}–167^{r}	211^{r-v}	80^{r-v}	131^{r-v}	144^{v}–145^{r}	89^{r}	
99. St Martha	167^{r}–168^{r}	211^{v}–213^{v}	80^{v}–81^{v}	131^{v}–132^{v}	145^{r-v}	89^{r}–90^{r}	285^{v}–287^{r}
100. Sts Abdon and Sennen	168^{r-v}	213^{v}	81^{v}	132^{v}–133^{r}	*146^{v}	90^{r}	287^{r-v}
101. St Germain	168^{v}–170^{r}	213^{v}–215^{v}	81^{v}–83^{r}	133^{r}–134^{r}	145^{v}–146^{v}	90^{r-v}	287^{v}–289^{r}
102. St Eusebius	170^{r}–171^{r}	215^{v}–216^{v}	83^{r-v}	134^{r}–135^{r}	*	90^{v}–91^{r}	289^{r}–290^{r}
103. Maccabees	171^{r-v}	216^{v}–217^{r}	83^{v}	135^{r}	*	91^{r}	290^{r-v}
104. St Peter in chains	171^{v}–173^{r}	217^{r}–219^{v}	83^{v}–85^{r}	135^{r}–136^{v}	*	91^{r}–92^{v}	290^{v}–292^{v}
105. Finding of St Stephen	173^{r}–175^{r}	219^{v}–222^{r}	85^{r}–86^{v}	*136^{v}	*	92^{v}–93^{r}	292^{v}–294^{v}
106. St Dominic	175^{r}–178^{v}	222^{r}–226^{r}	*86^{v}–88^{v}	*	*	93^{r}–95^{r}	
107. St Sixtus	178^{v}	226^{r-v}	*	*	*	95^{r}	
108. St Donatus	178^{v}–179^{v}	226^{v}–227^{v}	*89^{r}	*	*	95^{r-v}	
109. St Cyriacus	179^{v}–180^{r}	227^{v}–228^{v}	89^{r-v}	*	*	95^{v}–96^{r}	
110. St Laurence	180^{r}–183^{r}	228^{v}–232^{r}	*89^{v}–90^{v}	*137–138^{v}	*147^{r-v}	96^{r}–97^{r}	294^{v}–297^{v}

Volume 2 (*cont.*)

	E	H1	D	H2	A1	A2	L
111. St Hippolytus	183r–184r	232r–234v	*	138v–139r	147v–148r	97r–v	
112. Assumption of the Virgin	184r–194r	234v–245v	*91r–95v	*139r–146r	148r–152r	97v–103r	297v–309v
113. St Bernard	194r–198r	245v–250v	95v–99r	146r–150r	152r–155r	103r–105r	309v–314r
114. St Timothy	198r	250v	99r	150r	155r	105r–v	
115. St Symphorian	198r–v	250v–251r	99r	150r	155r–v	105v	
116. St Bartholomew	198v–201r	251r–254r	99r–101v	150r–152v	155v–157r	105v–107r	314r–317v
117. St Augustine	201r–205v	254r–259r	*101v–103r	152v–156v	157r–160r	107r–109v	317v–322v
118. Sts Felix and Adauctus	205v	259r	103r	156v	160r–v	109v	
119. Sts Savinian and Savina	205v–206v	259r–261r	103r–104r	156v–157v	160v–161r	109v–110r	
120. St Lupus	206v–207r	261r–v	104r–v	157v–158r	161r–v	110r–v	
121. St Mamertin	207r–208r	261v–262r	104v–105r	158r–v	161v–162r	110v	
122. St Giles	208r–209r	262r–263r	*105r–v	158v–159v	162r–v	110v–111v	322v–323v
123. Nativity of the Virgin	209r–212v	263r–267v	*35r–37r	159v–162v	162v–165r	111v–113v	323v–327v
124. St Cecilia I	212v–215r	267v–270v	37r–39v	162v–165r	165r–167r	113v–115r	327v–330v
125. St Adrian	215r–216v	270v–272v	39v–40v, 106r	165r–166v	*167r–v	115r–116r	
126. Sts Gorgonius and Dorotheus	216v–217r		106r	166v	*	116r	
127. Sts Protus and Hyacinth	217r–218r	272v–274r	106r–107r	166v–168r	*168r	116r–v	
128. Exaltation of the Cross	218r–220r	274r–277r	107r–109r	168r–170r	168r–170r	116v–118r	330v–333v
129. St John Chrysostom	220r–221v	277r–279r	109r–110r	170r–171r	170r–171r	118r–119r	333v–335r
130. Sts Cornelius and Cyprian	221v–222r	279r	110r–v	171r–v	171r	119r	
131. St Euphemia	222r–v	279r–280r	*110v	171v–172v	171r–v	119r–v	
132. St Lambert	222v–223r	280r–280v	*	172v	171v–172r	119v	
133. St Matthew	223r–225v	280v–284v	*111r–112v	172v–175r	172r–173v	119v–121r	335r–338r
134. St Maurice	225v–226v	284v–286v	112v–113v	175r–176v	*173v	121r–122r	
135. St Justina	226v–228v	286v–287v	113v–115r	176v–177v	*174r–175r	122r–v	
136. Sts Cosmas and Damian	228v–229v	287v–289r	115r–116r	177v–178v	175r–v	122v–123v	
137. St Fursey	229v–230v	289r–290r	116r–v	178v–179v	175v–176v	123v–124r	
138. St Michael, archangel	230v–232v	290r–292v	*116v	179v–181v	176v–177v	124r–124v	
139. St Jerome	232v–234v	292v–294v	*117r–118r	181v–183r	179v–180v	124v–125v	
140. Translation of St Remy	234v–235r	294v–295v	118r–v	183r–184r	180v–181r	125v–126r	
141. St Leger	235r–236r	295v–296v	118v–119r	184r–184v	181r–v	126r–v	
142. St Francis	*236r–240v	296v–302v	*119r–121r	184v–189r	181v–185r	126v–129r	338r–342v
143. St Pelagia	*	302v–303v	121v–122r	189r–v	185r–v	129r	
144. St Margaret Pelagia	*	303v–304v	122r–v	189v–190r	185v–186r	129r–v	
145. St Thais	*241r–v	304v–305v	*122v	190r–191r	186r–v	129v–130r	
146. St Dionysius the Areopagite	241v–243r	305v–308v	*123r–124v	191r–193r	186v–188r	130r–131r	342v–345r

Volume 2 (*cont.*)

	E	H1	D	H2	A1	A2	L
147. St Callistus	243$^{r–v}$	308^{v}–309^{r}	124^{v}–125^{r}	193$^{r–v}$	188$^{r–v}$	131$^{r–v}$	
148. St Leonard	243^{v}–245^{r}	309^{r}–311^{r}	*125$^{r–v}$	193^{v}–195^{r}	188^{v}–189^{v}	131^{v}–132^{r}	345^{r}–346^{v}
149. St Luke	245^{r}–248^{v}	311^{r}–315^{r}	*126$^{r–v}$	195^{r}–197^{v}	189^{v}–191^{v}	132^{r}–133^{v}	346^{v}–350^{r}
150. Sts Chrysanthus and Daria	248^{v}–249^{r}	315$^{r–v}$	126^{v}–127^{r}	197^{v}–198^{r}	191^{v}–192^{r}	133^{v}–134^{r}	
151. St Ursula and the 11,000 virgins	249^{r}–251^{r}	315^{v}–317^{v}	*127$^{r–v}$	198^{r}–199^{v}	192^{r}–193^{r}	134^{r}–135^{r}	350^{r}–352^{r}
152. Sts Simon and Jude	251^{r}–253^{v}	317^{v}–320^{v}	*128$^{r–v}$	199^{v}–201^{v}	193^{r}–194^{v}	135^{r}–136^{r}	352^{r}–354^{v}
153. St Quentin	253^{v}	320^{v}	128^{v}	201^{v}–202^{r}	194^{v}	136^{r}	
154. St Eustace	253^{v}–256^{v}	320^{v}–323^{v}	128^{v}–130^{v}	202^{r}–204^{r}	195^{r}–196^{v}	136^{r}–137^{v}	354^{v}–357^{v}
155. All Saints	256^{v}–260^{v}	323^{v}–328^{v}	130^{v}–133^{r}	204^{r}–207^{v}	196^{v}–199^{r}	137^{v}–139^{r}	357^{v}–361^{v}
156. All Souls	*260^{v}–264^{v}	328^{v}–333^{v}	*133^{v}–134^{v}	207^{v}–211^{v}	199^{r}–202^{r}	139^{r}–141^{r}	361^{v}–366^{v}
157. Four crowned martyrs	*	333^{v}–334^{r}	134^{v}	211^{v}	202^{r}	141^{r}	
158. St Theodore	*265^{r}	334$^{r–v}$	*134^{v}	211^{v}–212^{r}		141$^{r–v}$	
159. St Martin	265^{r}–269^{r}	334^{v}–339^{r}	*135^{r}–137^{r}	212^{r}–215^{v}	202^{r}–205^{r}	141^{v}–143^{v}	366^{v}–371^{r}
160. St Brice	269$^{r–v}$	339$^{r–v}$	137$^{r–v}$	215^{v}–216^{r}	205^{r}	143^{v}	371$^{r–v}$
161. St Elizabeth of Hungary	269^{v}–274^{r}	339^{v}–344^{v}	*137^{v}–140^{v}	216^{r}–219^{v}	205^{v}–208^{r}	143^{v}–145^{v}	372^{r}–376^{v}
162. St Cecilia 2	274^{r}–276^{v}	344^{v}–348^{r}	*141^{r}–142^{r}	219^{v}–221^{v}			
163. St Clement	276^{v}–281^{r}	348^{r}–353^{r}	*142^{r}–143^{v}	221^{v}–225^{r}	208^{r}–210^{v}	145^{v}–147^{v}	376^{v}–380^{v}
164. St Chrysogonus	281$^{r–v}$	353$^{r–v}$	*	225$^{r–v}$	210^{v}–211^{r}	147^{v}–148^{r}	
165. St Catherine	281^{v}–290^{v}	353^{v}–364^{v}	*144^{r}–148^{v}	225^{v}–233^{r}	*211^{r}–214^{v}	148^{r}–152^{v}	380^{v}–390^{v}
166. St Saturnine	290^{v}–291^{v}	364^{v}–365^{r}	148^{v}–149^{r}	233$^{r–v}$		152^{v}	392^{r}–393^{r}
167. St James Intercisus	291^{v}–293^{r}		149^{r}–150^{r}	233^{v}–234^{v}		152^{v}–153^{v}	390^{v}–392^{r}
168. St Pastor, abbot	293$^{r–v}$		150$^{r–v}$	234^{v}–235^{r}		153^{v}	393$^{r–v}$
169. St John, abbot	293^{v}–294^{r}		150^{v}	235$^{r–v}$		153^{v}–154^{r}	393^{v}–394^{r}
170. St Moses, abbot	294^{r}		150^{v}–151^{r}	235^{v}		154^{r}	394$^{r–v}$
171. St Arsenius, abbot	294^{r}–295^{r}		151$^{r–v}$	235^{v}–236^{v}		154$^{r–v}$	394^{v}–395^{v}
172. St Agathon, abbot	295^{r}–296^{r}		151^{v}–152^{r}	236^{v}–237^{r}		154^{v}	395^{v}–396^{r}
173. Sts Barlaam and Josaphat	296^{r}–301^{v}		*152^{r}–154^{v}	237^{r}–241^{v}		154^{v}–157^{r}	396^{r}–402^{v}
174. St Pelagius, pope	301^{v}–309^{v}		*155$^{r–v}$	*241^{v}–248^{v}		157^{r}–160^{v}	402^{v}–411^{v}
175. Dedication of the Church	309^{v}–314^{v}		*155^{v}–156^{v}	248^{v}–252^{v}		160^{v}–162^{r}	411^{v}–417^{r}
176. Advent	*314^{v}–315^{v}		*	252^{v}–256^{r}		167^{r}–168^{v}	417^{r}–421^{v}
177. Conception of the Virgin	*		*157^{r}	256^{r}–258^{v}			421^{v}–423^{v}
178. Adam and Eve	*316^{r}–319^{v}		*157^{r}–160^{v}	258^{v}–263^{r}		162^{r}–165^{r}	423^{v}–431^{r}
179. Five Wiles of Pharaoh	*320$^{r–v}$		*160^{v}–163^{r}	*263$^{r–v}$		165^{r}–167^{r}	431^{r}–437^{r}

T1 165 *Catherine*: *7^{r}–14^{v}, 5^{r}–6^{v}, 1^{r}–2^{v}; *Dorothy*: 2^{v}–4^{v}, 15^{r}–16^{v}; 20 *Anthony*: 17^{r}–20^{r}; 21 *Fabian*: 20$^{r–v}$; 22 *Sebastian*: 20^{v}–24^{v}; 23 *Agnes*: *24^{v}; 83 *Peter*: *25^{r}–28^{v}; 84 *Paul*: 28^{v}–39^{r}; 54 *George*: 39^{r}–40^{v}, 43^{r}–45^{v}; 146 *Dionysius*: 45^{v}–50^{v}; 148 *Leonard* 50^{v}, 41$^{r–v}$, 51^{r}–53^{r}; 116 *Bartholomew*: 53^{r}–56^{v}, 42$^{r–v}$, 57^{r}–59^{r}; 90 *Mary Magdalen*: 59^{r}–68^{r}; 110 *Lawrence*: 68^{r}–75^{v}; 111 *Hippolytus*: 75^{v}–77^{v}; 94 *Christopher*: 77^{v}–81^{v}; 2 *Nicholas*: 82^{r}–88^{r}; 80 *John Baptist*: 88^{v}–93^{v}; 151 *Ursula*: *94^{r}–96^{v}

T2 36 *Purification*: 30^{r}–35^{r}; 49 *Annunciation*: 35^{r}–39^{v}; 93 *James Greater*: 24^{v}–29^{v}; 112 *Assumption*: 39^{v}–48^{v}, 1^{v}–8^{v}; 165 *Catherine*: 9^{r}–24^{r}

K2 *Nicholas*: 93^{r}–96^{v}; 165 *Catherine*: 96^{v}–106^{r}; 87 *Margaret*: 106^{r}–107^{v}

Also **Du** contains (incomplete) 90 *Mary Magdalen*, **La** contains 154 *Eustace*, **M** contains part of 11 *Silvester*. For details including foliation of additional lives and other material in A1, A2, and L, see *Supplementary Lives*, pp. xiii–xvii.

In **A1** 100 *Abdon* and 101 *Germanus* were reversed, and the apparent hiatus in numbers at ff. 177^{v}–179^{v} is because of an added section on Michael; see *Supplementary Lives*, pp. xvi and 273–82.

4. AFFILIATIONS OF THE MANUSCRIPTS

A stemma for the manuscripts of GiL was devised for *Three Lives* (pp. 40–8, with the stemma itself on p. 46), in which full collation is supplied for 2 *Nicholas*, 54 *George*, and 116 *Bartholomew*; work on the preparation of the present edition has confirmed the results of that investigation. Full collations have been given in the apparatus of the present edition for 84 *Paul* and 155 *All Saints*, and these too support the relationships deduced in *Three Lives*. Since GiL is a close translation of LgD, it is easy in most cases to deduce by reference to the readings of LgD MSS P2SZ the original text written by s.w.

DH2

H2, written by the professional scribe Ricardus Franciscus,[12] is a close and careful copy of D, even retaining many of its spellings, though regularly substituting *th* for *þ* and tending to replace *ȝ*

[12] For Ricardus, see references given in description of H2 above, pp. 12–13.

variously by *y*, *g*, and *gh*. This relationship was first noticed by Butler, 73–4, and confirmed by Kurvinen, Thesis, 152–4. The accuracy of the copying is such that it is hard to find distinctive isolative readings for H2. The only examples in 84 *Paul* are 74 omission of *here*, 127 *prayere* for plural, 154 omission of *it*[1], 488 *ne* for *of*, and 482 *heth* for D *hey* (E *haye*), where Ricardus has mistaken a badly written *y* for *þ*; 155 *All Saints* has some eight trivial instances, such as 240 addition of *vs*, 241 *of* for *and*; and in Bartholomew (analysed for *Three Lives*) only three minor variants were found (p. 40). More tellingly, D was written by four scribes with somewhat differing spelling habits, and Ricardus generally follows their individual spellings.[13] H2 very occasionally corrects obvious errors in D, such as at 46.15 restoring *toke* where D has *to*, and 119.66 restoring *be* omitted by D. On the other hand, it retains D variants which make little sense, such as 123.129 *hele bi you* for *be hele yeue* in *and by hym shall be hele yeue to all the peple*, 124.132–3 *right so in obeyinge of derinite bene thre persones* for *right so in one beinge of diuinite be thre persones*, 145.9 *the* for *þis shillyng*; and in 146.214–7 H2 follows D in putting a paragraph mark before *And whan* and running the sentence on without punctuation into 217.

H1T1

T1 was copied from H1 after the many corrections and changes in that manuscript had been inserted, copying such altered readings as 29.35 *`my' mynde* H1 for *myn*, 83.421–2 *`bodeli' liȝt* H1 for *gostely derkenesse*, 84.284 *soule* changed to *Poule* H1, *poule* T1 for *saule*, and many less striking examples. T1 occasionally attempts corrections, such as 146.29 *Ambrose* for H1 *Andorose*, E *And Orose*. The T1 165 *Catherine*, however, was not copied from H1, but, as shown by Kurvinen in her thesis, belonged to a branch of the transmission of the Catherine life separate from GiL which it shares with Stonyhurst College MS 43; see pp. 39–41 below.

EH1T1A1(A2)

This is one of two main branches of the stemma (p. 30 below), easily identified in Paul by conjunctive errors or changes. 84 *Paul* gives EH1T1A1 84 *make* for *meue*, 283 *thinge* for *tunge*, 302 *diluvie* for *deluge*, 317 omission of *and his kindrede*, 399 *sithe* for *suche*, 404–5 omission of *but . . . worlde*, 429–30 omission of *ne archaungelles*, and numerous minor cases. T1 does not contain 155 *All Saints*, and for reasons that

[13] Hamer, 'Spellings of the Fifteenth-Century Scribe Ricardus Franciscus'.

will appear below A1 does not belong with EH1 at that stage; but conjunctive errors in EH1 include 148 *Verily* for *wherebi*, 207 *lowithe* for *louithe*, and 324 *ioyne* for *ioye*. In *Paul* E has several separative readings: *Paul* 17 *contre* for *kynrede*, 78 omission of *by fire*, 306 *places* for *endes*; in *All Saints* there are several minor instances and the unlikely reading 371 *grete* for *brede*. H1 has separative variants, which are shared by T1 (see examples from *Paul* above); cases from *All Saints* include 193 omission of *and of doctours*, 220 *seintes* for *synnes*, 305 *closeth* for *chesithe*. Corrections in H1 are often from the GDH2 branch, e.g. *Paul* 331, *wit* changed to *wel*, 365 *akinge* changed to *a thinge*, *All Saints* 101 addition of *thingis*. A1 has many individual readings, e.g. *Paul* 50 addition of *sight*, 64 *fully* for *truly* (DH2 *verrili*), 74 *court* for *corner*.

A2 is also linked to this branch in the earlier part of GiL (for instances in *Nicholas* and *George* see *Three Lives*, 41–3), but in *Paul*, although a number of cases could be attributed to this connection, none of them is individually conclusive, since they are of a type which could easily have been duplicated by the common ancestor (d) of A1A2 (for the link between which see below), and there are none in *All Saints* or *Catherine* (see Kurvinen, Thesis, 151 ff.). Occasional instances of corrections in A2 appear to be from other versions; for example, 132.23–5 *whom the frendes of the bisshop slowe as thei had deserued. And than Seint Lambert blamed*, which was omitted from all other manuscripts, must have been restored from LgA, since LgD omits *as thei had deserued*, LgA *sicut meruerunt*.

M

The 170 surviving lines of 11 *Silvester* in M offer sufficient evidence to show that this manuscript was closely related to EH1: EH1M have 125 *thanne us enforme* for *yeue us a forme*, 254 omission of *hillys . . . alle*, 310 *the* for *his*, 311 *pore peple and true* for *true peple*, 312 *of* for *and*, 323 *berest* for *lernydist*; EM agree in 280 *dye* for *dyer* and 339 omission of *in*; H1M share 324 addition of *þat*. From these one could deduce either that EH1M all descend from a common exemplar, or that E and H1 or an intervening exemplar were copied from M; in either case H1 would show obvious corrections at 280 and 339, while omission of the unnecessary second 324 *that* by E could be either a conscious correction or a careless omission. The meaningless 302 H1M *ours* and E *cours* for *curs* could be explained in various ways, as H1 mechanically copying M's error, or M and H1 copying the same exemplar, with E attempting a correction of the error in M or its exemplar, etc. The E spelling is apparently for 'course', since *MED* gives no instance of *cours* as a spelling for 'curse'. Context in this case would not have helped a scribe inclined to correct. The best hope of resolving the question is at 237, where *souereynli*, confirmed by G and LgD, is divided *so / uereynli* in M at the end of the line, E gives *so uereynli* in mid-line with a clear space, and H1A1A2 have the attempted correction *so verreli*. A line-ending division such as that in M must surely be the source of the E and H1A1A2 readings, so it seems on balance likely that M was indeed the source of these others; it is of course not impossible that M too was copying yet another manuscript with the word fortuitously in the same position. It is no doubt too much to hope that further fragments of M will be discovered and make it possible to establish with certainty its position. It has therefore been omitted from the stemma below.

GDH2A2

On the other main branch, there are numerous small agreements in 84 *Paul* between G and DH2, but few striking ones, notably the addition of 69 *pepul*, and between G and H2 where D is not running, including 414 and 416 *conuertid* for *coueited*. G is separated from DH2 by variants such as 342 addition of *and in Chastite*, 446 *medis* for *guerdons*, and 468 *trauayleris* for *trauayles*. DH2 have many separative variants, including 29 *wynter* for *yere*, 69 *gret* for *greuous*, 136 *brothir* for *bretheren*, 184 omission of *caste*. GDH2A2 share variants, including 29 *lif* for *Lyves*, 48 ff. *Patrik* for *Patrok*, 70 omission of *brought*, and DH2A2 are linked by many examples, such as 49 addition of *aȝen to lyfe*, 54 *mevinge* for *amonastinge*, 64 *verrili* for *truly*, and 92–3 *aweie* for *oute of my sight*. But since A2 does not share the isolative variants of G and DH2 noted above it cannot be directly descended from any of these manuscripts. A2 has, as in every part of the work, large numbers of its own variants, both large and small, well illustrated in the apparatus of both *Paul* and *All Saints*, e.g. *Paul* 213 addition of *for his grete trespace*, 217 addition of *as smalle as powdre*, *All Saints* 2 *offencis* for *defauutes*, 13 *did rebelle ayenste room* for *turned awey from his lordship*.

A1

At a certain point A1 stops sharing variants with the EH1 branch and thereafter joins DH2A2, as in many examples in *Catherine* (Kurvinen, Thesis, 151–6) and in 155 *All Saints*, for example 144–5 *Seint Augustine and Stephen seith* for *of Seint Stephen it ys saide*, 207 *sikirlie* for *secretely*,

247 *verite* for *vertu*, 331 *lightloker* for *sonner*, 353 add *companie*, 16 *ydollis* for *ymages* (A2 has *goddis*). The change appears to happen in 149 *Luke* between 92 and 94, though the immediate examples are rather tenuous: 87 H1A1 *vppon* for *in*, 92 H1A1 *that* for *as*, 94 EH1 *ny*, H2 *nygh vs*, A1 *in us*, 96 H2A1 *hem* for *hym*; more distinctively, 59 H1A1 *put on him* for *pitee of hem*, 122–4 H2A1 omission of *seruing, and that aperithe bi that whanne he went that oure Lorde hadde be a straunge man and receiued hym in his hous and dede hym.*

In 155 *All Saints* A1 has the following individual readings: 218–19 *withoute synne* for *hit shuld not be*, 267 *that they herde* for *in herte*, 295 *filth* for *flesshe*[1].

A1A2

In addition to their varying relationships to the EH1 and DH2 branches, A1 and A2 have shared variants throughout (for *Catherine* see Kurvinen, Thesis, 155, and for *Nicholas* see *Three Lives*, 41–2); in *George* and *Bartholomew* examples are shared with other manuscripts, but in 84 *Paul* and 155 *All Saints* there are many cases of just A1A2, e.g. *Paul* 40 *Senator* for *senate*, 281 add *seynt*, 447 *sorowes* for *tristesse*, *All Saints* 70 omit *Ierome*, 89 add *cause*, 130 *erthe* for *roche*, 139 *First* for *Fytheli*.

The following stemma is based on the arguments above. There are too many variables and uncertainties in the evidence for LK (see below) and the other minor manuscripts and M to make their inclusion useful. The copy used by Caxton for his *Golden Legend* is included with the sigil C*, for discussion of which see *Supplementary Lives*, p. xvii.

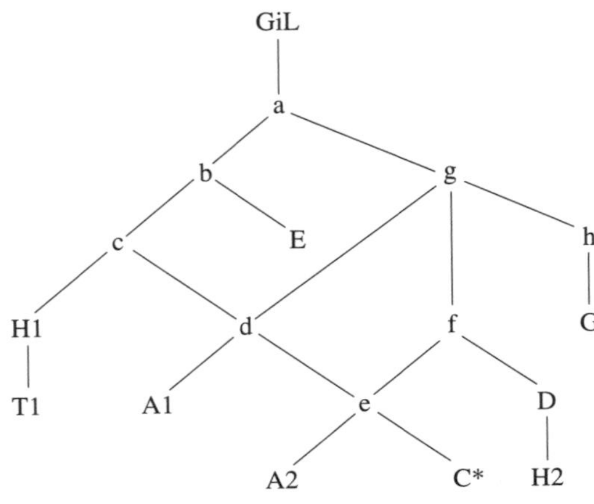

LK

L and K, the latter containing three GiL chapters, 2 *Nicholas*, 87 *Margaret*, and 165 *Catherine*, do not fit satisfactorily into this stemma. Kurvinen (Thesis, 158–9), who was unaware that these manuscripts were written by the same scribe, found in *Catherine* that they are basically on the EH1 branch, but that each has many readings from the D branch, though these are sometimes not shared; both have separative errors, and therefore K is not copied from L. She concluded that they are derived from the same exemplar, but that this contained some contamination 'in the form of interlinear and marginal notes, which the two scribes have adopted or rejected at will'. Her interpretation is compatible with the K and L variants in *Margaret*, and with those of K in *Nicholas*, which is missing from L.

However, clear cases of linked error would be needed to demonstrate the link with the EH1 group, but the only striking one in *Catherine*, 587 *ouer* EKL, *of* H1, for *of alle lordshippes and of* is not sufficient on its own.

Separative readings in 87 *Margaret* are numerous, including 26 *selfe* L for *beauute* EK, 56 *fygure* L for *forme* EK, 60 *downe to her feet* K for *to the erthe* EL, 82 *sone* K, *lightly* EL (the E readings are confirmed by LgD); shared LK variants in this short life are, however, few and minor, such as 84 *do sacrifice* for *sacrifice*. At 70 GLK share *dispisid*, which is perhaps the better reading, for *deposed*, *deboute* P2, *repellatur* LgA, the only sign of the link with the D branch postulated by Kurvinen; and there are no shared variants with the EH1 branch.

Some of K's variants in 2 *Nicholas* (which has been lost from L) are linked with EH1, e.g. 95 EK *chastised* for *chased*, 175 EH1K *blynded* for *illuded*, 292 EH1K *blessid* for *bisshop*; and throughout GiL L has a number of such agreements where correctness of the GD branch is confirmed by LgD, such as 24.95 EH1L *enflaumed* for G *enfamyned*, 84.331 EL *witte* for G *welle*, 117.105 EL *slepte* for D *wepte*, 129.68 EL *sawe* for D *saide*; these last three examples have all been corrected in H1.

At 87 *Margaret* 30–1 *Crist deliuered hymselff to dethe*, EH1K have *for* for *to*, but it is correct in L; it appears that the scribe copied the error in K but in copying L realized it must be wrong and corrected it; and as with the examples above, a corrector has changed it in H1.

In addition to the above, L frequently has readings agreeing with

LgD and LgA where GiL has changes resulting from either translator or scribal error, and L sometimes agrees closely with LgA when LgD and GiL share a mistranslation. Since none of the former seems particularly to suggest the reading of LgD, the probability is that the contamination referred to by Kurvinen in L's exemplar in both these types of correction resulted from use of the Latin.

Examples of the above in which GiL closely follows LgD (except as noted) and L follows LgA are: 55.189–90 *þrewen hym doun the seruaunt of God to the erthe, he crying to Seint Marke*, closely following LgD, *dei famulum sanctum Marchum inuocantem ad terram proiciunt* LgA, *threwe hym downe to the erthe hee cryeng fast to the seruaunt of god seynt Marke* L; 102.34–5 *shulde write her faithe* (add *et fist escrire* LgD) *to the bysshopp Denys of Melane and to .xxx.*[ti] *bisshopes*, *et Dionysium episcopum Mediolanum ac XXIX episcopos eidem fidei fecit subscribere* LgA, *and the bisshop Denys of Melan and .xxix. bisshoppis shuld subscribe to the same feith* L; 110.68–9 *Preue me that hast chose me couenable* (add *et me commeis* LgD), *Experire certe utrum idoneum ministrum elegeris cui commisisti* LgA, *Preve certeynly whether thow haste chose a couenabil mynyster to whom thow hast commyttid* L; 112.567 *vnnumerable*, *interminabilem* LgA, *interminabille* L; 149.66–7 *of the foregoer and of the natiuite* L, *percursoris et natiuitate* LgA, not in LgD or other GiL manuscripts; 156.206 *of the ministres*, *iniustorum* LgA, *that were vnrightwis* L, 207 *sum of that other*, *iusti* LgA, *þe rightwis* L; 176.143 *greuaunce to men*, *pressura in terris* LgA, *pressure in erthe* L; 176.272 *that is*, add *crux* LgA, add *þe crosse* L (which is in P1 but not in P2S).

There are also many other cases where L has a reading which represents that of LgD/LgA and which seems likely to have been the original version that s.w. wrote, but in which the other GiL manuscripts differ apparently as the result of scribal error; while these could in theory have been taken from a Latin (or indeed French) original, they often appear likely to derive from an early copy of GiL preceding the appearance of these errors. One passage in particular, because it does not come from LgA/LgD, seems to confirm this possibility: 79 Alban 1050–8 is omitted from all other manuscripts, but must surely have been included in the translation from its source; it does not seem credible that the scribe of L's exemplar or someone introducing marginal corrections would have inserted this as a result of comparison with the Latin original, and use of a copy of GiL better than any of the survivors seems more probable. Examples where L records a reading likely to be original to GiL but where the other manuscripts share variants which can easily be explained as scribal can be found in the apparatus on many pages of the text, and in many of these the changed meaning is not conspicuous in context, so that one would scarcely expect anyone to make the correction: 38.6 *bewte* L for *bonte*, 43.120 *pase* L for *place*, 45.144 *clerenesse* L for *clennesse*, 54.114 *woundes* L for *bowels* (where the other manuscripts have *bowels* picked up from the preceding line); and cases where replacement of an omitted clause makes no difference to the flow or sense: 41.2 *and asked hym*, 49.57 *oure Lorde the father is withe the*, 50.454 *and brought to Rome*, 51.1 *and sithe he was a noble knyght.*

If these changes result from use of a good early manuscript, as here suggested, it would follow that Kurvinen's suggestion of a connection to the D branch is unnecessary, since the early manuscript would also have shared the correct D readings. From the above information the following description of L's text is proposed: the LK scribe was not a slavish copyist, as is shown by instances where K and L differ despite being apparently copied from the same exemplar. A number of variants from the original shared with EH1, combined with cases where the exemplar was apparently derived from a manuscript with many original readings in cases where both the EH1 and D branches share variants, suggest that this exemplar had readings from two GiL sources, one close to EH1 and one closer to the original translation and free from some of the incorrect readings shared by both branches of the stemma. The matter is further confused by the cases already referred to where the text contains corrections based on LgA.

As a result of this analysis, in the text of the present edition numerous emendations have been adopted from L where its agreement with LgD and the likelihood that variants within the EH1 and D branches could result from subsequent scribal error suggest that L retains s.w.'s version. Where corrections in L to s.w.'s work appear to have been taken from LgA, this has not been used to emend the text, except in very rare cases for special reasons, and a few such instances have been recorded in the notes.

T2

Kurvinen (Thesis, pp. 154–5) showed that for 165 *Catherine* T2 is closely related to DH2, is copied from neither of them, but could have been copied from the same exemplar as D; further, it is not copied from A2, and there are no signs of relationship to other manuscripts. In 36 *Purification* the evidence is slight, with only 104

DT2 *kepte* for *kepest* suggesting a recurrence of that link. In 49 *Annunciation* there are a number of agreements of H1T2, including 92 *Pees of* for *Pers of*, which in H1 later changed to *wherof*, which cumulatively indicate some sort of link. In 93 *James the Greater* various agreements, mostly minor, again link H1T2, such as 123 *not drawe* for *todrawe*, 179 addition of *Thei said nay*, and omissions of 287 *came and* and 295 *sekirly*. In 112 *Assumption* a number of readings suggest a link with H2, or D when running, including 1 *rede* for *fynde*, 25 *aboue a* for *a bowe of*, 642 addition of *her in*, 907 *worship* for *lordshippe*, while only a few imply H1T2, such as 678 *lightly* for *likly*, 905 *continue* for *comune*. This mixture suggests that either two exemplars were being used, or, as suggested above for KL, a single exemplar containing corrections.

Du

Du contains about three quarters of 90 *Mary Magdalen*, and such indicators as there are suggest a link with GDH2, e.g. 2 DDu *kynne* for L *lingne* (EH1G *kingges*), 45 GDDu *þese wordis were* for L *this was* (EH1 *they were the wordes of*), 97 GDu *skape* for *parte* (but D as E), 259 GH2Du *drede* for *fere* (D missing). It was not copied from E, as 84 E omits *threst that for*, 143 E *brethinge* for *brayinge*, 145 E *lefte* for *loste*, 167 *goodes* for *thingges*, 289 E adds *to heuene*; nor from the group EH1T1, which has 65 *gouernours* for GDDu *gouernaunce*, 194 *aboute* for GH2Du *vpon*, 230 *lady* for GH2Du *Lazar*. Some minor agreements of DuT1, including 235 addition of *of God*, are inconclusive, and taken with the above disagreements with EH1T1 can be discounted. There are no readings which specifically rule out the possibility that it was copied from D, H2 or G.

La

La, which contains 154 *Eustace*, has very few variants linking it to any other manuscript. Apart from a few small similarities with DH2, the following may be mentioned: 36 omission of *Than saide oure Lorde* shared with E and with H1 before correction, 118 addition of *twoo* DLa, 119 DLa *It behoueth me* for *me behoued*, 173 *contre* as EH1 against D variant *toune*, 191 omission of *was* shared by EH1. The similarities with EH1 seem more significant than those with D.

66 St Malchus

The rubrics of the manuscripts announce this chapter as a Life of Jerome (L calls it an *example*). Its source is Jerome's *Vita Malchi Monachi Captivi*, at times loosely translated. It is not in A2 or Caxton, whose English source was closely related to A2. In A1 it was in a quire now mostly lost; calculation shows that this quire would have been too short without *Malchus*.

An edition of the Latin by H. Hurter ('The Text of the *Vitae patrum*', 1885) was reprinted in *Studies in the Text Tradition of St Jerome's* Vitae patrum, ed. Oldfather, 60–4.[14]

79 St Alban

The legend of St Alban first reached substantial form in *Alia Acta SS. Albani, Amphibali, et sociorum, anno DXC Anglice scripta, interpr. Guilielmo monacho Albanensi* (hereafter W) composed by a monk called William at St Albans between 1167 and 1178,[15] and this was substantially the source of all subsequent versions, including a *Tractatus de nobilitate, vita et martyrio sanctorum Albani et Amphibali, de quodam libro Gallico excerptus et in Latinum translatus* (hereafter Tr), which adds an account of the earlier parts of the lives of Alban and Amphibalus.[16] The Cotton MS of Tr appears to have been written under the direct supervision of Thomas Walsingham before September 1394. The statement that this work was excerpted from a French book seems almost as improbable as that of William that he was working from an English one; it is in fact based on W with some reference to Matthew Paris's *Chronica Maiora* and possibly other sources. The GiL chapter is derived from Tr (1–161 and 452–512) and W (162–452 and 516–end), as is Lydgate's *Life of Saint Albon and Saint Amphibalus*, written in 1439.[17] An account of these and all other

[14] The Latin citations in the notes to this edition are from a currently unpublished edition by Paul B. Harvey, Jr, which he has kindly made available.

[15] *AASS* June 22, pp. 129–38; for earlier accounts of Alban see *Saint Albon and Saint Amphibalus*, ed. Reinecke, pp. xviii–xxiv.

[16] London, BL MS Cotton Claudius E.iv., ff. 334^{v}–336^{r}; Oxford, Bodleian, MS Bodley 585, ff. 1^{r}–9^{v}. The text from the Cotton MS is given somewhat inaccurately in *John Lydgate, The Life of Saint Alban and Saint Amphibal*, ed. van der Westhuizen, 277–85, and relevant passages are quoted in the notes to Reinecke's edition. For the date see *The St Alban's Chronicle*, ed. Galbraith, pp. xxxviii and lxi.

[17] Editions by van der Westhuizen and Reinecke as above; the line numbers below relate to Reinecke's (much better) edition.

medieval versions is given by W. McLeod, who discusses their evolution and relationships.[18]

Clearly the GiL version's source is not Lydgate's poem, both from the close similarity of GiL to the Latin in some cases, and because, if we are to believe the D colophon, GiL dates from 1438. But since both not merely derive from a mixture of W and Tr, but also used the same passages of these in the same order, either Lydgate based his poem on GiL, or they both used a previous conflation of the two sources. McLeod argues for the latter, and says that this was probably Latin because 'there are indications that the compiler of [GiL] was working directly from a Latin text [since there are] passages in which it appears that the Latin was misread or misunderstood'. Further, 'there are occasional passages in which [Lydgate] reflects the Latin original more faithfully than [GiL]'. '[Lydgate] and [GiL] drew on an earlier life which was chiefly a compilation of [Tr] and W. This is the most likely solution. In confirmation we may cite some passages in which [Lydgate] and [GiL] render the Latin by essentially the same words, which are not, as it happens, the most obvious rendering.' 'Apparently [GiL] misread his Latin source from time to time, and [Lydgate] occasionally got it right where [GiL] blundered.'[19]

McLeod was, however, unfortunate in that the only manuscripts of GiL available to him were H2 and A2, and in the two substantial instances where GiL, but not Lydgate, is said to be incorrect, comparison with other manuscripts indicates that the error in H2 and A2 is scribal and not attributable to the translator: at 2 *subjugavit* Tr gives *Brouht . . . soget to them of Rome* Lydgate I. 113–15, *deuided* H2A2, *deliuered* EH1, *subdued* L; at 385 *remorderet* W gives *remors . . . hath cast* Lydgate II. 1033–4, *remotid hym* H2A2, *remorded hym* EH1, where L in the first case and EH1 in the second give the presumable GiL original reading and agree with both the Latin and Lydgate. However, two other examples given by McLeod, though less decisive, suggest direct use of the Latin by Lydgate: at 450 W *intolerabilis* gives *intollerable* Lydgate II. 1207, *vnsufferably* GiL; and for 821 *siknesse*, W *diutini morbi* is *old siknesse* Lydgate III. 387. Instances can also be found where Lydgate is closer to Tr, such as at 803 ff., Lydgate III. 323, where the events are said by Tr and Lydgate to have taken place at Lichfield. But a series of agreements in translation where GiL and

[18] 'Alban and Amphibal'. See too Hardy, *Descriptive Catalogue of Manuscripts*, i, nos. 8–31.

[19] 'Alban and Amphibal', 425–9.

Lydgate have either made the same change or selected one from a range of possibilities, including 154 *frenged* for *textis*, Lydgate II. 145; 423 *faylinge* for *fallacibus*, Lydgate II. 1127; 509 *sclavyne* for *chlamyde* Lydgate II. 1339 (both also use the same word at 345, Lydgate II. 877 for *caracallam*); 511 *cheste of lede* for *locello plumbeo* Lydgate II. 1338; 652 *to the grounde, to grounde* Lydgate II. 1864 for *in foveam*; 741 *the worde of God*, Lydgate III. 98, for *verbum vitae*, seem beyond the likelihood of coincidence, and Lydgate must surely have derived these from GiL.[20] Other examples can be added, such as 64 *manly desire*, *animositatem* Tr, 'courage', *deseeris* Lydgate I. 612; 104 *and to putte hym oute of mynde*, *memoratum* Tr, i.e. 'the aforesaid', Lydgate I. 745 *his name put out of mynde*, a mistranslation which GiL and Lydgate are unlikely to have produced independently; 108–9 *they slowe so many*, *tandem occidit* Tr, *He slouh* (. . .) *so greet noumbre* Lydgate I. 759; 121 *withe Maximien* GiL and Lydgate I. 794, not in Tr; 165 *ye durst*, Lydgate II. 180, *potuisti* W; 277 *withe his precious blood*, *pretio sanguinis sui* W, Lydgate II. 618, *with the pris of his precious blood*, suggesting use of both versions; 329 *that hadde espied hem*, Lydgate II. 813 *he did aspie*, not in W; 371 *Asclepiodote*, Lydgate II. 1001, not in W; 599 *We only worshippen oure goddes*, *nos deum Solem colimus* W, *It wer ther goddis and non othir wiht* Lydgate II. 1666; as a result of this error, *illi*, *hic*, and following singular verbs become plural in GiL, and the *goddis* continue in Lydgate's expanded version; 657 *the tormentour that slowe hym hadde smite that stroke*, *cum adhuc staret juxta corpus* W, Lydgate II. 1871–2 *He that smot of the hed of Seynt Albon*; 993 *mynde*, Lydgate III. 1067 *commemoracion* for W *commoratio*, 'dwelling'.

The development of the Life is also discussed by Reinecke (pp. xviii–xxxiv), who agrees that Lydgate and GiL used a common conflated Latin source; in particular he is inclined to accept (p. xxxi) the statement attached to the end of the poem, presumably but not certainly by Lydgate himself, that it was *translatid oute of frenssh and latyn* by Lydgate; though he does also suggest that the wording might have been influenced by the statement in the title of Tractatus quoted above, that it was *de quodam libro Gallico excerptus et in Latinum translatus*. He cites a number of passages where Lydgate appears to be nearer than GiL to the Latin sources. Like McLeod, he mostly referred to H2, though he did also compare with A2 and L, again causing difficulty with some of his examples, such as at 630 where manuscripts including H2 give past *bigan*, Lydgate II. 1787

[20] Though McLeod, ibid. 428 n. argues otherwise.

begonne, for the correct imperative *bigynne* as in L. But in other cases Lydgate and the Latin agree against GiL, such as at 613 where the latter omits *ad scelus de scelere transitum facientes*, Lydgate II. 1708 *For wikke to wers*.

Reinecke, however, has some reservations about this presumed intermediate source (p. xxxiii): 'But McLeod passes over the similarities between the *Legende* and Lydgate which are absent from the known Latin sources as just pointed out. He disposes of the possibility that Lydgate had by him and occasionally used the very recent English prose as well as the hypothetical version, saying merely that "the proximity of time makes this unlikely".' 'It is not impossible that the Gilte Legende was translated at St Albans. If this be true, then what could have been more likely than that Abbot Whethamstede should make available to the poet the year-old prose version?' 'That Lydgate should have used a Latin source . . . while occasionally referring to a vernacular version is not unlikely.'

It is indeed difficult to avoid the conclusion that, despite the statement about translating from French and Latin, the GiL version was a major source for Lydgate, and that he also consulted others. Materials on which to base it would surely have been supplied by John Whetehamstede, abbot of St Albans, who commissioned the poem, and, apart from the GiL life (which, of course, need not have been only a year old) these are likely to have included at least some of W, Tr, Matthew Paris's *Chronica Maiora*, and the French poem *La Vie de Saint Auban* (often also attributed to Paris). This could explain cases in which his version of the Latin appears more correct than or superior to the GiL version, and also the claim to translation from French. There is therefore no real argument for the existence of an intervening Latin conflation. The English version may have existed prior to GiL, and simply been incorporated by s.w. at the appropriate point, or it may have been produced specially as an addition; in the former case one can only speculate on whether s.w. or another compiler/translator was responsible, and there is no reason to suppose it was any different from the version we have.

80 St John the Baptist

John the Baptist is given two chapters in LgD/LgA, LXXXI *De nativitate Sancti Iohannis Baptiste* and CXXI *De decollatione Sancti Iohannis Baptiste*. In this GiL chapter the first 56 lines are a conflation of the LgA/LgD version of the Nativity with another source, 57–137 is entirely from elsewhere, and 138 to end consists of reduced and paraphrased excerpts from the Decollation interspersed with additional passages. The source(s) of the additions have not been identified.

EGDL all refer to *the natiuite* in the opening rubric, and EGD call it *the liff* in the closing rubric (L has no closing rubrics). This suggests that s.w. may have started to translate it before deciding that a conflation would be neater, and then forgot to correct the heading; but of course the heading could also have been changed back to the original by an early rubricator unaware of the conflation, who then failed to make a similar change to the closing rubric.

For an edition of another Life of St John the Baptist, compiled, almost certainly by a Brigittine, from various sources including LgA, and apparently dating from before the middle of the fifteenth century, see Claire M. Waters, *Virgins and Scholars*, 68–123, with discussion of the sources on pp. 23–5 and 425–36.

124 and 162 St Cecilia

For no apparent reason St Cecilia appears as Chapter 124 (Cec1) as well as in its correct LgA and calendar position at 162 (Cec2), where, however, it is not repeated in A1A2L. The two copies share many variations from LgD, and therefore must represent the same translation rather than its having been translated twice. Each version has separative errors, measured against P2; e.g. Cec1 is wrong at 35 *man* (Cec2 *men*), 127 omission of *and quickenithe*, 161 *not* (Cec2 *no beinge*), 178 *oure* (Cec2 *youre*), 203 *partithe* (Cec2 *puttithe*), and correct at 33 *way* (Cec2 *ile*), 185 *finde* (Cec2 *serue*), 273 *thi* (Cec2 *her*); and at 238–9 Cec2 has the substantial omission of *presumpcion . . . conscience*.

165 St Catherine

In her doctoral thesis Auvo Kurvinen studied four related versions *a*, *b*, *c*, and *d* of *The Life of St Catharine of Alexandria in Middle English Prose*. The versions contain different sections of the legend, and she demonstrated that *a* contains a basic core on which the other three were ultimately based, though they rewrote, added to, or omitted from it in various ways. Version *b* has two branches, *b1* with two known manuscripts, T1 and Stonyhurst College MS 43 (hereafter S2), and *b2* consisting of Cambridge, Fitzwilliam Museum MS McClean 129 (hereafter F) and the chapter in GiL. Version *c* derives from a manuscript of branch *b1*, and version *d* from branch *b2*. The *incipit* of one manuscript of *d*, Cambridge, Gonville and Caius College MS 390/610, states that the version was '*sent bi a discrete maister unto the kyng Henry the v.*[te].' If the statement is true, Version *d* was made before the king's death in 1422.[21] She suggests that *a* may have been composed in about 1420 in connection with the king's marriage to Catherine of France, and that the presentation of the *d* manuscript may have had a similar motive. This would place both *a* and *b* before 1422.

To summarize Kurvinen, Version *a* appears to be a translation from two texts, a Latin account of the youth and conversion of Catherine, and LgD. 'The author of Version *b* introduced a large number of verbal changes into the text and added new sections describing Catharine's genealogy and birth and the finding of her body. The additions are likely to be translations or adaptations of two different texts.' 'The added sections do not equal the original Version *a* in style.' 'In 1438 the text of Version *b* was incorporated into [GiL].' Since no precise sources have been identified for the non-LgD material in Versions *a* and *b*, the earliest dates for these versions cannot be more closely defined. The first part in GiL runs from 1 to 544, and is linked by a modified passage (see Note, p. 448) to the LgD/LgA chapter, of which, however, a substantial amount at the end is omitted.

For the purposes of the present edition, the part of the chapter that derives from LgD/LgA has been compared with P2, S, and P1. The only reading which might link the GiL version with P2S is the omission at 62 of *de diuersis prouinciis*, which is in P1 but not P2S; it is also in other manuscripts of LgD such as BL MS Royal 2.A.xviii, and thus may be indicative, in so far as omission of such a phrase can be. This suggests, but does not prove, that the copy of LgD used was the same as that used for the rest of GiL.

Manfred Görlach identified among extra Lives added to a copy of Mirk's *Festial* in Southwell Minster MS 7 another prose life of Catherine, and this has been edited by Nevanlinna and Taavitsainen, who show that it was compiled from versions *a* and *b* with some additions.[22]

A fragment of another late fifteenth-century manuscript of this life has come to light in an account book (numbered WAM 33329,

[21] Thesis, 216.

[22] Görlach (1972), 26; *St Katherine of Alexandria*, ed. Nevanlinna and Taavitsainen; see esp. pp. 21–35.

hereafter Wm) in the archives at Westminster Abbey, consisting of a bifolium of which one leaf is blank The Roxburghe Club volume in which the discovery is reported[23] supplies a plate (p. 57) giving one page of the text corresponding to Kurvinen's edition pp. 280–6 (even pages) ll. 486–525; the verso continues to l. 556, the whole corresponding to 464 *virgines* to 532 *assigned* in the present edition.

Wm belonged to the *b* version. It has several variants which show that it cannot be an ancestor of S2, T1, or F, including 494 (GiL 473–4) transposition of *suettest*, *blyssyd* as *blessed, swette*; omission of 512 (GiL 491) *and desiryth* and 518 (GiL 497) *all þat tyme*; 535 (512) *sith your departyng* for *þere of alle þis tyme*; 549 (GiL 525) *the causer* for *he þat was cause*; 552 (GiL 528) addition after *ayen* of *and sone after she rose ayene*; and it is not descended from any of these as shown by S2 493 (GiL 472) *face* for FT1Wm *visage*, 506 (GiL 485) omission of *grete* before *strook*, 533 (GiL 510) *ȝe perfyȝtly knowe* for FT1Wm *ye be perfitely taught*: T1 495 (GiL 475) *so fervently any thing as I do* for S2FWm *thing but*; 550 (GiL 526) *moche sorowe and* for S2FWm *gret*. In all these instances F agrees with GiL, but in the following it is alone: 505 (GiL 484) F *grete* for S2T1Wm *meche*; omissions of 545 (GiL 521) *or here it* (omit *it* GiL) and 551 (GiL 527) *þat* (*of* GiL) *oure lord*; 545 (GiL 521) *opinyd* for S2FWm *lifte up*. The only reading in this passage shared by S2T1Wm against Fb2 is 490 (GiL 469) *nobyl* for *newe*, where the latter is confirmed as original by the *a* version; but this by itself is not enough to confirm Wm as sharing an archetype with S2T1.

177 Conception of the Virgin

The immediate source of this chapter is a French version found as the third item of the *Festes Nouvelles*, a group of chapters, mostly saints' lives, added by Jean Golein to the end of the original LgD in about 1401, and found in ten of the surviving LgD manuscripts.[24] Golein is stated to have translated these from Latin, largely in fact from Vincent de Beauvais, but no single source for *Conception* has been identified.[25] The account of the Conception itself and the childhood of Mary (4–93) is a fairly close translation, with some minor

[23] Printed in *The Gardyners Passetaunce*, ed. Williams. The Westminster Abbey reference for the fragment is WAM 33329.

[24] Hamer, 'Jean Golein's *Festes Nouvelles*'.

[25] For the Conception, see Thurston, 'Abbot Anselm of Bury and the Immaculate Conception'; Bishop, *Liturgica Historica*, ch. 10: 'On the Origins of the Feast of the Conception of the Blessed Virgin Mary', pp. 238–59.

omissions, of the first part of a *Libellus de Nativitate Sanctae Mariae* derived from the *Evangelium* of Pseudo-Matthew.[26] The attribution in line 2 to Jerome has no justification and is abbreviated from a fictitious exchange of letters affixed to the beginning of the *Libellus*. The story of Abbot Helsin (96–126) is found in a *Tractatus de Conceptione Sanctae Mariae* wrongly attributed to St Anselm, but possibly the work of his nephew Abbot Anselm of Bury, and the miracle of the adulterous priest in the Seine (127–53) is in a *Sermo de Conceptione Beatae Mariae* also wrongly attributed.[27] No Latin version combining these elements and the two remaining miracles has been identified, though it seems more probable that there was such a one which Golein translated than that he was responsible for assembling them.

The use of this sole chapter from the *Festes Nouvelles* raises the question of whether the copy of LgD used by s.w. may have contained Golein's work as a whole, in which case s.w. must have decided not to add the rest of this large body of extra material to the work, 42–6 chapters depending on the manuscript used (some 109 folios in MS BN fr. 416, for example), but chose to include the Conception, celebration of the Feast of which seems to have originated in England, and was also strongly supported by the Benedictines. No separate copy of this item in French or English is known to have existed.

As with the main body of the text from the LgD, the French is translated closely, though there are a number of stylistic expansions similar to those described below (pp. 49–50), especially in lines 127–55 (cited in the Notes).

178 and 179 Adam and Eve and Five Wiles of Pharaoh

Adam and Eve and *Five Wiles* already existed in these versions when added as the last two chapters of GiL. Since a substantial portion of them is illegible in or missing from E, it has been judged best to use D, and H2 when D is lacking, as the base text for this edition, without attempting to eliminate the minor stylistic alterations typical of their practice. The texts here given should therefore not be regarded as representing the version supplied by s.w., or *a fortiori* a reconstruction of their originals. *Adam* has been edited from Wh by Mabel

[26] *Pseudo-Matthaei Evangelium textus et commentarius cura Jan Gijsel, Libellus de Nativitate Sanctae Mariae textus et commentarius cura Rita Beyers.*

[27] *PL* 159, cols. 324–5 and 321.

Day;[28] an edition of *Five Wiles* aiming to represent as closely as possible its original condition should presumably be based on MS Hb, or perhaps Cb.

The two chapters are complete in L and A2, but have suffered various amounts of loss and damage in E, D, and H2. Adam is also in Hb, Wh, Do, and Hc, but Do lacks a folio and Hc at an early stage lost a quire, the contents of which were replaced in an untidy cursive fifteenth-century hand which also made some 'corrections' to the surviving part of the text.[29] This replacement, however, was made from the B version (see below). Variants from this part of Hc, lines 34–270, have therefore not been noted in the apparatus. Do and Hc share an additional introductory section from the later Wycliffite version of Genesis, taking the story back to the creation; but as Day points out (pp. xxv and xxx), this cannot be part of the original as its presence results in a significant element of duplication.

In the Preface to her edition of the Wheatley Manuscript, Day gives a detailed account (pp. xxii–xxxii) of the prose versions in English of Adam and of their origins; she lists (p. xxii) the immediate sources of our version as: '(1) the Latin *Vita Adae et Evae*, (2) a Latin account of the traditional derivation of Adam's name, and of the materials of which his body was made, (3) connecting parts of the Bible narrative to make this into a continuous story.'[30] In addition to the copies referred to above is one in MS Bodley 596 (the B version), which lacks parts of the present version including the later Wycliffite beginning, and contains extra material.[31] She records that: 'In many passages the language is so similar that it is impossible that the two versions can be derived from independent translations even of the same Latin text; (. . .) B's readings are always the better' (p. xxix). It seems impossible to decide whether this version and B were separately compiled using the same translation from the Latin, or whether this was derived from the B version itself with other sources. Since some of the biblical connecting narrative, like that of the additional introduction in Do and Hc, comes from the later Wycliffite Bible of *c.*1388, compilation must have been between then and its insertion in GiL fifty years later. None of the manuscripts is datable,

[28] *The Wheatley Manuscript*, 76–99, Notes pp. 112–18.

[29] For the sigla of the manuscripts referred to in this section see pp. 19–20 above.

[30] For a fuller account, placing this version in the wider European context, see Murdoch, *The Apocryphal Adam and Eve*, esp. 97–112.

[31] B was edited by Horstmann, 'Nachträge zu den Legenden'. Another copy of this version is in Cambridge, Trinity College MS R.3.21; see *IMEP* XI, p. 27, item [30].

but they all appear to be towards the end of this period or somewhat later.

Hb and Do also contain *Five Wiles*, in Hb preceding *Adam*, in Do following it; as will emerge, these two manuscripts are apparently in different branches of the stemma. Since the two chapters are very different in character, *Adam* basically a narrative and *Five Wiles* an analysis of the nature of temptation, they do not sit easily together. Their relationship in the various manuscripts gives no answer to the question of whether they were from an early stage regarded as a pair.

It is apparent for *Adam* that none of the non-GiL manuscript versions was copied from GiL, since they agree with B in lacking a number of doublets and other minor additions found in GiL. The absence and illegibility of E for much of *Adam* makes this less easy to prove than it might have been, since D and L often make the same sort of addition independently, on top of any s.w. may have already made, but examples of E where it is legible are similar to those in D and L where it is not. Examples of GiL additions are: 211 *an aungelle oþere to*, 275 *thus longe*, 309 *ful ententifflie*; and of an inversion 284 *comforte ne merthe of the* for *myrþe of the ne comford*. The other manuscripts must therefore go back to an external archetype from which GiL also descends, and are not derived from GiL.

The 'addition' in Wh at 22 is probably original and omitted by an ancestor of the others, since it is in B, while 58 *children* for *chosen* indicates that Wh cannot be an ancestor, as does the addition at 192 of *in þe botme of þe watir*, which is not in B. Wh also contains a series of chapter headings, probably original, which the other manuscripts variously discard, though a few have survived down to GiL, in some cases having become incorporated in the prose of the text. At 421 HbWh correctly read *conuerte*, which is *converte* in the Vita, for DoHc and GiL *comforte*; likewise, the HbWh addition at 380 of *after the name of his sone* corresponds to Genesis and is probably original. Numerous other HbWh links in the apparatus confirm this relationship.

Several substantial omissions in Hc show that none of the others could have derived from it even before it lost much of its original central section, such as at 453–4, 499–500, 543–5; Do has rather less extensive omissions, as at 14, 47–8, and 104. DoHc have minor agreements, such as 354 omission of *nat* and 523 *kinde* for *kinrede*, which are suggestive rather than conclusive, and Do shares some readings with GiL, notably 549 *wrecchidnes* for HbWhHc *schrewidnesse*, so that any pairing within Hc, Do and GiL would be uncertain.

On this slender basis the following stemma is proposed:

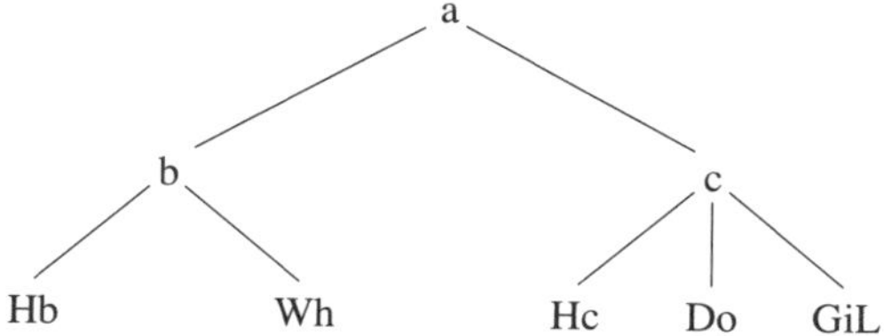

Relationships among the running GiL manuscripts are as usual (see p. 30 above). A small number of minor DL agreements where E agrees with the extraneous manuscripts probably result from the tendency to contamination by correction in L's exemplar (above, pp. 31–3), and some five minor agreements of L and Do in *Adam* and a further eight in *Five Wiles* can probably be similarly explained.

Five Wiles, in addition to the complete versions in L, A2, and Do, and in Hb which has lost one folio, is found in Cb and Ha; but in Ha only the first 126 lines survive. Two other manuscripts contain selections, Ca having two passages linked but in reverse order, and Ya two in different parts of the manuscript. These both have individual variants, Ya at 20, 21, Ca at 35, 44, 48, 52–4, and are closer to Hb than to any other manuscript; for Ya, see 1, 327, for Ca 44, 55. Ha has no very clear links with any other; HbHaCa agree at 46–7, 62, and HbHa share some omissions, as at 41, 52. Ha is not the source of any other, having 100–2 omission, 114 addition, 120 variant.

Since no source has been identified for *Five Wiles*, it is often impossible to decide which variants are original; Cb has numerous individual readings, a few of which are simple copying errors (258–9 *ignoraunt* for *I graunte*), but in many cases they are as likely to be original as those in the other manuscripts. Cases such as the omission at 136–7 eliminate Cb as a source of any other. However, the longest and most striking of Cb's variants, the additions at 397 and 460, certainly give the impression of being original rather than later additions. CbHb share variants, e.g. at 213 and 236 and omissions at 154–6. Hb has individual variants, such as 121–2, and an omission at 208–9, and Do at 30, 235, 392, and an omission at 474. There are no specific instances which prove that none of the others was copied from GiL, but equally none that suggest they were, and the comparable relationships in Adam with Hb and Do make the latter extremely unlikely. There are no apparently unoriginal readings shared by Do and GiL.

For the originally complete copies the following stemma is suggested:

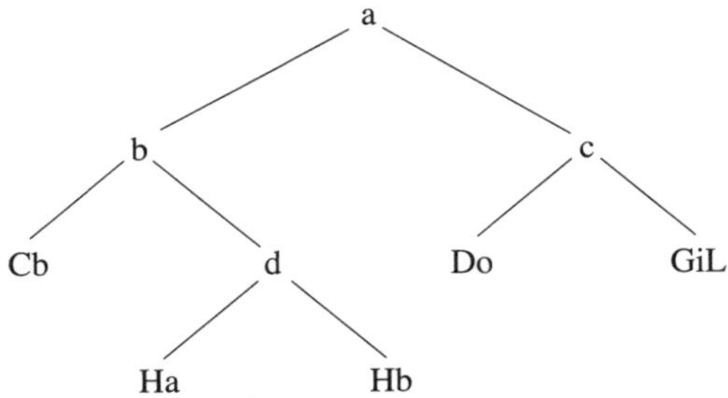

6. LANGUAGE

The spellings in the manuscripts generally seem to be typical of the south midlands and the region around London. *LALME* allocates E to Herts on the basis of a passage near the end written by Hand B, and H2 to Surrey using Horstmann's edition of *Adam and Eve*.[32] The latter localization is in fact more relevant to Hand D of MS D, since Ricardus Franciscus, the scribe of H2, was copying MS D almost literatim.[33] The only other manuscript of GiL whose language has been studied in any detail is A2, written in two hands, both of which contain a few spellings, but not the same ones in each hand, that might suggest a south-western, possibly Devon, origin.[34] But in view of the discrepancy between the south-western forms found and the general prevalence of forms typical of the home counties, it may be thought more likely that the two scribes were working from a south-western exemplar and variously eliminating some of its characteristic spellings.

The vocabulary of GiL exhibits a number of items of interest, having been available to *MED* only from the one or two chapters which had previously been edited, and from slips compiled by Sr Mary Jeremy from a reproduction of A2, a manuscript from which unusual forms and words tend to have been eliminated and more

[32] *LALME*, iii. 176, LP 6540 for E; iii. 497, LP 5770 for H2; Horstmann, 'Nachträge zu den Legenden'.

[33] For discussion of some of D's spellings, see Hamer, 'Spellings . . . of Ricardus Franciscus'.

[34] Hamer, 'Significance of Some Spellings'.

common ones substituted. GiL contains numerous words which are either unrecorded in *MED* or rare. Many of them are anglicized versions of the French, a few are technical terms not so far found in other texts, others merely extend the morphological possibilities of the language.

Among the many words taken directly from the French, conspicuous examples, some of which do not even attempt to conceal their French morphology, are *bruit*, *escrivans*, *forciblement*, *gendre*, *glorifiant*, *ioyouste*, *participans*, *pointerie*, *tesmonage*, *veynquor*; and s.w. recovered *bufones*, for which Vignay substituted the unexplained *botereaux*, directly from the Latin. Accurate specialist terms include *augustien* and *cesarien*, *azimes*, *mathesis*, *odoramenta*, *prunelles*, *solucion*, *sophistiques*, *supersubstanciel*, *vendeged*. Words with otherwise so far unrecorded morphological extensions are numerous, as one would expect in such a long work, such as *bemyred*, *childisnes*, *desiringly*, *enquirable*, *follissnesse*, *gerdonable*, *mellyngly*, *outragiousnes*, *sacrifisable*, *tariengly*, *vnagreabulte*, *vncondempnithe*. Details of these and other unusual words and usages are recorded at the appropriate point in the notes.

7. DATE AND PLACE OF THE TRANSLATION

The only precise evidence for the date of the translation is the 1438 given in the colophon to MS D quoted above. The extant manuscripts date from the middle of the fifteenth century or later. Kurvinen showed that the substituted version of *Catherine* was apparently put together before the death of Henry V in 1422.[35]

There is even less evidence for localization. The spellings and language of the manuscripts generally suggest the south midlands and the area around London, with no signs of northern or western provenance, except for a few spellings of possible south-western origin in two of the later manuscripts, A1 and A2, but it would be impossible to deduce the translator's dialect from the surviving copies, which all seem to be at several removes from the original.

One factor suggesting a probable place of origin is the insertion of an extremely long life of *Alban*, which seems likely either to have been compiled specially or inserted from an existing version because of some association with St Albans Abbey. Other accounts of St Alban,

[35] Thesis, 216.

such as those by the monk William, Matthew Paris, and John Lydgate, were either written at St Albans or at the instance of that house, and the same may well be the case here.[36]

8. CHARACTERISTICS OF THE TRANSLATION

Legenda Aurea, since it contains a wide diversity of types of subject matter and is derived, sometimes very directly, from numerous sources, is written in a variety of styles. Vignay, a hospitaller at the convent of St Jacques du Haut Pas in Paris, devoted his life to translating, a number of his works being commissioned by members of the royal family.[37] In most of these he was, in the words of Christine Knowles, 'assez médiocre', and 'un traducteur d'une fidelité extrême', which latter, indeed, in the Prologue to his translation of Vegetius's *De re militari*, he stated to be his intention. Knowles gives examples of Vignay's not infrequent errors, such as translation of *os* as *bouche* even when the context clearly requires *visage*, confusion of similar words such as *correptus* and *corruptus*, and failures to identify cases of nouns, tenses of verbs, and agreements of adjectives, and she notes that some of his mistranslations show him to have been ignorant in areas such as geography, history, and mythology.[38] Paul Meyer describes his LgD as 'un mot à mot inintelligent et dépourvu de style'.[39] Despite these shortcomings, his translations survive in numerous manuscripts, many of them of high quality and having belonged to royal and ducal libraries, and in due course appearing in print, in the case of LgD many times.[40]

[36] For further discussion, especially with reference to the provenance of H1, see Tracy, 'British Library MS Harley 630', and for a particular suggestion see below, pp. 52–6.

[37] But not this one, according to the rather disjointed statement in his own Prologue, *quant ie oi parfait le mireour des hystoires du monde & translatai de latin en francois, a la requeste de tres haute poissant & noble dame Madame iehanne de borgoigne roine de france par la grace de dieu, Ie fui tout esbahi a quel oeure faire ie me metroie . . . Et pour ce que il mest auis que ce est souuerain bien que de faire entendre as gens qui ne sont pas lectres . . . me sui ie mis a translater en francois La legende des sains qui est dite legende doree* (from P1). As a result of careless reading of the above, several of the later manuscripts including P2 have an additional preliminary passage incorrectly stating that the translation of LgD was made at the request of the queen, and these in turn have misled some recent writers, including myself, into the same mistake. See Knowles, 365–6; Hamer, 'From Vignay's *Légende dorée* to the Earliest Printed Editions', 71 n. 2.

[38] Knowles, 372–8.

[39] Meyer, 'Notice du MS Med. Pal.141 de la Laurentienne', 6.

[40] Dunn-Lardeau and Coq, 'Fifteenth- and Sixteenth-Century Editions of the *Légende dorée*'.

In translating LgD, s.w. likewise stayed in general very close to the original, often translating a French word by its anglicized equivalent rather than substituting a more commonly available word, and following fairly closely Vignay's word order even in sentences which would have benefitted from simplification or adjustment, and sometimes translating French idioms verbatim. Despite the clear evidence that s.w. had available a copy of LgA and made some use of it to correct LgD, as recorded in many cases in the notes in this volume, there remain a substantial number of uncorrected instances where the text of LgD seems so obviously wrong that one would have expected a translator with the Latin to hand to have corrected them. Misreadings by Vignay such as *oderant* for *aderant*, *geminatam* for *gemmatam*, *Iudeorum* for *inuidorum* (123.239, 114.6, 132.5) are duly followed by s.w. with strange results, and it is hard to believe that either translator could have made much sense of some of their own work, such as the sentence which has lost its negative at 84.305. Nor does s.w. fail to add to these inherited errors in various ways, such as by misreading a French word, or by choosing the wrong sense of a word with alternative meanings. Among the more extreme errors are: 101.3 *true kunnynge* for *science de droit*, *iuris scientiam*, 106.24 *of laughynge* for *deresie*, *heretica*, 175.52 *in wepinge* for *en plurier*, *in plurali*. Other examples will be found in the notes.

As stated above, several chapters of LgA and LgD are omitted from GiL. Whether these omissions were deliberate or the result of absence from the copy of LgD used is impossible to tell, but however that may be, in all these cases s.w. chose not to replace them from the LgA exemplar. In addition, quite substantial portions of some of the longer chapters were omitted, presumably deliberately, such as several miracles in 58 *Peter Martyr*, three stories in 1 *Andrew*, passages at the end of 12 *Circumcision* and 138 *Michael*, and sections of 117 *Augustine*, 106 *Dominic*, and 110 *Lawrence*; but in 161 *Elizabeth* a section which must have been lacking in the LgD manuscript used for GiL has been inserted later in the chapter, s.w. having translated it from the Latin.

In style the prose of GiL generally follows LgD, and is therefore simple and direct in narrative sections; but where the language is complex, as in passages of ratiocination or dialectic derived ultimately from Voragine's Latin sources, little or no attempt is made to disentangle it. Contributions by s.w. consist of the introduction of a number of doublets, sometimes explanatory but mostly stylistic, and the addition of affective adjectives, prisons being foul, torturers cruel, pits deep, and so on, and many other small additions, such as adverbs and adverbial phrases, designed to explain difficulties or to clarify or make a passage more vivid.

Perhaps the most striking feature is what may be called s.w.'s 'dramatic' tendency, a practice of enlivening speeches by adding introductory interjections or vocatives and other means: 17.9 *Allas*; 95.75 *Benedicite*; 165.696 *O thou most fole*; 173.462 *Sir kinge*; 124.86 *Truly my dere brother and suster*; 23.53 *I tell the pleinly*; 173.87–8 *Now dothe after my counsaile*; 164.8–9 *But this greuithe me sore*; 173.250 *Holde me excused*; 6.56 *Nay, thou hast misvnderstonde*; and many others.

9. THE TRANSLATOR

We must hope that the name of the 'synfulle wrecche' who, according to the D colophon (above, p. 2) translated and compiled GiL, has indeed been 'written in the boke of everlastinge life', but it is unlikely to become known for certain in this one. The only previously suggested candidate, Osbern Bokenham, a friar from Clare Priory and author of various works including a collection of *Legendys of Hooly Wummen*,[41] can now be dismissed. In his *Mappula Angliae*, Bokenham described a legendary he had 'compiled of legenda aurea and of oþer famous legendes', which he said contained many saints of England, including 'seynt Cedde, seynt Felix, seynt Edwarde, seynt Oswalde'. Carl Horstmann raised the possibility that this missing legendary was GiL, but then rejected it because he knew of no copy which included these lives.[42] Subsequent identification of A1 and A2 as copies of GiL containing a number of added English lives led to a tentative revival of Bokenham's claim by Sr M. Jeremy, but this was refuted convincingly by M. Görlach,[43] whose arguments have been vindicated by the identification in 2005 in Sir Walter Scott's library at Abbotsford House of a manuscript of a legendary based on LgA which also contains the lives named in the *Mappula* and other additional lives, including those from Bokenham's *Legendys of*

[41] ed. Serjeantson.

[42] Horstmann (ed.), 'Mappula Angliae von Osbern Bokenham', 5.

[43] M. Jeremy, Sr. 'The English Prose Translation of *Legenda Aurea*', and 'Caxton and the Synfulle Wretche', 427–8; Görlach (1972), 83–6, repeated in (1998), 133–5.

Hooly Wummen. The first hand of this manuscript is the same as that of BL Add. MS 11814, a copy of Claudian, *De consulatu Stiliconis* with translation, whose colophon states that it was written and translated at Clare in 1445, so that identification of the Abbotsford manuscript as the missing Bokenham legendary seems beyond doubt.[44]

A different account of GiL's composition is given at the end of H1, which concludes with 166 *Saturnine*, omitting the final thirteen chapters, and ends with the words *Here endeth the boke of the life of Seintes called in latyn legenda aurea compiled and drawen into englissh bi worthi clerkes and doctours of Diuinite suengly aftre the tenure of þe Latin*. The periphrastic avoidance of saying that it was translated from Latin is presumably deliberate, and perhaps refers to the corrections in GiL from the Latin mentioned above. In writing these words the scribe appears to envisage translation by a number of clerks and doctors, which is clearly at variance with the claim for single translation in the D colophon, and as it stands can scarcely mean simply that a number of learned men are responsible for the corrections. It seems best to regard it as an uninformed guess.

If we accept the D assertion of single authorship, all we can add about the translator must be derived from impressions in the text itself.

In addition to the stylistic traits mentioned in the preceding section, another characteristic of the translator is a tendency to use euphemisms, such as: 3.48–9 *siche oon as thou arte* and 86.58 *wicked woman* for *putain*; 93.223 and 140.49 *membres* and 173.409 *menbris* for *genitaires* and *membres dont il les engendra*; 133.18–19 *one of the kepers* for *vn chastre* (*eunuchum* LgA); 77.21 *had gote her with childe* for *lavoit corrumpue* (*se violasse* LgA); 135.79 *went to bedde to her* for *sailly desuergondeement ou lit*; 174.68 *misused* for *auoit charnellement a faire a*; 127.61 *praied hym to fulfell her wreched desire* for *luy pria quil couchast auecques luy charnelment*. GiL also omits at 106.195 the demon's statement that he gives the friars impure thoughts, and at 171.57 an account of a friar who covers his hands with his mantle while carrying his old mother across a river because touching her would provoke thoughts of other women. Such euphemisms and omissions perhaps suggest that the translator could have been a woman, as do occasional

[44] Horobin, 'A Manuscript Found in the Library of Abbotsford House'; for BL Add. MS 11814, see Watson, *Catalogue of Dated and Datable Manuscripts in the . . . British Library*, no. 63, p. 33.

additions of women to the text where they might be thought to have been gratuitously left out in LgD, such as 75.19 *and the moder*, 104.101 *and his wyff*, 173.304 *and my doughter*.

The only female English translator so far identified within this period is Dame Eleanor Hull, whose translation from the French of a *Commentary on the Penitential Psalms*,[45] as its recent editor writes, 'was probably made during the 1420s, after Dame Eleanor was widowed and while she was living, at least from time to time, at Sopwell Priory, a house of Benedictine nuns dependent upon the great Benedictine Abbey of St Albans' (p. xiv), though a later date is not excluded: 'She had completed her translations of *The Seven Psalms* and the *Meditations upon the Seven Days of the Week* before 1449–54 when Richard Fox, the steward of St Albans, had them copied into CUL MS Kk. 1. 6' (p. xxxi). Eleanor, née Malet, belonged to a substantial family who had held their estate at Enmore near Bridgewater in Somerset since shortly after the Conquest; her father had been a retainer of Henry Bolingbroke and later of John of Gaunt, and her husband was a retainer probably of Henry IV and certainly of Henry V, in each case involved in important ambassadorial work. She herself was from 1417 a servant of Queen Joan of Navarre, widow of Henry IV, and received significant income from St Albans Abbey under an agreement with the queen, and was admitted to the confraternity of the abbey in the same year. She took up residence at Sopwell Priory probably shortly after her husband's death in 1420 or 1421, and it seems to have been her main residence till about 1456, in which year she made the last of a number of recorded gifts by herself and members of her family to the abbey. However, when she made her will in October 1458 she was apparently living in the Benedictine Priory at Cannington in Somerset, two or three miles from her family estate. She died about the end of 1460.

While there is no evidence to identify Dame Eleanor with s.w., the above sketch shows that she would have been perfectly capable of this translation, and appears to have been at the right place at the right time. Other small and inconclusive facts can also be fitted into this putative attribution. The life of St Catherine in GiL is one of those for which a somewhat different version has been substituted, and as Kurvinen (Thesis, 216) showed, this was probably compiled early in

[45] *The Seven Psalms, a commentary on the Penitential Psalms translated by Dame Eleanor Hull*, ed. Barratt; for a detailed account of her career see pp. xxiii–xxxiii.

the 1420s, possibly with reference to the marriage of Henry V to Catherine of France in 1420, since one manuscript of version *d* of this life (see above, p. 40), contains the statement that it (the version rather than the manuscript) was sent to Henry V, who died in 1422. In her will Dame Eleanor requests 'that the almes of my lytel pursis be continued as long as is lefte eny good, that is to seye, vij*d* in worship of Seynt Kateryn and vij*d* to poure folkes'. Someone with a special interest in St Catherine might well have decided to substitute what they regarded as a better version of the life, or even one which they had themselves previously compiled; but it has to be said that Catherine was among the most popular saints in England at this time.[46]

Another coincidence, though interesting, may carry even less weight. Among Dame Eleanor's gifts to St Albans was one made in 1456 jointly with Roger Huswyf, a lawyer and later priest with whom she was associated in many of her dealings, consisting of a four-volume copy of the *Postillae* of Nicholas de Lyra written by the scribe Stephen Dodesham (now CUL MSS Dd. 7. 7–10).[47] As it happens, one of the GiL manuscripts, H1, which had been copied with a substantial lacuna, has had this omission replaced by insertion of a leaf written by Dodesham. Spellings of H1's main scribe, using criteria from *LALME*, suggest Hertfordshire, and Larissa Tracy's investigations indicate that the volume was in the St Albans area later in the century, making one wonder whether Dodesham might have supplied the replacement while in the vicinity working on the *Postillae*.[48]

It may also be significant that 'At some time during his first abbacy (1420–1440) John Whethamstede gave Eleanor Hull a silver cup worth £6. 13s. 4d. and another worth £3. 6s. 8d.'[49]

As well as the *Commentary on the Penitential Psalms*, Dame Eleanor translated a set of *Meditations on the days of the week*, both of which works are uniquely found in CUL MS Kk.1.6, written between 1449 and 1454 at St Albans. No source has been identified close enough to the *Commentary* to make possible a study of Dame Eleanor's translating practices, but Alexandra Barratt succeeded by combining the variously incomplete manuscript versions of the French source of

[46] Lewis, *The Cult of St Katherine of Alexandria*, esp. 40–4.
[47] Doyle, 'Stephen Dodesham of Witham and Sheen', 104.
[48] Tracy, 'British Library MS Harley 630'.
[49] *Seven Psalms*, ed. Barratt, p. xxxii.

the *Meditations* in making it possible to do so for that text. In a study of the style and translating techniques of the author she records the following characteristics.[50]

Whereas French gives pronouns gender on a purely grammatical basis, ME generally does so biologically; Dame Eleanor retains the French feminine gender in pronouns for *mescine*, 'sickness', *misericorde*, *mort*, and *huile* (the last of which had been treated as a feminine in one of the French manuscripts). In GiL many such gendered pronouns are found, including feminine for subjects as varied as a dish 45.39–41, pestilence 45.133, a wheel 48.82–3, St Paul's head 84.139, St Paul's tongue 84.499–500, patience 84.334, the flesh of Jesus 112.909–10, a dinner-table 142.119–20, an eclipse 146.28–9, a shrine 151.153; and masculine for a sound 65.234–9, money 95.109, a beak 149.51, a tree 159.144–8.

Like any translator of the period, Eleanor would often have been confronted by a French word for which an anglicized cognate was available as well as a word of English derivation. Barratt lists numerous examples of the use of each type, observing: 'She keeps a balance here, so that her text is neither uncomfortably Gallicized nor ostentatiously Germanic.' GiL shows the same sort of overall mixture, but perhaps tends more towards the Gallic, having, for example, a number of French-derived words which are shown by *MED* to have been rare, and sometimes are not recorded there at all. On the other hand, s.w. was more inclined to 'change' a word than was, for example, Caxton, though in some cases it was to a more familiar word of French derivation rather than to an 'English' one, as *chastite* for *continence*, *myght departe* for *distribueroit*, *priuily* for *secretement*.[51] For other examples of conspicuous French importations see p. 47 above.

A greater impression of gallicization is given in GiL by occasional adoptions of French syntactical constructions, such as 4.118 *examplis sensiblis*, 116.245 *remedies medicinables*, 171.81 *cisterne perced*, 2.15 *doughtres virgines*, 13.54 *citee riall*, 25.61 *a doughter only*, 28.29–31 *an eyre male*, 161.6 *delices reals*, but Barratt does not record instances of this sort.

Among expansions of the text Barratt includes two categories which, in her words, 'add nothing to the content but raise the emotional temperature'. The first of these is the addition of rather

[50] Barratt, 'Dame Eleanor Hull: The Translator at Work'.

[51] For a fuller account see *Three Lives from the Gilte Legende*, 21–2.

obvious adjectives of the type which has already been recorded above as appearing in GiL, *precyous blode*, *foule synnes*, *a bryght sterre*, etc. The second is the use of doublets, which are often mere synonyms, as *wykkydnes and foly*, *soryful and grevous*, *no stabilnes nor no suerte*, though sometimes they may have an explanatory purpose or introduce an additional sense, as with *lyghtly and corantly*, *so feyntful and so bitter*, *disawary or in dout*, each of which three examples, as it happens, includes a word unrecorded in *MED* which does not quite mean the same as its partner. As can be seen from the notes to this edition, examples of these sorts of doublet abound in GiL.

Sometimes such doublets add a moral significance, as with 43.143 addition of *wrecchid errour and* before *custume*, and sometimes such expansions are more substantial: 2.26–7 *hadde schewed to hym so gret charitee and hym brought oute of so gret mischeeff* for *auoit aidie a sa pourete*, as well as a large number of more basic pious additions, as 50.370 *moued by grace*. Other additions add substantially to the vividness of the action: 42.42–3 she *made as sche toke no hede of his crie but*; 50.498–9 *they toke hym away and bere hym ferre and threwe hym and* added before *plonged hym in a depe pitte*. There are also more plainly explanatory examples: 49.145 *that is to saye of a body sette before the light*. These longer additions are in line with similar ones cited by Barratt, 291: *and þat owyth euery cristyn man believe*; and *þat is to sey, lyght, mete, and medycyne*.

In her introductory statement to the *Meditations* Dame Eleanor says that their motive is *for-to enflawme the hert and the corage of hem that redyn it in the love of God and for-to make a man to know hym self*.[52] The introductory paragraph to GiL, which survives only in H2, rather similarly explains that the object of the work is *to excite and stere symple lettrid men and women to encrese in vertue bi the often redinge and hiringe of this boke. For bi hiringe mannes bileuinge is mooste stablid and istrengthid*. These both appear to be additions by the translator, who seems to favour supplying an edificatory justification which in neither case is found in the French.

Furthermore, the *Commentary on the Seven Psalms* begins with the words *Ihesu Cryst most mercyful, haue mercy on me sinful and helpe me as hyt is nedful*, not unreminiscent of the self-description as a *synfulle wrecche* in the GiL colophon, and I am grateful to Alexandra Barratt for the further information that on f. 148^{v} of the translation of the *Meditations* the meditator refers to 'me, synfull wrech full of syn'. But

[52] Barratt, 'Dame Eleanor Hull', 278–9.

again, one must acknowledge that such self-deprecations were not uncommon at the time.

The features discussed can of course be found in other writers of the period; the best one can say is that the practices of Eleanor and s.w. seem to have much in common. Finally one could add that the *Commentary* by its nature contains numerous quotations given in Latin, some of which are translated. In the absence of a precise source one cannot tell whether these had already been translated in the French, but in any case Dame Eleanor must, like s.w., have had some proficiency in these two languages.

This suggested identification can thus be presented as a possibility, but in view of the lack of solid evidence, no more. In short, s.w. seems to have been someone connected with St Albans, who was competent in French and Latin, and inserted into GiL substitutions of two chapters and additions of five more, which may have been simply available locally for insertion, or may have been earlier or *ad hoc* compilations or translations by s.w. which seemed suitable. Support for the idea that some lives may have been individually translated or compiled before GiL as a whole was embarked on is offered by the final paragraph of 117 *Augustine* 453–9, which is not in LgD or LgA and begins: *Mani a noble and glorious miracle this holy seint dede . . . whiche were to longe to be wretin in this litell volume for it conteynith more thanne alle this boke, wherfor y leue atte this tyme . . .* One could scarcely call *Gilte Legende* as a whole a *litell volume*, which suggests that this life may have been previously translated as a separate item and written in its own booklet. It is hard to see, however, that the last two chapters, *Adam and Eve* and *Five Wiles of Pharaoh*, are particularly suitable additions to GiL; possibly they were compilations which s.w. had previously made on broadly related subjects, and therefore included, along with the more appropriate *Conception*, in a sort of personal anthology.

BIBLIOGRAPHY

The bibliography is selective and limited to works directly related to the present edition and to a small number of the most important recent works on LgA and LgD. For fuller bibliographies, particularly dealing with the earlier and Continental developments, see especially Brenda Dunn-Lardeau's edition of *Légende dorée* and Barbara Fleith's study of the LgA manuscripts listed below. Voragine's sources are listed in detail in Maggioni's editions.

Text of Legenda Aurea

Jacobi a Voragine Legenda Aurea vulgo Historia Lombardica dicta ad optimorum librorum fidem recensuit, ed. T. Graesse (1st edn., Dresden, 1846; 2nd edn., Leipzig, 1850; 3rd edn., Breslau, 1890; *reproductio phototypica*, Osnabruck, 1969).

Iacopo da Varazze: Legenda Aurea, edizione critica, ed. Giovanni Paolo Maggioni, 2 vols. (2nd edn., Florence, 1999).

Iacopo da Varazze: Legenda Aurea, con le miniature dal codice Ambrosiano C 240 inf., con traduzione italiana coordinata da Francesco Stella, ed. Giovanni Paolo Maggioni, 2 vols. (Florence, 2007).

Modern Translations of Legenda Aurea

Apart from those by Boureau and Stella, the translations listed are all based on Graesse's edition. For a fuller list of translations, including selections, see the bibliography in Stace, pp. xxxiii–xxxiv.

Iacopo da Varazze: Legenda Aurea, con le miniature dal codice Ambrosiano C 240 inf., con traduzione italiana coordinata da Francesco Stella, ed. Giovanni Paolo Maggioni, 2 vols. (Florence, 2007).

Jacobus de Voragine: The Golden Legend, Readings in the Saints, trans. William Granger Ryan, 2 vols. (Princeton, 1993).

Jacobus de Voragine: The Golden Legend: Selections, trans. Christopher Stace (Harmondsworth, 1998).

Jacques de Voragine: La Légende dorée, trans. Alain Boureau (Bibliothèque de la Pléiade; Paris, 2004).

Die Legenda Aurea des Jacobus de Voragine aus dem lateinische übersetzt, trans. R. Benz (Jena, 1917; 9th edn., Heidelberg, 1979).

La Légende dorée de Jacques de Voragine nouvellement traduite en français, trans. J.-B. M. Roze (Paris, 1902; reissued in 2 vols. without original Introduction, Paris, 1967).

Texts of Légende Dorée

Hamer, Richard, and Russell, Vida, 'Four Chapters from the Légende dorée', *Mediaeval Studies*, 51 (1989), 130–204 (contains Nicholas, George, Bartholomew, and All Saints).

Jacques de Voragine: La Légende dorée, ed. Brenda Dunn-Lardeau (Paris, 1997).

Texts of Gilte Legende

Barlaam and Josaphat: A Transcription of MS Egerton 876 with Notes, Glossary and Comparative Study of the Middle English and Japanese Versions, ed. Keiko Ikegami (New York, 1999).

Barlaam and Josaphat, eine Prosaversion aus MS Egerton 876 fol. 301, ed. Carl Horstmann (Sagan, 1877).

Horstmann, Carl, 'Nachträge zu den Legenden', *Archiv*, 74 (1885), 353–65 (contains Adam and Eve).

The Life of St Catherine of Alexandria in Middle English Prose, ed. Auvo Kurvinen (D.Phil. thesis, Oxford University, 1960).

Rösler, M., 'Die Fassung der Alexius-legende', *Wiener Beiträge zur Kulturgeschichte und Linguistik*, 21 (1905), 113–17.

Supplementary Lives in Some Manuscripts of Gilte Legende, ed. Richard Hamer and Vida Russell, EETS 315 (2000).

Three Lives from the Gilte Legende, ed. Richard Hamer (Middle English Texts, 9; Heidelberg, 1978) (contains Nicholas, George, and Bartholomew).

The Wheatley Manuscript, ed. Mabel Day, EETS OS 155 (1921) (contains Adam and Eve).

Zupitza, Julius, 'Das Leben der heiligen Maria Magdalena', *Archiv*, 91 (1893), 207–24.

Other Primary Sources

Barlam and Iosaphat: A Middle English Life of Buddha Edited from MS Peterhouse 257, ed. J. C. Hirsh, EETS 290 (1986).

Capgrave, John, *Ye Solace of Pilgrims*, ed. C. A. Mills (London, 1911).

Deonise Hid Diuinite, ed. P. Hodgson, EETS 231 (1955).

The Gardyners Passetaunce, ed. F. B. Williams, Jr with notes by H. M. Nixon (Roxburghe Club, 1985).

Garmonsway, G. N., and Raymo, R. R., 'A Middle-English Prose Life of St Ursula', *RES* NS 9 (1958), 353–61.

Gregory the Great, *Moralia in Job*, ed. M. Adriaen, i (CCSL 143; Turnhout, 1979).

Hurter, H. (ed.), 'The Text of the *Vitae patrum*', in *Sanctorum Patrum Opuscula Selecta*, 49 (Innsbruck, 1885), 259–72, repr. in William Abbott

Oldfather (ed.), *Studies in the Text Tradition of St Jerome's* Vitae patrum (Urbana, Ill., 1943), 36–64.

Jean de Mailly, *Abrégé des gestes et miracles des saints*, trans. A. Dondaine (Paris, 1947).

John Lydgate, The Life of Saint Alban and Saint Amphibal, ed. J. E. van der Westhuizen (Leiden, 1974).

Love, Nicholas, *The Mirror of the Blessed Life of Jesus Christ, a Full Critical Edition*, ed. Michael G. Sargent (Exeter, 2005).

Mozley, J. H., 'The Vita Adae', *JTS* 30 (1929), 121–47.

Osbern Bokenham: Legendys of Hooly Wummen, ed. M. S. Serjeantson, EETS 206 (1938).

Pettorelli, J. P., 'La Vie latine d'Adam et Eve', *Archivium Latinitatis Medii Aevi*, 56 (1998), 5–104 and 57 (1999), 5–52.

Pseudo-Matthaei Evangelium textus et commentarius cura Jan Gijsel, Libellus de Nativitate Sanctae Mariae textus et commentarius cura Rita Beyers (Corpus Christianorum Series Apocryphum, 10; Turnhout, 1997).

The St Alban's Chronicle, ed. V. H. Galbraith (Oxford, 1937).

Saint Albon and Saint Amphibalus by John Lydgate, ed. G. F. Reinecke (New York and London, 1985).

St Katherine of Alexandria: The Late Middle English Prose Legend in Southwell Minster MS 7, ed. Saara Nevanlinna and Irma Taavitsainen (Cambridge, 1993).

The Seven Psalms, a Commentary on the Penitential Psalms Translated by Dame Eleanor Hull, ed. Alexandra Barratt, EETS 307 (1995).

Sulpicius Severus, *Gallus: Dialogues sur les "vertus" de Saint Martin / Sulpice Sévère*, ed. Jacques Fontaine (Sources chrétiennes, 510; Paris, 2006).

—— *Vie de Saint Martin*, ed. Jacques Fontaine (Sources chrétiennes, 133–5; Paris, 1967–9).

Talamo Atenolfi, G., *I testi medioevali degli Atti di S. Matteo l'Evangelista* (Rome, 1958).

Three Alliterative Saints' Hymns, ed. Ruth Kennedy, EETS 321 (2003).

Three Fifteenth-Century Chronicles, ed. J. Gairdner (Camden Society Publications, NS 28; London 1880).

Waters, Claire M., *Virgins and Scholars: A Fifteenth-Century Compilation of the Lives of John the Baptist, John the Evangelist, Jerome and Katherine of Alexandria* (Turnhout, 2008).

Secondary Sources and Studies

Barratt, Alexandra, 'Dame Eleanor Hull: The Translator at Work', *MÆ* 72 (2003), 277–96.

Bishop, Edmund, *Liturgica Historica: Papers on the Liturgy and Religious Life of the Western Church* (Oxford, 1918).

Blake, N. F., *Caxton's own Prose* (London, 1973).

Boffey, Julia, and Thompson, John J., 'Anthologies and Miscellanies: Production and Choice of Texts', in J. Griffiths and D. Pearsall (eds.), *Book Production and Publishing in Britain 1375–1475* (Cambridge, 1989), 279–315.

Boureau, A., *La Légende dorée: Le système narratif de Jacques de Voragine* (Paris, 1984).

Braswell, Laurel, *The Index of Middle English Prose Handlist IV: A Handlist of Manuscripts Containing Middle English Prose in the Douce Collection, Bodleian Library, Oxford* (Cambridge, 1987).

Brown, Peter, and Higgs, Elton D., *The Index of Middle English Prose Handlist V: A Handlist of Manuscripts Containing Middle English Prose in the Additional Collection (10001–14000), British Library, London* (Cambridge, 1988).

Burton, T. L., 'Drudgery, Bludgery and Fludgery: Lexicography for Editors of Middle English Texts', in T. L. and Jill Burton (eds.), *Lexicographical and Linguistic Studies: Essays in Honour of G. W. Turner* (Cambridge, 1988), 19–30.

Butler, Pierce, *Legenda Aurea—Légende Dorée—Golden Legend* (Baltimore, 1899).

Cassan, Stephen Hyde, *Lives of the Bishops of Winchester from Birinus, the First bishop of the West Saxons, to the Present Time*, 2 vols. (London, 1827).

de Hamel, Christopher, 'Phillipps Fragments in Tokyo', in Takami Matsuda, Richard A. Linenthal, and John Scahill (eds.), *The Medieval Book and a Modern Collector: Essays in Honour of Toshiyuki Takamiya* (Cambridge, 2004), 19–44.

D'Evelyn, Charlotte, 'Saints' Legends', in J. Burke Severs (ed.), *A Manual of the Writings in Middle English 1050–1500*, ii (Hamden, Conn., 1970), 410–57, 553–649.

Doyle, A. I., 'Stephen Dodesham of Witham and Sheen', in P. R. Robinson and Rivkah Zim (eds.), *Of the Making of Books: Medieval Manuscripts, their Scribes and Readers. Essays Presented to M. B. Parkes* (Aldershot, 1997), 94–115.

Dunn-Lardeau, Brenda, and Coq, D., 'Fifteenth- and Sixteenth-Century Editions of the *Légende dorée*', *Bibliothèque d'Humanisme et Renaissance*, 47 (1985), 87–101.

—— (ed.), *Legenda Aurea—la Légende dorée (XIIIe–XVe siècle). Actes du Congrès international de Perpignan* (Le Moyen Français, 32; Montreal, 1993).

—— (ed.), *Legenda Aurea: Sept siècles de diffusion* (Montreal, 1986).

Eldridge, L. M., *The Index of Middle English Prose Handlist IX: A Handlist of Manuscripts Containing Middle English Prose in the Ashmole Collection, Bodleian Library, Oxford* (Cambridge, 1992).

Faye, C. U., and Bond, W. H., *Supplement to the Census of Medieval Manuscripts in the United States and Canada* (New York, 1962).

Fleith, Barbara, *Studien zur Überlieferungsgeschichte der lateinischen Legenda Aurea* (Société des Bollandistes; Brussels, 1991).

—— and Morenzoni, Franco (eds.), *De la sainteté à l'hagiographie: Genèse et usage de la Légende dorée* (Publications romanes et françaises, 229; Geneva, 2001).

Görlach, Manfred, 'A Second Version of the Huntington Prose Legend of St Ursula', *RES* NS 24 (1973), 450–1.

—— *The South English Legendary, Gilte Legende and Golden Legend* (Brunswick, 1972) (revised and included in next item).

—— *Studies in Middle English Saints' Legends* (Anglistische Forschungen, 257; Heidelberg, 1998).

Gover, J. E. B., Mawer, Allen, and Stenton, F. M., *The Place-names of Hertfordshire* (English Place-name Society, 15; Cambridge, 1938).

Hamer, Richard, 'From Vignay's *Légende dorée* to the Earliest Printed Editions', in Dunn-Lardeau (ed.), *Legenda aurea—la Légende dorée*, 71–81.

—— 'Jean Golein's *Festes Nouvelles*: A Caxton Source', *MÆ* 55 (1986), 254–60.

—— 'The Significance of Some Spellings in British Library MS Additional 35298', in Katja Lenz and Ruth Möhlig (eds.), *Of dyuersite & chaunge of langage: Essays Presented to Manfred Görlach on the Occasion of his 65th Birthday* (Heidelberg, 2002), 353–63.

—— 'Spellings of the Fifteenth-Century Scribe Ricardus Franciscus', in E. G. Stanley and Douglas Gray (eds.), *Five Hundred Years of Words and Sounds: A Festschrift for Eric Dobson* (Cambridge, 1983), 63–73.

Hardy, T. D., *Descriptive Catalogue of MSS Relating to the Early History of Great Britain*, 4 vols. (RS; London, 1862–71), i, nos. 8–31.

Horobin, Simon, 'A Manuscript Found in the Library of Abbotsford House and the Lost Legendary of Osbern Bokenham', *English Manuscript Studies*, 14 (2008), 130–62.

Horstmann, C. (ed.), 'Mappula Angliae von Osbern Bokenham', *EStn* 10 (1887), 1–34.

James, M. R., *A Descriptive Catalogue of the Manuscripts in the Library of Corpus Christi College Cambridge*, i (Cambridge, 1912).

—— *A Descriptive Catalogue of the Manuscripts in the Library of Lambeth Palace: The Mediaeval Manuscripts* (Cambridge, 1932), 116–17.

—— *The Western Manuscripts in the Library of Trinity College, Cambridge: A Descriptive Catalogue*, iii (Cambridge, 1902).

—— and Jenkins, Claude, *A Descriptive Catalogue of the Manuscripts in the Library of Lambeth Palace* (Cambridge, 1930–2).

Jefferson, Lisa, *The Medieval Account Books of the Mercers of London*, 2 vols. (Aldershot, 2009).

Jefferson, Lisa, 'Two Fifteenth-Century Manuscripts of the Statutes of the Order of the Garter', *English Manuscript Studies 1100–1700*, 5 (1995), 18–35.

Jeremy, M., Sr., 'Caxton and the Synfulle Wretche', *Traditio*, 4 (1946), 423–8.

—— 'The English Prose Translation of *Legenda Aurea*', *MLN* 59 (1944), 181–3.

Keiser, G. R., 'Patronage and Piety in Fifteenth-Century England: Margaret, Duchess of Clarence, Symon Wynter and Beinecke MS 317', *Yale University Library Gazette*, 60 (1985) 32–46.

Ker, N. R., 'Archbishop Sancroft's Rearrangement of the Manuscripts of Lambeth Palace', in E. G. W. Bill (ed.), *A Catalogue of Manuscripts in Lambeth Palace Library: MSS 1222–1860* (Oxford, 1971), 1–51.

—— *Medieval Manuscripts in British Libraries*, ii: *Abbotsford-Keele* (Oxford, 1977).

Knowles, Christine, 'Jean de Vignay, un traducteur français du XIVe siècle', *Romania*, 75 (1954), 353–83.

Kurvinen, Auvo, 'Caxton's *Golden Legend* and the Manuscripts of the *Gilte Legende*', *NM* 60 (1959), 353–75.

Lancashire, Ian, 'Law and Modern English Lexicons', in R. W. McConchie et al. (eds.), *Selected Proceedings of the 2005 Symposium on New Approaches in English Historical Lexis* (Somerville, Mass., 2006), 8–23.

Lewis, Katherine, *The Cult of St Katherine of Alexandria in Late Medieval England* (Woodbridge, 2000).

McLeod, W., 'Alban and Amphibal: Some Extant Lives and a Lost Life', *Medieval Studies*, 42 (1980), 407–30.

Maggioni, Giovanni Paolo, *Ricerche sulla composizione e sulla trasmissione della Legenda Aurea* (Spoleto, 1995).

Meyer, Paul, 'Notice du MS Med. Pal.141 de la Laurentienne', *Romania*, 33 (1904), 1–49.

Mooney, Linne R., *The Index of Middle English Prose Handlist XI: Manuscripts in the Library of Trinity College, Cambridge* (Cambridge, 1995).

Murdoch, Brian, *The Apocryphal Adam and Eve in Medieval Europe: Vernacular Translations and Adaptations of the* Vita Adae et Evae (Oxford, 2009).

Nagy, M. von, and Nagy, C. de, *Die Legenda Aurea und ihr Verfasser Jacobus de Voragine* (Berne, 1971).

Nall, Catherine, 'Ricardus Franciscus Writes for William Worcester', *Journal of the Early Book Society*, 11 (2008), 207–12.

Pächt, O., and Alexander, J. J. G., *Illuminated Manuscripts in the Bodleian Library*, iii (Oxford, 1973).

Parkes, M. B., 'The Compilation of the Dominican Lectionary', in *Literarische Formen des Mittelalters*, ed. Kaspar Elm (Wiesbaden, 2000), 91–106.

Pickering, O. S., and O'Mara, V. M., *The Index of Middle English Prose Handlist XIII: Manuscripts in Lambeth Palace Library, Including those Formerly in Sion College Library* (Cambridge, 1999).

Poole, Reginald L., 'The See of Maurienne and the Valley of Susa', *EHR* 121 (1916), 1–19.

Rand, Kari Anne, *The Index of Middle English Prose Handlist XX: Manuscripts in the Library of Corpus Christi College, Cambridge* (Cambridge, 2009).

Reames, S. L., *The Legenda Aurea: A Re-examination of its Paradoxical History* (Madison, Wis., 1985).

Routh, E. M. G., *Lady Margaret: A Memoir of Lady Margaret Beaufort Countess of Richmond and Derby, Mother to Henry VII* (London, 1924).

Rud, Thomas, *Catalogi Veteres Librorum Ecclesiae Cathedralis Dunelmensis* (Surtees Society, 7; 1838 (1840)).

Russell, Vida, 'Evidence for a Stemma for the De Vignay MSS', in Dunn-Lardeau, ed., *Legenda Aurea: Sept Siècles de Diffusion*, 131–54.

Scott, Kathleen L., *Later Gothic Manuscripts 1390–1490*, 2 vols. (A Survey of Manuscripts Illuminated in the British Isles; London, 1996).

—— 'A Mid-Fifteenth-Century Illuminating Shop and its Customers', *Journal of the Warburg & Courtauld Institutes*, 31 (1968), 170–96.

Seybolt, R. F., 'The "Adriatic Port" in the *Legenda Aurea*', *Speculum*, 21 (1946), 500–4.

—— 'Fifteenth-Century Editions of the *Legenda Aurea*', *Speculum*, 21 (1946), 327–38.

—— 'A Troublesome Mediaeval Greek Word', *Speculum* 21 (1946), 38–41.

Shailor, Barbara A., *Catalogue of Medieval and Renaissance Manuscripts in the Beinecke Rare Books and Manuscripts Library*, iii (Binghamton, NY, 1993).

Stace, Christopher, *St George: Patron Saint of England* (London, 2002).

Thomson, R. M., 'Serlo of Wilton and the Schools of Oxford', *MÆ* 68 (1999), 1–12.

Thurston, Herbert, SJ, 'Abbot Anselm of Bury and the Immaculate Conception', *The Month* (1904), 561–73.

Tracy, Larissa, 'British Library MS Harley 630: Saint Alban's and Lydgate', *Journal of the Early Book Society*, 3 (2000), 36–58.

—— *Women of the Gilte Legende: A Selection of Middle English Saints' Lives* (Woodbridge, 2003).

Walter, Christopher, *The Warrior Saints in Byzantine Art and Tradition* (Aldershot, 2003).

Watson, Andrew G., *Catalogue of Dated and Datable Manuscripts c. 435-1600 in Oxford Libraries*, 2 vols. (Oxford, 1984).

—— *Catalogue of Dated and Datable Manuscripts c. 700-1600 in the Department of Manuscripts, the British Library* (Oxford, 1979).

NOTES ON THE TEXT

SIGLA FOR MANUSCRIPTS OF LÉGENDE DORÉE AND LEGENDA AUREA

Fb	Paris, Bibliothèque nationale de France, MS fr. 416
P1	Paris, Bibliothèque nationale France, MS fr. 241
P2	Paris, Bibliothèque nationale de France, MS fr. 244–5
Re	Vatican, Biblioteca Apostolica Vaticana, MS Reg. 485
S	Rennes, Bibliothèque municipale, MS 266
Z	London, British Library, MS Egerton 645

These notes consist largely of a record of changes to the text from its French and Latin sources, excluding paraphrasing and other minor changes and imprecisions. For example, LgA *legitur*, and with references to parts of the mass *cantatur*, often appear in GiL as *is saide*, the change being variously attributable to Vignay or s.w.; heathen gods are often rendered *ydoles*; s.w. consistently gives *catholique* as *cristen*, and for some reason *glaive* as *spere*; both Vignay and s.w. generally ignore the distinction between slaves and servants; *prouost* is indiscriminately used for prefects, proconsuls, and other high officials; *gloire/gloria* is usually translated as *ioye* (see 1.266 below); and *Francorum* becomes *of France*. Such changes are not recorded. Also the many place and personal names which have become garbled by the time they reach GiL are noted and corrected only if the result is misleading; otherwise their identifications are given in the index.

As far as possible, French and Latin citations are arranged to correspond to the syntax of the GiL text. LgD is usually cited from P2 (which was in fact written after the date of composition of GiL) because it is more complete and accurate than S, and generally spells more conventionally. S would otherwise have been preferred, since occasional readings indicate that it was somewhat closer in the stemma to s.w.'s exemplar. Where P2 lacks a passage or has an individual error or a spelling likely to mislead, S is used, or more rarely the closely related Z. LgA is cited from Maggioni's text, but the copy of LgA used by Vignay was not the version in that edition, having come from an earlier stage of LgA's development. Vignay's exemplar was somewhat closer to the early printed edition used by Graesse for his edition. The differences are not usually substantial, and the same is true of scribal alterations in the transmission of LgD between the original and s.w.'s exemplar. But where such changes in the intermediate stages of the transmission explain a significant development, additional citations are sometimes given from variants recorded in Maggioni's edition, from Graesse, from P1 (the earliest and best of the LgD MSS), and from Batallier's 1476 edition of LgD.

To simplify and shorten the notes, the following conventions have been used: following the lemma, (a) when GiL differs from LgD, but LgD agrees with LgA, only LgD is cited; (b) when GiL agrees with LgD, but LgD differs from LgA, only LgA is cited; (c) when all three differ, all three are cited; (d) when GiL has been corrected from LgA when LgD differs, all three are cited. Examples:

(a) 4.94 **grauntid**: *reuele* P2 (i.e. LgA *ostenderet* is as P2)
(b) 4.184 **.iiij. ensamples**: *triplici exemplo* LgA (i.e. P2 *quatre exemples* is as GiL)
(c) 4.101 **schal suffise**: *sera conuerti* P2, *commune erit* LgA
(d) 3.53 **creatour**: *creance* P2, *creatorem* LgA

Where a lemma is followed by the statement 'not in P2', or 'not in S', this should be taken to imply 'not in s.w.'s exemplar', without prejudice to whether it is in P1. References in the form 4.94 are to chapter and line number.

1 ST ANDREW

Maggioni, ch. II, p. 24; Dunn-Lardeau, ch. 2, p. 107.

12 **anoþir**: *alio* LgA, the same one as in 11.

19 **Petir**: *Symon* P2.

26–7 **schippe and nettis and all þat þay hadde**: *tout* P2.

29 **apostlis**: add *duquel appel maty dit ou .iij.*[e] *chapitre il apella a lui ceulx quil voult etc*. P2. LgA correctly attributes this to Mark.
so þat: only GiL.

31 **Morgundie**: *Margundiam* LgA; Margundia has not been identified.

33 **prison**: add *post paucos dies occidere eum disponentes* LgA.

43–4 **worshipid . . . brother**: *aoura* S.

45 **bi his gret miraculis**: only GiL.

53–5 **And whanne . . . to be so**: *Et ce que lon dit de laueuglement de saint mathieu* (add *et restitutione duorum luminum per Andream* LgA) *ie ne cuide pas estre voir* P2.

55 **apostul**: *euuangeliste* S.

56 **but þat he myȝt liȝtly haue gete**: *que il ne peust empetrer a soy* P2.

59 **for dispite þerof**: only GiL.

66 **enforce . . . aȝens hym**: *uos stulto labore consumitis* LgA.

66 and 67 **hym**: *eulx* P2

70 **.xv.**: *.l.* P2

at oo tyme and were buryid in oo pitte: *et furent mis en vng monument* (*moment* S) P2. Benz records variant *momento* for LgA *monumento*.

GiL here omits three stories, Maggioni, 26–8 (32–73), Dunn-Lardeau, 109–11.

83 **Nice**: add *Et dont dit au pere di celui, que me donras tu se ie le resuscite, et il lui dist, Je nay sy chere chose comme lui. Je le te donray* P2.

87 **hauyng envi vnto hem**: only GiL.

90 **liff**: add *Et ilz distrent tout ce quil leur estoit aduenu* P2.

95 **Egie**: add *le preuost* P2.

98 **pretendist**: *as desserui* P2.

105–6 **the contrarie**: *ces choses* P2.

115 **did**: *fist faire* P2.

118 **furste**: neither LgD nor LgA numbers these reasons.

123 **the þridde day**: only GiL.

aȝen: add *quant il dit. Jay poeste de mettre mon ame et de la reprendre de rechief* P2.

125 **at his maunde**: only GiL, add *et sy ne lescheua il pas* P2.

142 **shuld stroght**: *shuld streight* H1, *scholde strecche* GH2, *estendist* P2; *MED strecchen* records no forms with infinitive in *-ght*, nor indeed any forms with *o*. It seems likely that *shuld* was added before an original past form in an early copy and retained in EH1, and that GH2 show an attempt to correct this.

145 **eisell and**: *viande de* P2.

147 **mortalite**: add *Car se ihesu crist neust este mortel homme neust pas este fait immortel* P2.

148 **to tho that leven the**: *aux tiens* P2.

148–9 **to almyghti God**: *aux dieux tous poissans* P2.

153 **know it**: add *Et Egee dist, Je te demanderai assauoir ceste chose par tormens* P1; P2S omit *Et Egee dist*, so s.w. omitted the now meaningless reply of Egias.

154–5 **til . . . brought**: *et au matin il vint* P2.

155–6 **ledde . . . do**: *mene au* P2, *Egeas eum iterum inuitare cepit* LgA.

158–9 **with . . . part**: *sicomme il le menacoit de moult de tourmens* P2.

160–1 **and thou . . . receyue hem**: only GiL.

165 **fete**: add *affin quil eust plus long tourment* P2.

170–1 **O worschipfull . . . blesfull crosse**: *Dieu te sauf, croix* P2, *salue crux* LgA.

174 **thou art loue of heuen**: *amorem celestem obtinens pro uoto susciperis* LgA
O blessid crosse: only GiL.

180 **loued**: add *et que mon couraige tant desire et couuoite* P2.
fro . . . prison: *de cy* P2, *ab hominibus* LgA.

184 **hangyng on the crosse**: only GiL.

199 **Confessiouns**: *liure de penitence* P2.

203 **yef it liked thi gret goodnesse**: only GiL.

204 **obedience**: add *et estre oste de ceste agreable charge* (*grauissimo indumento* LgA) P2.

204–6 **For . . . refreynyng**: *Recordor quantum in portando onerosum, in domando superbum, in fouendo infirmum, in coercendo letum laboraui* LgA, 'I recall how much I have laboured in carrying its great weight, in taming its pride, in supporting its infirmity, and in coercing it from indolence.'

209 **thi**: *son* P2.

212 **myght of thi grace**: *ton euure* P2.

214 **comaunde**: *commandes* P2, *commendes* LgA; *MED commaunden* sense 6(b) gives 'entrust or commend'.

215 **that thou hast take me**: *ce que tu mauoies baillie* P2.

215–17 **and comaunde . . . laboure**: *commenda alii quam illo ultra non impedias et resurrecturum seruet et reddat ut et ipsum quoque meritum sui laboris recipiat* LgA.

219 **vndefaillynge**: add *anxiantem non iam retrahat nec impediat.' Hec Augustinus* LgA; *MED* gives no *un-* forms related to *defailen*, and the positive gerund is recorded only for Chauliac.

220 **environde**: *ouer houyd* G, 'hovered above', *MED hoven* v. (1).

221–2 **for gret . . . hym**: only GiL.

232 **was born**: *translatum esse perhibetur* LgA.

235 **thyng . . . wold saye**: *toutes ses euures il lamentoit tousiours et disoit* P2.

245 **whanne . . . allone**: only GiL.

247 **in gret delites**: *delicieusement* P2, *delicate* LgA.

248 **straunge abite**: *peregrino habitu* LgA.

250 **erthely**: *delit de* P2, *lit de* P1.

251 **Crist**: add *a tousiours* P2.

251–2 **other spouse**: *charnel couple* P2.

254 **pore and**: only GiL.

254–5 **lese my virginite**: *corrompre la foy a mon espoux* P2.

266 **ioye**: *gloire* P2; *ioye* is the standard translation of *ioie/gaudium*, but s.w. frequently also used it for *gloire/gloria* (*MED joy(e* sense 5 (b)). For a discussion of *ioie/glorie*, see the text at 7.54–61.

268–9 **and it schall be redy to you**: only GiL.

275–6 **the bisshop . . . before hym**: *sistrent lun contre lautre et les autres sistrent de ca et de la* P2.

279 **The fende . . . hym**: *Et lancien ennemy quant il la regardoit naura le cueur de lui dun grief dart. Et ce dyable* P2.

281–2 **yef he hadde hadd tyme and place**: *quant il pourroit* P2.

283 **inne**: add *et len ne li vouloit ouurir sy que il crioit et feroit de plus fort en plus fort* P2.

285 **question**: add *assez griefue* P2.

286 **inne**: add *et se il ne la scet si soit boute hors si que il ny entre comme non saichant et non digne* (add *episcopi presentia* LgA). *Et tous obeirent a celle sentence* P2.

288 **that wolde purpoos it**: *trouue souffisant* P2.

295 **men**: add *comme il a este des le commancement du monde et sera iusques a la fin* P2.

296 **thyng**: add *et si mist dieu tous les sens du corps* P2.

296–7 **of his gret wisdom**: *et distrent Cest vray et tres bonne response de la question* P2.

299 **highest**: *plus haulte que tout le ciel* P2.

300 **imperiall**: *emperial* P2, *empyreo* LgA; *MED empirial* has only one instance, cited as 'adj. as n.', 'the highest of the heavenly spheres', *c.*1450; its spelling here indicates that the French was taken to mean 'imperial', which *MED* records with both initial *i* and *e*. See too 64.249, 250.

301 **is**: add (*que*) *le corps ihesu crist qui est forme de nostre char est plus hault que tout le ciel* P2. This answer is expanded in other LgD MSS and LgA, Maggioni, 35 (203–6), Dunn-Lardeau, 118.

301–2 **of . . . gretly**: *de sa response quant le message la rapporta et loerent merueilleusemant sa sagesce* S.

303 **hardest of all**: *tres griefue et occulte et forte a souldre. Sy que sa sagesce soit tierce fois esprouuee et quil soit digne destre receu a table deuesque* P2.

306–9 The feminine pronouns are all masculine in LgD and LgA, to signify Andrew's awareness that the woman is in reality the devil.

324 GiL here omits one story, Maggioni, 36–7 (223–8), Dunn-Lardeau, 119.

2 ST NICHOLAS

Maggioni, ch. III, p. 38; Dunn-Lardeau, ch. 3, p. 119.

1 **was borne in**: *cytoien de* P2.

1–2 **noble and riche**: *riches et sains* P2.

9–10 **putte it in werke after his powere**: *mettoit a euure* P2, *memoriter retinebat* LgA.

15–17 **This . . . lucree**: *mais pour la pourete deulz ensemble elles estoient constraintes daler a pechie, Sy que du gaing de leur infamete il fut soustenu et nourry* P2, *ob inopiam prostituere cogitur, ut sic infami earum commercio aleretur* LgA.

22 **was fulfilled . . . and**: only GiL.

26–7 **schewed . . . mischeeff**: *aidie a sa pourete* P2.

28–9 **inne priuely . . . to done**: *en la maison di cellui* P2.

31 **For Goddes loue**: *Sire* P2. **so faste**: only GiL.

34 **deuied**: *deuea* P2SP1; *deveer/devier*, 'refuse', is frequent in LgD, and it seems clear that s.w. translated it as *devien*. Its sense is similar to that of Fr. *denier*, ME *denien*, and scribes in either language may have employed either word, it being in many cases impossible to distinguish between *n* and *u*. The open top of *u* is generally clear in P2SP1, but in most of the GiL MSS, including E, the scribes made no consistent distinction. Here G seems to write *n* in *denoydid*, while H2 seems to have a clear *u* in *deuoid*. *MED* records no verb which would account for either of these forms. *MED* records the verb *devaien* only for two instances from *Sir Gawain and the Green Knight*, but others may be concealed because editors have not recognized the possibility of *u* in this word. For this edition it is assumed that s.w. translates *devier* as *devien*, but where the base text writing looks like a probable *n* this is noted in the apparatus.

39 **hangged**: G has *honyd*, H2 *houed*. *MED* gives no sign of the former, and none of the senses of *hoven* v.(1) (related to *hover*) or *hoven v.*(2) (shortened form of *bihoven*) seems to fit.

46–7 **Right . . . hym**: *Ce fut merueilleuse chose car* P2.

49 **he anone . . . ansuered**: *cellui qui estoit simple comme coulon enclina le chief* P2.

50–2 **Thanne . . . ioye**: *et ilz li menerent en leglise* P2.

53–7 **but he most . . . governaunce**: *Et il ensuy ainsy comme deuant humilite et honnestete de meurs en toutes choses* P2.

61–2 **were in the see in gret perile**: *perissoient* P2, *periclitarentur* LgA.

62 **cried**: *prierent* P2.

63 **proue**: *espreuue* P2, *experiamur* LgA.

64 **thi gret . . . praiere**: *si les espreuue maintenant* P2.

66 **Called ye me not**: *Vocastis enim me* LgA.

67–8 **And thanne . . . away**: only GiL.

69 **tellyng of any creature**: *demonstrer* P2.

72 **wold sette it**: *lattribuassent* P2; the sense 'attribute', also found at 112.94 and 149.26, is not recorded *s.v. MED setten*.

75 **allmost**: only GiL.

79 **schip**: add *au moins* P2.

81–6 The wheat should have been coming *from* Alexandria, but Vignay mistranslated the Latin: *quia mensuratum est Alexandrie, oportet in horrea imperatoris nos reddere*, and *eandem mensuram quam Alexandrie acceperant redidissent ministris imperatoris*.

85 **hadd deliuered hym**: *leurent baille* P2; *hym* should refer to the wheat, but is perhaps thought of as dative 'to hym'.

87 **and[2]**: *in* LgA.

91–2 **the fals goddes Dyane**: *le faulx ymage de lexcommeniee Dyane* P2, *pre ceteris nefande Dyane simulacrum* LgA.

93 **mony**: add *rustici* LgA.

95–6 **all tho trees**: *cest arbre* P2.

96–7 **was . . . ordeyned**: *fust courroucie contre lui. Sy fist* P2.

97 **oyle**: *oleum mydiacon* LgA. Seybolt, 'A Troublesome Mediaeval Greek Word', shows that this derives from a form like *Mediacon*, 'of the Medes', and that 'Median oil' was an early name for Greek fire, whose main ingredient, naphtha, came principally from that region.

100 **And whanne sche neighed hem**: only GiL.

101–2 **Al heile . . . God**: *Je aymasse mieulx aler a lomme dieu auec vous* P2.

107–8 **a reuerent persone lik to**: *vng tres semblable a* P2.

114–15 **the bisshop . . . londed**: only GiL.

117 **hondes**: *agais* P2.

118 **emperour**: so S, *empire* P2, *impero* LgA.

120–1 **the port of Adrian**: *portui Adriatico* LgA, = Andriaca on the Lycian coast; see Benz 561–2 and Seybolt, 'The "Adriatic Port"', who shows that Andriaca was often called 'the Adriatic port'. The term Adriatic was applied to a larger area of the eastern Mediterranean than now.

122 **hym[1]**: add *car il vouloit garder ses gens de leur rapine que ilz faisoient* P2.

And . . . hym[2]: *Et si comme le saint ny estoit pas* P2.

123, 132, 133 **consult**: *consulte* P2, *consul* LgA. Spellings with *t* are standard in GiL and LgD, including Batallier's edition, but are not recorded in *MED*; see *s.v. consul.* At 123 GH2A1A2 give various spellings of *counsel*, but at 132 H2 has *counsult* and at 133 GH2 read *consult*.

126 **thei**[2] **. . . bihedid**: *ceulx a decoler estoient* P2.

127 **man**: *decoleur* P2.

loftyng: *liftyng* GH2, *lyftyng* T1; *MED* has no verbal forms with *o*, so the E spelling may be influenced by *loft n.*

128–9 **sette afere**: *embrase* P2. *MED* records no verb to which G *affreynyd it*, H2 *offreyned it* could belong.

129 **putte . . . hem**: *sembati hardiement contre le decoleur* P2.

131 **her eyghen . . . innocentis**: *les Innocens et les amena* P2.

132 **iugement**: *pretorium* LgA.

136 **or misauenture**: only GiL.

145–7 **ymagened treson ayenst hem and (. . .) thei were falsli accused to the emperour of treson ayenst his mageste**: *distrent en traison a lemperiere et* (. . .) *ilz furent accusez faulcement du blasme de sa mageste* P2, *prefecto imperatoris* (. . .) *suggesserunt ut eos apud imperatorem de lese maiestatis crimine accusaret* LgA.

150 **priueli hadd told hem**: *les gardoit* P2.

157 **cause**: *mesfait* P2.

159 **many batayles**: *bataille* P2, *bellum* LgA.

160–1 **hauyng . . . merveil**: only GiL.

163–5 **with that . . . hym**: *ainsy espouenta le preuost disant* P2.

164 **the provost**: see note to 145–7 above, where Vignay and s.w. had lost the provost.

169 **manast** appears to be a reduced form from *manacen*, but is not recorded by *MED*. H2 has *manest* here and *maneth* at 184 for E *manace*.

171 **and therwith he vanished away**: only GiL.

173 **the princes . . . come**: *ces enchartrez. Et* P2.

175–6 **coude . . . craft**: *nestoient pas enchanteurs* P2.

184 **youre**: *de nostris* LgA.

194–5 **and thanne . . . worlde**: not in P2, *statimque in terra se proiciens et signo crucis se muniens* LgA.

199 **the**: *vne* P2.

202 **holi lyff**: *bonne volente* P2.

207 **.iiij.**[1]: *XLII* LgA.

210 **.xv.**: *sept* P2.

218 **be his wile and malice**: *en or* P2, *auro minuto* LgA.

222 **toke . . . Iue**: *lui demanda le baston. Et le iuif qui ne scot pas la malice lui rendi* S.

223 **went quite**: *sen alla* P2.

224 **karfoke**, 'cross-roads'; the word is apparently unfamiliar to several of the scribes. *MED karfouk* has no records for variants *cartesclade*, *cartesoke*, *karfont* (E at 265 below), etc., and no entries under *slade* or *soke* which might help to explain these forms.

232 **the miracles**: *les vertueux miracles* P2, *uirtuosam potentiam in miraculis faciendis* LgA.

236 **vpon the**: *par vous battre et tormenter* P2.

240 **I hadd putte you**: *nonne* (. . .) *uos posueram* LgA.

244 **tormentis**: add *et refraindray ma forsennerie en toy battre* P2.

246 **al forwounded**: *aussy comme sil eust en soy tous les batemens* P2.

247 **hem**: add *hec uel similia uerba* LgA.

249–50 **those thinges and the goodes**: *tout* P2.

260–1 **went to scole. And**: *aprenoit a lettre* (*ses lettres* P1). *Vne foys que le pere ot appareillie son disner et conuie moult de clercs* P2.

261 **that . . . deuocion**: only GiL.

264–5 **dede . . . almesse and**: *sy le suiuy sicomme il sen alloit. Et* P2, *Properat puer, sed peregrinum non inueniens* LgA.

268 **chaumbre**: add *et commenca a crier de douleur* P2.

270 **haue**: add *sy longuement* P2.

274 **wolde be mene**: *impetrast* P2.

276 **with hym**: *lui* P2.
after his desire: only GiL.

278–9 **the shappe therof**: only GiL.

280 **towarde**: add *leglise de* P2.

296 **Nicholas**[1]: add *et lapella dieu donne* P2, add *quem Adeodatum uocauit* LgA.

298–9 **so it happenyd . . . seruage to**: *fut depute a seruir* P2, *Adeodatus ergo quadam uice ab Agarenis capitur et in seruitutem* (. . .) *deputatur* LgA.

306 **now**: *auec nous* P2.

309 **his fadris ȝatis**: *les portes la ou les parens faisoient la solennite du saint* P2, *fores ecclesie ubi parentes agebant sollempnia* LgA.

311 **ouer þe Grete See**: *oultre mer* P2.

313 **Day**: add *et il eust este apres mis en chartre* P2.

315 **sodeynly**: not in LgD, *subito* LgA.

317–19 **where . . . Nicholas**: only GiL.

3 ST LUCY

Maggioni, ch. IV, p. 49; Dunn-Lardeau, ch. 4, p. 129.

3 **sche . . . here**: not in P2, *sepulcrum eius adiit* LgA.

8–9 **hath . . . hire**: *a tousiours celui presentement auec elle* P2, *illum semper habere presentem* LgA, 'is always in the presence of him'.

17 **be ȝe of good comforte for**: only GiL.

21–2 **lete me deie . . . biddist me**: *puis fay ce que tu vouldras* (add *de facultatibus* LgA) P2.

23–4 **mowe . . . þanke**: *ne le peulz porter auec toy* P2.

30 **wif**: *espouse* P2, *sponsa* LgA; s.w. translates *espouse*, which can mean either wife or betrothed, as the former.

49 **siche oon as thou arte**: *putain* P2.

52 **Ȝe amongis ȝou**: *Entre vous estes corrompeurs de corps et de pensee* P2, *Corruptores mentis uos estis* LgA.

53 **creatour**: *creance* P2, *creatorem* LgA.

55 **goodis**: *vices* P2, *viandes* P1, *epulis* LgA.

63 **God and of**: only GiL.

64 **bordel**: add *si que tu soies la corrompue* P2.

69 **þat þou canst deuyse**: only GiL.

72 **ribaudis and lecherous**: *lenones* LgA, 'procurers'.

72–3 **goo . . . dede**: *Amonnestez tout le peuple daller a ceste et soit tant despite que len me demonstre* (*nuntietur* LgA) *que elle soit morte* P2.

75 **and**: add *lui* [*la* S] *fist lier piez et mains mais ilz ne la peurent oncques mouuoir. Et donc adiousta auec les mil hommes* P2.

82 **now**: add *Et Paschasien cuida selon la sorcerie daucuns que malefice fut oste par pissat. sy len fist arrouser. mais elle ne fut pourtant oncques meue* P2.

83 **was . . . and**: not in P2, *angustiatus nimis* LgA.

85–6 **a terme**: *indutias* LgA, delay; *terme* here seems from context to mean 'end', as it does at 106.217 for LgA *termino*; but elsewhere, as at 174.567 (*inducias*), context makes clear the sense 'limited period of delay'.

87 **þe weyis of ioie**: *la voix de excaulcement* P2, *uocem insultationis* LgA.

94 **defenderesse**: *MED* has only one citation, for a1456 from Lydgate.

98 **emperoure, prouost**: *cesarem*, *cesar* LgA.

102 **smyten**: add *et ne rendi oncques lesperit* P2.

103–4 **sche . . . sche and**: *elle ot faicte soroison* P2.

105–6 **And now . . . Venyse**: *et ecclesia fabricata* LgA; the reference to Venice was substituted by Vignay.

107 **Maxymyan**: *Maxentii* LgA.
thre hundrid and ten: Lucy died in 304.

4 ST THOMAS APOSTLE

Maggioni, ch. V, p. 53; Dunn-Lardeau, ch. 5, p. 133.

10–11 **to seke a crafty man**: only GiL.

18–19 **þe prouost and Thomas**: *Abannes et le roy* P2, *Abanem et apostolum* LgA.

19 **among oþir**: *y* P2.

19–20 **amongis oþer mynstrellis**: only GiL.

20 **mayden**: add *hebree* P2.
tabur: *frestel* P2, i.e. GiL substitutes a drum for a sort of flute.

26 **þat**: add *il ne mengoit point ne ne buuoit mais auoit tousiours les yeulx au ciel* P2.

27 **vndir**: *en* P2.

29 **be punyschid now and**: only GiL.

38 **and resseyuyd cristen faith**: only GiL, after which GiL omits Maggioni, 55–6 (33–46), Dunn-Lardeau, 134–5.

39–40 and 43 **ȝong mariage**: *lespoux et lespouse* P2; the apparent sense here, 'married couple' for *mariage*, is not recorded by *MED*.

42 **eche of her handis**: *la main de lespoux* P2.

51 **purite**: *entierete* P2.

53 **of klennesse**: *de luxure* P2, *libidinum* LgA.
lordschip: *tropheum* LgA.
discomfiture: *expugnatio* LgA.

54–5 **Luxurie is engendrid of corrupcion**: *De libidine autem corruptio gignitur* LgA.

58 **like**: *gardez* P2.

62 **husbond**: add *Denis par nom* P2.

71 **that he hadde**: only GiL.

71–2 **and purposid . . . bothe**: *Sy que apres ce il les fist escorcher et ardoir* P2, *ut postmodo uiuos excoriatos ultricibus daret flammis* LgA.

76 **to brenne and scle**: *escorcher et ardoir* P2; s.w. perhaps wrote *fle*, but in that case the transposing of the verbs is hard to explain.

83 **here**: *en cellui* P2.

89 **hauen**: *cuident auoir* P2, *cupiunt habere* LgA.

94 **grauntid**: *reuele* P2.

95 **a prynce**: *participes* LgA. In LgD/LgA the apostle is addressing both brothers, so the plural should continue.

101 **schal suffise**: *sera conuerti* P2, *commune erit* LgA.

108 **brouȝt forth**: *apart* P2.

111 **lay as dede**: *cuidoient estre cheuz du coup de la fouldre* P2.

113 **vs alle**: *nous* P2, *uos* LgA.

116 **þe**[2]: add *duodecim* LgA.

121 **þat that þou hast lernyd**: *ut quod non didicisti inuenias* LgA (some MSS omit *non*).

122 **it**[1]: *que didiceris* LgA.

122–3 **fele . . . teche it**: *entens ce qui peut estre demonstre* (add *et* S) *enseigne* P2.

125–6 **ther . . . þyngis**: not in P2, *quatuor sensibus constat* LgA.
heryng: add *gouster* P2.
smellyng: add *et sont ces choses plusieurs* P2.

131–2 **þyngis þat ben nedefull**: *es choses a faire* P2.

132 **God**: add *et requeissent* (*complerent* LgA) *ces choses par euure* P2.

136 **þre skore .M^{li}.**: *xl.^{M}* P2, *nouem milia* LgA, variant *XI milia*.

141–2 **Y desire . . . wise**: *Cuides tu que ie le puisse veoir* P2.

143–4 **in womannys clothyng**: only GiL.

150 **colere**: in *MED s.v. collirie*.

159 **ordeynyd that**: *impetra que* P2, *a rege impetrauit et* LgA.

163–4 **fro þis cristen religion**: only GiL.

167 **his**: *ses* P2, *ces* P1, *hiis* LgA.

168 **.iiij.**: *tribus* LgA.

171 **wher**: *pour quoy* P2.

176 **come in the kingis bedd**: *coupler au roy* P2.

184 **.iiij. ensamples**: *triplici exemplo* LgA.
thei aught not obeie to hem: *il ne lui* (*le* P1) *deuoit pas faire* P2, *hoc facere non deberent* LgA. LgD changed this to singular, implying that just the king's wife is meant. GiL restored the plural, referring to the two wives, perhaps from the sense of the preceding sentence, or remembering Eph. 5: 22.

188 **sithe thou louest this**: only GiL.
how: *comme* P2, *Quanto magis* LgA.

189–90 **labour and**: only GiL.

190 **that God . . . louithe**: *a aimer dieu de ses seruans que il aime* P2, *deum amare . . . in seruis suis, quod diligis et in tuis* LgA.

191 **hym**: add *et* (*en* P1) *ses seruans* P2, not in LgA.

192 **toure**: *terram* LgA.

198–9 **with atempre cold that**: *que lautre iour* P2.

200–1 **one of oure goddes**: *vng des dieux seul* P2, *deo solis* LgA.

202–3 **to the kyng**: *Roy* (vocative) P2, *regi* LgA.

205 **peinture**: GiL omits remainder of his speech, Maggioni, 61 (153–7); Dunn-Lardeau, 140–1.

206 **comparisons**: *choses pareilles* S.

206–7 **Do . . . dye**: only in GiL.

215–16 **whanne . . . rennen**: *dont tous les prestres vindrent* (*muirent* P1) *comme bestes. Et leuesque du temple leua le glaiue et tresperca* P2.

224 **no man herburith**: *nul homme ny heberge* P2, *nul herege* P1, *nullus hereticus* LgA.

224–5 **ne no tiraunt**: only GiL (from next).

225 **there**: add *nul tiraunt ny peut la viure* (*nuire* P1, *nocere* LgA) P2.

231 **of Seintes**: *patrum.* LgA.

233 **harde of byleue**: *mescreans en oyant* P2, *audiendo incredulus, uidendo fidelis* LgA.

233–4 **in the parties . . . Brachiens**: *aux pertes* (*partes* S, *perthes* P1) *aux medes aux hirques* (*hyrcans* P1) *aux brachiens* P2, *Parthis, Medis et Persis Hircanisque et Brachianis* LgA.

236 **bodi**: add *de glaiues et sacosta* (*occubuit* LgA) P2.

5 NATIVITY

Maggioni, ch. VI, p. 63; Dunn-Lardeau, ch. 6, p. 142.

The three ways in which the Nativity is revealed to man are stated at 64–5 as A *mervailously*, B *multiplyingli*, and C *profitably*:

A *mervailously* 65–6:
- (i) applies to the mother, as virgin in conceiving, virgin after the birth, and virgin in giving birth 67–93;
- (ii) applies to the child, as everlasting, ancient, and new 94–108;
- (iii) applies to the birth itself 109–121.

B *multiplyingli* by five manners of being 122–7:
- (i) those with only being, as stones 127–88;
- (ii) those with being and living, as plants 189–91;
- (iii) those with being, living and feeling, as animals 192–200;
- (iv) those with being, living, feeling, and discerning, as mankind 201–30;
- (v) omitted by GiL, those with being, living, feeling, discerning, and understanding, as angels.

C *profitably* 231:
- (i) confusion of the fiend 231–55;
- (ii) forgiveness of sins 256–66;
- (iii) cure of infirmities 266–73;
- (iv) reduction of pride 274 to end.

Some inaccuracies in presenting this scheme are indicated below, especially at 64.

1 **Crist**: add *selon la char* P2.

3–4 **In . . . emperour**: ends previous sentence in LgD/LgA, but all GiL MSS as here.

4 **emperour**: add *le compte de .vj.M ans fut trouue de methodien plus par temps vertique que par croniques* (*mistice quam chronice* LgA) P2.

4–5 **into this worlde**: *en terre* P2, *in carnem* LgA.

5 **the only emperours**: *le seul empereur* P2, *unicus* (. . .) *imperator* LgA.

6 **lordschipped**: add *pacifice* LgA.

8–9 **for the dignite of the emperial honour**: *imperator a dignitatis honore* LgA.

13 **Cesar**: add *adonc auguste* P2.

15 **Stories**: *hystoriis scholasticis* LgA, variant *hystoria scholastica*.

17 **siluer**: add *qui ualebat decem nummos usuales unde et denarius decebatur* LgA.

18 **prouince**: add *se subditum Romano imperio profiteretur* LgA.

24 **opin confession**: *confession* (*fassio* LgA) *de propre bouche* P2.

26 **money**: *cens* P2, *censi* (. . .) *id est denarium illum qui sic uocabatur* LgA.

28 **Cirin**: add *Prima dicitur, ut in eisdem hystoriis scholasticis habetur, quantum ad Cirinum* LgA. In what follows LgA is concerned to explain the use of the term *Prima*.

30 **after . . . aboute**: *apres par les contrees dentour et puis par les autres apres* P2, *deinde per circumstantes regiones et alii presides prosequerentur* LgA.

30–1 **And . . . universall**: *Vel prima dicitur id est uniuersalis* LgA.

31–2 **the other were made bi parties**: add *auant* P2, *alie precesserunt particulares* LgA, i.e. previous ones had been partial and not universal.

32–4 **either . . . Cesar**: *ou pource que la premiere cheuetaine fut faicte en la cite au preuost. La seconde fut faicte des citez en la contree deuant le messaige cesar* P2, *Vel forte prima capitum in ciuitate fiebat a preside, secunda ciuitatum in regione a legato cesaris* LgA.

34 **Cesar**: add *tertia regionum in urbe coram cesare* LgA.

40 **Bartilmew**: Bartholomew of Trent.

41–2 **in . . . Crist**: *et de libro infantie saluatoris sumptum est* LgA, the Gospel of Pseudo-Matthew, which Vignay and s.w., by losing *et*, attribute to Bartholomew.

50 **comon place**: *communi transitu* LgA.

53 **tyme**: *temps* (*aeris* LgA, i.e. weather) *la ou ioseph auoit fait vne cresche a vng beuf et a vng asne* P2.

56–8 **And thanne . . . hous**: only GiL.

59 **befell**: add *nocte media* LgA.

61 **Maister of Stories**: *lystoire escoliere* P2, *hystoriis scholasticis* LgA, i.e. Peter Comestor's *Historia Scholastica*. The GiL form of words here suggests that *the Maister* is the author, but more typically the three words are treated as the title of the book, as at 130 and 155 below. *MED s.v. stori(e* n.(1) gives '*clerk* (*maister*) *of* (*the*) *stories*, Peter Comestor, author of the Historia Scholastica'.

63 **after . . . theron**: not in LgA.

64–5 **done . . . profitably**: *mirabiliter facta, multipliciter ostensa et utiliter exhibita* LgA. In losing this triple balance, Vignay also lost the complex framework underlying the rest of the chapter, which is additionally obscured by errors and omissions by later scribes of LgD, and further in GiL by frequent substitution of *Also* for numerical adverbs and by omissions such as those noted at 122 and 124 below. The LgA *mirabiliter facta* section begins in

GiL at 65 and is subdivided into *ex parte generantis* (66), *ex parte geniti* (94), and *ex parte modi generandi* (109). The second LgA section, *multipliciter ostensa*, starts at 122, and the third, *utiliter exhibita*, at 231. Subdivisions within these are easier to identify, and where necessary are given in the notes below.

MED does not record *multipliingli*, nor are the participle and gerund forms recorded in the sense here required, 'in many ways'.

66 **child**: add *tum ex parte modi generandi* LgA.

67 **in**: *ante* LgA.

68 **and after**: only GiL.

70 **Secoundly**: add *par mesure* P2, add *per figuram* LgA.

71 **and bare fruit**: *sans nulle humaine estude* P2.

74 **in**: add *compilatione Bartholomei habetur et* LgA.

76 **Ioseph**: add *ne cuida pas que dieu naistroit de la benoite vierge marie* P2. **of women**: only GiL.

78 **myde**: *tasta et enquist* P2, *considerans et inquirens* LgA; *myde* appears to be a past form of *MED mien*, 'crumble (of bread), grate', *etc*., perhaps with extended sense 'touch' or 'probe'.

83 **Innocence**: *Innocentius papa tertius* LgA.

85 **of Rome**: *Romuli* LgA.

93 **chirche of seint Marie the Nwgh**: now Santa Francesca Romana. See Capgrave, 22, 'That place whech is cleped Sancta Maria le noue þat was þe temple of concorde and pite.'

94 **child**: add *Car sicomme saint bernard dit* P2.

98 **Andrewe saithe hereof: God hathe made . . .** : *Et si dit encore andry* (*audui* S, *au iour dui* P1) *cellui dieu fist . . .* P2, *Iterum, sicut idem dicit, hodie* (. . .) *fecit deus* LgA; *idem* refers to Bernard, reference to whom GiL has omitted at 94 above.

99 **merveylously**: add *singulieres que oncques celles ne furent faictes ne jamais ne seront* P2.

101 **erthe**: *le monde terre* P2, *limon de terre* P1, *limus* LgA.

102 **filthe**: *vice* P2, *uilitas* LgA.

103 **erthe**: *lymon* P2.

108 **childynge**: add *Hec Bernardus* LgA.

110–11 **wherfor . . . sithe that**: *par ce que* P2.

111 **that sche schuld bere**: *il fut raison pource que elle enfanta* P2.

117 **.v.**: *quarte* P2.

manere: add *mirabilem* LgA.

122 **shewed**: *multipliciter ostensa. Ostensa est enim* LgA; LgA gives five categories, *pure corporea, uegetabilia, animalia, homo, angelus*, which LgD and GiL altered and reduced as in 124–6 below.

124 **stones**: *la pure creature* P2, *pure corporea* LgA.
trees: *la deitant* P2, *la deuant* S, *la degetant* P1, *uegetabilia* LgA (and so some MSS of LgD), add *et arbores* Graesse. Dunn-Lardeau reads P1 as *vegetant*, and it appears that a badly written *v* at an early stage has been misread as *d* and then copied by subsequent scribes.

125 **bestis**: add *quedam que habet esse, uiuere, sentire et discernere, sicut homo* LgA.
and the .iij.: *vne* P2.

126 **feling**: add *deuiser* P2.

127 **Lord**: add *La premiere creature la pure corporel. cy est triple. cest obscure trespassant* (*tresparent* P1) *et lurant* P2, add *Prima autem creatura, scilicet pure corporea, triplex est, scilicet opaca, transparens siue peruia et lucida* LgA. This omission has obscured the beginning of a series which should continue at 189, 192, and 201. 'Fifthly' has been lost after 230.

127–8 **furst be stones**: *Elle fut premierement demonstree par la pure corporel obscure* P2.

129 **Rome**: *romulle* P2, *Romuli dei Romanorum* LgA.

131 **Ieconie**: *ierome* P2, *Ieremie* P1, *Ieremias* LgA.

135 **temple**: add *et laouroient illec* P2.

136–7 **that the grettest . . . profit**: *paterne traditionis hoc esse misterium quod a sancto propheta eorum maiores acceperant* LgA.

138 **And so**: *ainsi* belonging to the preceding sentence in P2, which begins this one *Secondement*.
purete of the erthe: *pure corporelle transparant* P2.

141, 143 **Tybre**; spellings *tymbre* with *m*, as here in E and at 45.82, are also variously found in LgD MSS, in this case in P1, but not P2S. It seems that this intrusive *m* must have been accepted by s.w., so it should not have been emended here (it has not at 45.82). The church is Santa Maria in Trastevere.

146 **Also**: *Tiercement elle fut demonstree par la purte corporelle luisant sicomme par le corporel sur le celestiel* P2, so and add further *Nam in ipsa die natiuitatis, secundum aliquorum relationem* LgA.
Orose: *Chrysostomus* LgA.
kyngges: *magis* LgA.
of the orient weren: *oroient* P2.

147 **beholdyng vp to heuene**: only GiL.

thei seen appere to hem a woman: *vne femme estoit apparue decoste eulx* P2, *vne estoile apparut apres eulz* P1, *stella quedam iuxta eos apparuit* LgA.

147–8 **withe . . . arme**: *qui auoit la figure dun tresbel enfant* P2.

148 **a crosse**: *et la croix estoit* (*splendebat* LgA) P2.

149 **kynggez**: *trois roys* P2, *magis* LgA.

152 **of the Trinite and of God appered**: *de la trinite et de vng dieu apparoit* P2, *trini et unius dei* (. . .) *imminebat* LgA.

156 **before the tyme**: *auant par aucun temps* P2, *ante per aliquod tempus, scilicet* LgA.

157 **saiethe**: *le dit* P2. The sentence should end after *Cronicle*.
Innocent also: *Innocent pape dit* P2.

159 **that the peple**: *il pleust tant au peuple* (*senatui* LgA) *que ilz* P2.

162 **enordinat**: not in LgA.

165 **her chaumbre**: *la chambre* (add *imperatoris* LgA) P2.

167 **virgine**: add *sur vng autel* P2.

168 **arme**: *giron* P2.

171 **only**: only GiL.

173 **Virgine . . . Heuene**: *Sancta Maria Ara Celi* LgA.

177 **houre of tierce**: *hora tertia* LgA. GH2 spelling *oueir* for *houre* is not recorded in *MED*.

179 **made**: add *et regeret* LgA.

179–80 **In this same . . . Eutrope**: *Hec Orosius, idem ait Eutropius* LgA, followed by a short quotation from Albumasar, Maggioni, 70 (104–5). *Timothe* should begin a new sentence.

180 **of stories that is found**: *hystorien dit que on trouua* P2.

181 **.xxv.**: *XXXV* LgA.

182 **curiously**: add *a diis* LgA.

189 **Also**: *Secondement* P2; see 127 above.

190 **For as the seintes seine**: *In hac enim nocte, ut Bartholomeus in sua compilatione testatur* LgA.

192 **Also**: *Tiercement* P2.

194 **and an asse**: only GiL.

195 **money**: *les cens* P2, *censum* LgA.

196 **the**[1]: *vng* P2.

198 **a**[1]: *sa* P2.

200 **schalle defend**: *deficient* LgA.

oxen: *les bles proffiteront* P2, *segetes proficient* LgA.

201 **And**: *Quartement* P2.

202 **man**: add *fut par les pasteurs* P2.

211–12 **with . . . herd**: *dont fut auec cellui ange grant* P2.

212–13 **and right high thingges**: *es tres haultes choses* P2, *in altissimis* LgA.

213 **of good wille**: *en terre* P2.

220–1 **a cronicle**: *vnes croniques* P2, *quibusdam* (. . .) *chronicis* LgA.

225 **þis cause**: *celle cause* P2, *cele clause* P1, *illud* LgA.

230 **lothed**: *delaissa* P2, *fere desiit* LgA.

flesche: add *Quintement par la creature qui a estre viure sentir deuiser et entendre, sicomme ange. Les autres* (*angres* P1) *noncierent aux pasteurs sicomme dit est* (add *superius* LgA) *la natiuite nostre seigneur* P2, add further *Qui quidem apparuerunt in multitudine cum claritate et cum iubilatione* LgA.

231 **Also**: *Tiercement* P2.

235 **profete**: *prophetes* P2.

237 **from benethe**: *de humo* LgA.

239–41 **to take . . . oute**: *a tolir leur deuocion et leur cuida faire croire a sa leccon, lors le chaca hors du refretouer et du dortouer le vil estraing, pascience du chapitre* P2, *ipsum ab oratorio deuotio, a refectorio lectio, a dormitorio stramenta uilia, a capitulo patientia reiecit* LgA.

247 **come**: add *aussy comme* P2.

253–4 **with charite and fervense**: *de charite de seruans* (*feruans* S) P2, add *impedimentis: caritate scilicet seruientium* LgA.

256 **Also this fest**: *Secondement elle* P2. The *furst* to which this relates is at 231.

257 **the**: *vng* P2, *quodam* LgA.

257–8 **sinfull . . . mysgouernaunce**: *femme folieuse sy reuint touteffoys* (*tandem* LgA) *a son cueur et se desperoit de pardon* P2.

259 **peynes of helle**: *iugement* P2.

260 **hem alle**: *a estre tourmentee en enfer* P2.

262 **to apere tofore his woundes**: only GiL.

264 **the goodnesse of**: only GiL.

264–5 **that he wolde haue mercy on her**: only GiL.

266 **Also**: *Tiercement* P2.

272 **was clene**: *fut ne* P2, *fut nez* S, *natus est* LgA.

273 **oure dethe**: add *Hec Bernardus* LgA.

274 **Also**: *Quartement* P2.

279 **stynk**: *paour* P2, *tumor* LgA.

280 **oure saueoure**: *premier homme* P2, *Christi* LgA.

287 **goddes knowyng good and euell**: *dieu* P2, *dii* LgA.

289 **sone of God**: add *secundum Iohannem Damascenum* LgA.

290–2 **in . . . virgine**: *iusques aux hommes, sur les hommes. Pour les hommes, car ce fu a leur prouffit et a leur salut; iusques aux hommes pour vne semblable maniere de naistre; sur les hommes, aussi par vne autre semblable* (*dissimilem* LgA) *maniere de naistre. Selon aucun cas elle* (*eius natiuitatis* LgA) *nous fu semblable car il fu nez de famme par vne meismes porte. Et selon aucune chose elle nous fu dessamblable car elle fu nee de vierge* S.

292 **of a virgine**: *de spiritu sancto ex Maria uirgine* LgA.

6 ST ANASTASIA

Maggioni, ch. VII, p. 75; Dunn-Lardeau, ch. 7, p. 152.

2 **Fauste**: add *crestienne* P2.

2–3 **cristenly taught**: *entroduite* P2.

8–10 **so he purposed . . . of her**: *la vouloit ainsi occire* (*obscure* P2) *pour soy esbattre de ses tresgrans deulx* (*dueilz* P2, *douleurs* P1, *possessionibus* LgA) S, *Volebat enim eam sic perimere ut posset in eius latissimis possessionibus lasciuire* LgA; Batallier, no doubt correctly, substituted *douaires*. Faced by confusion in the exemplar, s.w. chose to improvise.

22 **and horrible to beholde**: only GiL.

23 **servauntes**: *serui* LgA; servants and slaves are rarely distinguished in LgD, which occasionally uses *serf*, and never in GiL. The distinction seldom matters to the narrative except in situations such as 26.65–7, where a threat is made to sell a slave unless he keeps a secret.

28 **and**: *alii lutum et puluerem in eum proiciebant, alii* LgA.

29 **all this tyme**: *les yeulx de lui estoient tenus que* P2.

32 **he**: add *et tous les autres* P2.

38–9 **and slept . . . stering**: *de celle merueille si que il ronfloit et ne pouoit estre esueille de ceulz qui le boutoient* P2.

41 **to the provost**: *cuidam prefecto* LgA.

52 **saide**: add *priuatim* LgA.

56 **Nay . . . for**: only GiL.

60 **slayn**: *tourmentee* P2.

67 **pelere**: *pel* P2, *palos* LgA.

68 **one**: *vng* and 69 **she**: *Il* P2. This unnamed male martyr is wrongly assumed by s.w. to be Anastace.

69 **dispoiled**: add *de ses richesces* P2.

70 **Take . . . inow**: only GiL.

71 **Seint**: not in LgA.

74 **thre score**: *octante* P2.

7 ST STEPHEN

Maggioni, ch. VIII, p. 78; Dunn-Lardeau, ch. 8, p. 155.

1–2 **were . . . apostelis**: *ab apostolis in ministerium ordinatus* LgA.

4–5 **olde women**: *vefues femmes* P2.

5 **serue**: add *Huius autem murmuris causa dupliciter potest intelligi, aut quia uidue eorum in ministerio non admittebantur* LgA.

6 **seruise**: add *car les apostres pource que ilz feussent plus despechez aux predicacions* (add *ministrationem commiserunt* LgA) *aux vefues* P2.

7 **for the**: add *mutacion des* P2, add *administratione* LgA.

11 **you**: add *.vij.* P2.

13 **werke**: add *Glossa:* LgA.

18 **hym**: *eulx* P2.

20 **manased hym**: *les menerent* P2, *lenuierent* P1, *Inuidentes* LgA.

27 **marterdom**: add *en chascune bataille il eust trois choses. lassaillir en bataille. laide donnee et la victoire* P2.

29–47 *cf.* Acts 6: 8–15.

29 **thyngges**: *signa* LgA.

32 **libertynes**: add *vne region* (*a regione* LgA) *ainsi dicte ou de ceulx qui estoient filz des liberacins* (*libertorum* LgA) S.

36 **of hem of the citee**: *Alixandrinorum* LgA.

37 **Dasee**: *dase* P2, *Asia* LgA.

38 **And thanne . . . victorie after**: *deinde subiungit triumphum* LgA.
seithe: only GiL.

39–40 **for . . . hym**: *Et au derrenier il met laide et a lesperit qui parloit* P2, *postremo ponit adiutorium et spiritum qui loquebatur* LgA.

41–2 **in no wise**: *par ceste maniere* P2.

42 **malicyously**: *callide* LgA.

45 **of God**: *en dieu* P2, i.e. God and Moses were the first two.

46 **in the tabernacle and in the temple**: *ou tabernacle et ou temple* P2, *et in tabernaculum siue templum* LgA.

46–7 **This . . . bataile**: *ecce prelium* LgA.

48 **aungell**: add *cest laide* P2, add *ecce auxilium* LgA.

49 **For . . . saide**: *cum falsi testes de hiis omnibus confutantur* LgA.

50–1 **Now it is thus, what saiest thou now**: *or est ainsy* P2, *si hec ita se haberent* LgA.

51 **of al**: *de illis quatuor* LgA.
excused: *MED* records neither E *aclused* nor H1 *conclued*, and one cannot tell from context what the scribes thought they meant.

52 **blame**: *blasphemia* LgA; *MED* records the sense 'blasphemy' neither for the noun nor the verb, though it is clearly required in a number of cases later in this chapter and throughout GiL.

55 **in trebel wise**: *trebuchement* P2, *tripliciter* LgA.
the yever of lawes: *donneur de loys* S, *collatiuus glorie* LgA.

56 **Bokes of Kyngges**: *Regum II* LgA.
see my name: *mon nom verra* P2, *monorera* P1, *honorificauerit me* LgA.

58 **Prouerbes**: add *.viij.* P2.

59 **to**: add *I Tim. I 'Regi seculorum immortali etc.'* LgA.

60 **glorifiant**: *glorificatiuus* LgA; s.w. adopts the French participial form. Neither this nor the G variant *glorificant* is recorded in *MED*.

61 **glorified**: (*a* P1) *glorifier* P2, *glorificandus* LgA.

62 **the**: add *secunda* LgA.

64 **for he smote the Ebrew**: *percutientem* LgA.

66 **in the desert**: follows 65 *Egipte* P2.

74 **tesmonage**, 'testimony' (*tesmongnage* P2), is not recorded in *MED*, the nearest noun being *testimoigne*, which has only two citations, one early 14th c., one for 1416.

76 **of that**: *deument du signe qui* P2, *de crimine sibi obiecto rationabiliter* LgA.

78–9 **atte the laste**: *au moins* P2.
no: only GiL. It is likely that s.w. translated correctly, and the error and addition of *no* to compensate are due to subsequent scribes; the text here should therefore have been emended.

81 **Lorde**: add *de* (add *fraternel* P1) *correction* P2.
enforsed hym to refreyne hem: *eos conatus est corrigere et a tanta malitia coercere* LgA.

83 **hertis**: add *et lamour* (*la mort* P1, *necem* LgA) *des sains* P2.

84 **that is to saie withe opstinat spirites**: only GiL.

86 **oure Lorde**: *iusti* LgA.

87 **foure**: *tres* LgA.
malice: add *tenus* P2, add *des Juis* P1, add *eorum* LgA.

88 **slowe**: *persecuterent* P2.

89 **encresed**: add *et le occistrent* P2.
the ferthe that: *et* P2. GiL adds this to correct the numerical error at 87.

90 **in her last malice**: only GiL.
wicked woman: *folieuse femme* P2, *mulieris meretricis* LgA.

96 **aduersarie**: *aduersaires* P2.

104–6 **wenyng . . . castelles**: *in hoc secundum legem se agere arbitrantes, que blasphemum extra castra mandauerat lapidari* LgA.

107–8 **for to be . . . stones**: *que ilz ne feussent touchiez* (*conchies* P1, *coinquinatur* LgA) *de la touchement de dieu* (*illius* LgA) *si que* (*uel* LgA) *il feussent plus despechiez a le lappider* S.

112 **seigh that he**: only GiL.

115 **for hem**: add *Pro se quidem orauit* LgA.

116 **abak and**: add *sic ipsi rei noxa maiori tenerentur. Pro ipsis autem orauit* LgA.

117 **hym stonyng . . . seyeng**: '*Lapidabant,' inquit, 'Stephanum inuocantem et dicentem* LgA.

120 **for**[1]: *orando per se stetit* LgA.

121 **hymselff**: add *et que il couuoitast plus estre espinchie* (*essaucie* P1, *exaudiri* LgA) *pour eulx que pour soy* P2.

123 **praiere**: add *In hoc etiam martyr Christi Christum imitatus est* LgA.

131–2 **that weren . . . cristen**: *qui estoient entour les conseulz des Juifz pour les crestiens* P2, *qui erant pro christianis in omnibus consiliis Iudeorum* LgA.

137 **provinces**: *prouince* P2.

147 **chapitre**: *liure* P2.

152 **Gendre**: perhaps *sone in lawe* was an inserted gloss which became incorporated, *gendre*, which is not recorded by *MED*, then being taken as his name; but at 174.634 *gendre*, meaning 'son-in-law', is correctly used.

154 **vnder . . . hede**: *au cheuet son sire* P2, *ad caput soceri* LgA.

157–9 **whan . . . anone:** *il lui dist que il creoit en dieu. Et il le baptisa* S.

180 **astrayeng**: *MED* has only one entry for *astraien* from Mannyng in the military sense 'break formation'; forms without *a-* are common.

185–7 **and thanne . . . helpe**: only GiL.

187 **chirche**: add *de saint estienne* P2.

193 **of eni part of hym**: *et nen eust puis point* P2.

200 **bothe**: add *Ore* (*Orosius* LgA) *quant il reuint de Iherusalem* (*Ieronimo* LgA) *il apporta a saint augustin des reliques de saint estienne aux quelles plusieurs miracles ceulx et autres* (add *furent faiz* S) P2.

205–6 **the festes**: *hec tria festa* LgA.

212 **virgine and**: only GiL.

8 ST JOHN EVANGELIST

Maggioni, ch. IX, p. 87; Dunn-Lardeau, ch. 9, p. 163.

4 **emperour**: add *Domitianus* LgA.

5–6 **before hym**: *deuant porte latine* P2.

11–12 In LgA the senate did the repealing, but who slew him is not stated.

18 **Neuenys and Orfelius**: *et les nepueux* (*veuues* P1) *et les orphelins* P2.

30 **two**: add *ditissimos* LgA.

34 **in thre maners**: only GiL.

35–6 **he . . . man**: *pource quil est homme* (*loe* P1) *des hommes* P2.

39 **gerdonable**: 'deserving of reward', not recorded in *MED*.
pore: add *sicomme dieu dit* P2.

48 **and folued the apostell**: only GiL.

55 **went**: add *plusieurs fois* P2, *per septem dies* LgA.
goldesmithes: add *et aux pierriers* P2.

66 **richesse**: add *et nudus et sine diuitiis moritur* LgA.

67 **benefices**: add *sic et inter homines omnibus omnia communia esse deberent* LgA.

69 **pursuithe, pursued**: *possidet, possidetur* LgA.

72–3 **miche . . . lesyng**: *ilz ont trauail en acquerant et paour en gardant* P2.

76 **dampnacion**: add *et encores est ce en perte double bien cest en present de grace et du bien auenir qui est gloire pardurable* P2.

78–9 **the moder of his wiff**: *mater, uidua* LgA.

85 **many**: *multa* LgA, i.e. many things.
of helle: *que il auoit veues* P2.

87 **the fende laugh**: *les dyables esioissans* P2.

103–4 **parted the game betwene hem**: *hanc disiunctam proposuit* LgA; the English amounts to: 'devised a competition between them'.

114–15 **What . . . apese the**: *Quid tibi uis? Faciam ut placeris* LgA.

136 **tellithe**: add *sicut* (. . .) *inuenitur* LgA, i.e. Clement is quoted in *Historia Ecclesiastica*.

137 **and it is founde bi other**: not in LgA; it is an attempt by Vignay to make sense of LgA *inuenitur* recorded in the previous note.

138 **goodli**: *bel et cruel* P2.

145 **Truly**: *par mon ame* P2, *in anima* LgA.

147 **clothes**: add *et se fery des poings ou chief* P2.
feble: *bonne* P2. GiL does not translate the sarcasm.

157 **kessed hem**: *lui commenca a baisier* (add *manum* LgA) P2.

161 **aboue said**: *ecclesiaste et* P2, *eadem* (. . .) *et habetur* LgA. Omission by GiL of *et* conceals the fact that two sources are being cited.

161–2 **the Cronicle**: *secundam canonicam* LgA, i.e. Apocalypse.

163–4 **La Chernice**: *Cherintum* LgA. At 165 both GiL and P2 have *Chernice* without preceding article.

166–7 **And as . . . downe**: only GiL.

168 **Cassiadore**: *Cassianus* LgA, variant *Cassiodorus*.
Dolacionis: *in libro Collationum* LgA.

169–70 **plaied . . . lust**: *lapplanissoit aussy comme en apriuoisant* P2.

191 **and comonly . . . to hem**: *il ne pouoit plus dire de paroles fors* P2, so and add *ad quamlibet pausam hoc dicebat* LgA.

198–9 **wrought . . . place**: *ora en tres secret lieu ou il estoit ales escrire les choses diuines* P2.

201 **place**: add *Hec Helinandus* LgA.

202 **fyue score**: *nonante* S.

215 **I bede . . . and**: *inuitatus ad conuiuium tuum* LgA.

217 **herte**: Two similar sentences follow in LgA, Maggioni, 95 (147–9).

223 **Edward**: *eaumont* P2, *eadmont* P1, *Eadmundus* LgA. GiL correctly attributes this story to Edward the Confessor (see *ODS*, 124; *Supplementary Lives*, 22–3). Maggioni identifies its source as Bartholomew of Trent, *Liber epilogorum in gesta sanctorum, XIX*, which also has Edmund for Edward.
and confessour: *dangleterre* P2.

223–4 **hadde suche a deuocion to Seint Iohn that he**: only GiL.

227 **aumenere**: *chambellan* P2.

232–3 **and thi thanke . . . vnderstode well**: *dont il apparut clerement* P2.

9 INNOCENTS

Maggioni, ch. X, p. 97; Dunn-Lardeau, ch. 10, p. 171.

2 **owne fame**: *infamie* P2.

4 **born**: add *et a quo pueri occisi sunt* LgA.

6 **prison**: add *Vnde de hoc extant uersus:*
Ascalonita necat pueros, Antipa Iohannem,
Agrippa Iacobum claudens in carcere Petrum LgA.

7 **furst**: add *et briefment* P2.

8 **Antipater**: add *Ydumeus* LgA.

10 **after**: add *ce dit* P2.

12 **thre**: *.vj.* P2.

13 **Aristobole**: add *Archelaus, Herodes Antipas et Philippus* LgA.
they: *Alexandrum autem et Aristobolum* LgA.
Most of the LgD MSS have lost three of the sons but failed to alter 'six' to 'three'.
in Iudee: *Iudea* LgA, 'a Jewess'.

14 **they**: i.e. Alexander and Aristobole.

15–16 **and duelled withe her fader**: only GiL.

19 **the twayne conceyuyng this treted priuely**: *sicomme ilz traictoient* P2.

26 **verray**: *ueterorum* LgA.

39 **Ioseph**: add *cum puero et matre* LgA.

47 **perfides**: LgA *persidis*, but it appears variously with *s* or *f* in LgD MSS, with *perfidis* in P2 and P1, *persidis* in S. H1 appears to have corrected it. It is recorded by *MED s.v. persidis*, 'a kind of tree, ? the Persea or Persea-tree of antiquity, a sacred tree of Egypt and Persia'.

51 **Crist**: add *Hec Cassiodorus* LgA. GiL and LgD here omit another short miracle, the provision of water by the roots of a palm tree, Maggioni, 99 (34–9).

55 **passed ouer the kyngges**: i.e. *magos* (. . .) *transuexissent* LgA.

60 **yeue**: add *le regne* P2.

63 **yere**: add *et de moins selon le temps que il auoit enquis des roys. Et ceste chose contient double entente. si que ce que il dit de moins contient de temps des enfans de .ij. ans* P2.

64 **the natiuite . . . appered**: *ea die qua stella apparuit eis dominum natum esse* LgA.

65–6 **annother yere**: *lautre annee et aucuns iours estoient passez* P2, *dominum anniculum et aliquorum insuper dierum esse credebat* LgA.

67 **yere**: add *et infra usque ad unius noctis* LgA.

68 **yere**: *puer* LgA.

69 **age**: add *uel infra faciem* LgA.

71 **witheinne**: *infra* LgA.

76 **and**: add *unde pueros bimos occidit* LgA.

77 **he dede moche persecusyon**: *et non pas les mineurs de .ij. ans* P2.

77–8 **they haue euydence . . . saie**: *fait la foy* P2, *fidem facere uidetur* LgA.

84 **bochers**: *MED bocher* gives only one citation for sense 3, 'one who slaughters human beings'; it is frequent in this text for those directly or indirectly responsible for the killing and torture of martyrs.

85–7 **The voise . . . heuene**: '*Vox, ploratus et ululatus*', *piarum scilicet matrum, 'audita est in Rama', id est in excelsum* LgA.

97 **thei saide**: (*il*) *dit* P2.
kembithe: *blanchissoit* P2, *tingeret* LgA.

99–100 **ordeyned Antipater . . . after Antipater**: *Antipatrem autem futurum regem instituit, sed ipsi Antipatri Herodem Antipam in regnum substituit* LgA. The Latin is not entirely clear, so Vignay's incorrect attempt at clarification, followed by GiL, is excusable, apart from the substitution of Agrippa for Antipas.

101–2 **that . . . Aristoboll**: *quos ex Aristobulo susceperat* LgA. Herod took care of his executed sons' five children. This was in 7 BC.

102 **for**: add *ceste* P2.

103 **double**: *mortel* P2, *intolerabile* LgA.

106 **Herodes pigges**: *Juif* P2, *pourcel* P1.

107 **for . . . pigges**: *car il est juif si espargne ses prochains* (*les pourciaus* P1) P2, *quia cum sit proselitus, porcis parcit* LgA.

108 **thanne**: add *cestui Herodes auoit ja lxx ans* P2.

109 **his body roted**: *pourreture de corps* P2, *prurigine corporis* LgA.

109–11 **his hede . . . sighyng**: *tourmens continuelz du col vers orde puantise souuent toussir par souspirs entrerompus et tourment* (*le tourmentoient* P1) P2, *colli continuis tormentis,* (. . .) *uermescentibus testiculis, intolerabili fetore, crebro anhelitu et interruptis suspiriis torquebatur* LgA.

112 **in fyre and take out**: *en fut oste* P2.

114 **most**: add *nobles* P2.

117 **there shall be**: *ie pourrai bien auoir* P2.

sorugh: *auoir nobles exeques* P2.

118–19 **sende . . . men**: *occir tous ceulx que ie tiens en chartre* P2.

121 **appel**: *poire* P2, *pomum* LgA.

123 **lette hym**: add *se il se feroit* P2.

128 **anone . . . prison**: *les decoleurs* P2.

130 **vnfortunat**: *enfortune* P2.

134 **Iues**: *uinctos* LgA.

10 ST THOMAS OF CANTERBURY

Maggioni, ch. XI, p. 103; Dunn-Lardeau, ch. 11, p. 176.

8 **made hym**: *le voult faire* P2.

11–12 **called the hayre**: only GiL.

23 **for to go**: only GiL.

28 **restabled**: *restablen*, 'restore', is not recorded in *MED*. It occurs fourteen times in GiL, usually in the past; DH2 sometimes substitute *restablisshed*, which *MED* records with one citation from Lydgate, a1475(?a1430), and then not till a1500.

29 **he**[1]: *le roy* P2.

36 **to . . . goodly**: *et Senonis a papa Alexandro susceptus* LgA.

37 **chirche of Clyny**: *monstier de clugni* P2, *in monasterio Pontiniacensi* LgA; *MED* first records *monasteri(e* for *c*.1400, the usual term having previously been *chirche*, *MED* sense 3. Both are frequent in GiL. Vignay also sometimes gives *eglise* for monastery, e.g. at 139.107.

39 **to defende**: *qui deffendissent* P2, *qui* (. . .) *diffinirent* LgA, 'who should decide'.

42 **kynne**: add *nequaquam deferens conditioni uel sexui, ordini uel etati* LgA. LgD puts this into the next sentence after **lefte neuer** as *pour condicion nulle*, which GiL omits.

45 **payne**: *palma* LgA.

50 **voide**: add *entre les apostres* P2.

51 **it was saide to hym**: *angelus respondit* LgA.

52 **the**: *vng* P2.
Thomas: only GiL.

53 **symple**: only GiL.

54–5 **and fonde hym in symple connyng**: only GiL.

55 **ydiote**: add *et inscius* LgA.

56 **of his masse and**: only GiL.

61–2 **and it is sowed . . . leid it**: *de soye rouge que il auoit laissiee la* P2, *et setam rubeam de qua illud consuit ibidem reliquit* LgA.

62 **bi this token**: only GiL.

68 **wold turne**: *flectitur* LgA.

70 **into the chirche**: *et demandoient en riant* (*criant* P1) P2.

71 **He herde it and**: *il* P2, *Monachis autem ecclesiam claudentibus, ipse illam reserauit* LgA.

72 **with cruel voys**: only GiL.

73 **as thou shalt wete**: not in P2, *et ultra uiuere non ualebis* LgA.
mekely: only GiL.

75 **but**: *Se vous me querez* P2.

78 **Marie**: add *et sanctis omnibus* LgA.

80 **men**: add *sacra capitis corona preciditur* LgA.

84 **the aungels**: *angelorum chori* LgA.
were redy and: *estoient la qui* P2, *ut aiunt* LgA.

85 **singgers**: *clercs chantans* P2, *cantantium* LgA.

93 **religious prestis**: *sacerdotum et religiosorum* LgA.

94 **Goddes enemys**: *autres* P2, *persequentium* LgA.

101 **for to . . . peple**: *pour estre plus belle* [*et*] *plus jolie* P2, *ob lasciuiam et maiorem pulchritudinem* LgA.

103 **had made her**: *fut agenoullee en* P2.

104 **aperseyued her defauute and**: only GiL.

105–8 **to restore . . . sight**: *que elle neust pas vers yeulx mais lui rendist les siens. laquelle chose elle empetra* P2, *sed saltem suos sibi redderet. Quod tandem cum multa difficultate uix ualuit obtinere* LgA.

109 **his lorde**: add *conuiuanti* LgA.
symple water: add *in pixide* LgA.

113 **boxse**: *boite* P2, *pixidem* LgA; the nearest sense given by *MED* is 'jar (for salves etc.)'.

126 **he**: *i.e.* the sickness.

129–30 **one . . . nayles**: *les vngs derompoient par pieces* (add *dentibus* LgA) *leurs doys* P2.

130–1 **the tother . . . erthe**: *les autres cheirent par pourreture* P2.

132–3 **And . . . martir**: only GiL.

11 ST SILVESTER

Maggioni, ch. XII, p. 108; Dunn-Lardeau, ch. 12, p. 180.

1 **of a ryghtwys quene**: *de iuste royne* S, *a matre re et nomine Iusta* LgA.

2 **loued**: *hantoit* P2, *exercebat* LgA.

7 **hym**[1]: *les* P2, i.e. the *richesse*.

13 **worship**: add *Siluestri igitur carceri traditur et Tarquinius ad prandium inuitatur* LgA.

14 **a mossel of**: *los dun* P2.

20 **cristen**: *catholique* P2.

21 **cite**: add *de rome* P2.

24–6 **He fasted . . . Sonday**: *Hic quartum, sextum diem et sabbatum ieiuniis instituit observandum, quintum uero quasi dominicum celebrandum* LgA.

26 **Iues saide to the cristen**: *Grecis uero christianis dicentibus* (. . .) *respondit* LgA, i.e. 'to the Greek Christians who said (. . .) he answered'.

48 **piteously**: add *toutes escheuellees* P2.

49 **chayere**: *MED* records *char* as a spelling for *chaiere*, 'sedan chair, litter', but does not record *chaier(e* for *char*, n.(2) 'chariot', which it is here and at 80.273, 104.9.

50 **to heryng . . . wise**: only GiL.

51–2 **takithe hede what I shall saie to you**: *Oyez moy* P2.

59, 60 **in this bataile, in this bataile**: *in illis preliis, in his* LgA.

61 **who**: i.e. 'whoever'.
bataile: add *le vaincu* P2.

62 **he**: *victor* LgA.
the victorie[2]: *pitie* P2.

66 **This is my conclusion**: only GiL.

67 **the worship of**: not in LgA.
receyue: *recouurasse* P2.

68 **lyff**: add *par la mort diceulx P2*.

68–9 **and yet . . . cruelte**: *quam recuperare incertam est, cum tamen certum sit quod sic recuperata crudelis est* LgA.

71–2 **other caryage . . . home**: *porteurs sans nombre* P2.

83 **that thou hast destroied**: only GiL.

87 **come**: add *tout seur* P2, *intrepidus* LgA.

106 **al holy Chirche**: *tous les euesques* P2.

107 **be kepte . . . disese**: *ab omnibus seruetur immunis* LgA.

108–9 **and specialli in Rome**: *et especiaument dedens la cite de rome* P2, *intra muros alicuius ciuitatis* LgA.

121 **on his side**: only GiL.

125 **fourtie**: *.xlj.* P2.

132 **the**: *lune des* P2.

143 **sone allone**: *si seul* P2.

144 **oure**: *uestris* LgA.

150 **vnite**: *lumilite* P2, *unitatem* LgA.

153 **plites**: add *et puis les desploia* P2, add *dicens: 'Ecce uidete tre plicas.' Et explicans* LgA.

157 **God**[1]: add *sicomme nostre seigneur ihesu crist se voult affermer estre dieu* P2.

159 **to**: *en* P2. Dathan and Abiron rebelled against Moses, Num. 16.

162 **Iues**: *juges* P2.

174 **diuision**: *distinctionem* LgA.

178 **deied**: not in LgA.

185 **counsailed**: *loua* P2.

190 **the tyrauntes**: *vous tirans* (*crians* P1) P2, *clamantes* LgA.

201–2 **Yef . . . another**: *Si alium non dederit* LgA.

206 **halowed . . . after**: *sainctifie* (*baptizari* LgA) *pour estre de rechief saintifie* P2.

208 **begynnyng**: add *de nostre sanctifiement* P2.

221 **he**: add *qui* P2.

222 **ouercome**: add *Adam* P2; the insertions in H1 are correct.

225 **Beniamyn**: add *septimus* LgA.

227 **atte the ende**: *en la fin* P2, *in fame* LgA.

235 **temptacions**: here GiL and most LgD MSS omit one sentence, Maggioni, 115 (131–2), which Dunn-Lardeau, 188, records from P1 in apparatus.

236 **another**: *octauus* LgA.

239 **the sone of God**: *uerbum* LgA.

245 **bi his owne rightwisnesse**: only GiL.

246 **dethe**: add *quia in sua deitate non ad patiendum aptus non erat* LgA.

247 **perfeccion**: add *si in sua non erat deitate passibilis* LgA.

248 **that worde . . . sone**: *filium uerbum dici* LgA.

250 **sone**: add *extitit. Filius enim eius* LgA.
wisdom: *sapientia eius, uirtus eius. In patre autem semper fuit uerbum* LgA.

251 **Dauid**: *illud* LgA; Psalm 44.

259–60 **ne vncondempnithe . . . blamithe it not**: *ne descondempne point mariage ne ne les maudit* P2, *nec eis maledixit* LgA; **vncondempnithe** must be intended as 'approve', but the word is not recorded by *MED*.

260 **not**[2]: only GiL.

266 **receyued**[1,2]: *assumptus* LgA.
hym: add *a quo* LgA.

268 **but**: add *acceptamus* LgA.

272 **suffered dethe**: *patitur* LgA.

274–5 **so is he . . . God in Crist**: not in LgA.

281 **was deyed**: *teneretur digitis* LgA.

282–3 **either . . . manhede**: *ou ce qui estoit laine auant que il fut fait pourpre* P2.

285 **the passion . . . manhede**: *passioni in nullo subiacuit* LgA.

285–6 **And . . . ouercome**: not in LgA.

300 **fende**: *dyables* P2.

302 **knotte**: *veu* P2, *neu* P1, *nodo* LgA.

307 **oyle**: *lait* P2.

308 **hony**: add *et fontes nobis mellifluos aperiret* LgA.

309 **dede**: add *et rendist vie aux mors* P2, add *surrexit ut mortuis uitam redderet* LgA.

312 **alle that other peple**: *iudices et Iudei* LgA.

318 **I schalle preue hem**: *cilz sont* P2.

324 **knowe**: add *ce mistere* P2.

345 **I lefte the up**: *tibi dicitur* LgA.

347 **thanne**: add *regina* LgA.
iuges: add *et tous les autres* P2.

350–1 **a thousand**: *plus de .iijC.* P2.

365–6 **and . . . lanternes**: *in foueam per gradus CL duas secum ferens laternas* LgA.

366 **saide**: add *draconi predicta* LgA.

367 **mouthe**: add *stridentis et sibilantis* LgA.

368–9 **the ende**: *si usque ad draconem descenderent* LgA.

374 **ydoles**: *dyables* P2.

376 **clergy**: add *de tribus* LgA.

378 **shepe**: *assemblee* P2, *gregem* LgA.
he taught and saide and: only GiL.

379 **Crist**: add *circa annum domini CCCXXX* LgA.

12 CIRCUMCISION

Maggioni, ch. XIII, p. 120; Dunn-Lardeau, ch. 13, p. 192.

3 **name**: add *portant salu* P2.

5 After **natiuite** GiL omits Maggioni, 120 (4 to 9 *domini*), Dunn-Lardeau, 192–3.
we beseche: *supplemus* LgA, 'we fill in', rendered by Vignay as *nous supplions.*

8 After *etc.* GiL omits Maggioni, 120–1 (11–13), Dunn-Lardeau, 193.

14–16 **rennythe . . . anointeth**: *decourt comme huille et celi preschie repest celi pourpense aliege et celi apelle oint* S, *instar olei lucet predicatum, pascit recogitatum, lenit et ungit inuocatum* LgA. Translators and editors differ in the allocation of the verbs to the participles. Probably: 'It illuminates like oil, it nourishes when preached, it soothes when contemplated and anoints when invoked.'

19 **of God**: *de deo deus* LgA.

19–21 **Ihesus . . . humanite**: *Christus in quantum est homo a persona diuina quantum ad humanam naturam assumptus, Ihesus in quantum est deus humanitati unitus* LgA.

26 **he**[1], 27 **He**: impersonal, translating French *il* in *il nestoit, il estoit.*

27 **somme**: add *en partie* P2, add *coniecturaliter* LgA.
fewe: here Maggioni, 121 (part of 26 to 28), Dunn-Lardeau, 193–4, is shortened in LgD and omitted from GiL.

29 **cominitee**: *diffusionem* LgA, perhaps *MED communite* sense 3, 'the totality of the people'.

31 **most**: not in P2, *recte* LgA.

34 **it**[1]: add *car il le dist de soy meismes* S.

35 **knewen it**: *le congnoissent en sa passion* P2.
denyden: *nient* P2.

37 **procession**: *professione* LgA.

39 **participans**: *particibus* LgA. This form, taken directly from the French, is not recorded in *MED*, but see *participant* adj.
he seith: *dicitur* LgA.

39–40 **he shewith**: *insinuatur* LgA.

43 **pees**: *paix* P2, *pais* P1, *patris* LgA.
named: add *de* P2.

43–4 **And for . . . Crist**: *Ab hoc secundo nomine denominamur, quia a Christo dicimur christiani* LgA.

45 **purete**: *entierete* P2.
pacience: add *castitatis* LgA.

47 **appropred to the**: *et uindicas* LgA.
in whiche . . . thingges: *cui de tam plurimis rebus nec pauca subsistunt* LgA.
notable: *plus seures* P2.

48 **werke**: add *Hec Augustinus* LgA.

49 **is of suche vertue that**: *dicitur cibus, fons, medicina et lux. Hic autem cibus multiplicem habet effectum; est enim cibus confortatiuus, inpinguatiuus, roboratiuus et uegetatiuus. De hiis sic dicit Bernardus: 'Est cibus hoc nomen Ihesus* LgA. All this is missing from S; P1 and P2 have lost different parts of it.

51 **defendethe from ydell thougthes**: *deffent les folles pensees* P2, *exercitatos reparat sensus* LgA; GiL *from* shows that *defendethe* is from *MED defenden* sense 3, 'protect', but LgD *deffent* requires sense 7, 'forbid'.

51–2 **comfortithe . . . fende**: *reconforme les assailliz* P2, *uirtutes roborat* LgA.

53 **drawithe to hym**: *attrait* S, *acroist* P1, *uegetat* LgA.

55–6 **seled . . . stremes**: only GiL.

56 **seled**: add *uite* LgA.

59 **absolucion**: *ablutione* LgA.

60 **redemptor**: *redemptio* LgA.

61 **quik spryngges**: *tres riui* LgA.

62 **confession**: add *sang despersion ou quel affliction est signifiee* P2.

64 **Also**: *Tiercement* P2.

67 **fere**: *fluxum* LgA.

70 **Also**: *Quartement* P2.
saiethe: add *Vnde* LgA.

73–4 **afore the gentiles, and the voys therof was lyght brennyng fulle of suetnesse**: *deuant les gens et les voix* (*rois* P1) *aussy comme la lumiere fut* (*sus* P1) *vng chandelabre. Et ce nom ihesus est de grant souuenance. dont saint bernard dit. se tu es crist il ne me sent* (*ser* P1) *riens. se il ny a ihesus se tu desputes il ne me sent* (*sert* P1) *riens se ihesus nest nommez* P2, *coram gentibus et regibus tamquam lucernam super candelabrum.' Hoc iterum nomen Ihesus est multe suauitatis, unde Bernardus: 'Si scribas, non sapit mihi nisi legero ibi Ihesum, si disputes ac conferas, non sapit mihi nisi sonuerit ibi Ihesus.'* LgA.

77 **Also**: *Secondement* P2.
vertue: *virtuositas* LgA.
saith: add *tu apelleras le nom de lui ihesus* P2.

80 **fendes**: add *des corps assegiez* P2.

81 **Also**: *Tiercement* P2.

83 **flesche**: add *de mon sang* P2.

84 **merveylable**: *MED merveilable* has only one citation, from Walton's Boethius, dated *c.*1450 (1410).

85 **inestimable**: add *et est plus merueillable que nom inextimable et plus gracieux de cellui que agreable* P2.

88 **Ioseph**: *Ihesus* P2, *Ioseph* SZ, corrected in S in the margin.
saueoure: Here GiL omits Maggioni, 124 (76–83), Dunn-Lardeau, 196.

91–2 **in .v. maners and**: only GiL.

92 **circumcision**: add *Et ce fut commencement de nostre sauuement* P2.

93 **tofore . . . water**: *et ce fut en demonstrant le desir de nostre redempcion* P2.

94 **scourgyng**: add *et ce fut la merite de nostre redempcion. car nous sommes gariz par son sang* P2.
crucifieng: add *et ce fut le pris de nostre redempcion* P2, add further *tunc enim que non rapuit exsoluit* LgA.

106 GiL here omits Maggioni, 125–8 (101–62), Dunn-Lardeau, 197–201, including the remaining 'causes'.

109 **it was translated**: *il la translata* P2.

110 **Chartres**: *Carosium* LgA, i.e. Charroux.

111 **chirch that is called Sancta sanctorum**: according to early pilgrim guides, this was the chapel of Sancta Sanctorum in the church of St John Lateran, which has subsequently been burned down and rebuilt more than once.

112 On St Gregory's appointing of the 'stacions', see Capgrave, 85.

113 GiL omits from here to the end, Maggioni, 129–30 (168–82), Dunn-Lardeau, 201–2.

13 EPIPHANY

Maggioni, ch. XIV, p. 131; Dunn-Lardeau, ch. 14, p. 202.

2–4 **the .iij. kyngges . . . Bethelem**: *Christum magus adorat* LgA.

4–5 **oure . . . Iordane**: not in LgA.

7 **thre**: *.xiij.* P2.

9 **as . . . aboue**: *sicomme il est dit en lexposicion par dessus* P2, *ab epi, quod est*

supra, et phanos, apparitio, quia tunc desursum stella apparuit LgA. Vignay, misled by *supra*, forgot there was no introductory etymology to this chapter.

12 **yere**[1]: add *car il auoit .xxix. ans et .xiij. iours et estoit aussy commencant de .xxx. ans* P2.
after Beede: *sicomme lucas dit ou selon bede* P2.

12–13 **and the Chirche . . . holde**: *quod et Romanam ecclesiam tenere asserit* LgA.

18 **yere**: add *et .xiii. iours* P2.

24 ***Illuminas***: *illuminans* P2.
she: i.e. the day.

25 **mete**: *mengier* P2, *bucca siue manducare* LgA.
this: add *quarto* LgA.

27 **Iohn**: *Iohannes VI* LgA.

29 **thries**: *quatre foys* P2.

32–3 **of the .iij. kyngges**: only GiL.

38 **Magus**: add *sy a tripple significat. Magus* P2.

38–9 **an enchauntour, a scornere**: *enchanteur. escharnisseur* P2, *illusor, maleficus* LgA.

40 **scorners**: *escharnisseurs* P2, *illusores* LgA.

41 **scorned**: *mocquerent* P2, *illuserunt* LgA.

42 **thei . . . hym**: *il estoit mocquie des roys* P2.

43 **troubled**: add *Et magus est a dire enchanteur maleficie car les maistres maleficiez de pharaon estoient ditz magi* P2, as P2 without *enchanteur* LgA; but the Latin word *maleficus* generally implies involvement of the black arts.

44 **wicked doers**: *maleficos* LgA; see above.

48 **for . . . scribe**: *nam Perse magus, Hebraice scriba* LgA.
philosophie: *phylozophe* P2.

50 **thre**: add *sages* P2.

59 **not**[1]: add *excuser ne* P2.

67 **sterre**: add *secundum Remigium* LgA.

68 **her fader**: in some traditions the three kings were regarded as descendants of Balaam.

71–2 **of heuene**: not in LgA.

72 **for to take continuelly hede**: only GiL.

75 **.xij.**[e]: add *chascun an* P2.
an high hille: *montem Victorialem* LgA, add *et demouroient la par trois iours* P2.

77 **that**: add *vne foys* P2.

79 **another sterre**: *et auoit vne estoille* (*crux* LgA) P2.

82 **fynde**: add *nez* P2.

94 **more (. . .) thanne**: *autant* (. . .) *comme* P2.
dayes: add *et le dromadaire est expose vertueux de courre* P2, add *unde dicitur dromedarius a dromos quod est cursus et ares quod est virtus* LgA.

112–15 **wherof . . . dignite**: In LgA this follows 120 *apered*.

115 **hille**: *culmine* LgA.

116 **Iues**: *romanis* LgA.
the emperour: *Augustus* LgA.

117 **ordeyned**: add *sic enim ordinauerant Romani ut nullus deus uel rex sine sui licentia et imperio diceretur* LgA.

118–19 **was wrothe. What meruaile for**: *turbatus est, nimirum quia* LgA; Knowles (pp. 356–7 n. 5) comments on Vignay's rather frequent use of the phrase *quelle merveille*, 'qui semble le plus souvent (mais pas toujours) traduire le mot latin *quippe*'.

119, 120 **was confounded, apered**: *confunditur, aperitur* LgA.

122–3 **the comyng . . . empire**: *la venu de cellui juste ilz ne peuvent joir de leur empire* P2, *impii gaudere nequeunt de aduentu iusti* LgA.

131–2 **of the lawe**: only GiL.

138–9 **worschip hym . . . slee hym**: *aorer cellui que il vouloit occire* P2.

142 **enquere**: add *de la natiuite di celui si que ilz feussent certains dicelle. tant par* P2.

144 **as sone as**: *pource que* P2.

146 **true peple**: *infidelibus data sunt secundum apostolum, sed prophetia fidelibus* LgA.

146–7 **of withedrawyng of the sterre**: only GiL.

148 **Iues**: add *mescreans* P2, add *fideles* LgA; add further *Et la glose cy endroit touche trois raisons* P2.

168 **and**: add *en mouuement car elle* P2.

169 **gyde**: add *Et nestoit pas menee* (*meue* P1) *par maniere de mouuement de cercle. mais aussy comme par maniere* (*motu* LgA) *de beste. qui alast deuant* P2.

170 **Mathew**: *Mathei II, que incipit 'Hec stella dominice natiuitatis etc.'* LgA.
makyng of the sterre: *naissance* P2, *origine* LgA.

173 **Genesis**: *Genesis I* LgA.

178 **ioie**: GiL here omits Maggioni, 137–8 (96–114), Dunn-Lardeau, 207–8.
hous: *maisonnette* P2.

178–80 **and thei . . . childe**: *chascun sagenoulla* P2.

182 **is**: add *Es dras du quel* R, *ad cuius pannos* LgA; many MSS, including P2SP1, write *Esdras*.
preisen: *touchent* P2, *couchent* P1, *excubant* LgA.

183 **dreden**: add *Les ensuiteurs de saigesce sagenoullent* P2.

184 **Seint Ierome saiethe**: not in LgA, add *o ciel. ou quel lumiere nest pas mais estoille* P2, add *O beatum tugurium, o sedes dei secunda post celum, ubi non lucerna, sed stella* LgA.

185 **duellith**: *tu habites* P2, *habitat* LgA.
a kyng not crowned: *non rex gemmatus* LgA.
corporat: *encorpore* P2, 'incorporated', i.e. incarnate; *MED corporaten* v. sense 1 'incorporate or assimilate' gives only three citations, all from Trevisa, but none with this specific contextual extension.

186–8 **an hard crache . . . seruice of sterres**: *dure cresche* (. . .) *pour nobles vestemens et pour mol lit. et pour* [*t*]*rez dorez. Tu as haultesce de maison enfumee. mais elle est ennoblie par seruice destoilles* P2, *pro mollibus toris dura presepia, pro laquearibus aureis fumea culminum tecta, sed sideris obsequio decorata* LgA. P2 *trez* (MS *crez*) = *trefs*, 'beams', 187 *she* is the *hous*.

188–9 **in the tone side, in that other side**: only GiL.

196 **semed**: *furent fais* P2.

198 **childe**[2]: *lenfantement* P2.

199 **hym**: add *les drappellez ordissent. dieu en est aoure* P2.

200 **pershed**: *preschee. Et veez cy que les choses humiliables et enfermes ne furent pas tant seulement en dieu* (*Christo puero* LgA) *mais les treshaultes de diuinite* P2.

201 **Ebrewes**: *Ephesios* LgA.

204 **philosofers**: *pharisei* LgA.

206 **God**: add *tonnant* P2.

210 **was**: add *ut dicit Remigius* LgA.

211 **kyng**: add *Perse* LgA.

212 **yeftes**: add *et si comme il est dit en lystoire escoliere. Ceulx cy vindrent des fins de perse et de caldee ou le fleuue de sabba est. dont la region* [*est*] *dicte sabee* P2.

219 **dethe**: *mortalitas* LgA.

221 **Crist**: add *La quinte car par ces .iij. choses sont signifiees trois choses qui estoient auant en ihesucrist* P2.

229–30 **The name . . . Crist**: *La manne signifie de la natiuite ihesucrist* P2, *la* *maniere segnefie la manne de ihu crist* S, *La manne senefie la magne de la diuinite ihesucrist* P1, *manna (significabat) diuinitas* LgA.

235 **corrupte**: *non corrompue* P2.

237 **region**: add *per aliam viam* LgA.

241–2 **oure bretherin**: *ordinis nostris, scilicet fratrum predicatorum* LgA.

14 ST PAUL HERMIT

Maggioni, ch. XV, p. 141; Dunn-Lardeau, ch. 15, p. 211.

S lacks one folio covering Paul Hermit and first part of Remy.

1–2 **saiethe . . . witnessithe that**: *qui escript la vie de cellui tesmongne* P2.

4–5 **Decyen was of Galile and hadde double name**: *Decius* (. . .) *fuisse Gallienus, qui fuit binomius* LgA. Decius was emperor 249–51, Valerianus 253–60, and Gallienus at first jointly with his father 253–68. There is no sign that Decius was ever called Gallienus. Voragine tries to sort out this name in a passage in the life of St Lawrence, Maggioni, 760–2; see note to 110.12.

23 **deserued victori of preysing**: *tropheum laude dignum promeruit* LgA.

25–6 **duelled . . . hermytage**: *primum se inter monachos heremicolam cogitaret* LgA; the necessary sense of *hermytage*, 'being a hermit', is not recorded by *MED*.

28 **and wildernesse**: only GiL.

30 **palmers**: *MED* has only two citations for *palmer*, 'palm-tree', one for *c.*1400, one for *c.*1500.

33 **a satirell, lorde of the wodis**: *Satyr, deum siluarum* LgA. GiL takes *satirell* from LgD; it is not recorded by *MED*, which, however, has *satire* in this sense.

15 ST REMY

Maggioni, ch. XVI, p. 143; Dunn-Lardeau, ch. 16, p. 213.

15 **reclusage**: state of being a recluse, not recorded in *MED*.

16 **erchebisshop**: add *Remensis* LgA.

25 **gret . . . nombre**: add *destranges gens* P2, *infinitus exercitus Alemannorum* LgA.

27 **straunge peple**: *Alemannis* LgA.

32–3 **toke . . . and**: only GiL.

36 **Genebaude**: add *uir prouidus* LgA.

37 **moder**: *niepce* P2.

40 **bicause of visitacion**: i.e. for the purpose of instruction.

48 **it**: i.e. the news.

51 **And**: *quod cum sanctus Remigius prohibuisset et* LgA.

69 **fiftee**: *D* LgA.

16 ST HILARY

Maggioni, ch. XVII, p. 146; Dunn-Lardeau, ch. 17, p. 215.

7 **heresies**: *hereges* S.
in: i.e. into.

8 **maister**: *fautor* LgA.

9 **heresyes**: *hereges* P2.

10 **alle**: add *episcopi* LgA.

11 **of .x.**: *des diz* P2, *dictorum* LgA, i.e. the 'two' referred to in 7 above.

13 **to go**: *redire* LgA.

15 **chased . . . lokyng**: *omnes serpentes ex sui uisione fugabat* LgA.

17 **the whiche**: *tamquam* LgA.

18 **is**: *sit* LgA.

18–19 **a dede childe (. . .) was releued (. . .) and restabled to lyff ayein**: *vng enfant mort* (. . .) *fut resuscite* (. . .) *et restabli a vie* P2, *infantem defunctum* (. . .) *ad uitam restituit* LgA; *MED releven* sense 4 (b) gives 'arise from the dead', and 4 (c) 'restore to a previous condition', but not precisely 'resuscitate' as required here and in several later instances.

20 **orison**: *la pouldre* P2.

24 **stabeled**: add *pource que elle ne fut tournee aucunes fois* P2, add *ne aliquando flecteretur formidans* LgA.

32 **heresies**: *hereges* P2.

33 **vnsent for**: 'uninvited'; *MED* has two entries, the first for *c.*1440 Scrope.

36–7 **I am not Galle, but I am a bisshop of Fraunce**: *Non sum Gallus, sed de Gallia, id est non sum in Gallia natus, sed de Gallia episcopus* LgA. The pun on *Gallus*, 'domestic cock', is not attempted in GiL, and subsequent wordplay on *iudex/Iuda* is also lost in LgD.

37 **Thanne saide the pope**: not in P2, in LgA.
And: add *si tu es Hylarius de Gallia* LgA.

37–8 **iuge . . . Rome**: *Romane sedis apostolicus et iudex* LgA.

39–40 **and thou iuge . . . mageste**: *si iudicans resides, sed non in sede maiestatis* LgA.

54–62 Hilary died *c.*368, and Leo I became pope in 440. The pope here should be Liberius, 352–66. For 61 *Constaunt* LgA gives *Constantino*, but since Constantine died in 337, this emperor must be Constantius II, 337–361, who, although Christian, fell out with Liberius on a number of issues. See Boureau, 1117–18, nn. 11–13.

56 **cronicle**: it is not clear what chronicle is here referred to.

74 **four hundred and fourti**: *CCCXL* LgA.

78 **hym**: add *et lautre vint a cellui* P2.
loef: add *Tunc ille confusus ingemuit et munera maiora obtulit* LgA.

17 ST MACARIUS

Maggioni, ch. XVIII, p. 149; Dunn-Lardeau, ch. 18, p. 218.

1 **Makarie**: add *abbas* LgA.
oute of a place of desert: *de Syti* LgA, i.e. Scete in Upper Egypt.

1–2 **in the sepulture of a dede man**: *dormir en vng monument ou la sepulture des corps des paiens estoient* P2.

2 **the**: *lun* P2.

3 **fende**: *dyables* P2.

9 **Allas**: only GiL.

13–14 **And . . . doest**: *quidquid tu facias et ego facio* LgA.

27 **violes**: add *Et il dist* P2.

31 **halowed**: add *et nul ne sest accorde a moy* P2.

31–2 **and he . . . drinke**: only GiL.

33 **gretly**: only GiL.
holy: only GiL.

33–4 **exhortacion**: *coniuration* P2, *exhortatione* LgA.

50 **roser**: *rosel* P2, i.e. 'small reed'. *MED* cites only three instances of *rosel*, the unfamiliarity of which doubtless accounts for substitution of more familiar *roser*, 'rose-plant'.

64 **flies**: *scabronibus* LgA, 'insect-bites'.

65 **myracles**: *vertuz* P2.

18 ST FELIX OF NOLA

Maggioni, ch. XIX, p. 152; Dunn-Lardeau, ch. 19, p. 220.

1 **Enpinces**: *in pincis* LgA; the chapter is basically about St Felix of Nola,

the soubriquet being taken from the presence of a church in his name on the hill called Pincio in Rome (26 below), for which probably the first story has been devised. See Boureau, 1120–1, Maggioni (2007), 1494.

2–3 **pinche is to saie greef**: *pinchee est a dire greffe* P2, *pinca subula dicitur* LgA; Voragine glosses the unfamiliar late Latin *pinca* as 'awl'; *MED* defines *grefe* as 'a writing or engraving instrument, a stylus', but does not record *pinche*.

9 **ydole**: add *et il souffloit encontre et tantost elle tresbuchoit* P2.

10 **And**: *Il est leu en vne autre legende que* P2.

Mychine the bisshop and Valerien: *Micheme* (*Maxime* P1) *euesque et Valerien* P2, *Maximus, Nolanus episcopus* LgA. Vignay seems to have identified the former wrongly as the Maximus celebrated (14 April) with Tiburtius and Valerian, brother and husband of St Cecilia, and therefore substituted Valerian for *Nolanus*, i.e. 'of Nola'.

12 **as halff dede**: only GiL.

14 **to comforte hym**: *quil lui peust donner* P2, *cibi* LgA.

15 **honycombe**: *roisin* P2, *racemum* LgA, 'bunch of grapes'.

15–16 **the hony . . . mowthe**: *si quil lui espraint* (add *uinum* LgA) *en la bouche* P2.

16 **toke . . . and**: only GiL.

26 **was**: add *reddita* LgA.

Lorde: add *et fut enseueli empres la cite en vng lieu qui est dit pincees* P2.

31 **stale**: *vouldrent oster* P2.

32 **but . . . gardine**: only GiL.

35 **wolde haue hadde**: *vindrent pour prendre* P2.

36 **passion**: add *manus eorum* LgA.

and rore like madde bestis: only GiL.

44 **confermed**: *instruxisset* LgA.

19 ST MARCELLUS POPE

Maggioni, ch. XX, p. 154; Dunn-Lardeau, ch. 20, p. 222.

1 **preste**: not in P2, *pontifex* LgA.

2 **cristen**: here GiL, LgD, and some MSS of LgA omit Maggioni, 154 (3–5), *imperator . . . argueretur*.

3 **that . . . chirche**: *in ecclesia consecrata* LgA.

20 ST ANTHONY

Maggioni, ch. XXI, p. 155; Dunn-Lardeau, ch. 21, p. 222.

S lacks a folio, containing *Antony* 104 to end, all of *Fabian*, and *Sebastian* 1–4.

2 **gospell**: *eglise* P2.

4 **the fende**: *dyables* P2.

17 **thei come ayein**: *de la vertu de lui il les esmouuoit a lui* P2.

18–19 **withe her hornes and nayles**: *aux dens, aux ongles, et aux cornes* P2.

34 **he shulde haue herde the sowne in the falle**: *utique pre sui magnitudine latere non posset* LgA.

37 **it was as**: *il fuy aussy comme se* P2.

41 **besette with snares**: *entretenant ensemble par la terre* (*laceures* P1) *de las* P2, *laqueis sese inuicem connectentibus plenum* LgA.

47 **faste**: only GiL, 'by all means'.

50–58 **I . . . cristen**: in LgA the direct speech ends at 54 **awaye**.

54 **Crist**: add *et membati contre lui* P2.

57–8 **these cursed cristen**: *maledicunt christiani* LgA.

59 **malice**: *vision* P2, *insidiis* LgA.

60 **wrathe me al togederes**: *se courroucent ensemble* P2.

62 **felawship**: *ses compaignons* P2, *fratribus* LgA.

62–3 **and lowgh hym to scorne**: not in P2, *et ei displicuit* LgA.

69 **restresse**: *relacher* P2; *MED restressen* has only one entry, for a1500(?a1400), glossed 'restrain'.

70 **confused**: *edificatus* LgA.

76–7 **Antony?' And he saide**: *et anthoine dit* P2.

81 **deyen from thaire holy purpos**: *cest hors de leurs propos* P2, *a quietis proposito resoluuntur* LgA.

83 **sight**: *ranqueur* P2, *uisus* LgA.
and fighting: *il se combat* P2.

86 **saide: 'Bretheren**: *dit aux freres* P2.

87 **and thei saide: 'Ye'**: only GiL.

93 **in to moche talkyng**: only GiL. EH1G *into* obscures the sense.

98 **houndes**: add *et aues* LgA.

100 **witheholde**: *veulent auoir* P2.

103 **thoughtez**: add *et dont se leua et entra seul ou desert* P2.

110 **defended**: add *et auoit les mains estendues* P2, add *extensis manibus* LgA.

114–16 **the acorde of soules . . . witholde hem**: *laccort des ames et les dyables* (*le deable* P1) *qui les deffendoit aler hault. et detenoit aucunes en ses las. et se douloit de ce que celles des sains sen voloient que il ne pouoit retenir* P2, *animarum* (. . .) *conscensum* (variant *consensum*) *et dyabolum prohibentem qui quasdam obnoxias retineret et de sanctorum uolatu, quos retinere non poterat, sic doleret* LgA. Finding *consensum* for *conscensum*, 'ascension', Vignay understandably linked the souls with the devil.

117 **praied**: *ouuroit* P2, 'worked'; confusion between *ouuroit* and *ouroit* is frequent.

122 **felony**: add *qui* P2.
afore: add *estoit a auenir ou siecle* P2, *seculis immineret* LgA.

124 **spores**: *calcibus* LgA.

125 **shal . . . tormented**: *par grant tourment* (. . .) *sera bestournee* P2, *magno turbine* (. . .) *subuertetur* LgA.

128 **abhominacion**: the variant *abhortacion* in EH1 is recorded in neither *MED* nor *OED*.

129 **baptime**: *baptisterium et ecclesias* LgA.

130 **the cristen sacrified**: *sacrifioient les crestiens* P2.
bestes: *ouailles* P2.

131 **duke**: add *arianus* LgA.

131–2 **tormented . . . comune**: *ita ecclesiam infestaret ut uirgines et monachos nudatos publice uerberaret* LgA.

138 **come**: add *quoque* LgA.

140 **and al torent . . . same**: *par les mors dicellui* P2.

141 **hors**: add *et eust rongiees et desrompues les cuisses* P2.

151 **Olde**: only GiL.

153–4 **Constant**: *Constantino* LgA; in fact Constantine died in 337, St Anthony in 356.

21 ST FABIAN

Maggioni, ch. XXII, p. 161; Dunn-Lardeau, ch. 22, p. 227.

2–3 **to the register . . . it**: *rei exitum scire uolens* LgA; Vignay and s.w. apparently take *registre/register* as 'official recorder', a sense first given in *MED s.v. register(e* for a1443.

7 **and brought hem to hym**: not in LgA.

14 **two hundered**: *CC.iiijxx. et .iij.* P2, *CCLIII* LgA. He died in 250.

22 ST SEBASTIAN

Maggioni, ch. XXIII, p. 162; Dunn-Lardeau, ch. 23, p. 228.

2 **citezein**: *eruditus* LgA.

4 **felawship of knyghtes**: *cohortis* LgA.

5 **alwaye**: *tant seulement* P2.

8 **bretherin**: *gemini fratres* LgA.

12 **and suffre for you**: *ne pleur sy fort a souffrir* P2.

14 **I wolde . . . dethe**: *a force je les suiuroie de bataille, se ilz feussent enclos en chartre ie la romproie et deussent morir* P2.

15 **to me**: not in LgA.

15–19 **the yougthe . . . lyue**: paraphrasing Maggioni, 163 (13–14), except that GiL follows P2S, which read *viollence* for P1 *viellesce*, LgA *senectus*.

19 **fader**: add *qui estoit ainsy* (*ancien* P1) P2.

30 **before my sight**: *par glaiue* P2.

33 **and oure children**: *a qui seront ces enfans qui leur donra larges possessions* P2, *qui erunt horum infantium domini, quis uestras largas diuidet possessiones?* LgA.

45–6 **defoulen . . . in hym**: *et conchie ceulx qui si actendent et despit ceulx qui y ont prescripcion* P2, *se expectantes decepit, de se presumentes irrisit* LgA.

47–8 **to be a theef . . . madde**: *furem ut rapiat, iracundum ut seuiat* LgA.

58 **chasithe**: *enchante* P2S, *en chauce* P1, *insultat* LgA; *enchaucier* for *enchalcier* can mean 'pursue' or 'pursue with reproaches'.

61 **other**: add *nimio splendore illustratus est; apparuitque sibi iuuenis pallio candido indutus dans ei pacem et dicens: 'Tu semper mecum eris.'* LgA.
the whiche kepte: *in cuius domo* (. . .) *custodiebantur* LgA.

65 **mouthe**: add *et les croit. sy lui ouure la bouche qui apparut* (*aperuit* LgA) *la bouche* P2, i.e. 'let him open her mouth who opened the mouth of Zecharia'.

88 **bi any occasyen**: *hac occasione* LgA, 'in such an event'; *MED s.v. occasioun* sense 4b (a) records the phrase but with the sense 'for any cause'.

95 **light**: *disciplina* LgA.

97 **pais**: *pondera* LgA, doubtless intended as a substantial sum of money; this usage is not recorded in *MED*; see *s.v. peis* sense 6.

109 **Tyberien**: *Tiburtius* LgA, i.e. *Tyburcien* as at 100 above.

110 **sone**: add *et lui* P2.

116 **do sacrifice**: *que il donnast encens* P2.

132 **accused . . . emperour**: *denonca les faiz de* (add *sebastien a* P1) *dyoclecien empereure* P2.

135 **haste now abaied and cried**: *hactenus latuisti* LgA.

142 **so thikke . . . side**: only GiL.

143 **two**: *paucos* LgA.

145 **emperour** and 146 **hym** are plural in LgD and LgA, so 145 *he* is Sebastian; at 146–7 *emperour* and *I comaunded* are singular in LgD, plural in LgA; and at 150 all have singular, even LgA.

148 **refused**: *resuscite* P2; and similarly at 122.79. GiL has *resussytynge* gerund at 43.50 and pp. *resuscite* at 95.155; probably s.w. used it here but an early copyist did not recognize it. *MED* records *resusciten* with only two citations from *Knight of La Tour-Landry*, *c*.1450, and also *resuscen*, with one citation from one MS of *Cursor Mundi*, regarded as an erroneous form of *resusciten* or an error for *rescouen.*

152 **preuey**: *chambre quoye* P2, *cloacam* LgA; the Latin is more precisely 'sewer', but Vignay and s.w. translate thus on each of its occurrences.

154 **Luce**: *Lucine* LgA.

156 **and**[1]: add *il* P2.

167 **preest . . . fende**: *dyable assailly cellui prestre* P2.

168 **saide that thei shulde speke to**: *distrent aux* P2, *duxerunt autem eam* (. . .) *ad* LgA.

169 **shuld enchaunte**: *suis incantationibus* (. . .) *effugarent* LgA.

170 **right wisdom**: *iugement* P2.

175 **Gilbert**: *Gumberti* LgA.

177 **Romas**: *rome* P2.

179 **make hem departe**: *cedem faceret* LgA.

180 **deied oute therof**: *mors en estoient mis hors* P2.

183 **Petre**: add *qui est dicte aux lyens* P2.

184 **from thennes born to**: *la apportees de* P2.

187 **the stabilnesse**: *leur fermete* P2, *infirmitate* LgA.

188 **oure**: *voz* P2, *nostris* LgA.

188–9 **towardes the**: *a prece* LgA.

189 **thine enemyes**: *infirmis* LgA, variant *inimici.*

23 ST AGNES

Maggioni, ch. XXIV, p. 169; Dunn-Lardeau, ch. 24, p. 235.

2 **her liff and**: only GiL.
.xiiij.: *xiij*[e] P2.

4 **aunsien . . . wisdom**: *senectus mentis immensa* LgA.

9 **sheparde**: *pasture* P2, *pabulum* LgA.
begynnyng: *fomes* LgA.
felones: *felonnie* P2.

12 **manere**: *decore* LgA.

19 **comforted**: add *par son atouchement* P2.

20 **continence**: *sanctitas* LgA.
assembelyng: *unio* LgA.

21 **auctorite**: add *dicens* LgA.

21–3 **of whom . . . other**: these are rhetorical questions in LgA, *Cuius generositas celsior, etc.*; Vignay gives them as statements, *duquel la noblesce est plus haulte . . .*

26 **byndeth**: *signat* LgA.

27 **bi the passion of his blode**: *passionis sue sanguine* LgA.

36 **that mowen not be nombered**: *incomparabiles* LgA.

45 **blandishe**: 'flattering', not as adj. in *MED*, but cf. *blaundice* n.

46 **What wilt thou do**: *Quidquid uis age* LgA.

47–8 **I praise . . . manasing**: *Je ne te prise pas plus par bel parler que par menacier* P2.

49 **to oure goddes in the clothyng of goddes**: *a noz dieux en vestement de deesse. ou se ta virginite te plaist* P2, *cum uirginibus dee Veste si tibi uirginitas placet* LgA.

53 **I tell the pleinli**: only GiL.

67 **miracle**: add *et sen retournerent et* P2.

78 **lyff**: add *Tamen quia tempus est ut uirtus domini manifesteretur, egredimur foras* LgA.

79 **and praied hertely oure Lorde**: not in LgD, *apparuit ei angelus domini et ipsam flentem et orantem a terra eleuauit* LgA.

85–6 **he durst . . . peple**: *proscriptionem metuens* LgA.

86 **ordeyned . . . Aspasien**: *estably vng vicaire* P2, *uicarium dereliquit* LgA.

88 **nwe**: only GiL. **vicarie**: add *qui auoit nom aspasien* P2.

89 **and whanne . . . middell of the fyre**: *mais* P2.

90 **misbeleuers**: add *et eam minime contingebat* LgA.

94 **Constant**: *Constantini* LgA.

112 **Constant**: *Constantini* LgA.
siknesse: *lepre* P2.

130 **and kepte the rynge faste**: only GiL.

140 **Ther nys no more**: *nul nest plus* P2.

141 **of men**: *ab omnibus* LgA, variant *hominibus*.

141–2 **wherfor . . . marter**: *car tant hommes comme crieurs qui preschent ceste matiere* P2, *quot homines, tot precones, qui martyrem predicant dum loquuntur* LgA.

147–8 **that nature hadde a strong striff of the victorie**: *que nature ia forte a estrif de victoire* P2, *iam matura uictorie, certare difficilis* LgA; *difficilis* can perhaps be rendered 'not well equipped for'.

153 G *desoxenyd* for *deserued* is hard to account for and not found in *MED*.

156–7 **and endelesly to ioie with hym**: only GiL.

24 ST VINCENT

Maggioni, ch. XXV, p. 174; Dunn-Lardeau, ch. 25, p. 240.

3 **he hadde a lettyng in**: *il estoit plus despechiez de* P2, *impeditioris erat* LgA.

3–4 In these lines 'he' is the bishop.

5 **of**: add *preuost* P2.

6 **drawen**: add *Valentiam* LgA, i.e. 'to Valencia'. Valerius was bishop of Saragossa.

17 ff. In this passage Dacien is both the *iuge* and the *prouost* (*iudex* and *preses*).

23 **eculee**: The description comes from LgD, but is not in LgA; *eculee* is also described at 51.59, 54.109, and 118.9–10, and is said to be *frenshe* at 109.59. At 71.25 LgD supplies a description which GiL omits, and at 38.59–60 LgD omits the word but gives a description, which s.w. translates. Caxton's adaptation of the example from 51 (Secundus) is the only citation in *OED*; it is not in *MED*.

26 **saiest**: *voys* P2.

27 **is al torent**: only GiL.

30–1 **O thou cursed creature**: *O felicem me* LgA.

35 **more mow suffre**: *pouoir plus quant je seray tourmente* P2.

43 **you all**: *voz tormens* P2.

60–1 **the lemes . . . moyster**: LgD and LgA have an extended account of this burning, including in LgA the sprinkling of salt, Maggioni, 176 (45–6), Dunn-Lardeau, 242.

61–2 **till he was made**: *Inter hec ille manet* LgA.

73 **softenesse and**: only GiL.

78 **creueys**, 129 **trewens**: both represent LgD *creuaces* (LgA *rimas* 78, *lacunas* 129); at 78 variants are *greues* H1, *greneys* A1, *grenyes* A2; DH2 omit *the creueys of*. 129 *trewens* is so spelt in EH1DH2, but *krenys* G, *creves* L, *crevais* A1, *creveons* A2. In these hands *n* and *u* can be ambiguous even when apparently distinct, and *c* and *t* are sometimes very similar, including in E and H1. *MED s.v. crevace* records no forms with initial *g* or *t* or medial *n*; the word *crani* is likely to be irrelevant. In view of the L spelling, the reading should probably also be *creueys* at 129.

82 **softe clothes**: *stramentis mollioribus* LgA.
glorious: add *sy que* (add *par* P1) *auenture il ne defaille es tourmens* P2.

87 **.CCC.**: *.CC.* P2.
.viij.: *VII* LgA.

95 **briddes**: add *greigneurs de lui* P2.

103 **fishes**: *belues* P2.

105 **of Ihesu Crist**: *ipso* LgA.

110–11 **for the loue of God**: *pour hanter dieu* P2, *ut exerceatur* LgA.

120 **vnouercome**: *oon ouercome* GL, and so G but not L at 133.

123 **.viijC.**: *CCC* LgA.

125 **hokes drawyng, the fire brennyng**: *les ongles les destraignans flambez* P2, *ungule, stridensque flammis lamina* LgA.

127 **ouerdrawe**: *retordez* P2.

128–9 **that his brethe . . . membres**: add *retorsez et que le gisier begaie* P2, *ut per lacunas uulnerum iecur retectum palpitet* LgA. For **trewens** see note to 78 above.

134 **more . . . other**: *plus fort des plus fors* P2.

25 ST BASIL

Maggioni, ch. XXVI, p. 180; Dunn-Lardeau, ch. 26, p. 244.

1 **Philesiene**: *amphilesien* P2, *Amphilocius* LgA.

2 **of Dyaconye**: *diconie* P2, *Yconii* LgA.

7 **tuelfe day**: *le iour de la typhaine* P2.

only for to see this man: *ut tantum uirum uidere posset* LgA.

8 **fayre**: *blanc* P2.

11 **of colde and of hunger**: *du iour et du chaut* P2.

25 **strokyng**: add *la queue* P2.

27 **The emperour**: *Valens imperator* LgA.

30 **yeuithe rightwisly**: *ayme droicture* P2.

33 **What hast thou to do therwith**: *car il tapartient* P2, *non decet te* LgA.

35–6 **flateryng wordes**: *vne fallace de double parolle* P2, *barbarismum* LgA.

37 **potage**: 'cooked meals'; the specific senses, variously thick soup, stew, or simply vegetables, are here generalized.

43–4 **to the Arryens thei**: *a tous. les arriens* P2.

51 **gret**: *moult de* P2.

56 **saide that he**: *sicomme il dit illec* P2.

76 **praieth**: *postulo* LgA.

77 **ye glorifie**: *tu te glorifies* P2, *glorier* LgA.

80 **panyme**: add *et apella la les dyables* P2.

102 **myn inwarde sorugh**: *mes* (*tes* P1) *entrailles* P2, *uisceris tuis* LgA. In Latin this means 'your own flesh and blood, offspring', but, having been taken literally by Vignay, produced poor sense, so other LgD MSS assigned the 'entrails' to his daughter.

111 **wrechidnesse**: *amour de joliuete* P2.

117 **moche of**: *toute* P2.

119 **wedded**: only GiL.

133 **husbond**: add *et a elle* P2.

137 **confessed**: from *MED confessen* v., sense 3, 'acknowledge, avow one's faith in', correctly recorded by L. The other MSS add 'to' on the mistaken assumption that this is the more usual sense 1.

145 **comest**: *venis* P2.
the: add *Et le saint dit. Ne te doubtes pas filz croy tant seulement* P2, add further *dans ei modicam escam* LgA.

148 **I herde**: *Iay oy* P2, *audio* LgA.

149 **seigh**: *voy* P2.

153 **seigh the**: add *huy* P2.

157 **visiblie**: *inuisibiliter* LgA.

163 **myn**: *mon dieu* P2.

165 **preiudice**: here GiL and P2 omit three sentences, Maggioni, 185 (121–6), Dunn-Lardeau, 249 apparatus.

181 **and**: add *elle* P2.

203 **He praied hym taste**: *et fist aussy comme sil amast son ouurage et cil tasta* P2.

pounce: 'pulse'; *MED s.v. pouse* gives this spelling as 'error', so this is perhaps for *pouuce*.

211 **saide**: add *Cest impossible sire. et basille dit. se ie suruis iusques a demain heure de nonne que feras tu. Et ioseph dit* P2.

26 ST JOHN ALMONER

Maggioni, ch. XXVII, p. 188; Dunn-Lardeau, ch. 27, p. 251.

5 **God**: add *de celo* LgA.

16–17 **a merye tale . . . seten and**: *que les poures qui* P2.

20 **that hight Theolonair**: *thelonarius* ('tax-farmer') *nomine Petrus* LgA. For the rest of the passage LgD and GiL several times refer to him by this name, e.g. substituting *Tholonayre* for *Petre* at 57.

26 **and turned . . . gate**: *en la maison de cellui* P2.

28–9 **wolde . . . nothyng**: *ne trouua nulle pierre a lui getter* P2.

31 **threwe . . . hede**: *en feri le poure a grant forsennerie* P2.

35 **and as . . . sperit**: only GiL.

36 **som**: *Mauros quosdam* LgA.

43 **blacke fendes**: *noirs* P2, *Mauri* LgA.

47 **al naked**: *naufragus* LgA.

65 **one . . . on**: *son notaire* P2.

67 **straunge men**: *barbaris* LgA.

68 **citee**: *saincte cite* P2.

71 **the servaunt**: *illo* LgA, see 65 above.

74 **the price for hym**: *triginta numismata* LgA.

76–7 **was . . . kichin and**: only GiL.

78 **and despised**: *de tous et estoit souuent batu des autres sergens* P2.

79 **clothyng**: add *et numismata* LgA.

81 **worthi men**: *ilz* S, not in P2, *quidam uicini eius* LgA.

82 **was**: add *pour visiter les lieux sains* P2.

83–4 **on . . . saide**: *ilz sentredisoient lun a lautre en loreille* P2.

84 **yonge man**: *enfant* P2, *puer* LgA; *puer* here means 'slave', misunderstood by Vignay.

85 **they**: *lun* P2.

86 **Late . . . hym**: *Je me leueray et le prendray* P2.

101 **stirre . . . ayeinst hym**: *a saint iehan aquelir ne aleuer aucune male esclandre* S, *sibi uerbis persuaderi et ad scandalum facile inclinari* LgA.
ayeinst hym: i.e. against Vitall.
and: add *saint iehan* P2, LgA as GiL. Vignay misunderstood this part of the story, although it becomes obvious at 112 that Vitall is the active party.

102 **a citee**: *ciuitatem* LgA, i.e. Alexandria.

102–3 **went . . . women**: *omnes publicas meretrices conscripsit* LgA.

104 **an hous of hers**: *la maison dicelle* P2, i.e. 'of each one'; *Intrabat ergo ad illas per ordinem* LgA.

108 **the olde man**: *saint iehan* P2, *sene* LgA, i.e. Vitall.

109 **cursed**: only GiL.

111 **He**: *ce tres mauuais* P2.
fornicacion: add *et non pour autre chose* P2.

114 **as though he hadde be wrothe**: only GiL.

118 **made hym wrothe**: *fingens se iratum* LgA.

119 **to defame**: *scandalizari* LgA.

125–6 **it were not . . . defamed hym**: *non imputaretur in peccatum hiis qui in eum scandalizantur* LgA.

129 **gaue hym a bofette**: i.e. the man struck Vitall.

133 **of a man**: *dun mor* P2, *Mauri* LgA; the mistake is probably that of a GiL scribe and not s.w., so this should perhaps have been emended.

138 **his**[2]: *ceste* P2.

138–9 **to his disciples**: not in LgA.

140 **God**: add *Et saint iehan le louoit mesmement disant: Pource que celle buffe que cellui receust, ie leusse receue pour moy* P2.

142–51 The G variant *disposer* for *dispenser* in these lines, based on *MED disposen*, sense 2, 'to make provision', 'to look after (someone's) welfare', is not recorded.

151 **putte to his lorde priuily**: *bouta* P2.

155 **patricyen**: 'high official'; *MED* has only one entry *s.v. patricion* ?a1475(?a1425) Higden.

156 **of the contrey**: *ecclesie* LgA.

157 **but**: add *vouloit* P2.

173 **strength of vertues**: *vertu de pensee* P2.

176 **before**: *Je feray telle chose en lui que toute alixandrie sen merueillera* P2.

182 **was ordeyned**: *fut amoneste* P2, *precepit* LgA.

183 **whiles**: i.e. 'whenever'.
clergie: add *a vne haulte feste* P2.

187–8 **vpon hym and vpon his bedd**: *en son habit* P2, *in stratu* LgA.

190 **in a nyght**: *illud nocte* LgA.

194 **bemyred**: *incenati* LgA, 'without dinner'; *MED* does not record the word, for which context suggests 'befouled' or 'in a desperate situation', *cf. mire* n. 1, sense 3 (b).

197 **.xxvj**: *triginta sex* LgA.

210 **gerdon**: *bon guerredon* P2, *mercedem non modicam* LgA.

221–2 **hym, he, he**: i.e. the gospel.

222 **any**: *vng* P2.

227 **not**: only GiL.

228 **fourti**: *.lx.*P2.

228–9 **may not suffre**: *non portabo* LgA, intended as a question, but not seen as such by Vignay.

253–5 **thou haste enhaunsed . . . goodes of other**: *exaudisti miseriam meam rogantem bonitatem tuam ne inueniretur morienti mihi nisi unum tremisse. Hoc igitur pauperibus dari iubeo* LgA; a *tremis* was a late empire coin worth the third part of a solidus.
enhaunsed: *exaulcie* P2.
drede: add *et tremble* P2.

259 **the place**: *locum medium* LgA.

273 **a bisshop**[2]: *deux euesques qui se reposoient auec lui* P2.

282 **he was ennobled**: *claruit* LgA, 'he lived his excellent life'; *MED s.v. ennobeled* ppl. 'refined, noble', records one instance for *c.*1475, but does not record a verb *ennoblen*. At 29.5 *was ennobled withe many vertues* translates *multis uirtutibus clarus*; and at 55.26–7 *Oure Lord hath ennoblid hym with so gret gracis* the verb loosely translates *prerogauit*, 'previously granted', but must here mean 'has made him great'.

27 CONVERSION OF ST PAUL

Maggioni, ch. XXVIII, p. 198; Dunn-Lardeau, ch. 28, p. 260.

3 **naturel, aperyng**: A *naturel yere* is a calendar year; an *aperyng* year (LgA *emergenti*) means twelve months starting from any time.

5 **.iij. dayes**: *tiers iour* P1.

August: add *Et estienne* (*pol* P1) *fut lapide* (*conuerti* P1) *en le viij.*^{e} *kalende de feurier* P2.

17 **hurte**: *treper* P2.

24 **bolwyng**: *MED* gives only one citation for *bolwen*, 'to swell', from *Ancrene Wisse*, and several for *bollen* and *bolnen*; other MSS here read: *bollyng* H1, *bolning* A2, *boluing* L, *boluyng* with an unusually big *u* G, *boluing* or *bolning* A1. At 117.16 *bolnithe* may equally be *boluithe*, *n* and *u* being frequently indistinguishable.

27 **thisteles**: *squamas* LgA, 'scales'.

28 **signified**: *est signifiee* P2.

32 **in avauntyng hymselff**: *en soy batant* P2, *quasi se ingerens* LgA; *avauncyng* would better have translated LgA (the French being somewhat arguable), and was perhaps s.w.'s original.

38 **dispositiff**: Maggioni records *dispositiua* only as a variant addition in one MS. *MED* gives one citation, from Chauliac, ?a1425, defined 'Contributory, secondary', with one later citation for the adverb from *Boke of Noblesse* with similar sense. Latin and French dictionaries suggest rather 'regulated, controlled'.

41 **enuye**: *zelo* LgA.

43 **sighyng al full of manasez**: *souspirant et plain de menaces* P2, *spirans minarum etc.* LgA.

entent: *intelligentia* LgA.

46 **bi thy witte of a Iwe**: 'according to your Jewish understanding'.

53 **done**: add *Car ces .iij. choses furent faictes en lui par dehors merueilleusement* P2.

59 **leuer**: add *elisus est lupus et factus est agnus* LgA; *MED s.v. lever* n.(2) has only one citation, from *Cursor Mundi*.

66 **dressed**: *esdrecie* P2, *unctum* LgA.

72 LgA ends the quotation from Augustine at *aduersitees*, and introduces the next thus: *Chrysostomus:* '*Tyrannos ac populus* . . . Vignay misread *Chrysostomus* as *tourmenteurs* and combined the two quotations.

72–3 **and ouercome**: *extimabat* LgA.

28 ST PAULA

Maggioni, ch. XXIX, p. 201; Dunn-Lardeau, ch. 29, p. 263.

1 **Paula** is *Pauline* in the GiL MSS except *Paula* in L (where, however, she

is *Paulyne the lady* in the rubric), *Pole* or *Paule* in the LgD MSS, but *Pauline* in the initial and final rubrics in P1, *Paula* in LgA.

3 **membres**: *artus* LgA.

12–13 **she lefte her pore the most pore of all**: *Omnes suos pauperes pauperior ipsa dimisit* LgA, i.e. 'she left her people/family poor, herself being even poorer'.

21 **This same here**: *ceste cy* P2.

22 **Paule**: *eam* LgA. Having substituted *Paule*, Vignay omitted the next name, *Paulinam*, and neither he nor s.w. noticed that this leaves the passage one child short.

22–3 **the whiche . . . thingges**: *Paulinam, que sanctum et admirabilem uirum et prepositum rerum suarum Pammachium reliquit heredem* LgA.

24 **to**: only GiL.

25 **in holy places**: *es sains lieux* P2, 'in the Holy Places'.
in the chirche of virginite: *uirginitatis et ecclesie* LgA.
Eufyne: *Rufinam* LgA.

27 **Thoroch**: *Toxotium* LgA.

29 **obeied**: *abeyid* G. *MED obeien* records no forms with initial *a*.

29–30 **an eyre male**: *mares* (. . .) *liberos* LgA.

32–3 **she desired . . . hadde**: *ut mortem eius uideretur optasse* LgA, i.e. she might have seemed to have wanted his death.

34 **houses**: *domus* LgA, singular.

38 **I**: add *Descendit ad portum* LgA.

39 **Here, her, hir**: The spelling variations are probably deliberate (see Hamer, 'Significance of Some Spellings', 362).

41 **her**: i.e. his.

43 **his**: i.e. her. GiL and LgD here give the correct form of *Rufine* (*Eufyne* at 25 above).

44 **eyen**: add *siccos* LgA.

44–5 **and trowyd felonye in her sones and pitee in God**: *impietate in filios pietate in Deum sperans* LgA, 'regarding lack of dutifulness towards children as piety towards God'.

45–51 **And she vnknowe . . . the loue of God**: *et ne sauoit pas que elle fust mere pource quelle sappareilloit estre ancelle de dieu. Et elle estoit tourmentee es entrailles aussy comme se len lui traist hors des membres. elle se combatoit auec douleur et souffroit planiere creance contre les drois de nature. Et comment que son esioyssant courage couuoitast la mort* [*lamour* S] *des filz greigneur selon nature elle deprisoit pour lamour de dieu* P2, *Nesciebat se matrem ut Christi se probaret* *ancillam. Torquebantur uiscera et, quasi a suis membris distraherentur, cum dolore pugnabat. Hoc contra iura nature plena fides patiebatur, immo gaudens animus appetebat et amorem filiorum maiore in deum amore contempnens* LgA; s.w. translated the French, which itself contains some misunderstanding, literally and without comprehending, making it worse by adding *hem* and translating *drois* as 'right' rather than 'laws', and not recognizing *plenier creaunce*, adopted directly from LgD. As it stands, the English can be translated thus: 'And she did not recognize herself as a mother, for she arrayed herself as the servant of God, and she was tormented in her bowels as if her entrails were being drawn out, and she fought with sorrow, and her complete faith suffered against the law of nature; and though her rejoicing heart longed for the love of children to be the greatest in nature, yet she left them all for the love of God.'

49 **though**: all MSS except L have forms which appear to represent 'thou', *thow* E, *þou* G, *þu* H1, *þ*[u] D, etc., but equally all except *þu* are included in the numerous forms recorded for 'though' in *LALME* iv. 56–9.

52 **Eustace**: *estace* P2, *Eustochio* LgA.

54 **behylde**: *regardoient* P2; all MSS except L read *besiled*, which cannot be from *MED besilen*, a rare verb meaning 'destroy' or 'steal', 15th-c., mostly found in Lydgate.

54–5 **to heuene and turned hem fro**: *tournez que elle ne veist ce que* P2.

56 **place**: *lieux* P2.

57 **the worthinesse of her**: only GiL; this seems to be a mistranslation corrected by the next phrase but mistakenly retained.

peple: *gent* P2, *familiam* LgA.

59 **euery day**: *cuncta* LgA.

65 **beclipped**: *auironnoit* P2, not in LgA.

66 **and drowe**: *quasi* (. . .) *lambebat* LgA.

71 **the holi place**: *sacrum uirginis deuersorium* LgA.

74–5 **the sterre . . . bestis**: *stellam fulgentem desuper, matrem uirginem, nutricium sedulum, pastores nocte uenientes* LgA. The *nutricium sedulum* is Joseph.

75 **the sone of God**: *uerbum* LgA.

76 **for to deie, thanne . . . Euangeliste**: *pour dedier adonc le commancement de iehan leuuangliste* P2, *et iam tunc euangeliste Iohannis principium dedicarent* LgA. Vignay translated *dedicarent*, which must here mean 'announced', as *dedia*, 'dedicated', for which s.w. presumably wrote *dedie*, and an early scribe who did not recognize the word in a sentence which by now made little sense substituted *deie*. *MED* has only two citations for *dedien*, one for c1450(c1400), and one for c1450.

78 **sleyng children**: *et les enfans occis* P2.

80 **of pes**: *panis* LgA.

82 **of the whiche plente**: *de laquelle dieu est plente* P2, *cuius fertilitas deus est* LgA.

in this wise: Verrely: *fiablement* P2.

83 **worship**: add *ou* P2.

85 **cried full litell**: *brest petit* P2, *paruulus uagiit* LgA.

98–9 **and þat . . . continued**: *Et touteffoys elle joignoit ce repos. Et repos doit estre dit iour et nuyt a oroisons a bien pou continuee* P2, *si tamen illa quies dicenda est que iugibus pene orationibus dies noctesque iungebat* LgA.

104 **coloures**: *purpurisso et cerussa et stibio* LgA.

106 **recompensed**: *MED* has no word corresponding to the G and H1 spellings *recompellid* and *recompessed*.

110 **I wolde . . . chastite**: *castitatem in illa uoluero predicare* LgA; *predicare* here means 'praise' rather than 'preach'.

116–19 **It apertenithe . . . alwaies do**: *'Non ut aliis refrigerium sit uobis autem tribulatio, sed ex qualitate in hoc tempore ut uestra abundantia sit ad illorum inopiam et illorum abundantia sit ad uestram inopiam' et prouidendum esse ne, quod libenter faceret, semper facere non posset* LgA. The scarcely comprehensible English is close to LgD except as below. The passage is based on 2 Cor. 8: 13–14, from which it is clear that *qualitate* should be *equalitate* (so Graesse); P2S read *dequalite*.

118 **of hem**: add *et la leur habondance soit a nostre souffraite* P2.

121 **receiued**: *corrompoit* P2, *dissoluebat* LgA, 'refuted'.

I calle: *en apelle* P2, *inuocans* LgA, i.e. in LgD and LgA Paula is the subject.

123 **to her owne body**: *que elle* P2.

124 **suayre**: *sindone* LgA; the GiL spelling follows the French, but is not recorded in *MED s.v. sudari(e*, the nearest being *suarie*.

124–5 **And . . . asked her**: *et disoit. se ie le demande* P2, *Ad extremum inferebat: 'Ego, si petiero* LgA.

126 **of other**: *etiam de alieno* LgA.

129 **be founde**: *sont tournees* P2, *uoluuntur* LgA.

132 **mete**: add *exceptis* LgA.

132–3 **so that . . . faste fro**: *sy que de ce vne chose fut estriuee* [*estimee* S]. *cest que elle pouoit jugier de* P2, *ut ex hoc uno extimaretur quid de* (. . .) *iudicaret* LgA.

133 **licoures**: *liquamine* LgA; 'sauces' fits the context, but is not recorded as a sense by *MED*.

134 **of this**: only GiL.

136 **thei wene**: add *tutam pudicitiam* LgA.

136–9 **he be . . . norished**: *ilz cuident que ce soit vng despiteux homme qui lui dit que le lignage des hommes estoit vil et sy debonnaire que pour la tresgrant ardeur de vertus il estoit aduis a aucuns que cestoit forsennerie. Et que le ceruel dicelle deust estre soustenu et nourri* P2, *tutam pudicitiam suspicantur. Noui susurronem quendam, quod genus hominum uel perniciosissimum est, quasi beneuolum nuntiasse ut pre nimio feruore uirtutum quibusdam uideretur insana et cerebrum illius diceret confouendum* LgA.

140 **tresoure beholding**: *regard* P2, *Theatrum* LgA, variant *spectaculum.*

142 **many**: only GiL.

143 **oure**: *uirorum* LgA.

149 **wolde reherce**: *racordoit* P2.

152 **be dissolut**: only GiL.

155 **sike**: add *et* P2, add *et* (. . .) *quoque exhiberet* LgA.
of fleshe and of metes: *et des viandes de char* P2.

160 **Iulit**: so E and G, *Iulet* L , *Julij* H1. The EGL spellings reflect LgD *juillet. MED s.v. juil* records no spellings with final *-t.*

163 **I**: add *clam* LgA.

165–7 **she felt . . . tolde hym**: *Et tantost elle senti ce que iauoie espie et me dist ce que il lui diroit* S, *statim sensit insidias et subridens meum esse quod ille diceret intimauit* LgA.

171–2 **She was debonaire to her husbonde and in weping milde, and she breke myghtly her sensualite, and moste ayeinst her children**: *Elle etoit debonnaire vers son mary et vsoit de senonemens vers ses enfans. meismement* P2 (P1 punctuates after *meismement,* S no punctuation), *In luctu mitis erat et suorum mortibus frangebatur, maxime liberorum* LgA, 'She was gentle in mourning and devastated by the deaths of her relatives, especially the children.' Vignay's mistranslation appears to result from misreading *luctu* as *iunctu*, interpreted as 'married state', and *suorum mortibus* as *sermonibus*, the latter appearing in various inaccurate guises in the LgD MSS, and 'corrected' to *sermonemens* by Batallier. It seems that s.w., confronted by this intractable passage, consulted LgA sufficiently to substitute *she breke* for *vsoit*, neglecting its passive form, and guessed in translating *senonemens* as *sensualite*, which is given three senses by *MED*, 'the natural capacity for receiving physical sensation *etc.*', 'physical desire, . . . a sinful, passionate emotion', 'the body'. The passage might then be tentatively rendered: 'she strongly subdued her natural emotion, especially with regard to her children'. But it seems unlikely that s.w. should have looked at LgA sufficiently to abstract *breke* and not have also corrected the rest of the sentence; one might alternatively suggest a misreading of *vsoit* as *brisoit*. I am grateful to Graham Edwards for the foregoing explanation (private communication).

175–8 **the impression . . . ouercome**: *limpression de la croix sefforcoit contre la douleur de la mere pour assouager et surmontoit le couraige la croiable et la pensee de mere. et les entrailles estoient acrauentees et ainsy vainquoit en courage la fragilite du corps et estoit vaincue* P2, *matris dolorem crucis niteretur impressione lenire, superabat affectum et credulam mentem parentis uiscera consternabant animoque uincens fragilitate corporis uincebatur* LgA.

182 **And she speke another tonge**: *Loquar et aliis* LgA.

183 **lyght**: *creable* P2.
lerned: *volt aprendre et aprist* P2, *discere uoluit* LgA.

185 **for pite**: *ex parte* LgA.

186 **leste she lefte me er I her**: *que ie ne la delaisse et que elle ne me delaisse* P2, *ne ipse ab ea deserar* LgA.

191 **right passing**: *tresspassantes* S, *trespuissantes* P2, *recrespissantes* P1, *crispantia* LgA, 'rippling'.

192 **in estaffys that bene litell shippes**: *in scopulis* LgA, 'onto the rocks'; *MED s.v. scaf(fe* n. (1) (a) 'boat; small boat, skiff, dinghy'. French has *estaffes* P2S, *escafes* P1. Greimas gives *escafe* as 'Chaloupe, navire d'une seule pièce de bois', from Lat. *scapha* from Greek.

194 **that**: *ce que* P2.

200 **this vers**: *ces vers* P2.

203 **beyng**: *lestre* P2, 'the dwelling',which s.w. has taken for its more familiar homograph.

206 **to me crieng and soruyng**: *clamanti an doleret aliquid* LgA.

208 **pesible and in quiete**: *paisiblement* P2, *quieta et tranquilla* LgA.
this: *ces* P2.

209 **closed**: add *quasi humana despiceret* LgA.

214–15 **in the pitte beside the chirche**: *subter ecclesiam et iuxta specum domini* LgA.

216 **moder**: add *aussy comme se elle lalaictast* P2, add *quasi ablactata* LgA. LgD: 'as if she were suckling her'; LgA: 'as if weaned'.

219 **but money of straungers**: *fors monnoie destranges* S, *sed magnum es alienum* LgA, 'but a big debt'.

221 **Oure Lorde saue the**: *Vale* LgA.

29 ST JULIAN HOSPITALLER

Maggioni, ch. XXX, p. 209; Dunn-Lardeau, ch. 30, p. 270.

1, 4 **of Emans**: *du mans* P2, i.e. of Le Mans.

4 **Lorde**: Here LgD and GiL omit Maggioni, 209 (7–9).

5 **ennobled**: *clarus* LgA.

6 **Lorde**: Here LgD and GiL omit Maggioni, 209–10 (11–13).

28 **dragon**: *dyacre* P2.
shepe: add *ecclesie* LgA.

35 **Seint Gregor**: *gregoire* P2, *Gregorius Turonensis* LgA.

36–8 **anone . . . out of his hondes**: *il fust tantost contrait des dois des mains. et la coingnie a quoy il vouloit nectoier le soc ardi* (*aerdy* S) *a sa main destre* P2, *protinus contractis digitis manubrium securis, cum qua uomerem mundare uolebat, eius dextre adhesit* LgA. GiL *share of his sool*, 'cutting edge of his plough'.

39 **Iulian**: add *par les prieres de lui* P2.

40 **Iulien**: *iulin* P2, *Iulii* LgA.

47 **Iulyn**: *Julin* P2, *Iulius* LgA.

58 **Iulyn**: *Julin* P2, *Iulium* LgA.

76 **wete well that**: only GiL.

84 **with grete lordshippes that longithe therto**: *pour son douaire* P2.

99–100 **in verrey wodenesse of ielosie**: *tout souef* P2, *silenter* LgA.

101 **chaumbre**: *maison* P2.

104 **with gret gladnesse**: only GiL.

118 **perisched**: *periclitabantur* LgA.
litell: not in LgD, *maximum* LgA.

120 **hem**: only GiL (see next).

120–1 **and mynster to hem after her power**: *tous poures* P2.

123–5 **cried . . . colde**: *appelloit Iulien a lui passer a voix piteuse* P2.

129 **warmthe**: add *et se doubta que il ne deffaulsist par froit* P2.

137–8 Julian, nephew of Constantine the Great, though brought up as a Christian, early rejected Christianity privately, but for fear of Constantine and his successor Constantius he did not declare his apostasy until himself becoming emperor in 361.

143 **bifore**: i.e. in the presence of.

144 **many of thother**: *aucuns* P2.
monkes: add *et ne demonstra point autremant que il y eust eu or* P2.

144–6 **hadde . . . loked**: *prist ces pos* P2.

154, 166 **so haunsed**: *soubzhaucie* P2, i.e. he became emperor. GiL often translates *soubzhaucie* thus.

158 **that his maister . . . as**: *cum puer adhuc esset et recedente magistro suo* LgA.

160 **coniuremente**s: *MED* has only two citations, one for a1333 meaning 'exorcism', one for *c.*1450 with the sense 'magic spell', as here.

178 **alwayes**: *per decem dies* LgA.

182 **that**[1]: add *quant il vendroit la* P2.

196 **men**: Here LgD and GiL omit Maggioni, 216 (112–16 *uigilantibus*).

202 **Crist**: add *et in eadem ecclesia erat sepultus* LgA.

207–8 **hem, hym**[1], **hym**[2]: *cil, les, les* P2.

209 **he was there as men kepte hym**: *ilz estoient la ou en les gardoit* P2.

218 **cursidly**: add *Ab omnibus autem suis insepultus relinquitur et a Persis excoriatur et de corio suo regi Persarum substratorium efficitur* LgA.

30 SEPTUAGESIMA

Maggioni, ch. XXXI, p. 219; Dunn-Lardeau, ch. 31, p. 277.

1–2 **that . . . waye**: only GiL.

3 **renouacion**: *uiduationis* LgA.

7 **Sonday**: *samedi* P2.

8 **thre resones**: i.e. 10 ff. *redempcion*, 25 ff. *signifyeng*, 45 ff. *representacion*.

11 **ascension**: *diei ascensionis* LgA.
kinde: *nature humaine* P2, *natura* LgA.

13 **fifte day**: i.e. Thursday.

14 **furste begynnyng of the Chirche**: *leglise premitiue* P2.

16 **and**: *ou* P2.

21 **to the Chirche**: only GiL.

23 **ordeyned**: *adiousterent* P2.
lik to: *a la* P2.

27 **is ledde**: *est demene* P2, *peragitur* LgA.
turnyng ayen: *retournement* P2, *reuolutione* LgA.

28 **Septuagesme**: *septuaginta enim dies* LgA.

29 **.lxx.**: *.lxx.C* P2.

35 **bothe stoles**, 44 **double stole**: These are no further explained by

Beleth, whom Voragine is following fairly closely; a clearer account is given by Gregory the Great: *Ante resurrectionem quippe stolas singulas accepisse dicti sunt quia sola adhuc mentis beatitudine perfruuntur. Binas ergo accepturi sunt quando cum animarum perfecto gaudio etiam corporum incorruptione uestientur* (Gregory the Great, *Moralia in Job*, ed. Adriaen, i, *Praefatio* 10.20.) I am grateful to Simon Tugwell, OP, for directing me to this quotation.

38 **pees**: *patrie* LgA.

40 **Tracte**: chant that replaced the Alleluia during mass from Septuagesima until Easter.

45 **Another**: *Lautre* P2, see 8 above.

47 **songges**: *organa* LgA.

50 **into Ciro**: *de tir* P2, *a Cyro* LgA, i.e. 'having been permitted by Cyrus'.

51 **were**: *chantons* P2. It seems unlikely that *were* is the rare sense 4 of *MED weren* v. (2), 'make use of', but no other explanation suggests itself.

54 **after**: add *alleluia* LgA.

58 **in**: only GiL.

60 **were** should be present tense; *sic et nos in sexta mundi etate* LgA, with verb understood.

79 **in fleing**: *brauium* LgA, i.e. 'the prize', caught by Vignay from 82.

31 SEXAGESIMA

Maggioni, ch. XXXII, p. 222; Dunn-Lardeau, ch. 32, p. 279.

9 **of**: *a* P2.

11 **for her**: *dicelle* P2; text should have been emended to *of her*.

12 **the fruit of .lx.**[ti]: *le fruit soixantime* P2, *fructus sexagesimus* LgA, sixtyfold being interpreted as the widow's share, Matt. 13: 8, 23.

done: *deu* P2; probably an early misreading of *due*, the scribes taking *done* as 'performed', and thence 'given'. Text should perhaps be emended to *due*.

14 **wingges**: *euures* P2, *ale* LgA.

.vij.: *.vj.* P2.

17 **vnderstonde**: add *les .vj. euures de misericorde. et par les dix soient entendus* P2.

is: add *propter representationem* LgA.

20–1 **man . . . orderes**: the tenth lost piece of silver in Luke 15: 8–9 represents man, the nine orders are the angels, partly destroyed by the Fall (Ryan, 134; Boureau, 1152 n. 5).

24 **alle**: *nous* P2, read by s.w. as *tous*.

35 **his spouse**: i.e. the Church.

46–7 **for it semithe hem as though he slepte**: *cum dormire uideantur*, *ipsos non eripiendo* LgA, so Graesse; the passage is hard to translate as it stands. Maggioni and Benz record variants with singular *uideatur*. Benz, Ryan and Boureau translate as singular, Roze as plural: 'alors qu'ils paraissent endormis en ne les soustrayant pas à leur position'. Maggioni and Graesse give 45–50 thus: *Clamat ergo ecclesia ut exurgat. Quantum ad primos, ipsos confortando cum dormire uideantur, ipsos non eripiendo clamat ut exurgat. Quantum ad secundos, ipsos conuertendo, a quibus uidetur faciem auertisse, ipsos quodammodo repellendo clamat ut exurgat. Quantum ad tertios, ipsos in prosperis adiuando et liberando.* Roze, Benz, Ryan, and Boureau agree in taking *Clamat* each time as the beginning of the sentence, which seems preferable.

46 **she** and 49 **he**[1] are both for 45 *the Chirche.*

32 QUINQUAGESIMA

Maggioni, ch. XXXIII, p. 224; Dunn-Lardeau, ch. 33, p. 281.

13 **that**: add *aussy* P2.

14 **the comon peple**: *illos quattuor* LgA, i.e. 'those four days'.

16 **And . . . saiethe**: *et hoc papa Telesphorus ordinauit, ut ait Ambrosius* LgA; omitting the first part, Vignay attached the attribution to Ambrose to the next sentence.

for significacion: not in LgD, *propter significationem* LgA.

21 **of synnes**: *peccatorum* LgA.

22 **of the fende**: *demonum* LgA.

36 **made**: *facit* LgA.

37 **the mynde of the passion**: *memoria passionis facilia* LgA, i.e. the memory of the passion makes works of penance easy, balancing 36 *stedfast beleue made his werkes acceptable.*

38 **mynde of the**: only GiL.

39–40 **but that . . . wille**: *que len ne seuffre onniement a bon courage* P2, 'which cannot be borne with a calm spirit'.

40 **She continuethe charite**: *elle fait estre charite continuee* P2, *Caritas facit esse continua* LgA.

40–1 **þe same clerke**: *il* P2, *Gregorius* LgA.

46 **hope**: add *propter penitentiam* LgA.

51 **confermed**: add *in ipsa gratia* LgA.

52 **defence**: add *ut in ipsis tribulationibus protegantur* LgA.

33 LENT

Maggioni, ch. XXXIV, p. 227; Dunn-Lardeau, ch. 34, p. 283.

9 **yere**: add *Annus enim habet CCCLXV dies, quorum XXXVI sunt decima* LgA.

17 **the nombre of fourti**[1]: *quinquagenarium* LgA.

18 **peny**: *denier* P2, *denarius* LgA. Vignay took the Latin, meaning 'tenth', in its monetary sense, and s.w. translated this as *peny*, and again at 27 below (where the MSS give it correctly); EH1G *payre* and L *payne* must result from English scribal misreadings.

22 **Maister**: add *Prepositiuus* [*sic*] LgA, also *he*[2] at 41 below. This is Praepositinus of Cremona.

27 **peny**: *denier* P2; see 18 above.

28 **bi foure and foure**: *per quaternarium* LgA.

33 **lightnesse for to do synne**: *leaue* P2. GiL has caught this from 43 below.

35–6 **in the tonge . . . delit**: *in lingua et auribus scurrilitas, in genitalibus uoluptas* LgA.

42 **lecherie and**: not in LgA.

43 **synne**: add *Hec Prepositiuus* LgA.

56 **yere**: add *Hec Gregorius* LgA.

59 **baptime**: add *mais la continuons iusques a pasques* P2.

61 **so moche**: only GiL.

70–1 **for . . . remedie**: only GiL.

72 **in . . . sacrement**: only GiL.

34 EMBER DAYS

Maggioni, ch. XXXV, p. 230; Dunn-Lardeau, ch. 35, p. 285.

14 **herbes**: *germina* LgA.

14–15 **freshe and grene and suete smellyng**: only GiL.

15 **Whitsonday**: *penthecouste* P2, *septimana pentecostes* LgA.

29 **reported**: *raporte* P2, i.e. figuratively related. *MED* has no such sense under *reporten*, and no *e* spelling for *raporten*, of which this is sense (b). It is translated as *lykened* at 48 below. See too 64.60, 61.

37 **hatefull**: *uersutus* LgA, 'deceitful'.

40 **moiste**: *hebes* LgA, 'dull'.

49 **wexen in age**: *croissance* P2, *adolescentiam* LgA.

50 **gret age**: *viellesce* P2.

51–2 **stable . . . encresing**: *fermes par bonne croissance* P2, *iuuenes per constantiam* LgA.

60 **yere**: *mense* LgA.

64 **oure**: *leur* P2.

35 ST IGNATIUS

Maggioni, ch. XXXVI, p. 233; Dunn-Lardeau, ch. 36, p. 287.

1 **the Euuangelist**: only GiL.

4–7 **I (. . .) newe frende . . . mervayles**: *moy nouuel amy de Iehan et ton disciple deusses tu auoir conforte et estre conforte de Ihesucrist ay ie tant apperceu de merueilles adire* P2, *Me neophitum Iohannisque tui discipulum confortare et consolari debueras; de Ihesu enim tuo percepi mira dictu* LgA.

11 **confessin**: *confirmentur* LgA.

12–13 **the frend . . . servaunt**: *dilecto condiscipulo humilis ancilla* LgA.

17 **certefie**: *uisere* LgA.

26 **is as miche name of loue as of dileccion**: *non esse nomen amoris quam dilectionis* LgA; the Greek word *agape* was widely adopted by Christians to avoid the sensual connotations of *eros*, and similarly Latin *amor* was replaced by *caritas* or *dilectio*.

will: *voult* P2.

29 **rede**: add *en* P2.

36 **was**: *cepit* LgA, 'began to reign'.

40–2 **manassing . . . Rome**: not in P2, in LgA.

48 **wolues**: *liepars* P2.

48, 49 **oure, we**: *nostris*, *ego* LgA.

50 **felonye**: *felonnies* P2.

O . . . bestis: *comme cest sauue chose que ces bestes* P2, *O salutares bestias* LgA.

53 **I shall enforce**: *Inuitabo* LgA.

68 **his backe**: *uulnera* LgA.

70 **was . . . plight**: *estoit tout sans soy mouuoir* P2.

74–5 **for . . . not**: picked up from 76.

75 **but . . . mych**: *que il seuffre tant et ne veult consentir* P2, *quod tanta patiens non consentis* LgA.

76 **vse not enchauntementes**: *ne sommes pas malefices* P2.

77 **that thei be not**: *que les malefices ne viuent* P2.

do thou awaye thi wickednesse: *oste ces malefices* P2, *uos malefici estis* LgA.

79 **his backe**: *les plaies* P2.

105–6 **the secounde prouost**: *Plinius secundus* LgA, i.e. Pliny the Younger.

109 **felle**: i.e. into the hands of the authorities.

119 **loued**: add *martyr et ipse* LgA.

121 **Crist**: add *egregius plane titulus dignitatis et commendatio honoris immensi* LgA.

36 PURIFICATION OF THE VIRGIN

Maggioni, ch. XXXVII, p. 238; Dunn-Lardeau, ch. 37, p. 291.

7 **Leuitique**: *Leuitici XII* LgA.

9 **wokes**: *diebus* LgA.

21 **as . . . *Scolastica***: not in P2, in LgA.

22 **philosophers**: *physici* LgA.

.xlvj.^{ti}: *xl.^{e} P2, XLVI* LgA.

37 **left**: i.e. 'omitted'.

42 **the corse**: *la maleurete de la femme* P2.

45 **furst and**: only GiL.

55 The **.iiij. resones** are at 56, 100, 111, and 118. In each case Mary is the implied subject of an *ut* clause with a subjunctive verb. For the last three, Vignay supplied a masculine subject, and s.w. substituted the indicative. At 100 **he hymselff** is for LgD *il*, LgA *dominus*.

59–60 **that . . . similitude**: only GiL.

62 **sone**: *pere* P2, *filii* LgA.

63 **but**: only GiL.

64 **circumcision**: add *ut pauper et peccator, sed hodie* LgA.

73 **Victore**: *saint victor* P2.

98–9 **was circumcised**: *se laissa circoncire* P2.

100–1 **as . . . saiethe**: only GiL.

107 **as moche . . . may**: *bien* P2.

109–10 **in ensaumple^{1} . . . pouerte**: *a lexemple doblation en exemple de humilite et de pourete* P2, *legi oblationis ad exemplum paupertatis* LgA.

115 **in suche wise**: *per fidem* (. . .) *secundum quod dicitur in Actibus*: '*Fide purificans corda eorum.*' LgA.

115–16 **the faders be not bounde to solucion**: 'the fathers are not held to payment', i.e. to fulfil their obligation by purchase of a sacrificial oblation. *MED s.v. solucioun* cites this sense once, *c.*1525.

123 **refusing of**: not in LgA.

125–6 **whiche . . . wight**: not in LgA.

129 **furst**: *primogenita* LgA.
Leuytes: add *que nunquam redimebantur* LgA.

129–30 **last age**: *adultam etatem* LgA.

131 **that were clene**: *qui nestoient pas mondes* P2, *mundorum* LgA.

132 **chaunged**: i.e. 'substituted'.

141 **and**: add *pource ne voult pas dieu loffrir en son sacrefice* P2.

144 **haue**: add *achate* P2.

151 **in**: add *diuine* P2, add *misticam* LgA.

152 **of hym**: i.e. 'for him'.

158–66 LgA gives these avian properties in verse, Maggioni, 244.

159 **Ver**: *son masle* P2, *uer* LgA, Vignay having taken *uer* as *uir*.

162 **felawship**: add *il escheue charongnes* P2.

163 **and cherisithe**: not in LgD; GiL may have been influenced by LgA *sociumque per oscula tangit.*

164 **sparhauuke**: *hostem in flumine uisam* LgA.

171 **also it**: *anti quod* LgA.

173 **thre . . . mevyngges**: *triplex obumbratio siue exinanitio* LgA.

174 **furste**: add *est exinanitio* LgA.

175 **hymselff**[2]: add *qui est vita* LgA.

182 **he saiethe**: *il est dit* P2.

185 **Glorie**: add *du peuple disrel* P2.

187 **levyng and in foryeuyng**: *remittendo* LgA.

190 **peple**: add *ou* (*en* P1) *donnant gloire* P2.

191–2 **furst, secound, .iij**: i.e. 'names', 185 above.

193 **Temple**: *altare* LgA.
procession: *profession* P2, *processionem* LgA.

194 **thirdely**: *et* LgA.

195 **ferthely**: *tertio* LgA.

196 **synginge**: *cum canticis* LgA.
For: *Quartement* P2; this follows 193 *Thirdely*.

199 **that is presentacion**: not in LgA.

201 **Israel**: add *Et donc acourons nous en lencontre ihesu crist en lair* P2.

202 **pees**[1]: add *salu* P2.

203 **conditor**: *doctor* LgA.

208–9 **vsed (. . .) to go aboute**: *lustrabant* LgA.

211 **he . . . sones**: *son filz leur donnast* P2.
enemyes: add *du quel ilz aouroient la mere* P2.

212 **that is . . . lyght**: not in LgA.

213 **Pluto**: *februs* P2, *Februo, id est Plutoni* LgA.
the god of hell: not in LgA.

213–14 **in that tyme**: *Februario* LgA.

214–15 **they deden . . . of hem**: *hoc pro animabus antecessorum suorum ut ergo propitiarentur eorum* LgA.

225 **custume**: add *des paiens* P2.

227 **cristen**: add *omni anno* LgA.
shulde . . . chirche: *totum mundum* (. . .) *illustrarent* LgA.

236 **puretee**: LgD and GiL here omit Maggioni, 247 (126).

237–8 **she was conceyued . . . moder**: *Vere enim purificatione non indigebat que ex suscepto semine non conceperat et in matris utero perfectissime mundata et sanctificata erat* LgA.

239 **no spotte ne**: only GiL.

261 **Temple**: add *et le portons iusques en leglise* P2.

265 **coniunccion**: *commixtione* LgA.

268 **wasting**: *degastant* P2, *consumens* LgA.

268–9 **Wherof . . . vers**: *Vnde quidam omittens tamen de lichino sic ait* LgA; *omittens tamen de lichino* is itself omitted by Graesse. GiL's final verse is not in LgD or LgA, and a different version is given by Graesse, *Lychnus est anima carne latens preopima*, but not recorded by Maggioni in any other MS or by Benz.

306–7 **thei come**: *vint* P2, i.e. the *one* of 304.

308 **queresters**: *ceroferarios* LgA.

317 **preestis**: *prestre* P2.

324 **wise**: add *mais le tendroit en deuocion* P2.

345 **by her moste holi merites**: only GiL.

37 ST BLAISE

Maggioni, ch. XXXVIII, p. 252; Dunn-Lardeau, ch. 38, p. 303.

6–7 **hadde paued hem . . . blessed hem**: *les eust aplainez et beneis* P2, *imponeret manum eis benedicens* LgA. The medial consonant in *paued* looks like *n* in G and L, but is ambiguous in E and H1. *MED* gives *panen*, with only two citations, meaning 'line (a mantle)', or 'decorate with alternating panels'; *pauen* with only one, defined as '? touch or strike (sb.) with the paw'; and *paven*, 'cover' or 'pave' with paving stones or the like.

16 **other . . . founde**: *les crestiens* P2.

17 **hym**: add *ter* LgA.

25 **deied**: *se mouroit* P2.

29 **for that disese**: only GiL.

30 **and lyued**: only GiL.
woman: add *paupercula* LgA.

33 **Be not wrothe**: *noli contristari* LgA.

37, 38 **prince, prouost**: *principis*, *preses* LgA; these are different characters, not that it affects the story.

46 **Thenke wel**: only GiL.

48 **hede**: *queue* P2, *caput* LgA.

49 **mekely**: only GiL. **her**: add *et en mengea* P2.

62 **the middes of**: not in P2, in LgA.

66 **in the**: *ou parfont du* P2.

79 **of . . . kyngdom**: *celestiel* P2, *regni celestis* LgA.

82 **melke**[1]: *nix* LgA.

92 **not . . . do**: only GiL.

104 **O thou wrechid**: only GiL.

38 ST AGATHA

Maggioni, ch. XXXIX, p. 256; Dunn-Lardeau, ch. 39, p. 307.

5–6 **in takyng . . . drede**: *fut doubte en prenant vne noble dame* P2, i.e. in the hope that he might be feared or respected.

12 **that weren . . . vnclene**: not in LgD, *eiusdem turpitudinis* LgA.
that: add *per triginta dies* LgA; Vignay adds the reference to thirty days at 22 below.

12–13 **bi thaire filthe and foly and wyckednesse**: not in LgA.

16 **and myn entencion**: only GiL.

19 **iapes**: *friuoles* P2, *flumina* LgA.

49 **whan**: only GiL.

49–50 **her cruelte will assuage**: *ilz sassouageront* P2.

59–60 **the crosse . . . erthe**: *eculeum* LgA; see note to 24.23.

64 **take away**: *redacta* LgA, i.e. 'separated'.

67, 68 **drawe of, drawen**: *torses, torses* P2.

81 **turnyd hym to**: *lui tourneront en* P2.

87 **Wherfore schold y**: *Je ne puis* P2, *unde* (. . .) *possum* LgA.

92 **þyngis**: add *Hic si uult potest me curare* LgA.

96 **fill doun prostrate**: *sagenoulla* P2, *procidens* LgA.

106 **þy goddis**: *lapides* LgA.

113 **of shellis . . . flore**: only GiL.

114 **colis**: *feu* P2, *carbones* LgA.

116 **turmentid**: *concussit* LgA.

117 **sclewe . . . counsellouris**: *tourmenta sy les conseilliers de quincien et agrauanta* P2, *duos consiliarios Quintiani opprimeret* LgA.

133 **disapperid**: *desaparut* P2; L shares G *þeron apperid*; perhaps an early copyist substituted *vnapperid*, which being rare (only one *MED* citation) was subsequently altered.

134 **Holy mynde of good wille**: *mentem sanctam, spontaneam* LgA.

136–7 **sche offrid frely worschip to God**: *elle souffry de volente. elle donna honneur a dieu* P2, *spontaneam se obtulit, honorem deo dedit* LgA.

141 **as he passid by hem**: *et a getter des pies* P2.

146 **brente**: *fondoit* P2.
come: add *a grant force* P2.

156–7 **and at . . . schynyng**: *et les glorieux seruices denterrer tes membres resplendissent* P2, *sic humandi artus gloriosa fulgent obsequia* LgA.

157 **felaschip**: *chorus* LgA.

158 **schewyng**: *demonstra* P2.
holynesse: add *mentis* LgA.

39 ST VEDAST

Maggioni, ch. XL, p. 262; Dunn-Lardeau, ch. 40, p. 312.

1 i.e. Vedast was ordained as bishop of Arras by Remy.

13 **.v.C**: *.vjC.* P2, *DL* LgA; he died in 539.

15 **man**: add *pre senio* LgA.

40 ST AMAND

Maggioni, ch. XLI, p. 263; Dunn-Lardeau, ch. 41, p. 313.

1, 2 **chirche, monasterie**: both are *monstier* in P2; s.w. usually translates this as *chirche*, but also often uses *monasterie*, including for St Albans at 79.81. See too note to 10.37.

8 **oon of þe keperis**: *la garde* P2, *custos* LgA.

24 **of Troies**: *in Traiectensem* LgA, 'in Maastricht'.

38 **he wende to haue ben sclayne**: *ilz le cuidoient occire* P2.

44–5 **by . . . Lord**: only GiL.

41 ST VALENTINE

Maggioni, ch. XLII, p. 265; Dunn-Lardeau, ch. 42, p. 315.

2–3 **Art þou Valentyne**: *Qui es tu valentin* P2, *Quid est Valentine?* LgA.

4 **wikkid lawe**: *superstitionem* LgA.

13 **comune goodis**: *res publica* LgA.

19 **chaungid**: *immutatum* LgA.

22 **prince**: *prefectus* LgA.

26 **prouost**: *imperator* LgA.

42 ST JULIANA

Maggioni, ch. XLIII, p. 267; Dunn-Lardeau, ch. 43, p. 316.

1 **weddid**: *espousee* P2, *desponsata* LgA; the sense required is 'betrothed' (see 8 below), which is not however recorded by *MED s.v. wedden*.

2 **consente to hym**: *coupler a lui* P2.

4 **be**: add *despoillee et* P2.

15 **all a day**: *demi iour* P2.

17 **vnbounde hir of hir**: *la lya de* P2.
aȝen: only GiL.

25 **whanne**: add *elle le tint et* P2.

32 **his ocupacion . . . tempte hem**: *il eslongnoit forment des crestiens* P2, *maxime a christianis elongabatur* LgA.

42–3 **made . . . but**: only GiL.

44 **grete . . . foule**: *latrinam* LgA.

49 **.vC.xj.^{xx}. and ten women**: *.v.C hommes .xj.^{xx} et .x. femmes* P2, *uiri quingenti et mulieres CXXX* LgA.

61 **.xxiiij.^{ti}**: *XXXIV* LgA.

43 CHAIR OF ST PETER

Maggioni, ch. XLIV, p. 270; Dunn-Lardeau, ch. 44, p. 319.

3 **.iiij. causes**: here and at 111, 131, and 150.

14–15 **Y . . . bataile**: *ie suy prest qui aidera a ta maleurete* P2, *Presto est qui tue subueniat miserie* LgA.

32 **curyosite**: *curialitas* LgA, 'courtliness'.

37–8 **owte at ȝoure wille**: *a ta* (*sa* P1) *volente* P2, *libertate* LgA.

43 **men seide**: *ilz dient* P2.

47–8 **þat he . . . sounde**: *et incolumem eum reddam et liberum* LgA.

51 **to þe**: only GiL.

60 **pepul**: add *In qua septem annis sedit, sed postmodum ueniens Romam in Romana cathedra sedit xxv annis* LgA.

66–7 **militacion, malignancion and trivmphancion**: *des cheuauchans des malfaisans et des victorians* P2, *militantium, malignantium et triumphantium* LgA. L ends all three in *-ium*. At 78 and 80 below, GiL has *of victoriaunce* for *des victorians* P2, *triumphantium* LgA. *MED* has one citation *s.v. malignacion*, 'hatred', from Hardyng Chron. B., 1543(1464), one for *militatioun*, '? military service', from Vegetius (a1460), and none for *trivmphancion* or *victoriaunce*.

71–2 **of Seint Petir**: only GiL.

74 **brekyng hire and wastyng hire**: *degastant* P2, *dissipando* LgA.

78, 80 **of victoriaunce**: see 66–7 above.

82 **mony**: add *autres* P2.

84 **othir**: add *apostolis* LgA.

99–100 **Or . . . Chirche**: *Ou ce benefice peut estre tripple. lequel le pecheur a en leglise. par la vertu des clefz* P2, *Vel istud beneficium potest esse triplex beneficium aliud quod uirtute clauium peccator in ecclesia consequitur* LgA, i.e. 'Or this benefit can be (seen as) another triple benefit which the sinner acquires in church by the virtue of the keys.'

101 **absolucion of synnys schewid**: *demonstrance de labsolution de pechie* P2.

103 **peynys**: add *en partie* P2.

112 **boke**: *itinerario* LgA.

121 **ten**: *vij*. P2.

134–5 **the .iij.^{e}**: *certo* LgA.

140 **wikkid**: s.w. misread LgD *mannes* (LgA *manes*) as *mauues*.

143 **wrecchid errour and**: only GiL.

145–6 **falce errour and custume**: *chose* P2.

156 **the furste is**: *scilicet* LgA.

161 **here**: add *ou a la rature* P2.

166 **queynte and curiouse**: *coint* P2, *formabilem, id est* (. . .) *exquisitum* LgA.

170 **foule**: *foles* P2, *superfluas* LgA.

171 **eere**: add *preste et appareilliee* P2.

174 **endyng**: add *par quoy il est donne a entendre que les clers sont ministres de dieu qui na ne fin ne commencement* P2.

176 **heris ben**: *il y a angle* P2.
gladly: only GiL.
Seint Bernard seith: *ut dicit Bernardus* LgA, 178 **And Ierome seith**: *sicut dicit Ieronimus* LgA, in each case belonging to the preceding sentence.

185 **Poule**: *illud* LgA. The reference is to Matt. 10: 16.

186 GiL and LgD omit Maggioni, 276 (97–9).

44 ST MATTHIAS APOSTLE

Maggioni, ch. XLV, p. 277; Dunn-Lardeau, ch. 45, p. 325.

11 **y trowe þat**: not in LgD, *ceu puto* LgA.

20 **yle of Skariot**: it seems probable, however, that Judas was named from his village of origin in Judea, itself not identified.

24 **child**: add *de belle forme* P2.

26–7 **I schold not . . . aftir me**: *ne regni mei successore priuarer* LgA.

41 **þe kyngis sone**: add *que il cuidoit son frere* P2, add *fratrem suum putatiuum* LgA.

46 **cher**: though fairly well attested (*MED chere* sense 6(a), 'kindness, friendliness' etc.), this troubled some scribes; L substituted *love and favour*.

69 **most vnhappi**: *plus desloyalle* P2, *infelicissima* LgA.

79 **to rede**: *recitanda* LgA.

80 **reder**: add *licet sit potius relinquenda quam asserenda* LgA.

94 **hymselff**: add *a vng las* P2.

106 ***in cenaculo***: *en vng disner* P2, LgA as GiL.

132 **vncorded**: *descordassent* P2, an unrecorded negative verb based on *MED corden* v. (1), sense 2 'agree, consent *etc.*', with G *encordid* and L *oone acorded* resulting from the unfamiliarity of this word.

147 ***thearticum***: *vne seignourie de dieu* P2, *thearchicum* LgA, i.e. by divine gift. In LgA the whole sentence reads: *Videntur enim mihi eloquia sortem nominare thearchicum quoddam donum demonstrans illi thearchico choro a diuina electione susceptum.*

151 **places**: *liures* P2.

153–4 Some of his supposed relics were removed to Trier in the 11th c. (185–6 below); but cf. Capgrave, 85: 'In þe hie auter of þe cherch [Sancta. maria maior] restith þe body of seynt mathie þe apostil.'

155 **it**: *qui* P2, i.e. the legend rather than the body; this sentence belongs with the next.

157 **And**: only GiL.

161 **and þat**: *ut* LgA.

169 **bisshop**: *pontifice* LgA, i.e. High Priest; also at 172.

169–70 **he ansuered . . . saide**: *respondit: 'De obiectis que crimina dicitis'* LgA, 'about the accusations which you call crimes'.

170–1 **the name . . . glorie**: *christianum esse non est criminis, sed glorie* LgA.

173 **by apostasie**: not in LgD, in LgA.

174 **found**: add *ne ne soye renye* P2, not in LgA.

194 **lawe**: *cultum* LgA.

197 **that ye tormented**: *Quem* (. . .) *afflixerunt* LgA.

199 **mowed**: *dentibus* (. . .) *fremebant* LgA.
durst: *pouoient* P2.

202 **and lete hym oute of prison**: only GiL.

45 ST GREGORY

Maggioni, ch. XLVI, p. 285; Dunn-Lardeau, ch. 46, p. 332.

5–6 **thenking . . . God**: *Sed dum longius conuersionem protraheret et tutius se Christo famulaturum putaret* LgA.

7 **.vij. yere**: not in LgA.

8–9 **so that . . . mynde**: *sy que il estoit au retenir et par esperance et par pensee* P2, *ita un non tantum specie, sed in eo retineretur et mente* LgA.

10 **.vij.**: *.vj.* P2.

11 **.vij.**: *septimum* LgA.

12 **and one**: not in LgA.

18 **upon**: *in prologo super* LgA.

19 **O thou**: *mon* P2.

19–20 **putte . . . that**: *occupationis sue pulsatus uulnere meminit qualis* LgA. 'He' is Gregory's soul in these lines.

20 **whanne**: *comment* P2.

21–2 **how . . . yeuen**: *quantum rebus omnibus que uoluuntur eminebat* LgA.

22 **yef**: *sy que* P2, *quod* LgA.

28 **vnnethe . . . mete**: *subsistere uix ualeret* LgA.

29 **diuerse tymes**: *par heures* P2.

so gret anguishe: *incisionem uitalium, quam Greci syncopim uocant,* (. . .) *crebris angustiis* LgA.

31 **devine**: *daucunes* P2.

32 **pore man**: *naufragi* LgA.

37 **sorer thanne he dede before**: *forment* P2.

39–40 **that his moder . . . she**: *remansisse* (. . .) *quam mater sua* LgA.

45–6 **of faire . . . beauute**: *les cheueulx donneste beaute et honnorables* P2, *capillorum nitore perspicuos esse uenales* LgA.

47 **marchauntes**: *marchant* singular P2, and so thereafter.

55–6 **in Latin . . . men**: *angloys* P2, *Anglici uocantur* LgA.

59 **Of Irlonde**: *yrois* P2, *Deiri* LgA, the Northumbrian kingdom of Deira.

61 **the name**: *lire* P2, *nomine* LgA.

69 **that . . . hennes**: *Gregorium demisisti* LgA; the Latin is a neat triplet: *Petrum offendisti, Romam destruxisti, Gregorium demisisti.*

70 **repele**: the literal sense, 'call back', is not recorded in *MED*.

73 ***locusta*, that is a maner grassope**: *langoustre qui est apellee aousterolle* P2, *locusta* LgA. P1 and S spell as P2, Batallier gives *sousterelle*, *cf.* modern *sauterelle*, 'grasshopper'.

74–5 **that is saide . . . place**: not in LgA.

77 **or they myght remwe**: only GiL.

82 **Tymbre**: add *vng fleuue de rome* P2, not in LgA.

87 **the corrupte . . . hem**: *ilz corrompirent lair par leur pourreture* P2.

88 **pestilence**: add *quam inguinariam uocant* LgA.

88–9 **men sawen . . . luste**: *corporali uisu sagitte celitus uenire et singulos quosque percutere uiderentur* LgA.

92 **citee**: add *et que plusieurs maisons demouerent vuides en la cite* P2.

95 **herte and**: only GiL.

96 **destroied**: add *tout le peuple* P2.

97 **processiones**: *processionem* LgA.

101 **into tyme that**: *jusques a tant que* P2.
party: *pitie* P2; this was perhaps thought to be for *MED parti(e* sense 5. (a) 'a group of people'.

105 **for the same cause**: *pour ce* P2, *propter eum* LgA.

107 **and so . . . citee**: *Et tantost comme il fut hors* P2, *Qui mox* LgA.

110 **descended**: *pendoit* P2.

111 **aungell**: *anges* P2.

116 **Anarace**: *a narse* P2, *ad Narsum* LgA; at 166 he appears as *Narracien.*

117 **me**[2]: add *le pleur de* P2.

119 **cure**: *culmen* LgA.

120 **dewed with teres of sorugh**: *arrose de tristesse* P2, *percussum merore* LgA.

121 **faire but bitter**: *Noemi, id est pulchrum, sed uocate me Mara* LgA; Ruth 1: 20.

122–3 **knowen and writen**: *congnoissiez et sauez* P2, *cognoscitis* LgA; s.w. misread *sauez* as *scrivez.*

123 **of apostel**: *dapostole* P2, *episcopatus* LgA, *apostolatus* Re.

126 **nedes**: *negoces* P2.

127–8 **after the faire forme of her reste**: *post tam pulchram quietis sue speciem* LgA, 'après avoir été si beau en son repos', Boureau.

128 **beholde**: *regarde que ie seuffre et regarde* P2.

131 **furst**: *prioris* LgA.

135 **teres and wepingges**: *litaniis* LgA.
and[3]: only GiL.

137 **was**: *adhuc est* LgA. **Rome**: Graesse and some MSS of LgA add *in ecclesia quae dicitur Sancta Maria major*. See too Capgrave, 85.

137–8 **the apostell**: not in LgA.

138 **peintour . . . phisician**: *medicus et pictor egregius* LgA.

141 **derkenesse**: *infectio* LgA.

144 **all . . . was**: *mira serenitas et aeris puritas remanebat* LgA.

145 **herde**: add *delez celle ymage* P2.

166 **Narracien**: see 116 above.

166–8 **Ye . . . name**: *Quod cause et nominis similitudinem faciendo per scripturas clausulas declamationesque formatis* LgA, 'for in equating the name to the thing you make rhetorical conclusions and declamations in your writings'.

169 **us**: *uos* LgA, but Graesse reads *nos*, in which case the clause amounts to 'as we ourselves do'. Other MSS substitute *uocatis* for *uocamus*. Without one of these adjustments translation is difficult.

170 **scabbes whelpe**: *chiens rongneux* P2, *scabiosos catulos* LgA, 'mangy puppies'. *MED* records adjective *scabbi(e*, but no form *scabbes* or, as G, *schabbes*.

178 **me**: add *Sed queso, uir sancte, nobis aliquid de hoc certamine nostro conueniat, ut si non quod dicitis ita est, sic ita quia dicitis* LgA.

181 **writinge**: *prefatione* LgA.
olde peinted: *voulu empraindre* P2.

184 **more thanne reson requirithe** belongs with the previous sentence, i.e. 'we are ourselves diminished in unreasonably praising others'. The new sentence should begin: *I wil not to be enhaunsed of wordes but of maners . . .*

189 **of the senatoures**: *fraudolenter a synodo* LgA, the synod of Constantinople 587–8. For a succinct account of this dispute see *ODCC* under John the Faster, St (d. 595).

192–3 **Wolde God he were verrely one true membre of the chirche that coueitithe to be called vniversall**: *Par ma volente soit il lun diceulx quil couuoite estre le tout* P2, *Vtinam uel sine imminutione sit unus qui esse appetit uniuersus* LgA. The sentence has caused difficulty and published translations vary: Stace: 'Who seeks to be universal so that he alone can reign supreme?' Ryan: 'so that without lessening [the status of other bishops] he may be number one and yearns to be universal'. Roze: 'comme le ferait quelqu'un qui, sans vouloir rabaisser altrui, veut être seul au-dessus des autres quand il aspire à être universel'. Boureau: 'Que celui qui aspire à l'universalité commence par ne pas rabaisser sa propre personne.' Maggioni (2007): 'come farebbe qualcuno che, anche senza volerne diminuire i meriti, desidera essere "universale"'.

193–5 **Also . . . me**: *il vouloit estre dit parolle de commandement des euesques ses compaignons* P2, *Verbum etiam iussionis sibi a coepiscopis dici nolebat* LgA, 'he did not wish his fellow bishops to speak of his "commands"'.

195–200 **wherof . . . hym**: *En sur que tout* P2, *Et sus tout ce* P1; this passage is in LgA, from which s.w. translated it directly.

198–9 **In open places**: *Loco* LgA, i.e. 'in position, status'.

202 **or handemaydenes**: only GiL.
the wiff of Patrice: *femme du patricien* P2, *patricie* LgA.

203–9 All pronouns referring to Rusticana are singular in LgD and LgA.

211 **other**: i.e. his successors.

216 **ye . . . for**: *tu nous a voulu enuoier* P2, *uobis transmitti uoluistis* LgA.

217 **youre desire**: *nostre estude* P2, *uestro studio* LgA.

219 **youre contreyeman**: *nostre compaignon* P2, *compatriote uestri* LgA.

221 **dedely prison**: *chartre* P2, *carne* LgA.

223 **sertainly in a boke**: *in quodam libro* LgA.

225 **the holy . . . aposteles**: *apostolorum limina* LgA.
the[2]: *leglise des* P2.

228 **as hym aught**: *si comme il disoit* P2, *ut decebat* LgA.

242 **that he wolde haue yeue water to**: *duquel il nauoit pas voulu prendre leaue* P2, *in cuius manibus aquam fundere uoluerat* LgA.

252 **propre**: not in LgA.

257 **pore shipman**: *poure qui perdi tout en la mer* P2, *naufragus* LgA; see 32 above.

262 **to be**: *preesse* LgA.

267 **loued**: *aplainoit souuent* P2.

268 **lappe**: add *aussy comme sa compaigne* P2, add *quasi cohabitatricem* LgA.

270–1 **be . . . heuene**: *auoir esperance dauoir mencion du guerredon auenir* P2.

272 **that he shulde be guerdoned**: *que ce seroit* P2.

273 **Rome**: *que il deuoit esperer dauoir mansion auecques lui* P2.

279 **only**[1,2]: only GiL.

281 **handelest and**: only GiL.

290 **witheoute his name**: *apocrisiario* LgA, i.e. 'to his deputy'.

294 **his**: *sa* P2; English should be plural following 292 *men* translating *la gent*.

301 **that . . . gretly**: *quanto me ei male seruientem affligitis* LgA.

302 **and**: only GiL.

317 **and so Foce**: *car vng pou de temps apres foce lun de ses cheualiers* P2.

330 **abide**: *demeures* P2, *mortuus fueris* LgA.

338 **to rechelesly**: only GiL.

342 **tyme**: add *apres la mort de troye* P2.
he: *et* LgA.

346 **Lo**: add *que iay acompli ta requeste. Car* P2.

354 **fynably**: *finablement* P2, *finaliter* LgA, 'finally'; *MED* has two citations, for *c.*1485 and 1500, both meaning 'in perpetuity' rather than 'finally' as here, and one of the adjective *finable*, 'final, ultimate', for *c.*1450.

361 **other**: *les autres* P2; since all GiL MSS have *ther*(*e*), the error must go back to an early copy.

363 **foryeuithe**: *concedit* LgA.

371 **abideth and is withholde**: *est retenue* P2.

386 **gret**: add *mais elle nest pas sy lante que elle ne departe ne sy tresgrant* P2.

391 The H1 correction, 'singing bread', is defined in *MED s.v. singing(e* as 'large wafers to be used by the priest for consecrating at mass'.

402–3 **was conuerted**: *retourna* P2.

407 **domatyk**: error for *dalmatik*, which has three citations in *MED*, starting in 1415, two of them in mostly Latin lists.

409 **despite**: add *comme* [*s*]*e ce feussent vilz reliques* P2.

410–11 **of the pointerie**: *des pointures* P2; *pointerie* is not recorded by *MED*.

414 **communyalte of Rome**: *communione* LgA; *MED s.v. communalite* does not record the sense 'communion', giving senses 'people of a city, community', etc., so a contemporary reader might have interpreted this as exile rather than excommunication.

416 **maistres of sorsery**: *ars magiques* P2, *magorum* LgA.

419 **shuld perische**: *periclitaretur* LgA.

420 **and the fende made**: *enuoierent vng dyable et firent* P2.

429 **called**: add *a Grecis* LgA.
Lymo: the Greek name *Leimon*, 'meadow', was given to a book of stories and anecdotes about monastic life by Iohannes Moschus (d. *c.*619).

429–30 **of that . . . Gregorie**: *ou monstier gregoire pape sy lui denonca* P2.

431 **tresoure**: *numismata tria* LgA.

433 **sori**: *moult yre* P2.

439 **stronge**: only GiL.

444 **and . . . God**: only GiL.

446 GiL here omits Maggioni, 300 (225–6), Dunn-Lardeau, 345.

450 ***sumptum***: add *&c.* P2. LgA adds a further five lines, Maggioni, 301.

457, 459 **hem**: add *tousiours* P2.

460–1 **blamed . . . spekynge**: *le corriga troys foys de ce quil estoit trop tenant et que il targoit trop moult doulcement* P2, *ter blande de sua tenacia et detractione corripuit* LgA.

472 **ensaumples**: *exemplaires* P2; error for *ensaumpleres*, 'copies of a book'.

473 **parties of the worlde**: *citez* P2, *mundi partibus* LgA.

479 **be**: *nestoit* P2.
yef[2]: *et que* P2.

479–80 **he graunted . . . bokes**: *ipse quoque combustoribus manus daret* LgA, *i.e.* he would help them.

482 **thanne**: add *cum apparatu diaconi* LgA.

484 **and suore**: only GiL.

486 **strange . . . dethe**: *a dolore mortis extraneus* LgA, i.e. without feeling the pain of death.

488–9 **a company of ribaudes**: *peculium* LgA, 'a sum of money'; likewise 490–1 **foule companye**, 493 **foule felawship**.

496 **sigh**: *souspir* P2, *flatum* LgA.

497 **in the laste ende**: not in LgA.

498 **that was . . . anone and**: *continuo reuiuiscens* LgA.

501 **be**: add *en vng temps* P2.

502 **goode bretheren**: only GiL.

504 **and praiethe for hym**: not in LgA.

507–8 **abiecciones, abieccion**: G *obieccionys*, *obieccioun*, which should have been recorded in apparatus. *MED abjeccioun* gives only senses relating to humility and degradation; this should have been emended to [*o*]*biecciones* (as at 44.169).

519 **gret langoure of**: only GiL.

521 **for . . . susteyned**: *de ce que autres peussent bien mourir* P2, not in LgA.

525 **anone**: add *cil qui ne pouoit mourir* P2.

528 **Rome**: add *nomine Adrianus* LgA.

530 **vnyuersely**: *proffitablement* P2, *uniuersaliter* LgA.
þe kyng: *empereur* P2.

543 **of auctorite**: only GiL.

552 **God**: add *et sic usque hodie obseruatur* LgA.

559 **lawghyng**: add *inflatis buccis* LgA.

560 **and**: not in LgA.

572–3 **a man of Ynde**: only GiL; see note to 133.1–17.

577 **her**[1]: *illec* P2.

LgA has a further paragraph, Maggioni, 305–6 (287–95), which is absent from some MSS and from Graesse.

46 ST LONGINUS

Maggioni, ch. XLVII, p. 307; Dunn-Lardeau, ch. 47, p. 349.

3 **and tokenys**: only GiL.

4 **in the deying of hym**: *fais* P2.

15 **braste doun**: *rompi et froissa* P2.

28 **siȝt**: add *et sante* P2.

47 ST BENEDICT

Maggioni, ch. XLVIII, p. 309; Dunn-Lardeau, ch. 48, p. 351.

12 **the waye was longe**: *iter non esset* LgA.

24 **for it is Ester Day**: not in P2, *quia hodie pascha domini est* LgA.

25–6 **in that . . . from men. But yet**: *et que iay deseruy a toy veoir de loing qui suy mis pres des hommes. Mais* P2, *quia uidere te merui.' Longe quippe ab hominibus positus quia* LgA.

28 **Lorde**: add *il ne te conuient pas faire abstinence* P2.

28–9 **for . . . refeccion**: only GiL.

31 **As . . . tellithe that**: only GiL.

32 **in Latin *merula***: *vng merle* P2, *merula* LgA.

35 **hym**: *les yeulx de sa pensee* P2.

37–8 **and goodnesse**: only GiL.

38–9 **and whanne . . . hymselff**: not in P2, *se exuit* LgA.

41 **towounded**: see *MED s.v. to-* for verbs with this prefix. This word is not recorded.

42 **mynde**: add *et ainsy vainqui le pechie que il mua son ardeur* P2.

45 **of the**: *dun* P2.

46 **fader . . . gouernour**: *maistre* P2.

50 **repented and**: only GiL.

52 **and felte**: only GiL.

53 **vncustumed thingges noyed hem**: *illicita non licere* LgA; *MED*

records *uncustumed* only in the sense 'without imposition of duty or tax', not 'unaccustomed' as required here.

54 **maliciously**: only GiL.

56–7 **as . . . caste**: *qui estoit loing au get* P2, *quasi iactu lapidis* LgA.

63–4 **he encresed . . . signes**: *et la les signes crurent* P2.

68 **wordely**: add *et transitoire* P2.

75 **same**: *alia* LgA.

77 **for his blyndenesse**: *pource quil ne sauoit quil faisoit* P2, *pro sui cecitate* LgA.

79–80 **but . . . hym**: only GiL.

81 **As . . . wretin**: only GiL.

84 **wolde come and visite**: *mutaret* LgA.

84–5 **and . . . hem**: only GiL.

92 **moyst and**: only GiL.

96 **mowed doune**: *fauchoit et couppoit* P2.

96–7 **the place . . . duelled**: *le monstier de lomme de dieu* P2.

97 **place**: *lacum* LgA.

98 **tree**: *manche* P2; *MED* sense 2b (g), 'the wooden part of something'.

100 **ouer the place**: *in lacu* LgA.

102 **water**[1]: *fleuue* P2.

121 **twies thries**: *encore et encore* S.

123 **and bere it forthe**: only GiL.

127 **daunce**: only GiL.

128–9 **to synne and to vnclennesse**: *a luxure* P2.

130 **his enemye**: *lenuie* P2.

134 **knowing this**: only GiL.

136, 137 **as wel, as**: *ou, ou* P2.

138 **hem, they, her**: singular P2.

141 **purpose**: *ennemy* S.

145 **enforced hym**: *se forsenoit* P2.

148 **cursed and not blessed**: *maloit et non pas benoit* S; the pun on Benedict's name is lost in English.

149–50 **to putte . . . that**: *qui gisoit a terre en vng edifice et* P2.

154 **hadde made it so heuy**: *seoit la qui ne la laissoit mouuoir* P2.

157 **hym**: *leur* P2.

162 **lyff**: add *par son oroison* P2.

166 **as hym thought**: not in LgA.

185 **rich**: *royal* P2.

194–5 **he was . . . orders**: *il sen fut garde par aucun temps et il vit quil auoit este mis es mineurs ordres* P2, *hoc aliquo tempore custodisset, sed minores suos sibi preponi in sacris ordinibus cerneret* LgA; i.e. he could see his juniors being put above him in holy orders; *kepe* should have been emended to *kepte*.

199 **flaskons**: *flacons* P2, *flascones* LgA, not recorded in *MED*. Unfamiliarity no doubt led to the substitution of the also rare *flaskettis* found in G; the misreadings *flaskowse* and *flascouse* in E and H1 are not made to look like plurals as context demands. See next.

206 **flaken**: *flacon* P2, *flascone* LgA; *MED s.v. flagon* (first citation 1442) records *flakon* but not this spelling.

212 **leue that hert**: *signa cor tuum* LgA.

215 **be . . . reste**: *ad monasterium recedere et quietum sedere* LgA.

216–73 These sections are not in Maggioni's text, but supplied from Re in his critical apparatus, pp. 316–17; they are also in Graesse.

216 **of Goche**: *des gothes* S.

218 **the faithe of holy Chirche**: *les religieux de la foy catholicque* P2.

222 **of the courte**: only GiL.

228 **before hym**: *ante equum suum* LgA.

231 **sitting**: add *et lisant* P2.

236 **take**: *rens* P2.

256 **wrothe and troubeled**: *courrouciez* P2, *contristatos* LgA.

264 **gretly ne sodeinly**: only GiL.

267 **chine**, G *chynne*; *MED* gives *chin* as a possible though rare spelling for 'skin'.

268 **was . . . beholde**: *ne pouoit estre muciee* P2.

269 **that . . . faithe**: only GiL.

277–8 **to a monke (. . .) whiche he hadde ordeyned aboue other as prouost**: *monacho quem illic preposuerat atque eius preposito* LgA. Vignay reduced these two monks to one, but retained the original plural pronouns in the rest of the passage.

279 **goodly and**: only GiL.
sotelly: in LgA this goes with 278 *shewed*, *subtiliter designauit*.

285 **a**: *la* P2.

288 **to laugh**: *a ire* P2.

291 **not in pronounsynge but in assaienge**: *non proferendo* (. . .) *sed intentando* LgA. Vignay took *intentando*, 'threatening', as *in tentando*, perhaps 'putting them to the test'.

294 **comithe**: *commenie* P2, *communicat* LgA; P1 has the more usual spelling *communie*.

298 **her**: only GiL.

299 **for**^{2}: *et* P2.

300–1 **They laye in pees and**: only GiL.

304 **two tymes**: *vne foys ou deux* P2, *semel et bis* LgA.

311 **he**: add *fut courroucie et* P2.

313 **gretly aferde**: only GiL.

319 **to the peple**: *egentibus* LgA, 'to the needy'.

336 **downe and helde vp**: *et* P2, *in* LgA.
priue: only GiL.

337 **done and**: only GiL.

339 **ther . . . hous**: *il ne peust oncques mouuoir le pie* P2.

340 **þat she hadde praied**: only GiL.

345 **nyght**: add *ilz furent sans dormir et* P2.

346–7 **of the loue . . . Lorde**: only GiL.

349 **heuene**: *les secrez du ciel* P2.

356 **of a companye**: *de capuenne* P2, *episcopi Capuani in sphera ignea ab angelis* LgA.

360 **the tyme and**: only GiL.

360–1 **.viij. daye after**: *vj.*^{e} *iour auant* P2.

366 **disciples**: add *et leua les mains au ciel* P2.

369 **encortined**: *MED encurtinen* has only one citation, from Gower, with the *en-* prefix.

374 **servaunt and the**: only GiL.

48 ST PATRICK

Maggioni, ch. XLIX, p. 321; Dunn-Lardeau, ch. 49, p. 362.

1 **beganne to preche**: *cepit* LgA.

1–2 **.CCCC..iiij.**^{xx}.: *iij.C .iiij.*^{xx} P2, *CCLXXX* LgA; Patrick lived *c.*390–*c.*460.

16–17 **ne none . . . openly**: only GiL.

19 **blede**: *beellast* P2; EH1G agree, but s.w. doubtless wrote *blete*, so this should have been emended.

23–4 **His . . . praied**: *a suis admonitus a deo cur non uiderit precibus dum requireret* LgA.

36 **harme**: *purgatorium* LgA.

38 **another**: add *et dont moult de ceulz* (. . .) *y entrerent qui nen reuindrent puis* P2.

40 **a**: add *noble* P2.

44 **the whiche . . . kaye**: *cum claui que in quadam abbatia seruatur* LgA.

48–9 **sadde . . . faithe**: *ferme* P2.

50 **remedye and**: only GiL.

52 **saie**: add *et crie* P2.

Dei uiui: *dauid* P2, not in LgA. At 59–60 and 69 LgD reads *de dieu vif*, giving the prayer in French each time.

54–5 **and made . . . it**: *premierement par promesses et par belles parolles* P2.

67 **in this fere brennynge**: *ardoir dedens ce feu* P2.

72–3 **tobeten . . . appered**: *laminis ferreis candentibus a demonibus usque ad uiscera flagellari* LgA.

74 **and**[1]: *aliosque* LgA.

77 **bufones**: *botereaux* P2, *bufones* LgA, 'toads'. *MED* does not record the word. Roze, 247, observes: 'on ne saurait concevoir comment des crapauds pourraient arracher des entrailles avec des instruments aigus', but it is clear that is just what one is asked to imagine.

78 **brennyng**: not in LgD, *ignitis* LgA.

80 **but**: *et fut tourmente de ces pieces de fer et de ces peines. mais il dit adonc. ihesucrist filz de dieu vif ayes pitie de moy pecheur. et* P2.

81 **by lemes of fere**: *par motes* P2, not in LgA; at 84 below, *vne mote de feu* P2, *globum igneum* LgA.

82 **fere**: *uncinis igneis* LgA.

90 **depe**: *le* P2 , 'wide'.

100 **foryete**: add *inuocare* LgA.

105–6 **polisched as glas and as sleper as yse yfrosen**: *aussy poli comme glace et tout estoillant* P2, *instar glaciei politus et lubricus* LgA.

113 **forthe**: add *et dont mist lautre pie apres* P2.

121 **sorugh . . . disese**: *douleur ne pueur* P2.

123 **ayein**: add *premierement* P2.

49 ANNUNCIATION

Maggioni, ch. L, p. 326; Dunn-Lardeau, ch. 50, p. 367.

From 30 to 202 this chapter is based substantially on Bernard, *Homiliae super Missus est* (*in laudibus virginis matris*), and consists largely of a close commentary on the account in Luke.

5 **for . . . assembeling**: *ordinis connotandi* LgA, 'pour conservir un certain ordre' (Roze).

6 **vnbeysaunce** has only two citations in *MED s.v. unobeisaunce*, for (a1382) and *c.*1425; the spelling without *o* (not recorded in *MED*) is given by EH1GH2T2, but LA2 have *o*; A1 is defective.

6–7 **that is . . . fader**: not in LgA.

7 **woman**: add *pour traire la* S.

to drede: *doubter* P2, *dubitationem* LgA; *MED dreden* sense 5, 'be in doubt', has only three citations, the latest for a1425, but there are many in this text (see Glossary). However the related noun, which is considerably earlier and more frequent, can carry this sense, as can the adverb *dredeles.*

16 **falle of aungels**: *decheement et le pechie de lange qui chey* P2, *lapsus angelici* LgA.

20 **no more** begins a new sentence in LgD and LgA, adding after **resurreccion**: *non est le message de lange. dieu denonca par lange lune et lautre a la femme* (*utrumque . . . mulieri* LgA). *cest assauoir lincarnation a la Vierge et la resurrection a la magdaleine* P2.

24–6 **God . . . yerde of Ioseph**: *nisi deus aliter disponeret, eam Ioseph desponsauit domino reuelante et Ioseph uirga frondente* LgA.

31 **of the floure**: not in P2, *de flore* LgA.

34–6 **Bernarde sterithe . . . salutacion**: *Et lexemple de gabriel nous amonnesta a saluer marie et la joye de iehan et le proffit du salu* P2, *Bernardus: 'Inuitat nos ad Marie salutationem Gabrielis exemplum, Iohannis tripudium et resalutationis lucrum'* LgA. *exemplum*, *tripudium*, and *lucrum* are the joint subjects of *Inuitat*, 'Gabriel's example, John's rejoicing, and the reward of a returned greeting'.

38 **foure**: *.iij.* P2.

46–7 **that**[2] **. . . ordinatly**: *ut per uirum genealogie series texeretur* LgA.

48 ***Dominus tecum, et c.***: *&c.* P2, not in LgA. Bernard gives it as a phrase by phrase commentary, but LgD and GiL do not entirely follow this.

53 **tho . . . chetiuyte**: not in P2, *captiui* LgA.

redempcion: add *egri curationem* LgA.

56 **of mankinde**: *de char humaine* P2, *humane caritatis* LgA, *humanae carnis* Graesse.

56–7 **Oure Lorde is with the**: GiL compounds the error of the incorrect insertion at 48 above by failing to translate this back into Latin; LgD has it all in French.

60 **as**: *ainsy* P2.

61 *et c.*: only GiL.

62 **virgine**: *mater, uirgo mater* LgA.

63 **before that tyme**: only GiL.

65 **conceiued**: *conceuent* P2.
saide: add *quant elle ot les enfans* P2, not in LgA.

67 **cours**: *maudicon de tourment* P2; this spelling with *ou* (also at 65) not recorded in *MED s.v. curs* n., though it is for the verb.

68 **he . . . Genesis**: *genesis dit* P2.

69 **woo and**: only GiL.

75 **deuocion**: add *de* P2.

76 **reuerence**: add *de* P2.
sadnesse: *maceree* P2, *martyrium* LgA.

81 **.iiij.**: add *autres* P2.

87 **Virgine**: add *en oyr. en vouloir. en penser* P2.
heringe: add *est* (. . .) *louee* P2.

87–8 **in heringe . . . temperaunce**: *en oyr en vouloir en penser. En oyr est son attrempance loee* P2.

89 **for**: *unde* LgA.

96–7 **for . . . troubled**: *et ce que elle ne fut pas troublee moult luy vint de force* P2, *quod non perturbata, fortitudinis* LgA.

98 **prudence and discrecion**: *sagesse* P2, *prudentie et discretionis* LgA.

102 **he saiethe**: i.e. the angel; see Luke 1:31.

111 **of that she dradde**: *et qui interrogat dubitat LgA.*

112 **Zakarie**: add *solus* LgA.
deef: *muet* P2.

114 **priuetees . . . herte**: *pechiez* P2, *peccatorum* LgA.
only: *auant* P2.

115 **she sheued**: *demonstra* P2, *iudicauit* LgA. The subject should still be *He* from 113.

116 **demaundes**: *demandans* P2, i.e. the motives of those questioning.
hope: *especes* P2, *species* LgA, *spes* Graesse.

117 **dred that was kyndely**: *doubta par nature* P2, *dubitauit pro natura* LgA.

117–18 **She asked the ordinaunce holy**: *hec integre ordinem querit* LgA.

118–19 **dradde . . . vndone**: *ordonna ce que dieu voult ne puisse estre fait* P2, *que deus uult fieri non posse prescribit* LgA.

119–20 **by ensaumples sheued**: *impellentibus exemplis* LgA, i.e. despite compelling examples.

121–2 **he . . . mariage**: *ille de conceptu disputat coniugali* LgA.

134–5 **that of only . . . man**: *que ce soit par grace* (add *sola* LgA) *que nulle merite domme nestoit auant faicte* P2.

137–8 **cause mouyng to**: *cause mouuant de la* P2, *motiuum* LgA.

138 **concepcion**[1]: add *et cest la raison hue de saint victor* P2.

139 **he**: i.e. Hugh of St Victor, omitted in preceding line.

144 ***obiecto***: *deiecte* S, *obiecto* LgA.

145 **that . . . light**: only GiL.

146 **as pure man**: i.e. being entirely human.

148 **body of mankinde**: *humanitatis* LgA.

149 **the lyght of**: only GiL.

151 **shadowes**: *membres* P2, *umbra* LgA.

152 ***obiectum***: *contraire* P2, *obiectum* LgA.

154 **brightnesse**: *cereum* LgA.

159–60 **doctour whiche is auutour**: i.e. teacher who is himself the doer.

161 **But**: not in P2, *Vel* LgA.

164 **Loo here**: picking up 162 *see here*.
a gret nouelte: *magnum nouum uicinum* LgA.

165 **causes**: add *secundum Bernardum* LgA.

166 **perfeccion**: *perfusio* LgA.

168 **bareyne**: *MED* offers no word which could explain the variants in the other MSS.

171 **where . . . Virgine**: *Sy que la vierge le sceust* P2.

174 **doune in erthe**: not in LgD, *in terris* LgA.

179 **profite**: i.e. John Baptist.

180 **and . . . miracle**: *et mirabilius fiat miraculum de miraculis* LgA.

181 A: *Item* P2.

185 **confession**: *deuocion* P2, *confessionem* LgA.

186 **and**: add *les yeulx esleuez* P2.

192 **by**[2]: *ou* P2, *in* LgA.

195 ***Ecce ancilla Domini***: only GiL.

198 **priuely**: *espirituelment* P2, *silenter* LgA.

204, 205 **ioye, ioyed**: *saluer, salua* P2.

207 **was the furste that**: only GiL.

208 **As . . . Men**: In LgA this concludes the preceding sentence.
in the Boke of Rightwise Men: *in libro iustorum* LgA; the *Liber Justorum* refers to the lost (and unidentified) Book of Jasher mentioned twice in the Bible, at Josh. 10: 13 and 2 Kgs. 1: 18 (i.e. 2 Samuel).

209 **as the cours hathe ronne aboute**: *par moult des cours des temps* P2.

211–19 T2 leaves a space for the verses, which have not been inserted, as is also the case with many of the Latin quotations.

211 ***coheres***: *coherces* P2, *coerces* LgA; the GiL substitution is unsatisfactory, since *cohaero*, 'stick together', can only be intransitive. At whatever stage the misreading happened, s.w. was unaware of it and adopted *restreined* from Vignay *as restraint* as at 220–7 below (*MED restreinen* sense 2. (a) 'prevent or staunch bleeding') for *coerces* 'enclose', whence 'bind up'.

212 ***et***: so S, not in P2 or LgA.

214 ***ob ense***: *ab ense* P2 and LgA.

219 ***cum Christo***: *per Christum* LgA.

220 **This is the Englishe of these vers**: *Et pource que ces vers sont mis en mettre en latin. Je frere iehan qui translate ce liure les vueil aussy mettre en francois. en la maniere qui sensuit* P2, one of Vignay's rare personal statements.

220–7 Vignay's translation, in the spelling of P1:

Ie te salue iour tres saint.
qui nos plaies nous as restraint.
Langre fu enuoie ce iour.
Diex i souffry mort sanz seiour.
A ce iour fu fait Adam homme.
& a ce iour mordi en la pomme.
Abel fu occis pour la disme.
de son propre frere meisme.
Melchisedech offre al autel.
Abraham fist dysaac autel.
Et herode par son meschief.
coupa au baptiste le chief.
Pierres sa prison remua.
& herodes Iaques tua.
Auec dieu en sa compaignie.

suscita cors sains grant partie.
Le larron qui out en memoire.
ihesucrist fu mis en sa gloire.

228 **Here . . . Lady**: only GiL.
a[2]: add *riche et* P2.

230 **monkes**: add *orent honte que sy noble personne fut mise entre les lays* P2.

232 **duelled**: *demourast* P2 (subjunctive).

232–3 **for . . . hym**: *quant il eust este longuement a maistre* P2.

235–6 **with herte . . . mouthe**: only GiL.

246–7 **hadde . . . he**: only GiL.

247–8 **worship . . . aungell**: *la* (. . .) *saluoit* P2.

257 **some**: *aucun* P2.

267 **.xliij.**: *xiij* P2, *XIIII* LgA.

276–7 **and lyued . . . Lady**: only GiL.

280 **neuer . . . disese**: *ne nuyses* P2, *nocere presumas* LgA.

281 **seruithe ne**: only GiL.

50 PASSION

Maggioni, ch. LI, p. 336; Dunn-Lardeau, ch. 51, p. 375.

The Passion was A painful, B humiliating, and C profitable 1–2:

A painful:
- (i) it was shameful 3–22;
- (ii) it was unjust 23–39;
- (iii) it was brought about by his friends 40–54;
- (iv) it was painful through the tenderness of his body 55–62;
- (v) it affected all his parts and all his senses 63–150: (a) by sight 64–71; (b) by hearing 71–122; (c) by smell 123–8; (d) by taste 129–37; (e) by touch 138–50.

B humiliating; the scorn was suffered on four occasions 151–2:
- (i) the house of Annas 152–7;
- (ii) the house of Herod 157–75;
- (iii) the house of Pilate 176–95;
- (iv) on the cross 196–205. Summary by Bernard 206–12.

C profitable:
- (i) in three ways, remission of sins, getting of grace, the gift of glory 213–26;
- (ii) for four reasons (not five as in text) 227–30: (a) reconciliation of man

with God 231–61; (b) healing of man's ills in time, in place, and in like and different ways 262–98; (c) drawing man to the love of God 299–317; (d) chasing away the fiend from mankind 318–36.

1–2 **by dispitfull, by illusion**: *despite par illusion* P2, *ex illusione despecta* LgA; s.w. has turned the triple division into four, in the process using the rare adjectival form *dispitfull*, 'miserable', which has only three citations in *MED*, as a noun.

12 **that**²: add *primo* LgA.

14 **it is**: *dicitur* LgA.

16 **payne**: here Vignay supplies six verses in Latin followed by his own rhyming translation; see Dunn-Lardeau, 376.

18 **nedes**: *negoces* P2.

19 **messanger**: *paranymphum* LgA, 'bridesman', or more generally 'supporter', referring to St John.

23 **she**: i.e. *the Passion*, see 3 above. So too 63 below.

23–4 **ne gile**: only GiL.

31 **thanne**: *leur* P2; the text should be emended to *hem*, as G.

40 **by despite**: not in LgA.

42 **and**: *uel* LgA.

43 **for to suffre**: *il souffry touteffoys* P2, *tamen patitur ab amicis, id est* LgA.

45 **that shulde be**: only GiL.

47 **after**: *apres ce* P2, *Item* LgA.

48 **moche good to and**: only GiL.

56–7 **worme eten**: *pourry* P2, *uermiculus* LgA.

58 **a persing soune**: *le terme* P2, *tinnitus* LgA.

59 **boillethe oute**: *sy en yssist* P2, *ebullit* LgA.

61 **was hidde**: *comprenant* P2.

65 **the apostell**: *Heber* P2, *Hebr. V.* LgA. This belongs to the preceding quotation, and is followed in LgA by *Bernardus*: introducing the next.

66–7 **added . . . teres**: *plora auecque les lermes* P2, *clamori lacrimas addidit* LgA.

71 **tho here**: *hee tertie* LgA.

78 **waye . . . lyff**: *voye verite et vie* P2.

82 **perfitely good**: *bon parfait* P2, *bonus* LgA.

82–3 **In these . . . blasphemes**: not in LgD, in LgA.

86 **the name of**: *Beelzebub* LgA.

87 *.xxvij.*: *.xvij.* P2, *XXVII* LgA.

90 **sought**: add *et quamt ilz orent respondu* P2.
and: only GiL.

94–5 **What shal he do whan he iugethe, sithe he ferithe so hem þat iugen hym**: *que fera celuy a estre iugie que fist il a iugier* P2, *Quid iudicaturus faciet, qui iudicandus hoc fecit?* LgA; the only possible sense of *ferithe* seems to be 'frightens', perhaps caught from LgD *fera*.

99 **waye . . . trouthe**: *voye verite et vertu* P2, *uia, ueritas et uita* LgA.

102 **of**: i.e. concerning.

103 **that . . . trouthe**: *a oyr labsolution de verite* P2, *solutionem audire* LgA.

105 **it**[1]: *quest verite* P2, *illam questionem* LgA.

106 **one**: add *malfaicteur* P2, not in LgA.

115 **whanne she iuged tho thingges**: *que iudicatur ab hiis* LgA.

118 *.ix.*[o]: not in LgD, *XXIII* LgA.

125–6 **nakednesse . . . hede**: *os capitis humani nudum* LgA, i.e. the bare skull.

127 **called**: add *lieu de* P2.

130 **gall and eisell**: *fiel* P2.

134 **felinge**: *olfactus* LgA.

141 **tremble**: add *fut point de plente despines* P2.

145 **clamour**: *insultus* LgA.

147 **crosse**: add *les mains qui fourmerent les cielx furent estendues et fichees de cloux en la croix* P2.

152 **maners**: *fois* P2.

155 **orible**: only GiL.

156 **his eyen**: *le* P2.

157 **And after**: *Secundo* LgA.

164 **Herode**: add *pour toy en blanche vesteure* P2.

166 **wise**: add *in gaudium* LgA.

172 **Pilate**: add *et Iudeis* LgA.

178 **in scorne**: only GiL.
Heille: *dieu te sauf* P2, *Aue* LgA.

181 **in gret plente**: only GiL.

182 **multitude of**: not in P2, *multiplici* LgA.

187 **Iohn**: *illud* LgA; John 19:30.

188 **anone . . . hem**: *Hanc triplicem opinionem Iudei saltem ipso facto uidentur sciuisse* LgA.

194 ***Agios***: add *etc.* P2.

203 **moste apperinge**: 'most visible, uppermost'.

209 **in wakinge**: *les veilles que il fist* P2.

209–10 **in wepinge**: *des pleurs que il fist par pitie* P2.

210 **spekinge**: *parlemens* P2.

211 **tresones**: *subsannationum* LgA, 'derisive gestures'.

215 **yefte**: *exhibitio* LgA.

221 **withdrawinge**: add *les hommes de pechie* P2.

224 **come**: *uocati* LgA.

225–6 **a good contre**: *patriam* LgA.

227 .v.: *quatuor* LgA, variant *quinque*; there are four, at 231, 262, 299, and 318.

230 **and . . . God**: not in LgA, but in one MS as variant.

236 **Paule . . . Ephisens**: *Eph. III* LgA.

236–7 **He toke hymselff in oblacion:** *Tradidit semet ipsum oblationem* LgA.

238–9 **he . . . God**: 'he became a sacrifice, making peace for and reconciling us to God'.

241 **For**: *Et* LgD, *Vt, quoniam* LgA.
oure: *omni* LgA.

243–4 **that one and that other**: i.e. God and man.

244–5 **abode one with hymselff to whom he offered**: *pource est vng seul auec luy quant il soffroit* P2, *unum cum ipso maneret cui offerebat* LgA; add further *et que il fist vne seule chose en soy ceulx pour qui il offroit* P2, *unum in se faceret pro quibus offerebat* LgA, i.e. he made himself one with those for whom he was offering.

245–6 **was hymselff alone the whiche offered and was offered**: *et ce quil offroit* P2, *unus ipse esset qui offerebat et quod offerebat* LgA. LgD omitted the first part of this, which GiL restored from LgA. The sense of the whole passage should be: 'He remained one with him to whom he was offering, he made himself one with those for whom he was offering, he himself was both the one who was offering and the thing he was offering.'

249 **reconsiled**[1]: add *dieu a qui nous sommes reconsiliez* P2.

252 **and**: *quant* P2.

260 **Al . . . suffered**: only GiL.

261 **and . . . me**: not in P2, *et tu diuideris a me* LgA.

266 **and the .vj.[te] houre**: not in P2, *et hora sexta* LgA.

267 **same**: *iour* P2.

274 **was beried**[1]: *passus est* LgA; Abraham acquired a burial place for Sarah in a cave at Hebron, and was later himself buried there (Gen. 23 and 25: 8–10). A tradition arose that this had also been Adam's burial place. See too 178 Adam 621–2.

276 **Iosue**: add *IV* LgA, in fact Josh. 14: 15.

280 **same tree**: *meismes maniere* P2, *eodem* LgA.

280–1 **The .iij. maner of the partie of curinge**: *de la partie de la maniere du cueur* P2, *Tertio ex parte modi curandi* LgA.

284–5 **man**[1] **. . . dethe**: *lomme deliura les hommes il mortel deliura les mortelz et les mors par sa mort* P2, *homo homines, mortalis mortales, morte mortuos liberauit* LgA; GiL substitution of *the childe* for P2 *les mors* is hard to explain.

286 **he, this**: *lun, lautre* P2, *ille, hic* LgA.

287 **follissnesse**: 'stupidity', not recorded by *MED*.

290 **man**: add *secundum Gregorium* LgA.

295–6 **humylinge . . . torment**: *humilitationem, diuine uoluntatis impletionem et afflictionem* LgA; *MED humilien* has only one citation, for ?c1450, Knight of La Tour Landry, but no gerund.

296 **saiethe the apostell**: *Phi. II* LgA.

298 **dethe**: add *etc.* LgA.

299 **she**: i.e. redemption.

299–300 **the fre will saued**: *saluo libertatis arbitrio* LgA, i.e. without violation of free will.

301 **drowe**: *actrait* P2.

304 **myghtely**: *legerement* P2; probably s.w. wrote *lyghtely*, so this should have been emended.

306 **hastely**: add *et uehementius afficit* LgA.

307 **anentisshed**: *anientas* P2; see note to 88.65.

308, 309 **lyghtnithe, stremithe**: *esclercy*, *raya* P2.

309–10 **As . . . truste**: *Qualiter uero ad fiduciam, dicitur Rom. VIII* LgA.

312 **how . . . hymselff**: *quomodo non etiam cum illo omnia nobis donauit?* LgA; this has become detached from *all* at the end of the previous sentence; *And Bernard saiethe* introduces the next.

316 **loue**: add *les piez lun deuant lautre a mouuoir auec nous* P2, *pedum affixionem ad nobiscum commanendum* LgA.

318 **he**: redemption is here masculine; *cf.* 299 above.

320 **proude**[1]: add *et ultimus: 'Numquid poteris capere Leuiathan hamo?'* LgA.

321 **mete**: *escam* LgA, which in this context carries the sense 'bait', also at 326 and *flesshe* at 323.

322–3 **whan . . . manhede**: *dyabolus capere uolens escam carnis captus est ab hamo diuinitatis* LgA, 'the devil wishing to take the bait of the meat was caught by the hook of divinity'.

324, 325 **beyer**: *racheteur* P2.

325 **the**[2]: *nostre* P2.

327 **not of**: i.e. not that of.

331 **sirograf**: a formal document; *MED* has four records of this word, the last for *c.*1390, all spelt with initial *c*.

337 **his**: *ceste* P2.

338 **we . . . ayein**: *nos de inimici potestate reduxit* LgA.

338–9 **by . . . saide**: *dicit in persona Christi* LgA.

340 **that . . . done**: *et tu ne le feis* P2, *et non feci* LgA.

345–6 **Whi . . . right**: *Ceterum si neque tam multiplici iure debitum a uobis est elicere famulatum* LgA, 'but if it is not possible to recover from you the service owed by such a multiple obligation'.

346–7 **al thingges leffte**: *omissis omnibus* LgA, i.e. apart from anything else.

347 ***conuenite***: *conuenir* P2, LgA as GiL, i.e. come to terms.
of[1] **. . . day**: *ex diurno denario* LgA, i.e. for a penny a day.

350–1 **of brynginge forthe**: *et origine* LgA.

354 **wreten**: *leu* P2.

362 **atte the balle . . . games**: *a la pelote et a moult dautres fais* P2, *pugno* LgA.

365 **of playes**: *destrif* P2.

370 **moued by grace**: only GiL.

378–9 **and wrathe**: only GiL.

382 **Romaynes**: add *et dontera les cous des outrageux* S, *et colla ferocium hostium ferox ipse domabit* LgA.

391 **veynquor**: 'conqueror', not in *MED*; *OED* gives *vainquer* for 1456 and 1481.

393 **beyng kyng**: only GiL.
wisdom: *industriam* LgA.

396 **whanne . . . to hym**: only GiL.

397 **vpon**: add *Judee et* P2.

406 **Galile**: *garizim* P2, Mount Gerizim, east of Nablus.

407 **his**: add *et se doubtoit que il deceust aussi touz les siens* (*iuis* P1) S, add *timens ne similiter Iudeos seduceret* LgA.

422 **.viij.**: *xiiij.* P2.

425–6 **anone . . . lamentacion**: only GiL.

431 **here**: *ca et la* P2.
was alwayes: *laissasse moult enuis que ie ne feusse* P2.

436 **my**: *la* P2.

436–9 **and whanne . . . say**: *et il me rendy semblable a son honorable face tout figure* P2.

457 **zeme**: 'seam'. *MED s.v. sem(e* n.1 records no forms with initial *z*.

485 **ioyned hem to**: *si sesioirent du* P2.

486 **wiked**: add *et puant* P2.

487 **the wawes**: *inundationes in aquis* LgA.

488 **tempestes**: add *et pluies* P2, add *et grandines* LgA.

489 **so**: only GiL.

489–90 **that . . . askaped**: only GiL.

491 **and**[1]: add *derisionis causa* LgA.

492–3 **that . . . helle**: not in LgA.

493 **cursinge**: add *uel potius dicitur Bienna eo quod, ut dicitur, quasi biennio sit constructa* LgA.

495 **tormentes**: *infestationem* LgA.

496–7 **depe pitte of Losenge**: *terrouer de losanne* P2, *Losanne ciuitatis territorio* LgA.

498 **tempestes**: *infestationibus* LgA.

498–9 **and bere hym ferre and threwe hym**: only GiL.

501 **maculaciones**: *machinations* P2; *MED maculacion*, 'defilement', has only two citations, both from *Ludus Coventriae*, dated a1475.

502 **Stori**: add *apocrypha* LgA; see 354 above.

508 **Corbonan**: *tronc* P2, *corbonam* LgA, *MED s.v. corban*, 'the treasury of the Temple at Jerusalem'.
and: add *en* P2, add *inde* LgA.

517 **verrely**: *tant seulement* P2.

51 ST SECUNDUS

Maggioni, ch. LIII, p. 370; Dunn-Lardeau, ch. 53, p. 405.

1 **noble**[1]: *strenuus* LgA.
noble knyght[2]: *athleta egregius* LgA.

3 **is ennoblisshed**: *illustratur* LgA; the word also occurs at 84.340 (for *decoratus* LgA), and similarly at 161.3, but is not in *MED*. For the related *ennobled* see note to 26.282.

5 **Calotero**: *alexien* P2, *Calocero* LgA (dative).

8 **Terdonensi**: *victoire* P2, *Terdonensi* LgA.

9 **as . . . disport**: 'as though for diversion'.

15 **herde**: *uidit* LgA.

17 **in the**: not in LgA.

17–18 **thou . . . ydoles**: *tu nyras pas faire ainsy les cultiueurs des ydoles* P2, *sic super ydolorum cultores ambulabis* LgA; it is difficult to make sense of GiL, other than by some extension of the normal meanings of *folw*, such as 'drive out'.

18–19 **me thinkithe**: only GiL.

21 **same**: *similiter* LgA.

23 **yet**: only GiL.

24 **verrily on**: *a la verite de* P2.

25 **of the**: only GiL.
And anone . . . pees: not in LgA.

31 **of oure Lorde**: only GiL.

33–4 **the whiche . . . prison**: not in P2, in LgA.

38 **Secound**: add *ut ad Marcianum deferret* LgA.

39 **riuer**: *riue* P2.

39–40 **whiche . . . contre**: not in LgA.

44 **and**: add *il le prist et* P2.

47 **hous**: *hostel* P2.

49 **and so . . . done**: only GiL.

55 **more sharpely**: *potius* LgA.

58 **beter . . . before**: only GiL.

60–1 **It . . . erthe**: not in LgA.

72 **hym**: *eis* LgA.

80–1 **and . . . sentence**: only GiL.

84 **or clere wyne**: *ou tressouef vin blanc* P2, not in LgA.

52 ST MARY OF EGYPT

Maggioni, ch. LIV, p. 374; Dunn-Lardeau, ch. 54, p. 408.

2 **desert**: add *quam circa annos domini CCLXX tempore Claudii intrauit* LgA. **doynge her penaunce**: only GiL.

2–3 **And . . . desert**: not in LgA.

3 **holy fader**: *abbe* P2.

9 **as moche . . . myght**: *hastiuement* P2.

22–3 **and houered in the eyre**: only GiL.

29 **pitously**: only GiL.

31 **venemous**: only GiL.

32 **charged . . . wyse**: *la hastoit forment* P2.

50–1 **as . . . sorugh**: only GiL.

51 **I behelde . . . there**: *regarday au portail et* P2, *respiciensque* LgA.

64 **long**: add *instar lapidis* LgA.

65 **.xvij.**: *XLVII* LgA.

68–9 **and my clothes . . . agone** precedes 65 **I haue bene** in LgD and LgA.

69 **werkes**: here P2 ends the chapter with the words: *Et apres ce il sen party et la demoura longuement et fut saincte en paradis.*

77, 83, 91, 100, 103, 111 **holy** is for *ancien* or *viel* S, *senex* LgA.

81 **as sone . . . hym**: only GiL.

83 **her**: *ce* S, *ceste chose* P1, *Quod* LgA.

95 **to God ne**: only GiL.

98 **sepulture**: *puluerem* LgA.

99 **kalende**: *die* LgA.

101 **lyff**: add *Et Zozimas estoit apaines alez a ce lieu parmi le desert par .xxx. iournees et elle y ala en vne seulle heure et feni sa vie* (*migrauit* LgA) S.

106 **I**[1]: add *qui suis viel ne puis fouir ne ie* S.

107–8 **withe . . . wherinne**: only GiL.

108 **I may**: *possimus* LgA.

112–13 **and wrote . . . all**: not in LgA.

53 ST AMBROSE

Maggioni, ch. LV, p. 378; Dunn-Lardeau, ch. 55, p. 412.

P2 omits this chapter.

1 Ambrose, son of Aurelius Ambrosius, the pretorian prefect of Gaul, was born at Trier.

2 **a place . . . iugementes**: *atrio pretorii* LgA.
iugementes: add *et si se dormoit* S.

5 **propre habitacion**: *alueolum* LgA, 'small cavity'.

8 **mervayled gretly**: *fut tout espouente* S.

9 **and a mervaylous**: only GiL.

10 **holy suster**: *sororem sacram uirginem* LgA.

13–14 **She . . . refused it**: *illa uero ut adolescentem et nescientem quid diceret respuebat* LgA, 'she rebuffed him as a child not knowing what he was saying'.

15–17 **And . . . wherfor**: *Rome igitur litteris eruditus cum causas pretorii splendide peroraret* LgA.

18 **Emurie**: *Emiliam* LgA; H1 has *Enjurie*, other GiL and LgD MSS including S and P1 appear to read *Eniurie*.

28–30 **he went . . . chirche**: *ut eos a se terroribus remoueret, ecclesiam exiens tribunal conscendit et* LgA, i.e. to frighten them out of choosing him.

34 **wolde . . . philysophie**: *philosophiam profiteri uoluit* LgA, i.e. wanted to devote himself to philosophy.

38–9 **he coude . . . hym**: only GiL.

40 **the citee of Cyenin**: *Ticinum* LgA, Pavia.

46 **his . . . required**: *les iuges qui estoient enuoiez de lui feussent requis* S.

47 **the good prouost**: *Probus prefectus* LgA; Probus was prefect of Illyria, see Boureau, 1206 nn. 7 and 10.

50 **foryeue . . . crosse**: *ut episcopus* LgA.

58 **emperour**: *empereris* S, 'empress'; the error is repeated at 72.

59 **none**: *aliquis* LgA.
his: *sua* LgA, i.e. 'their'.

60 **went vp**: *tribunal conscendit* LgA.

67 **so it felle atte**: only GiL.

68 **conueyed**: add *la* S.

69 **worshipp**: *grace* S.

71–2 **moche . . . awayte**: *moult dagais* S.

72 **emperour for he**: *empereris et* S.

he: LgD does not supply the pronoun, which might have alerted s.w. to the continuing mistake in Iustine's gender.

88 **But . . . hym**: only GiL.

90 **withe . . . saide**: only GiL.

91 **the merites of**: only GiL.

93 **depe . . . water**: *piscinam* LgA.

102 **and saide**: add *a lui et lui distrent que* S, what follows being in indirect speech.

104–5 **we . . . therof**: *il estoient bien loing. Et encore le doubtoient il* S, *etiam longe positi urerentur* LgA.

108 **the chirche of**, 109–10 **of the chirche**: not in LgA.

112 **in a tyme**: *nocte* LgA.

113 **spere**: *glaiue* S.

121 **coude not bollen the withe pride**: *nescit inflari* LgA.

136 **sauf**: add *dimenche et* S.

137 **hadde or myght gete**: *pouoit auoir* S.

158–9 **to torment . . . todrewe**: *tout a desrompre* S.

161 **as . . . togedre**: only GiL.

175 **to his meyne**: only GiL.

180 **vice**: *radicem* LgA.

182–3 **they solden all her werkes for mede**: *il vendoient tout et faisoient par pris et par loier* S, *omnia pretio uendebantur* LgA.

187 **to the resureccion of oure Lorde**: i.e. until Easter Day.

188–9 **endited . . . psalme**: so all versions, but doubtless he was dictating a commentary, of which an uncompleted version survives (Boureau, 1207 n. 36.).

189 **.xviij.**: *.xliiij.* S.

190 **a litell**: *petit a petit* S.

192 **and abide**: only GiL.

206 **be**: add *bon* S.

207 **one . . . named**: *nominassent* LgA.

209–10 **But, Bon, Bon**: *Senex, sed bonus* LgA.

210 **hym**: *le viellart* S, *Quod* LgA.

211 **they chase . . . named**: *il neslurent fors que celui bon quil auoit nomme* S, *nonnisi illum* (. . .) *elegerunt* LgA.

218 **.iiijC. .iiij^{xx}.x.**: *.iij.^{C} .iiij.^{xx} et .x.* S, *CCCLXXX* LgA.

219 **Day**: *nocte* LgA.

221 **vp**: add *es cieulx* S, not in LgA.
and[2]: add *plusieurs* S.

228 **toke . . . but**: only GiL.

234 **chirche**: add *et est in decreto XXIII. q. VIII* LgA. In LgD and GiL this reference is transferred to 241 below.

242 **my lyff**: *animam* LgA; for LgD *lame* misread as *la uie*.

245 **whanne . . . chirche**: *de basilica non tradenda* LgA, i.e. the title given to the epistle.

246 **Valentinyen**: *de valentunien* S, *Valentiniani* LgA, i.e. Valentinian's official.

249 **folyes**: *felonnie* S, *tela* LgA.

253 **quene**: *regine* LgA, i.e. Justina, see 58 and 72 above.

257 **deuocion and**: only GiL.

261 **it is**: *Paulin* S.

270 **.xj.**: *II* LgA.

271 **Lucyne**: *Iustina* LgA.
moder[2]: *alumpna* LgA.

274–5 **Generall . . . Arienes**: *Ariminensis concilii* LgA, Synod of Rimini 359.

275–6 **Ambrose . . . her**: *ecclesie murum et turrim ualidissimam pulsabat Ambrosium* LgA, 'she (Justina) battered Ambrose, the most mighty wall and tower of the Church'.

276 **certainly**: not in LgA.

281 **the yocke of thi seruice**: *ton seruice* S, *tuo iugo* LgA.

282 **Eghtely**: *Secundo* LgA. Having misunderstood Voragine's scheme, which divided 268 *stronge perseuerance* into *Primo*, *Secundo*, and *Tertio* at GiL 269, 282, and 307, Vignay renumbered *Secundo* and *Tertio* as *huitiesmement* and *nouiesmement* to follow the *Septimo* of the larger scheme at 268; he then put *dixiesmement* for 374 *Octauo*, which P1 gives as *Nouiesmement* and S as *Meismement*, and s.w. 'corrects' to *Tenthely*.
defence: add *de la franchise* S.

283–4 **and . . . lordshipp**: not in LgA.

285–6 **by an erle**: *a comitibus* LgA.

287–295 The obscurity of this passage results from a combination of misreadings and unsuitably literal translations by Vignay. The gist of the original is: If you want my patrimony, come and take it; if you want to imprison or kill me, that is what I desire, I will hand myself over and not surround myself with defenders or cling to the altar praying for my life, and will happily be sacrificed for the sake of the altars. I am urged by royal commands to hand over a basilica, but we are strengthened by the words of Scripture: 'You speak like one of the foolish women.'

287–8 **the heritage of his moder**: *patrimonium* LgA, i.e. 'my patrimony', variant *matrimonium.*

288–9 **I will . . . prison**: *si lasaillez se ie met mon corps encontre et vous voulez mettez le en lians et amort se vous voulez* S, *inuadite*; *si corpus, occurram. Vultis in uincula rapere? Vultis in mortem?* LgA. In expanding the translation of *lasaillez* to account for the addition of *of his moder*, s.w. reversed the sense of this part of the sentence.

291–2 **but . . . auuter**: *mais hairroie ma vie se ie nestoie sacrefie pour lautel gracieusement* S, *uitam obsecrans, sed pro altaribus gratius immolabor* LgA. Vignay mistakes *obsecrans* as *exsecrans.*

293 **we be anoynted . . . reaws**: *Nous sommes donques oins par les royaux commandemans* S, *urgemur igitur preceptis regalibus* LgA. Vignay took *urgemur* as *unguemur. MED* does not record the spelling *reaws* under *real* n. or adj. (1).

294 **confermed**: LgA *confirmamur*, 'we are strengthened', but having mistaken *urgemur* as *unguemur* Vignay, followed by s.w., adopted the sense 'confirmed' to balance *anoynted.*

299 **the chirches right**: *ses choses* S, *uites suas* LgA.

300 **wolde . . . lingne**: *ne bailla pas sa vigne* S; though it appears from the previous note that neither Vignay nor s.w. had recognized the Naboth story, it may be that s.w. wrote *vigne* and the reading of the MSS results from subsequent scribal error.

307 **Ninthely**: *Meismement* S, *Nouiesmement* P1, *Tertio* LgA, see 282 above.

310 **Theodore**: *theodosien emperere* S.

315 **gate**: *porte* S.

318 **synne**: add *il appartient que tu vainques ta poeste par ton vice* S, *Decet te ut uincat ratio potestatem* LgA.

an emperour: *O emperere* S; this should probably have been emended, since misinterpretation of O as 'one' and thence 'an' must surely be an English scribal error.

318–19 **but . . . conseruatour**: not in S, *sed conseruorum* LgA, i.e. 'but of fellow-slaves'.

319–20 **communion . . . Lorde**: *communis domini templum* LgA.

320 **on**: add *le pauement du* S.

322 **oure rightwysse**: *non droiturier* S, *iniustus* LgA.

340–1 **shulde not drede . . . reconsiled**: *le tourneroit bien* S.

345 **obeye**: *abeie* G, *abaye* L; *MED s.v. abaien*, 'bark', records spellings with initial *o*.

348 **haue . . . and**: only GiL.

358–9 **Thou . . . felonye**: *tu qui as fait* (*ensui* P1) *la folie, ensui la correction* S.

363 **the place of the quere**: *interiora loca* LgA.

365 **in the chirche withoute**: only GiL.

368 **helde . . . benethe and**: only GiL.

374 **Tenthely**: *Meismement* S, *Nouuiesmement* P1, *Octauo* LgA, see 282 above. Voragine divided this into *altam profunditatem* (375 *high dipnesse of wisdom*), *Firmam soliditatem* (omitted after 378 *stabelnesse* by LgD and GiL), *Elegantem uenustatem* (380 *high noblesse*), and *Magnam auctoritatem* (386 *gret and noble auctoritees*). Vignay did not recognize this structure, and tried to incorporate the categories into the various quotations.

376 **science**: *pinna* LgA, 'flight'.

377–8 **into . . . thingges**: *en parfont* S. The sentence in LgA reads: *Ambrosius super profondorum pinna raptus et aeris uolucer quamdiu in profundum ingreditur, fructum de alto carpere uidetur*, rendered by Roze as 'Ambroise plane au-dessus des profondeurs comme un oiseau qui s'élance dans les airs; c'est dans le ciel qu'il cueille ses fruits'.

378 **stabelnesse**: *fermete afremee* (*afermee* P1) S, *fructum* LgA. LgA ends the quotation at *fructum* and adds: *Firmam soliditatem*; *Ieronimus ibidem*:.

378–80 **for . . . noblesse**: *car toutes les sciences* (*sentences* P1) *de lui dittes de la foy de leglise et de toutes vertus sont fermes coulompnes et tres haulte noblece* S, '*Eius omnes sententie fidei et ecclesie et omnium uirtutum firme sunt columpne.' Elegantem uenustatem*; LgA.

380–1 **Austin . . . heretykes**: *augustin ou liure des mauuaiz et contre pellagien maistre des hereges* S, *Augustinus in libro de nuptiis et contractibus: 'Pelagius heresiarcha* LgA; the book was in fact *De nuptiis et concupiscentia*.

381–2 **and . . . bokes**: *et le dit saint et que es liures dicelui* S, *ut dicat: 'Beatus Ambrosius episcopus, in cuius* (. . .) *libris* LgA.

383 **escriuans**; *escripuans* S, *scriptorum* LgA; *MED* does not record *escrivan*, though it records *escrivener*, *scrivein*, and *scrivener*, but none of them in this sense, 'authors'.

384 **full of suetnesse**: only GiL.

384–6 **Of whom . . . auctoritees**: *du quel la foy et le tres pur sens est es escriptures. Si que lanemi nose reprendre sa grant auctorite* S, '*Cuius fidem et* *purissimum in scripturis sensum ne inimicus quidem ausus est reprehendere.' Magnam auctoritatem*, LgA.

is abidden: *MED abiden* sense 9. (a) 'remain in existence'. There seems to be no good reason why s.w. did not put this in the present.

388–9 **why he faste**: *cur* (. . .) *non ieiunaretur* LgA.

389 **whanne he was**: not in LgA.

392 **sclaundred**: add *et non pas de toy* S, add *nec quemquam tibi* LgA.

54 ST GEORGE

Maggioni, ch. LVI, p. 391; Dunn-Lardeau, ch. 56, p. 424.

1 **iuge**: *tribunus* LgA.

3 **a ponde**: not in LgD, *instar maris* LgA.

11 **they . . . that**: not in LgA.

12–13 **and all . . . from hym**: *mesmement que ilz ne peurent auoir nulles herbes pour les bestes* P2, *maxime cum harum copiam habere non possent* LgA.

15 **so ferforthely that**: *Cum* LgA.
hym: add *par sort* P2.

32–3 **seest that**: only GiL.

36–7 **to haue . . . kynrede**: *auoir de toy et nourrir royal lingnie* P2, *de te filios in regali gremio nutrire* LgA.

37 **devowred** is confirmed by L and LgD. A1A2 read *solowed*, 'swallowed', the original reading of H1 before it was replaced by *wirowed*, 'slain', from the GD branch (*MED s.v. wirien*). T1 *deuouryd* for once does not follow H1, but it would have been an easy substitution.

38 **to haue sommed my richesse**: *a semondre mes princes* P2; neither *sommed*, 'calculated' or 'collected together', nor LH1 *somond*, 'invited' or 'called upon', correctly translating the French verb, is contextually satisfactory with *richesse*. *MED* records *sommed* as a spelling for *somned*; *MED somnen* sense 4. (a) 'assemble' may be the intended sense, though that is not recorded for this sort of context.

39 **but . . . manere**: *et que tu feusses aornee de royaulx vestemens et de pierres precieuses et auoir tymbres et tabours et orgues et tu ten vas estre deuoree au dragon* P2, *palatium margaritis ornare, tympana et organa audire, et nunc uadis ut a dracone deuoreris* LgA.

43 **her**: add *en plorant* P2.

46 **and what . . . allone**: only GiL.

47 **Syr . . . waye**: *bon iouuencel. cheuauche hastiuement* P2.

58 **allone**: add *car tu ne me pourroies deliurer mais periroies auec moy* S.

63 **shelde**: *lance* P2.

64 **and his spere**: only GiL.

70 **as . . . wode**: only GiL.

90 **toke . . . of**: *baisa* P2.

91 **waye**: add *Et toutesfoys list len en aucuns liures que sicomme le dragon aloit deuorer la pucelle. george se garny de la croix et ala occire le dragon* P2.

93 **Dacyen**: many martyrdoms in Iberia in the early fourth century are attributed to a persecution under Dacianus, governor of Spain, but he is unlikely to have been responsible for that of George at Lydda. It seems that this Dacianus (Dadianus in some sources) was an otherwise unidentified Middle Eastern monarch for whom the more familiar persecutor has been substituted. See Stace, *St George: Patron saint of England*, 15 ff. and Walter, *The Warrior Saints in Byzantine Art and Tradition*, 131.

94 **.xx.^{ti}**: *.xxij.* P2, *XVII* LgA.

100–1 **and erthe**: only GiL.

105 **frely**: only GiL.

106 **suerly**: *franchement* P2.

108–10 **a torment . . . erthe**: *vng tourment qui est aussy comme vne croix fichee* (add *enterre* P1) *par ses deux boutz* (*bras* P1) *et est nommee eculee* P2, *in eculeum leuari* LgA.

116 **Seint Peter**: *dominus* LgA.

124 **to helpe hym**: only GiL.
whanne . . . do: *puis* P2.

136 **witheinne and witheoute**: *de .ij. pars* P2.

140 **goodly**: only GiL.

154 **withe the contrary**: *departir de sa loy et sacrefier* P2, *tandem credere et sacrificare* LgA.
full of ioye: *Ornata* (. . .) *pre gaudio* LgA.

156 **to beholde hym**: *joyeux et lye* P2.

158 **atte**: translating LgD *a*, LgA *ad*, 'for the purpose of'.
hym: i.e. God.

164–5 **he gouerned . . . priuely**: *christianitatis professio silentio tegeretur* LgA; s.w. adopted Vignay's mistranslation, but no sense can be made of *gouerned* in this context.

171 **reynynge**: *regne* P2.
shewing: *demonstrance* P2, *portenta* LgA; the Latin can carry the sense 'monster, monstrosity', as here.

176 **thow**: *toy* S, *roi* P1, *rex* LgA; Dacian was previously a *preses* at 93 and 107, and perhaps the *iudex* at 133.

188 **with what sorugh**: *quelle douleur* P2, exclamatory.

197 **condampned**: add *de* P2.

200 **she had**: *espandue* P2; the English perhaps results from an early scribal misreading of *shedde*.

201 **heuene**: add *Hec Ambrosius* LgA.

211 **vengeaunce**: *dieu* P2.

216 **hadde**: add *laissie* P2.

220 **hem**: add *ses* P2.

224 **in the middes**: only GiL.

227 A2 f. 36ra adds the following: *And from Ramys is .ij. myle vnto a chapel of Seint George, the which is nowe desolate and the rofe downe, and there is a prety towne, and the moost parte thereof is cristen of the Grekes. And there liethe the body of Seint George, but not his hed, and þer lye his fader, his moder and his vncle, not buried in the chapelle but vnder the walle of the chapelle. And the kepers wolle not suffre pylgryms to come in þer but if thaye paye .ij. dokettis, and þerefore there came but fewe pilgryms there, but thaye offre withoute the chaple at an auter, and þer is .vij. yeres and .vij. lentis of pardon. And in the mydille of the quere of the saide chapel there is a tombe wherein Seinte George lyeth, and þerin is a hole that a man maye put in his honde, and whan any Sarazyn is brought theder mad, anone as he hath put his hed in that hole he is made perfitly hole and hath his wytte ayen.* Caxton included this with some modifications in the *Golden Legend*, notably altering *from Ramys is .ij. myle vnto a chapel* to *bytwene Jherusalem and porte Japhe by a towne called Ramys is a chapel.* He further added a brief passage on George as patron of England, the foundation of the Order of the Garter, and the presence of some relics of St George at Windsor; see Blake, *Caxton's own Prose*, 89–90.

55 ST MARK

Maggioni, ch. LVII, p. 399; Dunn-Lardeau, ch. 57, p. 431.

1 **ordre of dekens**: *leuiticus genere* LgA.

5 **prayid . . . hem**: *lui prierent que le benoist marc leur escripsist* P2, *rogauerunt* (. . .) *beatum Marchum ut* (. . .) *deberet conscribere* LgA; in expanding *lui* to *Seint Petir* s.w. fortifies Vignay's error that the request to Mark was made via St Peter.

18 **bisshoprich and the office**: *pontificatus officio* LgA.

26–7 **hath ennoblid**: 'has made him great', loosely translating *prerogauit*; see note to 26.282.

32 **ensamplis**: here GiL omits further quotation from Damian, Maggioni, 400–1 (22–4), Dunn-Lardeau, 433.

39 **of deth**: *de vie* P2, *mortuis* LgA.

42–3 **and no moo**: only GiL.

43–4 **hath . . . my**: *ma fait* (. . .) *acomplir bon* P2.

53 **dispisid**: add *le sacrifice de* P2.
lay in awaite of hym: *lespierent* P2, *ei insidias posuerunt* LgA.

54 **he hadde baptisid**: *curauerat, qui dicebatur Anianus* LgA.

57 **ymultiplyed**: add *Qui etiam iuxta mare in rupibus ecclesiam construxerant in loco qui dicitur Bucculi, id est Bubulci* LgA.

58 **tempul**: *temples* P2.

60–1 **bocher, bocherie**: *bouuier, lieu de la bouuerie* P2, *bubalum, loca Bucculi* LgA; *bubalum* is 'wild ox', and *loca Bucculi* gives a latinized form of *ta Boukolou*, 'the pastureland', the name of an area in the eastern part of Alexandria, according to some versions the location of Mark's martyrdom and burial.

61 **And . . . hym**: only GiL.
hangid: *demouroit* P2, *fluebant* LgA.

63–4 **aungellis . . . Crist**: *lange. Et lange mesmes* P2, *ab angelo confortatur dicente sibi: 'Ecce, nomen tuum in libro uite ascriptum est sociusque factus es supernarum uirtutum.' Sed et ipse dominus Ihesus Christus eum uisitauit* (*et*) LgA.

68 **mekely**: only GiL.

70 **vndir Nero**: add *qui cepit* LgA.

76 **eyen**: add *recaluaster* LgA, i.e. rather bald in front.
of faire gretnesse: *habitudinis optime* LgA, 'of excellent physical condition'.

79 **by**: add *innumeris* LgA.

84 **dide his labour**: *labori contradidit* LgA, 'returned to his work'.

84–5 **He . . . myracle and**: *Illius cuius nempe predicabat euangelium simul imitatur miraculum,* (. . .) *uidelicet* LgA.

85–6 **fro her birthe**: not in P2, in LgA.

87 **.iiijC.lxvij.**: add *tempore Leonis imperatoris* LgA, apparently Leo V, 813–80; Boureau (p. 1213 n. 17) and Maggioni (2007) (pp. 1543–4) suggest that Voragine has erroneously supplied a date more compatible with Pope Leo I,

440–61, but since the reference is to an emperor the confusion is more probably with the Byzantine emperor Leo I, 457–74.

90 **Certeynly summe merchauntis**: *Quidam namque mercatores* LgA.

108–9 **by . . . weri**: *par tourmens. et que les notonniers estoient lassez* P2, *et naute tempestate quassati* LgA.

116 **the peple . . . by**: *les gens du pays* P2.

124–5 **and the precious corseint**: only GiL.

128 **þe more surely and**: only GiL.

130 **body**: *thesaurus* LgA.

139–40 **And . . . comfortid**: only GiL.

145–6 **the wiche . . . peynys**: *sy que vers le rongoient a grant tourment* P2, 'so that worms gnawed him painfully'.

149 **as . . . doo**: only GiL.

152 **hertily and pitously**: only GiL.

154 **sore**: *malade* P2.

160 **weren wente**: *aloient* P2.

168 **cristen pepul**: *autres* P2.

174 **callid**: *fut appelle* P2.

177 **heithe**: add *et fut tout desrompu membre a membre par tout le corps* P2.

188 **tyrauntis**: *satellites* LgA.

189–90 **þrewen . . . Marke**: *dei famulum sanctum Marchum inuocantem ad terram proiciunt* LgA. L has corrected this, *threwe hym downe to the erthe hee cryeng fast to the seruaunt of god seynt Marke*.

191 **with . . . make**: *par nulle force riens faire* P2.

193–4 **but whanne . . . greued hym**: *et les pies auec. mais le fer qui est non amoliable sans feu. fut tantost conuerty en molete de plomb* P2.

196–7 **of hardenesse**: only GiL.

201 **but by a litell skinne**: only GiL.

202 **leches**: add *et les amis* P2.

202–3 **for there was none other remedy**: only GiL.

207 **dreieng up of the wounde**: *cicatrix* LgA.

208–9 **he went . . . seint**: not in LgA.

212 **shulde drowne**: *nistroit iamais de la par sa propre force* P2.

221 **This . . . but**: *et il* P2.

227 **other**: add *sy qui les veoit tous* P2.

229 **to God . . . seint**: *a dieu* P2, not in LgA.

238 **borne of Fauentyne**: *natione Fauentinus* LgA, 'a native of Faenza'.

56 ST MARCELLINUS POPE

Maggioni, ch. LVIII, p. 411; Dunn-Lardeau, ch. 58, p. 440.

3 **sacrifice**: add *Cum autem non assentiret et ex hoc diuersa tormentorum genera sustinere deberet* LgA.

6–7 **for . . . releued**: *car elle fut ferue par le chief qui fut malade. mais les plus fors membres se resordirent* P2, *Verumptamen infirmato capite fortiora membra resurgunt* LgA.

9 **Marcellyn**: add *souuerain euesque* P2.

10 **correccion**: *conseil* P2.

57 ST VITALIS

Maggioni, ch. LIX, p. 413; Dunn-Lardeau, ch. 59, p. 441.

1 **knyght and consult**: *miles consularis* LgA, officer of high or consular rank.

10 **voyde**: only GiL.

12–13 **in as moche as**: *tant pource que il retraist vrsin de sacrefier comme pource que* P2, *Ille uero nimium indignatus, tum quia ad se uenire noluit, tum quia Vrsicinum sacrificare uolentem retraxit, tum quia* LgA.

17 **comfort**: *liberare* LgA.

20 **quik**[1]: *enuers* P2, *uiuum et supinum* LgA.
quik[2]: add *sub Nerone qui cepit* LgA.

58 ST PETER MARTYR

Maggioni, ch. LXI, p. 421; Dunn-Lardeau, ch. 61, p. 448.

P2 concludes this chapter at 368.

2 **Nerone**: *neronne* P2, *uerone* SP1, *Veronensi* LgA.

12 ***Deum***: add *creatorem celi et terre* LgA.

13 **heuene**: add *et terre* LgA.

17 **and slowe hymself**: *quant quil pouoit. mes lenfant plain du saint esperit tourna toutes ses auctoritez contre luy et loccist* P2.

23 **lawe**: *foy* P2.

23–4 **sithe . . . And**: *Qui* (i.e. his uncle) *nesciens uerum dixit dum* LgA.

24 **he prophecied . . . Cayphas**: see Acts 4.

30 **it was not**: *il faisoit mauuais* P2, *non esse tutum* LgA. *MED not* n. gives 'nothing, nothingness, nought'; here an adjectival sense 'worthless' is required. *MED s.v. nought* n. gives senses 'evil, worthless conduct'.

31 **dispisinge**: add *le monde et* P2.

33 **he . . . pesibly**: *comment il y vesqui loablement* P2.

37 **made . . . felawship**: *fultus caterua* LgA, 'supported by a troop'.

39–40 **as in an hote fire of loue**: only GiL.

42–4 The wordplay on *Petrus/petra* is lost in English translation.

44 **worthely**: E *wordely*; *MED* records one spelling of the adjective with *d*, but suspects it is a mistake. E elsewhere writes *worthely* for this word, using *wordely* exclusively for 'worldly'.

50 **spared hymselff fro**: *restraint sa char par continuee espargne de* P2.

52 **rightwisnesse**: *iustificacions* P2.

54 **he . . . awaite that**: only GiL, 'he conducted himself in the case of such a trap so that'.

55 **wickednesse of sperites**: *esperis de mauuaistie* P2, *spiritualibus nequitiis* LgA.

63 **amyable**: *predicabilis* LgA.

64 **well ordeyned . . . condicions**: *bien ordonne en toute meurte de bonnes meurs* P2.

65 **to highe . . . ensaumple**: *par arrousemens dongnemens de vertus* P2, *profusis uirtutum aromatibus* LgA.

76 **examyned**: add *a Milan* S.

83 **wenen . . . and**: only GiL.

84 **as thou doest**: only GiL.

88 **heresies**: add *et fidem catholicam recepturum* LgA.

107 **Seint**: only GiL, incorrectly.

109 **knee**: *gueule* P2.

113 **was nyghe dede**: *cuida bien morir* P2.

116 **al rough**: *et pilorum densitate uillosum* LgA.

117 **and**: *sueque lingue soluto ligamine* LgA.

120 **entamed**: *touchie* P2, *infecisset* LgA, 'infected'; Batallier substituted *conchie*, which was doubtless what Vignay wrote, and s.w. gives *entamed*, with the more general sense 'injured'.

al the: *moult de* P2.

121 **visytours**: *inquisitores de ordine predicatorum* LgA; this stretches the sense of 'visitor', more normally a bishop or his representative conducting a visitation.

123 **they**: i.e. heretics.

134 **enquisitour**: *MED s.v. inqusitour* has only one citation, for a1402, Trevisa, of uncertain meaning. Here, an official authorized to conduct enquiries relating to heresy.

146 **peyne**: *palmam* LgA.

153 **felon**: *ferus* LgA.

162 **sacrilege** as agent noun, here taken from the French, is not recorded in *MED*; the recognised form is *sacrileger(e*.

164 **mekely**: *en souffrant tout paisiblement* (*patienter* LgA) P2.

167 **that cursed whiche that**: *celluy excommenie qui* P2. *MED* records spellings *wicche* and *whiche* for both the pronoun and the noun; *whiche* here is for *MED wicch(e* n. sense (b), 'idolater'.

171 **witheoute pitee**: only GiL.

174 **confessour**: add *confesseur pource que entre les tourmens il confessa tres fermement la foy ihesu crist. et que il se confessa auant ce mesme* (*ipsa die* LgA) *si comme il est acoustume et rendy a dieu sacrefice de louenge* P2.

175 **that**: add *cum* LgA.

176 **quarteyne**: add *et* P2.
he[1]: *ilz* P2.

193 **.xxx.**[ti]: *quadraginta* LgA.

205 **heretikes**: add *et de leurs faicteurs* P2, add *et fautores* LgA; *faiteur* 'deceiver' and *fauteur* 'adherent' are often confused.

211 **suetely**: *pleinement* P2, so and add *sic plenius* (. . .); *sic granum sinapis contritum uirtutem suam multipliciter demonstrauit* LgA.

right so: *sic* LgA, from the omitted clause, and now attached to the following section.

213 **souerein bisshop**: i.e. Innocent.

220 **seint**: *saintete di cellui* P2.

220–3 **in that . . . sore and**: *prist vng morsel en disant que ja ne le peust il passer se cestoit voir que il mentist. Et tantost il senty que le morsel se prist sy au gosier que il ne le pouoit ne gloutir ne getter. pourquoy il se repenty tantost et auoit ja la couleur muee. aussy comme sil sentist la venue de mort. Et dont* P2.

226 **come**: add *auxilio uiri* LgA.

228 **God**: *luy* P2.

231 GiL here omits three short miracles, Maggioni, 428 (92–5), Dunn-Lardeau, 456.

232 **Innocent**: add *quartus* LgA.

238 **tapit**: *magnum pulpitum* LgA.

248 **that**[1]: add *se* P2.
he[3]: i.e. the cloth.

252 **fire**: add *et reuint arriere sus les charbons* P2.

254 **vnder**: *sur* P2.

260 **Florence**: add *cum quibusdam aliis iuuenibus* LgA.

278 **hideous and**: only GiL.

279 **in grete sorugh and drede**: only GiL.

288 **this glorious marter**: *le benoit pierre* P2.

289 **of the shippe hange**: *en quoy la voille de la nef pent* P2.

295 **gladde**: add *a iennes* P2, i.e. 'to Genoa'.

302 **brought it to the feet of**: *se mist a deprier* P2.

306 **sodenly . . . hymselff**: *le prestre sans ce quil eust sceu quel non il deuoit dire* P2.

310 **prouince**: i.e. of the Dominican order.

327 **of nygromancye**: *de gramaire* P2.

331 **loues**: *amies* P2; this is a plural form of *MED lef* n. (2).

335 **dethe**: add *prochaine* P2.

339 **And**: *Mira res* LgA.

341 **prioure**: *soubzprieur* P2.

355 **gret**: *quatuor* LgA.

365 **Peter**: add *et sen alla a lautel di celluy* P2.

367 **or**: *que* P2, *Sicque factum est quod* LgA.
sesed: add *du tout en celle nuyt* P2.

371–2 **and wolde haue helpe**: only GiL.

385 **the strete of Corteyne**: *de loco Cortiongo* LgA; this seems to be Cuorgnè in Piedmont, southwest of Ivrea.

388 **peple**: add *par la bouche dicelle* S.

389 **Mariable, perot**: *mariole, perot* S, *Mariola, Petrine* LgA; on the use of contemptuous diminutives of saints' names by demons, see Boureau, 1286 n. 29.
he went oute: *issirent* S.

392 GiL here omits two miracles, Maggioni, 433–4 (173–86), Dunn-Lardeau, 461.

401 **.xxxiiij**: *XIV* LgA.

401–2 **and so . . . mynde**: only GiL.

403 **Peter**: add *Et ce fu merueilleuse maniere* S, *Mirum in modum* LgA.

412 GiL here omits five miracles, Maggioni, 435–7 (194–234), Dunn-Lardeau, 462–4.

424 **brake a veyne**: *se rompi* (. . .) *en laine* S, 'ruptured his groin'.

427–8 **the erthe . . . God**: *celle terre mais tu qui par les merites de saint pierre* S.

431–2 **in the yere . . . .lix**: This belongs with the next paragraph, but all GiL MSS put it here.

434 **suolle**: add *in modum utrium* LgA, 'like a wineskin'.

434–5 **as . . . toswolle**: *uentrem tumentem instar pregnantis* LgA.

435 **suellynge**: add *totumque corpus inflatum* LgA.

436 **oute of kinde**: only GiL.

449–51 **wherfor . . . Peter**: only GiL.

59 ST PHILIP APOSTLE

Maggioni, ch. LXII, p. 443; Dunn-Lardeau, ch. 62, p. 465.

1 **.xxj.**: *XX* LgA.

5 **iuges**: *tribunos* LgA.

5–6 **of whiche the mynistres**: i.e. whose servants.

8, 9 **these fals ymages, hem, her**: singular LgA.

13 **these ydoles**: singular P2.

16–17 **to hem . . . dede**: *aux .iij. mors* P2.

17 **after**: add *par vng an* P2.

19 **Ebronitarum**: *hebionites regnoit* P2; the Ebionites were an early heretical sect who denied the divinity of Christ and the virgin birth; see *ODCC* under Ebionites.

20–1 **into . . . peple**: not in LgA.

21 **he destroied hem**: *il la destruisist* P2, i.e. the heresy.

22 **ther wer**: *la estoient* P2.

24, 26 **.viij.**: *sept* P2.

34 **to the Galiens**: *Gallis* LgA; probably, as Maggioni (2007, p. 1549) suggests, a confusion in Voragine's source between Gallis and Galatis.

35–6 **the peple . . . feithe**: *les estranges gens qui estoient prochaines a tenebres* *et la grant mer* (*tumenti oceano* LgA) *a la lumiere de science et a port de la foy* P2.

37 **of Frise**: *Phrigie* LgA.

40 **day**: *yde* P2.

41 **his**: add *tres* LgA.

42 **he . . . Ephesim**: *quarta apud Ephesum requiescit* LgA.

46 **saiethe**: *uideatur dicere* LgA.

60 ST JAMES THE LESS

Maggioni, ch. LXIII, p. 446; Dunn-Lardeau, ch. 63, p. 467.

5, 7 **thousande, thousand**: *millisme, milliesme* P2.

5 **called**: add *iaques alphey* (. . .) *car il fut* P2.

10 **token**: *signum osculi* LgA.

14 **Iustice**: *juste* P2.

30 **alle**: add *ces autres* P2, *ceteris apostolis* LgA.

31 **of**: add *iaques* P2, add *Iacobi Zebedei* LgA.

35 **holinesse**: add *Et sy fut dit iaques le iuste pour la merite ḍe sa tres excellante saintete* P2.

40 **witnessith**: add *et Ieronimus in libro de uiris illustribus attestatur* LgA.

41 **Iustice**: *iuste* P2.

of Alpheie: *de tous* P2.

45 **he wered neuer lynen**: *sindone, id est ueste linea, semper indutus* LgA; apparently wearing linen was modest to Voragine but luxurious to Vignay and s.w.

47 **rightwisse continuaunce**: *droicture continuee* P2, *incessabili et summa iustitia* LgA.

49 **garnison and defence**: *munimentum* (. . .) *et iustitia* LgA.

50 **entered**: *laissie entrer* P2.

50–1 **whiche . . . sacrified**: not in LgA, but add *Hec Egisippus*.

58 **aposteles**: add *et* P2.

59 **takin of**: 'understood to stand for', *MED taken* sense 22. (b).

60 **songe**: *celebre* P2.

60–1 ***in pontificalibus***: *comme euesque* P2, LgA as GiL.

63 **perduringe**: *MED* has only one citation for *perduren*, from *Ludus Coventriae*, a1475.

64 **Ayeinst Puynyen**: *contra Iouinianum* LgA.
and: add *si comme* P2.
Iosephus: add *le iour que nostre seigneur fut mort. Et ierome le tesmongne* P2.

66 **before**: add *que il verroit* P2.

67 **a**: *le* P2.

77 **Caiaphas wolde haue**: *uellent* LgA.

78 **ye good**: only GiL.

81 **wicked**: only GiL.

86 **Cesar hadde called hym**: *Cesarem appellasset* LgA.

94 **that . . . Crist**: not in LgA.

97–8 **This . . . men**: *Virorum iustissime* LgA.

111–12 **'Stone we . . . thanne**: *'Lapidemus Iacobum iustum'. Qui deiectus non solum mori non potuit, sed* LgA.

117 **perche**: *perche a foulon* P2, 'fuller's rod'.

120 **.liij.**: *LVII* LgA.

130 **by Iamys the same**: *maxime per Iacobum* LgA.

135 **spere**: *glaiue* P2.

136 **ȝere**: *air* P2, *annum* LgA.
and also . . . brennyng: *exitialibus flammis ardere* LgA.

136–7 **in a feste of her azimes**: *In quodam festo azimorum* LgA; *azimes*, 'unleavened bread or cakes', is not recorded in *MED*.

139 **a bole**: *vne beste* P2, *uitula* LgA.

140 **of hym þat offrid . . . forth**: *du sacrifiant* (. . .) *enfanta* P2, *ministrorum* (. . .) *est enixa* LgA.

143 **with yren and**: not in LgA.

145 **unpouruoiedly**: *despourueuement* P2, 'unexpectedly', is not in *MED*; but *unpurveied* used adverbially is recorded *s.v. unpurveien*.

148 **erthe quake . . . lightnynge**: *aucuns esmouuemens* P2.

149–50 **for or . . . bataile**: *Ante quartum etiam annum belli* LgA, beginning the next story.

156 **al tomanglid**: G divides this as *alto manglid*. *MED* does not record *tomanglen*; the prefix is *to-* (2), ('In the great majority of the verbs and gerunds . . . the prefix has the sense of separation, division, pulverisation or destruction.' *MED to-* pref.(2) A).

175 **torment of the see**: *naufragium* LgA; *MED torment* sense 4, 'tempest'.

185 **an harde**: only GiL.

190 **I dare saie it**: only GiL.

195–8 **And thanne . . . leue**: *Petita igitur a cesare licentia Iherosolimam cum manu armata pergam et omnes proditores huius et occisores funditus euertam* LgA. The speech is continuous from 194 **I am sertayne.**

201 **comen ayein**: *destruendi Iudeam et Iherusalem a cesare licentiam impetrauit* LgA.

202 **and so as**: *cum* LgA.

214 **of that cursed citee**: *tam de urbe sacrilega quam de populo scelerato* LgA.

216 **was**[1]: add *princeps et dux* LgA.

218 **citee**: add *imminere* LgA.
sisterne: *sousterrin* P2, *subterraneam domum* LgA; *MED cisterne* sense (b) 'cave or cavern' gives one instance, from the Northern Passion a1500.
.ix.: *.xj.* P2.

224 **pleased and**: only GiL.

224–5 **the cronicles**: *la cronique* P2, *quadam chronica* LgA.

227–8 **he ordeyned**: *sy establi* P2.

229 **be tweine and tweine**: *entre deux et deux* P2.

231–2 **And . . . another**: *cum quo Iosephus sortes missurus fuit. Tunc* LgA.

232 **another**: *lautre* P2.

233 **worthi**: *noble* P2, *strenuus* LgA.
manly: *legier* P2, *agilis* LgA.
lightly: only GiL, picked up from preceding.

247–8 **My . . . trouthe that**: only GiL.

252 **winter**: *dies* LgA.

258 **went forthe and**: only GiL.

259 **And**: add *sicomme len list en celle hystoire apocriffe* P2.

268–9 **considered . . . thingges**: *ex paucis multa coniecit* LgA, 'from this small information inferred many things'.

271 **ofte**: only GiL.

275 **thanne . . . wete that**: *sceust que* P2, not in LgA.
one: *vng sergent* P2, *seruus* LgA.

282–3 **to Titus . . . fest**: *cito prandium fieri precepit* LgA.

285–6 **sorugh and anger**: *tristesce* P2, *molestia* LgA.

287 **seke**: *infrigidatus* LgA.

294–6 **faders . . . men**[2]: *parentes filiis et filii parentibus, uiri uxoribus et uxores uiris cibos non tantum e manibus, sed etiam ex ipsis dentibus rapiebant* LgA.

296 This sentence is paraphrased, and has lost the balanced *parentes filiis et filii parentibus.*

297 **and lyghter**: not in LgA.

298–9 **dede . . . domme**: *simulacra* LgA.

301 **but**: *ex publico sumptu ipsa sepeliebant, sed deficiente sumptu et uincente cadauerum multitudine* LgA.
aboute: *de* LgA.

303 **walles**: *valees* P2, i.e. ditches outside city walls.

307 **gerdelys of leder**: *courroies* P2, 'shoe-laces'.

313 **rentinge**: *desrompement* P2, *direptione* LgA, 'plundering'; Vignay loses the specific sense of the original, and *rentinge* here needs a more general sense than *MED* offers, such as 'destruction'.

314–15 **a praie . . . worlde**: *matri cibus, predonibus furor, seculis fabula* LgA, 'a meal for your mother, a source of scandal for the robbers, a fable for posterity'.

322 **What ailethe you**: only GiL.

323 **that other partie**: *qui lay porte* P2, *quem genui* LgA.

324 **I that am his moder**: *matre* LgA.

325 **I that am a woman**: *les femmes* P2.

327 **quaking for orrour**: *espouentez* P2.

330, 331 **solde, solde**: *achate*, *vendi* P2.

332–3 **.xj. thousande**: *.xj.^{CM}* P2.

336–7 **auncien . . . chere**: *ancien homme honnorable de caniture et de regart* P2.

343 **was risen he**: *resurgens* LgA.

345 **thei . . . hym**: *et il ne laissoit point* P2.

345–6 **but . . . ayenne**: *que il fut de rechief enclos par les juifs* P2.

351 **hym**: add *au soir* P2.

352 **this day . . . partie**: *iay perdu ce iour* S.

353 **the**: *aucuns* P2.

355 **Josephus**: *Miletus* LgA.

360 **strangeled and ouercome**: *estains* P2, *exusti* LgA.

61 FINDING OF THE CROSS

Maggioni, ch. LXIV, p. 459; Dunn-Lardeau, ch. 64, p. 479.

9–10 **of whiche . . . yere**[2]: *anni tantum V milia CIC et XXXIII fluxisse* *credantur* LgA, i.e. from (the death of ?) Adam to the Passion is 5199 + 33 = 5232 years; GiL, not clearly expressed, appears to give 5500–233 = 5267. According to chapter 178.571–4 below, from the death of Adam to the Passion is 5228 years.

22 **sauf . . . Sauxe**: *en sauf en la maison des saulx* P2, *in domo saltus* LgA; s.w. takes *sauxe* as a name. Roze refers to 3 Kgs. 7: 2, *Aedificavit quoque domum saltus Libani*, 'He built also the house of the forest of Lebanon'.

24 **shorte**: add *si quando uero secundum loci exigentiam ipsam rationabiliter decurtassent, adeo breuis uidebatur quod omnino incongrua habebatur* LgA.

30 **And**: *tamen* LgA.

31 **of Saux**: see 22 above.

35 **of probacion**: *probatica* LgA, 'of sheep' (Greek *probatike*), which Vignay did not recognize, and s.w. followed him. The reference is to the pool of Bethesda; see John 5: 2.

36 **men**[1]: *Nathinei uel subdiacones* LgA.

41 **And**: *autem* LgA.
Lorde[2]: add *sicomme len tesmongne* P2.

42 **oliue**: *liben* P2, *oliue* LgA.

42–4 **wherof . . . cipresse**: not in P2, *Vnde dicitur: ligna crucis palma, cedrus, cypressus, oliua* LgA.

46 **the mortays**: *le tronc* P2.

47 **inne**: add *Ou selon gregoire de tours. la table de trauers qui fut dessoubz les piez ihesucrist fut dautre, sy que chascun membre peust bien estre de vne des dictes manieres* P2.

48 **Paule**: only GiL. 'The apostle Paul appears to refer to the difference of woods'; s.w. has followed the French word order.

55–8 **in whiche . . . hem**: not in P2, in LgA.

57–8 **to hope . . . hem**: *sperare celestia, sacramenta non profanare* LgA.

63, 66 **Danibe** (Danube) seems to be the reading in E and H1 at 66, but it could equally be *Dambe* in all MSS at 63 and in G and L at 66.

75 **manly**: only GiL.

80 **tolde . . . crosse**: *ei sancte crucis misterium et fidem trinitatis plenius enarrauerunt* LgA.

82–3 **bisshop**: add *de* P2; for discussion of the identity of Constantine's baptizer see Boureau, 1228.

88, 91 **Constantine**[1], **Constantine**[1]: *Constantius, Constantio* LgA. From the first appearance of Constantine at 61 to the last at 265, LgD gives both him and his father Constantius as *Constant*, except at 145, where they are correctly distinguished; GiL gives *Constantine* for both before 145, where again each is given correctly, but thereafter GiL gives both indiscriminately as *Consta(u)nt.*

95–6 **in this wise**: *autrement* P2.

97 **Albynum**: *malurie* P2, *Malbinum* LgA, i.e. the Milvian Bridge.

112 **right side**: *destre* P2, 'right hand'.

112–13 **he had worshipped**: *munierat* LgA.

115 **tyrauntes**: *tyranno* LgA.

116–18 **And thanne . . . ouer**: *Maxentius autem iussit nauibus ad decipulam compositis fluuium sterni et suppositis pontibus exequari* LgA, 'Then Maxence, as a deception, ordered boats to be spread out across the river and false bridges to be laid over them'.

126 **stori**: add *assez* P2.

137 **cronicles**: *cronique* P2.
was: add *fait* P2.

140–1 **the Stori of Ecclesiast**: *hystoires ecclesiastiques* P2. This is based on various ecclesiastical histories, but not Eusebius, as GiL singular implies.

142 **Chirche**: *eglises* P2.

145 GiL here and at 149 correctly gives *Constant* instead of usual substitution of *Constantine.*
is not: *non videtur* LgA.

147 **beyende the see**: *en ierusalem* P2.

151 **well I wote**: only GiL.

154–5 **misknewe . . . stable**: *illum stabularium non ignorauit qui uulnera curauit a latronibus uulnerati* LgA, 'who was not ignorant of the innkeeper who cured the wounds of the man wounded by thieves'. Luke 10: 30–5.

155–6 **acounted . . . laboure**: *ama mieulx reputer toutes choses aussy comme fiens et ordure pour gaingner lamour nostre seigneur ihesu crist* P2.

157–8 **fro this foule place to his endeles blisse**: *du fiens a son regne* P2.

162 **witnessen**: add *licet alibi legatur, quod fuerit Treuirensis* LgA.

167 **I wote**: *sciatis* LgA.

168 **kinrede**: *peres* P2.
anientised: see note to 88.65.

169 **fader**[1]: add *symon* P2.

171 **shewe it to noon**: *illam manifesta* LgA.

175 **youre**: *noz* P2.

177 **his fader**: *il* P2.

178 **was . . . and**: only GiL.

183 **prouable**: *probabilis* LgA; the required sense here, 'probable, credible', is not recorded in *MED*. See too 112.14.

205 **depe**: *tout sec* P2.

206 **.vij. dayes he beesought**: *six iours. il requist au vij.*[e] P2.

207 **the place of**: only GiL.

212 **Maister of Stories**: *ecclesiasticis hystoriis* LgA.

217 **to be worshipped**: *aouurir* P2 'to be opened up', *inarari* LgA 'to be ploughed up'; s.w. misread the French as *aourer*.

218 **Iudas**: add *sescourca et* P2, 'stripped and'.

223 **Iudas**: add *feretrum tenuit et* LgA.

231 **al hole**: *les yeulx ouuers* P2, *apertis oculis sanata* LgA.

240 **yef y may**: only GiL.

242 **and**: add *cum tormentis* LgA.

245 **and**: add *il le fit* P2.

247 **strongly**: *fermement* P2, *constanter* LgA.

249 **and**: add *quant leuesque de ierusalem fut mort* P2.

256 **crosse**: add *filio* LgA.

257 **bare . . . Ierusalem**: *reliquit in loco* LgA.

258 **and . . . sone**: not in LgA; replaces *filio* omitted at 256.

260 **Cesariens**: *eusebe de cesariense* P2.
sette hem in a bridell: *fist faire vng frain* P2.

267 **a deluge and destruccion**: *uorago* LgA.

273 **backe of the hede**: *uertice* LgA, i.e. top rather than back of the head.

274 **the witte appered**: *sensus premineat* LgA, 'intelligence was prominent'.

286 **God**: *Christum* LgA.

290 **made . . . froted**: *le fist arrouser* P2.

301 **body**: *pis* P2, 'chest'.

302 **notarie**: *escriuain* P2, *notario* LgA.

306 **suerdes**: *lances* P2.

309 **the Ethiope**: *demon* LgA.

309–10 **Will he, his, hym**: *uis, tuum, te* LgA.

318 **turne . . . side**: *ex parte dextera stare* LgA.

62 ST JOHN BEFORE THE LATIN GATE

Maggioni, ch. LXV, p. 471; Dunn-Lardeau, ch. 65, p. 489.

6 **destroier of the ydoles**: *deorum contemptor* LgA.

12 **hurtinge**: add *non adustus, sed unctus. Quod uidens Domitianus obstupuit et ipsum occidere timuit* LgA.

16 **emperour**: *empereurs* P2.

17 **they²**: i.e. the Romans.

19 **not**: not in LgA.

20 **of any**: *de Nerone* LgA.

21 **of**: i.e. regarding.
that . . . consent: *et que tyberien se consenti* P2.

29 **coueitous of the worlde**: *auari et ambitiosi* LgA.

30 **that**: i.e. the approval of the senate.

30–1 **for . . . pouer**: *pource quil ne fut ordonne estre subget a lumaine puissance* P2, *ne hoc humane potentie ascriberetur* LgA.

33 **wolde . . . but**: only GiL.

38 **men**: *les autres dieux* P2.

41 **moder of that Seint Iohn**, Mary Salome, wife of Zebedee and one of the three Marys; she is the patron saint of Veroli, and her reputed bones are held in the basilica dedicated to her there.

47 **Iohn**: *Iaques* P2.

63 LITANIES

Maggioni, ch. LXVI, p. 473; Dunn-Lardeau, ch. 66, p. 491.

7 **blacke crosse**: *noires croix* P2.

9 **Seint**: *le grant* P2.

17 **the throte**: *inguine* LgA, 'the groin'.

22 **used**: add *Car quant nous oyons vng homme qui esternue nous disons dieu taist* P2.

23 **yaned**: *MED s.v. yenen*, sense 1(e), hesitates to accept the sense 'yawn', but here, translating French *bailloit*, Latin *oscitabat*, and linked to *galpinge*, it seems beyond doubt.
whiche . . . galpinge: only GiL.

25–6 **And it is founde in the liff of Seint Gregorie**: see 45.82–102.

32 **continentes**: 'chaste unmarried women'; the adjective used as a noun is

not recorded in *MED* (but *continent* n., 'content(s)', has two citations from Chauliac). The sense here must be feminine, but not necessarily at 155.350 and 175.284.

40 **heled or**: only GiL.

41 **or sackes or heires**: only GiL.

44 **Seint Mamertine**: *beatus Mamertus* LgA.

47–8 **Procession . . . cause**: *la mineur letanie et rouuoisons et procession et est dicte la mineur letanie a la difference de lautre* P2.

50 **a grete erthequake**: add *et souuent* P2, *frequentes et maximi terremotus* LgA.

54–5 **pigges . . . houses**: *demones porcos intrauerunt* LgA.

58 **were . . . contre**: *cotidie fierent* LgA.

66 **in that tyme**: *in uere* LgA, 'in Spring'.

67 **the frutes . . . erthe**: *teneros adhuc fructus conseruando* LgA.

69–70 **and the vnordinat . . . encresen**: *in uere enim sanguis magis feruet et illiciti motus magis pullulant* LgA.

71 **and holily**: only GiL.

71–2 **honestly . . . praiers**: *nam per ieiunium magis habilitatur et per rogationes dignior redditur* LgA.

73 **Davenne**: *dauenne* P2, *daucerre* P1, *Altissiodorensis* LgA, i.e. d'Auxerre. **thre**: *.ij.* P2.

82 **and may . . . none**: *bene uolare non potest, sicut patet in struthione* LgA.

90 **travelinge**: *cheuauchant* P2, *militanti* LgA; *MED* records *militaunt* only in the context of the Church Militant, and only once before this date, and not as used by LgA here; s.w. has modified Vignay's attempt at translation, whereas Batallier reverted to *militant*.

92 **that**: *ualde timeret, qui* LgA.

95 **baners**: add *id est cruces* LgA.

100–1 **eueri creature wote**: only GiL.

102 **that is to come and**: only GiL.

107 **deuell, he**: *dyables, ilz* P2.

109 **bere . . . chirches**: *porte hors la croix daucunes eglises* P2.

110 **fende, he**: *les dyables, ilz* P2.

115 **shewinge**: *uictoriam* LgA.

120–1 **songe, song, preising**: *chans, chans, louenges* S.

125 **.ij. the furst**: *les deux premiers* P2.

127 **was**: *in hoc mundo regnauit* LgA.

127–8 **before the law, vnder the lawe**, i.e. before and under Mosaic law.

130 **þe response . . . that**: not in LgA.

134 **and oure nede**: only GiL.

135 **and the reuerence of God**: not in P2, *et dei reuerentiam* LgA.

139 **and nede . . . nede**: *cest pour la pourete que nous auons en deseruant* P2, i.e. for our lack of merit.

141 **beholdinge her ioye**: *contemplando* LgA.
sethe we: *sy que nous qui* P2.

144–5 **sonner . . . herde**: *en a greigneur talent* P2, not in LgA.

146–7 **we haue . . . merites**: *quant nous auons par leurs aides ce que nous requerons* P2.

149–50 **makithe . . . hym**: *puisse impetrer laide de ses amis* P2.

150 **And**: add *en* P2.

153 **Damacyen**: *Damascenus in liber tertio* LgA.

157 **Sane**: *sane* P2, *synodo* LgA. This spelling is not recorded by *MED s.v. sene* n.3; s.w., as reflected by L, apparently adopted it from his exemplar, the LgD MSS having *sane* rather than the more usual *sene*. The Synod of Chalcedon was held in 451.

158 **Damacien**: not in P2, *Damascenus* LgA.

159 **this clause**: *la clause* P2, *la cause* P1, *ita* LgA.
We . . . songe: *Nos autem ita aimus* LgA.

160 **restrenithe . . . hem**: *et si demones rescindantur* LgA.

163 **Sidon**: *sane* P2, *synodus* LgA; see 157 above.

164 **and fleen it**: not in LgA.

64 ASCENSION

Maggioni, ch. LXVII, p. 480; Dunn-Lardeau, ch. 67, p. 496.

Seven questions are raised by the Ascension 1–6:

A Whence he ascended 7–38.

B Why he delayed ascending 39–41:
(i) to prove the fact of the Resurrection 41–54;
(ii) to comfort the apostles 55–9;
(iii) because of the mystical relationships of the times and numbers 59–71.

C How he ascended (misnumbered *Ferthely* in the text):
(i) mightily by his own strength 72–86;

(ii) openly 87–95;
(iii) gladly 95–100;
(iv) hastily 100–22.

D With whom he ascended, i.e. with men and with angels 123–38, Whereof Denis wrote that the angels raised three questions 139–43:
(i) the superior angels asked each other who he was 144–64;
(ii) they also asked Christ why he was clothed in red 165–86;
(iii) the lesser angels asked the superior angels who was this king of glory 187–98.

E By what merits he ascended 199–205.

F The heavens above which he ascended 206–8:
(i) material, of seven kinds (of which GiL omits three, see note below) 208–10;
(ii) reasonable 210–19;
(iii) intellectual 220–40;
(iv) supersubstantial (*substancial* in GiL) 241–93.

G Why he ascended 294–5:
(i) divine love 295–9;
(ii) greater knowledge of God 300–4;
(iii) our faith 305–17;
(iv) our security 318–27;
(v) our dignity 328–43;
(vi) stability of faith 344–9;
(vii) to show us the way 350–3;
(viii) to open the heavenly gate 354–7;
(ix) preparation of the place 358–62.

5 **whos merites**: *quel merite* P2.

12–13 **aboue . . . or**: not in LgA.

17 **.xij.**: *.xj.* P2.

17–18 **in the *cenaculo***: in LgA but not LgD.

18 **aposteles with the disciples**: *disciples tant apostres comme autres* P2.

22 **shulde dine for**: *appareillast* P2.

23 **disciples**: add *et mulieres* LgA.

32 **Ierusalem**: add *et habetur in Glossa* LgA.

33 **abode long after**: *estoient* P2.

35 **hym**: *ceulx* P2.

35–7 **he saithe . . . ascension**: *Calcati etiam pulueris a domino hoc dicit esse documentum quod uestigia impressa cernuntur* LgA, 'he says it is proof that this dust was stood on by the Lord that the footprints can be seen'.

41 **certainte**: *certefiance* P2.

42 **is**: *estoit* P2.

48 **pope**: add *in sermone de ascensione* LgA.

51 **faithe**: add *de la ressurrection* P2.

51–2 **bi good and profitable techinge**: *documentis necessariis* LgA.

59 **debonaire**: *misticam* LgA.

60 **be reportid**: *sont raportees* P2, *comparantur* LgA; *comparentur* appears at 61 as *likened*, P2 *acomparagie*. See note to 34.29.

60–2 **be . . . day**[1]: *superabundant. Consolationibus comparantur enim tribulationes sicut annus ad diem, dies ad horam, hora ad momentum* LgA.

63 **.xlj.**[ti]: *LXI* LgA.

70 **thei sene me**: *Il me jut* P2, *il iut* S, 'he lay'; s.w. must have read *iut* in his exemplar as *uit*.

71 **erthe**: add *Quod uero comparentur sicut hora ad momentum, insinuatur Ys. LV: 'In momento indignationis mee abscondi faciem meam etc.'* LgA.

72 **Fertheli**: *Tiercement* P2, *Circa tertium, qualiter scilicet ascendit* LgA. s.w. attached this to the preceding sub-series to follow *Thirdely* at 59. It belongs, however, to the seven questions laid out at 2–6.

73 **.xlvj.**[ti]: *.lxvj.*[e] P2, *LXIII* LgA.

74 **Edom**: add *etc.* P2.

75 **Seint . . . Euuangelist**: *Ioh. III* LgA.

84 **Ennok**[2]: add *per coitum* LgA.

85 **engendered**[1]: add *le second fut* P2.

91 **he**: *nul* P2.
sithe ye: *ce que il* P2.

92 **before you**: only GiL.

94 **gladly**: only GiL, caught from 95.

96–7 **that is to saye ioiously**: not in LgA.

98 **songen**: *plaudunt* LgA.

99 **felawship**: *compaignies des anges* P2, *chori* LgA.

103–4 **eueri cercle of heuene and of eueri planete**: *chascun cercle ou ciel de chascune planette* P2.

108 **heuene of Saturne** translates LgA *concauum celi saturni*, and 110 **concauete** translates *concauum celi*; *MED concavite* is recorded only for anatomical usages and in the senses 'valley or depression' and 'excavation'.

110 **.viij.**: *a vint* P2, *avint* P1. s.w. misread this as the roman numeral; and a

predecessor of EH1, whose exemplar perhaps read *eight*, attempted a correction to *hight*. Vignay, followed by GiL, omitted some detail and lost the clarity of Moses Maimonides's exposition, for which see Maggioni, 483–4 (53–5).

117 **thingges**: *saulx* P2.

130 **.xliij.**: *LXIII* LgA.

131 **coloure**: add *de Bosra* LgA.

133 **passion**: add *et resurrectionis* LgA.

135 **was ministred to hem**: *admirantur* LgA.

136–7 **What is this he**: *Qui est cestui* P2.

137 **he saiethe**: *dit il ainsy* P2, *similiter* LgA.

139 **saiethe**: *insinuare uidetur* LgA.
Aungels: add *c. VII* LgA.

146 **aduersarie or ellis**: only GiL.

150–1 The citation should end after *hele*, but punctuation of LgD and GiL MSS shows that they consider it ends at *mankinde*.

155–6 **and saiethe . . . it**: only GiL.

159 **the gloser**: *commentator* LgA, identified by Maggioni as Maximus Confessor, *Scholia in Dionysium Areopagita*.

160 **and aske**: only GiL.

162 **precognicion**: *procession* P2, 'advance'; *precognicion* has only one citation in *MED*, for a1500(a1450).

165–6 **that is to saye the lasse aungels**: *supremi* LgA.

166–7 **alle . . . pressure**: *ainsy comme de ceulx qui foulent au pressouer* P2. Taking *foulent* as passive, s.w. gives *defouled* 'made dirty', *MED* sense 3, instead of sense 1 'trampled'. See Isaiah 63.

177–8 **bene defouled in**: *foule* P2. See previous note.

180 **largely . . . hym**: *aussy comme en vne bataille* P2.

183 **withoute the man but vice**: *seulement* (. . .) *la rappe, cest lordure des pechiez* P2, *solum uinatia* LgA, the skin left after pressing grapes.

190 **that**: *desquelles la responce* P2.

194 **they**: *les deables* P2, *alii* LgA.
is: add *celuy* P2.

195 **had . . . fairenesse**: *neust en la croix repoz ne beaute* P2, *non habuit speciem neque decorem* LgA.

195–6 **feble and sike on the crosse, stronge in dispoiled, vile in the body**: *fort en despoulle. vil en la croix* P2, *infirmus in ligno, fortis in spolio, uilis* *in corpusculo* LgA. *MED* records only two instances of *despoile* as noun, both later, with senses 'booty, pillaging', etc., rather than the required 'state of being stripped of clothing'; the apparent participial form *dispoiled* is hard to account for.

198 **blewe in reproues**: *fuscus in obprobrio* LgA.

199 **whos merites**: *quel merite* P2.

200–5 In LgA the quotation (Ps. 44: 5) is broken up, with Jerome's interspersed comments in the second person, to which LgD switches at 204 (see Maggioni, 487 (110–11)); s.w. simplified the conclusion.

204 **only**: only GiL.

204–5 **for . . . heuene**: *et ie tay doubte ta puissance et ta vertu te menra ou ciel* P2, *'Et deducet te mirabiliter dextera tua'*: *potentia siue uirtus deducet te, hoc est in celum* LgA.

207 **heuenes**: add *et dit sur* (*sus* P1) *tous les cieulx* P2, add further *secundum quod dicitur. Eph. IV: 'Qui descendit ipse est et qui ascendit super omnes celos* LgA.

209 **entendible**: *entendible* P2, *intellectuale* LgA; neither *entendible* nor *intendible* is recorded by *MED*, which, however, gives *entendable*, with one citation only, from Gower, meaning 'zealous', a sense related rather to *MED entenden* sense 2. (b) 'devote (oneself)' than to sense 3. (b) 'understand', as at 65.300 *intendibles* below. Here s.w. has adopted it from the French, which can perhaps be regarded as a mistranslation by Vignay, who at 220 and 268 gives *intellectuel(z)* for LgA *intellectuale(s)*, and is in those cases followed by GiL. At 65.300 Vignay has correctly translated *intelligibiles* as *entendibles*.

209–10 **supersubstancial, *ignium, siderium, christallinum et empirium***: *substanciel* (*susustanciel* P1). *Ciel materiel est en moult de manieres. Cest ciel aerin de lair. Ciel etherin. Ciel olimpin. Ciel fouin de feu. ciel estele. Ciel crestelin. ciel emperial* S, *supersubstantiale. Celum materiale multiplex est, scilicet celum aereum, ethereum, olimpium, igneum, sidereum, cristallinum et empireum* LgA. *MED* does not record *supersubstancial*, but has one instance of the adverbial form, meaning 'above the material world'.

210 **eueri**: only GiL.

212 **Ysay**: *Ys. LXVI* LgA.

218 **God**: *les sains* P2.
his: only GiL.

220 **aungels**[1]: *ange* P2.

221 **of reson . . . excellence**: *par la raison de dignite et dexcellence* P2.

223–4 **Aboue . . . thought**: *Diuine mentes sunt super reliqua existentia et uiuunt super reliqua uiuentia* LgA.

226 **soule that may be**: *existentia* LgA.

227 **beauute . . . goodnesse**: *celluy* P2.
Thei be made: *ilz sont tres* P2, *Secundo sunt pulcherrimi* LgA.

228 **beauute**: add *desquelz* P2.

231 **of gode fourme, the fourme of God**: *de bonne forme formee de dieu* P2; in contrast to 195–6 above, s.w. has taken the participle as a noun.

237 **Of two the furst**: *des deux premiers* P2.

238 **and**[2]: *de tertio* LgA.

239 **.xvij.**: *.xxvij.* P2, *XXXVII* LgA, some other MSS as LgD. LgA is correct.

239–40 **thre thingges with hym**: so LgD, *etc.* LgA, i.e. Job 37:18 *caelos, qui solidissimi, quasi aere, fusi sunt.*

241 **substancial**: *supersubstantiale* LgA.
the qualite: *lequalite* S, *equalitas* LgA.

245 **substancial**: *supersubstantiale* LgA.

249, 250 **imperial**: see note to chapter 1.300.

250 **high**: *sublunarem* LgA.
region: add *mais il ne la passa pas oultre. mais fut transporte en paradis terrestre qui est sy hault quil appert quil ioingne a la haulte region* P2.

256 **passed**: *passa oultre parmi* P2, *transcendit* LgA. Vignay misunderstood *transcendit*, 'transcends', as 'moved past', and therefore used the past tense. E fortuitously restored the present.

259 **called . . . vnmeuable**: *uniforme, immobile, luminositatis perfecte* LgA.

260 **bene and**: only GiL.

261 **wrought rightwisly**: not in LgA.

265 **Canticles**: *Cant. II* LgA.

266–7 **hilles, mountaynes**: GiL has reversed these each time.

269–70 LgD gives the quotation only in French; GiL restores the Latin and then offers a translation, in which *his* for *tuum* suggests use of the French, which has *sa*.

274 **substancial**: *supersubstanciale* LgA.

275, 278 **the qualite**: *lequalite* S, *equalitas* LgD; also 241 above.

275–6 **Seint Matheu**: *Mc. ult.* LgA.

277 **his disciples**: *eulx, cest assauoir aux disciples* P2, *eis* LgA.

282 **disperpeled**: *despareille* P2, 'unequal'.

284–5 **and that was . . . guerdon**: *scilicet locali, remuneratione premii,* *cognitionali et uirtuali* LgA. Vignay's compression, followed by s.w., loses the fourfold division of the list.

287 **also . . . Ephesiens**: *Phil. II* LgA.

292 **aboue cherubin and**: not in LgA.

293 **seraphin**: add *Eph. III* LgA.
which . . . science: '*Scire etiam supereminentem scientie caritatem Christi*' LgA.

294 **whanne he asked**: *quant il est demande* P2, not in LgA.

296–7 **Seint . . . Euuangelist**: *Ioh. XVI* LgA.

300–1 **Seint . . . Euuangelist**: *Ioh. XIV* LgA.

304 **as God**[1]: not in LgA.

308–9 **the lightnesse**: *lapeticement* P2.

309 **substaunce**: add *qua patre minor est, non egere* LgA.

321 **Seint . . . chapitle**: *Ioh. prima, II* LgA.

322 **to praie for us and**: *et ipse est propitiatio* LgA.

325 **shewithe**: add *filio* LgA.

327 **tokenes**: add *de charite* P2.

331 **Apocalipes**: add *XIX* LgA.

333 **conservaunt**: *sergent* P2, *conseruus* LgA.

336 **aboue**: *super se* LgA.

338 **humanite**: *humilite* P2.

341–3 **with the thingges . . . reuerence**: *cum remotis a conspectu hominum, qui merito reuerentiam sui sentiebatur indicere* LgA, 'since, having removed from the sight of men what is felt by its merit to indicate respect for them . . .'. In LgA this follows *mirabilior*, 340 *more mervailous*, and precedes 340–1 *so that feithe . . . colde*.

345 **Ebrewes**: add *IV* LgA.
Ye haue: *Habentes* LgA.

346 **holdinge**: *teneamus* LgA.
of: add *vostre* P2, *nostre* LgA.
confession: in LgA a further citation follows from Hebr. 6: 18–20, Maggioni, 492 (198).

349 ***etc***: *eo spes tendit et corporis* LgA.

350 **Michee**: *Mich. II* LgA.

352 **hathe made**: *test fait* P2.

352–3 **thou hast well whedir**: *tu as bien ou* P2, *habes quo* LgA. The Latin idiom, 'you know the way', is literally translated; see *MED haven* v. sense 4d.

355 **of hell**: *du ciel* P2, *inferni* LgA.
secound: *adam ouury le premier* P2.

358 **reperacion**: *preparation* P2.

65 PENTECOST

Maggioni, ch. LXVIII, p. 493; Dunn-Lardeau, ch. 68, p. 507.

Eight questions are raised about the sending of the holy spirit (GiL here omits the sixth) 1–7.

A By whom 8–31; Ambrose shows four ways by which the holy spirit is known to be God 32–50.

B In how many ways does it appear? 51–4:
(i) invisibly 54–74;
(ii) visibly 75–94: (a) as a dove 94–116; (b) as a cloud 117–34; (c) like breath 135–56; (d) as fire 156–7; (e) as tongues of fire (omitted by GiL).

C At what time (and why)? 158–62:
(i) for the perfection of the law 162–71;
(ii) for everlasting reward 171–5;
(iii) for the remission of sins 176–92.

D How many times? 193–6:
(i) before the passion 196–209;
(ii) after the resurrection 210–19;
(iii) after the ascension 220–31.

E How? 232–4:
(i) by sound 234–70;
(ii) in tongues of fire 271–5: (a) why tongues of fire? 275–83; (b) why fire? 283–345; (c) why tongues? 346–68;
(iii) sitting upon the disciples 369–82.

F To whom? 383–425 (omitted by GiL in the initial list).

G Why? 426–56 (numbered *.vj.* in the initial list).

H By what means? 457–66 (numbered *.vij.* here and in the initial list).

6–7 **the .vj. . . . sent**[2]: *sexto in quos missus est, septimo propter quid missus est; octauo per quid missus est* LgA.

14 **lowe thingges**: *inferioribus* LgA, i.e. earthly.

15–18 LgD numbers these three *Premierement* etc, but GiL follows LgA.

16–17 **vertue, vertue**: *uirtutem, iurisdictionem* LgA. The first carries the basic sense 'power', the second is *MED* sense 14(a) 'legal authority', though probably Vignay carelessly repeated the first *vertu* and s.w. merely adopted it.

21 **auctorite**: add *in operando* LgA.

21–2 **Seint . . . saithe**: *uidetur insinuari Joh.XVI cum dicitur* LgA.

25–6 **oo substaunce . . . will**: *vne substance et non diuisee en euure. acordable et acompaignie en volente* P2, *una est in substantia, indiuisa in opere, consors in uoluntate* LgA.

26 **myght**: *toute poissance* P2, *omnipotentia* LgA.

27–8 **shulde be to us debonayre**: *propitiaretur* LgA.

28 **make hym debonayre**: *propitiaret* LgA.

29 **enchaufe . . . loue**: *igniret* LgA.

30–1 **he is saide . . . hymselff**: *ideo recte dicitur se ipsum dare* LgA.

38 **gaue**[1,2]: *exhibuit* LgA.

40 **the holi . . . adopcion**: not in P2, in LgA.

42 **hymselff gaue**: *se donna* S.

44 **pris**: add *de nostre raencon* P2, LgA as GiL.

47 **Corinthees**: *I Cor. XII* LgA.
to sum wisdom: not in P2, *Alii* (. . .) *sermo sapientie* LgA.

55 **Seint . . . Euuangelist**: *Ioh. III* LgA.

61 **brekithe**: *corrompt* P2; this approximates to *OED* sense 30, but is not offered by *MED*.

64 **enquirable**: not recorded by *MED*.

64–5 **and I . . . truly**: *Certes* P2.

65–74 This passage shows clear signs of checking by s.w. against LgA, most strikingly in substituting a translation of *occultorum* for Vignay's *yeulx* (probably for *oculorum* in his exemplar) and in the correction at 71.

66 **of vices**: not in P2, *uitiorum* LgA.

68 **inwarde mynde**: *yeulx* P2, *occultorum* LgA, variant *oculorum*.
gretnesse and: only GiL.

69 **maners**: *choses* P2, *morum* LgA.

71 **sperit of my mynde**: *saint esperit* P2, *spiritus mentis mee* LgA.

72 **beholding . . . togeders**: *regart des autres hommes tous* P2, *contuitu horum omnium* LgA.

73 **mervailed and**: only GiL.
and[2]: only GiL.

81 **Seint . . . Euuangelist**: *Mt. XVII* LgA.

82 **cloude**: add *lucida* LgA.
hym: *eos* LgA.

83–6 **right . . . cloude**: *Sicut baptizato domino sic et clarificato. Misterium sancte trinitatis ostenditur: spiritus sanctus ibi in columba, hic in nube lucida* LgA.

92 **myght be likened to**: *operatur* LgA, 'puts to work'.

96 **fulfellith . . . hem**: *illos quos replet facit* LgA.
Ysaie: *Ys. LIX* LgA.

97 **dovues**: add *qui sapense* P2.

99 **Also**: *Secundo* LgA.

100 **or bitternesse**: *damerete* P2; H1 has corrected to *of*.

100–1 **boke of Sapience**: *Sap. XII* LgA.

101–2 **that same boke**: *eodem VII* LgA.

104 **debonaire**: add *ou cueur* P2.

106 **that be colde**: not in LgA.
Canticles: *Cant. II* LgA.

107 **up**: add *ma mie* P2.
spouse: add *et ueni* LgA.

108 **that is to wete**: not in LgA.
infusion: *remplissemens* P2, *infusione* LgA.

109 **in . . . woundes**: '*In foraminibus petre'; Glossa: 'In Christi uulneribus'*. LgA.
And . . . saide: *Thren. ult*. LgA; Lam. 4: 20.

113 **and oure flesshe**: *quia est os nostrum et caro nostra* LgA.

116 **we lyuen . . . peple**: *uiuemus per iugem memoriam* LgA, 'we will live through perpetual memory'.

120 **.vij.°**: not in P2, *VIII* LgA.

121–2 **Also Ezechiel *primo***: *Sicomme Ioh. dit* P2, LgA as GiL.

123 **the sperit . . . whelys**: not in P2, LgA as GiL.

124 **Bernard**: *Gregoire* P2.

125 **Secoundely he yeuithe**: *Et sy donne la nue refroidement. aussy donne le saint sperit* P2, LgA as GiL.

126 **enbrasinge**, 'kindling'. *MED*'s only citation of the gerund, Lydgate (?a1439), is defined as 'an aureate term for the heat of the sun'; *embrasen* v. 'set on fire', both figuratively and literally, is first recorded for Lydgate (a1420).

130 **refressheth . . . strengthe**: *habet uim regeneratiuam* LgA; context requires sense of *refressheth* to extend to 'purifies'.

130–1 **And of that . . . Euuangelist**: *Ioh. VII* LgA.

132 **waters**: add *hoc autem dixit de spiritu sancto quem erant accepturi credentes in eum* LgA.
And therwith as: *Tertio* LgA.

133 **water**: *pluie* P2.

136 **swifte, light**: *legier, legier* P2, *leuis, lenis* LgA.

139 **tariengly**: *MED tariingli* has two citations, for 1530(c1450) and c1475(c1445).

139–40 **he canne . . . goste**: LgD and LgA end the sentence after *goste*.

140–1 **and . . . Euuangelist**: *Luc. XII* LgA.

141–2 **to brenne . . . will**: *sy que ce que ie vueil arde* P2, *quid uolo, nisi ut ardeat* LgA.

143 ***Canticles***: *Cant. IV* LgA.

144, 145 **lyghtly, lyghtnesse**: *lenis, lenitatem* LgA.

145 ***Iohannis tercio***: *Jehan leuuangeliste* P2, *I Ioh. III* LgA; in fact, 1 John 2: 27.

146 **vs**: *uos* LgA.

147 **singeth**: *dit* P2, *cantat* LgA.

148 **.xix.**: *III Reg. XIX* LgA.

148–9 **Also . . . Lorde**: not in P2, LgA as GiL.

151 **fro man**: *ad horam* LgA, i.e. 'for an hour'.

153–4 **And . . . elliswhere**: not in LgA.

155 **And . . . saieth**: *Ioh. VI* LgA.

156 **fire**: add *Quinto in specie lingue* LgA, the fifth of the *.v. maners* at 91.

162 **the Chirche**: *leglise* P2, *la glose* SP1, *glossam* LgA.

164 **to Moyses**: not in LgA.
brennynge fire: *buisson ardant* P2, *igne* LgA.

165–6 **Ihesu . . . descended**: *que ihesu crist descendy le saint esperit* P2, *Christi descendit spiritus* LgA.

166 **in the mount of Syon**: not in LgA.

171 **that . . . loue**: only GiL.

176–7 **wherof . . . place**: not in P2, LgA as GiL.

177 **it . . . as**: not in LgA.

177–8 **that right . . . Rome**: *quia indulgentia fiebat in iubileo* LgA.

182 **seruauntes**: *cerfs* (*serfs* S). *cest a dire les hommes soubzmis a pechie* P2.

183 **seruages**: add *Et ce dit la glose* P2, having lost which GiL assumes the next clause belongs to this list.

184 **apostell . . . Romaynes**: *Rom. VIII* LgA.

185 **lyff**: add *ou* P2, i.e. in.
and of dethe: not in LgD, in LgA; add *les debtes des pechiez sont delaissiees* P2.

188 **contre**: add *cest esperit* (*Hereditas* LgA) *qui estoit perdu est rendu* P2.

188–9 **apostell . . . Romaynes**: *Rom. VIII* LgA.

190 **his sones**[1]: add *et de dieu* S, *filii dei* LgA.
and[2]: i.e. 'we are also'; *Si autem filii, et heredes* LgA.

191 **apostell . . . Corinthiens:** *II Cor. IV* LgA.

192 **heritage**: *libertas* LgA.

196 **yeue to hem** add *premierement a faire miracles. secondement a relachier pechiez. Tiercement a confermer leurs cueurs* P2.

199 **Seint Mathew**: *Mt. XII* LgA.

200 **But . . . conuenient**: *Non tamen consequens est* LgA.
though a man: *quiconques* P2.

205 **abilite**: *habilitationem* LgA, 'ability, aptitude', perhaps 'what is inherently possible'. On the nature and functions of angels see *ODCC s.v. Angels*.

212 **eueri prest may not**: *chascun ne peut pas* P2, *Non tamen potest quis* LgA.

215 **the holi goste**: *grace* P2.

220 **conserued**: *conferma* P2, *solidata* LgA.

222 **is**: add *toute* P2.

224 **or heuinesse**: only GiL.

229 **thingges**: *dona* LgA.

230 **but**: *car* P2.

230–1 **and plente therof**: only GiL.

232 **thei were**[1,2]: *il fut* P2.

233–4 **to the disciples in sittynge**; i.e. sitting upon them.

The subdivision on *soune* begins here, obscured by substitution of *and* for LgA *autem*.

234 **hasti**: *uehemens* LgA.

237 **hasti and dredfull**: *Vehemens* LgA.

237–8 **and . . . loue**: *uel quia eternum ue adimit unde uehemens quasi ue adimens, uel quia mentem ab omni carnali amore uehit unde uehemens quasi uehens mentem* LgA.

241 **for to be full**: *plenitudinis* LgA.

242 **withholdith**: *retinte* S; s.w. has translated *retinte*, for LgA *resonare*, as if it were from *retenir*.

Iob: *Iob VII* LgA.

243 **Whanne . . . not**: *Numquid mugiet bos, cum presepe plenum steterit?* LgA.

244–5 **crieng . . . inpacience**: *locum non habet mugitus impatientie* LgA.

246–7 **withehelde . . . inpacience**: *per impatientiam non resonabant* LgA.

248–9 **whanne . . . full**[1]: add *ne lomme quant il est saoul* P2, *siue satietam habere* LgA.

250 **other**: add *Et aussy lomme qui est saoul ne couuoite plus viande* P2.

252 **Isaye**: *Ys. I* LgA.

256 **Grete See**: *oceano* LgA.

260 **Ecclesiast**: *Eccl. XXIV* LgA.

261 **that it is that**: *cest ce qui* P2.

262 **properly after the lettre**: in LgA this introduces the following explanation.

262–4 **in ouer aboundinge . . . aboute hym**: *effluere et circumadiacentia irrigare* LgA.

264–5 **to renne . . . hem**: *tantost a arrouser et a courre* P2, *effluere* LgA.

266–9 **The grettest . . . ouer all**: *ce fut signe destre plains quant le vaissel deulx sen alla par dessus.et mist hors le feu ou fleuue et ne se pot mucier et se commencierent tantost a arrouser entour eulx* P2, *Ecce signum plenitudinis; plenum uas erumpit, ignis in sinu non potest occultari, ceperunt iterum circumadiacentia irrigare* LgA.

270 **.iiij. thousand**: *.iijM.* P2.

272–5 GiL has reversed the order of the second and third questions, but the original LgA numbers are retained at 284 and 346.

278 **loue**: *dieu* P2, *amoris* LgA.

281 **by**: *parler en* P2.

284 **secound**: this should be 'third', the second having here been postponed to appear at 346 below.

288 **the blinde**: *les obscures* P2.

289 **tho . . . vices**: *les decourables* P2, *fluida* LgA; the Latin has the secondary sense 'lax'; by inserting *by vices* s.w. adds an explanation to *rennen*, 'flow' (*MED rennen* v. (1) sense 8a).

291 **thingges**: *metalla* LgA.

292 **makithe . . . vpwarde**: *les fait tendre en hault* P2, *sursum tendit* LgA.

296 **yeuinge of her**: only GiL.

296–7 **shewinge of her hinesse**: *la haultesce de sa demonstrance* P2, *sublimitatis in situatione* LgA.

297 **vigorosite**: *vertueusete* P2, *uigorositatis* LgA; *MED* does not record this word.

299 **defiled**: *incoinquinatus* LgA, i.e. undefiled.

300 **intendibles**: *entendibles* P2, *intelligibiles* LgA; see note to 64.209.

301 **of wisdom**: *Sap. VII* LgA.

302 **ayenst . . . hym**: *ou multipliable estat de luy* P2, *penes eius multiplicem efficaciam* LgA, 'in its many sorts of effectiveness'.

303 **.iiij. resones**: *Hanc rationem* LgA.

306 **Her**: *Et ce dist* P2.

307 **Zakarie**: *Zach. XIII* LgA.
Brenne: *uram* LgA.

310 **Ysay**: *Ys. IV* LgA.

310–11 **þe synnes**: *sanguinem* LgA.

312–13 **Thou . . . hem**: *Torporem excutit* LgA; this balances *Exurit peccata* and *Purgat corda* above (*He brennithe the synnes* and *He purgithe the hertis*), but Vignay has attached it to the quotation from Isaiah.

313 **the aposteles . . . Romaynes**: *lapostre dit aux romains* P2, *dicitur* (. . .) *Rom. XII* LgA.

314 **fulfellithe**: add *eschaufans ou saint esperit etc. Et saint gregoire dit* P2.
apperithe: *apparut* P2.

315 **hertes**: add *quil raemplist* P2.

317 **Boke of Wisdom**: *Sap. IX* LgA.

319 **Corinthiens**: *I Cor. II* LgA.

322 **to fire**: *par feu* P2.

327 **formable**: *mesmement* (. . .) *formable* P2, *maxime formale* LgA; Voragine's own definition is the best possible for this context, *modicum habet de materia et multum de forma*. *MED* has three citations for *formable*, for ?*c*.1475, 1479, and *c*.1443, offering the senses 'in correct form', 'orderly', and 'of ideas: capable of being developed . . . from a proposition'.
hathe: add *pou* P2.

328 **and of beaute**: not in LgA.

331 **fleschely . . . thingges**[2]: *charnelment mais* (add *potius* LgA) *espirituelment* P2.

332 **loue**: add *la char* P2.

333 ***carnaliter***: *charnelment* P2; it is unclear why s.w. has substituted the Latin.

333–4 **The .iij. hathe**: *Tiercement car* P2.

334–5 **strechithe . . . thingges**[1]: *tendre hault* P2.

335 **thingges that flowen abrode**: *fluida* LgA.

336 **ouneth** is from *MED onen*, 'unify', though no *ou* spellings are recorded; GL have *onyth*, H1 appears to have *ounth* with an abbreviation mark after the *n*.

337–8 **of Names: 'The devine**: *des noms diuins* P2 , i.e. 'the Book of the Divine Names'.

338, 340 **ordening/ordenyng, ordeineth**: *coordinatiuam, coordinat* LgA.

341 **thingges**: add *Et ce dist saint denis* S.

346 **the .iij.**: this is in fact the second of the three listed at 266–7 above.

348 **stronge**: *fort* P2, *difficile* LgA; this is *MED* sense 12 (b) 'arduous, difficult'; it is given as *harde* at 351.

349 **whanne . . . governed**: *et droicturier* P2, *bene rectum* LgA.

351 **goste**: add *dont saint iaques apostre* (*Jac. III* LgA) *dit: Nostre langue si est entouchee du feu du saint esperit etc.* P2.

357 **into the sperit**: *en espece* P2.

360–1 **sadde . . . drede**: *fermement et sans nulle doubte* P2; in LgA these words introduce the next citation.

361–2 **boke . . . Aposteles**: *Act. IV* LgA.

363–4 **multiplyingly . . . hem**: in LgA these words introduce the next citation.

365 **.ij.º**: not in P2, in LgA. **thei . . . speke**: *ce fut proffitablement* P2, LgA as GiL.

366 **to profite . . . herers**: *Vtiliter ad edificationem et utilitatem* LgA; in LgA these words introduce the next citation.

367 **.lxij.**: not in LgD, in LgA.

369 **sittyng**: i.e. on the apostles.

370–1 **that is . . . peple**: not in LgA; the definition is supplied by Vignay.

371 **peple**: add *Il est neccessaire aux presidens et aux juges* P2.

372–3 **Seint . . . Euuangelist**: *Ioh. XX* LgA.

374 **wisdom**: add *a juger* P2. **Isay**: *Ys. XLII* LgA.

375–6 **He . . . suetnesse**: *Je mettray mon esperit sur le jugement et ma grace pour debonnairete a estaindre jcellui* P2, '*Ponam spiritum meum super eum, iudicium gentibus proferet.' Mansuetudinem ad supportandum:* LgA.

376–7 **Boke of Nombres**: *Num. XI* LgA.

380–1 **He yeuithe . . . enfourme**: *Il donne aornement de saintete pour enfourmer* P2, *Ornatum sanctitatis ad informandum* LgA.

381 **Iob**: add *XXVI* LgA.

383 and 384 **thei were**: *il fut* P2.

384–6 **pure . . . goste**: *nez a luy receuoir et conuenables* P2, *receptacula munda, secundum quod de eis cantatur 'Fuerunt receptacula munda', et habilia ad susceptionem* LgA.

387 **all thingges**: *animo* LgA.

388–9 **day, was, day**: plural P2.

390 **a day of**: only GiL.
Ysay: *Ys. LXVI* LgA.

393 **will**: *ame* P2.

399 **charite**: *diuinite* P2.

400 **place**[1]: add *Et cest signe par ce que il dit en vng* (*in eodem* LgA) *lieu* P2.

400–1 **that**[2] **. . . ete**: not in LgA.

401 **Osee**: *Os. II* LgA.

401–2 **hem, of hem**: *le, dicelluy* P2, *eam, eius* LgA. The quotation refers to Gomer, the wife of Hosea.

407 **Boke of Wysdom**: *Sap. VII* LgA.

408 **called**: add *dieu* P2, LgA as GiL.

409 **Seint Iohn**: *Ioh. XIV* LgA; (John 14:16).

409–10 **ayein the holy goste**: *vng autre paraclit* P2.

413–14 **like . . . before**: *et* LgA.

418–19 **and . . . hem**: *Ioh. XX, ubi primo pacem obtulit dicens* LgA.

419–20 **he was amonges hem**: *leur embati en eulx le saint esperit* P2, *insufflauit* LgA.

422 **the souerein parte of the senacle**: *superiori cenaculo* LgA, i.e. the upper room.

423–5 **he most . . . mynde**: *carnis domicilium mentis contemplatione transcendens calcat* LgA, 'rises above the fleshly dwelling and tramples it by spiritual contemplation' (Ryan).

430 **goste**: add *qui* P2.
Isay: *Ys. LXI* LgA.

431–2 **and bringithe**: *Vt ponerem* LgA.

434 **hope**: add *de pardon* P2.
and waylen: only GiL.
filth: *fait* P2, *perpetratione* LgA.

435 **releuen**: *relieue* P2; GiL substitution of the plural, confirmed by the other MSS, loses the sense of the passage.

436 **saieth**: add *lesperit* P2.

437 **Ezechiell**: *Ezec. XXXVII* LgA.

439 **to signifie**: *ad sanctificandum* LgA.

440–1 **for right . . . clensithe**: *sicut enim dicitur spiritus quia uiuificat, ita sanctus quia sanctificat et mundat* LgA.

442–3 **reioysith and gladith**: not in LgA.

443 **the comynge . . . aboundynge**: *la venue du fleuue surondant et habondant en esperit* P2, *inundans et abundans gratia spiritus sancti* LgA.

447–8 **he saide . . . you**: *il est dit pere. Il est dit pere pource quil nous ayme* P2.

448 **Iohn . . . Euuangelist**: *Joh. XVI* LgA.

449–50 **and we . . . betwene bretheren**: *Si pater et nos filii eius et fratres ad inuicem et inter fratres perfecta amicitia perseuerat* LgA.

451 **he saide**: *dicitur* LgA.

453 **saueour**[1,2]: *salu* P2.

456 **he saide**: *dicitur* LgA.

457 **And . . . .vij.**: *La huitiesme* P2.
furst: *premitiue* P2.

458 **and**: not in LgA.

459 **Luke . . . Euuangelist**: *Luc. III* LgA.
Ihesu praied and: *Orante Ihesu* LgA.

460 **reson herde**: *auditionem* LgA.

461 **Dedis of Apostelis**: *Act. X* LgA.

464 **saieth**: *est dit* P2, *notatur Act. VII* LgA.

465 **And this**: *uel* LgA.

66 ST MALCHUS

For this additional life, see above, Introduction, p. 35. Citations from the *Vita Malchi Monachi Captivi* (VMalc) are from the unpublished edition by Paul B. Harvey Jr, kindly supplied by the editor.

Rubric The GiL MSS, both here and in the concluding rubrics, call this a life (in L, an *example*) of Jerome rather than Jerome's life of Malchus.

1–4 GiL severely reduces Jerome's introductory paragraph.

10 **same contre of birth**: *Syrus natione* VMalc.

15–16 **be rage . . . oure Lorde**: *matrimonii, sanguinis an spiritus* VMalc.

21–2 **He ansuered . . . Athenes**: *'Ego,' inquit, 'mi nate, Nisibeni agelli* *colonus'* VMalc, 'He replied: "My child, I was once a farmer of a plot at Nisibis."' The unfamiliar name of Nisibis in Mesopotamia, modern Nusaybin, led to various attempts at 'correction' including 'Athens', found in several MSS of the Vita.

26–7 **and serue . . . wyff**: only GiL.

32–4 **ne into . . . to passe**: *propter vicinam Persidem et Romanorum militum custodiam* VMalc.

36–7 **hermitage . . . desert**: *eremum Chalcidos quae inter Immas et Beroeam magis ad austrum sita est* VMalc. *MED hermitage* has two instances with the sense 'wilderness', one for a1425(?a1400), the other for a1500. Chalcis is modern Quinnesrin in Syria, Beroea is Aleppo; Immae was east of Antioch.

39 **and with praiers**: only GiL.

41–2 **for to see . . . moder and**: *et dum adviveret mater* (*iam enim patrem mortuum audieram*) VMalc.

45 **I wolde store . . . lerned**: *monasterium construerem* VMalc; the English appears to mean 'I would equip a cell where I would study'.

46–8 **And whanne . . . thinge**: only GiL.

50 **thinge**: VMalc gives the abbot's attempts at persuasion in greater detail.

52–4 **but what . . . ensaumples**: only GiL.

60–1 **and alle the bretheren**: only GiL.

63–4 **And atte . . . was**: only GiL.

66 **aspied**: *notatum cauterio* VMalc, 'marked with a branding iron'.

69–70 **Thanne I went . . . Edise**: *De Beroea Edessam pergentibus vicina est publico itineri solitudo* VMalc; having been incorrectly transferred to *desert*, *comune* must mean 'not owned by, and therefore open to, anybody'.

71–4 **ther duelled . . . entered**: *per quam Sarraceni, incertis semper sedibus, huc atque illuc vagantur. Quae suspitio frequentiam in illis locis viatorum congregat ut inminens periculum auxilio mutuo declinetur. Erant in comitatu meo viri, feminae, senes, iuvenes, parvuli, numero circiter septuaginta. Et ecce!* VMalc.

75–7 **bering . . . erthe**: *crinitis vittatisque capitibus ac seminudo corpore, pallia et lata ciliciola trahentes* VMalc, 'with long hair bound in fillets and with half-naked bodies, wearing tunics and wide cloaks'. Harvey substitutes *ciliciola* for various other readings such as *caligas*, *calliculas*; 'wide boots' would be, as he says, absurd here.

82 **Bitwene a woman and me**: *cum altera muliercula in unius heri servitutem sortitus venio* VMalc, 'with another, a young woman, I came having been won by lot into the servitude of one master'.

84 **that we wost not what to do**: only GiL.

85–7 **in such peyne . . . neckes**: only GiL.

88 **and suche . . . before**: only GiL.

90 **gret**: *interiorem* VMalc.

90–1 **we founde . . . seruage**: *dominam liberosque ex more gentis adorare jussi, cervices fleximus* VMalc.

92 **as alle other dede**: only GiL.

92–3 **and sauf . . . no clothing**: *nam aeris intemperies praeter pudenda nihil aliud velari patiebatur* VMalc; other MSS read *temperies* and *pudicitiam*, as translated in GiL.

94 **bestis**: *oves* VMalc.

96 **his meyne**: *conservos* VMalc , 'fellow slaves'.

96–7 **and ther . . . bestis**: only GiL.

99 **that was made of the bestes þat I kepte**: only GiL.

100 **said**: *canebam* VMalc.

101–2 **sithe . . . do**: only GiL.

102–4 **But . . . you**: *agebamque Dei iudicio gratias quod monachum quem in patria fueram perditurus in eremo inveneram. O nihil umquam tutum apud diabolum! O multiplices et ineffibabiles eius insidiae! Sic quoque me latentem invenit invidia* VMalc.

105 **whos bestes I kepte**: only GiL.

117–20 **The dethe . . . wille**: only GiL.

126–7 **in myn age . . . was yong**: *incanescente iam capite* VMalc, 'now grey-haired'.

130–1 **And thanne . . . soule**: only GiL.

132–3 **deye . . . will**: *proprio mucrone confodimur? Verte in te gladium* VMalc.

141 **in my gilte**: *sed sanguinem meum* VMalc.

144 **fro hennes forward**: *quam me captivitas docuit* VMalc.
deye: add *antequam perderem* VMalc.

153–4 **sadnesse and**: only GiL.

154–5 **And thanne . . . desire**: *coniuge plus amavi* VMalc.

159–60 **and hadde . . . maried**: *Nulla fugae suspicio* VMalc.

166–7 **my fader and of my moder . . . wrechidnesse**: *vultum patris mei, qui me erudierat, tenuerat, perdideratque* VMalc.

168–70 **a gret hill of emptes . . . mervaylously**: *formicarum gregem angusto calle fervere* VMalc.

171 **that other . . . sedes**: *alii herbarum quaedam semina forcipe oris trahebant* VMalc.

173 **eyren**: *corpora* VMalc.

184 **the wille of my corage**: *tristitiam animi vultu* VMalc.

186 **yef she wolde graunte therto**: only GiL.

186–8 **and I required . . . gladly**: *Peto silentium. Fidem tribuit. Et iugi susurro inter spem et metum medii fluctuamus* VMalc.

188 **oxen**: *hirci* VMalc, 'he-goats'.

190–1 **in suche wise . . . water**: only GiL.

197–8 **But . . . aboute**: only GiL.

202–3 **and thus we parted fro the ryuere**: only GiL.

204 **as tho that were euer in drede**: only GiL.

206 **for fere . . . us**: *propter insidias late vagantium Sarracenorum* VMalc.

209 **on horsbacke vpon two cameles**: *duos camelis sedentis venire concite* VMalc.

214–15 **we were pursued**: *vestigiis per harenas nos proditos* VMalc.

229–30 **We helde us stille**: only GiL.

232 **not . . . lenger**: *Quid statis? Quid moramini?* VMalc.

234 **al alowe**: *MED aloue*, adv., 'below', here translating VMalc *intro*.

235–6 **And what trowe . . . Ierom**: *Iesu bone!* VMalc.

237 **before us**: *perire* VMalc.

242–4 **But . . . anone**: *a fera tentus est quam nostras latebras praeteriet* VMalc.

248 **al that nyght in . . . morw**: *praestolamus eventum rei inter tanta pericula, pudicitiae tantum conscientia pro muro saepti* VMalc, 'we await the outcome amid such great perils, guarded merely by our consciousness of chastity as by a wall'.

254–6 **that thei that were dede . . . coude**: *quos ob nimiam velocitatem dromedas vocant, praeteritos cibos in ore volvere et in alvum missos iterum retrahere. Quibus ascensis et nova sitarchia refocilati* VMalc, 'who are called dromedaries because of their great speed, chewing the cud; and having mounted them and being revived by a fresh supply of travelling provisions'.

257 **.xiiij.**: *decima* VMalc.

259–60 **for to . . . auenture**: only GiL.

260–1 **and he . . . worthe**: only GiL.

263–6 **And this . . . lyff**: *Hanc trado virginibus, diligens eam ut sororem, non tamen me ei credens ut sorori* VMalc.

269 **me**: add *adulescentulo* VMalc.

270 **olde**: only GiL.

275–7 **be disseuered . . . Amen**: *superari* VMalc.

67 ST GORDIAN

Maggioni, ch. LXIX, p. 509; Dunn-Lardeau, ch. 69, p. 522.

3 **oure Lordes grace**: *predication* P2.
wyff: add *nomine Marina* LgA.
.lij.: *LIII* LgA.

10 **this felle**: *sepelitur* LgA.

68 STS NEREUS AND ACHILLEUS

Maggioni, ch. LXX, p. 510; Dunn-Lardeau, ch. 70, p. 523.

1–2 **chaste . . . chamberleynes**: *chastes* (*chastres* P1) *et estoient chambellans* P2, *eunuchi cubicularii* LgA.

3 **the whiche**: *Lesquelz* P2, *i.e.* Nereus and Achileus.

4 **was maried**: *nupta esset* LgA, 'was about to be married'.

6 **comended**: *loeren*t P2, *commendauerunt* LgA.

8 **cosin to seintes**: *cousine aux hommes* P2, *hominibus innatam* LgA; this is *MED* sense 1 (e), as in *ben cosin to*, 'be akin to'.

9 **ofte tyme**[1]: not in LgA.

9–10 **ofte tyme**[2] . . . **chyldren**: *mettoit hors souuent les enfantemens* P2, *deformes partus sepius procreari* LgA.

15 **but**: *Numquid* LgA.

16–17 **Thenke . . . debonayre**: *tant comme on les voit bel parler len cuide que ilz soient debonnaires* P2, *Quamdiu sunt sponsi uidentur esse benigni* LgA.

17 **haue her entent and**: only GiL.

18 **many tymes**: *aucunes fois* P2.

25 **halowed and**: only GiL.

26 **husbond**: *mary* P2, *sponsus* LgA; see 4 above.

35 **.CCC.**: not in LgA.

38 **whiche . . . servauntes**: *auec lesquelz domicile sestoit acompaignee* P2, *quibus Domitilla adherebat* LgA.

38 **they**, 39 **her**, 40 **they**: singular LgA, i.e. Aurelyen.

40 **hogges mete**: *cantabrum* LgA, 'bran'.

46 **for this miracle**: only GiL.

49 **to serue her**: *collactaneas eius* LgA.

50 **teche her and to**: only GiL.

52 **husbondes**: *maris* P2, *sponsis* LgA; see 4 above.

53–4 **to make . . . force**: *ut eius nuptias celebraret et ipsam saltem uiolenter opprimeret* LgA.

54 **as . . . wolde**: only GiL.

55 **whanne . . . he**: *aurelien* P2.

57 **to daunce and**[1]: not in LgA.

57–8 **and to syngge**: only GiL.

59–60 **alle . . . syngge**: *les jongleurs furent lassez de chanter et les autres de baler et de saillir* P2.

62 **of the emperour**: not in LgA.

65–6 **al hole and vntamed**: *tous entiers* P2, *illesa* LgA; *vntamed* 'uninjured' is related to *MED tamen* v. 2, sense I. (b) 'injure', and is not recorded by *MED* with this sense or derivation.

69 ST PANCRAS

Maggioni, ch. LXXI, p. 513; Dunn-Lardeau, ch. 71, p. 526.

2 **Fryse**: *Phrygiam* LgA.
vncle: add *relictus est* LgA.

3 **commen**: *reuindrent* P2.

5 **that**: *donc* P2.

6 **was lefte**: *moritur* LgA.

7 **to the kynge Cesar**: *cesari* LgA.

8 **that tyme**: *aussy comme* P2, *quasi* LgA.
Dyoclician: add *cesar* LgA.

9 **that . . . that**: *ne* LgA.

12–13 **and cherisshe the**: only GiL.

13 **this holy childe**: only GiL.

17 **corumpours**: *MED* records *corruptour*, but no forms with *mp*-.

19–20 **haddest . . . governaunce**: *les feroies tantost occire* P2.

23 **hygh waye**: *voye aurelienne* P2.

24 **.CC. and .iiij^{xx}.**: CCLXXXVII LgA.

29 **a**: add *grant* P2.

33–4 **of the dede**: *aliquo iudicio* LgA.

35–6 **al ful . . . dede**: *eius malitie conscius zelo accensus iustitie* LgA.

36 **I dar saye that**: *je forsenne ou* P2.

38–9 **that . . . trouthe**: not in LgA.

39 **auuter**: *tumulum* LgA.

70 ST URBAN

Maggioni, ch. LXXII, p. 515; Dunn-Lardeau, ch. 72, p. 528.

7 **engroged**: *si se forsenoit* P2; no such verb is recorded in *MED*, though the H1G spellings *engregged* are from rare *engreggen* (*aggreggen* is more common) meaning 'oppress' etc.; or it could be a form of *grucchen* (L has *grucchyd*) with a unique prefix, for which *MED* records many spellings, but not this one.

9 **and Karpesien her mynistre**: *procurante Carpasio quodam ministro* LgA, following 8 *pitte*.

12 **conuerted**: *deceu* P2.
Seint: *sacrilegia* LgA, i.e. blasphemer.

13–14 **of the chirche**: *Cecilie* LgA.

16 **but . . . that**: only GiL.

19 **thanne**: add *subridens* LgA.

22 **hym**[1,2]: plural P2.

30 **to another ydole**: *ad sacrificandum* LgA.
hem: *luy* P2, *ipsum ydolum* LgA This should not have been emended; substitute *hym*.

31 **kessed togedres**: *sentrebaisierent de la paix* P2.

32 **beganne**: add *circa* LgA.

33 **and Almaciene**: *dalmacien* P2, not in LgA; 33–5 **were, her, hem, they were** are accordingly single in LgD and LgA.

36 **Marmenye and his wiff**: *eius uxor Marmenia* LgA.
thei: *elle* P2.

37 **doughter**: add *Lucina et tota* LgA.

38 **holy**: only GiL.

71 ST PETRONILLA

Maggioni, ch. LXXIII, p. 517; Dunn-Lardeau, ch. 73, p. 529.

4 **this day**: only GiL.

6–7 **for ye . . . hole**: *affin que vous ne cuidez que ce soit impossible a moy et que ie mescuse par mes parolles* P2, *meis sermonibus excusari* LgA.

8 **up**[1]: add *tost* P2.

9 **hym**: *leur* P2.

16–17 **and the feste for Pernell, she**: *et sa feste a faire peronelle* P2, *Petronilla* LgA.

22 **he**: *prefectus* LgA.

25 **eculee**: add *cest vng tourment fait en maniere dun sautouer* P2, not in LgA.

29 **of Rome . . . so**: *de Rome* P2, not in LgA.

30 **his clerke**: *clerico* LgA.

72 ST PETER DEACON

Maggioni, ch. LXXIV, p. 519; Dunn-Lardeau, ch. 74, p. 530.

1 **Deken**: *exorcista* LgA, one of the four orders of the subdiaconate, the others being porters, lectors, and acolytes; s.w. has followed Vignay in substituting the more familiar albeit higher status.

prouost: not in LgA. Archiuyen is the gaoler, not the provost; see below 19–22.

3 **ofte and sore**: *forment* P2, *sepius* LgA.

10 **the**: add *et filiam meam sanauerit* LgA.

11 **atte . . . Petre**: not in LgA.

13 **of the crosse . . . hym**: *du saint esperit et de la croix* P2, *crucis* LgA.

14 **he fell**: *arthemien sagenoulla* P2, *ille* (. . .) *prostrauit* LgA.

19 **prouost**: add *oy ce il* P2.
alle: add *incarceratos* LgA.

22 **al quite**: *sans nulle laidure* P2, *illesus* LgA.

25 **glas**: add *et neust ne eaue ne lumiere* P2.

26 **putte in a streite prison**: *mis ou cep destroictement en vne autre chartre* P2, 'attached tightly to a stake in another prison'.

32 **to be enmured**: *obrui* LgA. The sense required is 'entombed'; *MED* has only one instance *s.v. enmured*, 'Fig. surrounded as with a protective wall', from Lydgate *c.*1410.

34–5 **Seint Marcelline . . . was**: *in illa cripta Sanctus Marcellinus christianis se protegentibus missam celebrauit* LgA.

37 **wolde haue**: not in LgA.

39 **Archevien**: add *gladio* LgA.

wiff: *matrem* LgA.

43 **.iiij^{xx}.**: *.iiij^{xx}. & .vij.* P2.

45 **sight**: only GiL.

73 STS PRIMUS AND FELICIANUS

Maggioni, ch. LXXV, p. 521; Dunn-Lardeau, ch. 75, p. 532.

1 **Dioclucian**: add *et Maximianum* LgA; accordingly 2 *hym*, 2 and 3 *he*, and 4 and 6 *emperour* are plural in LgA.

7 **torent**: add *et departis lun de lautre* P2.

8–10 **To whom . . . that**[1]: *tu as ja bien quatre vins ans. voire dit il que* P2, LgA as GiL.

10 **that**[1]: *viure en* P2.

14 **to bete**: add *longuement* P2, *torqueri* LgA.

15 **neither . . . drinke**: only GiL.

17–18 **of princes**: *des empereurs* P2.

22 **bete**: *ars* P2.

23 **mouthe**: add *cernente Feliciano, ut sic terreri posset* LgA.

25 **nygh madde for angger**: *moult courroucie* P2, *iratus* LgA.

26 **to deuoure hem**: only GiL.

29 **.CC.**: *XII* LgA.

74 ST BARNABAS

Maggioni, ch. LXXVI, p. 523; Dunn-Lardeau, ch. 76, p. 533.

6 These three strengths are elaborated here and at 31 and 54, each containing three subsets; the second and third of each are numbered in LgA and LgD, but GiL is inconsistent, sometimes substituting *also* as recorded below.

7 **coueytous and irous**: *concupiscibilem et irascibilem* LgA; Ryan notes (p. 319): 'The concupiscible appetite, according to Thomas Aquinas, has as its object good or evil as agreeable or repellent in itself. The irascible appetite has as its object the good perceived as subject to some condition of difficulty or danger.'

was: *ot force raisonnable* P2.

8 **.xiij. chapitle**: not in P2, *XIII* LgA.

9 **Thei were in Antioche**: *Erant autem in ecclesia que erat Antioche* LgA.

11–12 **Dedes of the Aposteles**: *Acta IV* LgA.

14–15 **In . . . fote**: *il enseigne a defouler lor et les richesces et aprengne a touchier a la deite* P2, *Destituendum probat quod tangere deuitat et docet calcandum esse aurum* LgA, 'he proves that what one avoids touching should be set aside, and teaches that gold should be trampled on'. It seems impossible to make sense of the first part of s.w.'s attempt to restore LgA.

16 **Also**: *Tiercement* P2.

16–20 **he hadde . . . contrary thingges**: s.w. over-literally translates the French, which is a fair representation of the Latin: *habuit irascibilem, roboratum magnitudine probitatis et hoc uel uiriliter aggrediendo ardua uel perseueranter agendo fortia uel constanter sustinendo aduersa* LgA.

20 **So as it shewithe**: *Viriliter aggrediendo ardua* LgA.

22 **Aposteles**: add *IX* LgA.

25 **opinly**: *Perseueranter* LgA, starting the next sentence, referring back to 16–20 above. P2S and GiL MSS punctuate if at all after *thingges*.

26 **tormented**: *macerauit et afflixit* LgA.

27 **Aposteles**: add *XIII* LgA.

28 **and suffered**: *Et en souffrant* P2, referring back to 19 above.

29–30 **that . . . men**: '*Cum carissimis nostris* (. . .) *hominibus qui tradiderunt animas suas* LgA; no GiL MS punctuates to indicate this as speech, but P2 does, beginning *Ce furent*.

30 **Crist**: *add cest assauoir pol et barnabe* P2.

31 **thei were**: *il fut* P2.

34–5 **it is saide**: *dieu dit* P2, not in LgA.
wher the holy goste saide: not in P2, in LgA, a fairly detailed correction by GiL from LgA.

35 **Aposteles**: add *XIII* LgA.

36 **and hem in**: *et les enuoyez en* P2, *in* LgA.
office: *opus* LgA.

37 **Also**: *Secondement* P2.

38 **Apostelis**: add *XIV* LgA.

39 **done . . . goddes**: *actribuer a yceulx la maieste diuine* P2.

40 **furst**: *priorem* LgA, i.e. senior.

45 **God**[1]: add *uiuum* LgA.
Also: *Tiercement* P2.

46 **boke aforesayd . . . saide**: *fait des apostres. Car sicomme ilz disoient* P2, *Act. XV* LgA.

47–8 **of the Iues**: add *conuers* P2.

52–3 **that errour**: *lerreur diceulx* P2.

54 **Also thei were**: *Tiercement il fut* P2.
ayeinst her neyghboures: *quant a soy* P2, *quantum ad proximum* LgA.

57 **Apostelys**: add *XV* LgA.

58 **semithe**: *appert* P2, *patet* LgA.

59 **that**[2]: *Et sy que* P2, *adeo ut* LgA.

60 **Also**: *Secondement* P2.

61 **byholdinge**: *speculum* LgA.

62 **thingges**: *son* P2, *suo opere* LgA.
strong, noble are paired in LgD and LgA as the first of the four, but lack of punctuation makes this ambiguous in P2S.

64 **Apostelis**: add *XV* LgA.

67 **Also**: *Tiercement* P2.

72 **Apostelis**: add *XI* LgA.

74 **sende**: add *pour administrer* P2.

76 **olde men**: *anciens* P2, *seniores* LgA, i.e. the elders.
that . . . spare: not in LgA.

81 **hym**: add *a prendre de rechief en disciple* P2.
departie, 'separation', not in *MED*, which has only one instance of *depart* in this sense, from Lydgate (a1449).

83 **of mercye**: not in P2, *misericordie* LgA.

85 **Glose**: *Glossa Act. XV* LgA.

86 **fro the hete of charite**: only GiL.

88–9 **not . . . synne**: *faicte par esmouuement de pechie* P2, *non est facta ex commotione uitii* LgA.

90 **in diuerse places**: only GiL.

94 **so haunsed**: *le soushaucie* P2, *excelsus* LgA.

95 **this . . . seest**: *a nul ce que tu verras* P2, *cuiquam quod uidisti* LgA.

98 **thi frendes and thiselff**: *amis* (*a mis* S) *ton ame* P2, *animam tuam* (. . .) *tradidisti*. LgA.

103 **also**: *sic* LgA.

117 **they founde**: *leur fut* P2, *inuenerunt* LgA.

117–18 **the ile of**: not in LgA; Paphos is not an island.

120 **wher . . . inne**: not in LgA.

121 **partie**: add *eius* LgA.

124 **hasted hym**: *festinabant* LgA.

129 **torent**: *combusserunt* LgA.

130 **membres**: *ossa* LgA.

133 **pitte**: *cripta* LgA.

135 **hundered**: add *et vng* P2, LgA as GiL.
And . . . saiethe: in LgA this follows 136 **founde**.

136 **and was founde**: *et furent ses membres trouuez* P2, *reperta fuerunt* LgA.

75 STS VITUS AND MODESTUS

Maggioni, ch. LXXVII, p. 529; Dunn-Lardeau, ch. 77, p. 539.

1 **noble**: *egregius* LgA.

7–8 **the prouostes . . . hym**: *brachia autem uerberantium et manus prefecti statim aruerunt* LgA.

9 **bothe armes and hondes**: *la main* P2.

16 **songes**: *manieres de chans* P2, *generibus* LgA.

19 **and the moder**: only GiL.

23 **citee of Luke**: *ciuitas Lucana* LgA. This seems to mean 'a city (unspecified) of Lucania', a region of southern Italy consisting more or less of modern Basilicata. For differences in Voragine's source about this location see Boureau, 1257 n. 5; for the probability that two groups of saints have become confused, see *ODS*, 394 and Maggioni (2007), 1565.

26–7 **and thorugh . . . sight**: not in LgA.

59 **foule**: *tout* P2.
afraied: add *pugnis se percutiebat* LgA.

63 **aungeles**: *aigles* P2.

64 **of Florence**: *Florentia* LgA, i.e. it is her name.

76 STS QUIRICUS AND JULITTA

Maggioni, ch. LXXVIII, p. 532; Dunn-Lardeau, ch. 78, p. 541.

1 **of**[1]: add *julite* P2.

2 **Quiryne**: since L always, and the other MSS mostly, spell this with *n*, except for *Quirice* in EH1 here and in EH1G at 24, the misspelling must originate with s.w. or soon after. Caxton adopted the *n* form.

3 **Cesile**: *silicie* P2.

6 **iuge**: i.e. the provost, who is *preses* throughout in LgA.

14 **hym**: add *ungulis* LgA.

17 **by the ere . . . hede**: *es cheueulx et luy esrachoit* P2, *in scapulis* LgA.

18 **so . . . and**: *indigne et tourmente* P2.

19 **shedde**: add *au siege du juge* P2.

23 **wasshe**: *arousee* P2.

25 **whanne he blamed hym**: *minantem* LgA.

26 **after**: *selon* P2.

27 **was**: *loquebatur* LgA.

29 **childe**: add *necdum temporis circulo trimam* LgA.

30–1 **Ner . . . me**: *la diuine sagesce de dieu* P2.

33 **more strengthe and more**: *forces* P2, *totiens uires* LgA.

39 **thei**: *horum corpora* LgA.

77 ST MARINA

Maggioni, ch. LXXIX, p. 534; Dunn-Lardeau, ch. 79, p. 543.

In this chapter GiL differs quite substantially from LgD, in which the monks generally act corporately, the abbot is scarcely mentioned, and bells are not magically rung. The abbot has been developed into something of a 'character', and the whole tone is more dramatic and emotional. One cannot therefore decide between variants among the GiL MSS on the basis of LgD, and readings from E have generally been retained.

1 **noble**: only GiL.

1–2 **was^{1} . . . suster**: *fut vne seule fille auec son pere* P2, *unica erat patri suo* LgA.

2 **after . . . moder**: not in LgA.

7 **goodly**: *et fut receu en moyne* P2. From here on there is much variation and inconsistency in all versions on whether pronouns for Marina are masculine or feminine.

11 **vpon his blessinge**: only GiL.

12–14 **And . . . woman**: only GiL.

18 **frankeleyne**: *homme* P2.

21–5 **Whanne . . . asked hym**: *Et dont demanda len* P2.

31 **born**: *seure* P2, i.e. *sevré*, weaned.

32–4 **and bade . . . pouere**: *a nourrir et demoura la de rechief auec marin* P2.

37–43 **and preied . . . therto**: *et le receurent ou monstier* P2.

47–52 **Than the brethren . . . wosshe her**: *Et en la parfin en lauant le corps dicelle ilz auoient en propos que il seroit enterre en vng lieu vil. Et quant* P2.

53–73 **and ronnen . . . beryed**: *Et distrent quilz auoient moult pechie contre la chamberiere de dieu. Et dont vindrent tous a ce grant regart et requeroient pardon de leur ignorance et de leur meffait. Et dont mistrent le corps honnorablement en leglise* P2.

75 **alle . . . assembeled**: *populi undique confluunt* LgA.

76 **and preised . . . virgine**: only GiL.

78 **day**: *kal.* LgA.

78 STS GERVASE AND PROTASE

Maggioni, ch. LXXX, p. 536; Dunn-Lardeau, ch. 81, p. 555.

1–2 **that . . . tyme**: only GiL.

6 **I wote neuer**: *forte per anticipationem accipitur* LgA.

12 **Celce**: *ipsum* LgA, i.e. Nazarius.

13 **see**: add *et menerent geruaise et prothaise a Milan* P2.
Makary: *Nazarius* LgA.

15 **hem of Maresne**: *ceulx de la marche* P2, *Marcomannos* LgA, a Germanic people from north of the Alps.

21 **bete** add *plumbatis* LgA.

24–5 **Thou . . . me**: *Quis est miser, ego qui te non timeo aut tu qui me timere probaris?* LgA.

29 **goddes**: add *car se tu* (add *ne* P1) *doubtoies que ie te feisses mal tu ne me constraindroies pas* (add *a sacrefier* P1) *a tes dieux* (*ydoles* P1) P2.

33–4 **I . . . brother**: *la debonnairete* (add *du sauueur* P1) *me puisse auec mon frere venir a lencontre* P2, *cum fratre meo* (. . .) *possit occurrere benignitas saluatoris* LgA.

44 **two**: add *tresbeaux* P2.

44–5 **one clothinge**: *blans vestemens* P2.

45 **hosen**: *chauciez de chausses* P2, *caliculis calculati* LgA, 'wearing small boots'.

46 **vp to heuene**: only GiL.

53 **Petre**: *Paulo* LgA.

57 **peces**: *piez* P2, *pedum altitudine* LgA.

59 **her lyff**: only GiL.

60 **neygheboures aboute**: *uicinis coepiscopis* LgA.

made hem: *commenca le premier* P2.

62 **yere**: add *et ultra* LgA.

68 **emperour**: *empire* P2.

72 **the boke**: *libro XXII* LgA.

75 **Prothase**: add *mais len ne scet pas se cest le deuant dit auugle* P2.

76–7 **a towne . . . Victorien**: *uilla que dicitur Victoriana que ab Yporegio triginta milibus distat* LgA.

77 **strangeled**: *uexauit* LgA.

78 **dede**: *tout mort* P2, *tamquam mortuum* LgA.

79 **this dede man**: *il* P2,.

80 **He sterte . . . to**: *qui chantoient. et entra* P2.

82 **thennes**: add *aussy comme sil y fut lie* P2.
wroth: *coniure* P2.

86 **lyke thredes**: only GiL.

92 **the felawshipp of the fende**: *la compaignie du dyable tres felon* P2, *nequissimi hostis uitiorum aciem prosternentes* LgA.

96 **the striff of a wombe**: *vng seul ventre destrif* P2, *unus uterus maternus* LgA.

79 ST ALBAN

For sources of this life see Introduction above, pp. 35–8.

Quotations from the Tractatus (Tr) are from Reinecke's edition of *Saint Albon and Saint Amphibalus by John Lydgate*, checked against Oxford, Bodleian Library, MS Bodley 585, and those from Willliam of St Albans's *Alia Acta SS. Albani, Amphibali, et sociorum* (W) are from the *Acta Sanctorum* checked against Oxford, Bodleian Library, MS Digby 172.

1 **so**: not Tr.

9 **vnworship**: add *ignauia* Tr, 'by cowardice'.

14–15 **Seuerus . . . whiche was after emperour of Rome**: Sextus Julius Severus, governor of Britain, *c.*130–3, but in saying he was later emperor Tr has confused him with Septimius Severus, emperor from 193 to 211, who made an expedition to Britain in 208.

27 **sent**: add *romam* Tr.

30 **sixty**: *quinquaginta* Tr.

35 **Albon**: add *pro recipiendo ordine militari* Tr.

61 **dedyen**: *MED dedien*, 'dedicate', is first recorded for c1450(c1400);

dedifien is first recorded for a1475, though a citation is also given for a1500(c1386).

64 **manly desire**: *animositatem* Tr, 'courage'; the English is perhaps 'ambition'.

65 **I canne . . . desire and**: not in Tr.

72 **and by**: *contra* Tr.
Ficulues: *siculos* Tr, 'Sicilians'.

74 **and deden in armes worthely**: *per multos dies* Tr.

75–7 **and aboue . . . name of victori**: *precipue tamen sancto Albano* Tr.

81 **in the monasterie of Seint Albone**: *eidem sancto albano et eiusdem monasterio* Tr.

89–90 **whanne ye wyll**: not in Tr.

90 **abide in oure seruise and**: not in Tr.

104 **and to putte hym oute of mynde**: *memoratum* Tr, i.e. 'the aforesaid'.

108–9 **they slowe so many**: *tandem occidit* Tr.

109–10 **that of his name they called it Walbroke that time**: so also Tr. Ekwall (p. 491) derives Walbrook from **walabroc*, 'brook of the Welshmen or serfs'.

114 **Romaynes**: add *qui missi fuerant* Tr.

121 **withe Maximien**: not in Tr.

123 **hym**: add *Quem etiam dominus prius inuestiuit creans eum dominum Verolamie ciuitatis* Tr.

128 **his**: add *et infinitos alios* Tr.

133 **kingdom**: *imperio* Tr.

140 **he ordeined**: *ordinauerunt* Tr.

141 **withholders**: *detentores* Tr; *MED* gives only one example in this sense, 'one who declines to give something up', for *c*.1450. The only other citation is for a1382 with the figurative sense 'possessor'.

146 **Rome**: add *et* Tr.

159 **signe of a clerk**: *signa* (. . .) *clericalia* Tr.

160–1 **witheoute . . . hospitalite**: *qui semper cunctis peregrinis et pauperibus fuerat hospitaliter* Tr.

161 After **clerke** the source switches from Tr to W.

165 **ye durst**: *potuisti* W.

172 **What is that ye afferme that God shulde be bore**: *Quid est quod Deus natus esse asseritur* W.

186 **the holy gost . . . in the**: *concipies* W.

195 **nobelnesse**: *insignia* W, 'distinguishing marks', and by extension 'status'.

longe tyme before: *futurum fuisse* W.

200 **the blynde, the lame**: *debilibus, aegrotis* W.

204 **God**: *Christum. Idcirco hanc urbem ingressus sum, ut in ea praeco tuae fierem passionis* W.

210–11 **what talkest thou?**: *nescis quid discis* W.

214 **punisshed**: add *secundum publicas legum sanctiones* W.

216 **place**: *habitaculo* W.

229 **scourges**: add *et graviter laniatur* W.
holy: *saucium* W, 'wounded'.

230 **crosse**: add *per transversum ligni robur manus expanduntur* W.

240 **and done**: not in W.

247 **Takynge his myghtes**: *resumptis viribus* W.

250 **he come**: *venerant* W.
syngers: *candidatorum* W.

256 **is not . . . telle**: *nec volo nec licet ulli mortalium indicare* W.

264–5 **to obeye hymselff to**: *subire* W.

277 **withe his precious blood**: *pretio sanguinis sui* W.

284 **with a gret sperit**: *in haec verba* W.

305–6 **so (. . .) hondes and the fete**: *sic pedes sic vulnerum loca* W.

320 **true doctrine**: *solicitudinem* (. . .) *doctoris* W, 'care of a teacher'.

325 **was called Tugurium**: *tugurium vulgo solet appellari* W; *tugurium*, 'hut, peasant dwelling', mistaken as the name of the building; also 359 *Tigurium*.

326 **alle the nightes**: *totam noctem* W.

327 **lyuers**: *leuers* H1A1, *lyvers* H2, 'believers'. Singular *leuer* is found at 27.59, the same spelling as the only citation in *MED s.v. lever* n.2.

327–8 **vntreue . . . faithe**[2]: *infidelibus; qui cultores Christianae religionis, non in fide sequi, sed pro fide persequi contendebant* W, 'who strove not to follow the adherents of the Christian religion in the faith, but to persecute them because of the faith'.

329 **that hadde espied hem**: not in W.

330–1 **alle that he hadde herde**: *quod factum fuerat* W.

331 **vntamed**: *intactum* W, 'untouched'. *MED* records no sense which corresponds to the Latin or fits this context.

338 **slayne**: *jugulandos* W.

339 **sacrifice**: *victimae* W.

340 **go before**: *praevenire* W, 'forestall', an over-literal translation.
of þe princes: *principis* W.
made: *hortatur* W.

341 **clothe of golde**: *chlamydem auro textam* W.

344 **an oste of men**: *cuneos hostium* W.
vndesesed: MED has only one citation, s.v. *undisesed*, 'untroubled', dated ?*c*.1450.

360 **kneling**: *precibus incumbentem* W.

366 **cruelte**: add *mox ei manus injecerunt* W.

368–9 **and treted**: *tractantes* W.

371 **Asclepiodote**: not in W; he has not been named since 116, so this is a useful reminder.

375 **went before**: *praeerat* W, 'presided over'.

379 **ansuered**: add *tantum* W.

380 **frely**: *libera voce* W.

382–3 **that is entred . . . beiape**: *qui nuper a Christo nescio quo huc directus, ut* (. . .) *illuderet* W.

385 **remorded**: *remorderet* W.

386–7 **and as a worthi maister aleged hym for his disciple**: *ut pro se suoque disciplo magister egregius allegaret* W, 'as a worthy master would present the case for himself and his disciple'.

401 **synne**: add *criminibus indulgentiam* W.

422 **Shortely**: not in W.

427 **and multitude of noyse**: *insultationis* W.

439 **in verrey sacrifice**: *in holocaustum libenter* W.

445 **wokes**: *mensibus* W.

449 **erthe**: add *venti non spirarunt* W.
but euer . . . sone: *sed in dies singulos omnis regio sub sole ardentissimo torrebatur* W; the mistranslation in EDL appears to be by s.w., only A1 and a corrector of H1 having put it right.

452 **wicked men/but**: here the source switches back from W to Tr.

456 **conuersion**: add *Interea Albanus in carcere seruabatur a mense Decembri usque ad mediam mensem Junii, id est per sex menses* Tr.

459 **peple**: add *persecutioni occiduarum* Tr, i.e. the persecution of those abandoning their pagan religion.

463 **hym**[2]: add *penis* Tr.

471 **slayne**: add *ante eius oculos* Tr.

474 **Asclepeodot**: not in Tr.

492 **Verolamye**: *burgenses verolamij et walyngcestrenciam et londoniensium seu trinouancium et omni villarum uicinarum* Tr. Wæclingaceaster, an earlier name for St Albans, is first recorded from Bede (*The Place-names of Hertfordshire*, 86–7); Augusta Trinobantum, an alternative name for London, goes back at least to Ammianus Marcellinus.

504 **do derogacion**, 'disparage'; the first citation of the noun in this sense in *MED* is for *c.*1443.

509–10 **The crosse . . . beryed**: *Crux quem adorauit cum clamide quam gestauit mittatur* Tr; if *dede were* is here a periphrastic past, it is unusual for this text, and led to various scribal attempts at correction.

512 **goddes**: ends interpolation from Tractatus, summarizing the end of W before reverting fully to W at 516.

516 **toke hevily**: *graviter* (. . .) *accipiens, vehementer coepit formidare* W.
he: add *ad martyrium praeparatus* W.

522 **boldenesse**: add *virtus decidat in defectum* W.

523 **What abide ye? Whom susteyne ye**: *Quid sustinetis* W; the sense of the Latin, 'defer', is not recorded in *MED*. The sense of the English is not clear.

530 **dyuinite**: add *cum sint opere manuum hominum* W.

539 **ydoles**: add *et vae cultoribus idolorum* W.

547 **goddes**: add *nonnulli, evulsis oculis post magistrum suum dirigendum esse decreverunt* W.

548–9 **be . . . emperoure**: not in W.

549 **iugement**: add *vinculis iterum constrictus* W.

554 **go on faste**: *Vade* W.

564–5 **many one . . . pitously**: *dum alter alterum praeire contendit; nulli facilem transitum pontis angustia concedebat* W.

566 **dede of her clothes and**: not in W.

567 **that coude not swymmen**: not in W.
and: add *ab aquis vehementibus intercepti* W.

576 **peple**: add *sanus et incolumis* W.

577 **water**: *alveus* W, 'river bed'.

578–9 **His orison . . . riuere**: *orationis virtus flumen exhaurit* W.

579 **a way**: add *inter undas* W.

580 **encrese**: add *et virtutibus virtutes dum succedunt* W.

581 **be the myght of Crist**: *in populo* W.

583 **in the depenesse of the riuere**: not in W.

587 **God dede for hym**: *fiebant ab eo, poenitentia ductus* W.

590 **almyghty**: *verus* W.

591–2 **and therfor . . . servaunt**: *In illum me jam noveris credere, illum mihi tecum pro Deo vendicare* W.

595 **wickidnesse**: add *invidiae stimulis agitantur, et homines acerrimi fiunt acriores* W.

596 **Albone**: add *sicut asseris* W.

599 **We only worshippen oure goddes**: *nos deum Solem colimus* W. As result of this error, *illi*, *hic*, and following singular verbs become plural in GiL.

601 **for oure ease**: *propter nos* W.

602–3 **alle . . . sounde**: *sani et numero integri* W.

603 **beholde**: *cerneremus* W, i.e. *we* understood, not *the multitude*.

613 **sondes**: add *ad scelus de scelere transitum facientes* W.

614–17 **this most . . . blodye**: *cum per dura lapidum loca, per vepres et aspera quaeque, B. Albanum homines crudelissimi ducerent et reducerent: spinae quoque et radices arborum etiam de pedibus avulsa secum frusta diriperent, et saxa pretiosus sanguis inficeret* W.

620–1 **nye . . . thruste**: *siti aestuantes; extremum spiritum jam trahebant* W.

621–2 **grynted . . . tethe**: *fremebant* W.

626 **withe gret affeccion**: *intimo affectu* W.

631 **thruste and**: not in W.

634 **welle**: f. 162ᵛ ends at this point in H1 and another hand has written below the column: *next after this shuld folow þat is þe begynnyng of þe next lefe saue oone at this sign*. On f. 164 the scribe omitted 651 *atte one* to 726 *we that*. This has been supplied on an inserted folio following f. 162 in the hand of Stephen Dodesham.

and: *in medio* W.

645 **Venus**: *Soli* W.

647 **nede**: add *ut aquarum rivulus subito de terra prosiliens, nobis occurreret ad salutem* W.

saide: add *ad fundendum sanguinem populi furor accenditur* W.

648 **and hys hede to a bowe**: not in W or EH1, but it is in L, in modified form in D, and also in Lydgate combined with the next clause as *First his*

lokkys that wer longe and large / Maliciously thei bounde hem to a stake (II. 1857–8).

649 **dede**: add *pro omnibus* W.

652–3 **þe body . . . redy to heuene**: *Cadit in foveam cadaver exanime, praeparatam caedi* W.

657 **that slowe . . . stroke**: *cum adhuc staret juxta corpus* W.

669 **seruise**: add *nec dubium quin servi sui manibus celerem conferat medicinam* W.

670 **charitee**: *fidei* W.

671–2 **he . . . mercy**: *ad clementiam possit perducere salvatoris* W.

698–9 **felawe . . . consolaciones**: *consors passionis, gloriae quoque consortia non amisit* W.

711–12 **Albon . . . marter**: The Latin is used as a refrain by Lydgate, *Albanus vir egregius martir extat gloriosus.*

719–20 **fendes . . . hem**: *potius probantur esse portenta quam numina; quippe quibus virtus nulla, nulla divinitas inesse facile deprehenditur* W.

737–8 **they hoped to fynde**: *manere putabatur* W.

740 **by the . . . holinesse**: *famae celebritatae* W.

741 **of God**: *vitae* W.

744 **taken**: *commendaverat* W.

745 **vpon hym**: i.e. upon the proffered cross.
to Amphiball: not in W.

750 **supersticion**: the EH1A1 readings *superfeccion* here and *superficience* at 788 below are not recorded in MED, but *superficite*, with the sense 'outer surface', is. The scribes are copying an earlier misreading.

752 **bapteme**: *signaculum quod in Christo est* W.

754–5 **came . . . hereof**: *per loca singula convalescens* W.

755 **Verolamye**: add *vario sermone replevit* W.

759 **who went**: *qui abierint* W, i.e. 'had gone'.

760 **were anone wretin**: *mox jubentur annotari* W.

761–2 **Thanne . . . warde**: *Adversum quos nimio furore commoti, totis viribus se praeparant ad insequendum: instructique armis bellicis cum ingenti strepitu iter ineunt, acsi essent ad praelia processuri* W.

762 **holy**: *celebre* W.

763 **come**: add *fama ducente* W.

766 **thou . . . men**: *seductor pessime* W.

769 **presumed hem**: *praesumperunt* W.

771 **Thou . . . ease**: *tibi non cedet in prosperum* W.

773 **vngilty**: add *coram diis et hominibus* W.

775 **into oure contre**: *ad propria* W.

776 **presumptuouse**: *pertinacia* W.

781–2 **that he . . . God**: *cultorem esse veri Dei* W.

782 **sight**: add *more solito* W.

783 **And wete it well**: not in W.

788 **supersticions**: for the variant see note to 750 above.

791 **God . . . Lorde**: *Deus autem et Dominus noster Jesus Christus* W.

793 **purpos**: add *Quid inaniter et superflue laboratis?* W.
Wetithe wel that: not in W.

799 **fader**: add *cives a civibus* W.

800 **ne mercy to kinrede**: *non parentum miseratio dura carnificum corda molllivit* W.

801–2 **obeyed . . . tyrauntes**: *certatim cervices suas gladiis objiciunt: et dum prior trucidatur, moras arguit secuturus. Ex hoc sacro collegio unus omnino superfuit, qui in via corporis infirmitate detentus adesse non potuit* W.

803 In Tr, which summarizes these events, they are said to have taken place at Lichfield, which is also named by Lydgate at this point.

804 **withe . . . victorie**: *laetus* W.

807 **hym**: *inimicum deorum suorum* W.

809 **on . . . horses**: *sublimes in equis* W.

811 **waye**[1]: add *Carnifices vero semper ad locum caedis respicientes, seria jam poenitentia ducti, super cognatos amicos suos, quos in furore suo trucidaverunt, amarissime flere incipiunt* W.

812 **whiche . . . Amphiball**: *secus viam jacere* W.

812–14 **By fortune . . . felawshipp**: not in W.

818–19 **not movinge bere**: *non ferentes* W; for *movinge* see *MED mouen* v. sense 2a, 'to be able'.

823 **done myght be not conseled**: *diu celari non potuit* W.

830 **and her . . . hem**: *telluri* W.

838–9 **they hadde . . . after**: *eos, pro quibus ierant, incolumes ad patria revocassent* W.

844–5 **the brother . . . neighebour**[2]: *cives a civibus se queruntur destitutos:*

hic fratrem, ille propinquam se deflet amisisse: matres quoque, cognita filiorum nece, sparsis crinibus W.

848 **vpon vs**: W and Lydgate here include a lament of the townspeople at the fate of their kindred in another country.

Vndedly God: *Dii immortales* W.

849 **oure²**: *vestris* W.

850 **in hym**: add *et mala, quae in nos commisit, in caput proprium retorquete* W.

856 **of frendes**: *parentes a filiis* W.

857–9 **and namely . . . sorugh for hem**: *nec nos quidem abnuimus: sed illis multam* [*nullam* Digby] *de se materiam gaudendi posteris derelinquunt. Istis nequaquam condolendum est, imo magis congaudendum* W. The contrast between the afterlife expectations of pagans and Christians is obscured by the GiL paraphrase.

859 **whiche**: *quos semper beate victuros constat in caelo* W.

862 **blisse**: add *Non sunt quasi mortui plangendi in terris, qui feliciter cum Christo vivunt in caelis. Damna deflere, humanum quidem est; sed dolori nolle modum ponere, insaniae proximum est* W.

865 **tale**: add *ad omnem multitudinem* W.

867–8 **into Walys**: *tandem in Walliam fama ducente pervenimus* W.

871 **frendes**: *parentes* W.

871–3 **by monicions . . . thenkke**: *nunc monitis, nunc minis eos coepimus convenire* W.

873 **sadnesse**: *pertinacia* W.

874 **one hole oure**: *ad horam* W, 'at that time'.

875–6 **the iniurie of oure contemptes**: *iniuriam nostri contemptus* W.

879 **the fader . . . sone**: *filii in patres, patres in filios insurgerent, prosternerent, interficerent* W.

881 **this**: *quod dicturi sumus* W.

sorugh: W adds two graphic sentences about the slaughter.

882 **Whanne . . . done**: *Dum haec agerentur* W.

886 **we**: add *qui caedem exercuimus* W.

888 **and oure kynne**: not in W.

890 **citezenis**: *concives* W.

894 **.ixC. and .xxx.^ti^**: *nongenti nonaginta novem* W.

896 **another**: add *propter vulnera et sanguinis copiam qui prefluxerat* W.

901–2 **This . . . fourme of man**: *Factumque est ut agnitionem humanam* W, 'so it came about that our human perception'.

904 **peple**: *populus terrae* W.
the worse parte: *sinistra interpretatione* W.

905–6 **denyed . . . in alle wise**: *et ne in suis finibus mandentur sepulturae, qui fidem Christi susceperunt, vehementer obsistit. Supremum naturae debitum defunctis negatur, et devorandi bestiis ac volatilibus exponuntur* W.

907 **deth**: add (*et*) *dura furentium corda mollivit* W.

908 **hem**: add *Ut enim liquido daretur intelligi, divinam Christi cultoribus non deesse custodiam* W, 'For as may be clearly understood, the divine guardianship of Christ was not lacking to the worshippers.'

910–12 **and whanne . . . mervaile**: *ut eos ad illorum missus esse praesidium facile sensus humanus intelligeret. Quibus perspectis* W.

917–18 **now . . . berienge**: *nec pati poterant ut eos terra susciperet; nunc versa vice miris laudibus extollunt, et habere desiderant* W.

920 **men**: add *Ad perpetuandam quoque memoriam occisorum, ab ipsis incolis eorum numerus et nomina describuntur* W.

921–2 **we be . . . witnesse**: *nobiscum testis extitit* W.

932 **of you**: not in W.

943–4 **he may . . . hym**: *ab omnibus sibi vindictam sentiat irrogari. Dicant omnes quod voluerint: sed nos nostrae civitatis injuriam negligere vel inultam relinquere non debemus. Hoc mandatum postquam in civitate divulgatum est* W.

945 **ranne**: add *hinc inde* W.

946 **faste**: add *et in suum sese invicem excitant inimicum* W.

948 **nombered**: add *nec poterant plateae multitudinem capere confluentem: et quia stipatis agminibus incedebant prae densitate sua lento gradu iter agere cogebantur* W.

950–1 **one of hem, He, he**: plural W.

953 **bowel**: add *ejus ferro* W.

957 **turmentours . . . wodenesse**: *illi acriores effecti eum quasi ad signum statuunt* W.

958–60 **suerdes . . . stake**: *cultellis lanceolique quod reliquum erat corporis confodiunt* W.

967 **hym**: add *et quam se jam videre perhibebant* W.

969 **princes, thei**: singular W.

973–4 **withe gret ioye**: not in W.

975 **most wicked**: *crudelissime* W.

977 **peple**: add *et perversis ac feralibus tuis monitis irretitos a cultura deorum submovisti?* W.

978 **so cruelly**: not in W.
peple: add *Diligenter attende, vir bone, quid feceris. Tuorum subtilitate verborum parentes et amici nostri in perditionem abierunt* W.

978–9 **this peple**: add *tu eos ad mortis laqueum impulisti. Hinc justis odiis te persequimur: maxime cum ipse quoque justitia justitiae adversarius jubeat adversari* W.

982–3 **sorowe and forthenkinge**: *poenitendo* W.

984 **secte**: add *quam hucusque tenuisti* W.
thou[2]: add *ignorans forsitan* W.

985–7 **for oure . . . bodie**: *quia mox rerum omnium affluentiam consequeris; insuper omnes quo neci nuper tradidisti, per suae divinitatis potentiam dii nostri a mortuis revocabunt* W.

993 **mynde**: *commoratio* W, 'dwelling'.

1000 **turmentis**: add *talium quippe cultores numinum talis decet retributio meritorum* W, 'for indeed such retribution for their faults is fitting for the worshippers of such divinities'.

1005–6 **Rennithe . . . haste**: not in W.

1026–7 **and sayd . . . truly**: *Vox etiam coelitus hujusce modi ad eum facta est: Amen dico tibi* W.

1029 **soule**: add *niveo candore fulgentem* W.

1032 **witheoute soule**: *corpus exanime et in vinculis constitutum* W.

1035 **debate and striff**: *certamen* W.

1035–6 **eueri . . . bodi**: *usque ad conflictum gladiorum contentio nefanda procedit. Agmine denso pars utraque cucurrit; et supra membra beatissima gravis pugna committitur* W.

1039 **for**: *Dum enim tumultus incresceret, et inter se Pagani turbarentur* W.

1042 **beganne to be shewed**: *desaevit* W.
peple: add *distorquentur labia* W.

1044 **other diuerse turmentis**: W gives these in more detail.

1045 **suffered**: add *sic demum a praelio quieverunt* W.

1047 **Amphiball**: add *et tamen periculum evasisse* W.

1050–1 **for . . . abrode**: *Exciti rumore vicini accurrunt; quod auditu perceperant, oculis comprobantes. Mox* W.

1054 **defautes**: add *fatentur errores, undamque lavacri expetunt salutaris* W.

1061–end. William's fictitious attribution of composition of this Life to a writer preceding the Anglo-Saxon conversion is translated into English without comment. The injunction that those who would name him must call him 'most wretched and most sinfull' (*me miserum, me peccatorem*) is reminiscent of s.w.'s self-reference as a 'synfulle wrecche' recorded in the D colophon (see p. 2).

1062 **Albone**: add *nec jam de eis multum tractant homines aut loquuntur* W.

1063 **abidethe endelesly**: add *sed ejus laudabile meritum, si quid mea carmina possunt, longe lateque per orbem diffundetur* W.

1064 **men**: add *viri Christiani* W.

1065 **Bretaigne**: add *Isti cum venerint, Dei magnalia hoc modo libris adserta reperient, legent et ad notitiam deferent plurimorum* W.

1067–8 **of grace of visitacion**: *visitationis et gratiae* W, looking forward to the arrival of St Augustine.

1070 **a true man and**: not in W.

80 ST JOHN THE BAPTIST

Maggioni, chs. LXXXI and CXXI, pp. 540 and 873; Dunn-Lardeau, ch. 80 and 120, pp. 544 and 821.

The chapter is a conflation of two chapters in LgA and LgD, with additional material. See Introduction, pp. 38–9.

10 **encence**: add *et grant multitude de peuple lactendoit dehors* P2.

11 **and**: add *Zacharie se doubta de la vision di celluy. Lange adonc luy* P2.

11–12 **thou . . . Lorde**: *ton oroison est oye* P2.

14 **syder**: *siceram* LgA, 'strong drink'; this not uncommonly appears as 'cider' in ME texts, but here GiL is following LgD.

32–5 **Withe . . . cosin**: *et que elle nestoit mais brehaigne. et conforta celle en sa viellesce et vint a elle* P2, *congratulans uirgo fecunda ablate sterilitati et compatiens senectuti uenit ad Elizabeth* LgA.

35–7 **And anone . . . ioye**: *Et quant elle la salua le benoit iehan qui estoit ia raemply du saint esperit senty le filz de dieu venir a soy. et commenca a trepper de joie ou ventre de sa mere. et salua celluy par mouuement que il ne pouoit saluer par voix. il sesdreca aussy comme efforcant soy le saluer. et soy leuer encontre son seigneur* P2.

37–53 **and . . . graunted her**: only GiL.

56–62 **and wosshe . . . moder**: not in LgD, *ut habetur in hystoria scholastica, et quasi morem gerule officiosissime peregit* LgA.

The remainder of LgA LXXXI, Maggioni, 543–51 (46–191), is omitted.

128–9 **What . . . thiselff**: *Dixerunt ergo ei: Quis es? ut responsum demus his qui miserunt nos; quid dicis de teipso?* John 1: 22.

138 The rest of the chapter consists of excerpts from LgA CXXI, Maggioni,

873–85, interspersed with other material, sometimes substituting details which do not agree with the LgA/LgD version.

138–9 **In . . . wrongfully**: this summarizes a rather fuller account in LgA/LgD of the marital misconduct of Herod Antipas.

148–76 **And . . . hym**: only GiL.

156 **pore men and symple prechen**: *pauperes evangelizantur* Luke 7: 22.

186 GiL omits Maggioni, 874–5 (20–32), Dunn-Lardeau, 822–3.

186–7 **O . . . Seint**: only GiL.

187–90 **the scole . . . faithe**: *schola uirtutum, magisterium uite, sanctitatis forma, norma iustitie, uirginitatis speculum, pudicitie titulus, castitatis exemplum, penitentie uia, peccatorum uenia, fidei disciplina* LgA.

191 **souerayne of the gospels** *euangelii sanctio* LgA.

192 **sawer of faithe**: *legis summa* LgA; GiL has changed the order of the list.

wey: *uox* LgA.

stintinge: *silentium* LgA.

193–5 **was putte . . . auouuterere**: *datur incestui, traditur adultere, addicitur saltatrici* LgA.

194–5 **the doughter . . . auouutere**: *lauoultre saillant* P2.

195 **was not punisshed**: *ne sen alla pas impugny* P2; 195–7 inaccurately summarizes an account of the later history of the family from *Historia Scholastica*, which does not mention devouring by beasts, Maggioni, 875–6 (37–51), Dunn-Lardeau, 823.

197 **as . . . tellithe**: this belongs to the next sentence in LgA, beginning a section which GiL omits; the section starting at 198 begins: *Sicut enim legitur in XI libro hystorie ecclesiastice*, so it appears the omission was by eyeskip.

212 **fonde**: *reposuit* LgA; in LgA Theophilus purged the temple and then dedicated it as a basilica in honour of John.

214 **that**: add *Beda et* LgA.

215–16 **and arraied withe precious stones**: *en jennes* P2, 'at Genoa'.

217 **priuileges**: here GiL and LgD omit Maggioni, 878 (62–7).

220–2 This refers to 29 Julian 209–18. Paula comes between the Conversion of Paul and Julian, so it may indicate a stage of LgA at which Voragine had not yet included Paula.

Here GiL omits Maggioni, 878–81 (70–111), Dunn-Lardeau, 825–8.

230 **.CCC.liij.**: *CCCCLII* LgA.

231 **.iij.**: *deux* P2.

237–9 **a pore man . . . Misse**: *vng potier de la cite de misse qui sen aloit par pourete* P2.

242 **the same night**: only GiL.

243–4 **and bere . . . worshipped it**: *et honnoroit le saint chief en vne fosse* P2.

246 **assuraunce**: i.e. pledge of secrecy.

246–7 **as longe as . . . it**: add *aussy comme il auoit fait* P2, *secundum eundem modum sibi inuicem successores* LgA.

253–5 **And . . . cussed hym**: in P2 this follows 252 *come to hym.*
nye hym: add *et eius pedibus se prostrauisset* LgA.
cussed hym: *dedit ei osculum pacis* LgA.

256 **The nexst night**: *quadam alia nocte* LgA.

275–6 **for aught . . . drawe**: *combien que len y menast des beufz et pour ce le conuint il laisser la* P2, *quantumcumque boues stimulis urgerentur ideoque ipsum ibidem deponere sunt coacti* LgA.

277 **a noble lady**: *matronam uirginem* LgA.

280 **that he . . . tyme**: *quil ne se laissast oster* P2.

282 **chirche**: add *et ce dit lystoire partie en .iij.* P2.

283 **in Fraunce**: only GiL; this was Pepin I, king of Aquitaine 817–38, son of Louis the Pious and grandson of Charlemagne.

284 **Fraunce**; add *en poitou* P2.
many . . . done: *moult de mors sont resuscitez* P2.

285 **and Herodien were**: *fut* P2.

286–7 **the wreched doughter . . . hym**: *fut herodienne qui conseilla a la pucelle quelle demandast le chief de iehan et la pucelle qui le requist* P2.

287–9 **for as . . . wrechidly**: LgD and LgA report various accounts of the fates of the two women, ending with one that the earth swallowed the daughter alive.

292–3 **whanne . . . *mundi***: only GiL.

294 **Seint Tecle**: also Tigris or Tigra; see *AASS* 25 Jun., 73 ff. For her *Vita* see Poole, 'The See of Maurienne and the Valley of Susa', 7–10; see too Maggioni (2007), 1631 and note to 296–7 below.

294–5 **ouer the mountaynes**: *inter Alpes* LgA.

295 **of Seint Martin**: *Maurianensi* LgA, now St. Jean-de-Maurienne; variants are *Sancti Martini*, *Sancti Maximi*.

296–7 **into Normandye**: *qui comburi non potuit de ultra marinis partibus in Mauriennam* (variant *Normanniam*) LgA. Waters, 115, note to 680, identifies St Thecla as 'the legendary travelling and preaching companion of St Paul', from the *Acts of Paul and Thecla* in the New Testament Apocrypha; there seems, however, to be no reason to associate her with Normandy, though that must have been named here in Voragine's source. Its replacement by *Mauriennam* in the later redactions of LgA indicates that he associated this story with Maurienne.

299 GiL omits three miracles, Maggioni, 884–5 (160–75), Dunn-Lardeau, 831–2.

81 STS JOHN AND PAUL

Maggioni, ch. LXXXII, p. 552; Dunn-Lardeau, ch. 82, p. 559.

1 **prouostes and maisters**: *primicerii et prepositi* LgA; it is difficult to say exactly what these terms mean; Ryan's 'high officials' seems the best translation of the Latin.

6 **labour and payne**: *peine* P2, *laboris* LgA.

12–13 **content herewithe**: only GiL.

13 **sent**: *manere permitteret* LgA.

15–16 **in hope . . . her**: *sibi concederet in specie quasi firmitatis maioris* LgA, variant for *in specie*, 'under the appearance', *in spe*.

16–17 **she . . . deuoutely**: *elle prioit* P2.

18–19 **This . . . herde**: *ceste promesse pleut a tous* P2.

22 **Chichens**: *chicheiens* P2, *Scithicarum* LgA, i.e. Scythians, the *men of Siche* at 3 above.

27 **spere**: *glaiue* P2.

29 **alle**: *uniuersum exercitum* LgA.
hym: add *seulement* P2.

31 **comforted**: *confirmabant* LgA.

36–7 **because . . . also**: only GiL.

37 **for his doughters**: *et due filie Gallicani* LgA.

39 **Crist**[1]: add *en pourete* P2.

39–40 **his . . . that**: only GiL.

43 **that londe**: *orbe terrarum* LgA.
come: add *ab oriente et occidente* LgA.
beholde: *oyr* P2, *veoir* P1.

43–4 **and to here hym**: only GiL.

44 **paynyme**: *pacient* P2, *ex patricio et consule* LgA.

46 **and ministred . . . lyvinge**: only GiL.

47 **al lowly seruice**: *tous ces autres seruices dessusdiz* P2, *cetera sancte seruitutis officia* LgA.

49 **heretyk**: add *ariana* LgA.

49–52 **sothely . . . cesarien**: *Et le pere constancien auoit vng frere qui auoit nom constant. Et dont constancien fist* (add *Constant* Z) *son oncle cesarien* P2, *uerum cum Constantius frater Constantini duos filios, scilicet Gallum et Iulianum, reliquisset, Constantius imperator dictum Gallum Cesarem fecit* LgA. The earlier emperors carried both the titles Caesar and Augustus; but from the time of Hadrian a distinction was made between the Augustus, the reigning emperor, and the Caesar, the heir; this development is described in the text at 104.123–7. All occurrences of Caesar in this sense are accusative *cesarem* in LgA, and in GiL and LgD appear as *cesarien*; *MED* does not record this word, nor *cesar* in this sense. The modification is due to Vignay, who probably did not think of it grammatically but adjusted the Latin to a more French form.

54 **whanne . . . laboure**: *apres* P2.

57 **vnder religious**: *moult religieux* P2.

60 **for . . . cheueteynes**: *urgentibus negotiis* LgA.

66 **there**: *ab infidelibus* LgA.

85 **princes**: *premiers* P2.

86 **shall not longe**: *nen pourray estre despit* P2; *longe*, perhaps 'delay'. An H1 corrector felt this was unsatisfactory and added *suffer yowe*, taking *longe* as adverbial.

96 **praiers and in**: only GiL.

98 **image**: add *aureum* LgA.

101 **priuely** modifies *beheded* in LgD and LgA.

103 **depe**: only GiL.

103–4 **and he saide to alle the peple (. . .) for her renome**: *famam faciens* LgA, 'creating a rumour'.

108 **atte . . . seintes**: not in LgA.
he: i.e. Terencien; in LgA this clause follows *felonye*.

109 **.iiij^{xx}. and .xiij.**: *CCCLXIV* LgA.

123 **oure**: *vng seul* P2.

82 ST LEO POPE

Maggioni, ch. LXXXIII, p. 556; Dunn-Lardeau, ch. 83, p. 562.

6 **bi whiche he was hurt**: *se scandalizantem* LgA.

15 **celebred**: 'performed, held'; *MED* gives only two instances, both from Spec. Sacer., a1500(?c1425) and both specifically related to a religious rite.

16 **in ordre**; i.e. as a religious.

22 **thanne . . . and**: not in LgA.

23 **anone**: *tantost quil veist le benoist Leon* P2.

25–6 **alle . . . prison**: *les enchetiuez* P2.

35 **That**: *ce que* P2.

44 **imposicion of honde**: i.e. for ordination.

47 **.xl.**: *LX* LgA.

83 ST PETER APOSTLE

Maggioni, ch. LXXXIV, p. 559; Dunn-Lardeau, ch. 84, p. 564.

S lacks the last few lines of Leo, and Peter up to about 157.

5 **name**: add *car sicomme crisostome dit. sil leust nomme pierre se fust tantost leue et leust desrompu* P2.

6 **he rered**: *a susciter* P2.

7 **balaunce**: *staterem* LgA, a Jewish coin, which Vignay misread as *stateram*, 'scales'.
wombe: *ore* LgA.

8–9 **He toke . . . Crist**: *pascendas oues a Christo suscepit* LgA.

10 **predicacion**: add *claudum cum Iohanne sanauit et tunc quinque milia conuertit* LgA.

25 **was**: *uidebatur* LgA.

29 **his**: should be *her*; French *sa* is ambiguous, LgA reads *cum uxor Petri ad passionem duceretur.*

32 **fourty**: *.xx.* P2.

46 **God**: add *et que len luy donroit communement honneurs* P2, add *diuinis donabor honoribus* LgA; Vignay had converted this citation into indirect speech.

50 **and saide**: *que Ierosme dit* Z.

51 **I am a spouse**: not in LgA, but one MS gives *sponsus* for *speciosus* (GiL *right faire*); perhaps Vignay's exemplar incorporated both.

52 **the soule**: *omnia* LgA, variant *anima*.
of iren: *darain* P2, 'of brass'.

53 **of iren**: *darain et de pierres* P2.

63–4 **debates . . . pees**: *batailles naissent de pechiez et la ou peche nest fait il est paix* P2.

65 **It is not as**: *ce nest riens que* P2.

66 **divinite**: add *ut repente adores me* LgA.

68 **I**[1]: add *puis* P2.

69 **malices**: *malefices* P2.

71 **by cause**: only GiL; the sense must be 'in order to prevent', for which *MED s.v. bi cause, because*, has only one citation, from Malory.

72 **to the peple**: only GiL.

73 **Rome**: add *ut ibi deus habeatur* LgA.

76 **two**: add *episcopos* LgA.

80 **chastite**: add *et la mettoit auant* P2.

81 **maydenes**: *concubinas* LgA.

85 **with the**: add *ut eruam te* LgA, 'that I will shield you'.

87 **knewe**: *ut ait Linus* LgA.

98 **Nero**: add *sicut idem Leo refert* LgA.

104–5 **vpon . . . foyson**: *la tout aglutine* P2.

109 **Leon**: add *pape* P2.
And . . . that: *Hec Leo* LgA.
The *Leon* named as a source in this chapter was Pope Leo I, subject of the preceding chapter, to whom a *Passio SS. Petri et Pauli auct. pseudo-Marcello* (*BHL* 6657) is attributed; for sources to this chapter see Maggioni, p. lxiii.

115 **enchauntementz**: *maleficia* LgA.

122 **sheuithe his diuinite in gret thingges**: *demonstre sa diuinite es choses et laferme* P2, *diuinitatem suam rebus affirmat* LgA.

129 **Now saye, Simon**: *Or dye symon qui se fait dieu* P2; s.w. has translated the French subjunctive as an imperative.

130 **done**: add *Respondit Symon: 'Petrus magis dicat quid cogitem ego.' Dixitque Petrus: 'Quid cogitet Symon me scire docebo dum quod cogitauerit fecero.'* LgA.
Simon: add *indignatus* LgA.

131 **horrible**: *tres grans* P2.

135 **thought**: *pensoit* P2; *MED thinken* v.2, sense 8, 'intend (malice)'. All GiL MSS have *wrought*, probably a misreading by an English scribe rather than a substitution by the translator.
only: only GiL.

138 **aungelles but fendes**: *anges diuins mes chiennins* P2.

139 **ye shull come**: *nous yrons* P2.

140 **bothe**[2]: add *Haec Leo* LgA.

141 **Egisippe**: *et Lin* P2, i.e. Linus.

146–8 **he enforced . . . meued hym**: *uisus est a circumstantibus caput agitare defunctus* LgA.

151 **speke**: add *ou autrement saichiez que* P2.

151–2 **ye . . . meue**: *le chief dun mort se meuue* P2.

166 **Marcell**: add *discipuli eius* LgA.

167 **will come**: *ingredi poterit* LgA.

168 **Seint Peter and Seint Paule**: *pol et puis pierre* P2, *Petrus* LgA.

173 **in the body**: *et canis quidem corpus eius non lesit* LgA.
into lytell: *a bien pou* P2, *penitus* LgA.

174 **withe**: *et mesmement* P2.

177–8 **that . . . Simon**: not in LgA; Vignay had omitted this information at 166.

186–7 **as Leon . . . capitaille**: *sicomme lin . . . capitole* P2, *turrim excelsam uel, secundum Linum, Capitolium conscendit* LgA.

187 **from pilour to pilour**: *de couronne en* (*de* P1) *couronne* P2, *coronatus lauro* LgA.

189 **gete**: *impetrer* P2, i.e. command.

190 **God**: only GiL.

194 **of hell**: *du diable* P2, *Sathane* LgA.

197 **necke**: *ceruel* P2, *ceruicibus* LgA.

199–200 **Ye . . . me**: *Suspecto animo me fecistis* LgA.

201 **and**: add *paulin* P2.

204 **Paulyn**: add *post passionem apostolorum* LgA.

210 **gate**: add *ad locum* LgA. The gate is the Porta Appia, and the church there is now called Domine Quo Vadis?.

216 **full . . . departinge**: only GiL.

221 **Thou art**: *Tune es* LgA.

228 **Timothee**[1]: add *de morte Pauli* LgA.

229 **batayles . . . ende**: *agones consummationis* LgA, 'the strife at their last end'.

232 **felawshippe**: *tombes* P2, *tourbes* P1; *MED* does not give the sense required here of a (hostile) crowd.

237–8 **This . . . art**: *Pax tecum* LgA.

239 **lambe**: *aigneaux* P2.

241 **And**: add *quant* P2.

249–50 **late . . . to me** *crucem meam girate* LgA.

252 **slayne, deliuer**: GiL has retained part of the French syntax: *vouloient occire . . . et deliurer.*

254 **Leon**: *Egesippus* LgA.

256–7 **and oure Lorde**: only GiL.

259 **in this wyse**: *Et dont pierre commenca a dire en la croix* P2, so and add *ut testatur idem Egesippus* LgA.

260 **right**: add *et hault* P2.

263 **and condicion**: *de la generation* P2.

264 **bowynge to the erth by effecte**: *proni in terram* (. . .) *effundi* LgA, 'spread out prone on the ground'; *by effecte*, translated from LgD, appears to have no real function.

265 **good, euell**: *dextrum, sinistrum* LgA.

267–9 **withe . . . of the**: *de tout lesperit par quoy je vif par quoy jentens par quoy ie ent[r]eprens les choses* P2, *spiritu toto quo uiuo, quo te intelligo, quo te interpello* LgA.

280 **.xv.**: *.xxv.* P2.

282 **after that as**: *selon ce que* P2.

286 **of this worlde**: only GiL.

287 **into**: *es portes de* P2.

288 **withe baners**: *luminis* LgA.

292 **shull write**: *mettons* P2.

293 **techithe in a storie**: *ut in quadam hystoria* (. . .) *legitur* LgA.

293–4 **that as Senek lokede and**: *que sicomme senecque* P2, not in LgA.

294–5 **the payne . . . hym**: *laboris sui* LgA.

299 **it faste**: *la* (. . .) *fort et souuent* P2; LD share the H1G reading *his fest/ fist*, probably derived from an early English copying error which E has intelligently corrected.

305 **whanne . . . childe**: not in LgA.

309 **witheinne the bathe**: *des .ij. bras dedens* P2.

314 **Gylyan**: *julien gal* P2, *Iulius Gallio* LgA, variant *Iulianus Gallio*, which is also in Graesse.

318 **stori of**: *dicte hystoire* P2, *eadem hystoria apocrypha* LgA.

324 **trauaile and payne**: *douleur et le nourry a sy grant trauail et curieusement* P2.

327 **of childe**: add *et crioit* P2.

330 **kynde**: add *ne ce nest pas chose a sauoir qui nest consentante a raison* P2.

334 **contrarie thingges**: *nature contraria* LgA.

338 **sorugh and**: only GiL.

339–40 **for . . . labour**: *puis je a peine alener ne auoir mon alaine* P2.

341 **brake**: *vomir* P2.

346 **suche one in**: *tel ne du* P2, i.e. 'born thus from'.

347 **fruit**: *fetus* LgA.

348 **in the creveis of a stone**: *testudini lapidum* LgA, 'in a stone vault'.
be well redde: *non leguntur* LgA.

351 **distruccion**: *succensio* LgA.
Troye: *rome* P2, *Troie* LgA.

351, 352 **.viij.**: *.vij.*P2.

353 **solempne garnement**: *habite enfle* P2, *turgido habitu* LgA, 'in a bombastic manner'.

354 **Holyade**: *Helyade* P1, *Iliadem* LgA.

356–7 **þat is . . . syngingges**: not in LgA.

357–8 **he wedded . . . husbonde**: *uirum in uxorem duxit, ipse a uiro ut uxor acceptus est* LgA, i.e. two separate men.

358 **not**: add *plus* P2.

362 **cursed**: only GiL.

364 **in an hole of a walle**: *en vne pierre creuse* P2, *in testitudine latitantem* LgA.

365–6 **toke . . . Lateren**: add *aussy comme alaite rayne* P2, *ut aliqui dicunt, ubi rana latuerat, Lateranensis a latente rana nomen accepit* LgA. Vignay mistranslated *latuerat*, 'lay hidden', as *alaite*, 'suckle'.

375 **Catacombes**: *catacumbas* LgA, originally the name of the subterranean cemetery of St Sebastian on the Appian Way; it was later taken as a plural and applied to other similar cemeteries.

378 **as they went**: *sicomme* P2.

389 **mayde**: add *paralitica* LgA.

390 **hadde . . . fete and**: *dissolutis renibus* LgA.

392 **praied**: add *sanitatem* LgA.

395 **sought**: add *soudainement* P2.

396–7 **Oure sheparde (. . .) and oure norissher**: *Je suys peue et nourrie et nostre* P2, *Pastor et nutritor noster* LgA. Vignay has taken *Pastor* and *nutritor* as 1 pr. sg. passive.

401 **Dialoge**: *liure* P2.

403 **consult**: add *et patricien de rome* P2.
to Patricien of Rome: only GiL.

403–4 **a lytell space of tyme**: *unius anni spatio* LgA.

404–6 **And after . . . rychesse**: *Quam dum ad iterandum thalamum etas et opes uocarent* LgA.

410 **complexcion**: *corps* P2, *conspersio corporis* LgA.

414 **she deserued to be**: *ne desserui elle pas pource que elle estoit enlaidie de ceste chose que elle ne feust* S.

415–16 **that . . . soule**: only GiL.

421 **hadde**: *haioit* P2.

422 **in a nyght**: only GiL.

423 **chaundelers** add *ante eius lectum* LgA.

434 **I come to you**: *Je vois ie voys* P2, *Venio, uenio* LgA.

436–7 **hym mervaylinge**: *en soy merueillant* P2.

442 **and**: add *fere* LgA.

444 **Leon**: add *uel Maximus* LgA.

451 **persecucion**: *persecuteur* P2.

458–60 s.w. renders Vignay's attempt at verse translation:

pol fut couronne dune espee.
pierre eust la croix reuersee.
neron fut duc sicomme len nomme.
le lieu fut la cite de rome.

460 **Rome**: add *Item alius: Ense sacrat Paulum par lux, dux, urbs cruce Petrum* LgA.

465 **furste the principalite**: *primatum* LgA.

84 ST PAUL APOSTLE

Maggioni, ch. LXXXV, p. 576; Dunn-Lardeau, ch. 85, p. 579.

3 **of Philip**: *in Philippis* LgA.

6–7 **he . . . wallys**: *per sportam a muro deponitur* LgA.

10 **there**: add *occisus* LgA.

14 **lyff**: add *qui estoit cheut dune haulte fenestre* P2.

Milite: *Mitilenem* LgA; whereabouts of this island is disputed, the main candidates being Malta and Mljet in Croatia; Voragine names Mytilene, the chief city of Lesbos.

15 **assailled . . . honde**: *manum eius inuasit* LgA.

15, 16 **she, her**: so SP1, masculine in P2.

17 **kynrede**: add *de cel homme* P2.

20 **was**[1]: *est* P2.

23 **prechinge**: add *sy que plusieurs foys il tenoit son sermon iusques a la nuyt* P2.

24 **praie**: here LgD and GiL omit a similar quotation from Remigius, Maggioni, 577–8 (27–8).

25–6 **not for that**: *toutes foys* P2, *etiam* LgA.

28 **suerly**: *libere* LgA.

35 **of**: add *Haec Ieronimus* LgA.

40 **hymselff**: i.e. itself.

41 **Paule**: add *circa uesperas* LgA.

50 **that was dede to**: *auec* P2.

51 **come and . . . gate**: *uiuens adesse pre foribus nuntiatur* LgA.

57, 58 **worldes**: *siecles* P2, *MED* sense 6 (b).

60–1 **Go . . . hym**: *Ergo militas illi regi?* LgA.

61 **I am fully withe hym**: *je y cheuauche* P2, *milito* LgA.

68 **any demaunde**: *autre demande* P2, *interrogatione* LgA; *MED* records 'interrogate' for *demaunden* v., but does not give this sense for the noun *demaunde*.

71 **that . . . before me**: *mihi autem uinctus* LgA.

72–3 **makest . . . foly**: *les acqueil auec toy* P2.

76 **fayle**: add *et qui mettent hors toute deffaulte* P2.

81 **his**: *Christi* LgA.

82 **gilty of his mageste**: *maiestatis reum* LgA; the reduced form of *laesae maiestatis* adopted from LgA by LgD and GiL is not recorded by *MED*; *lese majesty* is not recorded for English till 1536.

85–6 **whanne . . . Nero**: *proclamaret* LgA.

86 **amende . . . maners**: *oste ta maniere* P2, *Pone modum* LgA.

88 **defended**: *deffendent* P2.

94–5 **the deceiuour of wittes, the chaunger and the strangeler of thoughtes**: *sensuum alienatorem* (. . .) *mentium immutatorem* LgA.

the strangeler: *lestrangeur* P2; *MED* records neither 'estrange' nor the related agent noun; it appears s.w. concluded that *strangler* in the general sense 'destroyer' was intended.

96–7 **shall lyue**: *viuray* P2; T1 *beleue* shows that that scribe at least could be confused by variant spellings for 'live', 'believe'. See vol. 1, p. xiii.

100 **wete that**: add *apres la mort* P2.

105 **were there**: *le menoient* P2.

112 **abidinge, a true**: *bon et loyal* P2, *legitimus* LgA.

114–15 **and berie it**: (*gardez* P1) *en cel lieu ou ilz le mettront* P2, *Vos autem locum notate* LgA.

123 **thou hast wonne**: *meruisti* LgA.

124 **gate**: add *hostiense* P2, add *Ostiensi* LgA.

135 **in . . . contreye**: *patria uoce* LgA, 'in his own language'.

139 **she**: i.e. the head.

141 **it**[3]: *Christum uel Ihesum uel utrumque* LgA.

146–7 **of Paule**: *de morte Pauli* LgA.

148, 152 **bochers**: *boucher* P2.

151 **sorugh**: add *et sans contrainte* P2.

154 **plied**: *explicuit* LgA, 'unfolded', which Vignay mistranslated as *plia*. **blode**: add *et le lya* P2.

155–6 **whanne . . . bocher**: *reuerso militi carnifici dixit Lemobia* LgA.

158 **citee**: add *in ualle pugilum* LgA.

161–2 **more . . . sonne**: *fulgentes luce radientes* LgA, ending the speech here.

162 **and . . . kercheef**: *et protulit uelum* (. . .) *et monstrauit eis* LgA.

168 **and**[1]: only GiL.

170 **not ouercome** relates to **kinge**, *regis eterni et inuicti miles* LgA.

171 **wicked**: *eterna* LgA.

175 **many**: only GiL.

176 **Longis**: *Longinus magister* LgA.

177 **Paule**: add *et la virent .ij. hommes orans. cestoit lucas et titus et ou milieu pol estoit* P2.

178 **flee**: add *et pol se desapparut* P2.

184 **vale,** 187 **valey**: *valee, fosse* P2, *uallem, fouea* LgA; s.w. seems to take these to be the same.

200 **thanne**: *si come il plot a touz* S.

203 **Paule**: add *Hec Dionysius* LgA.

204 **Gregori**: add *de tours* P2, add *Turonensis, qui tempore Iustini iunioris claruit* LgA.

208 **purposed**: add *Et en appareillant le laps il disoit tousiours saint pol aide moy* P2.

214 **Seint**: only GiL. LgA begins: *Gregorius in registro: 'Ex catenis beati Pauli multa miracula demonstrantur* . . . and the quotation, from Gregory the Great, *Registrum epistolarum*, continues till 219 *gete*.

215 **Sum . . . asken**: *Et quant aucuns demandent* P2.

218 **laboure**: *demeure* P2.

220 **a**: *celle* P2, *eadem quoque* (. . .) *que supra dicta est* LgA.

221–2 **myn, my**: *noz* P2.

222 **prunelles**: *pupillis* LgA; *MED* has only one citation, for which the sense is 'small plum, (?) sloe'. It had early acquired the subsidiary sense 'pupil of the eye' in French.

224 **vyle clothes**: *lugubribus* LgA.

227 **debonayre . . . peple**: *gentium familiaris, consolator parentum* LgA.

230 **harpe**: *frestel* P2, a sort of flute.

232–3 **he . . . us**: *delessa touz les esperiz de laide fourme et nous* S, *spiritus deiformis omnes nos dereliquit* LgA; Vignay's understandable difficulties with the passage have been compounded by his misreading of *deiformis* as *deformis*.

234 **despised and wicked** go with **worlde**.

235 **al hys loue**: *son amy* P2.

236 **thi maister, thi fader, and alle thi loue**: *ton pere amy de mon maistre* P2, *pater tuus, magister, amator?* LgA.

242 **litell . . . lytell**: *modicus* LgA.

245 **hem**: add *ne qui expose les paraboles ne les signifiances des parolles diceulx* P2, *parabolarum et paradigmatum et eloquiorum ipsorum* LgA.

248 **of the**: *tuorum* LgA.

249 **the**: *nos* LgA.

250 **the noble**: *noz* P2.

252 **God by**: *dieu et* P2, not in LgA.

253 **Sothely . . . children**: *ne ne les exposeront* P2, *Vere ue hiis filiis* LgA.

254 **fader**: *pere* (*patribus* LgA) *de quoy toute lassemblee est priuee* P2.

255 **maister**: *maistres* P2.

258 **cours**: 'race', alluding to 2 Tim. 4: 7.

261 **glori and ioye and worship**: *gloire et honneur* P2.

266–7 **thi . . . Chirche**: *ta voix frestel des eglises hault sonnant* P2, *uocem tuam, fistula ecclesiarum et fistula altisona* LgA.

267 **þe**: add *plectre de ton* P2.

272 **serued**: *seruit* LgA.
he: i.e. Jerusalem.

273 **he**: i.e. Rome.

280 **shul fle to**: *ce seroit* P2.

281 **hym**: *eis* LgA, i.e. the friends.

282 **Paule**: add *et le loue moult en disant ainsy. Cil na de riens folie qui a lame de pol vng personnage noble de vertus* P2.

285–6 **but more . . . after**: *Et qui plus est et des anges ne nous recordons pas pource* (*pour* P1) *ceste chose que nous ne dions bien apres* P2, *sed etiam, quod est amplius, angelorum? Nec tamen idcirco reticebimus, quin potius pauca dicemus* LgA.

Here GiL omits Maggioni, 586 (191–4), Dunn-Lardeau, 588–9.

287 **but**: add *se* P2.

292 **to God**: not in LgA.
alle the worlde: *aussy comme en volant la terre et la mer de grece et toute la region estrange* P2.

299–300 **And vnnethes . . . dethes**: *Vis autem eius innumeras tibi ostendi mortes* LgA; Vignay took *Vis* as *Vix* and altered the rest of the clause.

302 **more . . . deluge**: *plus cruel fleuue qui surondoit par deluge* P2, *multo seuiore inundante diluuio* LgA.

303 **that pershed . . . worlde**: *tout le monde qui perissoit* P2, *uniuersum orbem periclitantem* LgA.

304 **bordes**: *tables* P2. GiL loses the play on the two senses of *table*, 'plank', 'writing-tablet'.

305 **shippe**: i.e. the epistles.
that he made: not in LgA; *he*, here refers to Paul, contrasted with Noah.
a place: *vng lieu* P2, *non uno loco* LgA; it is hard to tell what sense the rest of this sentence made to Vignay and s.w. following the loss of this negative.

307 **thei**: *les tables* P2.

308 **In this doinge**: i.e. in writing his epistles.

309 **to folue aungels**: *imitatores*
in conuersacion: only GiL.

310–11 **hadde . . . ayenne**: *coruum recipiens coruum rursum emisit* LgA; i.e. it was still a raven. Voragine is contrasting the changes wrought in men by the 'ark' of Paul's writings with the unchanging natures of the beasts in Noah's ark.

313 **the egles**: not in LgA.

314 **cruelte**: add *et mist en eulx la debonnairete du saint esperit* P2, add (*et*) *mansuetudinem spiritus introduxit* LgA.

315 **Some folke**: *omnes* LgA.

322 **deliuered**: add *le filz de* P2; on the rescue of Lot, Abraham's brother's son, see Gen. 14: 12–16.

328 **the well**: *les puis* P2; see Gen. 26: 12–22.

328–9 **not . . . beten**: *ne veoit pas les puis. mes veoit ses gens tuez et agravantez de pierres et ne batoit pas tant seullement son propre corps* S, *non puteos cernens lapidibus obrutos, sed proprium corpus, non solum, sicut ille, cedebat* LgA.

333 **debonairte**: *longanimitate* LgA.

337 **moche tempest**: *moult tempestes* P2, *temptationes mille* LgA.

339–40 **of the hondes . . . mouthe**: *ex dyaboli faucibus* LgA.

340 **ennobelisshed**: *decoratus* LgA, 'honoured'; not in *MED*; see note on *ennobled* at 26.282.

345–6 **and who was witheoute eny stiringe as the dede body to the dede**: i.e. he responded to beauty no more than a dead man would to a corpse.

348 **gret agonye**: *sa lignie* P2, *agone* LgA.

349 **bright and**: only GiL.

350 **euery day**: *souuent* P2.

351 **alle**[1]: not in P2, *innumeras* LgA.

351–2 **and alle . . . companies**: *et contre les compagnies* P2, not in LgA.

352 **more sufferable**: *plus dur* P2, *tolerantior* LgA.

355–6 **Job . . . hospitaler**: *Job si estoit grant hospitalite* P2, *illi erat magna hospitalitas* LgA.

gret besinesse: *cure* P2.

360 **bestes**: *ouailles* S.

361 **posseded**: *poursuioit* P2, *possidens* LgA.

362 **nedes**: *besongneux* P2.

362–3 **sum . . . writinge**: *aucun autre lieu* P2, *alicubi* LgA.

364–5 **and rotones . . . Iob**: *atque uulnera seuos sancto Job inferebant dolores* LgA.

and akinge: only GiL.

366 **the prisone**: *chartres* P2, not in LgA.

367 **straungers**: add *a cetero* (. . .) *orbe* LgA.

367–8 **as moche . . . other**: *sollicitudinem quam pro ecclesiis, ustionem quam pro scandalizatis singulis perferebat* LgA.

370 **ademond**: *MED adamaunt* records no spelling in *ond* (confined to E). L *ayemant* is probably nearer to s.w.'s spelling; *MED s.v. aimant* has only two instances, spelt *aymont, aymant*; P2 has *aymant.*

372 **hardefull**: *mesfaisant* P2. Not recorded by *MED*, perhaps for *harmful.*
Paule: add *de singulis quibusque labentibus* LgA.
suete: *iuges* LgA, 'continual'.

374 **thanne . . . creature**: *que de plaies en chascun homme* P2, *Omnique muliere parturiente* LgA.

375 **I haue bore**: *parturio* LgA.

378 **only**: only GiL.
his kynne: *ses parens* P2, *pereuntibus* LgA.

379 **he wolde**: *ne voult* P2, *uoluit* LgA.

383 **gouerned hymselff**: *se tournoit* P2, *uersatus est* LgA, 'conducted his life'.
middes: add *strepitu* LgA.

385–7 **and withe . . . prechinge**: *Il laissoit aucunes fois la viande de fourment pour lestude de preschier* P2, *ac necessario quidem indulgens cibo, feruenti studio predicandi* LgA.

388 **not only**: *vng ne* P2.

391–2 **of whiche . . . obeyen**: *in quibus magnificum predicamus, quia* (. . .) *obediuit* LgA, 'in which things we preach that he is magnificent, because he obeyed'.

398 **he purged it**: *se combatoit* P2, *purgauit* LgA.
yet . . . heuene: *nondum celum iste sortitus est* LgA, 'he was not yet destined for heaven'.

400 **and**: *qui estoit encore* P2.
A Lorde: only GiL.

401 **we see**: only GiL.
to be: *sont* P2.

402–7 **Ne . . . nature**: *Non enim aliam est ille sortitus naturam nec dissimilem nactus animam nec alterum habitans mundum, sed in eadem terra eademque regione, sub eisdem etiam legibus nutritus et moribus cunctos qui nunc sunt homines uel fuerunt animi uirtute transcendit* LgA.

407–8 **this thinge, only**: the juxtaposition *hoc solum* in LgA makes the sense clearer.

410 **recompensed . . . guerdon**: *etiam quod uirtutem ipsam pro mercede pensauit* LgA.
Here GiL omits Maggioni, 590 (244–5), Dunn-Lardeau, 592.

413 **for grace**: *ob studium* LgA.

414 **a gret feste full of ioye**: *bonorum oblectamenta* LgA, 'the delights of good things'.

416–17 **and in hys reste**: *Et apres le repos* P2, *post laborem* LgA.

417 **of rest**: only GiL.

418 **for her frendes**: *contre leur anemis* P1 (P2S have various errors).

421–3 **he refused . . . erthe**: *Et ne me dictes pas quil couuoitast loyers gens effors peccunes prouinces puissaunces. toutes ces choses il reputoit autant comme fil daraignes* P2.

426–7 **tho thingges . . . was of**: *ce que greigneur chose est Il vsoit de* P2, *quod enim erat maius omnibus,* (. . .) *fruebatur* LgA.

428 **blessed of alle**: *beatiorem* (. . .) *cunctis* LgA.

429–30 **ne aungeles ne archaungelles**: not in LgA.

430 **man**: *ou du nombre* P2, *immo etiam ex numero* LgA.

434 **hym**: add *peine* P2.

435 **rewme**: add *ce luy estoit promesse* P2.

437 **And so**: *il desprisoit si* S.

437–8 **men . . . leef**: *len seult despriser vng pou derbe pourrie* P2.

439 **as in greuaunce**: only GiL.

448 **He was enbraced withe right gret wepingges**: *Il estoit embrase de tres grant pleur* P2, *Merore* (. . .) *maximo urebatur* LgA; from the context s.w. may have taken LgD *embrase*, 'inflamed', as though from *MED embracen*, sense 3b(a) 'afflict', rather than *embrasen*, of which *MED* records only seven instances, five of them from Lydgate.

449 **Who is desclaundred and I am not brent**: *Quis scandalizatur et ego non uror* LgA; *MED disclaundren* sense 2 'bring into disgrace', correctly represents the Latin.
he canne saye: *se aucun dit* P2.

450 **and yet**: only GiL.

452 **it . . . greuaunce**: *se dueillent plus* P2.

455 **other . . . familiers**: *estranges* P2.

455–6 **for right as**: *Quemadmodum* LgA, 'to the extent that'.

465 **preciouste**: From this point GiL omits substantially, as follows: Maggioni, 591–7 (269–73, 283–8, 295–340, 344–9), Dunn-Lardeau, 594–9.

465–6 **and more precious**: only GiL.

469 **one body**: *non corporel* P2.

478 **basketis**: *peaulx* P2.

479 **trouth**: add *les romains* P2.

480 **Iudayes**: *Indos* LgA.

483 **ledde**: add *lye* P2.
the Grete See: *tam uastum pelagus* LgA.

484 **to see an empire**: *in maximum imperium* LgA.

492–3 **bete . . . wordes**: *les* (*le* P1) *batoit il de parolles et les reprenoit* (*prenoit* P1) P2, *tamen uerberantes ipsos sermone capientem* LgA.

493 **and yet**: *dont pour certain* P2.
and techinge of hym: only GiL.

495 **seinge and**: not in LgA.
techinge and spekinge: *parler habondamment* P2.

496–7 **token . . . enemies**: *prenoient ilz en eulx plus certaine joyeusete et en estoient plus hastiuement portez contre leurs aduersaires* P2, *abundanter auderent sine timore uerbum dei loqui.' Tunc certiorem alacritatem et ipse capiebat ac uehementius in aduersarios ferebatur* LgA; Vignay transferred *abundanter* to the previous clause.

498 **diuerse maneres and withe**: not in LgA.

500–1 **to what thinge . . . thing**: *a quelconques chose que elle fut esmeue elle se transportoit tantost a jcelles* P2, *quibuscumque fuisset admota ad se eos continue transferebat* LgA; 'whomever it was directed towards, it at once brought them to him'. Vignay took *quibuscumque* to be 'things' rather than 'people'.

501 **that she vndertoke**: *ceulx qui le reprenoient* P2, *Impugnatores* LgA.
pastoure: *pabulum* LgA; the English is a possible if ambiguous spelling for *pasture*.

85 SEVEN BROTHERS

Maggioni, ch. LXXXVI, p. 598; Dunn-Lardeau, ch. 86, p. 600.

1 **weren**: add *filz* P2.
Felice: *felicite* P2, *Felicitatis* LgA; also at 18 and 21.

2 GiL has omitted *Felix* from the list, changed the order somewhat, and followed P2SZ in *Aluanie* for *siluain* P1, *Siluanus* LgA.

7–8 **betraie . . . not**: only GiL.

11 **bethe sadde and**: only GiL.

12–13 **his loue**: *luy* P2.

13 **knightes to**: *en lamour de* P2.

15 **paumes**: *paumees* P2, *alapis* LgA; *alapus*, a slap on the cheek or ear; *paumees* also means 'slaps'. Probably s.w. took this as *paumes*, 'palms (of the hand)', and a copying error *pannes* was repeated by most of the MSS; L substituted *dyvers paynes*.

24 **prison**: *carne* LgA.
frendes: *parens* P2, *parentes* LgA; s.w. has apparently taken this as the later extended sense 'kinsfolk', *MED frend* sense 4.

24–5 **in prison**: *auant* P2.

26 **brought**: *enfantast* Z.

27 **seigh**: *sauoit* P2.

30 **rightwisely**: *par droicture* P2, *Recte* LgA.

31 **so ofte desired dethe**: *a este tant de foys estaincte* P2; L *suffred* may be original or an intelligent correction.
desiringly: *MED* has only one citation, for a1500.

35 **.C.l. and .x.**: *.C. et .x.* S, *CLX* LgA.

86 ST THEODORA

Maggioni, ch. LXXXVIII, p. 611; Dunn-Lardeau, ch. 87, p. 601.

1 **Theodore**: *Theodora* LgA.

8 **enchauntoure**: *magam* LgA, and so feminine including pronouns to 18.

11 **he ioyned . . . to her**: *malefica adiunxit* LgA.

23 **beaute of my name**: *regart de ma beaute* P2, *aspectum decoris mei* LgA.

28 **was**: *elle auoit* P2.

34 **oute**: add *comam suam precidit et* LgA.

38 **Theodore**: *Theodorum* LgA.

40 **oxen**, 46 **cameles**: this metamorphosis, which goes back to LgA, remains unexplained.

41–2 **gretly dredinge**: *ploroit moult fort et se doubtoit* P2.

43 **erly**: only GiL.

44–5 **waye . . . Paule**: *uia martyrii Petri* (*et Pauli* Re) *apostoli* LgA.

58 **wicked woman**: *putain* P2; likewise at 86–7 below.

60 **that be dredfull and tremble**: *a doubter qui sont tremblables* P2, *tremendas* LgA.

61–2 **saye . . . I**: *non dicas quia ego sum* LgA, 'you can say I don't exist'.

67 **another . . . childe**: *vng* (*alterum* LgA) *qui gisoit en lostel* P2.

72 **toke . . . childe**: *mist lenfant entre les bras* P2.

73–4 **and bade . . . shame and**: *Illa autem eiecta per* LgA.

78 **al my ioie**: *ma lumiere* P2.

85 **and**: *car les dyables* P2, *demones* LgA.

89 **worshipped her**: *laouroit P2*, *eum* (. . .) *adorabant* LgA.

99 **thou dedest**: *fecit* LgA.

103 **hys bretherin and**: only GiL.

107 **cleped**: since elsewhere consistently spelled *clipped*, this is doubtless scribal and should have been emended.

117 **a**: add *seule* P2.

121 **The**: *ses* P2, *Ces* S, *VII* LgA.

127 **that . . . defamed**: *de ta fille* P2.

128 **they toke awaye**: *osta* P2.

129 **seen or**: only GiL.

87 ST MARGARET

Maggioni, ch. LXXXIX, p. 616, Dunn-Lardeau, ch. 88, p. 605.

9 **bounde**: *ancelle* P2.

18 **Wost thou thanne**: *dont scez tu* P2, *Vnde scis* LgA.

19 **Ye**: only GiL.

20 **might**: *pena* LgA.

23 **mankinde**: add *sed nunc eum in eternum uiuere affirmaret* LgA.

25 **voyde and**: not in LgA.

26 **goddes**: add *ut bene tibi sit* LgA.

28 **obeyen**: *craignent* P2.

31 **the loue of**: only GiL.

33–5 In LgD and LgA she is put onto the *eculee* first and then beaten.

34 **bete**: add *primo uirgis deinde pectinibus ferreis usque ad nudationem ossium* LgA.

38 **beleue**: *mescreandise* P2.

38–9 **yet . . . thiselff**: *croy aumoins orendroit* P2.

42 **hounde**: add *leo* LgA.

49 **so cruelly vexed her and**: only GiL.

52–3 **opened . . . mouthe**: *luy mist la bouche soubz la teste et la langue soubz les piez* P2.

53–4 **and by . . . made**: *mais quant il la vouloit engloutir. elle fist le signe de la croix et* P2.

55 **sounde**: add *Istud autem quod dicitur de draconis deuoratione et ipsius crepatione, apocryphum et friuolum reputatur* LgA.

60 **here**: *caput* LgA.

61 **thou enemye**: *superbe demon* LgA.

62 **and bete hym**: not in LgA.

63 **bete**: *uinceret* LgA.

67 **whi**: add *uenisset. Qui se uenisse ait ut sibi consuleret quod monitis presidis obediret. Coegit quoque ut diceret cur* LgA.

69 **to hem . . . vertues**: *contre les hommes plains de vertu* P2.

70 **putte abacke . . . deposed**: *deboute* P2.

84 **to her goddes**: not in LgA.

89 **and the . . . hideous**: *et fist tresfort temps* P2, *cunctis uidentibus* LgA.

96 **deuoutely and**[1]: not in LgA.
deuoutely[2]: *doulcement* P2, *deuote* LgA.

98–9 **withoute . . . cristendom**: *sans nulle bleceure et demourast la femme toute saine* P2, *illesam* LgA.

101 **and . . . Lorde**: not in P2, *Surgensque ab oratione* LgA.

104 **.xij.**: *.xiij.* P2.
Iuill: *Augusti ut in eius hystoria inuenitur. Alibi legitur quod III idus Iulii* LgA.

106–8 **sadde . . . pacience**: *ferme de la paour de dieu ennoblie de religion aornee de componction arrousee donnestete loable par sangle pacience* P2, *timoris dei instantia predita, religione comperta, compunctione profusa, honestate laudabilis, patientia singularis* LgA.

108 **thing**: add *a la religion crestienne* P2.

109 **frende and loue**: *aime* P2, *dilecta* LgA; *aime* and *amie* are virtually indistinguishable in P2 and other MSS.

88 ST ALEXIS

Maggioni, ch. XC, p. 621; Dunn-Lardeau, ch. 89, p. 609.

The scribes and probably the translator seem to think this is *Calixt* rather than *Alexius*. Even L, who always begins this name with *A*, usually ends it with *t*. The spellings in E, G, and L are as follows: Rubric *Calixte* E, *Kalixte*

G, *Aalixt* L; 1 *Calixte* EG, *Aalixt* L; 42 *Calex* E, *Calixte* G, *Alex* L; 56 *Calixt* E, *Alex* G, *Alixt* L; 80 *Calixt* E, *Alix* GL; concluding rubric *Calixt* E, *Kalixte* G, not in L. H1 has *Calixte* changed to *Alexien* in rubric with *Alexus* in margin and *Seynt Alexis* above column; it also has *Alexis* in another hand above the column on f. 192ra; at 42 and 56 H1 has *Calex* and at 80 *Calix*, all with *C* marked for deletion.

1 **Eufemyen**: add *Romani* LgA.

4 **clothes . . . and of**: only GiL.

8 **was**: add *de ce propos et* P2.

9 **relygion**: *region* P2, *religionis* LgA.

11 **continence and**: only GiL.

12 **scole**: *ars liberaux* P2.

16 **in the loue and**: only GiL.

17 **of virgines**: *et uirginite* P2.

18 **all . . . hadde**: *les aornemens que il auoit* P2, *caput baltei quo cingebatur* LgA.

19 **the**^{1}: *a dieu* P2.
the^{2}: *nous* P2.

20 **went**: add *ad mare* LgA.

27–8 **that men . . . lyued**: *il retenoit ce qui luy suffisoit* P2.

34 **for thi loue**: only GiL.

35 **ayein**: add *au pere* P2.

36 **wyse**: *lieu* P2.

40 **allone**: add *comme turtre* P2.

41 **my**: add *tresdoulx* P2.

42 **.xv.**: *.xvij.* P2.

42–3 **in the citee aforesayd (. . .) in the porche witheoute**: *en lestre deuant dit* P2, *in predicto atrio* LgA.

49 **witheoute**: add *en* P2.

56 **sayde**: add *intra se* LgA.

57 **I will seke no further**: *nec alteri onerosus ero* LgA.

60–1 **for the loue of God**: only GiL.

62 **borde**: add *sy que dieu daigne auoir pitie du tien pelerin* P2.

64 **euery day**: only GiL.

65 **borde**: add *et ordonna pour son propre ministre* P2.
amentised: *amegrissoit* P2; this should have been emended to *anientised*

(as at 61.168 and 174.178); *ni* and *m* are often indistinguishable in these MSS, and indeed in this case L was sufficiently misled to give *aventysyd*. *MED amentisen*, 'diminish', gives only one citation, which is for H2 from this instance, taken from Rösler, 'Die Fassung der Alexius-legende'. These instances belong to *MED s.v. anientisshen*, 'bring to nought' etc., which recognizes spellings in *-is(s)en*. It also seems likely that the one *MED* instance of *amentissement* is a similar case, from *Letters of Queen Margaret of Anjou and Bishop Beckington and Others*, ed. C. Munro (Camden Society, 86/91 (1863).

67 **water**: *les laueures* P2, *aquam utensilium* LgA.
hym[2]: *le chef* P2.

67–8 **in scorne**: not in P2, *et multas ei iniurias irrogabant* LgA.

69 **.xviij.**: *.xvij.* P2.

73 **herde**: add *in sanctuario LgA*.

76 **Praiethe**: *Querite* LgA.

79 **Effemyen**: add *Requisitus ille se nihil scire de hoc dicebat* LgA, so and add further *Et dont les empereurs archadien et honnore auecques leuesque Innocent vindrent en la maison de eufemien* P2.

81 **youre**: *nostre* P2.

87 **emperoure**: *empereurs* P2.

93 **peple**: add *et patre ipsius* LgA.

97 **cried . . . saide**: *super filii sui corpus corruens exclamabat* LgA.

101 **counsaill**: *consolationem* LgA.

103–4 **madde . . . herselff**: *leonesse rompt la roys aussy rompi elle ses vestemens et tiroit ses cheueux* P2.

104 **hondes**: *oculos* LgA.

105 **saide**: *pource que elle ne pouoit aller au corps saint pour la grant multitude des gens elle crioit disant* P2.

108 **eyen**: add *pour quoy nous as tu ce fait* P2.

109 **me**: *nous* P2.
many a tyme: only GiL.

112 **full mekely**: only GiL.

113–14 **as . . . loue**: *se laissoit cheoir et recheoir sus le corps et maintenant elle estendoit ses bras sus luy et manioit a ses mains le voult de luy semblable a ange et le baisoit et crioit* P2.

116 **my**: add *seul* P2.

117 **rebuked . . . smiten hym**: *le lesdengoient et le feroient de joees* P2, 'insulted him and slapped his face'.

121 **departed**: *desolee* P2, 'left alone'. *MED* does not precisely record this as a sense; perhaps the nearest is 'separated'.

126 **worshipfully**: *honnorable* P2.

126, 133 **emperour**: *empereurs* P2.

129 **seke . . . bere**: *malade atouchoit au corps saint* P2.

135 **they**: *imperatores* LgA.

136 **place**: *places* P2, *plateis* LgA; *MED* does not record the sense 'public street' for *place*, which s.w. here adapts as 'main square'. See too 166.64.

141 **the chirche of Seint Boneface the marter**: now the church of Sant'Alessio, on the Aventine.

147 **.xvij.**: *XVI* LgA.
.iiijC.: *.ccc.* P2.

89 ST PRAXEDES

Maggioni, ch. XCI, p. 627; Dunn-Lardeau, ch. 91, p. 627.

1 **Seint Praxedes**: *Praest vierge* P2.

2 **Seint**: add *nouat et de saint* P2.
was: so P2, plural in P1 and LgA.

3 **the**[3]: *moult de* P2.

5 **.C.lx.**: *CLXV* LgA, variant *CLX*.

6 **Marke Antoyne**: *Marc antonin neron* P2, *Marcho Aurelio et L. Vero* LgA, variant *Marcho Antonino Nerone*.

90 ST MARY MAGDALEN

Maggioni, ch. XCII, p. 628; Dunn-Lardeau, ch. 90, p. 614.

17 **more, more**: only GiL.

20 **here in erthe**: *illec et ailleurs* P2.

23 **came**: *demoura derriere* P2.

26 **of that londe**: *du soleil* P2.

27 **verrey**: not in LgA.

29 **verrey pride**: *droicture orgueilleuse* P2.

33 **of**: add *sept* P2.

37 **suster**: add *qui disoit* P2.

40 **and**: add *cuius amore Martham* LgA.

43 **these suete wordes**: *ce tresdoulz et benoit mot* P2.

44 **But**: *Nam* LgA.

44–5 **it . . . chaumbrere**: *ce fut marthe qui le dit. Et ceste fut sa chamberiere* P2, *illa fuit Martha et hec eius famula* LgA, i.e. the former was Martha (who had the flux) and the latter the maidservant (who said the words).

46 **Lorde**: add *lacrimis* LgA.

48 **and was the furste that**: *toute la premiere. qui* P2. Punctuation and capitalization in H1GL (E has none here) show that they wrongly place this with the next clause, as suggested by s.w.'s addition of *and.*

52 **sepulcre**: add *et les disciples sen partirent* P2.

53 **she . . . aposteles**: *et apostolorum apostolam fecit* LgA.

56 **of that contre**: *des contrees de Judee* P2.

65 **gouernaunce**: *gouuernail* P2, *gubernator* LgA.

71 **discrete tunge**: *facie serena* LgA.

76–7 **were . . . withe**: *espiroit* P2, *uerbi dei spiraret odorem* LgA.

80 **reproued**: *contredit* P2, *dissuasit* LgA.

83 **pore seruauntes**: *poures* P2, *sanctos* LgA.

84 **and for threst**: only GiL.
colde: add *Addiditque minas nisi marito suo persuaderet ut sanctorum inopiam subleuaret* LgA.

86–8 **and manaced . . . repent her**: not in LgA.

89–90 **the thridd . . . visage**: *sapparut tierce foys par nuyt obscure a ycelle et a son mary froncant et yree et a visaige de feu* (add *ac si tota domus arderet* LgA) *et dit* P2.

93 **full**: add *de diuerses viandes* P2.

94 **perisshe**: add *de fam* P2, add *fame et siti* LgA.
Thou lyest: *Te gis tu* P2, i.e. a question.

96 **lyghtly**: only GiL.

98 **longe**: add *eis benefacere* LgA.

99 **sighed**[1]: add *et tremeret* LgA.

100 **and trembeled**: not in LgA.

101–2 **am sore aferde**: *en ay paour* P2, *pauere non desino* LgA, 'I can't stop trembling'.

102 **aferde**: add *quen ferons nous* P2.

106 **to . . . prince**: only GiL.

108 **lawe**: *fidem* LgA.

110 **oure**: *mei* LgA.

113–14 **For that it shall not abide**: *Propter hoc* (. . .) *non remanebit* LgA, 'it won't be that which causes delay'.

118 **merite**: *ueritas* LgA.

120 **yef God will**: only GiL.

121 **come**: add et *quant tu reposeras ie reposeray* P2.

128 **wicked**: *antiquus* LgA.

150 **Sufferithe . . . sufferithe**: *Parcite* (. . .) *parcite* LgA.

153–4 **yef . . . ayenne**: *estre respiree* P2.

157 **deuoured**: add *des belues de mer* P2.

166–7 **her and the childe**: *elle conceust et morust en lenfantement. Et sy conuient que ce que elle conceust qui est ne perisse car il nest nul qui le nourrisse* P2.

180 **to yeue lyff**: *de donner* P2, *dona dare* LgA.

180–1 **whom . . . youe**: *ce quil a donne et de restablir ce quil a oste* P2.

181 **al**: *ton* P2.

184 **preched**: add (*et*) *miracula fecit* LgA.

185 **places**: *locum* LgA.

187 **toke . . . and**: only GiL.

193 **whanne . . . goo**: only GiL.

194–5 **they come**: *applicuisset* LgA.

195 **they founde**: *il vit* S.

196 **come thedir**: *yssy de la nef* P2.

209 **an harde**: only GiL.

210 **in the sight of God**: only GiL.

212 **benignely serued me**: *acompli seruice de chamberiere* P2.

217 **suffered dethe**: *souffry et fut mort* P2.

226 **her**^{2}: add *pieds* P2, add *pedibus eius cum lacrimis* LgA.

235 **loue**: *contemplationis* LgA.
right . . . in: *vng tresaspre* P2.

241–2 **atte eueri Houre of the dai**: *a chascune heure canonial* P2, *septem horis canonicis* LgA.

248 **bowshotes**: *toises* P2, *stadia* LgA. A toise is about six feet, a stadium about a furlong.

256 **gret**: *audaci* LgA.

257–8 **his . . . bounde**: *ceperunt eius crura resolui* LgA.

272 **that . . . of**: *de marie* P2.

273 **named**: *renommee* P2.
and wosshe: not in LgA.

278–9 **witheoute . . . felawship**: *sans congnoissance de nul* P2; cf. 316, where the same phrase is correctly translated *withoute knowlage of any creature*.

283 **me**: add *de nostre seigneur* P2.

292 **oratorie**: add *solus* LgA.

295 **hyght**: add *stans in medio angelorum* LgA.

296 **And**: add *sicomme* P2.

297 **Come hedyr myn owne fader**: *Accede huc, pater, propius* LgA.

300–1 **as . . . sonne**: *ut facilius solis radios quam ipsius faciem intueri quis posset* LgA.

302 **body**: add *et le sang* P2.

306 **amonge hem**: *des entrans la* P2.

310 **after sum bokes and**: *uel secundum quosdam libros* LgA.
well: *assez* P2.

311 **for**: *Et* P2, *enim* LgA.

313 **that for sorugh . . . felt**: *et tedio quod habebat* LgA.

316–17 **in euery Houre**: *aux .vij. heures* P2.

320 **one**: add *et elle la vesti* S.

321–2 **and . . . Lorde**: *eleuatis in oratione manibus iuxta altare* LgA.

324 **.lxxj.**: *DCCLXIX* LgA.

326 **chirches**: add *et moult de monstiers* P2.

329 **suerte**: *compaignie* P2.

331 **sepulture**: add *car le sepulchre* P2, add *cuius sculptura* LgA.

336 **myle**: *lieue* P2.

341 **frendes**: *parentibus* LgA.

342 **suete**: *piis* LgA.

346 **sacrement**: *uiaticum* LgA.

348–9 **were . . . see**: *naufragium pertulit* LgA.

360 **husbond**: add *sen alla et* P2.

362 **of dedly synne and**: only GiL.

365 **delite**: add *deuant ces autres* P2.

365–6 **thei . . . hym**: *de iehan dient il quil lennobli* P2.

367 **delite**: add *Hec autem falsa et friuola reputantur* LgA.

368–9 **chirche . . . Mauudelein**: *monasterium Vizeliacum* LgA.

369 **be . . . pilgrimage**: only GiL.
her body: *corpus beate Marie Magdalene* LgA.

373 **and . . . clerely**: only GiL.

375 **of goodnesse**: only GiL.

378 **prison**: *fers* P2, 'irons'.

385 **he . . . here**: *non solum non facere, sed nec audire uolebat* LgA.

389 **woman**: add *lugubres gerens oculos* LgA.

392 **merites**: *prieres* P2.

399 **withe hem**: *es cieulx* (*ciex* P1) *a loenges* P2.

91 ST APOLLINARIS

Maggioni, ch. XCIII, p. 643; Dunn-Lardeau, ch. 92, p. 627.

1 **sent**: add *ab eo* LgA.

4–5 **wold haue made hym to do sacrifice to Iupiter**: *fut mene au temple Jupiter pour sacrifier* P2.

11 **and . . . heled**: *ut* (. . .) *curaret* LgA.

12 **deef**: *muet* P2.

12–13 **he . . . hym**: *domum ingrederetur, puella quedam immundum spiritum habens* LgA.

15 **thorugh**: *hors de* P2.

17 **ayeinst this enemye**: *super mutum* (. . .) *et curatus fuisset* LgA.
.v.Ml.: *.vC.* P2.

22 **they sene . . . Crist**: *il preschoit encores ihesu crist tres fermement* P2.

32 **and . . . anone**: not in P2, in LgA.

35–6 **prouost of the iugement**: *prefectum pretorii* LgA.

39 **to be hangged**: *tendre* P2.

41 **woundes**: add *qui estoient nouuelles* P2.

48 **the tempest of the see**: *periculum tempestatis* LgA.
and the clerkes withe hym: *auec .ij. clers* P2.
.CC.: *duobus* LgA.

49 **the .CC.**: *ipsos* LgA.

54 **hem that were**: *son filz qui estoit* P2.

55 **kepinge**: *garde* P2, *predio* LgA, 'estate'.

57 **he shulde sacrifice**: *satisfaciat* LgA, variant *sacrificaret*.

58 **For**: add *non* LgA.

59 **and**: *sed* LgA.

60 **yef hem luste**: *silz se courroucent* P2.

61 **Domestenis**: *Demosthenes patricius* LgA.

62–4 **they, hem, thei**: singular LgA.

63 **of Iewes and**: not in LgA.

65 **.viij.**: *.vij.* P2.

67 **aboute . . . Vaspasyen**: *sub Vespasiano qui cepit circa annos domini LXX* LgA.

68 **The**: *Apolinaire* P2.

71 **vertues**: add *a eulx qui croioient ihesucrist* P2.

72–3 **tormentes, but he, perfite in the loue of Ihesu Crist, shewed gret miracles**: *batemens de flaiaulx. Et son corps ia viel fut desrompu par felons et redoubtez tourmens. Mais pource que les bons crestiens ne tremblassent de ses trauaulx. il parfist en la vertu du nom ihesucrist les dapostre* (*signa apostolica* LgA) P2.

76 **heled . . . infirmitees**: *gary les enfermes de mortel maladie* P2, *dissoluta morbo sanat pestifero membra* LgA, 'healed the damaged limbs of one sick with a plague'.

80 **that . . . tormentis:** *qui estoies ja reffroidy par aage eschauffe* (add *constanter* LgA) *par peines* P2.

92 ST CHRISTINA

Maggioni, ch. XCIV, p. 646; Dunn-Lardeau, ch. 93, p. 630.

1 **Tiry**: there seem to have been two saints Christina, one of whom was said to have been martyred at Tyre in Phoenicia, the other in the lake Bolsena area. Tiro is recorded in some accounts as a settlement on the hill of Civita not far from the lake, destroyed in the late eighth century. Voragine places his saint in Italy. It is likely that accounts of the two have become confused. See Boureau, 1296–7 and Maggioni (2007), 1589.

4 **her fader**: *ses parens* P2.

6 **dredde**: *abhorrebat* LgA.

18 **vncunynge**: add *de la verite* P2.

19 **thre . . . God**: only GiL.

29 **seest . . . faylen**: *ceulx qui me batent deffaillent* P2.

30 **and strength**: only GiL.

40 **and so she was**: only GiL.

57 **the name of**: not in LgA.

58 **my name**: *me* LgA.

68 **terre**: *resine* S.

86 **Art . . . serpentes**: *nestu pas enchanteur? esmeuz ces bestes* P2.

100 **is**: *estoit* P2.

93 ST JAMES THE GREATER

Maggioni, ch. XCV, p. 650; Dunn-Lardeau, ch. 94, p. 633.

1 **preched**: add *apres* P2.

2 **resureccion**: *ascensionem* LgA.

5 **.xj.**: *.ix.* P2.

6 **ix.**: *.vij.* P2.

9–10 **his . . . came**: *enuoya philete son disciple* P2.

11 **alle**: *Iudeis* LgA.

12 **hym**[1]: add *raisonnablement* P2.

20 **a couer of hys hede**: *son cueurechief* P2.
sayde: add *Dis luy que il prengne ce cueurechief et que il die:* P2.

20–1 **O Lorde, lefte up (. . .) vnbynde**: *Nostreseigneur esdrece (. . .) deslie* P2, i.e. indicative.

21–2 **he hadde sayde**: *de sudario tactus est* LgA.

22–3 **he . . . gladde**: *solutus a uinculis. magicis artibus Hermogenis insultauit et ad Iacobum properauit* LgA.

24 **Hermogenes**: add *fut courroucie et* P2.

25 **Iames**: add *uinctum* LgA.

27 **dresse hem ayeinst**: *insultare* LgA.

28 **and to cryen**: only GiL.

36 **me**: add *lie mais* P2.

38 **hym**:add *ainsy* P2, add *sic uinctum* LgA.

39 **bounde**: *incensi* LgA.

43–4 **though . . . hym**: *plus que a vng fourmiz qui est en ta couche* P2.

45 **us**: add *Hermogenes te ligauit* LgA.

57 **repentaunt**: add *et cil que tu as soustenu jusques cy mesdisant de toy* P2.

61 **by her**: *par leurs* P2; this is Vignay's rendering of *cum eis*; however, the

clause reads *cum eis per scripturas aduentum et passionem Christi euidenter probasset.*

63 **bisshop**: *pontifex* LgA.

68–9 **whos loue**: *lequel* P2, *cuius fide* LgA.

71 **necke**: add *et le traynoit* P2.

79–80 **and . . . hym**: only GiL.

83 **þe crowne of marterdome**: *par auoir le chief couppe* S.

84 **Auerell**: add *in annuntiatione domini* LgA.

85 **born into Constantinenople**: *transporte en compostelle* P2, *Compostellam translatus* LgA.

86 **.viij.**: *III* LgA.

88 **halowed**: add *uniuersaliter* LgA.

90 **made**: *exequitur* LgA, i.e. Beleth wrote a detailed account of the translation.

92–3 **it to the devine gouernaile**: *a la voulente diuine la sepulture de luy et monterent en la nef sans nul gouuernail* P2. Because of the omission, *gouernaile* has acquired the alternative sense 'governance', though at 104 it means 'rudder', as it does here in LgD. L substituted *gouernaunce*.

95–6 **that is . . . wolff**: only GiL.

99 **sepulcre**: *sarcophagum* LgA.

105 **this**: add *ut dicit idem magister Iohannes Beleth* LgA.

106 **and . . . writen**: *uel secundum alios* LgA.

114 **in that contrey**: only GiL.

119 **my**: not in LgA.

121 **verray cursednesse**: *pensee louuine* P2.

122 **and**: add *cuidoit que* P2.

123–4 **wolde . . . body**: *courroient ca et la et romproient le char et getteroient le corps* P2.

124 **wyle**: *sagesce* P2.

125 **thought not her wyckednesse**: *dolum eius non cogitantes* LgA.

127 **he departed euene atweyne**: *il party parmy* P2, *per medium uentrum scindunt* LgA.

129, 131 **wylde**: only GiL.

136 **lyued and ended**: *feny* P2, *uitam finiuit* LgA.

139–40 **atte the laste**: only GiL.

145 **Seint Bede**: *bede* P2. EGL leave a space, A1 omits the clause, H1 has

Seint Calixte inserted by a corrector, D has *Kalyxt* inserted in a hand not unlike that of the H1 corrector; H2 copies the D correction; T2 has *Iames*, A2 and Caxton *Bede*.

153 **Loreine**: add *ut ait Hubertus Bisuntinus* LgA.

154 **.M^{l}.lxxiij.**: *MLXX* LgA.

155–6 **that . . . couenaunt**: not in LgA.

158–9 **abode still withe hym and**: only GiL.

160 **And . . . night**: *sed aduesperascente die moritur* LgA.

163 **trauelinge man**: *cheuaucheur* P2, *equitis* LgA.

164 **Take**: *baille* P2.

165–6 **And . . . night**: *Sicque illa nocte ante solis ortum dietas XV peragentes* LgA.

166 **the mountayne**: *la mont Joye* P2, Monte del Gozo near Compostela.

170 **was not**: *ne valoit riens* P2.

172 **in so shorte tyme**: only GiL.

175 **.M^{l}.iiij^{xx}.iij.**: *MXC* LgA.

176 **oste,** 177 **osteler**: *osteler* (*MED s.v. hostiler*) could mean 'innkeeper' or 'innkeeper's servant'. In using different words s.w. seems to have intended the latter in contrast to *oste*; but in LgD and LgA they are clearly the same person.

185 **before, before**: *pour, pour* P2.

188 **to that place . . . hangged**: only GiL.

192 **euer sethe**: only GiL.

193–4 **was . . . ioye and**: only GiL.

194 **dede . . . that**: not in LgA.

195 **see . . . thanne**: only GiL.
sone: add *tout sain* S.

205–6 **come . . . ayenne**: *occurrit et ereptum ad thronum iudicis deduxit et accusantibus demonibus ut uite restitueretur obtinuit* LgA.

207 **An**: *Hue* P2, *Hugo* LgA.

211 **Whost**: only E includes *h*, (H1 *Woost*, G *Wotist*, L *Woste*); among a number of spellings for past forms *MED witen* v. (1) gives only one with *h*, *inwhat* for *ich ne wot*, so this should perhaps have been emended.

216 **For**: *il nappartient pas ainsy faire mais* P2.

217 **synnes**: add *prius* LgA.

218 **contricion**: add *et par pelerinage soy repentir* P2.

227 **slow hymselff**: *se feri parmy le ventre* P2.

229 **anone**: add *que ilz ne feussent souspecionez de cel homicide* P2.

235 **withe me to come**: *et venismes* P2.

249 **his**, 250.
one: *quosdam, quosdam* LgA.

260–1 **and . . . become**: not in LgA.

265 **and woke hym**: *et veilloient* P2, *uigilantibus* LgA.

268 **frely . . . wolde**: *tout deslie* P2.

271 **Lyon**: add *ut ait Hubertus Bisuntinus* LgA.

273 **her**[1]: add *sacculum* LgA.

273–4 **anone . . . hors**: *il la porta* P2, i.e. the lady in GiL and P2, her bag in LgA.

274 **man**: add *in uia deficientem* LgA.

275 **also**: only GiL, *ars* EH1G. Since it is not in LgD or LgA one cannot tell which is the original GiL reading, though *also* seems the more probable. The nearest sense cited by *MED* to *ars* is from Ipomedon (3), *He smote him thurgh the shuldre and bare him ouer his hors ars to the erthe.*

burdon, 'pilgrim's staff'; this word, *MED burdoun* n. (1), is always spelled with *d*, but 'burden', *MED s.v. birthen*, is recorded with *th* or *d*, and with *u, o, ou*, or *e*. The error of the common archetype of EH1G is therefore not surprising, but is rectified below at 288 and 289 as context suggests.

277 **his laboure of his fete**: *lerrer a pie* P2, *labore itineris* LgA.

278–80 **his . . . to hem for**: *quant ses compaignons le prierent du salu de lame* P2.

281 **speche**: add *et ses compaignons actendoient sa mort* P2.
.iij.: *quarta* LgA.
woke and: only GiL.
sayde: add *sociis eius mortem expectantibus* LgA.

287, 288 **right, lefte**: *sinistra, dextra* LgA.

290 **anger**: add *et leua le bourdon du poure pelerin* P2, *eleuato baculo* LgA.

296–7 **And . . . deyed**: *Et donc morut* P2, not in LgA.

297–8 **his felawes . . . contre**: *ses compaignons retournerent* P2, not in LgA.

298 **one of hem**: *lautre* P2, *ille* LgA.

304 **so . . . shame**: only GiL.

311 **Iames**: add *enuiron lan de grace mil et cent* P2.

320 **to by**: *racheter* P2.

322 **hym**: add *in testimonium huius miraculi* LgA.

lond: *terres et par les chastiaulx* P2.

323 **miracle**: add *Car quant aucun le vouloit prendre tantost comme il veoit la chaienne il estoit espouente et senfuioit. Et quant le lyon et les autres bestes se vouloient esdrecier contre luy par les desers ou il aloit. et il veoient la chaienne. ilz auoient trop grant paour et senfuioient tantost* P2.

327 **by sympelnesse . . . shrewe**: *de simplesce par conseille dune vielle* P2, *rustica quadam simplicitate* LgA, 'by a certain rustic simplicity'.

328 **of his maister . . . kept**: *du tuteur qui le deuoit garder* P2, *tutoris sui* LgA.

328–9 **he wolde haue away**: i.e. the *maister* wished to deprive him of it.

330 **drawe**: add *ad caudam equi* LgA.
he: add *confessa son pechie et* P2.

336 **the apostell**: *populo* LgA.

337–8 **and . . . deliuered**: only GiL.

94 ST CHRISTOPHER

Maggioni, ch. XCVI, p. 663; Dunn-Lardeau, ch. 95, p. 644.

5 **and obeye hym**: *secum moraturus* LgA.

21 **the**[1]: only GiL.

22 **hym**: *ipsum dyabolum* LgA.

30 **and gladde**: only GiL.

31 **servaunt**: add *et le prist a estre son seigneur* P2.

36 **he**[1]: add *sesmerueilla et* P2.
what hym ayled that: *pourquoy* P2.

37 **aferde**: add *et auoit laissie la plaine voye et estoit alle par sy aspre desert* P2.

41 **as ferre as y may**: not in P2, *territus* LgA.

42 **hym and**: only GiL.

43 **Now see I well that**: only GiL.
haue not: add *encores* P2.

44 **lorde**: add *mundi* LgA.
go thi way: *ualeas* LgA.

44–5 **will no lenger serue the**: *te vueil laisser* P2.

47–8 **into . . . an**: *en vng desert a vng* P2, *ad quendam* LgA.

52 **wake and**: not in LgA.

55–6 **And . . . there and**: *in quo multi transeuntes periclitantur et pereunt?' Cui Christophorus: 'Noui.' Et ille* LgA.

58 **God**: *regi Christo* LgA.

60–1 **truly to God**: only GiL.

65 **that wolde come**: only GiL.

70 **called**: add *ab eodem ut prius* LgA.

72 **benignely**: *obnixe* LgA.

73, 77 **necke**: *espaules* P2.

91–2 **floure and fruit**: *frondes et dactilos* LgA, 'leaves and dates'.

93 **into**: add *Samon* LgA, i.e. Samos.

95 **and so he dede**: not in LgA.

100 **Cristofore**: add *uultum discooperiens* LgA.

110 **And**: add *quant ilz le virent ou voult* P2.

117 **lede hym**: add *lye* P2.

121 **Reproued**: *Reprobus* LgA.

122 **Cristofore**: add *Ante baptismum Cananeus, nunc autem christianus* LgA.

123 **God**: *Christi* LgA.

125 **withe thi wichecraft**: *maleficie* P2.

126 **Dagarus**: *Dagnus* LgA; the point of this apparent verbal play is lost.

127–8 **be . . . hem**: *sont fais des mains des hommes* P2.

130 **thou spekest so madly**: *ne peuz tu dire que sauuages paroles et qui sont mescongneues aux hommes* P2.

132 **peynes and**: only GiL.

132–3 **in no wise**: only GiL.

133 **streite**: only GiL.

134 **he hadde conuerted**: *auoient este auecques cristofle* P2, *ad Christophorum missi fuerant* LgA.

136 **putte**: *in carcerem recludi* LgA.
to: *auecques* P2.

140 **iapinge**: *lesioyssement* P2, *plausu manuum* LgA.

146 **to**: *par* P2.

154 **stone of a**: only GiL.

156 **a flavme of**: only GiL.

166 **.xl.**: *CCCC* LgA.

169 **dressed . . . towarde hym**: *cum eidem insultaret* LgA.

172–3 **and thanne . . . erthe**: *fay vng pou de boue de mon sang* P2, *lutum de* *sanguine meo facies* LgA, 'make a paste with my blood' (Ryan); referring to this at 192, LgA gives *cruor cum terre*, LgD *sang*, GiL *blode*.

174 **as he sayd . . . after**: *apres ce* P2.

183 **lawe**: *errore* LgA.

185 **comune atte bordell**: *au bordel commun* P2.

194 **gate . . . siknesse**: *luy impetra vers toy pensee chrestienne et eust en suppliant grace doster maladies et enfermetez* P2, *mentem; nam apud te ueniam impetrauit atque ut morbos et infirmitates repellat supplicanter obtinuit* LgA.

95 SEVEN SLEEPERS OF EPHESUS

Maggioni, ch. XCVII, p. 670; Dunn-Lardeau, ch. 96, p. 650.

5 **lete bringe hem bounde**: *lier* P2, *uinctos . . . compelleret* LgA.

10 **persecucion**: only GiL.

15 **comynge**: *reditum* LgA.

21 **seke hem**: add *ad sacrificandum* LgA.

22 **hem**: *ses compaignons* P2.

31 **pore men**: *christianis pauperibus* LgA.

32 **cristen**: only GiL.

37 **with hem**: add *sy que parce que dieu le voult ainsy* P2.

38 **caue**: add *ou ilz habitoient* P2.

39 **sorugh**: *mesaise* P2, *inopia* LgA.
that[1]: not in LgA.

42 **.CCC.lxxvij.**: *CCCLXXII* LgA.

49 **geue**: *confirmare* LgA.

56 **Malk (. . .) saide**: *interrogauerunt Malchum* LgA.

58 **or . . . deye**: *cest ce que lempereur a enpense de nous* P2.

59 **to deye**: only GiL.

62 **redely**: only GiL.

70 **crosse**: add *et la cite garnie* P2, add *et mutatam ciuitatem* LgA.

72 **confermed hymselff**: *se aduisa et conforta* P2, *se confirmans* LgA.

75 ***Benedicite***: only GiL.

78 **bylded**: add *cest vne autre cite* P2.

89 **we . . . counsaill**: *te celerons bien car autrement tu ne peuz estre cele* P2.

94 **hidde**: only GiL.

95–6 **he wolde . . . tresours**: *uolebat eis satisfacere quod nihil inuenerat* LgA.

97 **in that other syde**: only GiL.

99–100 **wherfor . . . meruaile**: only GiL.

100 **mased**: *aussy comme forsene* P2.

109 **kynrede**: add *Et len luy demanda de quelle cite il estoit* P2.

110 **Ephesim**: add *Et le iuge li dist fay venir tes parens qui tesmoigneront pour toy. il les nomma maiz nul ne les congnoissoit. Et ilz distrent que il se faingnoit pour eschaper en aucune maniere* S.

113 **.lxvij.**: *.lxxvij.* P2, *LXXII* LgA.
it went: i.e. it was current; this is an earlier instance than either of the two in *MED s.v. gon* sense 15d (a).

115–16 **myght . . . now**: *peuent auoir este tes parens de tant de temps* P2, *parentes tui ante tantum tempus fuerunt* LgA.

121 **axse you**: add *et je vous diray ce que iay ou cueur* P2.

134 **folued . . . thedir**: only GiL.

139 **sittynge**: add *en celle cauerne* P2.

143–4 **And . . . message**: only GiL.

145 **wepte**: *lugebat* LgA.

152 **thi loue**: *toy* P2.

153 **beleue**: add *que* P2.

154 **that be to come**: *est* P2.

156 **or dysese**: *lesion* P2, *lesionem et uiuit* LgA.

157 **any disese**: *riens* P2.

158 **they hadde**: *il eust* P2.
sayde: add *uidentibus cunctis* LgA.

162 **and syluer**: not in LgA.

166 **nobly withe**: *inauratis* LgA, 'with gilded'.

167 **done**: *doubte* P2.

168 **.CCC.lxxvij.**: *.CCCLXXII.* LgA.

170 **.iiij.**: *tribus* LgA.

171 **.C.iiij.^{xx}.xiij.**: *CXCVI* LgA; LgA is correct.

96 STS NAZARIUS AND CELSUS

Maggioni, ch. XCVIII, p. 676; Dunn-Lardeau, ch. 97, p. 655.

5 **contreye and**: *et contraire* P2.

6 **relygion**: add *et que sa mere tenoit la loy de baptesme et son pere tenoit la loy du sabbat* P2.

8 **lawe**: *volente* P2.

9 **that . . . afterward**: *pape* P2.

12–13 **but . . . purpose**: *Et ce que len dit que il fut baptizie de saint lin pape nest pas a entendre que il fut adonc pape mais lestoit encores a estre* P2.

14 **by that**: not in P2, *infra* LgA.

16 **after**: add *la mort* P2.

19 **towne**: *urbe Roma* LgA.

20 **into Itayle**: *par les citez dytalie* P2.
that good as he went: only GiL.

22 **the**: add *x*[e] P2.

24–5 **And he went . . . hem**: not in LgA.

31 **Iumylly**: *Gemellus* LgA; Maggioni (index, p. 1349) identifies this as Cimiez, near Nice.

33 **that was . . . stature**: *elegantem* LgA.

33–4 **and . . . hym**[3]: *en requerant que il le baptizast et menast auec luy* P2.

34–5 **of Fraunce**: *Galliarum* LgA.

39 **after . . . goddes**: *deos omnipotentes uindicare presumeret* LgA.

40 **seintes**: add *mais il les amonnesta* P2.

51–2 **withe good wylle**: only GiL.

53 **Celce**: add *plorantem* LgA.

54 **hym, he**[1]: *les, ilz* P2.

54–5 **into . . . deye**: *tant quil eust pourpense les tourmens de quoy il les occirent* P2.

57 **and . . . and**: *et rompirent tout et* P2, *erumpens* LgA.

58 **men**: add *et en desrompirent* P2.

59 **that**: *quil sen vint a peine au palais* P2.

64 **Nazarien**: add *des talons* P2.
childe: add *de verges* P2.

66 **to haue be scorned**: *phantastice deludi* LgA.

76 **and the see was before**: *la mer estoit* P2.

77 **to retorne**: *periclitari* LgA.

78 **wyckednesse**: add *quilz auoient fais aux sains* P2.

82 **preched**: add *diutius* LgA.

83 **prouost**: add *Anolin* LgD, *Anolinus* LgA.

90 **constreyned**: add *cum iniuria multa* LgA.
bysshoppes: add *des temples* P2.

91 **exile**: add *a Rome* P2.

92–3 **there . . . houndes**: *dont fut mene oultre la porte romaine en vng lieu qui est dit .iij. murs et fut decole auecques lenfant celse* P2.

96 **for**: *propter* LgA.

99 **he**: *ilz* P2.

108 **.lxvij.**: *LVII* LgA.

108–15 LgD and LgA quote Ambrose at greater length. GiL reduces it to Maggioni, 680: 57, 62, first phrase of 63, 64, Dunn-Lardeau, 659–60.

97 ST FELIX POPE

Maggioni, ch. XCIX, p. 681; Dunn-Lardeau, ch. 98, p. 660.

1 **of**: *en lieu de* P2.

5 **pope**: add *loco eius* LgA.

6 **after the**: *assembla vng* P2.
bisshoppes: add *et* P2.

7 **the eretik . . . emperour**: *arrien et herese empereur* P2, *imperatorem arianum et hereticum* LgA.

9 **repeled**: 'called back' or 'reinstated'; the necessary sense is not recorded under *MED repelen*.

10 **shulde be partenere withe**: *participeroit auecques* P2, *communicaret* LgA, 'should give communion to'.

98 STS SIMPLICIUS AND FAUSTINUS

Maggioni, ch. C, p. 682; Dunn-Lardeau, ch. 99, p. 661.

S has lost a folio after 13 *as*, resuming at Martha 75.

7 **disportinge aboute**: *jouant entour* P2, *ambiret* LgA. The Latin word could mean either that he was walking near the property, or that he wished to acquire it, but from context must here be the latter.

8 **sawe her and**: not in LgA.

9 **sawe that and**: only GiL.

17 **the martyres**: add *et as vaincu* P2, not in LgA.
wete thou well that: only GiL.

18 **of fendes**: *du dyable* P2.

19 **in the same houre**: not in LgA.

20 **so horribly**: *sy* P2.
withe the: du P2.

24 **vnder Dioclusian**: only GiL.

99 ST MARTHA

Maggioni, ch. CI, p. 683; Dunn-Lardeau, ch. 100, p. 662.

S resumes after missing folio at 75 *(ui)ues auec ton maistre.*

3 **parties**: *oreilles* P2, 'coastal regions'.

4 **castelles**: *oppida* LgA.

7–9 **and . . . oste**: *et sa seur ne vouloit administrer car il luy estoit aduis quelle nestoit pas souffisant a administrer a sy grant hoste et non pas tout le monde* P2, *et sororem pariter ministrare uolebat, quia uidebatur sibi quod ad seruiendum tanto hospiti non sufficeret etiam totus mundus* LgA. Vignay having translated *sororem uolebat* as though it were *soror nolebat,* GiL tried to improve the sense by omitting the last three words.

10 **passion**: *ascensionem* LgA.

11 **the lazar**: *le ladre* P2, *Lazaro* LgA; at 95 Seven Sleepers 151 GiL gives *Lazar* for these LgD and LgA readings. *MED s.v. laser* n. (1) records several instances of Lazarus, brother of Martha, with definite article as though a common noun. He is not recorded as having suffered from leprosy, but the other Lazarus, mentioned above at 8.64, from the parable of Dives and Lazarus (Luke 16: 19–31), was widely believed to have been a leper, which became the usual sense of the word.

14 **witheoute . . . sayle**: *ablatis remis, uelis et gubernaculis* LgA.

15 **Iues**: not in LgA.

16 **holy goste**: *dieu* P2, *domino* LgA.

18 **in the sight of alle**: *a tous* P2.

19 **vnder**: *sur* P2.

20 **any**: *vng* P2.

21 **wyngges**: *dens* P2.

22 **horned**: *ut tortua* (. . .) *munitus* LgA, 'armed like a tortoise'.

24 **of Galacie**: *de Galatia Asye* LgA.

25 **Lamecana**: *leuiatan* P2.

26 **snake**: *onace* P2, *onacho* LgA, a mythical monster of that region.

27 **by . . . tyme**: *per spatium iugeris* LgA, 'over the space of an acre'.

28 **shyninge as a mirrour**: *uelut spiculum*, LgA, 'like a dart'. Vignay read *spiculum* as *speculum*.

30 **founde hym**: add *in nemore* LgA.

33 **slayne**: add *du peuple* P2.

34 **Carasture or Taracle**: *Tarascurus* LgA.

36 **the blacke place**: *noirlus cest a dire noir lieu* P2, *Nerluc, id est niger lacus* LgA.

41 **companye**: *couuent* P2.
chirche: *magna* (. . .) *basilica* LgA.

42–3 **they ledde**: *duxit* LgA.

44 **botre**: only GiL.

46 **man**: add *qui estoit oultre le rosne* P2.

50 **presented**: add *pour estre resuscite* P2.

53 **byholde**: add *mi hospes care* LgA.

56 **the**[1]: add *quint* P2.

56–7 **that woman**: *mulier emorroissa* LgA, 'woman with haemorrhage'.

58 **and . . . frenges**: *cum ueste et fimbria* LgA.

69 **the day before**: *ante octauum diem* LgA.

71 **felawshippe**: *couuent* P2.

72 **that haue . . . togederes**: *et longuement nourris ensemble* P2, *et dulcissimi alumpni* LgA.

74 **blesse of heuene**: *sieges polis* P2, *sedes pollicitas* LgA.

76 **passinge**: add *prochaine* P2.

81 **dere**: add *hely* P2, *ely* follows *pater* LgA.

82 **hondes** add *scripta* LgA.

86–7 **in this mene tyme**: only GiL.

87 **saide**: add *Veni* LgA.

89 **I shall enhaunse**: *exaudiam* LgA, 'listen to'.

100 **whanne**: add *circa corpus eius* LgA.

102 **satte**: *dormoit* P2.

109 **and**: only GiL.

110 **to saye**: *petens* LgA.
sodenly: *a peine* P2.

114 **gloues and my crismatorie**: *gans et mes crisces* P2, *cyrothecas criseas* LgA, 'gold-coloured gloves'; no explanation for the LgD reading has so far

been forthcoming. Batallier omitted *et mes crisces*; see Dunn-Lardeau's note, p. 1296. *MED* has only one earlier citation of *crismatorie*, for a1425.

119 **sexstayne**: *segrestain* P2.

125 **of evell**: *de mal oyr* P2.

126 **ouer all**: *cunctis foliis* LgA.

128 **late**: only GiL.
cristin: add *et baptizie* P2.

131–2 **on euery syde and gaue gret fraunchise to her place**: *dune part et dautre du rosne.* (add *tout* P1) *entour* (add *auec* P1) *les chastiaux et les villes et franchi cestuy lieu* **P2,** *ex utraque parte Rodani terram, uillas et castra dedit locumque illum liberum fecit* LgA.

133 **Marcell . . . maistresse**: *Marcilla uero eius famula uitam conscripsit ipsius* LgA. The only indication LgD gives of Marcelle's gender is *elle* (GiL *he*) at 135.

100 STS ABDON AND SENNEN

Maggioni, ch. CII, p. 688; Dunn-Lardeau, ch. 101, p. 666.

1 **Dacyan**: *decien* P2, *Decius* LgA. In this chapter Decius is consistently spelt with *a* in all MSS, as opposed to the random spellings in most MSS in 95 Seven Sleepers.

4 **bounde**: not in LgA.

10 **pesibly**: *franchement* P2.

13 **place of . . . marterdom**: *theatrum* LgA.

101 ST GERMANUS

Maggioni, ch. CIII, p. 689; Dunn-Lardeau, ch. 102, p. 667.

3 **true kunnynge**: *science de droit* P2, *iuris scientiam* LgA.

4 **to Fraunce**: *ad Gallias* LgA.

5 **of the dignite**: *de la dignite du duchie* P2, *ducatus* LgA.

7 **pyne appell tree**: *pin* P2, *arborem quandam pinum* LgA.

9 **that he toke**: only GiL.

17–18 **He . . . madness**: *sy donna lieu a celluy forsenant* P2, 'yielded to this angry man'.

18 **Augustinense**: *augustin* P2, *Augustodunum* LgA.

20 **and sacrid**: *tonsurans* LgA.

26–7 **ne[3] . . . that**: *et* P2, *nunquam uel* LgA.

27–8 **suche . . . vsed**: only GiL.

30 **vtterly**: not in P2, *nimiis* LgA.

33 **cote**: *tunicam* LgA.
gowne: *cucullam* LgA, 'cowl'.

38–9 **neuer . . . gurte**: *il ne portoit nautre vestement. il sechaucoit pou et portoit pou cainture* P2, *numquam uestimentum, raro calceamenta et raro cingulum detrahebat* LgA.

40–1 **but . . . incredyble**: *que cestoit miracle de sa char et estoit aussy comme chose non credible* P2, *si miraculis caruisset, incredibilis uideretur* LgA.

47–8 **atte sertayne houre**: *vit* P2.

53–4 **And . . . hem**: *Et dont furent les gens merueillez et dirent que cestoient dyables qui se mocquoient ainsy des hommes* P2, *Adiurati igitur se demones esse dixerunt qui sic hominibus illudebant* LgA, 'put to the oath, they admitted that they were demons who thus deceived men'.

56 **walles**: *porte* P2.

59 **Lowe**: *le leu* P2, *lupus* LgA.
bestes: *gregis* LgA.
and of chastisinge: only GiL.

65 **heresyes**: *hereses* P2.

68 **diuerse**: *assegiez* P2.

71–2 **that same strete**: *totus ille uicus* LgA.

76 **for the heresyes**: *pour les hereses* P2, *ut hereticos confutaret* LgA.

77 **by the way**: *en vne cite* P2, *apud Cormadorum* LgA, which has not been identified; Boureau, 1316 n. 7, suggests it may be a bad reading for *Tornadorum*, Tonnerre.

79 **how**: *que* P2.

85 **and hys felawshippe**: *et a ses compaignons* P2.

86 **cowherde**: *subulcus* LgA, 'swineherd'.
pasture: Gil omits the rest of the section, Maggioni, 692 (46–52), Dunn-Lardeau, 670–1, possibly because it was thought disparaging to Britain. Caxton supplies the omission, but in his version the cowherd becomes not king but governor, and a comment that all subsequent kings of Britain descended from him is omitted.

91 **brennynge charite**: *ardeur* P2; LgA makes it clearer that they propose to fight unarmed.

93 **hastely**: *hardiement* P2.

101 **wher he was**: *cunctis audientibus* LgA.

115 **came**: add *de son hostel au palais* P2.
laboure: *ieiuniis et laboribus* LgA.

118 **meruaylous high**: *mirae mansuetudinis* LgA.

126 **.viij.**: *.vij.*[e] P2.

128 **.xx.**: *.xxx.* LgA.

139–40 **in dede**: *mort* P2; EH1L are likely to be correct and this should not have been emended.

141 **the gret Eusebe**: subject of the next chapter, and bishop of Vercelli in the preceding century, d. 371.

144 **but**: *ergo* LgA.

102 ST EUSEBIUS

Maggioni, ch. CIV, p. 695; Dunn-Lardeau, ch. 103, p. 673.

5 **aungeles**: add *custodientibus* LgA.

9 **the aungeles serued hym**: *inter manus eius ministerium angelicum appareret* LgA.

10 **heretik Ariene**: *leresie arrienne* S, *ariana pestis* LgA.

11 **was consentant**: (*en* P1) *estoit consentant* P2, *eidem heresi fauente* LgA. L *consentyng to the same heresy* is so close to LgA that it must surely derive from it. EH1D follow P2S, so must reflect s.w.'s translation.

14 **chirche**: add *at Eusebius urbem ingressus ante ostium maioris ecclesie* LgA.

17–18 **right a good man**: *vng homme catholique* P2.

18 **chirches**: *leglise* P2.

19 **heresye**: add *arrienne* P2.

21 **not God**: only GiL.

21–2 **that he hadde a begynninge**: *quil estoit et quil nestoit mie* P2, *quod erat, quando non erat* LgA, 'that there was a time when he was not'.

24 **of Nyce**: *de Luques* P2, *Nicenum* LgA.

26 **hys boweles . . . procession**: *uiscera et intestina per secessum* LgA, i.e. 'in a privy'.

31 **come**: add *et suam senectutem opposuit* LgA; this is the *excusacion* of the next sentence.

32 **was ordeyned**: *seroit celebre* P2.

34 **write her faithe**: *eidem fidei* (. . .) *subscribere* LgA; all forms of *write* from 49–57 also represent forms of LgA *subscribere*.

34–5 **to the . . . bisshopes**: *et fist escrire a denis euesque de milan et a xxix* *euesques leur foy* P2, *et Dionysium episcopum Mediolanensem ac XXIX episcopas*. See too note to 49 below.

38–9 **he called . . . and**: only GiL.

43–4 **yeftes nor by prayers**: *blanditiis* LgA.

49 **sayden . . . als**: *ce que Denis y auoit escript et distrent que il y escripsist* P2, *cui Dionysius subscripserat* LgA.

51 **I . . . anewe**: *escriuez se vous voulez au nouuel que iescripray* P2.

56 **to her wrytinge**: *a y escrire* P2, not in LgA.

59 **fro the**: add *aliorum* LgA.

63–4 **they bonde . . . necke**: *le traynoient vne corde ou col* P2, *per collum cum fune ipsum trahebant per* LgA; GiL transposes this with the preceding clause.

66 **confession . . . Chirche**: *deffence de la foy catholique* P2, *confessione fidei catholice* LgA.

68 **Denis**: add *et paulin* P2.

69 **to withestonde . . . wyckednesse**: only GiL.

70 **Ierapolyn**: *Scitopolim* LgA.

72–3 **ne[1] . . . hede and**: *Et auoit le chief estraint sy quil ne pouoit mouuoir tant seulement* P2.

78 **repayred**: *aperiri* LgA.

84 **and[2]**: add *extra domum ipsum supinum trahentes* LgA.

103 MACCABEES

Maggioni, ch. CV, p. 699; Dunn-Lardeau, ch. 104, p. 676.

4 **for**: only GiL.

13 **thou it be so**: *ja soit ce que ilz descendissent en enfer. La premiere raison est pource que ilz eurent prerogatiue de martire car ilz souffrirent tourmens non oys et oultre ce que nul des sains du viel testament ne souffrirent. Et pource sont ilz priuilegiez que leur passion soit celebree par leur merite. Et ceste rayson est mise en lystoire escoliere. La seconde rayson est pour la representation du mistere. car le nombre de .vij. est vniuersel et general. Et donc par ceulz sont signifiez tous les peres du vielz testament dignes destre celebrez. Et ja soit ce que* P2.

14 **for as moche, but for as moche**: *tant pource que, tant pource que* P2. **helle**: *limbum* LgA.

18 **ensaumple**: add *des bons crestiens pour deux choses. Cest pource que par la fermete deulx ilz soient* P2.

19 **the lawes**: *la loy* P2.

21 **that**: *car* P2.

22 **suffered**: add *autelz tourmens* P2.

23 **gospell**: add *Et maistre iehan beleth assigne ces .ij.* (*tres ultimas* LgA) *raisons en la somme de loffice* P2.

104 ST PETER IN CHAINS

Maggioni, ch. CVI, p. 701; Dunn-Lardeau, ch. 105, p. 677.

6 **cause**: add *est ou memoire* P2.

8 **familyer with**: add *Gayen nepueu de* P2. Gaius became the emperor Caligula.

10 **the**[2]: 2 sg. personal pronoun accusative.

15–16 **dyuine thingges**: *deuinemens* P2, 'divinations'.

17 **enemyes**: *amicos* LgA.

26 **day before Estre**: *deuant le iour des azimes* P2, *ante diebus azimorum* LgA, i.e. before the Passover.

27 **in the Day of Estre**: *au iour des azimes* P2, *in diebus azimorum* LgA, the seven days from Passover, Exod. 12: 15.

28 **to sle hym**: *le* (. . .) *monstrer au peuple et occire* P2, *producere eum populo* LgA.

33 **diuerse**: *diris* LgA.

37 **boke . . . Aunysens**: *XIX antiquitatum libro* LgA, 'book 19 of the Antiquities'.

39 **iugement**: *theatrum* LgA.

40 **of . . . riche**: *tyssu merueilleusement dor et dargent* P2.

42 **more gloriously**: *sy que elle donnoit double lumiere aux regardans et estoit la resplendeur comme de metail rouge* (*uibrantis* LgA) P2.

43 **gret reuerence and**: only GiL.

43–5 **the pride . . . nature**: *plus aliquid de eo quam humane nature est artifex arrogantia mentiretur* LgA.

49 **ouer**: *sur le trecouer de* P2, 'headband'.
sawe: add *lange et* P2, add *angelum id est* LgA.

51 **lorde**: *deus* LgA.
in haste: only GiL.

56 **delyueraunce**: add *tam mire* LgA.

58 **wrete**: *chantee* P2.

60 **done**: add *Et selon ce doit elle estre apellee saint pierre aux lyans* P2.

61 **ordenaunce**: i.e. establishment of the *feste*, 1–2 above.

64 **places**: EH1D *bondes* comes from misreading of *lieux* as *liens* by s.w., and therefore should not have been emended.

67 **prouoste**: *prefecture* LgA. L substitutes *office*. *MED* records two occurrences, both from Proc. Privy C. for 1443, of *provostee*, 'area under jurisdiction of a government-appointed administrator' rather than 'office of provost' as required here.

75 **prison**: *custodiam* LgA.

76 **and vpon . . . ouer you**: not in LgA.

79 **sette . . . hem**: *doubla les gardes* P2, *fecit quod dixit* LgA.

85 **syke of the gowte**: *gutturosam* LgA, 'goitered'.

94 **therby**: only GiL.

98–9 **and whanne . . . anone**: *et dont les bailla a sa fille a baiser. Et tantost quelle les eust baisiez* P2, *easque cum inuenisset filie sue osculandas dedit. Illa mox cum osculata est uincula* LgA.

101 **and his wyff**: only GiL.

104 **cheynes**: add *et la nomina saint pierre aux lyans* P2.
sollempnite: add *a celle eglise* P2.

112 **toke**: add *a femme* P2.

115 **away**: add *vaincus* P2.

117 **of the prouince**: *prouinciam* LgA.

119, 123 **the profite (. . .) comune**: *rempublicam* LgA.

120 **gladly**: only GiL.

121 **batayles**: *les batailles des gens* P2, *ciuilia bella* LgA.

127 **Cesariens**: *cesares* LgA; see note to 81.49–52.

128 **Sextillys**: add *quia a Martio sextus erat* LgA.
he: *le peuple* P2.

130–1 **of the yere**: *chascun an* P2, not in LgA.

133 **.CCCC.xxvij.**: *CCCC.xxvj* P2.

136 **the cheynes**: *duas (. . .) catenas* LgA.

142 **shulde not be vsed so**: *sic staret* LgA.

143 **Petre**: add *et que tout le peuple nommeroit celluy iour saint pierre* P2.

143–4 **that same day**: *de ce* P2, not in LgA.

146 **of Romaynes**: *des paiens* P2.

150 **he**: *lapostre* P2.

152 **miracle**: add *tout aussy comme selle eust este vne seule et celle mesme. Et*

dont le pape et la royne establirent que lonneur de la folle religion deulx faisoit a vng paien dampne fut muee en mieulx et fut faicte a pierre prince des apostres P2.

157 **these cheynes**: *celle chaienne* P2.

158 **.CCCC.xliiij.**: *DCCCCLXIV* LgA.

162 **the cheynes**: *la chaienne* P2.

168 **Theodorik**: add *euesque de mez* P2.

169 **in his honde**: only GiL.

173 **cheyne**: add *episcopo* LgA.

176–8 **the bisshoppe before named made the sygne of the crosse byfore his mouthe and thorughe vertu therof he spette the dragon in the mouthe and he deyed anone**: *leuesque donat nombre* (*noble* P1) *par vertu luy* (*Il* P1) *cracha en la bouche et il morust tantost. mais leuesque fist auant le signe de la croix a ses doys* P2, *in cuius ore Donatus episcopus uirtute insignis expuens mox occidit, prius tamen ante eius faciem digitis crucem designans et eidem ostendans* LgA. All three versions are given in full to show an attempt in GiL to clarify a somewhat confused French passage; but in turning the sentence round s.w. misplaced and mistranslated *par vertu*, and misread *donat nombre* or emended it to *deuant nomme*, apparently without looking at the Latin.

179 **.vij.**: *octo* LgA.
might not draw: *trainerent a peine* P2.

181 **stinke**: add *Et milet dit la mesmes* P2.

182 **before hym**: *de* P2.

183 **vpon . . . hyll**: *delez la mer sus le coupel dune tresgrant montaigne* P2, *super magnum montis precipitium iuxta mare* LgA.

185 **Beheste**: add *et en apella sans nombre* P2, add *innumeros enecauit* LgA.

185–6 **euell wille of þe Iwes**: *loccasion du Juif* P2.

187–8 **And . . . hem**: *sy que quant ilz furent sus ce trebuchement de celle montaigne il en noya sans nombre et se venga deulz* P2, *de eis se taliter uindicauit* LgA.

GiL here omits three sentences, Maggioni, 707 (94–6), Dunn-Lardeau, 682–3.

190 **Petre**: add *des lyans* P2.

196–8 **bothe . . . synne**: *tu voys que lepistre recorde labsolution des lyens faicte a lapostre. et leuuangille recorde la puissance qui lui fut donnee dabsouldre. Et loroison de la iournee dui le requiert que labsolution nous soit faicte de luy* P2; EDL have the ambiguous barred *ll* in *pistell* and *gospell*; H1 has *pistelez*. The plural form, perhaps wrongly adopted in the text here, might have resulted from the erroneous thought that this refers to the two Epistles of Peter; the correct singular, as in LgD and LgA, refers to the epistle appointed for the Feast of St Peter in Chains; see Acts 12: 3–11.

GiL omits the rest of the chapter, Maggioni, 708–9 (102–25), Dunn-Lardeau, 683–4.

105 FINDING OF ST STEPHEN

Maggioni, ch. CVIII, p. 711; Dunn-Lardeau, ch. 107, 684.

1 **holy**: only GiL.

2 **.xvij.**: *VII* LgA.

3 **and**: *linuention de luy la translation et la conionction fut trouuee* P2, *Reperitur autem eius inuentio, translatio et coniunctio. Inuentio ipsius* (. . .) *facta fuit* LgA. For the 'conjunction' (with St Lawrence) see 120 ff. below.

5 **holy**: *nobles* P2.

9 **golde**[1]: add *chaucie de chausses brodees dor sapparut* P2.

12 **go a Thoursday**: *va jeudy* P2, *Vade igitur, dic Iohanni* LgA.

18 **lawe**: add *a mes piez* P2.

19 **for Goddes loue**: only GiL.

20 **bestes**: add *et des oyseaulx* P2.
he kepte hym: *cil len garda* P2, *hoc omnino ille prohibuit* LgA.

21 **varienge**: *corrompre* P2.
diligence: *reuerentia* LgA.

25–6 **the drede of us**: *pour nous* P2, *ob nostri reuerentiam* LgA.

32 **.xv.^{e} yere**: *XX* LgA.

34 **bapteme ne**: only GiL.

36 **ellwhere**: *MED elleswhere* records some spellings without *s*, but they are rare. Here *ell* is at the end of the line with barred *ll*, which may be intended for *elles*.

44 **ayenne**: *tertio* LgA.

46 **deuyde**: *deuiser* P2, *discernere* LgA; this is an extension of *MED dividen* sense 3(b), 'classify'.

50 **saferon**: *dencens et de mirre blanc* P2, *croco* LgA.

57 **syluer**: add *plain dencens et de mirre* P2, add *croco plenus* LgA.

60 **after**: add *de* P2.

72 **of Seint Stephen**: only GiL.

74 **inuencion**: add *de saint estienne* P2.

89 **ordeyned**: *transporta* P2.

94 **he beried hymselff**: *il se fist enseuelir* P2.

100 **fulle welle**: *bien* P2, not in LgA.

111 **prince**: EH1 *prve*, a spelling for *prou*, 'proud'; *MED prou* records only one instance in this sense, from one MS of Chaucer, dated *c.*1410.

117 **alle**: add *sains* P2.

121 **by this ordenaunce**: *hoc ordine* LgA, 'in this manner'.

139–40 **that . . . ershebissop**: not in LgA.

140–1 **the Romaynes were come**: *uenissent* LgA.

143–4 **withe . . . voys**: only GiL.

147 **reioysinge**: add *de la venue* P2.

149 **and made hym place**: not in LgA.

151 **pope**: add *et les clercs* P2.

154 **Lumbardes**: *latins* P2.

160 **.ixC.xxv.**: *CCCCXXV*.LgA.

163 **dede**: add *sic* (. . .) *ut ei iam pollices ligarentur* LgA.

168 **deyed**: add *deuant tous* P2.

169 **by miracle**: *toute saine* P2, *stupentibus sanata LgA.*

175 **to lyff**: add *a linuocation de saint estienne* P2.

177 **maister of scole**: *stolatus* LgA, 'wearing a priestly garment'.

178 **pore clothes**: *drapellez* P2, *pannis* LgA, 'swaddling clothes', but Latin and French can also carry the sense 'rags', and s.w. has taken it as such.
furst: only GiL.

179 **blode**: *lapide* LgA.

182 **of faithe and**: only GiL.

182–3 **withe a maner of tongges**: *dunes tenailles* P2.

183–5 **in the furneys of the fere of the faithe he was destreyned, smiten harde, demened and beten, and yet his faithe encresed and was not ouercome**: *fide fundabilis igniebatur et pendebatur, feriebatur et producebatur, constringebatur et augebatur, cedebatur et non uincebatur* LgA; the passage is obscure, and translations have varied, the earlier ones following Graesse, who omits *et pendebatur* and reads *angebatur* for *augebatur*. One would expect the verbs either to agree in their general tendency until the final contrasting negative *non uincebatur*, or to work in contrasting pairs; the latter would be more convincing if the conjunction used had been *sed*. Taking Graesse's *angebatur*, one might offer: 'grounded in the faith, he was burned and hanged, beaten and arraigned, constrained and tortured, slain and (yet) was not defeated'.

186 **vpon this auctorite . . . vigour**: *sus ceste auctorite dur ceruel &c. Celluy ne fut pas blandy mais deboute. Il ne trembloit pas mais les enchassoit et il dit ainsy ailleurs* P2, *super illud, 'Dura ceruice etc.': Hic non blanditur, sed inuehitur, non palpat sed prouocat, non trepidat sed instigat.' Idem*: LgA. *Dura ceruice* is the opening of Acts 7: 51, Stephen's rebuke to the Jews.

191 **profited in obeysinge or obeyenge**: *proffita en obeissant* P2, *perfecit obediendo* LgA.

106 ST DOMINIC

Maggioni, ch. CIX, p. 718; Dunn-Lardeau, ch. 108, p. 691.

GiL omits about three-fifths of the chapter, as detailed below.

12 **for to learn science**: *ad studium amore sapientie addiscende* LgA, 'for study, for the love of acquiring knowledge'.

16 **seculer chanon**: *chanoine regulier* P2.

17 **lyff**: add *aux hommes* P2, add *omnibus* LgA.

20 **euene cristene**: *prochains* P2; forms of *even* with *em-* are recorded, so the EH1 spelling should not have been emended.

24 **of laughynge**: *deresie* P2; s.w. has taken this as *de risee*.

25–6 **of . . . plente**: *de premices* P2, 'of the first fruits'.

32–3 **his faythe was not**: *leur foy nestoit que tricherie* P2, *eorum fides, imo perfidia, uera esset* LgA.

33 **was hys faithe good and**: only GiL.
he preched: *predicarent* LgA.

43 **harde malice**: *durte* P2.

46 **myracle**: add *Factum est autem hoc apud montem Regalem* (variant *Victorialem*) LgA, i.e. Montréal between Carcassonne and Fanjeaux.

47–8 **the hyll of Victorien in the temple of Iouis**: *Fanum Iouis* LgA, i.e. Fanjeaux. LgD *mont Victorial* has been transferred here from the previous sentence. The reason for the substitution of Victorial for Regal is unknown.

48 **amonge**: *contre* P2.

50 **Dawngeoys**: *dalbigois* P2, *Albigensium* LgA.

51 **of other parte**: *dune part et dautre* P2.

54 **amonge other**: *pre ceteris libellis catholicorum* LgA.

61 **secoundely**: add *ac tertio* LgA.

62 **harmynge or**: only GiL.

65 **of the Chirche**: *de catholiques qui saioindrent a luy* P2, *sibi adherentibus* LgA.

67 **filthe**: *boe et autres choses viles* P2.

75 **but**: *par plaies. mais petit a petit. et* P2.

78 **wamelynge**: *toullier* P2, *uolutari* LgA, 'twisting around'. The main sense of *MED wamelen* is 'feel nausea, vomit'; this belongs to sense (b), 'roll around', for which the only citation is dated a1450.

81 **seinge this**: only GiL.

94 **fast by**: *chiez* P2.

95 **occasyon**: *ostentationem* LgA, i.e. of the heretics.

96 **he seynge . . . compassion**: *dont* P2.

97 **his felaw also**: *vng sien compaignon* P2.

97–8 **that by the shadowe . . . errour**: *ut sic clauum clauo obtunderet* LgA, i.e. beat the heretics at their own game.

100–1 **by . . . ensaumple**: only GiL.

103 **and of what office he myght be**: *cuius officium esset* LgA, 'whose function it would be'.

104 **of holy Chirche**: *catholique* P2.

111–12 **as he . . . he**: le pape P2.

113–14 **in that one**: *de lautre* P2.

114 **and**: *humerisque suppositis* LgA.

120 **atte that tyme but**: only GiL.

122–3 **they . . . precheoures**: *re et nomine predicatores futuri unanimiter elegerunt* LgA.

131 **saide**: *disoient* P2, plural.

137 **.ij.**: only GiL.

138 **sayde that he**: only GiL.

139–40 **afore her sone**: only GiL.

140 **holdynge . . . hondes**: *les mains joinctes* P2.
besyly: *son filz* P2.

145 **slayne**: add *me et* LgA.
confessours: add *et docteurs* P2.

146 **will not therof**: *ne sy accordent point* P2.

147 **the**: add *aliquid* LgA.

148 **and yef . . . hem**: *ou autrement* P2.

149 Here GiL omits one story, as does Batallier, Maggioni, 724 (77–82); Dunn-Lardeau, 695 records it from P1 in apparatus.

154 **and**: *tenant* P2.
speris: add *en sa main et les* P2.

175 **we shull renne togederes**: *tu courras auec moy et serons ensemble* P2.

176 **aduersitee**: *aduersaire* P2.

178 **and**: add *commanderent a garder ceste amour a* P2.

Here GiL omits Maggioni, 725–35 (101–247), Dunn-Lardeau, 696–706.

186 **anone he confessed hym**: *confestim cognouit* LgA.

188 **made . . . his**: *froissie* P2.
silence: i.e. the rule of silence in a religious community after the last office of the day.

194–5 **abyde to long from her seruice**: *demeurent au diuin office jour et nuyt et ont entretant ordes pensees* P2, *a diuino officio remanere et interdum immundas cogitationes habere* LgA.

197 **vp and doune**: only GiL.
bordes: add *et disoit souuent vne foys plus vne foys moins* P2, add *'Plus et minue' sepius repetendo dicebat* LgA.

198–9 **sum . . . moche**: *aucuns freres de mengier plus sy que ilz pechent den prendre trop et aucuns qui en prennent moins* P2.

202 **and iangelyd faste**: only GiL.

210 **fast shet**: *enferme* P2, *infernus* LgA.

212 **place**: add *de maleicon* P2.

225 **that is to saye perfite**: *auoir* P2.

226 **And I . . . al thinge**: *et leur donna ce que il peust estroitement* P2; LgD and LgA give the rest of this speech as indirect.

231–2 **for drede lest**: *et ne doubtez car* P2.

236 **Celetre**: *celetre* P2, *cele cite* P1, *eiusdem ciuitatis* LgA.
as: add *in campanili fratrum* LgA.

238–9 **of which . . . other**: *desquelles Ihesu crist et sa mere tenoient le bout denhault* P2.

241 **synginge . . . ioye**: *chantant* P2, *iubilantes* LgA.
in . . . laddres: *In medio autem scalarum in imo* LgA.

243 **ladder**: *eschielles* P2.

255 **assigned**: *signa* P2, *notans* LgA; *MED* does not record the required sense, 'took note of, made a record of'.

256 **was**: add *adonc* P2.

262 **withe . . . opin**: *a peine a instrumens de fer et il fut ouuert et la pierre ostee* P2.

263 **solempnely**: *tresgrant* P2.

264 **place**: *celle* P2.

265 **more . . . aromates**: *nulle autre oudeur nestoit semblable a celle* P2.

266 **ne in the**: *du saint* P2.
pouder: add *ne en la chasse* P2.

268 **many . . . therof**: *loingtaines regions et retint apres ce celle oudeur longuement* P2.

270 **neither . . . aweye**: *combien que elles feussent lauees ou frotees elles retindrent plusieurs iours loudeur et porterent tesmoing de la flaireur* P2.

Here GiL omits Maggioni, 738–43 (299–363), Dunn-Lardeau, 709–12.

271 **Bendom**: *vendosme* P2, *Vindomensis* LgA; Boureau has identified this as Winchester, correctly *Vindoniensis*; Alexander was in fact bishop of Coventry and Lichfield from 1224 to 1238, and his Apostilles have not survived. For an account of him see Boureau, 1331 n. 71.
pisteles: *postilles* P2.

272 ***Misericordia . . . sibi***: Vignay gives this in French.

276 **as moche as he myght**: *dont* P2.

278–9 **Ryghtwisnesse**: *droicture* P2, *iustitia* LgA.

282 **and**: add *hurta a luys pour y estre. mais lostesse qui estoit dedens respondy. ie suis verite et tu nes pas veritable. si ne te receuray point. Et de la alla a la tierce maison oultre celle et* P2.

285 **therfor**: *pource que* P2.

291 **mercy**: *penitentie* LgA.

297 **habite**: add *ordinis* LgA.

298 **Domenik**: add *auant* P2. This extra narration, which Vignay declines to complete, is not in the earliest MSS of LgA, but recorded from Re by Maggioni, 744.

300 **Benyngnay**: *Vignay* P2.

301–7 **thus . . . Amen**: *dist que ceste vision mesmes fut faicte a vng moyne et de rechief a vng autre pour quoy je ne la vueil pas troys foys mettre cy* P2.

107 ST SIXTUS

Maggioni, ch. CX, p. 745; Dunn-Lardeau, ch. 109, p. 713.

4 **emperoures**: not in LgA.
disciples: *diaconibus* LgA.

4, 5 **Decyen, Dacien**: both for *Decius*; H1 has *Dacien*, A2 *Dacyen* for each. Decius died in 251, and Sixtus II was martyred under Valerian in 258.

11 **the**[2]: add *pro fide Christi* LgA.

11–12 **sone dekene**: *sousdiacre* P2, not in LgA.

14 **Valerian**: add *prefectus* LgA.

20 **hym saye so**: *parler des tresors* P2.
faste: only GiL.

22 **Transfiguracion**: add *du corps* P2, LgA as GiL.

23 **the blood**: *le corps* P2, *sanguis* LgA.
wyne: add *quant il peut estre trouue* P2.

24 **elles**: *saltem* LgA.
grape: add *aliquantulum in calice eliquatur* LgA.
in many places: not in LgA.

25 **taken . . . breed**: *inde communicat* LgA.

27 **withe you**: not in LgA.

32 **wyne**: add *non quod in hac die, ut quidam aiunt, transfiguratio sit facta, sed ab apostolis in hac die manifestata* LgA.

36 **that day**: add *Ita legitur in libro qui dicitur Mitrale* LgA.

108 ST DONATUS

Maggioni, ch. CXI, p. 747; Dunn-Lardeau, ch. 110, p. 714.

1 **of**: *cum* LgA.
emperour: add *Et a donc celui iulien fu ordonne en sousdiacre mais* P2.

4 **gret**: *moult de* P2.

5 **vexed**: *MED* records spellings with *w*, but this has been emended because E employs it in this word only here and at 174.317 (where by inadvertence it has been left unemended in the text).

16 **prison**: *tourmens* P2.
sone: *filiis* LgA.

24 **peple**: *clergie* P2.

24–5 **and so he was**: not in LgA.

26 **hym**: *communicatis* LgA.

27 **holy body**: *sanguinem* LgA.

33 **miracle**: add *Pagani autem hoc uiso miraculo conuersi sunt et LXXX baptisma susceperunt* LgA.

41 **he and his felawes were opressed**: *il auoit soif et ses compaignons* P2.

47 **and by . . . goo**: only GiL.

51 **smitethe so sore**: *sault* P2, *exit* LgA.

51–2 **I dare not goo oute**: *ignoro quo uadam* LgA.

52 **to goo oute**: *et jystrai* P2, *exeundi et exeo* LgA.

58 **.x. *libri***: *.CC. solz* P2.
tille . . . paied: *pour ce* P2.

64 **ouercome hym**: *conuainqui cellui* P2.

66–7 **reste in pees**: *dorme de rechief* P2.

71 **hym**: *Donatum* LgA.

72–3 **that . . . reyne**: not in LgA.

73–4 **And oure . . . reyne**: *et il* (add *en* P1) *donna grant habondance* P2.

76–7 **were wasted**: *se departirent* P2.

77 **And Dasyan**: *Enadecien* P2, *Euadracianus* LgA.

109 ST CYRIACUS

Maggioni, ch. CXII, p. 751; Dunn-Lardeau, ch. 111, p. 717.

4 **wher . . . caues**: *scilicet thermas, qui ibi construebatur* LgA; the LgD MSS appear to read *caues*, as does Batallier, though Vignay presumably wrote *eaues*.

5 **an olde man**: not in P2, *senex* LgA.

6 **hem**: only GiL.

19 **vexed and turmented**: *tourmentee* P2, *uexaretur* LgA.

31 **and**: only GiL.

35 **thedir**: *in Babyloniam* LgA.

36 **and baren withe hem**: *naui impositis* LgA.

39 **how . . . trauaile**: *Fatigatus es?* LgA.

44 **sore**: not in P2, *exire* LgA.

51 **hym**: add *nudum* LgA.

52 **after**: *deuant* P2.

53 **Valerian**: *galerien* P2. Galerius was emperor from 305–11; s.w. may have picked up *V* from 55 *Valery* below (although his full name was Gaius Galerius Valerius Maximianus).

58 **take . . . and**: only GiL.

58–9 **that . . . Frenshe**: only GiL.

61 This cannot have been before 305; see 53 above.

62 **asked**: *impetre* P2, which can also mean 'acquired (by asking)'.

63 **of Cyriake**: *des crestiens* P2.

65 **.xix.**: *xxx* P2, *XIX* LgA.

66–7 **loue and to drede**: *doubter et honnorer* P2.

110 ST LAWRENCE

Maggioni, ch. CXIII, p. 754; Dunn-Lardeau, ch. 112, p. 719.

2 **oute of that cuntree**: not in P2, *Romam* LgA.

3 **and . . . wise**: only GiL.

9 **Italye**: *Hyspaniam* LgA.

10 **reson of misterie Iohn Belette**: *raison de maistre iehan beleth* P2, *positioni Iohannis Beleth* LgA, i.e. the time of the martyrdom is incompatible with the opinion of John Beleth.

12 **Dacyen, Dacyene**: *Decien*, *Decien* P2, *decien, dacien* P1, *Decio*, *Daciano*. Vignay correctly distinguished the emperor Decius from Dacianus, a governor under Diocletian, which was indeed the whole point of Voragine's explanation of why Beleth was wrong, but their re-confusion by a predecessor of P2S was apparently not noticed by s.w. This is the only allusion to Dacianus in this chapter, and all others, however spelt, are to Decius. Here and elsewhere the spelling of Decien (Decius) is inconsistent in E, appearing in this chapter with *e*, *a*, and *y*. In LgD and L it is always correct, in D always *a*, and in H1 it generally agrees with E but some cases of *e* have been 'corrected' to *a*. The text here has not been emended, nor are these instances noted in the apparatus, apart from the H1 changes.

Lawence was in fact martyred in 258 under Valerian. Voragine tries to sort this out by reference to various authorities in a passage which GiL omits after 198, including the suggestion that it was not the Emperor Decius, but a *Decio iuniore, qui cesar, non imperator extitit*. However, the Decius who held this office was the son of Emperor Decius, and died with him in 251; and he was appointed Augustus towards the end of his life, reigning under the name Herennius Etruscus.

14 **Vincent**: add *iuuenili etate* LgA.

15 **thanne**: *geune* S.

24 **was rather sayd of**: *fut plus a* P2, *dicaretur* LgA.

25 **of playes**: *spectaculorum* LgA.

29 **sowde and submitte**: *oster le contens et pour sousmettre* P2, *subiugaret* LgA; GiL: 'unite it and subject it to'; LgD: 'remove the disaffection and subject it to'.

30–1 **submitted . . . victorie**: *ad libitum potitus uictoria Romam rediit* LgA.

35 **and thanne**: not in LgA.

36 **empire**: add *et de morte sui domini pertractare* LgA.

37 **his parlour**: *son pauillon* P2, *stratu suo sub papilione* LgA.

39 **praiers**: add *et promesses* P2.

45 **Chirche**: *eglises* P2.

47 **it is trwe**: *potuit esse* LgA.

48 **the**[2]: *aliquem* LgA.

50 **chirche**: add *licet dubitationem habeat uehementem utrum Sixtus tunc temporis fuerit, sicut infra dicetur* LgA.

51 **for drede of**: *et se muca pour* P2.

54 **for . . . idoles**: *pour lamour de ce quil auoit renye les ydoles* P2, *zelo ydolatrie* LgA.

68 **Hast . . . forlingne**: *mas tu veu deslinager* P2, *Numquid degenerem me probasti* LgA; GiL may be rendered: 'Have you found me unnatural or degenerate?' E *forlingne*, H1L *forlinge* belong to *MED forlinen*, 'degenerate', with two examples from Walton's Boethius, neither with these spellings; D *forlyvinge* belongs under *MED forliven*, sense 2, also 'degenerate', whose two examples are from Chaucer's Boethius.

68–9 **Preue . . . couenable**: add *et me commeis* P2, *Experire certe utrum idoneum ministrum elegeris cui commisisti* LgA; L reads *Preve certeynly whether thow haste chose a couenabil mynyster to whom thow hast commyttid*, a correction which can only have come from LgA.

70 **leue, will (. . .) leue**: *laisse*, *laisseray* P2, *desero*, *derelinquo* LgA.

72 **and**: *autem* LgA.

74 **me**: add *sacerdotem leuita* LgA.

79 **pore woman**: *femme vefue* P2.

88 **Holy Seint**: *Saint* P2, *pater sancte* LgA; L reads *holy Fader*.

91 **prouost Valerian**: *preuost* P2, *Partemio tribuno* LgA, P2 giving no name.

105 **taught**: *interrogasset* LgA.

119 **and ioye**: only GiL.

120 **he came ayenne**: *vindrent de rechief* P2, *ambo uenerunt* LgA.

121 **or space**: only GiL.

126 **neuer shull fayle**: *namenuiseront* P2.

126–7 **be departed . . . hymselff**: *sont espartis en chascun par soy* P2, *in singulis disperguntur* LgA.

129 **What . . . thingges**: *Quid variaris per multa?* LgA; 'Pourquoi tous ces détours?' (Roze).

150 **pelotes**: *plommees* P2, *plumbatis* LgA; both French and Latin can mean either 'lead balls' or 'whips with lead balls attached'. For *pelote MED* gives only pellets and various other globular objects.

153 **felonye**: *furore* LgA; at 106.161 s.w. renders LgD *felonnie*, LgA *furorem*, as *wratthe*; this sense is attested for the French by Greimas, but not for English by *MED*, though some citations for sense 4(a), 'ill will *etc.*', arguably approach it.

154–5 **neyther . . . hem**: *nec deos colit* LgA.

159 **Romanus**: *Laurence* P2, *Romanus* LgA, whence it has been corrected by L; s.w. followed the incorrect LgD reading, as retained in EH1D, and tried to adjust at 166 and 169 by translating P2 *romain* as *the Romayne*, in which L agrees with the other MSS.

161 **thi woundes and**: only GiL.

166, 169 **the Romayne**: *romain* P2, i.e. Romanus; see 159 above.

179 **my**: not in LgA.

183 **turned . . . fro**: *le fouloient encontre* P2.

187 **renyed**: the D substitution *revied* is from *MED revien*, 'to vie with or challenge', with three citations from two works, the earliest c1450.

189 **sayd**: add *hylari uultu* LgA.

194 **Tyberien**: *Tyberii* LgA.

197 **feled Beren**: *champ veren* P2, *agro Verano* LgA. This spelling of *feld* not recorded in *MED*.

198 Here GiL omits Maggioni, 760–2 (138–55); Dunn-Lardeau, 725–6.

219 **panier**: *clibano* LgA, 'bread-oven'.

224 **Mylen**: add *ut refert Vincentius in sua chronica* LgA.

229–30 **that**[1] **. . . chalice**: not in LgA.

ressoude: *resoude* P2, *solidatum* LgA; H1 spells as E, T1 *resowde*. It is not recorded by *MED*, but *souden*, 'to join together by soldering', is. L has *resownde*, but *resounden* is not in *MED*, though it has one example in a late text *s.v. resounen* of past *resounded*, which the same text also twice has without the *d*; the senses of this verb, relating to the making of sound, cannot be relevant here. A2 substitutes *make ayen*.

234 **.iij.**: *quatre* P2, *tres* LgA.

257 **Ragonde**: *Kunegundis* LgA; the earliest MSS, following Bartholomew of Trent, give this correct version of the queen's name, but later ones give

various spellings in *R-*, such as *Radegundis*, as do the LgD MSS and Batallier. The same happens at 174.578.

259 **paes**: so H1, but T1 substitutes *paces*; the EH1 spelling is not recorded in *MED s.v. pase*.

coles: *charbons et cendres* P2, *uomeres* LgA, 'ploughshares'.

260 **as**: add *nouisti* LgA.

264 **irnes**: *cendres* P2, *Totam* (. . .) *massam* LgA.

270 **hem, they, saiden**: *le, cellui, dit* P2.

273 **wyght**: add *Et quant nous cuidasmes tout auoir surmonte il getta ce pot en la balance* P2.

275 **that was**: *il apelloit ce pot vng calice* P2, *Ollam calicem uocabat* LgA, 'he called the chalice a pot'.

276 **geue**: *fait faire* P2.

chirche: add *de eniscense en lonneur* P2, *Einstetensi in honore* LgA, i.e. Eichstatt.

280–2 **to amende . . . ignoraunce**: *aucunes choses meilleurs au corps saint du benoit lorens. Mais touteffoys le corps saint lorens fut descouuert par ignorance* P2, *quedam ad corpus sancti Laurentii meliorare* (. . .) *et ubinam corpus eius esset nesciret, subito corpus eius ignoranter aperitur* LgA.

283 **other**: *mansionarii qui corpus eius uiderunt* LgA.

.ix.: *.x.* P2.

GiL omits Maggioni, 765–72 (198–303), Dunn-Lardeau, 729–34.

285 **he**: add *seul* P2.

287 **be many ordenaunces**: *par moult de desordonnances* P2, 'disorders', i.e. fasting has been substituted.

291 **straunge auentures**: *dauentures* P2, *de auoutieres* P1, *adulteria* LgA.

293 **abidethe**: add *et sont encores apellees vigilles* P2.

111 ST HIPPOLYTUS

Maggioni, ch. CXIV, p. 774; Dunn-Lardeau, ch. 113, p. 735.

For the merging of details from accounts of various saints of this name see Boureau, 1341–2.

2 **pees**: i.e. the kiss of peace.

6 **Dacyen**: *Decius cesar* LgA; use of the title *cesar* may mean that Voragine takes this as the younger Decius rather than his father (see note to 110.12).

7 **buried**: *emporte* P2.

14 **made**: not in P2, *effectus* LgA.

18 **thou manacest**: *tu oses nommer* P2; the H1 correction suggests access to LgD or LgA.

27 **diuerse**: *diris* LgA.

30 **before**: *pour* P2.

31 **And thanne Valerian**: *Cui Valerianus: 'Genus seruorum nisi cum suppliciis non emendatur.' Tunc* LgA.
present: add *et gaudente* LgA.

36 **to**: *extra* LgA.

40 **hondes and**: *par les* P2.

41 **to**: *aux colz de* P2.

43 **.CC.lxvj.**: *CCLVI* LgA.

43–4 **hym . . . hym**: *le corps di ceulx et les enseueli* P2.

60 **went . . . chayre**: *in currum aureum ascendit et pergunt ad amphitheatrum* LgA.

62–3 **hathe rauisshed . . . ledith me**: *catenis asperis uinctum me ducis* LgA.

64 **cheynes**: add *igneis* LgA.

64–7 In reality Valerian died as a captive of the Persians, and Decius died in battle.

72 **.xlvij.**: *XLVI* LgA.

75 **Seint Sixt**: *ou siege de rome* P2, *Sancto Sixto* LgA.

78 **Beren**: *veren* P2, *Verano* LgA; see note to 110.197.

GiL omits Maggioni, 776–7 (56–8), Dunn-Lardeau, 737.

81 **desired**: *maluit* LgA.

81–3 **the whiche duke to preue his knighthode put Seint Laurence in his kepinge. And this knight not only pursued Saint Laurence but rather mekely folowed hym**: *lequel duc des cheualiers le voult esprouuer sy quil ne persecuta pas le benoit lorens mis en sa garde mais lensuiuy* P2, *quam dux militum comprobari, beatumque Laurentium sue custodie mancipatum non persecutus est, sed subsecutus* LgA.

83–4 **he discuted**: *il debouta* P2, *discutit* LgA, 'investigated'; for this post-classical sense see Lewis & Short *s.v. discutio*. Vignay took it as the earlier sense 'dispersed'. *MED discuten*, first recorded from a1420 (Lydgate), gives senses 'investigate, discuss', the former of which s.w. is here restoring.

85 **tyrauntes**: *tyrant* P2.

87 **and asked**: only GiL.
fauour: *lamour* P2, *furorem* LgA. Ambrose reads *favorem* (Maggioni, 777).

88 **to be**: i.e. from being.

89 **withe**: i.e. by means of.

90 GiL omits Maggioni, 777–8 (63–75), Dunn-Lardeau, 738–9.

112 ASSUMPTION OF THE VIRGIN

Maggioni, ch. CXV, p. 779; Dunn-Lardeau, ch. 114, p. 739.

1 **boke**: add *apocriffe* P2.

is sent: *est attribue* P2; perhaps for *set*, as H1 correction; see 94 below and note to 2.72.

4 **cuntreyes**: *mundi* (. . .) *regiones* LgA.

14 **more prouable**: *plus approuuee* P2, *probabilius* LgA; context requires the sense 'probable', not recorded in *MED*. See too 61.183.

16 **yere**: add *cum apostoli totidem annis predicauerint in Iudea et circa partes illas, sicut ecclesiastica tradit hystoria* LgA.

19–21 **she hadde . . . tyme**: *elle nauoit pas egalment les confors de son filz qui luy estoient soustrais a temps* P2, *ad tempus subtracti filii equanimiter non ferret subtracta solacia* LgA, 'she could not with equanimity bear the loss of the consolations of her son taken away for a time'. In changing *equanimiter* to *egalment* Vignay gives it the sense 'in the same way' or perhaps 'in the usual way'.

foredrawe: 'taken away', a sense given in *MED* only with the qualification 'by force'.

and . . . longinge: only GiL.

23 **full of grace**: only GiL.

24 **the gretingges**: *salutem* LgA; Ps. 43: 5 *qui mandas salutes Iacob*.

30 **my sone**: *mes filz* P2.

38 **is dredfull and meruailous**: *admirabile est et magnum* LgA.

41 **to God**: *hors* P2.

42 **a moment**: *vne heure* P2, *momento* LgA.

47 **the tree**: *la verge* P2.

48 **morted**, a reduced form for *morwtide*, not recorded in *MED*.

53 **for ioye and**: *et pre gaudio* LgA.

55 **recomaundid**: *recoiue* P2, *commendauit* LgA.

57 **withe besy cure I recomaunde**: *ie creature esmeue* (. . .) *recommande* P2, *cura sollicita recommendo* LgA.

59 **in this wise**: *hommes et femmes* P2, *uiri fratres* LgA.

60 **And**: *igitur* LgA.

63 **alle**: add *les apostres* P2.

63, 64 **now, now**: only GiL.

70 **and wolcomed hem**: only GiL.

77 **atte the assumpcion . . . passinge**: *in dormitione* LgA. *MED* does not record *dormicion*, and when it is in LgD, s.w. renders it at 557 below as *partinge* and at 656 and 780 as *slepinge*, in the latter case LgA reading *obdormitio*.

78 **and weren togederes there**: *et se similiter interfuisse* LgA, i.e. Paul, see 151–2 below.

82–3 **of the moder of the prince of lyff**: *uite principis* LgA; having mistranslated *princeps*, here 'origin', as 'prince', Vignay restored sense by inserting *de la mere* before it.

84 **and[2]**: only GiL.

85 **me**: not in LgA.

86 **after her vertu**: *selon sa vertu* P2, *sicut unusquisque erat sufficiens* LgA.

90 **with songe**: not in LgA.

91 **and**: *les assemblees* P2.

92 **karoll**: *carolles* P2, *choro* LgA; it may be that the ambiguous crossed final *ll* is for plural, and simply repeats the LgD reading, which was apparently caught in error from the following phrase. In either case, none of the senses offered under *MED carole*, sense 1, 'a kind of round dance accompanied by singing; a group of people dancing and singing in a circle', 'a song used by carolers', 'a religious poem or song', is appropriate here.

92–3 **the karolles . . . ordeyned**: *Et auant les caroles des vierges les caroles* (*compaignies* P1) *des sains estoient ordonnees* P2, *et ante torum uirginis acies ordinantur* LgA.

94 **set**: *attribue* P2.

97 **the in**: *in te* LgA.

100 **in delite**: *in delictis* LgA; this is *MED delite* n. (3) 'crime, offence', with only one citation, from Scrope (1450).

101 **refeccion**: the citation is for Wisd. 3: 13, *habebit fructum in respectione animarum sanctarum*. Maggioni (p. 782) identifies the source of the misreading *refectione* in LgA as Bartholomew of Trent; the allusion is to the review of souls at the last judgement (see Lewis & Short *s.v. respectio*).

106 **I come**: *Je voys* P2, *uenio* LgA.

107 **of the boke**: *du quel* P2, *libri* LgA.

109 **so in the morwtyde the soule**: *Sicque Marie anima* LgA.

110 **also**: *autant* P2.

for sorugh: *de la douleur* P2, i.e. from.

120–1 **of hem**: *angelorum* LgA.

121 **came ayenne**: *vindrent a lencontre dicelle* P2; by omitting the object s.w. turns the preposition 'toward' by implication into an adverb; since *MED ayen* does not give the adverb with this sense, it seems that s.w. saw them as ascending and returning.

a kyng: *leur roy* P2.

122–3 **was ioyned to hym**: *super illum innixam* LgA, 'leaning upon him'.

124 **flowyng**: *plain* P2, *affluens* LgA.

ioyned to: *innixa super* LgA.

130 **none . . . ne**: only GiL.

133 **behelde and . . . þat**: not in P2.

135–6 **aboute to wasshe**: 'engaged in washing'.

141 **art**: add *esleu* P2.

145 **of grace**: *de son filz* P2.

147 **of chastite and**: not in LgA.

154 **performed**: *parsuirent* P2.

155 **bere**: add *et les apostres* P2.

159–60 **so mervaylous a suetnesse and**: not in LgA.

163 **to berie**: only GiL.

168 **troubled**: add *nous et* P2.

172 **might . . . he**: only GiL.

178 **by . . . how**: *quant la chambreriere qui estoit huissiere tacusa comment* P2, *qualiter aliquando tibi astiti et qualiter te accusante ancilla ostiaria* LgA.

182 **hope and wene**: *cuide* P2, *spero* LgA.

185 **abode**: add *es bras* P2.

188 **saide**[1]: *fait* P2.

196 **God of ioye be with the**: *Gloria tibi deus* LgA.

201–2 **the right syde . . . euerlastinge**: *ta dextre en pardurablete* P2.

204 **haste the**: *proxima mea* LgA.

206 **touchinge**: *atouchement* P2, *coitum* LgA.

208 **in suche wise**: only GiL.

209 **tourned up . . . eyre**: *fut retourne en la chambre de lair* P2, *sicque ad ethereum assumitur thalamum* LgA.

210 **felawship**: add *angelorum* LgA.

211 **there**: add *Et quant il vint il ne voult pas croire* P2.
so: *subito* LgA.

213 **bothe . . . soule**: *du tout* P2.

215 **Eustachien**: add *Ne forte si uenerit in manibus uestris illud apocryphum de transitu uirginis dubia pro certis recipiatis* LgA, omitted from some MSS.

217–9 **that þe . . . there**: *quod promissa sit et exhibita uirgini omnimoda consolatio, apostolorum omnium congregatio* LgA.

220–2 **and that . . . felawship**: *sepulture in ualle Iosaphat preparatio, exequialis deuotio, Christi et totius curie celestis obuiatio* LgA.

223 **of Iewes**: i.e. by the Jews.
the cleringe of myracles: *lesclaircissement des miracles* P2, *miraculorum in omni causa condecente coruscatio* LgA.

226 **that he dredde**: *quant il vint il doubta* P2.

228 **in the**: *ou tombel au* P2.

230 **of Romaynes**: *Normannorum* LgA.

232 **spere**: add *aussy comme vne lumiere* P2, add *more uexilli* LgA, 'like a standard'.

233 **and folowed hem**: *subsequente populo* LgA.

234 **and trembeled**: *stabatque totus corpore tremulus* LgA.

236 **aboue the devine shewynge**: *diuino iudicio superaddunt et* LgA, 'went beyond the divine judgement and'.

238 **vnapered**: 'disappeared'; *MED* records only one instance, for a1460, in the sense 'become invisible or undetectable'.

238–9 **the duke . . . bosom**: *uisum continuo hostis recepit* LgA, 'the enemy at once recovered their sight'.

242 **a toumbe or**: not in LgA.

246 **man**: add *de celis admirabilis et gloriosus* LgA.

252 **so he saieth**: *si dist il* P2, *Dicit* LgA, i.e. she.
this Reuelacion: *ces mesmes reuelations* P2.

254 **and soule**: not in LgA.
and that: *Nam* LgA.

260 **dayes**: add *apres* P2.

265 **so hadde**: so in all MSS; but *soushauciee* is usually translated *so haunsed*, so this may result from a miscopying in the lost manuscript that lies between the original and all surviving MSS.
worshipfully and excellently: *entierement honnorablement joyeusement excellentement* P2.

266 **holy**: *entierement* P2, *integre in anima et corpore* LgA.

debonairly: *pie* LgA; usual senses of *debonairly*, 'graciously', etc., seem not quite appropriate in this context.

279 **of Auguste**: not in P2, *Septembris* LgA.

280–1 **wol rather mekely drede thanne to define any devout cause**: *veult mieulx debonnairement croire que folement doubter* P2, *potius elegit pie dubitare quam aliquid temere diffinire* LgA, 'chooses rather to hesitate piously than to decide rashly'. Vignay misunderstood and reversed the sense, and s.w. partly corrected it from LgA.

281 **preuithe**: add *ainsy* P2.

282–3 **Sethe tho that arisen withe oure Lorde sayen that the euerlastinge resureccion is not fulfelled in hem**: *que* (*se* P1) *ceulx qui resusciterent auecques nostre seigneur ne dient que la pardurable resurrection ne soit ja acomplie en eulx* P2, *Si non desunt qui dicant in hiis qui cum Christo surrexerunt perpetuam resurrectionem iam esse completam* LgA.

284 **the Euuangelist**: *custodem uirginis* LgA.

288 **assembelinge**: add *de la char* P2, *unitas carnis* LgA.

289–90 **Rotones of wormes . . . Crist**: *pourriture de vers et reproche de condition humaine* P2, *Putredo namque et uermis humane est obprobrium conditionis* LgA; P1 and S are as P2; Batallier substituted *et vers sont* for *de vers et*.

294 **oure Lorde**: *domini celi* LgA.

295 **of heuene**: *du ciel* (*Christi* LgA). *et il est digne destre la ou il est* P2.

296 **able**: *digne* P2.

299 **with . . . sone**[3]: not in P2, but SP1 give *par son propre filz*. Given the scope for eyeskip in these phrases one cannot tell what s.w. wrote, so in the text the full LgA version has been given as reflected by L.

306 **aministresse**: *administreresse* P2, *amenistreresse* S, *ministratrix* LgA, female servant, not recorded in *MED*, though it has one citation for *ministresse*, 'a nun who serves at the altar', a1500, *Rule Minoresses*. E divides *a ministresse*, H1 spells *Amynystresse*.

309–10 Unusually Vignay gives these verses in Latin and also translates into French: *Vierge qui enfanta monta en lair tant a de Jesse vergete. non sans corps mais sans temps tendy a estre ens vierge pure et nette*.

311–12 **Seint Gerarde**: St Gerard, or Gellert, of Csanád, Hungary, 980–1046. Almost all his writings are lost, including this homily. See Boureau, 1347 n. 30.

312 **an omely**: *ses omelies* P2.

313 **Uirgine**: add *letando* LgA.

315 **princes**: *principatus* LgA; this sense, 'principalities, one of the orders of angels', is not given in MED. The usual form seems to have been *principate*; s.w. is following LgD.

316 **sungen**: add *loanges* P2, *hymnizando* LgA.

326 **with gret haste**: *hastiuement* P2, *festiue* LgA, variant *festinam*.

329–30 **that none . . . tell it**: *que nul ne peut racompter* P2, *ineffabili* LgA.

333 **in gret haste**: *hastiuement* P2, *totus festiuus* LgA.

336 **moder**: add *Hec Ieronimus* LgA.

341 **Gerarde**: add *euesque* P2.

343 **preise**: add *hanc* LgA.

346 **trones**: *thronorum iubilationibus* LgA.
songges: *tripudiis* LgA, 'religious dances'.

347 **mightes**: *principatuum* LgA.

348 **princes**: *potestatum* LgA.

349 **obeyed with the praisinges**: *circumstantiata hymnificationibus* LgA.

350 **alle tyme**: *undique* LgA.

351 **gladnesse**: *tripudio* LgA, see 346.

354 **her**[1]: add *ineffabili laude* LgA.

357 **full of envy**: *non volentif* P2.

358 **wicked**: *procacissimi* LgA, 'very impudent'.
dreden her: *sy luy crient mercy* P2, *conclamant* LgA.

360 **the**: add *dolorem* LgA, *sorugh of the* in L.

363 **his**: only GiL.
neuer entamid: *point atouchee* P2, *innupta* LgA; *entamid* strictly means 'wounded'; cf. 206 above, *touchinge*, for a similar euphemism.

364 **moder**: add *de lumiere* P2.

365 **praie . . . the**: *soyes pour nous, nous le te pryons, tousiours depriant nostre seigneur* P2.

368 **art thou troubeled**: *trembles tu* P2.

372 **wylde**: *moult yolis et trop escoleriable* P2, *lubricus* LgA.

373 **And as**: only GiL.
by: *deuant* P2.

377 **her**: i.e. the soul.
What do you here?: only GiL.

379–80 **soule . . . hers**: *eius animam* LgA.

380 **was take**: *estoit* P2, *finisse uitam* LgA.

388 **sextayne**: *secretain* P2.

391–2 **by . . . Lady**: only GiL.

394 **vnwisely**: *indiscreta liberalitate* LgA.

395 **to**: *a donner* P2.

400 **full of sorugh and of wepinge**: *amy de tristesce et de pleur* P2, *meroris amicum* LgA, 'appropriate to grief'; s.w. renders *amy de* as *full of* and transfers the phrase from the place to the knight.

404–5 **and hevinesse**: only GiL.

407 **euer thou dede**: *deuant* P2.

412 **atte suche a day**: not in P2, *tali die* LgA.

427 **the clothinge**: *semblable habit* P2.

428 **the bodi**: *la dame* P2.

448 **and asked . . . Lady**: only GiL.

451 **fende**: add *Et quant il reuint il trouua encores sa femme dormant et lesueilla et lui racompta tout ce qui luy estoit aduenu. Et quant ilz furent retournez a lostel ilz getterent hors toutes les richesses du dyable* P2.
abide: *demoureren*t P2.

452 **bothe . . . gostely**: only GiL.

453–4 **to whos . . . Amen**: only GiL.

455 **rauisshed**: add *en vision* P2.

456 **redy**: only GiL.

463 **duell**: *mori* LgA.

464–5 **Lete . . . hymselff**: *laisse lomme parler pour toy* P2, *Permittitur, homo, pro te loqui* LgA.

466 **She**: i.e. the soul.
prescripcion of tyme: legal right resulting from continuous possession.

474 **trembelinge**: add *et plorant* P2.

479 **hym**²: add *vertueusement* P2, 'effectively'.

481 **whan**: add *le viij.*ᵉ *iour fut venu* P2.

483 **gostely**: *infernel* P2.

485 **he**: i.e. it.

486–7 **deye . . . they**: not in LgA.

487 **in dethe**: *ignibus* LgA.

489 **dethe**²: *sanguinem* LgA.

493–4 **saide hym so wicked a seruaunt**: *seruoit a sy cruel seigneur* P2.

497 **Renne . . . mynde**: *recorde toute ta pensee* P2, *tota mente recurre* LgA.
Lady: *matrem* LgA.

498 **in what . . . beste**: *de* P2.

502 **to drawe in his partie**: *de tirer de lautre part* P2, i.e. of the balance.

505–23 is in S but omitted by P2.

516 **fader**: *Mater* LgA.

524 **walked**: *estoient* P2, *stabant* LgA.

526–7 **grete . . . warde**: *remiges per flumen impetu nimio nauigantes* LgA.

529 **stuarde**: *preuost* P2.
of Fraunce: *Francorum* LgA.

529–30 **was apostata . . . Seint Gal**: LgA follows Bartholomew of Trent. Ebroin and the then King Theodoric III of Neustria having been driven out of power, Ebroin was confined at Luxeuil, not St Gall, and took monastic vows, but on seeing a political opportunity renounced them and regained power. See *Annales Mattenses* in *MGH Scriptores*, i. 317.

533 **wolde haue deuoured**: *voulions desrompre* P2.

534 **ouer youre houre**: i.e. outside the times permitted by the Rule.

535–6 **and the helpe . . . Amen**: only GiL.

538–9 **many . . . her**: *y metoit moult de remedes* P2.

539 **water**: add *aspersionem* LgA.

540 **his malyce**: *il* P2.

542 **withe . . . herte**: not in P2, *protinus* LgA.

548 **made and ordeyned**: *compilato* LgA.

552 **endeles**: only GiL.

553 **named**: *surnomme* P2.
Vesture: *le vesteur* P2, *Vestitor* LgA.

554 **his beforegoers**: add *qui y furent* P2.
to be foryete: *omittendum* LgA.

555–6 **disposed to lede to hym the lyff of his moder he sent to her the custumed aungell for to shewe her**: *ordonna a soy de la vie de sa mere et de lamener a soy par lange acoustume et luy denonca auant la demonstrance* P2, *ad se uite genitricem disposuit adducere, per angelum consuetum ei prenuntiat (. . .) exhibitionem* LgA.

557 **partynge**: *dormicion* P2; see note to 77 above.
sodenly: *sans le sauoir* P2, *inopinate* LgA.

560–1 **to take . . . to me and with me**: *prendre ma mere auecques moy* P2, *te* *assumendi ad me matrem meam* LgA, i.e. these words in GiL and LgD are spoken as if to the angel, but in LgA as to Mary.

562 **shalt yelde ioyfully alle**: *rendras yoieuses* P2.

564 **world**: add *corrompable* P2.
but take: *adeptura* LgA, 'being about to attain'.

567 **vnnumerable**: *interminabilem* LgA; L has *interminabille*.

574 **of erthes**: *terre* LgA, singular.

577–8 **contricion of peyne**: *Contriction de detrenchement* P2, 'the harm of destruction'.

581 **thou gauest hym**: only GiL.

583 **none**: *lamour dun* P2.

585 **hem that be fletynge**: *fluctuantium* LgA, 'of those tossed by the waves'. Senses of *fleten*, *fleting* in *MED* carry more neutral senses of travelling on water.

586 **stiers**: 'those who ascend'; *MED* records only riders of horses, camels etc. for this word.

590 **fulfelle in thi persone**: *meam personam impleant* (*in*). LgA.

594 **dedlynesse**: *mortaille* P2; s.w. takes *mortaille*, 'funeral', as *mortalite* (see 642 below).

594–5 **whanne . . . done**: *dont* P2.

596 **neygheboures and**: not in LgA.

599–600 **devine aungeles**: *vertu diuine des anges* P2.

600 **gladly**: *ad morientis lectum* LgA.

601–2 **A whi dredest thou**: *tu doubtes* P2.

610 **father**: GiL here omits Maggioni, 799 (349–50), Dunn-Lardeau, 757.

617 **and þat I were not**: *quam* (. . .) *interessem* LgA; L *than that I weer* follows LgA.

621–2 **and sodenly . . . reyned**: *plus blanc que vne nue. et les apostres furent amenez deuant la porte aussy comme sil apleussent* P2, *quasi nubes candide generatur et apostoli ante ianuam domus uirginis instar imbrium collocantur* LgA.

624 **anounced**: add *par lange* P2.

627–8 **My dere . . . kepe you**: *Auete, filii unigenite mei* LgA.

634 **expositour**: *impetratio* LgA, i.e. that which I have requested.

635 **haue sein**: *voy* P2.

638 **born**: *transportee* P2.

642 **mortalite**: *mortaille* P2, i.e. funeral clothes; see 594 above.

643 **into**: *en* P2.

647–8 **spouce . . . derkenesse**: *celestium thalamorum sponsa et trifidum et triadici luminis candelabrum* LgA.

649 **only**: only GiL.

650 **Archebisshopp**: add *Germanus* LgA.
witnessithe: add *similiter* LgA.

652 **and the . . . wise**: *dicens* LgA.

653 **thou Goddes moder**: not in P2, *o dei genitrix* LgA.

654 **mankinde**: *humaine nature* P2.

654–5 **the yee . . . there**: *loeil qui vous regarde* (*garde* P1) P2, *qui nos custodit oculus tuus* LgA.

655–6 **and thi slepinge**: *ne ta dormicion* P2, *nec mendax dormitio* LgA, 'nor is your dormition a falsehood'.

656–9 The verbs with future auxiliaries are either understood or in present tense in LgA, in LgD *racomptent*, *crient*, and *preschent* (GiL *shall tell, shull crye, shull preche* are present, others future).

657 **ouer . . . shewe**: *en terre et de eulx sera demonstree* P2, LgA as GiL.

658–9 **shull crye worship to the and to hem that amynistre the fro hem**: *uociferant honorem qui ex eis tibi administratus est* LgA, 'proclaim the honour that by them was paid you' (Ryan).

659 **seruise of lyff**: *obsequium* LgA.

662 **as . . . they**: *ut nosti et ipse* LgA.

664–5 **noble doctour and right grete souueraigne of the noble theologens were present**: *noble et tresgrant souuerainete de theologiens estoient presens* P2, *dei locorum eximia et maxima theologorum summitas* LgA; *dei locorum*, which is omitted by Graesse, has variants *dialogorum* and *dei logorum* recorded by Maggioni.

667 **after . . . thought**: *prout unusquisque esset immense uirtutis, bonitatem uiuifice infirmitatis* LgA, 'according to the immense capacity of each, about the goodness of that life-giving weakness'.

668 **the**: *vng* P2.

676 **moder**: add *in uallem Iosaphat* LgA.
dayes: add *illecques diligemment* P2.

685 **the body**: add *ut ait* LgA.

687–8 **I am but a thinge feint and haue kept that thou tokest me**: *tuum sum figmentum et tuum seruaui depositum* LgA, 'I am your creature and have looked after what you entrusted to me'.

688 **awoke**: add *ut ait* LgA.

689–90 **make moche sorugh**: *furent forment courrouciez* P2, *contristari plurimum* LgA.

696 **gret bruit**: *impetu* LgA; *MED* records *bruit* in this sense, 'commotion', only from Merlin a1500(c1450?).

698 **to drawe doune**: *tangere* LgA.
hys hondes: *eius tactu* LgA.

703 **the bere**: *corpus* LgA.
blessed: *perpetue* LgA.

706 **and were al hole**: *dont elles estoient esrachiees* P2.

707 **leeff**: *date* P2.
of the palme: *de* (*du* P1) *palmier et luy donna* P2; see 592 above.

709 **place**: *predium* LgA.

710 **sepulcre**[2]: add *uiuifico* LgA.

712 **sydoyne**: this is the form in the French MSS; *MED s.v. sindon(e* does not record *sidoine*, but gives the latter as a variant French form. L *syndony* may show knowledge of the more usual ME form or follow LgA *sindone*.

714 **aposteles**: add *et discipuli* LgA.

720 **with right gret reuerence**: only GiL.

721 **Euuangelyst**: add *et theologi* LgA.
he was: only GiL.

723 **he**[2]: add *sen esmerueilla et* P2.

728 **and**[1]: not in LgA.
wrothe: *contristatus* LgA.

729 **youre**: *nostri* LgA.

731 **vestement**: *vestemens* P2.

735 **emperice**: add *Pulcheria* LgA.
in mynde of holy Chirche: *sancte memorie* LgA.
and: only GiL.

740 **that citee riall**, i.e. Constantinople, where the bishops were staying on the way back from the synod.
the same: *le sane* P2, *synodum* LgA; it is likely that *same* is an early scribal error for s.w. *sane*, and the text should have been emended.

743 **for kepinge of this citee**: *ad custodiam huius urbis* LgA, 'into the care of this city'.

743–4 **the blessed . . . Virgine**: *le corps de ceste vierge* P2, *corpus illud* LgA.

746 **withe her sone**: only GiL.

749 **there**: *in dicta ecclesia* LgA.

ordeyned: *mis* P2.

750 **saide and**: only GiL.

753–4 **the forsaide sermon**: i.e. the sermon of Cosmas Vestitor; see 553 above.

755 **for that tyme**: *et ipse* LgA.

757 **preised (. . .) and saide**: *oy* P2, *Ait* LgA.

759 **annuel**: *annuel* P2, *animel* P1, *animata* LgA, 'living'. ME *annuel* can mean only 'annual' or 'anniversary', which do not fit; the other MSS seem to have regarded it as a name.

761 **innocent**: add *et simple* P2.

762 **whiche God receyued**: *quod deum suscepit* LgA.

763 **vnknowen**: *non sachant* P2.

764 **shall not faile**: *non in terram abiit* LgA.

765 **annuel**: as 759 above.

766 **that**: add *naturaliter* LgA.

773 **tabernacles**: *secula* LgA.

773–4 **is lefte up the body**: *satapist soubz le corps de la lune* P2, *sublunari corpore latens* LgA, i.e. concealed behind a sublunary body.

776 **and thou**: *sic et tu* LgA.
verray: *perennem* LgA.

776–7 **withoute wastinge and perfit**: *sans degaster* P2, *inconsumptus* LgA.

780 **called**: *appellanda* LgA.

782 **and Ihesu Crist**: not in LgA.

784 **comynge**: *ascensum* LgA.

787 **is well . . . dethe**[2]: *est bien dicte mort* P2, *benedicitur* LgA, a surprising error by Vignay.

788 **makithe**: *exhibet* LgA.

788–9 **for . . . departinge**: *Car ta mort ne ta transmigration ou ta perfection ou ton departement* P2, *mors enim tua non beatitudo tua, nec transmigratio tua perfectio tua, sed nec recessus* LgA.

789 **ne makithe the**: not in LgA.

789–90 **eny point of**: *point* P2; s.w. has misunderstood *point*, which completes the French negative *ne . . . point*.

793 **haue made the blessed**: supplied by Vignay, the verb in Latin being understood, *Tua securitas, etc.*

794 **only**: not in LgA.

dethe: add *mais* P2; this omission is probably attributable to an early scribe rather than the translator, and should perhaps have been emended.

796–7 **and payne**: only GiL.

797 **in**: i.e. into.
For: *Si enim* LgA.

800 **euerlastinge**: *sine principio* LgA.

801 **faders**: *parens* P2, *parentes humani generis* LgA.

802–3 **and of glotenye**: *peccati crapula iam ferentes* LgA, 'already bearing the inebriation of sin'.

804–5 **putte oute alle the filthe of synne**: *totius passionis immissionem excussit* LgA, 'drove out the source of all suffering'.

806, 810 **ere**: *MED* records a small number of instances of 'ear' with initial *h*, some at least of them northern; since it appears here twice in E and T2, and in H1 before a corrector changed it, it should perhaps not have been emended.

813 **durst, might**: reversed in LgA.

814 **all**: *ipsam* LgA.

815 **saithe**: *Addit* LgA.
his owne: *ses mesmes* P2, *eisdem* LgA.

817 **preche to the peple**: *preschier* (*peschier* S) *des hommes* P2, *hominum piscationi* LgA.

818 **one holy word**: *vne saine parolle* P2, *vne saine* (or *same*) *de paroles* P1, *sagena uerbi* LgA, i.e. continuing the fishing image, the net of the word.

819 **weddinges**: *nopces* P2; s.w. adopts the idiomatic French plural. *MED* records plural forms from the Wycliffite New Testament for Latin *nuptiae*; L here substitutes the normal ME singular.
of God: *patris* LgA.

821–2 **in assembelynge hem betwene his wynges**: *ultra quasdam aquilas congregans et colligens* LgA; one MS and Graesse read *aquas* for *aquilas*; Ryan translates 'gathering and collecting them from beyond the seas'.

824 **seintes**: add *qui la estoit* P2, add *que corporaliter aderat* LgA.

828 **most comfort**: *glorieux* P2.

829 **vnordeyned**: *desestablis* P2, *destitutis* LgA, 'deprived'. This sense is not recorded in *MED* for *unordeinen*, but following the French can here perhaps be translated 'detached'.

832 **of . . . departinge**: *de la departie* P2, not in LgA.

834 **my**: add *dilectis* LgA.

836 **blessed Lorde**: only GiL.

839 **Lord**: *Sire filz* P2, *fili* LgA.

841–2 **vnto . . . erthe**: *Tibi et non terre commendo corpus meum* LgA.

849 **tabernacles**: *tabernacle* P2, *tabernaculo domini* LgA.

850 **and**[1]: *adimpleti* LgA.
of: *ex contactu* LgA.

850–2 **what . . . hadde**: not in LgA.

852 **Fendes**: *morbi et demones* LgA.

853 **assencion**: add *de lesperit* P2.

854–5 **for . . . water / And . . . bodi**: transposed in P2.

862 **hedes**: *ceruicibus* LgA.

863–4 **other . . . ronnen**: *et les anges aloient deuant les vngs et les autres suioient le saint corps et les autres le couuroient* P2, *angelis antecedentibus subsequentibus aliisque sacrum corpus uelantibus* LgA; s.w. misread *couuroient* as *couroient.*

868 **one**: add *Hebreum* LgA.

869–70 **assailed it wodely and**: *pour qui les anges tramblent et enforsenant* P2, *ad quod angeli trepidabant accedere ac* (. . .) *furibunde* LgA.

871 **any stocke**: *.ij. bastons* P2, *ligna* LgA.

872 **a drie stocke**: *vng tronc* P2.

874 **and made**: *donec* LgA.

877–8 **bywette . . . parties**: *gouttes et lermes de saincte sueur decouroient* P2, *lacrime, sudoris gutte fluentes* LgA.

880–1 **And . . . digged**: *et disoient que sainte fontaine de dieu non fouy* P2, *Decebat autem dei sacrarium, fontem indefossum* LgA.

882 **cutte**: *irrigatam* LgA.
olyue: D *holiffe,* but no spelling with *h* is recorded in *MED.*

886 **body**: add *post mortem* LgA.

891 **multeplienge resones**: *multipliablement* P2.

894 **sone**: *ame* P2.

897 **his writynge**: *ses escrips* P2, *ses auctoritez* P1, *actibus* LgA.
receyued and: only GiL.

899–900 **Sethe . . . thinkithe**: *dont lescripture nen recommanda* (*recommande* P1) S, *Vnde scriptura nihil commendat* LgA .

903 **We . . . mankinde**: *Nous recordans de la condition humaine* P2.

905 **of**: *et* P2.

907 **to the lordshippe . . . of God**: *tante aule dei prerogatiue* LgA, i.e. 'to the prerogative of so great a habitation of God'.

910 **she**: i.e. the flesh.

912 **woman**: add *eue* P2, not in LgA.

914 **Marie susteyned neuer suche sorugh**: *Erumpnam Maria sustinuit* LgA, 'Mary endured pain'.

916 **thou**: *se* P2. E *thou* is a possible spelling for 'though' (e.g. 8.158, 101.122), but all other MSS give forms such as *þu*, suggesting the pronoun, whatever their usual spellings for 'though'. The error must go back to a copy between the translator's copy and the common archetype of the extant MSS.
in sum thingges: *en enfantement* P2, *erumpnis* LgA.

917 **But**: *ergo* LgA.

918 **excepte . . . generalitees**: *exceptee et de aucunes autres generalitez* P2.

918–9 **for that . . . lordeship**: *pource que la dignite luy donne celle seignorie* P2, *quam tanta attulit dignitatis prerogatiua* LgA.

919–20 **we mowe not saie**: *nec tamen* LgA.

920 **dethe**: add *numquid impium erit* LgA.

923 **and**: only GiL.

925 **breke**: *soluere* LgA.

933 **man in**: *omnem* LgA, variant *hominem*.

933–5 **Yef verrily the nature of the moder be the sones hit is conuenient that the sones be the moders**: *Sil est filz de vraye mere couuenable chose est que elle soit mere de celluy filz* P2, *Si natura matris est filius, conueniens est ut sit et filii mater* LgA.

936–8 **Yef vnite may make grace witheoute properte of spirituel nature, how moche more may it make vnite of grace by bodely and spirituel natiuite**: *se grace sans propriete despecial et corporel nature peut faire vnite. Comment plus dont le peut faire vnite de grace et corporel et especial nature* (*natiuite* S) *peut faire vnite de grace* P2, *Si enim unitatem facere potest gratia sine proprietate specialis nature, quanto magis ubi gratie unitas et corporalis est specialis natiuitas* LgA, 'For if grace can create unity without the property of a special nature, how much the more when the unity of grace and the bodily birth is unique'.

939 **that they be**: *Vt sint* LgA, 'may they be'.

942 **iuges**: *iugiez en vng* P2.

943 **wheder**: *ou* P2.
be: add *fors* P2, i.e 'where should she be, if not'.

947 **conseiued and bare**: *conceust* P2, *genuit* LgA.

954 **vncorrupte**: *non corrompable* P2.

955 **for that that**: *pource que* P2.

957–8 **seith ofte tyme**: *dist aucune foiz* S.

959 **ministres**: *ministre* P2.

964 **her lyff**: *infantiam eius* LgA.

965 **dethe of the**: only GiL.

978 **grace**: add *pre omnibus* LgA.

979 **Nay God defende**: *nennil non* P2, *Absit* LgA.
for: add *se* P2.

980 **we . . . precious**: *Maria sane est pretiosissima. Confitendum igitur censeo* LgA.

981 **receiued**: *assumptam* LgA.

984 **humanite**: add *putredinis* LgA.
wormes: add *de pourreture* P2, not in LgA.

985 **yef**: only GiL.
sauioure: add *suum et* LgA.

986–7 **the clothes . . . fyre**: Dan. 3.

988 **a straunge clothinge**: *ueste aliena* LgA, i.e. 'clothing of one not related'.

990 **and by his only grace**: *sola misericordia* LgA, belonging to preceding clause.
vncorrupte: add *gratia* LgA.

991 **in a pitte**: *en la fosse* P2, not in LgA.

991–2 **is . . . kepe**: *non seruanda est* LgA.

992–3 **by so many yeftes of merites and of dignites**: *par tant de dons et de merites de dignitez* P2, *tantis donata meritis dignitatum* LgA.

994 **haue not kepte nature**: *naturam non seruasse* LgA, 'nature has not saved'.

998 **was**: *est* P2.

999–1000 **she is lyving . . . all**: *sic integraliter uiuens que omnium integram genuit uitam* LgA.

1002 **thine**: add *Hec Augustinus* LgA.

113 ST BERNARD

Maggioni, ch. CXVI, p. 811; Dunn-Lardeau, ch. 115, p. 769.

5 **she . . . be**: *futuros* LgA.

7 **had no cure**: *refugiebat* LgA, 'avoided'; *cure*, 'care, concern', etc., can come through context to mean 'liking', *MED* sense 1. (b), as in such citations as *He nad noo cure of delicate mettis.*

8 **but**: only GiL.

10 **goodnesse**: add *materni* LgA, i.e. her own.

11 **delite**: *la cours* P2, *curie* LgA, i.e. public life.

12 **harde**: *grosses* P2.

26–7 **to . . . loue**: *Pueruli* (. . .) *bono zelo* LgA.

31 **bering**: *naissant* P2, *iterum nascens* LgA. *MED beren* does not record this 'passive' sense.

36 **beginningges**: *initia* LgA, i.e. his early works.

41 **chastite**: *castitatis proposito* LgA, 'resolution of chastity'.

51–2 **the fende . . . to synne**: *le dyable trippoit et lesmouuoit* P2, (*illa*) *deinde palpans et stimulans nouissime* LgA; *MED trippen* gives 'dance, caper', etc.; the French and Latin appear to have more suggestive overtones.

52 **at the laste she**: *cum immobilis ipse persisteret, illa licet impudentissima esset* LgA.

57 **wrechidly**: *desuergondeement en secret* P2.

60–1 **leude wreche**: *maleureuse* P2.

61 **priueli**: only Gil.

67–8 **what . . . afraied**: only GiL.

69 **assailingges**: *agais* P2.

70 **tresour**: add *castitatis* LgA.

75–6 **holy purpos**: *conuersion* P2.

76 **in no wise**: only GiL.
demenid hym: *les mena* P2.

78 **brother**: add *noble cheualier* P2.

81 **on . . . yeue**: *jay vng seul trauail. il donnera* P2, *sola uexatio* (. . .) *dabit* LgA.

88–9 **for to . . . sene hym**: only GiL.

91 **wete wele**: *Scito* LgA.

104–5 **a litell plot**: *tant seulement la terre* P2.

105 **well deuided . . . euenly**: *deuise a droit* P2, *ex equo diuisio* (. . .) *facta* LgA.

106 **wrothe and was**: only GiL.

109 **sharpe to hymself**: *inspire* P2, *in spiritum absortus* LgA.

111 **there . . . wyndowes**: *domus haberet testudinem* LgA, 'the house had a vaulted ceiling'.

113 **ende of the yere**: *chief de leglise* P2, i.e. the apse.

116 **was**: *degebant* LgA; 117 *his* should also be plural.

117 **holme**: *fou* P2, *fagi* (. . .) *et panem de ordeo et milio et uicia comedebant* LgA; *holme* is either holly or holm oak; *fou/fagus* is beech.

118 **wolde**: *veilloit* P2.

121 **God**: here LgD and GiL omit Maggioni, 815 (62).

122 **drawen to**: add *menger* P2.

128 **sumtyme**: *aliquando* LgA.

129 **in stede of botre**: not in LgA; see 132 below.

131 **grasse**: *sang* P2, *sagimen* LgA, 'lard', variant *sanguinem*.

132 **botour**: *viure. Il disoit que leaue seule lui sembloit bonne. Car quant il la prenoit elle luy refroidoit la bouche et le gosier* P2, placed here in LgA and P1, but misplaced to follow 129 *errour* in P2S. P2 and S read *viure* for P1 *burre*, LgA *butyro*, but at 129 P2 has *beurre,* S *viure*. P2 *viure*, also in S here and at 129 above, seems to be no more than a copying of ill-written *burre*.

135 **holme**: *fou* P2, see 117 above.

137 **holi orison and**: not in LgA.

138 **fully expouned**: *exposee* P2, *suppositam uel expositam* LgA.

139–41 **that he putte amonge his wordes mellyngly . . . after that**: *cum interloquendum ex hiis que suggerebat spiritus etsi non infideli minus tamen fidenti animo reseruaret ut haberet quid diceret denuo tractaturus* LgA, 'while speaking he held back in his mind some of what the Spirit suggested, not through disbelief, but being less certain, so that he would have something to say when dealing with the subject again in the future'.

mellyngly: *mesleement* P2, 'in a mixed manner'; *MED* records *medlen* v. and *medling(e* ger., both with ll- spellings for dl-, but no adverbial forms.

144 **in clothinge**: add *sordes nunquam* LgA, 'but shabbiness never'.

144–5 **outrageous clothinge**: *ordures* P2.

146 **hem in**: only GiL.

148 **or wondre**: only GiL.

149 **and**: not in LgA.

152 **refreine hym**: add *et conuenoit plus la guillon a faire le rire que il ne faisoit au laissier* P2.

153–4 **in wronge . . . bodi**: i.e. in insults, damage to objects, harm to the body.

155 **ensaumple**: *hiis exemplis* LgA. There are three of these, of which GiL omits the first, Maggioni, 817 (80–2), Dunn-Lardeau, 774, in which Bernard reacts calmly to an intemperate letter from a bishop whom he had gently admonished in a previous letter.

159 **charge**: add *sed et illis, inquit, qui tulerunt, leuius est parcendum, tum quia hoc Romana cupiditas sustulit, tum quia magna pecunia magnam eis temptationis occasionem ingessit* LgA.

161 **monke**: add *et quant il ne luy voult accorder* P2.

162 **hous**: *eglise* P2.

169 **cheke**: add *tam grauiter* LgA.

170–1 **for to . . . smete hym**: not in LgA.

174 **whan thei entred**: *qui vouloient entrer* P2.

176 **and fastin you . . . within**: *Si ad ea qui intus sunt festinatis* LgA, preceding 175 *Leuithe*.

180 **perissed**: *perilloit* P2.

182 **brother**: *freres* P2.

183 **her bretheren**: *il* P2.

189 **God**: *Christus* LgA.

194 **it was not lefull to**: *il ne la pouoit pas* P2.

196 **the stappes**: *la forme* P2.

197 **strangly**: *fort* P2, *repente* LgA.

199 **ouercam . . . religion and**: only GiL.

200 **assoiled**: add *ab ipso* LgA.
mariage: add *et entra en vng monstier* P2.

209–10 **that he . . . that one**: *sy que il luy souffit auoir souffert lune* P2, *altero ipse contentus* LgA.

210 **and of his merci**: only GiL.

212 **the uision passed away**: *conuentus ille solutus* (*est*). LgA.

213–14 **trauaile . . . wakingges**: *abstinentia, labore et uigiliis* LgA.

214 **continuel**: *grauissima et fere continua* LgA.

215 **folw the couent**: i.e. live the conventual life.

216 **praied**: add *instanter* LgA.

219 **thus . . . praieres**: *maleurez hommes. vous estes plus fors et auez vaincu* P2.
saue me: *espargnez moy* P2.

225 **his bretheren**: *les hommes* P2, *Fratres* LgA.

227 **and comfort**: only GiL.

232 **it was . . . therof**: *le prieur le dit a lun des freres et celluy le dit a lomme de dieu* P2.

234–5 **in . . . he went**: *Il alla vne iournee* P2, *totius diei itinere pergens* LgA.

235 **lake**[2]: add *sy quil lapperceust* P2, add *aut se uidere non uidit* LgA.

238 **For**: not in LgA.

240 **of**: *ab* LgA.

241 **to alle**: add *quem sibi omnes, ipse se nemini preferebat* LgA.

244 **chaunged**: add *et reputoit luy plus estre deffaillant* P2.

245 **and bretheren**: only GiL.

247 **bifore the Houres**: *aut orans* LgA.

251 **A, lorde**: *Orez* P2,*Vere nunc* LgA.

252 **that here the**: only GiL.

256 **pesibly**: *silenter* LgA.

259 **iaper**: *ioueur* P2, 'gambler'; *iaper* has various senses, here 'trifler'.

264 **cheuisaunce**: *cheuance* P2, *capitale* LgA; *MED* sense 2, 'provision or arrangement for accomplishing something', i.e. in this case stake money.

266 **truly**: not in P2, *libenter* LgA.

268 **in hope**: only GiL.
withdrawe hym: *le retraire* P2, *eum iterum reuocare* LgA, 'bring him back'. *MED* does not record this sense; probably s.w. took it as *withdrauen* sense 4 'restrain'; compare 90.72.

276–7 **and so . . . man**: only GiL.

278 **rode**: add *sur sa jument* P2.

279–80 **to this man . . . stable**: *de cordis instabilitate* LgA, i.e. of general human inconstancy, not that of himself or the *vplondisshe man*.

287 **trouthe**: *par ta foy que se tu penses a autre chose tu ne le me celeras pas* P2.

287–8 **and behight . . . trouth**: only GiL.

290 **he thought**: *importuna cogitatio* (. . .) *cordi suo se ingerit* LgA.

295 **was sette**: *sy sestoit mis* P2.

296 **lete hym be there**: *dissimulauit* LgA.

300 **fro the reyne**: *et le mucier* P2, not in LgA.

301 **and handle**: *hardiement* P2, *ne formides* LgA; *handle* is perhaps from *MED hondlen* sense 3, 'deal with, act upon', but may result from an earlier scribal error.

304 **chartre**: *charite* P2.
moisture: *molestiam* LgA.

308–9 **hem to the Chirche**: *les eglises* P2, *ipsos cum ecclesia* LgA.

309 **he had done and**: not in LgA.
fro Melan: *a milan* P2, *Papiam* LgA, to Pavia.

312 **lekys**: add *et brassicas deuorans* LgA.
wenist . . . oute: *tu ne me osteras pas* P2.

313 **hous**: *anicula* LgA, 'little old woman'.

314 **Seint Sire bare worship**: *beatus autem Syrus* (. . .) *deferre uoluit* LgA.

314–15 **wolde . . . that night**: *ne fist a celle nulle garison* P2; *celle nulle* misread as *celle nuit*.

316 **chide**: *per os eius garrire* LgA.
Sire: *Syrulus* LgA, a contemptuous version of his name.
Bernard: *Bernardinus* LgA, 'little Bernard'.

319 **this place**: *hac anicula* LgA.

320 **y am**: *je y suys* P2.

324 **In his glorie**: '*In gloria.' Et sanctus: 'Et tu in gloria fuisti?' Quo respondente: 'Vtique.'* LgA.

325 **he fell oute**: *Nous encheismes moult* P2.

337 **fende**: add *qui habitoit a elle et la lassa merueilleusement* P2, add *petulante et incubo uexabatur* LgA.
.vij.: *.vj.* P2.
in . . . luxurie: *abusus est ea et incredibili uexauit libidine* LgA.
as God wolde: *dont* P2.

340–1 **most enemy**: *persecuteur tres cruel* P2.

347 **hym**: add *cruelment* P2.

353 **the**: *eadem* LgA.

358–9 **sette afere with charite**: *a face embrasee et les flambiaux* (*les iex flamboians* P1) P2, *ignea facie et flammeis oculis* LgA.

370 **Almayne the Gret**: *regnum Germanie* LgA.

378 **a monke**: omit and add *Nenin* (*Nenil* P1) P2, *monachus* (. . .) *Absit a me* LgA.

379–80 **And . . . that**: *Et* P2, *Quid multa?* LgA.

388 **pensif**: *temptatus* LgA.

388–9 **thanne . . . other**: *des autres autant comme il auoit este plus tristre* P2.

389 **blamid**: *amicabiliter improperaret* LgA.

395 **solempne sacrifices of helthe**: *sacrefice* (add *de but* S, add *de salu* P1) P2, *hostiam salutarem* LgA, 'his requiem mass'.

396 **the ioye of hym**: i.e. that he was in glory; s.w. usually translates *gloire* as *ioye*.

397 **chaunged the forme of his orison**: for the customary post-communion prayer, Bernard substituted that for the mass of a confessor-bishop; see Boureau, 1353 nn. 45–7 .

398 **saienge**: add *ainsy a joieuse voix* P2.
Seint: *beatum* LgA.

401–2 **herde . . . saide**: *innueret* LgA.

404 **his fete**: *sacra eius uestigia* LgA.

405–6 **Lentin . . . Shroftide**: *la quarantaine aprouche* P2. *MED Shrof-tide* is first recorded for 1433–4 , and *shrof-* before *dai* and various days of the week is not recorded till mid-century.

406 **diuerse knightes**: *multis tyronibus* LgA, 'many students'.

408 **wolde in no wise accorde to hym**: *lui accorderent en telle maniere* P2, *nullo modo acquiescentibus* LgA.

409 **he asked wyne**: *fist appareillier du vin* P2, *iussit eis propinari uinum* LgA, 'ordered wine for them to drink a toast'.

413–14 **neighed . . . blessidly**: *approuchant ala mort beneurement. dist* P2; s.w. has transferred the adverb.

415 **principali**: only GiL.

417 **sklaundre**: *scandalum facere* LgA, 'create a cause of offence'.
y haue kepte it: *ie lay cele* P2, *sedaui* LgA, 'settled'.

422 **.C.lxxj.**: *CLX* LgA.
ordeined: 'composed', a sense not recorded by *MED*.

424 **.M.C.lvj.**: *MCLIII* LgA.

425–6 **And . . . peple**: *Post obitum suum multis gloriam suam manifestauit* LgA.

429 **For y will**: *Discere uolo* LgA.

430 **What menithe this**: *Quid* (. . .) *uis discere* LgA.

432 **none**: add *Ceste congnoissance de voir est nulle* P2.
verrey kuninge and: only GiL.

435 **and the same hour**: only GiL.

436 **mani**: add *dautres* P2.
miracles: add *et a bien pou non nombrables* P2.

114 ST TIMOTHY

Maggioni, ch. CXVII, p. 827; Dunn-Lardeau, ch. 116, p. 784.

For discussion of the identity of Timothy see Maggioni (2007), 1625.

1 **that was prouost**: *du preuost* P2, *a prefecto* LgA.

1–2 **was taken (. . .) and was greuousli bete**: *grauiter torqueretur* LgA.

2 **in . . . throte and**: not in LgA.

3 **to God . . . herte**: not in LgA.

6 **doublid**: *gemmatam* LgA, 'jewelled'; Vignay translates *geminatam*.

9 **prouost**: *preuost* P2, *preses* LgA. Some modern translators agree with Vignay that this is the prefect of 1 above, but Roze and Benz seem to be right to distinguish them.

11 **.lviij.**: *cinquante sept* P2.

115 ST SYMPHORIAN

Maggioni, ch. CXVIII, p. 828; Dunn-Lardeau, ch. 117, p. 784.

2 **so gret . . . werkis**: *tanta morum grauitate* LgA.

3 **surmounted**: *anticipare uideretur* LgA.

5 **Eradien**: *Heraclium prefectum* LgA.

10–11 **therfor . . . of right**: *paions donc a dieu la vie que nous luy deuons payer de son droit. Tardiue repentance est a entendre* (*atendre* P1) *induces* P2, *Vitam quam Christo soluturi sumus ex debito, soluamus ex uoto. Sera penitudo est sub iudicis timuisse conspectum* LgA, 'let us pay the debt we owe to Christ because we wish to. Repentance resulting from fear of the sight of the judge comes too late.'

11 **blake**: *fucata* LgA, 'stained, coloured', and thence 'falsified'.

12 **hertis . . . beleuers**: *pensees malcreans* P2, *credulis mentibus* LgA.

13 **obliged**: *obligee* P2, *obligata* LgA, 'bound together', and *cf. compedibus* (*es lyans* P2) at the end of the clause. This sense is recognized for French, but not recorded by *MED*.

15–16 **whanne . . . glas**: so with *ilz* for *ye* P2, *in similitudinem uitri cum ceperint splendere franguntur* LgA.

18–19 **of his marterdom**: not in LgA.

19 **of her hous**: not in LgA.

28 **with tre**: *en tables de fust* P2.

29 **founde in**: *ostee* (. . .) *du* P2.

116 ST BARTHOLOMEW

Maggioni, ch. CXIX, p. 830; Dunn-Lardeau, ch. 118, p. 786.

4 **al maner siknesses**: *languoreux* P2.

10 **harde strened and bounde**: *constrictus* LgA.

11 **ones**: not in LgA.
sethe: add *ex illa hora* LgA.

13 **an nigh**: only GiL.

17 **glad**: *grandes* LgA.

20–1 **of rede**: *purpureas* LgA.

21 **clothes**: add *ne sa chausseure* P2.
empaired: *viellirent* P2.

26 **spekithe**: add *et entent* P2.

27–8 **ye shull finde hym**: *il se demonstrera a vous* P2.

31 **And . . . came**: not in LgA.

32–3 **that is . . . fende**: only GiL.

39 **and²**: *quia* LgA.

40 **al thinge**: *tous ceulx* P2.

41 **saide thei**: only GiL.

42 **here**: *ja* P2.

43 **vnbounde**: *desliee et deliuree* P2.

50 **erthely thinge**: add *ne riens charnel* P2.

53 **merueilous and couenable**: *mirabilem congruentiam* LgA. The four, *congruentiam, potentiam, iustitiam, sapientiam* follow, beginning at 54, 57, 63, 65.

58 **he**: *dyabolus* LgA.

60 **sent**: *enuoie* P2, present tense.

62 **fendes**: add *et (cultum) Christi statuant* LgA.

66 **ouercome**: *despit* P2.

67 **for**: *Car* P2, *ut* LgA.
toke: *raperet* LgA.

68–71 **For that . . . and yet**: *ut si ibi ieiunans non famesceret absque dubio deus esset, si autem esuriret ipsum ut primum hominem per cibum deuinceret. Sed cognosci deus non potuit quia esuriuit nec uinci quia* LgA.

76 **of ydoles**: *ydolo* LgA.

77 **paleys**: *placitum* LgA, variant *palacium*.

fendes: *demon* LgA.

81 **And . . . kingdom**: *Ille autem ipsam mortem que regina est nostra captiuauit* LgA.

88 **of**: *a* P2.

89–90 **there . . . man**: only GiL.

95–6 **But now . . . hym / that duelled . . . desert**: Vignay, followed by GiL, transposes and mistranslates.

But now . . . hym: *prius tamen eum uobis ostendam* LgA.

that duelled . . . desert: *et habitorem eius quem apostolus in desertum locum ire precepit* LgA.

99 **tempest**: *fouldre* P2, *fuligine* LgA, 'soot'.

100 **heres**: *cheueulx* P2; *MED s.v. her* n. acknowledges existence of spellings without *h*, but since there is no other example in GiL the spelling in the MSS must derive from a scribal error in an early copy.

strechinge: the H1 spelling *streggyng* is not recorded in *MED*, but past *streged* is.

101–2 **by his . . . brimstone**: *mettant hors par la bouche flambes ensouffrees* P2, *flammas sulphureas ex ore et oculis spirantem* LgA.

106 **thou noye no creatoure**: *il nabite homme nul* S.

107–8 **with a gret . . . lighteninge**: only GiL.

110 **wif**: add *et ses enfans* P2.

113 **compleined hem**: add *contra apostolum* LgA.

115 **conuersion**: *deceptione* LgA.

122 **beleve**: *sacrificare* LgA.

126 **entent**: *ydole* P2.

131–2 **And . . . ende**: *Et ainsi fut fait* P2, not in LgA.

134 **temple**: *temples* P2.

fende: *dyables* P2.

135 **fulfelled**: add *moult loyalement* S, add *laudabiliter* LgA.

141 **of Dalbane**: *dalbane* P2, *in Albana* LgA.

142 **same**: *benoit* P2.

hilt: add *Ambrosius dicit quod fuit cesus et excoriatus* LgA, but not in other MSS or Graesse.

sum: *multis* LgA.

144 **furst**: add *cesus et postea* LgA.

147 **.CCC.xxxiij.**: *CCC.xxxj.* P2; in fact 831. L and D begin the new sentence at *the sarisenes.*

148 **yle**: add *de liparite* S.

150 **Ynde**: add *ad hanc insulam* LgA.

151 **sepulcre**: *corpus* LgA.

155 **and threwe hem abrode**: *et degettez et ilz sen furent partis* P2, *illis recedentibus* LgA.

159 **hem**: *te* P2.
destroied: add *nec auxilium nobis impenderis?* LgA.

162 **may aske ne gete**: *nay peu impetrer* P2.

167 **maister cite**: *metropolis* LgA.

173 **and yet . . . vessell**: *ja soit ce que ilz touchoient au doy luille clere* P2, *Cum tamen digitos in uas mitterent et oleum liquidum omnino palparent* LgA.

179 **and . . . powere**: *et sefforcoient* P2, *intendens* LgA.

180 **and sawe**: only Gil.

181 **were . . . counsaile**: *parloient daucune chose* P2.

185 **tabernacles**: *habitaculis* LgA.

186 **by**: add *ferme* P2.

188 Here Gil omits one miracle, Maggioni, 836–7 (110–26), Dunn-Lardeau, 792–3, about which, as LgA acknowledges, *simile fere legitur de beato Andrea*; see 1.233–324, vol. 1, pp. 9–12.

190 **deynid**: D looks like *denyded*, but *MED* records no such word; nor does it offer any satisfactory sense for *dividen*.

190–2 **Ihesu Crist, thou hast . . . mageste**: *Discipulis Christi tui unica diuinitate personaliter predicantibus trinitatem, tuam mundo mirabiliter dignatus es ostendere maiestatem* LgA, 'you have deigned to reveal to the disciples of Crist as they prayed the trinity in its single divinity, and miraculously to show your majesty to the world'.

193 **thou**: *benigna tui prospectio* LgA.

193–4 **worshiped bi right gret prerogatif**: *magna uirtutum prerogatiua colendum* LgA.

194 **he**: i.e. the *peple*.

195 **bi**: add *laccroissement de* P2.

194–6 **tho . . . peple**: *populum* (. . .) *licet humana penitus conuersatione remotum, tibi tamen predicationum augmento meruit consignare uicinum* LgA, 'although these people were very remote from human affairs he succeeded with copious preaching in establishing them as close to you'.

199 **of the**: add *prochains* P2.
as in fleing: *alatis quasi uestigiis* LgA.

200 **temple**: add *demoniacum* LgA.

203 **hym**: add *O quam mira uirtutum ipsius insigna, dum humana uoce uerbosantem contra se aduersarium solo iussu laceratis diutissime uiris reddidit mutum* LgA.

the quene: *reginam* (. . .) *puellam* LgA; this must refer to the king's daughter, 36–43 above.

206 **to preise . . . miracles**: *ut miraculis fidem commodaret certissimam* LgA.

207 **soueraigne**: add *salle* P2, i.e. heaven.

cheynes: add *et tres lait* P2.

210 **of her citees**: *urbiumque duodecim accole te deum patrem corpore sequuntur et mente* LgA .

211 **relacion**: *delatu* LgA, 'denunciation'.

212 **apostell**: add *tres ferme en toutes manieres en la foy* P2.

213–14 **And as he . . . dethe**: *Qui tamen mortis uiriliter perferendo discrimen* LgA, 'who, however, manfully enduring the danger of death'.

215 **strif**: add *Hucusque Ambrosius* LgA.

219 **there**: add *premierement* P2.

221 **rede**: *cuide* P2.

222 **preche**: add *discipule meus* LgA.

take upon the þe gret: *enprens* P2, *capax esto* LgA.

223 **furst**[1]: not in LgA.

224 **Fille the vessell that is necessarie**: *uos* (*vas* Graesse) *quod necessarium est implete* (*imple* Graesse) LgA.

folu: *Imitare* LgA.

loue: *emulare* LgA.

226 **that . . . suffered**: *queque pro te sustinui* LgA.

227 **pacience**: add *entre ceulx qui perissent* P2.

228 **refusid**: *recula* P2.

229 **and**: not in LgA.

of God: *mundi* LgA.

he enlumined: *ut illuminaret* LgA.

230 **so as . . . his boke**: *sicomme monseigneur saint augustin le tesmongne en son liure* P2, *tamquam sal terre ut gentes insipidas saliret* LgA. Vignay's divergence destroys the structure of the passage, and must result from illegibility in his exemplar.

231 **of Ihesu Crist**: not in LgA.

he . . . tilthe: *ut spiritualem culturam perficeret* LgA.

235 **last**: add *Et a tant de miracles comme pierre se pot comprendre et* (*a* P1)

autant souffit barthelemy emprendre P2, add *Ad quot ualet Petrus misteria capessenda ad tot sufficit Bartholomeus penetranda* LgA.

236 **by the yefte . . . gost**: *pars les dons du saint esperit* P2, *equa lance habuit et cetera diuina carismata* LgA, 'and he received divine gifts of equal weight' (to those of Peter).

237–8 **And right as . . . vnite**: *Hic ex diuino duodenarii numero medius ab utraque parte sonum diuine sermocinationis dat, sicut in cithara harmoniam* LgA, 'he at the centre of the divine number twelve gave out the sound of the divine message from every part, like the harmony of a harp'.

239 **crioures**: *pretores* LgA, i.e. those who precede.

241–2 **And there**: *Igitur uide* LgA.

242 **unresonable**: *rationabilia* LgA.

244 **vyne . . . paradys**: *paradisos et uineas* LgA.

247 **thornes**: *sepes* LgA, 'hedges'.

248 **worship**: *loyer* P2, 'reward', s.w. misreading *loier* as *louer*.

250 **tribulacion . . . for lyf**: *pro requiescibili uita amarissimam mortem* LgA.

251–2 **hilt of hem**: *decoriatus in morem follis fuit* LgA, 'his skin was pulled off as if to make a bag'.

252 **He deied noght . . . slow hym**: *Nec postquam migrauit ex hoc mundo neglexit occisores suos* LgA.

253 **but . . . miracles**: add *et receuoit ses contraires et les perdus par demonstrances* P2, add *sed inuitabat miraculis perditos et prodigiis admittebat aduersos* LgA.

256 **medicine**: *medecines* P2, *medentem* LgA; see note to 133.235.

256–7 **citee . . . keper**: *la cite refusa ce qui la soustenoit* P2, *orbi manuducentem* LgA, 'the bereaved (forsook) their guardian'; Vignay misread *orbi* as *urbi*.

257 **hym that gaue hem sight**: *ductorem* LgA.
tho that perisshed: *ceulz qui perilloient* P2, *naufragi* LgA.

259–60 **in a cofre of lede**: not in LgA.

261 **marteres**: add *car aussy ilz faisoient miracles* P2.

266 **right a pore woman**: *pauperculam* LgA.

267 **these . . . margarites**: *pretiosissima margarita* LgA.
creatoure: add *le tres resplendissant homme luminaire vint a vne tres tristre* P2; the meaning of these lines appears to be that the coffins arrived in a region which had been lacking in holy relics.

269 **the**: *vne* P2.

270 **citee of Sesile**: add *Miles* LgA, Milazzo.

271 **Calabre**: add *Et enuoya gregoire en la cite de la colompne et enuoia achare* (*Archatium* LgA) *en la cite qui est dicte thale* (*Thale* LgA) *et encores auiourduy resplendissent ilz par leurs merites* P2; these cities have not been identified.

272 **gret preisingges**: *multis hymnis, laudibus et candelis* LgA.

274 **to hym**: *habitatoribus* LgA.

275 **receiued**: *emittebat* LgA.
by the merites . . . Bartilmew: only GiL.

278 **same day**: add *a ceulx qui le voient et la forme comment il sen fouy* P2, *quasi figuratio fugientis ignis* LgA.
I salue: *Je te salue* P2. All MSS read *sawe*, which must be an English copying error.

279 **fisshes**: add *dulcis fructus uiuide palmitis* LgA.

283 **holynesse**: *santez* P2.

284 **goingges vnremuables**: *alees non remuables* P2, *meabilibus gressibus* LgA; for *unremuable MED* records this instance and one other, for this one proposing '?not subject to alteration, pre-determined'.

117 ST AUGUSTINE

Maggioni, ch. CXX, p. 841; Dunn-Lardeau, ch. 119, p. 796.

2 **of Cartage**: *Tagastensi* LgA,variant *Carthaginensi*, also in Graesse. Tagaste is now Souk Ahras in Algeria.

3 **Demomark**: *Monica* LgA.

10 **and²**: *Item in eodem* LgA.

11 **diuisiones and . . . noumbres**: *diuisions des figures et de musique et des nombres* P2, *de dimensionibus figurarum et de musicis et de numeris* LgA. *MED divisioun* sense 8 'dimension' gives one (uncertain) example.

13 **strengthe**: *force* P2, *difficultate* LgA; the French can carry the sense 'difficulty', but *MED* does not record it for *strengthe*. For another example see 420 below.

15 **largesse**: *acumen* LgA.
of the: *de ton nom* P2, *donum tuum* LgA.
to the: add *Gramaticam prius in sua ciuitate, postmodum rhetoricam in Carthagine docuit* LgA, omitted by other MSS and Graesse, who therefore continue the previous quotation up to *inflat*, *bolnithe up*. LgD MSS, however, punctuate before *mais*, thus rearranging the sentence as in GiL.

16 **bolnithe**: this may equally be *boluithe*, with identical meaning; see note to 27.24.

19 **And**: omit and end sentence after *childe* LgA.

23 **of philosophe**: *dun phylozophe* P2, *cuiusdam philosophi, scilicet Ciceronis* LgA.

taught: *docebatur* LgA.

27–8 **with . . . powere**: only GiL.

29 **in a place**: *in quadam linea lignea* LgA, 'on a wooden rule'.

30 **a**: add *pulcherrimus* LgA.

32 **as**: *la ou* P2.

35 **she**: add *disoit* P2.

36 **it was not so saide to me but 'there y am thou art'**: *Non* (. . .) *mihi dictum est 'Vbi ille, ibi tu', sed 'Vbi tu, ibi ille'* LgA.

46–7 **abode . . . priuely**: *eam decipiens nocte latenter recessit* LgA.

48 **night and day**: *au matin et au vespre* P2.

58 **that**: *ne* LgA, i.e. whether.

58–9 **nor other eresye**: *ne leur heresie* P2, *uel pro ipsa* LgA.

60 **comaunded**: *condempna* P2, *confutauit* LgA.

65 **for the drede of thi loue**: *par la paour de bonne amour* P2, *amore et horrore* LgA.

67–8 **Y am mete . . . ete me**: *Je suis viande de croys ma joye et tu mengeras* P2, *Cibus sum grandium, cresce et manducabis me* LgA.

68 **of**: *tue* LgA.

70 **hit**: *la voye de ihesu crist* P2.

75 **as he dede**: *en laquelle lautre aloit* P2, *in qua alius sic, alius sic ibat* LgA, 'in which some went this way, some that'.

76 **for as moche as he dede displese**: *car tout quanque il faisoit luy desplaisoit* P2, *Displicebat enim ei quicquid agebat in seculo* LgA.

76, 77 **witheoute, withoute**: *pre LgA.*

78 **in his best wise**: only GiL.

81 **done**: *peuent faire en eulx mesmes et non pas en leur dieu* P2.

83 **cam . . . Victor**: *victorin vint la* P2, *memoria Victorini uenit in medium* LgA.

85–6 **deserued . . . lyknesse**: *trouua vng grant ymage* P2, *Rome, quod maximum tunc erat, statuam in foro meruisset* LgA.

86–7 **not for that**: *moult de foys* P2.

87 **wolde be**: *estoit* P2.

88 **hym**: *te* P2.

91 **Crede of the masse**: *simbolum fidei* LgA.

hym: add *comme a vergondeux tres secretement* P2.
to rede: *ad legendum et pronuntiandum* LgA.

98 **dede**: add *in Egypto* LgA.
Constance: *Constantin* P2, *Constantino* LgA, variant *Constantio*; Ryan points out that this was Constantius II, as Antony died in 356.

100 **saide (. . .) with gret corage**: *assailly* (. . .) *tant de voult comme de pensee et sescria* P2, *tam uultu quam mente turbatus inuasit et fortiter exclamauit* LgA.

101 **abide we**: *oions nous* P2.

102–3 **and for . . . hem**: *An quia precesserunt pudet sequi et non pudet nec saltem sequi?* LgA, 'Or are we ashamed to follow because they have gone ahead, or should we be ashamed if we do not at least follow them?'

104 **hymself**: add *en ce mesmes liure* (add *confessionum* LgA) P2.

106–7 **for that . . . to litell**: add *et nauoit point de maniere en soy* P2, *Quamdiu, quamdiu, cras et cras, sine modo, sine paululum. Modo non habebat modum et sine paululum ibat in longum* LgA.

108 **after**: add *en* P2.

110–13 **A, Lorde . . . cause**: *Sire. faiz et nous esmeuz et nous rapelle. sire, viens nous rauir. resplendiz et adoulcis tous noz empeschemens. et je doubtay estre ainsy empeschie comme il appartient a doubter* P2, *Age, domine, et fac et excita et reuoca nos Accende et rape et fragra et dulcesce. Impedimentis omnibus sic timebam expediri, quemadmodum impediri timendum est* LgA.

112 **enponchementis**: *empeschemens* P2; the English must be intended to mean 'punishments', which also fits the context. *MED* records *punishement* but no form with *en-* or *em-* prefix.

116 **y fille**: *irruebam* LgA, 'I rushed'.

118 **clered**: add *et chacie* P2.

120 **coueite**: *sitio* LgA.

122 **a boke**: *le liure apostolique* P2, Rom. 13: 14.

126 **tyme**: add *ut refert in libro soliloquiorum* LgA.

127 **that**: add *sicut ipse ait* LgA.

139 **pronouncer**: *premier annoncant* P2, *prenuntiator* LgA; *MED*, with only two citations, from the same passage in Chaucer's and Walton's Boethius, defines as 'one who makes a formal statement, an orator'.

140–1 **begynnynges, sum thingges, thei, hem**: *commencement, aucune chose, elle, luy* P2.

145 **paynim**: add *et phylozophe* P2.

146 **exortaciones**: *predicacions* P2.

146–7 **merites . . . Ambrose**: *meritis matris et predicatione Ambrosii sacrum baptisma suscepit* LgA.

153 **Austine**: add *compilatum* LgA.

153–4 **of holy Chirche**: *catholique* P2.

159 **mynde**: *entrailles* P2.
meruailous maners: *meurs* P2, *seruorum tuorum* LgA.

159–61 **the ensaumples . . . brenned me**: *les exemples de tes meurs que tu auoyes fait des mors luysans et des mors vifz. les assemblees des pensees mardoient tout forsene* P2, *exempla seruorum tuorum, quos de nigris lucidos, de mortuis uiuos feceras, congesta in sinum cogitationis mee urebant* LgA.

162 **into the hille**: *a conualle* LgA, 'out of the vale'.

162–3 **the songe of degrees**: i.e. one of the Gradual Psalms; these were the psalms (nos. 120–34) sung while mounting the steps to the Temple in Jerusalem.

164 **salowed**: *saoule* P2, 'satisfied'.

165 **besinesse**: *haultesce* P2.

166–7 **How ofte . . . sharpely**: *Quantum fleui in hymnis et canticis tuis suaue sonantis ecclesie uocibus commotus acriter* LgA.

171 **song and**: only GiL.

175 **berker**: *abayant* P2, *latrator* LgA. *MED* gives 'barking dog, one who scoffs', the only citation for the latter being this passage from St Augustine in the *Smaller Vernon Legendary*.

176 **medlid**: *mielees* P2, *mellees* S, *melleas* LgA, 'honeyed'.

177 **of grace**: *et je malentissoie sus tes escriptures* P2.

179 **was fere for me to leve**: *mestoit paour de perdre* P2.

180–1 **hast made thi soueraigne suetnesse entre into me**: *ta souueraine souefuete entroyes pour moy* P2, *uera tu et summa suauitas, eiciebas et intrabas pro eis* LgA, 'you, the true and highest sweetness, threw them out and entered in their place'.

181 **suetnesse . . . alle**: only GiL.
delites: add *sed non carni et sanguini* LgA.

183 **and none so high as he**; *et nas plus nul hault sur toy* P2, *sed non sublimibus in se* LgA, 'but not to those who exalt themselves'.

185 **Tyberin**: *Ostia Tyberina* LgA.

186 **debonayr**: *pia* LgA.

199 **and wepte sore**: *et ploroit* P2, not in LgA.

200 **saide to hym** add *aussy comme en le confortant* P2.

200–1 **that it**: *ja soit quil* P2.

200–2 **that it was . . . bisshopriche**: *quia et locus presbiterii, licet ipse maiori dignus esset, appropinquaret tamen episcopatui* LgA.

205 **in that tonge**: *en la langue et es lettres* P2, *in Latina lingua et litteris* LgA.

206 **preche**: add *coram se in ecclesia* LgA.

207 **hym**: i.e. Valerius.

209–10 **the preste . . . heretik**: *presbiterum manicheum* LgA.

210 **heretikes**: add *donastites et manitheiens* P2, add *precipue rebaptizatos, donatistas et manicheos* LgA.

210, 211 **ouercome, confounded**: *osta, confondy* P2, *abstulit, fugauit* LgA.

213–15 **And . . . founde**: *et il luy eust aucunes foys offert sil ne cuidast quil sen fut ale en plus secret lieu. si que il ne peust estre trouue* P2, *Nam sibi aliquando ablatus fuisset, nisi eum ad locum secretum transire curasset ita ut inueniri minime potuisset* LgA, 'for at one time he might have been taken from him if he had not taken care to put him in a secret place so that he could not be found'.

216 **ershebisshop**: *euesque P2, archiepiscopo* LgA.
cese: *laissast leueschie* P2, *cederet* LgA.

220 **bisshopriche**: GiL omits two sentences, Maggioni, 849–50 (137–8), Dunn-Lardeau, 804–5 .
oftin: *apres* P2.

222 **that**: add *cum* LgA.
to be sette: *poni ad remum posuit me ad aplustre* LgA, 'to be set at an oar he put me at the helm'.

224 **clothing**: add *et son chaussement* P2.

226 **I am**: *Jay honte* P2.

228 **plente**: *espargnablement* P2.

228–9 **but scarsly . . . hymselff**: only GiL.

229 **hadde**: add *plerumque* LgA.

230 **other, other**: only GiL.

232 **ayens . . . detraccion**: not in P2, *contra pestem detractionis* LgA.

234 ***vetitam noueris:*** *indignam nouerit* LgA.

235–7 **This is . . . atte alle**: *Qui ayme pour ses diz mesdire daucune ame qui cy deffaille. Ceste table ce peut il dire luy est deue sans faille* P2.

237–8 **a man . . . withe hym**: *quidam familiarissimi sibi coepiscopi ad detractionem linguam laxassent* LgA.

238 **hym²**: *eos* LgA.

239–40 **but . . . table**: *nisi desisterent aut uersus ipsos deleret aut a mensa* *recederet* LgA. *MED* records neither *afface* nor *efface*; *OED* first records *efface* from Caxton for 1490.

242 **familier**: *curieux* P2.

244–6 **what . . . with you.'**: *que nous auez vous appareillie au disner. Et Augustin dit. Je ne scay riens de telz viandes. Et cil luy dit. ie ne scay riens de disner auecques vous* P2, *quid ciborum pransurus ipse paterfamilias preparasset. Cui Augustinus nequaquam talium epularum curiosus respondit: Et ego uobiscum nescio.* LgA.

248 **make no mariage**: *quil ne demandast ja femme a nul* P2, 'not to seek a wife for anyone'.

249–50 **neuer counsaile . . . hymself**: *ne loast ya cheuaucher a nul qui ne le vouldroit faire* P2, *militare uolentem ad hoc non commendaret* LgA. It is not clear whether s.w. takes *cheuaucher* in its basic sense rather than the extended *serve as a soldier* intended by Vignay, which is given for *MED riden* sense 4.

250 **he shulde go to no festis**: *il nalast ja disner a convy* P2, *ad conuiuia inuitatus non iret* LgA.

251 **the maker**: *le* P2, *sibi* LgA, i.e. each other.

252–3 **the rider . . . councellour**: *que les cheuauchans nayent aucun mal et sen prengnent a luy* P2, *ne militantes calumpniam exerceant et in eum alii culpam refundant* LgA.

255 **attemperaunce of**: not in LgA.

256 **litell**: *pour nulz* P2, *nulla uel minima* LgA.

256–7 **acounted . . . and**: only GiL.

262 **fables**: add *poetarum sicut fabulam* LgA.

268 **gardin**: *perier* P2.
 vynge: 'vineyard'; this spelling not recorded in *MED s.v. vini*, which gives only one queried example of this sense rather than 'vine'.

269 **also**: *in eodem quoque libro* LgA.

272 **y go . . . nede**: *ie voys a repos de saoulete pour tristresce de besoing* P2, *ad quietem satietatis ex indigentie molestia transeo* LgA, 'I pass from the unpleasantness of hunger to the relief of satiety'.

276 **ioyouste**: not recorded in *MED*.

276–7 **the whiche aforcith her oft tymes to perisshe**: *qui sefforce souuent de perir* P2, *et plerumque preire conatur* LgA, 'and often tries to lead the way'. Both *aforcith* and *sefforce* can mean either 'try' or 'compel'; misreading of *preire* as *perire* must go back to Vignay.

277 **perisshe**: Here GiL omits Maggioni, 851–2 (part of 170, 171–2), Dunn-Lardeau, 807.

278 **his metes**: *metas necessitatis* LgA.

278–9 **preised his name**: *magnificet nomen tuum* LgA.

279 **sinful man**: GiL here omits Maggioni, 852 (177–80), Dunn-Lardeau, 807.
is: *ne doit estre* P2.

280 **is**: add *apellee* P2.
temptacion: here GiL omits Maggioni, 852 (part of 181, 182–6), Dunn-Lardeau, 807–8.

284 **withdrawe**: i.e. rescued.

286 **yefte**: GiL omits Maggioni, 853 (190–3), Dunn-Lardeau, 808.

288 **.iij. tymes**: *inter se* LgA.

289 **Austin**: add *et disoient que on le deuroit occire aussy comme vng lou. et affermoient que dieu perdonroit tous ses pechiez a ceulx qui locciroient* P2.

290 **that**: add *par la grace de dieu* P2. The sentence is much abbreviated.

292 **to breke**: *frangi et conflari* LgA, 'to be broken up and melted down'.

294 **hym**: add *pource que il disoit quilz appartenoient mieulx aux filz ou aux prochains des mors* P2.

295 **was content . . . chirches**: add *Et encores ny estoit il point ententif par amour des choses* P2, *In hiis quoque que ecclesia possidebat intentus amore uel implicatus non erat* LgA.

296 **his mynde and thought was in**: *pensoit des* P2.

301 **oute of rule**: *desattrempeement* P2.

302 **recorden**: for *recorded*, which should have been emended.

307 **y haue**: *habemus* LgA.

308 **meruailously**: GiL omits Maggioni, 854 (208–14), Dunn-Lardeau, 809.

309–10 **but yef it were bi necessite of gret counsaile**: *se ce nestoit de grant secret* P2, *nisi secretum aliquod interesset* LgA.

310–12 **He dede . . . pouerte**: *il ne fist oncques bien a ses cousins tant quilz habondassent en richesces. mais ne luy chaloit mais* (*fors* P1) *quilz neussent souffrante ou trop grant besoing* P2, *Consanguineis sic benefecit non ut diuitias haberent, sed ut aut non aut minus egerent* LgA.

312 **roght neuer**: only GiL.
neuer^{2}: *raro* LgA.
ani cause: *aucun* P2.

313 **withoute gret cause**: only GiL; GiL then omits Maggioni, 854–5 (part of 217, 218–19), Dunn-Lardeau, 810.

314 **manere of his enditinge**: *stilum* LgA.

320 **ayenst hym**: GiL omits Maggioni, 855 (222), Dunn-Lardeau, 810.

323–4 **one of the secte of Manithenes**: *vng des manicheiens* P2, *quodam manicheorum negotiatore* LgA.

328 **the fals . . . gretly**: *infideles christianis plurimum insultabant* LgA, 'the heretics greatly abused the Christians'.

330 **were destroied**: *premi* LgA, 'oppressed'.

337 **.CCCC.lx.**: *CCCCXL* LgA.

339 **of**[1]: *ne pour* P2.

343 **wedowes**: *uiduatas* LgA; *MED widwe* sense 1 (e), described as figurative, though in this case it descends directly from the Latin in its basic sense 'bereft'.

345–6 **Be thou not . . . downe**: *Tu ne seras pas grant en cuidant grans choses pource que les fus et les pierres tresbuchent* P2.

349 **to**: *a veoir* P2.

350 **oure Lorde graunted hym**: *il ot* P2, *obtinuit* LgA.

352–3 **the departing**: *dissolutionem* (. . .) *imminere* LgA.

353 **he made . . . before hym**: *il se fist escripre les .vij. pseaumes de penitance* P2.

365 **hym**: add *et sanitatem reciperet* LgA.

367 **sike folkes**: *energumenos* LgA, 'possessed of devils'.

368 **miracles**: GiL omits Maggioni, 856–7 (244–9), Dunn-Lardeau, 812.

369–70 **his bretheren . . . mynde**: *hoc memoriale* LgA.

372 **resseiuyng his saueoure**: *eucharestia* LgA.

372–3 **he felt hymself**: not in LgA.
of good understondinge: not in LgA.

375–6 **and leyde . . . praied**: *coram positis fratribus et orantibus migrauit ad dominum* LgA.

377 **.CCCC.**: add *obiit autem circa annos domini CCCCXL* LgA. In fact he died in 430.

378 **this**: *aussy* P2, *ainsi* P1, *Itaque* LgA.

378–9 **fyting in defence**: *combatant et deffence* P2, *propugnaculum* LgA, 'bulwark'.

379 **of feithe . . . Chirche**: *fidei munimentum* LgA, 'rampart of the faith'.

383 **Remy . . . saien**: *remy en recordant ierome et aucuns autres docteurs dit* P2.

388 **of whom**: *cui* LgA.

392 **grete**: *eruditissimis* LgA.
alle: add *clarte* P2.

394 **or by kunynge**: only GiL.

394–5 **is putte away . . . to the**: *est oste et desert* P2, *a te positum atque disertum est* LgA, 'has been put down and dealt with by you'.

396 **and kunning**: only GiL.

Here GiL omits Maggioni, 858 (263–71), Dunn-Lardeau, 813.

399 **the studie**: *uestro studio* LgA.

400 **thou . . . kunning**: *delicioso cupitis pabulo saginari* LgA.

400–1 **rede . . . Austin**: *lisiez ou paistis delicieux du chief du benoist augustin nostre compaignon* P2, *beati Augustini compatriote uestri opuscula legite* LgA.

401 **oure**: *vostre* P2, *nostrum* LgA.

402 **rye**: GiL omits Maggioni, 859 (275–80), Dunn-Lardeau, 814.

403 **saithe**: add *ou* (add *tertio* LgA) *liure de la vie contemplatiue* P2.

404 **softe . . . speche**: *souef par engin ysnel de beau parler* P2, *acer ingenio suauis eloquio* LgA.
letterure: *secularis litterature* LgA; *MED* observes that it is often hard to distinguish between *lettrure*, *lettre*, and *lecture*, the latter given by H2L.

405 **clere . . . day**; *in quotidianis disputationibus clarus* LgA.
day: add *et ordonne en tous ses faiz* P2.

406 **right opin**: *circumspectus* LgA.

408 **canon**: add *Et bernard sy dit que augustin est tres puissant mail a confondre les hereses* P2.
Here GiL and LgD omit Maggioni, 859–60 (285–97).

409 **this**: add *cum* LgA.

412 **passed**: add *ab eus obitu* (. . .) *circa annos domini DCCXVIII tempore Leonis tertii* LgA.
Lumbardie: add *audiens Sardiniam a Saracenis depopulatam* LgA.
noble: *sollempnes* LgA.

414 **doctoure**: add *et ilz donnerent grant pris* P2.

415 **came**: add *iusques a la dicte cite* P2.

418 **solempne**: only GiL.
avowe: add *que se il sen laissoit porter dillec* P2.

419 **the . . . corseint**: *lonneur de luy* P2, *sui nomine* LgA.

420 **thei lefte hym up**: *il en fut mene dillec* P2.
strengthe: add *et le roy acompli ce quil auoit voue et fist faire leglise en lonneur de luy* LgA.

421 **a miracle**: *idem miraculum* LgA.

424 **pleine**: only GiL.

425–6 **desired . . . desire**: *uiderat sancto complacere ut in suo nomine ecclesia fieret ubicumque mansisset* LgA.

427–8 **and the kinge . . . body**: add *et la faisoit vne eglise en lonneur de luy* P2, *in omni loco ubi de nocte cum corpore hospitabatur in honorem ipsius ecclesias construebat* LgA.

430 *Ciel Dore*: GiL omits Maggioni, 861 (309–14), Dunn-Lardeau, 815–16.

431 **in a night**: *vne foys* P2.

438–52 omitted by P2, but in S.

438 **good**: *peccune* S.

440 **and**[1]: *et celi* S, *sed ille* LgA.

442 **kepte . . . cherete**: *laouroit touz iours moult deuotement* S.

443–4 **strengid it reuerently**: *estraingnoit* S, 'pressed'; *MED strengen* v. (1) does not record this sense, and this should perhaps be regarded as an aberrant spelling for *streynid.*

445 **the proper**: *unum* LgA.

452 **sore**: GiL omits Maggioni, 862–72 (324–521), Dunn-Lardeau, 816–20. Maggioni, 867–72 (420–521) is also absent from Graesse and LgD including Batallier.

453–9 **Mani . . . writinges**: only GiL. P2 closes with the words: *Et est de quoy raison luy demanda. Et aussy plusieurs autres en parlent en plusieurs liures de la vie monseigneur saint augustin euesque*, but this is not in S, P1, or Batallier.

455 **this litell volume** suggests that this chapter originally had a separate existence, suggesting that s.w. had previously translated this life and later incorporated it in the larger project of GiL; see above, Introduction p. 56.

118 STS FELIX AND ADAUCTUS

Maggioni, ch. CXXII, 886; Dunn-Lardeau, ch. 121, p. 832.

8–9 **that is called**: only GiL.

9 **that**[1] **. . . sawtier**: not in LgA.

9–11 **which . . . hangged**: only GiL.

18 **sikerly . . . frely**: *franchement estre* P2.

20 **Hardy**: *Adauctum* LgA.

20–1 **went hardely with**: *auctus sit* LgA, 'was added to'.

24 **He suffred**: *Ilz souffrirent* P2.

119 STS SAVINIAN AND SAVINA

Maggioni, ch. CXXIV, p. 891; Dunn-Lardeau, ch. 122, p. 833.

3 **gave hem bothe that name**: *ex nomine suo ambos uocauit* LgA.

6 **kneled**: *prostratus iacebat* LgA.

9 **Turment . . . lenger**: *ne te tourmentes mie jusques a la mort* P2.

11 **thanne snawe**: not in P2, *niue* LgA.

14 **ofte tymes**: *forment* P2.

19 **he passed the water**: *super fluuium Secane uenisset* LgA, i.e. the Seine.

32 **cheines**: *uectibus* LgA, 'bars'.

36 **emperour**: *rex* LgA; this must still be the *imperator*, which LgA uses except here and at 48, where *regem* survives as GiL *kinge*.

38 **and**: add *in faciam suam cecidit et surgens* LgA.

47 **nouthe . . . deliuerithe the**: *or viengne et te deliure* P2, 'Now let him come and deliver you.'

51–2 **in the same**: *au saint* P2, not in LgA.

57 **watir**: add *uelut super petram* LgA.

68 **.CC.lxx in the .ix. kalendes**: *CCLXXV, iv kal.* LgA.

71 **sacrified**: *supplicaret* LgA.

72 **leue**: *derelinque* LgA, i.e. give away.

74 **woman**: *compaigne* P2, *collectanee* LgA, 'foster-sister'.

75 **madame**: add *car jay veu vng homme parlant a toy. mais je ne scay quil te dist* P2.

77 **luste**: add *mais ne te occis mie* P2.

78 **fader**: *empereur* P2, *pater* LgA.

79 **tyme**: add *et non inuenisset* LgA.
eyen: *manibus* LgA.

89 **dyne and**: not in LgA.

91–2 **so as**: only GiL.

92 **go deye**: *peregre mori* LgA, 'die in a foreign place'.

95 **sike**: *riche* P2.
was: add *quasi* LgA.

98 **is dede**: *moriatur* LgA.

104 **she wolde rest**: *ilz se reposassent* P2.

109 **brother**: add *longuement perdu* P2.

110 **slaine**: *decollatus* LgA.

125 **beheded**: *decole* S, *decolee* P2, *decollata* LgA.

126 **he**: *il* S, *elle* P2, transferring the beheading from Savine to Valentine.

120 ST LUPUS

Maggioni, ch. CXXV, p. 895; Dunn-Lardeau, ch. 123, p. 837.

2 **gret . . . vertues**: *cunctis uirtutibus* LgA.

3–6 **whanne . . . ansuered hem**: *et* (. . .) *plurimos ad conuiuia inuitasset cum uinum ad medium non haberet sic respondit ministro* LgA.

8 **cuys**: *muys* P2, *modios* LgA; Latin *modius*, OFr *mui*, was a dry measure, usually of corn; *MED mui* has two citations, one relating to corn and one to a large quantity of gold rings. It is not clear at what stage the word became used in Latin or French to refer to a liquid measure. Either s.w. or an early GiL scribe must have miscopied *cuys* for this unfamiliar word, and it should perhaps have been emended in the text here.

9 **the court**: *curia sibi* LgA.

10 **uirgine**: add *de dieu* P2.

13 **straunge and vnsittinge**: *estranges* P2, *aliena* LgA.

22 **Burgoine . . . come to**: not in LgA.

25 **gret doctrine**: *moult de doctrine* P2, *doctrina et miraculis ualde* LgA.

27 **praied**: add *rege* LgA.

28 **that dede**: *Quem* (. . .) *exilio tabefactum ita* LgA, 'so weakened by exile'.

29 **kneled doune**: *prostratus* LgA.

30 **chirche**: *ciuitati* LgA.

35 **the bellis of Seyns**: *les sains de saint estienne de sens* P2, *campana sancti Stephani* LgA, and thereafter singular.

37 **ofter**: *souuent* P2, *sepius* LgA.

39 **lost**: add *la doulceur de* P2.

41 **.viij.**: *.vij.* P2.

48 **in the night**: *clam* LgA.

49 **opinly**: only GiL.

50 **tyme**: *nocte* LgA.

51–2 **striuynge and chydinge**: *rechignans* P2, 'grimacing' or 'grinding their teeth'.

56 **in**[2]: *Claruit circa* LgA.
.CCC. and .x.: *.vjC. et .x.* P2, *DCX* LgA.

121 ST MAMERTIN

Maggioni, ch. CXXVI, p. 897; Dunn-Lardeau, ch. 124, p. 839.

In this chapter LgA combines two short lives of St Mamertin and St Marian from Jean de Mailly's *Abbrevatio*, chapters 50–1, and Voragine's own abbreviations and some ambiguous uses of pronouns led to confusion between the two in the latter part of the chapter, as noted below. See Boureau, 1371. For a translation of these two lives see Jean de Mailly, *Abrégé des gestes et miracles des saints*, trans. Dondaine, 167–70.

2 **eye**: *hyȝe* D, *highe* H2, in both followed by a space.

3 **to another**: *au* P2.

4 **man**: add *nomine Sauinus* LgA.

6–7 **to haue . . . disese**: *sy que ce que jceulx moult oste courrouciez jceulx debonnaires le me rendent* P2, *ut que mihi abstulerunt irati reddant propitii* LgA. S and P1 are in different ways as confused as P2.

8 **that**[1]: *car tu* P2, *si* LgA.

13–14 **so . . . sepulcre**: *se mist en la celle qui estoit sur* P2, *propter pluuiam nocte illa ad quandam cellulam super tumbam* LgA.

14 **Concorde**: *Concordiani* LgA; from 16 GiL uses the LgA form, which is, however, a corruption of *Corcodomus*, a companion of St Peregrine of Auxerre; see Maggioni (2007), 1367 n. 8.
that night: only GiL.

16 **he**: *il* P2, referring to St Concordian (LgA *Concordianum*, see above), whom s.w. thought was female, whence 18–27 *she* and *her*, which are masculine in LgD; since the GiL MSS except E correctly follow LgD in this line, it seems that s.w. took this to refer to Amadour, but in E the scribe substituted *she* as though for Concordian taken as female as below.

19–20 **from . . . hym**: *qui la habitoit* (add *qui ne le ceissent* S, add *quil ne locceissent* P1) P2, *ne a serpentibus qui hic habitant occidatur* LgA.

22 **was made**: only GiL.

23 **dekene**: *subdiaconem* LgA.
Viuiane subdekene: *Iuuianum acolitum* LgA.

31 **go**: add *tost* P2.

36 **hadde**: *excedebant* LgA.
and . . . and: *Cumque omnes diffugerent* LgA.

37 **shulde neigh**: *nuysissent* P2.

41 **after**: add *saint* P2.
of this: *Huius* LgA, i.e. Mamertin.
Marin: add *in eius monasterio* LgA.

41–68 In LgA Mamertinus is named for the last time in 42, where he acts as the abbot over Marianus, and all that follows relates to Marianus, whose Life begins here and who is named here in LgA (GiL *he*[1] at 60), though otherwise referred to by pronouns.

44 **yle**: *silua* LgA.

45 **wilde swyne**: *cynes sauuages* P2, *aues siluestres* LgA; *cynes* 'swans'. It seems likely s.w. wrote *swans* and that *swyne* is a scribal error.

54 Roze, Benz, and Ryan must be correct to assume that the robbers return to Marianus's cell, and to name him for 54 *his*, LgA *eius*.

58 **monkes**: *petis moynes* P2, *iuniores monachi* LgA.

58–9 **with Seint Mamertin**: *secum* LgA; they were 'with Marian' (rather than Mamertin) as fellow members of the monastery.

60 **he**[1]: *Sanctus Marianus* LgA.

61 **thou shrewe**: *maleuree* P2, 'unfortunate creature'; the French has the secondary sense 'rascal', which s.w. has adopted.

63 It is likely both were buried in this church; but *he* here must be Marian rather than Mamertin.
Angers: *Autissiodorum* (Auxerre) LgA.

122 ST GILES

Maggioni, ch. CXXIII, p. 887; Dunn-Lardeau, ch. 125, p. 841.

8 **and deyde**: not in LgA.

12 **of the worlde**: *humani fauoris* LgA.

16 **seide . . . Rome**: *audito quod Romam tenderet* LgA.

17 **and he wolde**: only GiL.

21 **an ermite . . . holinesse**: *Veredemio heremita sanctitate conspicuo* LgA.

22 **derthe**: *faulte des biens* P2, *sterilitatem* LgA.

23 **he had . . . miracle**: *uterque miraculis coruscaret* LgA.
peine: *peril* P2.

24 **of this worlde**: *humaine* P2.
that hermite: *laissa celluy* P2.

31–2 **she hidde her**: *se mucoit* P2, *muissoit* P1, *mugiret* LgA, 'bellowed'.

48 **holy**: *ancien* P2.

worshipfull: add *par chaynure et* P2, *canitie autem et* LgA, 'by white hair and'.

50 **wentin**: add *a pie* P2.
to hym: add *ceteris retro stare iussis* LgA.
asked hym: add *dont il estoit et* P2.

51 **so gret a thiknesse**: *tam densam uastitatem* LgA.

55 **yeftes**: add *ad ipsa etiam non respexit* LgA.

57 **is perfit**: *estoit parfaicte* P2, *perfici* LgA.

61 **might bene**: *uigeret* LgA, 'might thrive'.

62 **cure**: add *illius monasterii* LgA.

63 **the[2]**: add *lacrimis et* LgA.

66 **hertely**: not in P2, *dignanter* LgA.

67 **amonge . . . hele**: *entre les autres parolles de salu* P2.

68–9 **to no creature**: *a luy ne a autre* P2, *nulli unquam nec ipsi sancto* LgA.

70 **hertly**: not in LgA.

71–2 **synnes . . . were . . . thei were**: singular P2.

79 **Verence**: *Nemausensem* LgA, 'Nîmes'.
refused: *resuscita* P2; see note to 22.148.

81 **of the faithe**: not in LgA.

84 **the riuer that hight**: only GiL.
Tybre: *tymbre de rome* P2, *Tyberim* LgA.

87 **Childerne**: *Ciberonem* LgA; this seems to be Cavaillon, south-east of Avignon; see Boureau, 1368 n. 7.
And . . . chirche: not in P2, in LgA.

89 **kepte hem**: add *sans despecier* P2.
periles: add *maris* LgA.

90 **in[1]**: *aux lintiers de* S, 'in the threshold of'.

90–1 **for . . . to hem**: *ad decus ecclesie et monimentum pacti Romane sedis* LgA.

92 **hym**: add *en esperit* P2.

96 **he . . . God**: *Claruit* LgA.

123 NATIVITY OF THE VIRGIN

Maggioni, ch. CXXVII, p. 900; Dunn-Lardeau, ch. 126, p. 845.

1 **Marie**: add *duxit originem* LgA.

3 **the right generacion**: *generationem Marie* LgA.

8 **David**: add *car son pere proprement en fut* P2, add *quod precipue patet ex hoc* LgA.
holy: *sepe* LgA.

9 **that**: add *Ihesu Crist fut ne de celle seule vierge. Il est certain que* P2.

13 **Melchi bar Pantham**: *Barpanthera* LgA.

15, 16, 18 **Nathan**: *Mathan* LgA; P2 gives the first as *mathan* with the first minim of *m* subpuncted, the other two as *nathan*; S gives *mathain* for the first two and *nathain* for the last. Different versions of the ancestry of Mary are given in Matt. 1: 1–16 and Luke 3: 23–38. In view of correct Nathan, son of David, at 10 above, and the names in the Vulgate genealogies Mathan at Matt. 1: 15 and Nathan at Luke 3: 31, the confusion here is understandable. Voragine derives his version from John Damascene, *De fide orthodoxa*.

16–17 **the sone of Nathan**: *ex tribu Nathe* LgA.

17 **Leui**: *leur* P2, *Leui* LgA.
brother: add *autem* LgA. Only LgA *autem* and H2 *and* make it clear that Melchi rather than Leui was the brother of Panthem.

18 **engendered**: add *ex ea* LgA.

21 **Nathan**: *salmon* P2, *Nathan* LgA.
deyed: not in P2, *Defunctus est* (. . .) *sine liberis* LgA.
Iacob: add *frater eius* LgA.

22–3 **the husbonde of Marie**: only GiL.

27 **of hym**: *du mort* P2.
law: add *Hec Damascenus* LgA.

28 **Maister of Stories**: *ecclesiastica hystoria* LgA, i.e. Eusebius. *Maister of Stories* is standard in GiL for *lystoire escoliere*, Peter Comestor's *Historia Scholastica*, whichVignay has substituted.

29 **cronicles**: *sa cronique* P2.

30 **cofers**: *arches* P2, *archiuis* LgA.

37 **other**: *aucuns* P2.

41–2 **and Elyude engendered seint Neemynen and Seint Seruacien**: *et* (add *de* P1) *Heliud fut ne emineu et saint seruarien* S, *De Eliud natus est Emineu, de Emineu natus est sanctus Seruatius* LgA.

43 **castell of Troussiet**: *oppido Traiecti* LgA.

44 **hadde**: *habuisse dicitur* LgA.

51 **Rightwis**: add *qui fut nomme barsabat* P2, *qui et Barsabas* LgA.

53–4 **also that she called**: *que elle apella aussy* P2.

56 **Euangelist**: add *et de ce y a vers qui contiennent ce que cy dessus est dit* P2, add *Vnde et de hoc extant uersus*:

Anna solet dici tres concepisse Marias,
Quas genuere uiri Iohachim, Cleophas Salomeque;
Has duxere uiri Ioseph, Alpheus, Zebedeus.
Prima parit Christum, Iacobum secunda minorem.
Et Ioseph iustum peperit cum Simone Iudam,
Tertia maiorem Iacobum uolucremque Iohannem LgA.

The verses (Maggioni, 902, Dunn-Lardeau, 846) are omitted by LgD, but pasted into H1 as f. 1*; there is no mark on f. 264[ra] to draw attention to them.

63–4 **but it is to understonde that the kinrede and that of the prestes**: *se la ligne de juda et la ligne des prestres* P2, *Et donc ceulz de la lignee de leui. espouserent fames de la lignee de Iuda. se la lignee roial et cele des prestres* P1, *sed sciendum quod et ipse Aaron et Ioiada summus sacerdos ambo de tribu Iuda duxerunt uxores, unde tribus sacerdotalis et regalis* LgA.

66 **and so be norisshed furthe**: *fieri datis nuptui feminis* LgA, 'and women be given in marriage'.

69–70 **and so**: *enim* LgA.

72 **shuld be offered**: *se deuoit offrir* P2.

73 **he shulde defende**: *regeret* LgA.
good: *fideles* LgA.

77 **prestes**: add *et prophete* LgA.

77–8 **chosin for**: *appellez* P2.

78 **presthode**: GiL omits Maggioni, 903 (34–5), Dunn-Lardeau, 847.

79 **Thanne . . . Ladi**: only GiL, a link passage after the omission.

82 **recordithe that**: *se recorda* P2, *se ibidem legisse recoluit* LgA.

82–3 **he drow . . . frende of his**: *il le translata par prieres daucuns* P2, *rogatus transcripsit* LgA.

83 **and fonde therin that**: not in LgA.

84 **Galile**: add *de la cite de nazareth* P2.

87 **temple**: add *et templi seruitoribus* LgA.

92 **in . . . festis**: *et y alerent par .ij. ans* P2, *in tribus festis precipuis* LgA.

92–3 **feste day of the yere**: *iour des estraines* P2, *festo enceniorum* LgA, the Feast of the Dedication.

97 **sittinge ne**: only GiL.

98 **lawe**: *foy* P2, *legis* LgA.

98–9 **oure Lorde**: *domino legis* LgA.

101 **thus . . . this**: *sic confusum se uidens* LgA.

105–6 **and comforted hym**: not in LgA.

110 **reproef**: add *que tu es brehaigne* P2.

114 **sayne and**: only GiL.

115 **was barein**: *sterilitatis obprobrium pertulit* LgA.

116 **.iiij^{xx}.**: *nonantiesme* P2.

121 **children**: *enfantemens* P2.

123 **same**: add *comme vous lauez voue sera des son enfance sacree a nostre seigneur et* P2.

125 **and**: add *non pas* P2.

138 **came to her warde**: *reuenoit* P2.

139 **haddyn . . . other**: *furent fermes de la lignie promise et lyez de veoir lun lautre* P2.

145 **to stie up to**: *circa* LgA.
Temple[1]: add *iuxta XV graduum psalmos* LgA.

146 **sette**[1]: add *et pour ce que nul ne pouoit aller a lautel des sacrifices qui est dehors fors par degrez* P2.

151 **aungeles**: *anges* (*angelo* LgA) *et vsoit chascun iour de la vision diuine* P2.

155 **None**[2]: add *usque uesperas* LgA.

159 **houses**: add *ut uiris legitime iungerentur* LgA.

160 **alle**: add *ces autres* P2.

165 **Vowithe**: *venez* P2, *Vouete* LgA.
yeldithe: add *a dieu* P2, not in LgA.

166 **breke . . . peple**: *morem genti insuetum introducere* LgA.

167 **fest**: *imminentem festiuitatem* LgA.

171 **oratorie**: add *cunctis audientibus* LgA.

175 **shulde . . . Virgine**: *seroit celluy sans doubte a qui la vierge deuoit estre espouse* P2.

176 **it fell amonge other**: only GiL.

179 **yerdes**: add *a lautel* P2, not in LgA.

180 **so . . . that**: *sicomme nulle chose* P2.

184 **by . . . bisshop**: not in LgA.

184–5 **the holy . . . of**: only GiL.

185–6 **was . . . yerde**: not in P2, *in eius cacumine* (. . .) *consedisset* LgA.

188 **weddid**: *espousa* S, *Desponsata* LgA. The Latin means 'betrothed', and Joseph goes home to prepare for his nuptials. The French is ambiguous, the English means 'married'. *MED* does not record *wedden* in the sense 'betroth',

though it means 'pledge' in other contexts. To avoid the problem, LgD and GiL make the change noted for 189 below.
the[2]: *sa* P2.

189 **meyne and his hous**: *domum* LgA.

190 **to housholde**: *a ce* P2, *nuptiis* LgA.

192 **and . . . miracle**: *quas ob ostensionem miraculi a sacerdote acceperat* LgA.

193 **of God**: *Gabriel* LgA.

197 **.vij.**: *vj*[e] P2.

199 **gret**: *iocundissimam* LgA.

200 **tyme**: *iour* P2.

202 **moder of God**: only GiL.

204 **acordinge**: i.e. to correspond.

206 **orisones**: *ieunes* P2.

207 **auncien scriptures**: *scripturis et antiquitatum testimoniis* LgA.

208 **of alle the Chirche**: only GiL.

210 **.iiij.**: add *qui fut ne de iennes* P2, add *natione Ianuensis* LgA.

211 **Gregori**: add *IX* LgA.

212 **of Rome**[1]: not in LgA.
enclosed: add *in quodam conclaui* LgA.

226 **that**: add *es percreus* P2, 'for adults'.

227 **circumcision**: *contritionem* LgA.

228 **committed**: *toute* P2, *comptee* S, *tota* LgA.

228–9 **that . . . no**: *celle de Marie ne conuint pas auoir* P2.

230 **.viij. resurreccion**: i.e. octave of the resurrection.

234 **were . . . done**: *len dit messe apres autre* P2.

235–6 **thei . . . done**: *il yssy hors du monstier* P2.

237–8 **anone . . . sawe hym**: only GiL.

239 **hated hym**: *aderant* LgA, misread as *oderant*.
saide . . . day: *luy affermoient et tous luy crioient ensemble quil auoit tres noblement tournoie* P2.

247 **with souerayne deuocion**: only GiL.

248 **cumpany**: *choro* LgA.

250 **felawship**: *choro* LgA.

254–6 s.w. follows closely Vignay's loose verse translation: *Chantons a nostre seigneur compaignes. Chantons luy honneur. Chantons a bouche debonnaire. La doulce amour qui luy doit plaire.*

257 **thanne . . . beganne**: *chantoient deux et deux par ordre* P2, *Predicteque bine cantatrices* (. . .) *in ordine uersus subsecute sunt* LgA.

259 ***cum tumuit***: *continuit* P2, *cum tumuit* LgA.

Vignay translates: *Le premier orgueil trebucha au bas de la tres grant lumiere. Le premier homme qui succa la pomme trebucha arriere* P2.

262 **sone**: *unicum filium* LgA.

269 **and peinted**: only GiL.
she kneled her adoune: *se tint* P2, *stans* LgA.

272 **thou . . . praiers**: *tu ne mas point encores aide qui suis mere maleuree* P2.

278–9 **and bare it with her**: only GiL.

279 **right faste**: *tres diligemment* P2, *cum claui diligentius* (. . .) *bonum obsidem pro filio suo habere se gaudens et ipsum diligenter custodiens* LgA.

288–9 **with al . . . to me**: only GiL.

290 **by your . . . pitee**: only GiL.

292 **oure most blessed Ladi**: *et la saluoit souuent* P2.

293 **take**: add *furtim quedam rapiens* LgA.
hanged: *iugie a pendre* P2.

295 **hym**: add *a ses mains* P2.

298 **aboute his necke**: only GiL.

302 **than**: add *sesmerueillerent et* P2.

304 **hous of religion**: *monstier* P2.

306 **Mateins**: *heures* P2.

306–7 **his . . . had**: *ses parens moururent ilz nauoient* P2.

308 **wif**: add *et gouuernast son propre heritage* P2.

310–11 **that he vsed to do**: only GiL.

311–12 **his . . . Uirgine**: *ses heures* P2.

313 **in sharpe wise**: *vng pou cruelment* P2, *quasi seuerius* LgA.

313–14 **fole unhappi**: *stulte et infidelis* LgA.

315–18 **And . . . thanne he**: *Et donc celluy esmeu* P2.

318–19 **feined . . . mariage**: *faingnist tout et laissa a celebrer les nopces* P2.

320 **priuili**: *de la maison* S.

321–3 **as long . . . blysse**: only GiL.

324 **symple**: only GiL.

325 **coude sing**: *sciebat* LgA.

329 **gretly**: add *ainsy comme traitre* P2.
of presthode: only GiL.
that: *et luy entredist* P2.

330 **more**: *messe* P2.

332 **for**: *requisiuit* (. . .) *et cur* LgA.

332–3 **seruaunt and her chapelein**: *chapellain* P2, *cancellarium* LgA.

334 **of presthode**: *acoustumee* P2.

336–7 **and charged . . . wont to singe**: (*et* P1) *que il ne celebrast nulle messe fors celle de la vierge marie* P2, *nullam missam preter illam quam sciebat de beata Maria celebrare debeat imperauit* LgA.

339 **eueri day**: not in LgA.

340 **Matenes and Oures**: *heures* P2, *horas sanctas* LgA.

342 **this wreche**: *cestuy* P2, *illo qui uos aspicit* LgA.

349 **endeles**: only GiL.

350 **request**: add *pour sauoir se* (*si uel saltem* LgA) *ie verray sa correction* P2.

354 **werkes of oure Lorde**: *bonnes euures* P2.
.iiijC.xxxvij.: *DXXXVII* LgA.

354–5 **the yere . . . Sesile**: This belongs to the following paragraph, which in LgA begins *Apud Siciliam* (. . .) *fuit quidam uir*.

358 **thinges**: add *ecclesiasticas* LgA.

360 **vikership**: *MED vicariship*e, 'position of deputy', has only one citation, for *c.*1450.

361 **wolde . . . of**: *ayma meulx que vng autre fut soubzhaucie en* P2.

364 **he**[2]: *ille* LgA, i.e. the Jew.

366 **his cristendome**: *la profession crestienne* P2, *christiane professionis abrenuntiauit* LgA.

367 **of his owne blode**: *abnegationis* LgA.
seale: add *et la bailla au dyable toute seellee* P2.

368 **so bi . . . crafte**: *ainsy* P2.
seruice: *office* P2, *seruitio* LgA.

372 **mesure**: add *de ce quil auoit fait* P2.

373 **grace and of**: only GiL.

378 **that he was verily foryeue**: *du pardon que elle luy auoit jmpetre* P2.

381–2 **But . . . Theophile that**: *mais sesioist quil* P2.

383 **thanne Theophile**: *quant theophile loy* (*lot* P1, *recepto* LgA) *il sesioy forment et* P2.

384 **thanked**: *sesmerueillerent* P2.

386 **Amen**: only GiL, omitting the rest of the chapter, Maggioni, 913–17 (161–237). LgD includes (161–80), Dunn-Lardeau, 857–8, but the remainder is also omitted from some MSS of LgA and by Batallier.

124 ST CECILIA I

Maggioni, ch. CLXV, p. 1180; Dunn-Lardeau, ch. 164, p. 1083.

Cecilia appears both here and in its correct LgA and calendar position at 162; see above, p. 39. The notes to both versions are given together here, line numbers where they differ being divided by a forward slash, Cec1/Cec2.

In Cec2 but not Cec1, D writes Palmachien consistently for Almachien.

4 **praie to**: *parler de* P2.

7 **her . . . her**: *ses amis la donnerent a femme* P2, *autem desponsata fuisset* LgA.
noble: only GiL.

9/8 **come**: *fut establi* P2.

9 **tendre**: only GiL.

11 **songe**[1]: *chantoient* P2, *smeten* Cec2.
oure Lorde: add *en son cueur* P2.

12/11–12 **Mi . . . God**: *Sire* P2.

13/12–13 **be thi grace**: only GiL.

14 **thre dayes**: *biduanis ac triduanis* LgA.

15/14 **oure Lorde**: add *que elle doubtoit* P2.

16/15 **into the**: add *secreta silentia* LgA.

17/16 **whanne . . . allone**: only GiL.

18/17 **Lo**: *O* P2 and Cec2.

20/18 **not . . . me**: *que tu le garderas en secret* P2.

23/22 **loue and tendirnesse**: *amour* P2, *zelo* LgA.

25/23 **in suche a wise**: *tantost* P2.

26/24 **age**: *aggreable ieunesce* P2.

27/25–6 **his loue**: *gloriam suam* LgA.

29/28 **leue**: *croye P2*, *leue* Cec2, *loue* Cec1.

30/29 **require me**: add *et se cest* (*diligis* LgA) *vn autre homme ie occiray toy et li dun glaiue* S.

32/31 **well**: *bien* P2, omitted by EH1 and Cec2.

32–3/31–2 **but while . . . may not**: only GiL.

33/32 **wherfor y shalle sende you**: *va* P2.
way: *voye* P2, *ile* Cec2.

34/33 **which is a mile from Rome**: *in tertium miliarum ab urbe* LgA.

35/33 **pore man**: *poures* P2, *pore men* Cec2.

36/35 **the**: add *ancien* P2.

38/37 **doute . . . but**: only GiL.

39/37 **hym**: add *et redieris* LgA.

41/40 **of dede men**: *martyrum* LgA.

41–2/40–1 **for drede . . . religion**: only GiL.
was: add *thanne* Cec2.

44/43 **heuene**: add *cum lacrimis* LgA.

44/43–4 **of rightwys**: *casti* LgA.

45/44 **sede**: *fruit de la semence* P2.

46/45 **Crist**: add *pastor bone* LgA.

48/47 **toke**: add *cruel* P2.
to me: *a toy* P2.

48–9/47–8 **as a debonair**: *as debonaire as a* Cec2, but H1H2 as Cec1 and P2; so Cec2 text should be emended.

49/48 **betwene hem**: not in LgA.

53–4/52–3 **that . . . this**: only GiL.

55/54 **alle[1]/all[2]**: add *et per omnia* LgA.

60/59 **whanne . . . done**: only GiL.

62–7/61–5 **And whanne . . . loke ye**: *et bailla lune a cecile et lautre a valerien et dit* P2; Cec2 gives *thou* for *ye*, but at 68/67 reverts to *you*. The angel distinguishes between singular for Valerian alone and plural for the two of them.

68–9/67 **by . . . God**: *de dieu* P2.

71/69 **charite**: *castitas* LgA.

71–3/69–71 **for . . . graunte the**: *pour ce que tu as creu proffitable conseil demande ce que tu vouldras* P2.

73/71–2 **with soueraine gladnesse**: only GiL.

74–8/72–6 **Worship . . . trouthe**: *il ne mest riens tant doulce chose en ceste vie comme la bonne volente dun mien frere que jay. Sy que ie te prie que il congnoisse auec moy la voye de verite* P2.

80/78 **peine**: *palma* LgA.

82/80 **of his . . . entred**: *et* P2.
so gret a: *a gret* Cec2 E, but H1H2 as Cec1.

82/80–1 **of swetnesse**: only GiL.

83/81 **that . . . astonied**: only GiL.

84–5/83 **myn hondes were full**: *ie tenoie roses et lis en ma main* P2.

85/83 **of swetnesse**: not in P2, *suauitatis* LgA.

86/84 **Truly . . . suster**: only GiL.

87/85 **with this suetnesse**: only GiL.

87–8/85–6 **altered and chaunged**: *soudainement mue* P2; Cec2 retains *sodenly*.

88/86 **Dere brother**: only GiL.

90/88 **sauour**: add *par moy* P2; Cec2 adds *and maist not see hem*, and substitutes *shalt* for Cec1 *maist*.

90–1/89 **in God**: not in Cec2, LgD, or LgA.

91/89 **do**: not in Cec2.

96/94 **with thin eyen**: only GiL.

100/98 **of the holy gost**: *du ciel* P2.
worlde: add *et ses chambres* P2, add *cum thalamis* LgA.

101/99 **paine**: *palmam* LgA.

105–6/103–4 **These . . . Ambrose**: not in P2, in LgA.

107/105 **hem**: *ei* LgA.

108/106 **but**: not in P2 or Cec2, nor in Cec1 MS D.
deef and: only GiL.

109–10/107–8 **worse . . . beste**: *beste* P2.

110/108 **heringe . . . ioy**: only GiL.

111/109 **be**: *estre* P2, not in Cec2
brother: *cousin* P2, *cognatum* LgA, 'kinsman'.

113/111 **cosin**: *cognatum* LgA.

113–14/111 **my dere brother**: only GiL.

120/117–18 **yef . . . to hym**: only GiL.

121–2/119 **we shulle renne in**: *nous encourons* P2, *incurremus* LgA, 'we shall incur'.

122/120 **of tirauntes**: only GiL.

125/123 **they**: *toutes les choses* P2, *all the thinges* Cec2.

127/125 **cominge**: *comithe* Cec2.
fader: add *viuifia* P2, add *and quickenithe* Cec2.

128/125 **God**: add *venant ou monde* P2.

128/126 **techithe**: *demonstra* P2, *uerbis et miraculis monstrauit* LgA.

129/127 **Truli . . . that**: *certes* P2.

130/128 **now ye sheue us**: *comment tesmongnes tu* P2.

134–5/132–3 **the cominge . . . passion**: *laduenement* (add *filii* LgA) *et de la passion de dieu et a luy demonstrer moult de conuenabletez de la passion* P2. The emendation *blessed* is supplied from Cec2; L reads *preysid*.

136/134 **mannes soule**: *lumain lignage* P2.

139/137 **man**: *homme* P2, *men* Cec2.

140–1/138–9 **suffered . . . crowned**: *eust en son chief coronnes* (*coronam* LgA) P2.

141/139 **man**: *nobis* LgA.

142/140 **of dampnacion**: only GiL.

143/141 **oure**: *la* P2.

144/142 **fader**: *peres* P2, *parentum* LgA.

145/143 **the trespas and the outrage**: *preuaricationem* LgA.

146/144 **Whanne . . . he**: *Et dont tyburcien* P2.

146–7/144–5 **A my dere brother**: only GiL.

149/147 **aungell**: *anges* P2.

150/148 **of hym . . . desired**: *tantost* (add *omnia* LgA) *ce quil leur requiroit* P2.

151–2/149–50 **departed . . . largely**: *estoient en aumosnes faire* P2, *elemosinis insistebant* LgA.

153/151 **for cristen faithe**: only GiL.

153–4/151–2 **whanne . . . he**: *celluy preuost* P2, *Almachius* LgA.

157/155 **settist so litell by**: *appelles* P2, *dampnatos appellas* LgA.

159/157 **is not sayn**: i.e. 'does not seem'.

161/159 **not**[1]: *non estre* P2, *no beinge* Cec2.

162/160–1 **whiche is . . . ioye**: *et la peine des mauuais* P2.

163–4/161–2 **I trowe . . . thiself**: *ie ne cuide pas que tu parles de ta pensee* P2.

166/164 **I suppose . . . hymself**: *pource que ton frere ne parle pas de saine teste. par aduenture* P2.

167/165 **Thanne saide Valerian**: this should follow 169/167 *peynes*, the end of Almachius's speech; see next note.

169/167 **peynes. For**: *toutes choses contraires a yoie. Et dont valerien dit* P2.

169–70/167–8 **children . . . scorned**: *jouer les oyseux et se mocquoient des* P2.

170–1/168–9 **werkemen and laboreres**: *operarios agricolas* LgA.

171/169 **fruytes**: *fruis* P2, add *laborum* LgA, *fruit* Cec2.

172/170 **the laboreres**: add *qui putabantur uani* LgA.
that . . . hem: *qui uidebantur urbani* LgA.

173/171 **and so . . . for**: *Sic et nos nunc* LgA.

174–5/172–3 **whan ye shul . . . sorw**: *Et vous qui auez orendroit joye transitoire arez ou temps aduenir la mort pardurable* P2, following 175/173 *ioye*.

177/175 **euerlastinge²**: *pardurable* P2, *perpetuel* Cec2.

178/176 **men**: *homuntiones* LgA, 'little men'.
oure: *vostre* P2, *youre* Cec2.

180/178 **of lower degree**: only GiL.

183/181 **almighti**: *vray* P2.

185/183 **finde**: *trouuer* P2, *serue* Cec2.

186/184 **the name of a god**: *nomen dei* LgA.

188/186 **And . . . blynde**: *dont foloie tout le monde* P2.

189/187 **knowynge only**: *congnoissiez* P2, *shulde only knowe* Cec2.
the trouthe: *le dieu vray* P2.

193/191 **beauute of youthe**: add *voulente de fraternite germaine* P2, *flos purpureus, o germanus fraternitatis affectus* LgA.

194/192 **and that (that go therto Cec2) . . . a will**: only GiL.

194/192–3 **ye were bode**: *ce fust aler* S, *festinatis* LgA.

196/194 **us**: *gloriam animarum eorum* LgA, *eorum* because LgA is in indirect speech.

197–8/195–6 **y . . . power**: *Je soye ars en flambe de feu se ie ne confesseray celluy dieu seul* P2.

198/197 **Maxymien**: add *et tous les bouchiers* P2.

201–2/199–200 **cam . . . vois to hem**: only GiL.

203/201 **O ye**: *mout joie* P2, *Eia* LgA, *Ye* Cec2.
partithe awey: *ostes* P2, *puttithe* aweye Cec2.

206–9/203–6 **and whanne thei wolde in no wise do sacrifice thei were beheded in the same place. And Maximian swore truly that whanne the holy seintes were martired he sawe a gret multitude of aungels aboute hem and**: *Et dont maximin jura par son serment quil vit les anges a leure de leur passion car ilz furent decolez ensemble pource quilz ne vouloient sacrifier. Et dit plus maximin que il vist* P2, *et dum sacrificare nollent pariter* *decollantur. Tunc Maximus cum iuramento asseruit se in hora passionis eorum angelos uidisse fulgentes et* LgA; Vignay altered the order of the clauses, but s.w. restored LgA order, though translating *fulgentes* as *a gret multitude of.* The versions are given in full since it is rare for s.w. to revert to the Latin if the French effectively covers the ground, as here.

209/207 **of her bodies**: not in LgA.

210/208 **bring**: *emportoient* P2, *beringe* Cec2.
up: add *en leurs girons* P2.

212/210 **yelde**: *gaue* Cec2, but D *yeldid.*

213/211 **sperit**: add *et saincte cecile en trouua* (*entra* S, *enterra* P1) *le corps delez les corps de valerien et de tyburcien* P2.

214/212 **toke al her goodes**: *amborum facultates cepit inquirere* LgA.

216–18/214–16 **And . . . Ihesu**: only GiL.

218–20/216–18 **the peple . . . here**: *elle fut constrainte a ce des sergens qui ploroient forment pour ce que sy noble pucelle et sy belle se mettoit a mort* P2; the *sergens* urging her to sacrifice are those of Almachien; in GiL the *servauntes* seem to be Cecilia's.

221/219 **beth . . . for**: only GiL.

222/220 **into betir**: only GiL.
myre or fenne: *boe* P2, *lutum* LgA, 'clay'; *or fenne* is not in Cec2. Cec2 *myrre* is a rare spelling for 'mire' and perhaps thought to be 'myrrh'.

223/221 **abite**: *habitaculum* LgA.
clothing: only GiL.

224/222 **large . . . place**: *tres cler lieu* P2, *forum perlucidum* LgA.

224–5/222 **O good lorde**: only GiL; this is perhaps a colloquial way of addressing Almachien rather than a pious ejaculation.

226/224 **Whi . . . how**: only GiL.

228–9/226–7 **it . . . verily**: not in LgA.

230/228 **Cecilie sent priuely for**: *fut appelle leuesque* P2.

232/230 **the tyraunt**: only GiL.

236/234 **What wenist thou that y conclude . . . demande**: *qui cuides que ie conclue .ij. responces soubz vne demande* P2, *que duas responsiones una putat inquisitione concludi* LgA; for **What . . . that** Cec2 reads *that wenist.*

238–9/236–7 **presumpcion . . . verrei**: in Cec1 but omitted from all MSS of Cec2.

238/236 **me . . . wise**: only GiL.

241/238–9 **Yes . . . for**: only GiL.

242/240 **a litell**: only GiL.
or a pynne: only GiL, not in Cec2.

243/240 **fade**: add *et toute sa roideur courberoit* P2.
What: only GiL.

244–5/242 **Iniurie . . . wordes**: i.e. it is only an insult if the words are untrue.

246/243 **vtterly**: *faulsement* P2; *MED* gives the adjective *outreli*, but not the adverb, with sense 'out of line, amiss', which is, however, required here.

249/247 **As y . . . ere**: only GiL.

250/247–8 **sadnesse of feithe**: *fermete* P2.

252/250 **and saide**: not in Cec2.

256/254 **Holde thi tunge and**: only GiL.

259–60/257 **fele . . . see**: *apren en tastant ce que tu ne peuz veoir* P2.

264/260–1 **neuer disese of hete**: *oncques vng peu de sueur* P2.

264–5/261 **satte . . . floures**: *estoit la tout aussy comme en vng froit* (add *loco* LgA) P2.

269/265–6 **he left . . . blodi**: *eam semiuiuam cruentus carnifex dereliquit* LgA; *there* is only in Cec2.

269/266 **ouer that lyued**: *suruesqui* P2, *ouerlyued* Cec2.

272–3/269 **hem here to thi**: *ceulx cy a ta* P2, *hem to her* Cec2.

274–6/270–3 **And . . . court**: only GiL.

277/274 **dedied**: *dedya* P2, *halowed* Cec2.

278–9/275 **and . . . lyf**: only GiL.

279/276 **.CC. and .xxiij.**: *CCXXV* LgA.

280/277 **Alisaundre**: add *Et len list ailleurs que elle souffri mort ou temps de marc aurelian qui fut empereur enuiron lan de nostre seigneur deux cens et xx* P2.

125 ST ADRIAN

Maggioni, ch. CXXVIII, p. 918; Dunn-Lardeau, ch. 127, p. 858.

3 **and**[1]: not in LgA.

4–5 **for loue . . . money**: *par paour les autres par amour et les autres par promesse dargent* P2, *alii timore pene, alii amore promisse pecunie* LgA.

5 **his neighbore**: add *et le prochain son prochain* P2.

7 **the kinge**: Voragine and Vignay refer to Maximianus as *imperator, empereur* at 2, 90, and 122, but elsewhere as *rex*, *roy*; similarly s.w., except that GiL has *emperoure* at 101 for *rex*, *roy*.

9 **the comaundement of thi foly**: *et stultitie tue iussionem irrisimus* LgA.

12–13 **eueriche . . . prison**: *annotata uniuscuiusque confessione ferro uinctos in carcere recludi* LgA.

15 **the vertu of**: only GiL.

15–16 **vertu and**: only GiL.

16–17 **that ye suffre thus**: only GiL.

19–20 **hem . . . perfitely**: *diligentibus* LgA.

29–30 **that was . . . cristen**: only GiL.

38 **diligently**: only GiL.

41 **haste . . . passion**: *tempore passionis nostre accersiam te* LgA, 'at the time of our passion I will send for you'.

43 **in oure Lorde**: only GiL.

46 **kepers**: add *et leur bailla les autres sains en pleige* P2.

47 **his wyf**: only GiL.

48 **his**: *leur* P2.

51–2 **of charite**: only GiL.

52 **and þat**: *Non mihi contingat ut soluatur a uinculis et* LgA.

52–3 **God defende it**: *ja ce nauiengne* P2. not in LgA.

56 **shette**: add *hastiuement* P2.

57 **is take awey**: *cest oste* P2, *corruit* LgA.

58–9 **God and his**: only GiL.

59 **Lorde**: add *Et dont se tourna deuers luy et luy dit* P2.

61 **Alas**: *ou* P2.

61–2 **from hem**; *a conuentu pacis* LgA.

62 **cowarde**: only GiL.

63 **fighters fight**: *les bataillans* P2, *repugnantem* LgA.

65–6 **the men . . . wickidnesse**: *la gent des felons et sans dieu* P2, *gente sine deo et de genere impiorum* LgA.

68–70 **He . . . renogate**: *il ne mest pas donne que par vne seule espaice de temps* (*unius hore spatium* LgA) *je feusse appellee femme dun martir. mais seray dicte femme dun renye* P2.

73 **the gret sadnesse of**: only GiL.

76 **atte the laste**: only GiL.

86 **martirdom**: *martires* P2, *tormenta* LgA.

86–7 **and myn . . . lefte**: *ensemble et le mien* P2.

88 **hym**: add *et dont sentre acolerent* P2.

89 **.viij.**: *sept* P2.

90 **And thanne**: *Statuta autem die* LgA.

92–3 **was bound . . . ecule and**: *estoit vraiement lye les mains derriere et parloit a natalie et fut porte sur le tourment deculee et* P2, *uero retro uinctis manibus sequebatur. Deinde Adrianus portans sibi eculeum* LgA.

96–7 **and . . . heuene**: *mais seras tantost essaucie auecques les anges* P2, *sed continuo cum angelis exultabis* LgA.

99 **Natalye**: add *cum gaudio* LgA.

102 **that be noght**: *quia eos qui non sunt dii blasphemo* LgA.

103 **dispisist**: *blasmes* P2.

106–8 **And . . . said**: *Et natalie couroit aux autres a grant joye et disoit les paroles de son mary* P2.

111 **martirdomes . . . ansueres**: *martires et les responses et les peines* P2, *penas et interrogationes et responsiones* LgA.

113 **appered**: *effunderentur* LgA.

117 **in comforting of hym**: not in LgA.

119 **my dere husbonde**: *ma lumiere* P2.

121 **for whom thou sufferist**: not in LgA.

130 **an orrible turment**: *vne enclume* P2, 'anvil'.

131–2 **shulde . . . turment**: *eussent dessus les cuisses froissees* P2.

135 **thies**: add *confractis* LgA.

136 **And Natalye praied hym**: only GiL.

140 **of her owne fre wille**: not in LgA.

153 **yonge**: *riche* P2.

158 **fro hem**: only GiL.

168 **to hem**: *hiis qui erant cum Natalia* LgA.
in a shippe: *en vne nef de fantosme* P2, *cum naui phantastica* LgA.

172 **finde and saile more right**: *vous nagerez plus droit* P2, *rectius nauigetis* LgA.

174–5 **apered . . . waye**: *in nauicula sedens eisdem apparuit et eos nauigare sicut prius ceperant admonuit, asserens malignum spiritum fuisse qui sibi locutus fuerat* LgA.

175 **hym**: add *aller deuant eulx* P2.

178 **of the martires**: *ou les martirs estoient* P2, *ubi erant corpora martyrum* LgA.

184 **holy**: *les corps des* P2.

126 STS GORGONIUS AND DOROTHEUS

Maggioni, ch. CXXIX, p. 924; Dunn-Lardeau, ch. 128, p. 864.

16 **and so . . . to God**: not in LgA.

17 **to**: add *lupis et* LgA.

18 **and beried**: not in LgA.

21 **.CCC.xxxiij.**: *DCCLXIV* LgA.

23 **chirche of Gorgonien**: *monstier de gourgomense* P2, *Gorziensi monasterio* LgA, i.e. error for the monastery at Gorze, near Metz.

127 STS PROTUS AND HYACINTH

Maggioni, ch. CXXX, p. 925; Dunn-Lardeau, ch. 129, p. 865.

1 **yonge men . . . kinrede**: *damoiseaulx de noble lignage* P2, *domicelli* LgA, young men of high birth attached to serve in a noble household. In LgA they are specifically linked to Eugenia in both categories, *domicelli et in studio philosophie socii Eugenie.*

7 **liberall**: add *et es lectres* P2.

8 **her²**: *ces* P2, *omnium* LgA.

10 **the sone . . . Aquile**: *acquilin filz du consulte acquilin* P2.

12 **only**: only GiL.

14 **by all good condicions**: *par bonnes meurs* P2, not in LgA, picked up by Vignay from 11 above.

17 **a vers . . . that**: not in LgA. This is Ps. 95: 5.

18 **only**: *certes* P2, *autem* LgA.

20 **ouerpassed**: add *scrupoloso studio* LgA.

21 **yddes**: *ydees* P2, *ideas* LgA. *MED* has three citations for *idea*, one from Trevisa and two from Lydgate, and the term was probably unknown to s.w. A2 substitutes *hyd thynges.* Here it is for the 'Platonic idea', but used more generally as 'concepts'.

22 **philosofers**: *le poete* P2.

22–3 **as moche errour . . . thenkithe**: *quanque lerreur* (*orator* LgA) *et le phylozophe pense* P2.

23 **sentence**: add *Dominam me uobis usurpata potestas, sororem uero sapientia fecit* LgA.

28 **heretikes**: *vng herese* P2.

31 **shuld haue**: *habere probaretur* LgA.

34 **chased confused and**: not in LgA.

35 **from all other**: *de tous* P2, i.e. by all.

37 **for thou . . . vertuously**: *quia cum sis femina uiriliter agis* LgA.

41 **come**: add *domum* LgA.

55 **semelihede**: *grandeur* P2, *elegantiam iuuentutis* LgA.

59 **to haue pitee of her**: *se inuisere dignaretur* LgA.

60–2 **she was sike . . . cussed hym**: *elle estoit esprise de son amour. et comment elle ardoit en la couuoitise de luy. et luy pria quil couchast auecques luy charnelment. et tantost le prist et acola et baisa et lamonnestoit a pechie* P2.

64 **Melancie**: Greek *mélas*, *mélan*-, 'black'.

66 **norissher**: *nourrissement* P2, *dux* LgA.
suster: *fomentum* LgA.
lecherie: add *soror anxietatis perpetue* LgA.

67 **wofull**: *angoisseuse* P2, not in LgA.

69 **felonie**: add *uoluit ipsa prior detegere* LgA.

76 **officers . . . constables**: *apariteurs* S.

78 **before hym**: add *et establi vng iour que ilz deuoient tous estre deliurez aux bestes pour les deuorer* P2.

88 **of hem**: *dicelle* P2, *ex ore eius* LgA.

94 **seruaunt**: *seruos* LgA.

98–100 **bynethe her breste . . . brestes**: *jusques a la cainture par dessus et par dessoubz aussy et dit que elle estoit femme sicomme il apparut* P2.

105 **and kissed her**: only GiL.

106 **for ioye**: only GiL.

108 **heres**: i.e. her people.

110 **lefte provostie**: *propter hoc a prefectura depositus* LgA.

113 **went**: *retournerent* P2.

116 **necke**: not in LgA.

118 **furneis**: add *estaingny et* P2.

120 **apered to her**: *luy esclairoit* P2.

125–6 **turmentours were**: *decoleur fut* P2.

127–8 **secound day after**: *le dymenche apres* P2, *die dominica* LgA.

130 **to do sacrifice**: not in LgA.

133 **.CC.lvij.**: *CCLVI* LgA.

128 EXALTATION OF THE CROSS

Maggioni, ch. CXXXI, p. 930; Dunn-Lardeau, ch. 130, p. 869.

4 **gret filthe**: *vilte* P2, *uilitatis* LgA, 'cheapness'; but *vil* and related French and English words had only the extended senses 'despicable' etc. At 11 below this *filthe* is contrasted with *preciouste*, and, as here, extension of its usual senses to 'baseness, worthlessness' is required.

7 **for it**: *car il estoit tenebreux et sans nulle beaute. Il* P2.

8 **stenche**: *pueur* P2; s.w. read *pueur* as *pouoir*, giving EH1D *strengthe*, and the L reading here adopted was a correction from LgA.

11 **filthe**: see 4 above.

11–12 **Holy . . . saue**: *Salve crux pretiosa etc.* LgA.

13 **palmer**: add *etc* P2, add *et apprehendam fructum eius* LgA, Canticles 7: 8.

15 **bifore**: *ou front des* P2, 'on the foreheads of'.

19 **it is songe**: *il est dit ou preface* P2, *cantatur* LgA; the quotation is from the Preface for the mass of the Holy Cross.

21 **suetnesse**: *oyr* P2, *odoris suauitatem* LgA.

30 **not for that**: i.e. notwithstanding.

35–6 **thei casted . . . rayne**: *per subtiles etiam et occultos ductus quasi deus desuper aquam infundebat* LgA.

36 **in the laste stage**: *in subterraneo specu* LgA.
horses[2]: *charettes* P2.

37 **tour**: add *et faingnissent a faire tonner* P2.

38 **the cursed wreche**: *profanus* LgA, i.e. Cosdroe.

38–9 **his temple**: *tali fano* LgA.

41 **in the office of . . .**: *ou liure de loffice du mitre* P2, *in libro mitrali de officio* LgA, the *Mitrale* of Sicard of Cremona. A2 omits *of* and leaves no space, A1 supplies *his alkeron*, the Koran, for which *MED* has only five citations *s.v. alkaron*, none with this spelling, i.e. all *alkaron* or *alcoran*. The other MSS leave a space.
throne: add *tamquam pater* LgA.

42 **crosse**: add *aussy comme le filz* P2.

43 **cokke**: the common source of EH1A1 must have left a space which E supplies by reference to a Latin text, but for some reason does not translate; A1, in line with insertion of the Koran above, supplies *mamet*.

49–50 **and suorn**: not in LgA.

50 **shulde be dismembred**: *len luy couppast les cuisses et les bras* P2.

57 **wost nothing**: *ne sauoit pas la fin* P2.

58–9 **for he . . . tydingges**: *car il estoit aoure de tous comme dieu sy que nul ne luy osoit dire* P2, *quia cum ab omnibus odiretur sibi a nemine intimatur* LgA.

62 **crosse**: add *selon ta maniere* P2.

63–4 **y . . . while**: *ie te rendray et tendras encores ton regne a pou dostages* P2, *uitam et regnum paucis a te acceptis obsidibus obtinebis* LgA.

75–6 **on horsbacke araied like a kinge**: *in equo regio et ornamentis imperialibus* LgA.

81 **no . . . horsbak**: *non cultu regio* LgA.

90 **whanne**: *ce iour que* P2, *eodem die eodemque momento* LgA.

91–3 **flowed . . . sauour**: *et sestoit espendue en iherusalem par tant despace des terres, retourna en iherusalem en ce mouuement* (*moment* S) *et rempli tous de sa souefuete* P2, *Iherosolimis de Persarum prouincia per tam longa terrarum spatia fuerat illapsus, tunc rediit omnesque mirabili suauitate refecit* LgA.

95–6 **thanne . . . men**: *de toutes les estoilles, honneur du monde tres sainte et aimable a tous* P2, *cunctis astris mundi, celebris hominibus, multum amabilis, sanctior uniuersis* LgA.

98 **God**: *doulx fais* P2, 'sweet burden'.

99 **of the**: add *et est signee de ton signe* P2.

101 **renoueled**: add *Mortuus quidam uite restuitur* LgA.

102 **cured and**: only GiL.

107 **in a cronicle**: *es chroniques* P2.
he: *ilz* P2.

115 **sone**: add *Mendasse* P2, add *Merdasan* LgA.
And: add *quant* P2.

117 **alle . . . londe**: *les nobles* P2.

118 **strong bondes of yren**: *lyans* P2.

121 **with**[1]: add *le fust de* P2.

123 **crosse**: add *et postmodum Constantinopolim deportauit* LgA.

124–5 **Sibille . . . the paynime**: *De hoc autem ligno crucis sic dixit Sibilla apud paganos, sicut dicitur in historia tripartita: 'O ter beatum lignum, in quo deus extensus est!' Hoc forte dictum est propter uitam nature, gratie et glorie que ex cruce prouenit* LgA.

129 **necke**: *gorge* P2.
a gret quantite: only GiL.

134–5 **sum cursed dede**: *homicide* P2.

136 **hem**: *luy* P2.

138 **thus moche**: *tantost* P2.

141 **ymage**: add *ut fertur* LgA.

143 **whiche . . . yere**: *sub annua pensione* LgA, i.e. for a year.

147 **cosynes**: *contribulibus* LgA, 'compatriots'.

152 **other**: add *cum adhuc predictam ymaginem non uidisset* LgA.

152–3 **he neuer . . . wost of hym**: *illam de qua dicebat ymaginem penitus ignorabat* LgA.

153 **he had leued hym**: *il estoit apaisie* P2.

156–7 **rebuked . . . coude**: *distrent et firent moult diniures* P2, *contumeliis diris afficiunt* LgA.

159 **turnement**: *obprobria* LgA.

172 **of**[2]: i.e. by.

178 **only**: only GiL.
kalendes: *V kal.* LgA.

180 **ide**: *.v.*[e] *Ide* P2.

184 **and namely**: *etiam* LgA, which begins a new section with this sentence.

187 **to drawe meche to hym**: *hanter auecques luy* P2, *secum habitare* LgA.

195–6 **entre in . . . benche**: *qui aloient au deuant de lun aussy comme par subiection daucune puissance. Et dont vit seoir celluy qui estoit* (*preerat* LgA) *ou milieu des autres* P2.

200 **diuision**: *discussionis* LgA; Vignay and s.w. presumably take this to be the distinction between the accounts of the various spirits.

201 **lif of**: only GiL.

202 **the fende come**: *uidit Sathanam sedentem* LgA.

212–13 **tempestes and turmentes**: *tourmens* P2, *commotiones maximas* LgA.

218 **debate in mariage**: *tancons en vnes nopces* P2, *rixas in quibusdam nuptiis* LgA.

219 **husbonde**: add *et ueni nuntiare tibi* LgA.

220 **.xx.**: *X* LgA.

223 **.x.**: *XL* LgA.

224 **unnethe**: add *tandem* LgA.

229 **vision**: *discussionis* LgA.

230 **wolde**: *auoit fait* P2.

231 **corage**: *carnis temptationem* LgA.

232–3 **sethe . . . do**: *sy que il luy a donne vne buffe en elle applanoiant hier a vespres et que le pechie se feroit* P2, *addens quod heri hora uespertina usque ad hoc eius mentem traxerit, ut in terga eius blandiens alapam daret* LgA.

234 **maister**: *malignus spiritus* LgA.
go forthe and performe: *parfeist* P2.

237 **behelde . . . asked**: *commanda que on querist* P2.

238 **in the corner**: *ou temple* P2.

238–9 **and bade . . . to hym**: only GiL.

239 **sorugh and**: only GiL.

241 **with houge voys**: not in P2, *territi* LgA.

242 **he . . . marked**: *il est signe* P2.
with that: *a ceste voix* P2.

243–4 **al . . . fere**: *tout esmeu* P2.

246 **hous**: add *et de son voisine* P2.

251 **sodenly**[1]: *gloutement* P2.

255 GiL omits one story, Maggioni, 938 (141–4), Dunn-Lardeau, 877.

129 ST JOHN CHRYSOSTOM

Maggioni, ch. CXXXII, p. 939; Dunn-Lardeau, ch. 131, p. 877.

2 **was the secounde sone of his fader**: *fut second son pere et sa mere carchure* P2, *filius Secundi et Anthure* (. . .) *fuit* LgA.

7 **holde olde**: *seuerior habebatur* LgA.

7–8 **brenninge of loue**: *feruori* LgA.

8 **outwardes**: only GiL.

8–9 **for the rightwisnesse of his lyf he entended to thingges to come. He was demed**: *pour la droicture de sa vie cellui ententif aux choses a uenir estoit cuide* P2, *propter uite rectitudine incautus ad futura prospicere nesciebat.* (. . .) *putabatur* LgA. Ryan's slight expansion captures the sense of the Latin: 'He . . . was incapable of looking forward prudently to the consequences of his actions.' Vignay, having mistranslated, partly recovers the sense by combining this sentence with the next: 'he was so detached through his concentration on the afterlife that he appeared proud'; s.w. separates the sentences again.

9 **proude**: *confabulatione arrogans* LgA.

11 **in refreninge the veyn maters**: *a refraindre les meurs* P2, *ad mores coercendos* LgA, 'enforcing good morality'. Vignay somewhat changed the sense, and s.w. added the adjective to clarify.

14 **of Constantinople**: not in P2, *Constantinopolitanus* LgA.

correcte: add *la vie des* P2.

16–17 **an euell speker of alle men**: *en mesdisoient a tous* P2, 'disparaged him to everyone'.

20–1 **for . . . sore**: *pourceque lestomac luy douloit souuent et pour abstinence* P2, *propter abstinentiam et stomachum et caput sepe dolebat* LgA.

23 **enemyes**: *enuieux* P2, *emuli* LgA.

27 **counceillour**: *consulte* P2, i.e. consul; at 76 below 'consul' appears as *counsaile.*

35–6 **and yet . . . chidde**: *sed insuper non destitit obiurgare* LgA.

49 **thereabout . . . prouinces**: *in Phenice* LgA, Phoenicia.

53–4 **of the kinrede of Celique barbaryn**: *du lignage de celsique barbarien par conseil* P2, *genere celticus, consilio barbarus* LgA.

57 **he**[2], 58 **he**[1], the emperor, 58 **he**[2], John.

59 **he by**: *ainsy* P2.

63 **pesibly**: *taisiblement* P2.

68 **auctorite**: *vng oratoire* P2.

76 **ornament of counsaile**: *aournament de consulte* P2, *consulari toga* LgA.

77 **now**: add *et ta premiere pourete et ta richesce de maintenant* P2.

79 **vnagreable**: *ingratus* LgA, 'ungrateful'; *MED* gives only one citation, from Chaucer's *Boethius*, in the sense 'unpleasant'.

82 **nobly**: *strenue* LgA.

89 **the citee**: *les autres citez* P2.

94 **Trace**: *tierce* P2, *Traciam* LgA.

96–7 **betoke . . . legacion**: i.e. sent him on a diplomatic mission.

98–100 **that knewe the trouthe of hym** (. . .) **for he knewe that he came for pitee and compassion**: *agnoscens eius fiduciam proprietate assumptam* LgA, which is hard to translate; Re gives the easier *pro pietate assumptam*, which must have been the reading in Vignay's source.

99 **in the waye**: *longo itinere* LgA.

100 **and compassion**: only GiL.

101 **cussed . . . mouthe**: *sy prist sa main et la mist en* (*a* S) *sa bouche et a ses yeulx* P2, *suisque oculis dexteram eius circumposuit* LgA.

102 **hys knees . . . holy**: *les sains genoulx* P2.

103 GiL omits Maggioni, 942 (53–65), Dunn-Lardeau, 880–1.

104 **were done**: add *en egypte* P2, referring to events in the preceding omitted section.

107 **and**[1]: *tamen* LgA.

111 **one to be thre by his vertu**: *.J. seul estre trois choses par sa vertu* P2, *tria uirtute unum* LgA, i.e. that one is the same as three.

113–16 **shulde . . . faithe**: *feussent a nocturnez. si que la mauuaise euure des autres fut destruicte. et que la foy des bons fut affermee. et fist faire croix dor et dargent qui estoient portees auecques cierges ardans* P2, *nocturnis hymnis insisteret ut et illorum opus offuscaretur et fidelium professio firmaretur; fecitque cruces argenteas que cum argenteis cereis portabantur LgA*.

117 **to the vtterest**: *iusques a la mort* P2, i.e. 'ready to fight to the death'.

118 **chamberleyn of the emperoure**: *eunuchus auguste* LgA, i.e. of the empress.

121–5 GiL omits Maggioni, 942–8 (75–186), Dunn-Lardeau, 882–8, and supplies **And . . . Septembre** as a link, the date of John's death being taken from the last of the omitted sentences.

128 **with strengthe and withoute reason**: *iniuste* LgA.

129 **that was his enemye**: only GiL.

131 **doctour of men**: *docteur de toutes terres* P2, *omnium doctore* LgA; Vignay detached *terrarum* from the following phrase, *terrarum occidentales episcopi*.

135 **emperoure**: *Archadii* LgA.

136 **partie**: *pitie* P2, *pietatem* LgA.

142 **ignoraunce**: add *et ses parens estoient tous mors pieca auoit* P2, 'and his parents were dead long since'.

146 **devout chirche**: *monstier* P2.

148 **Eudochie**: add *laquelle fist moult de choses a herotreem poetrique* P2, *que heroico metro poemata multa confecit* LgA.

152 **CCC.iiij**^{xx}**.x.**: *CCCC* LgA.

130 STS CORNELIUS AND CYPRIAN

Maggioni, ch. CXXXIII, p. 949; Dunn-Lardeau, ch. 132, p. 889.

17 **of the counsaile**: *en consulte* P2, *proconsuli* LgA.

19 **called**: *rapelle* P2.
consult: *proconsule* LgA.

131 ST EUPHEMIA

Maggioni, ch. CXXXIV, p. 951; Dunn-Lardeau, ch. 133, p. 890.

1 **of an vsurere**: *senatoris* LgA .

3 **to**: add *Priscum* LgA.

11 **sacrifice**: add *dont il fu esioy* S.

13 **straunge men and vnknowen**: *ignotos et aduenas* LgA, 'nobodies and strangers'.

14 **Crist**: add *et ad promissam gloriam peruenire* LgA.

15 **haddest turned thi thought**: *feusses retournee en ta pensee* P2, *ad mentem redisse* LgA.

16 **recordest**: *te feusses recordee de* S.
noblesse: add *uel sero* LgA, 'even if tardily'.

33 **the barres . . . fire**: *les lyans de la roe qui estoient ou feu* P2, *exeunte igne uectes* LgA; it is not clear how this instrument of torture worked.

36 **brent**: *comminuit* LgA.

42 **Apulien**, *Appellianus* LgA, apparently the LgA *preses* of 55 ff., distinguished from Priscus the *iudex* referred to from 3 up to this point; see note to 55 below.

48 **and**: add *quant il eust le glaiue trait il* P2.

49 **for . . . her**: *et que les anges deffendoient que il ne la touchast* P2, *quam eam quam angeli defendebant contingeret* LgA.

54 **hem alle**: *le* P2.

55 **iuge**: *preses* LgA; also at 62 (where LgD has *empereur*, GiL *emperour*); at 67–8 **whan the iuge sawe that he was confused that he deied nigh for anguisshe** (so too LgD) represents *iudicem hoc uidentem uehementius confuderunt. Vnde cum preses fere pre angustia moreretur* LgA. Thus Priscus the *iudex* and the *preses* are two different persons, the latter presumably Appellianus, who appears without further explanation at 42 above. Vignay, Batallier, and some modern translators, however, have taken them to be the same.
virgines: *la vierge* P2.

56 **prison**: add *negato cibo* LgA.

58 **oyle of her**: *luille doliue* P2.

60 **right gret softenesses**: *tres molle cendre* P2.

60–1 **And . . . aungeles**: only GiL.

62 **emperour**: *iuge* P2, *preses* LgA, see 55 above.

67 **iuge**: *preses* LgA; for variants in 66–7, see 55 above.

69–70 **smote . . . suerde**: *gladium in latus eius fixit* LgA.

73 **that . . . but**: *du tout en tout. Et dont ses gens le quistrent longuement et apeine peurent ilz trouuer* P2.

75 **ete hymself**: *se menga luy mesmes* P2, *se ipsum comedens* LgA; the

implication of the Latin, 'consuming himself with grief', is not recorded for ME by *MED*.

78 **.CC.iiij^xx^.**: *CCLXXXVII* LgA.

79 **virgine**: add *en son preface. Saincte vierge* P2.

84 **and obeied . . . praiers**: *Et* (add *soubmistrent leurs colz et* S) *toutes peines de tourment sont surmontees par son oroison* P2.

85 **martered**: *confesse* P2, *confossa* LgA.

86–9 **Now . . . merites**: *Et ceste saincte vierge te recommande de ton eglise et vueille toy deprier pour nous pecheurs. Et ceste vierge sans corrupcion florissant nous doint noz desirs estre octroiez de toy* P2.

132 ST LAMBERT

Maggioni, ch. CXXXV, p. 955; Dunn-Lardeau, ch. 134, p. 893.

4 **of Trete**: *dutrect* P2, *du tret* S, *Traiectensis* LgA, Maastricht, but Vignay took it as Utrecht. Both are Latin *Traiectum*, but sometimes more helpfully distinguished, as with *ad Mosam* or *superius* for Maastricht, and *ad Rhenum* or *inferius* for Utrecht.

5 **of Iewes**: *inuidorum* LgA, variant *in iudeorum*.

9 **he lete passe wynde bynethe**: *il fist vent par dessoubz* P2, *in pauimento* (. . .) *sonum fecit* LgA. Vignay seems to have taken this as a euphemism; in other versions of this life which mention the incident the saint dropped a shoe. This appears to be the first recorded use of the expression 'pass wind'.

12 **barefote**: add *fixus* LgA.

21 **there**: add *sicut prius* LgA.

23–5 **whom . . . blamed**: omitted from all MSS except A2, this passage must have been restored by reference to LgA, since LgD omits *as thei had deserued*, LgA *sicut meruerunt*. An H1 corrector marked the omission by a large cross in the margin, but apparently merely noted the disruption of sense, since no correction is attempted. The resultant confusion is such that an editorial decision was made, perhaps wrongly, to breach the normal convention on this occasion and to supply the A2 correction rather than to leave the authorial text.

25 **king**: only GiL; he was in fact mayor of the palace.

29 **cosin**: *cousins* P2, *occisorum* LgA.

36 **comforted . . . hem**: *amonnesta ses gens* P2.

133 ST MATTHEW

Maggioni, ch. CXXXVI, p. 957; Dunn-Lardeau, ch. 135, p. 895.

1–17 **In the londe . . . made here**: *Mathieu apostre preschant en ethiope en la cite qui est dicte magdaber sy trouua deux enchanteurs zaroes et arphazath qui enchantoient sy les hommes par leur art que ilz leur faisoient mieulx* (*muer* P1) *ce leur estoit aduis leurs membres en ce quilz vouloient* (from *qui . . . vouloient*: *qui ita homines suis artibus dementabat ut quoscumque uellent membrorum officio et sanitate priuare uiderentur* LgA) *et estoient montez en sy grant orgueil que ilz se faisoient aourer de tous comme dieu* P2. The GiL version of this passage and of 92–133 below closely follows *Passio Matthei*, *BHL* 5960, for text of which see Talamo Atenolfi, *I testi medioevali degli Atti di S. Matteo l'Evangelista*, 58–60.

1 Substitutions in GiL of *Inde* for *Ethiope* here and at 152, and at 65 for *Egypte* show that, like many other medieval writers, s.w. does not generally discriminate between them; see too 45.573 and 136.99 *an Ethiope, a man of Inde*, and 139.50 *man of Ynde* for P2 *ethiopien*. But at 152.63–5 *Ynde* is differentiated from *Egipte* and *Perse*.

18–19 **one of the kepers**: *vn chastre* P2, *eunuchum* LgA.

19 **of**[3]: only GiL.

23 **had lerned**: *uolebant* LgA.

29 **.ij. men**: *vng homme* P2.

30 **and sulphre**: *en souffre* P2.

36 **yef . . . you**: *nisi dominum rogassem* (. . .) *in uos protinus retorsissent* LgA.
the malice: *ce que* P2.

40 **glorious**: *grant* P2.
the ioyes: *la gloire* P2.

44 **the songe**: *organa* LgA.

45 **thei**[1]: *aues* LgA.

53 **keper**: *chastre* P2.
of[2]: only GiL.

60 **behelde**: *compescuit* LgA, 'restrained'.

63 **by . . . wrought**: *de largent quilz auoient apporte* P2.

63–4 **and**[2] **. . . apostell**: *in qua triginta annis et tribus* LgA.

65 **the cuntre of Ynde**: *egypte* P2.

67 **.ij. noble**: *plus de .ijC.* P2.

69 **Cyriake**: *Hyrtacus* LgA; but he is *Yrtakus* at 130 below.

74 **how . . . rightwisse**: *quam bona sint iusta coniugia* LgA.

76 **the kinge**: *uirginibus* LgA.

86 **brake the mariage that was ioyned before**: *corromproit le mariage conioinct* P2, *eius matrimoniam uiolasse conuincitur* LgA.

88 **durst thou or**: only GiL.

92–133 **and thanne . . . swerde**: *Et lapostre sans paour et ferme conferma tous les autres a pacience et a fermete et beney ephigenne agenoullee deuant luy par paour et toutes les autres vierges aussy. Et apres les solennitez des messes le roy enuoya vng decoleur qui occist mathieu dun glaiue par derriere qui estoit delez lautel en oroison et tendoit les mains au ciel* P2. The source of the substantial GiL substitution is the same as in 1–17 above.

135 **for to haue slaine hym**: *incensurus omnia* LgA.

137 **solempnite**: *ioye* P2.

141 **her nonnes**: *ces autres vierges* P2.

144 **his sone**: *vng sien filz* P2, *unico filio* LgA.

152 **Ynde**: *ethiope* P2.

158 **alle**: *theloneum* LgA, 'custom-house'.

162 **Iulius**: *Iulianus* LgA, i.e. Julian the Apostate.

163–4 **there as the folysshenesse . . . like as thei**: *ou sotie de lystoire mentant ou la folie de ceulx qui* P2, *uel imperitiam hystorici mentientis uel stultitiam eorum qui* LgA, 'either the ignorance of a false historian or the folly of those who'.

164 **as hastely**: not in P2, *quasi irrationabiliter* LgA.

165–6 **But that is verrey untrewe for**: only GiL.

166 **bi his diuyne mageste**: only GiL.

168 **of . . . mageste**: *de majeste diuine occulte* P2, *et maiestas diuinitatis occulta* LgA.

168–9 **upon his face**: *en sa face* P2, *in humana facie* LgA.

170 **and bi will**: not in LgA.

171 **it will drawe stones to hym to and to**: *que elle prengne les festus .ij. et .ij.* S, *annulos et festucas sibi copulet* LgA, 'will draw to him rings and rods'.

172 **will**: add *Hec Ieronimus* LgA.

173 **and**: *ou* P2.

174 **most**: not in P2, *tantum* LgA.

175 **but**: add *primo*; 176 **also**: *secundo* P2; 181 **after**: *tertio* P2; 184 **And**: *quarto* P2; Vignay may have dropped the ordinals on this occasion to avoid possible confusion with the current wider numerical scheme.

only: *tant seulement* P2, *etiam* LgA.

177 **of the seruice**: *misterii* LgA, apparently misread by Vignay as *ministerii.*

179 **was fedde**: *pascitur* LgA.

182–3 **of mercy, as whanne he saide: 'Y will merci**: *de misericorde par desir* P2, '*Misericordiam uolo* LgA.

189 **that name in comune**: *leur nom commun* P2, *nomen uulgatum* LgA, 'the usual title'; the nearest senses offered by *MED* for *in comune* are 'generally' and 'in public'.

195 **a publican and**: only GiL.

200 **of hym**: *euangelii ipsius* LgA.

201 **gospellis bene**: *euuangille est* P2.
the techer: *ces autres* P2, *ceteris euangelistis* LgA.

204 **Iames**: *Iohanne* LgA, variant *Iacobo*, also in Graesse. The reference is to 1 John 2: 16.

211–12 **upon . . . crafte**: *en vng port de mer ou il receuoit les treux et les redeuances des nefz* P2, *thelonearius; est autem theloneum, ut dicit Ysidorus, locus in portu maris ubi merces nauium et nautarum emolumenta redduntur: thelos autem grece, ut dicit Beda, latine dicitur uectigal* LgA.

216 **of the Chirche**: only GiL.

218 **so . . . and**: only GiL.

224 **Ambrose**: add *super Lucam* LgA.

228 **knowithe**: *congneust* P2.

230 **he chaunged**: *immutare potuit* LgA.
sodenly and hastely: *hastiuement* P2, *tam subito* LgA.

235 **medicine**: *medecin* P2; *MED s.v. medicin*, 'physician', has two citations, both for *c.*1450, and the H1 corrector's *medycine`r´* has only one citation, from Chauliac ?a1425.

238 **heled**: add *scilicet in beato Matheo* LgA.

243 **ne . . . wynninge**: add *quant au premier* P2, *iam non porto Leui, exui Leui, postquam Christum indui.' Et hoc quo ad primum* LgA.
also: *quant au second* P2.

245 **woundes**: add *Et apres il dit quant au tiers* P2.

247 **As ho . . . nothinge**: only GiL.

GiL omits Maggioni, 963–4 (101–12), Dunn-Lardeau, 901–2.

248 **founde**: add *anno domini D* LgA.

251 **bi . . . and**: *par* P2, *tam fide Barnabe quam* LgA.

252 **And . . . .vC.**: not in LgA.

134 ST MAURICE

Maggioni, ch. CXXXVII, p. 965; Dunn-Lardeau, ch. 136, p. 902.

1 **region de Thebes**: *legion de thebes* P2, *legione que Thebea dicitur* LgA. Legend identifies this with Egyptian Thebes, which is not easy to reconcile precisely with the following geographical description; see also note to 7 below.

5 **semely**: *grant* P2.

7 **.vjC. yates**: *centum portas* (. . .) *et super Nilum fluuium qui de paradiso egreditur et Gyon dicitur sita fuit* LgA.

30–1 **Thei . . . knightz (. . .) and sent**: *Sy assemblerent adonc celle esleue legion des cheualiers* (. . .) *et les enuoierent* P2, *Congregantes igitur electam militum legionem* (. . .) *miserunt* LgA.

31–2 **emperour, hym, his**: plural in LgD, LgA.

34 **tho that gouerned the baners**: *ceulx qui gouuernoient soubz luy et portoient les signes* P2, *signiferi* LgA.

35 **Blane**: *blaiue* P2, *blanc* SP1, *Candidus* LgA.
Sophie: *souspire* P2, *soupire* P1, *Exuperius* LgA, also at 70 and 74 below, where he appears as *Solpide* and *Sulpice*.

36 **Constantine**: *constancien* P2, *Constantius* LgA.

37 **hem**: *luy* P2.

38 **with hem**: *luy bailla* P2; Diocletian is still the subject.

40 **before**: add *de saint marcel* (*Marcellino* LgA) *pape* P2; Marcellinus was pope from 296 to 304; Maurice is supposed to have died *c.*287, but the historical details of his life are very uncertain.

43 **mountaynes**: add *et ilz vendrent oultre* P2, add *Alpium* (. . .) *et Octodorum aduenisset* LgA; Octodorus, now Martigny, in Valais.

44 **thanne thei ronne**: *que on courust* P2, *coniurarent* LgA.

49 **in haste**: goes with *come* in P2 and LgA.

50 **that were there**: only GiL.

51 **were cristen and**: only GiL.

54–5 **these foled knightes**: *ce failly cheualier* P2, *contumax miles* LgA.

55 **by, by**: *a, a* P2.

60 **for the loue of God**: only GiL.

61–2 **to his felawship**: *entre les autres choses* P2.

62 **Reioise you with us**: *Congratulor uobis* LgA.
we be: *estis* LgA.

63 **We haue suffered**: *sustinui* LgA.

64 **slaine** add *car ie les* (*uos* LgA) *ay veuz apparesIles a souffrir mort pour Ihesucrist. Et iay garde le commandemant de dieu qui dist a pierre met ton glaiue en sa gayne maiz pource que nous sommez ia cloz des corps des cheualiers nos compaignons* S.

69 **herde that**: add *il commanda encores* P2.

73–4 **wherfor . . . wete that**: *ne* P2.

82 **his loue**: *luy* P2.
that . . . deuise: *ne nous departirons de sa foy* P2.

88 **.CC.iiij^{xx}.**: *CCLXXXVII* LgA.

89 **it . . . that**: not in LgA.

90 **her**: *autres* P2.

91 **hadden (. . .) victorie of marterdom**: *gloriosissime triumpharent* LgA.

101 **Wolde . . . deied**: *quil eust este du tout beneure sil eust este occis* P2.

105–6 **and thei ordeined . . . Galerien**: *sy que ilz osterent en vng iour leurs vestemens royaulx pour mener plus simple vie. et que les plus ieunes comme constancien et maximin et galerien quilz auoient fait cesariens* (add *imperarent* LgA) P2.
Maxymien and Galerien: *Maximinus Galerius* LgA; Galerius Valerius Maximinus was emperor 310–13.

109 **in Rome**: *ou rosne* P2.
founde and: not in LgA.

110–11 **of . . . Chirche**: *a Domitiano Genauensi et Grato Augustano et Prothasio eiusdem loci episcopis* LgA, 'by bishops Domitian of Geneva and Gratus of Aosta and Prothase of the same place'.

112–14 **but . . . masse**: *mais il nouuroit seulement que aux dimenches et a leure que on faisoit la solennite des messes* P2, *qui aliis die dominico sollempnizantibus solus opus suum exercebat* LgA.

115–17 **blamed . . . seruice**: *le rauirent et batirent et le pristrent pource quil faisoit son euure de maconnerie quant les autres entendoient au diuin seruice* P2, *rapitur, ceditur et arguitur quod opus suum profanus assumpserit et die dominica cum alii diuinis intenderent ipse operibus mechanicis inhiaret* LgA.

120 **of trouthe**: *des loyaux* P2.
comynge: add *tibi* LgA.

121 **whiche**: add *supplia bonnement et qui estoit auironnee de mort par le corps et par les espees de tant de cheualiers. et elle* P2.

122 **stable faithe**: *fermete esueillee* P2, *uigili constantia* LgA.

124 **assailed hem**: *decimauit* LgA.

125 **wolde not remeue but**: only GiL.

140 **after**: *de ta vie* P2.

146 **thei**: *il* P2.

151 **.ixC.lxiij.**: Maggioni (2007), 1653, note to 77, says that all LgA MSS give 963, but points out that, since Nicholas was pope from 858 to 867 and Charles the Bald reigned from 840 to 77, this should be 863.

152 **by the auys of**: *par laccord de* P2, *obtentu* LgA.
asked: add *a Nicholao papa* LgA.

156 **and laie hym**: only GiL.
of: *que* P2.

157–8 **And thei had graunt**: only GiL.

165–6 **loued and meked**: *humilie* P2.

166 **myself**: add *meis hostibus* LgA.

168 **thundreclappe**: *fouldre* P2, 'thunderbolt'.

135 ST JUSTINA

Maggioni, ch. CXXXVIII, p. 971; Dunn-Lardeau, ch. 137, p. 907.

2 **a preste[2]**: *Prelium diaconem* LgA.

12 **enchauntement**: add *et faisoit les femmes conuertir en jumens* P2.

18 **I haue**: *Jayme* P2.
virgine: add *de Galileis* LgA.

19–20 **sumtyme . . . power for to**: *ay peu* P2.

21–2 **thorugh . . . Abel**: *procuray que cayn occist son frere* P2.

22–3 **afterwarde . . . tyme**: only GiL.

23 **made . . . cursed**: *feiz aux* P2.

24–7 **also . . . plesaunce**: *troublay les hommes ne pourray pas faire que tu ayes vne pucelle et en faces a ton plaisir* P2.

30–1 **enforced her and meued her**: *incitare conatur* (. . .) *cor eius* LgA.

31 **vnordinate**: *non lisible* P2, *illicitum* LgA.

32–3 **and also her soule**: only GiL.

34 **the tokene and**: only GiL.

39 **lefte**: *dimisit* LgA.

39–40 **more . . . saide**: *plus fort. Et celluy luy dit* P2.

41 **and am come**: only GiL.

the noun power of my felaw: *le non pouoir de luy* P2, *illius impossibilitatem* LgA; in *MED s.v. non-pouer* n.

42 **hardely**: only GiL.

42–3 **thi commaundement and**: only GiL.

45–7 **al that . . . thingges**: *desmouuoir son cueur en amour et denflamber son couraige en chose non loisible* (*ad amorem illicitum* LgA) P2.

53 **y sawe her haue**: *je vey en elle* P2.

54 **strengthe and**: only GiL.

57 **powere and youre**: only GiL.
so yonge: only GiL.

59 **fires**: *fieures* P2.
brennyngly: add *et arrouseray tout son corps de hastiue ardeur* P2.

64 **oure laboure**: *nous garder* P2, *nostri certaminis* LgA.

69 **vnobediensers**: 'those who disobey'; *MED unobediencer* has two citations, dated ?a1425 and c1456, and one for *inobedience*, dated 1420.

71 **but**: add *encourons en* P2.

80 **went to**: *sailly desuergondeement ou* P2.

83–4 **she . . . feueres**: *dyabolus* (. . .) *febribus eam fatigans* LgA.

84 **he**: *i.e. dyabolus*.

84–5 **to hem that were vexed with fendes**: *par les demoniacles* P2, *per demones* LgA, variant *demoniacos*, which is also in Graesse.

86 **to hym**: *coniugio* LgA.

90–1 **she . . . one**: *mortem eidem omnes minarentur* LgA.

91 **.vj.**: *septimo* LgA.

96 **hym**: add *et alla a luy en la fourme dicelle et le voult baisier aussy comme se elle languist de son amour* P2.

100 **wexe or**: only GiL.

110 **how he might . . . hys necke**: *que il ne pouoit ne fouir ne saillir* P2.

111 **Iustine**: add *se doubta quil ne cheist et creuast et* P2.

113 **wyckednesse**: add *Et toutes ces choses estoient faictes selon les faintes du dyable* P2.

119 **in euery point**: only GiL.

120 **ouer you**: only GiL.

121 **Y . . . yef**: *se* P2.

122 **from me**: add *ie te monstreray la victoire de sa vertu* P2.

125 **fende**: add: *quasi securus* LgA, 'as if reassured'.

126 **she**: *celle pucelle* P2.

126–7 **we wexe, we lese, we melt**: *tabui*, *amisi*, *effluxi* LgA.

130 **and mightier**: only GiL.

130–1 **he deliuerithe . . . turmente**: *nous baillera tous ceulx que nous deceuons cy a tourmenter* P2, *nos et omnes quos hic decipimus tradet* (. . .) *cruciandos* LgA; LgD clearly and GiL unclearly (because of loss of *nous*) specify that the devils will torture those they have deceived, whereas in LgA both devils and deceived will be subject to eternal torture.

132–3 **It . . . frende**: *dont doy je estre fait amy* P2.

137–8 **the fendes of hell**: *tes dyables* P2.

138 **of the crosse**: *de salu au crucifie* P2, *crucifixi salutari* LgA.

145 **vnuincyble**: not recorded in *MED*, though *invincible* is.

151 **thanne**: *sepe* LgA.

157 **and therin . . . boyled**: only GiL.

161 **was brought forthe**: *vint deuant la chaudiere* P2.

162 **god of Ercules**: *deus Hercules* LgA.

136 STS COSMAS AND DAMIAN

Maggioni, ch. CXXXIX, p. 977; Dunn-Lardeau, ch. 138, p. 913.

1 **bretheren**: *freres germains* P2, *gemini fratres* LgA.

8 **gret**: *horribles* P2.

9 **with miche daungere**: only GiL.

17, 22 **iuge**: Lysias is *proconsul* in LgA; from 29–55 *iuge* (and 38 *provost*) are for LgA *preses*, apparently a different person.

25 **manacled**: *tors* P2, *torqueri* LgA.

27 **bothe . . . fote**: only GiL.

29 **come ayen afore the iuge**: *ante presidem statuuntur* LgA; see 17, 22 above.

30 **Ye . . . wichcrafte**: *Per deos magnos maleficiis uincitis* LgA.

32 **in . . . and**: *et in nomine dei Adriani* LgA; unidentified, possibly the emperor Hadrian, deified in 139.

34 **aboute the mouthe and**: only GiL.

38–9 **thei werkyn proudely**: *jndignez* P2, *il sont endaignies* P1, *dii indignati sunt* LgA.

39 **me**: add *quia* LgA.

40 **hem**: not in P2, *uos* LgA.

in this wise: only GiL.

43–4 **the turment that ys called eculee**: *eculee cest vng tourment qui est fait comme vng saultouer* P2, *eculeum* LgA.

44–5 **the turmentours . . . mesure**: *fatigatis admodum in cedendo ministris* LgA.

48 **upon the crosse**: not in LgA.

52–3 **to be . . . and**: *super crucem* LgA.

53–4 **as thicke . . . to hem**: *par quatre cheualiers* P2.

55 **the iuge . . . do**: *fistrent* P2.

56 **seintes**: add *martirs* P2.

60–2 **there . . . place**: *ecce subito camelus aduenit et humana uoce proclamans sanctos in uno loco sepeliri precepit* LgA.

71–2 **and . . . merites**: only GiL.

90 **suerte**: *serement* P2.

92 **the .viij. after**: *attauus* LgA, 'predecessor'; Graesse and Benz, but not Maggioni, record *octavus* as a variant.

99 **an Ethiope, a man of Inde**: the gloss is by s.w., see note to 133.1–17.

100 **chircheyerde**: *cymitiere saint pierre aux lyens. aporte nous de la char pour mettre cy. Et dont sen ala au cymitiere* P2.

100–1, 102, 103 **the dede man**: *mor* P2, *Mauri* LgA.

106 **nothinge**: add *mali* LgA.

113 **.CC.iiij^{xx}.vij.**: not in LgA, repeated from 62–3 above.

137 ST FURSEY

Maggioni, ch. CXL, p. 982; Dunn-Lardeau, ch. 139, p. 917.

1 **wrote**: *scripsisse creditur* LgA.

2–3 **as yt semed**: only GiL.

5 **shelde**: add *et gladio* LgA.

6 **and he herde . . . saide**: not in LgA.

7 **ayenst hym**: *ante faciem eius* LgA.

8 **venym and**: only GiL.

10 **reskewed hem**: *les receuoit* P2, *ea suscipiebat* LgA; it is unclear why, having misread *receuoit*, s.w. did not substitute singular *hym*.

18–28 **We shull . . . before God**: *il eust indulgence en son cueur. Mais acoustumance se teust. Et le dyable dit. Aussy comme il prist mal par coustume sy* *recoiue mal* (*uindictam* LgA) *par le souuerain juge. Et le saint ange dit. Nous serons jugiez* (add *ante dominum* LgA) P2; s.w. has rearranged the order. Insertion of 19–23 *Thanne . . . herte* by s.w. from a version close to the first Anonymous Life of Fursey, *AASS Ian. II*, pp. 36–41, ch. 2, improves the sense of the passage.

31 **ys worthi . . . wises**: *plagis uapulabit multis* LgA, 'will be beaten with many blows'.

33–4 **a yefte . . . man**: *dons des mauuais* P2.

35 **proued**: add *auant* P2.

37–8 **felle downe**: *succubuit* LgA.

44–5 **and is in will**: only GiL.

49 **fende**: *dyables* P2.

53–4 **For thou . . . brenne the**, *pourceque tu lembrasas il ta ars* P2, *Quod incendisti arsit in te* LgA.

55–6 **and this peyne . . . gowne of hym**: *Et hanc percussionem permittente deo pro receptione illius uestis recepit* LgA, i.e. in LgA this follows the end of the speech.

58–9 **And thanne . . . comaundid**: not in LgA.

60 **Goddes**: *bonnes* P2.

65 **werke**: *parolle* P2.

67–8 **be a passer of his owne worde**: *nest felon et le trespassement de sa parole ne luy desplaist* P2, *Si deus iniquus non est et uerbi illius transgressio ei displicet* LgA; *MED* has only one instance of *passer* in this sense, 'transgressor', dated a1456.

70 **he saide**: *est dit* P2.

74 **thei be**[2]: *cest* P2.

77 **malicious**: *callidas* LgA, 'subtle'.

77–8 **do not to wete**: *ne denonces* P2.

80 **and**: not in LgA.

81 **of the prechour**: only GiL.

84 **the withsaieng**: *omni* (. . .) *contradictione* LgA.

85–6 **so ferforthe . . . wicked**: *donec iudice domino triumphantibus angelis deuictisque aduersariis* LgA.

97 **veyne**: *vilaines* P2, *superuacuis* P1.

100 **wonder faste**: only GiL.

101 **For**: *sire* P2.

104 **brenne**: not in P2, *ardet* LgA.

105 **payne of dette**: *peine deue* P2, 'merited penalty'.

106–7 **weping his frendes**: *et ses prochains ploroient* P2, *plangentibus propinquis* LgA.

138 ST MICHAEL ARCHANGEL

Maggioni, ch. CXLI, p. 986; Dunn-Lardeau, ch. 140, p. 920.

Not in L, which substitutes a chapter derived from the *South English Legendary*; see *Supplementary Lives* 27, pp. 273–82.

1 **Michael**: add *archangeli* LgA.

9 **was right riche and**: not in LgA.

16 **was go so astraied**: *estoit ale la foloiant* P2, *soliuagus incederet* LgA.

17 **arwe**[1]:. add *entouchee* P2, 'poisoned'.

21 **praie**: *querendum esse* LgA.

24 **that . . . kepe it**: *locum hunc in terris incolere tutumque seruare statuens* LgA.

30 **of the tombe**: *Tumba* LgA, Mont-Saint-Michel.

33–5 **that he . . . mynde of hym**: *ibi memoriam sancti Michaelis archangeli celebraret* LgA.

39–40 **of the going . . . bole**: *taurum in circuitu pedibus protriuisse* LgA.

45–6 **Seint Michael . . . stode**: add *et la partie du chantel donc lautre estoit ou mont. et ilz les porterent en la dicte eglise et les mistrent sus lautel* P2, *de monte Gargano partem pallii quod super altare sanctus Michael posuit et partem marmoris supra quo stetit ad suam ecclesiam detulerunt* LgA.

48 **water**: add *ut dicitur* LgA.

50 **the said . . . in**[2]: not in LgA.
.xviij. day: *.xvij.*[e] *kalende* P2.

53 **place**: *mons* LgA.
Gret See: *la mer occeane* P2, *Oceano* LgA; unless *of occean* is specified, the *Gret See* generally refers to the Mediterranean (*MED gret* adj. sense 1b. (c), and *occean*, 'the circumferential sea surrounding the world' or specific parts thereof, here the Atlantic).
but: add *bis* LgA.

54 **peple**: add *Nam propter fluxum et refluxum maris qui ibi fit bis qualibet die dicitur aperiri* LgA.

56–7 **whanne . . . so that**: *ecce, magno impetu unda redit et* LgA.

64 **come**: *legitur accidisse* LgA.
pope: add *Rome* LgA.

66 **pestilence**: *pestem inguinariam* LgA.

67–72 The Castel Sant'Angelo was started by the Emperor Hadrian as a mausoleum for himself and his successors and completed after his death by Antoninus Pius in 139.

68 **was**[1]: add *jadis* P2.

69 **blody**: add *et in uaginam mittebat* LgA.

71 **of Seint Michael**: add *lange* P2, *angelorum* LgA.

72 **another apering**: *Hec autem apparitio cum illa que* LgA.

74 **.viij. day of Iuyn**: *viij.*[e] *yde de juillet* P2, *VIII idus Maii* LgA.

Here GiL omits the fourth *apering*, about hierarchies of angels, Maggioni, 989–91 (49–92), Dunn-Lardeau, 923–5.

75 **Another**: *La quinte* P2.
made: *celle que on list* P2.

77 **the same place**: *lonneur de saint michiel* P2.

78 **of Michael**: *des michaelz* P2.
bicause of: *Cum igitur* LgA.

79–80 **caused of gret habundaunce of rede colere**: *meue de rouges coles* P2, *rubeis coloribus mota* LgA, 'caused by red spots'. *MED colre* is 'bile' (Lat. *cholera*), likewise OFr *cole*, but Latin *color* does not carry this sense.

80–2 **hym . . . drinke**: *a celluy eschauffe vng beuurage. lequel il getta hors par la bouche sy que depuis il gettoit hors tout ce quil buuoit et mengoit* P2.

87 **as for his sauuce**: only GiL.

88 **And so he was**: *Et quant il eust ce fait il fut plainement gary* P2.

92 **Victoriest**: *victoire* P2. *MED* has no such spelling; it is apparently for *victorious.*

97 **Bonyvent**: add *qui quinquaginta milibus a Siponto distant* LgA.
So that: *Qui* LgA.

98 **token**: *petierunt* LgA.

105 **an houge tempest arose**: *fouldres volerent especement* P2.

107–8 **by the shotte . . . eyre**: *tam ex ferro hostium quam ex sagittis igneis* LgA.

108 **by vertu of the aungel**: GiL follows Vignay, who misplaced this from the next sentence.

113 **the Apocalipse**: *lapostre* P2, *Apoc. XII* LgA.

116 **Lucifer**: add *auecques toute sa suite* P2.

118 **the erthe**: *lair* P2.

119 **among vs**: *in terra nobiscum* LgA.

123 **soules**: *hommes* P2.

124 **grettest peyne of**: only GiL.

125 **us**: add *ad nostrum exercitium* LgA, 'in order to harass us'.

128 **sayen**[2]: *cuident* P2.
fendes: add *et de malins esperis* P2.

137 **apostell**: *Apoc. XX* LgA.

138 **fend**: add *et lenuoia en abisme. Et thobie* (*Tob. VIII* LgA) *qui dit que lange raphael lya le dyable* P2.
the souerein desert: *deserto superiori* LgA, i.e. Upper Egypt (Tob. 8: 3).

139 **that he wolde haue ouer vs**: only GiL.

140 **thei deliuer us**: *ilz nous deliurerent* P2.
refreyning: *refrigerando* LgA.

144 **in the Apocalips . . . chapitre**: *par lapostre* P2, LgA as GiL.

157 **saithe**: add *Apoc. XIII super illud 'Vidi unum de capitibus eius occisum etc.'* LgA.

161 **as though he stied up bi his owne vertu**: only GiL.

162–3 **And whan . . . Olyuete**: *Et en la fin il montera ou mont doliuet. Et quant il serra en son pauillon en son siege* P2, *Tandem in montem olIueti ascendens, ut dicit Glossa super illud II Thes. II 'Quem dominus Ihesus interficiet etc.', dum stabit in papilione et in solio suo* LgA.

165–6 **after Seint Gregorie**: not in P2, *secundum Gregorium* LgA.

166 **the whiche . . . Apocalips**: *ce que lapostre dit* P2, add *XII* LgA.

167 **Michael and his aungels**: not in P2, *Michael etc.* LgA.

168 **bataile**[1]: add *de michiel* P2.

171 **This**: *Tertio hec* LgA.
also: only GiL.
dedicacion: *ordination* P2, *dedicatio* LgA.

172–3 **was . . . wise**: *fut dedie a luy par sa reuelation* P2, *a se dedicatum fuisse Michael archangelus reuelauit* LgA.

179 **done in**: *donnee* P2.

185 **with praiers**: *patron de pierres* (*prieres* S) P2, *precibus* LgA.

186 **make hym her special patron**: *le sentirent especial* P2, *se specialem suum patronum sentirent* LgA; i.e. P2 and S have *patron* transferred to the preceding clause.

190 **gret peple**: *uniuersus populus* LgA.

192–3 **thei . . . manteles**: *estoit couuert tout entour dun mantel vermeil* P2, i.e. just the third altar.

197 **chirche**: *spelunca* LgA.

198 **the comune**: *post communionem* LgA.

200 **worship**: add: *sancti Michaelis et* LgA.

201 **aungels**: *esperis* P2.

GiL omits Maggioni, 995–1001 (150–243), Dunn-Lardeau, 929–35.

139 ST JEROME

Maggioni, ch. CXLII, p. 1002; Dunn-Lardeau, ch. 141, p. 935.

In L a different account of Jerome has been substituted; see *Supplementary Lives* 29, pp. 321–65.

1 **Bede**: *Eusebii* LgA.

2 **castell Discrodoni**: *chastel destridoine* P2, *oppido Stridonis* LgA; Stridon, Dalmatia, was not far from the border with Pannonia, but its precise location is unknown.

is in the ferrest ende of: i.e. is on the borders between.

Damaske: *damas* P2, *Dalmatie* LgA.

6 **aduocate**: *oratorem* LgA.

9 **Eustace**: *eustocien* P2, *Eustochium* LgA; GiL gives *Eustachien* at 44 below.

9–10 **on a day . . . Plato**: *il eust vng iour curieusement leu platon et la nuyt tulles* P2, *Quodam uero tempore* (. . .) *dum de die Tullium et nocte Platonem auide legeret* LgA.

10 **wordes**: *parole desordonnee* P2.

11–12 **take . . . dethe**: *sy corrompu dune soudaine et sy tres ardant fieure que il fut sy refroidy par tout le corps que il nauoit mais point de chaleur fors que en la poitrine* P2.

14–15 **what . . . condicion**: *de quelle condition il estoit* P2.

16 **Thou failest full vntruli**: *tu mens* P2.

17 **citronyen**: *cyteronien* P2, *ciceronianus* LgA. *MED* gives one citation for *Cicerones*, 'gifted orators', Bokenham a1457. Having failed to identify and therefore omitted LgD *tulles* at 9–10 above, s.w. adopted a misspelling from the French presumably without relating it to Cicero.

21 **and mekeli besought**: only GiL.

23 **y rede in any of tho**: *ie ay jamais ou lis* P2.

23–4 **And thanne . . . awoke**: *Et dont fut laissie en ces paroles par son serement* P2, *In huius igitur iuramenti uerba dimissus* LgA.

26 **betinge**: add *quil auoit eu deuant le juge* P2.

29 **.xxix.**: *XXXIX* LgA.
was[2]: add *ordonne* P2.

31 **was chose for to be pope**: *fut esleu a estre digne de la souueraine prestrise* P2, *dignus summo sacerdotio ab omnibus acclamatur* LgA.

34 **saithe**: add *et Vincentius* LgA, i.e. Vincent de Beauvais.

41 **And . . . malys**: *Quod ille uidens tante eorum uesanie locum dedit* LgA.

44–5 **the loue of**: only GiL.

47 **right a drie**: *horridum* LgA.

47–8 **and supposed**: only GiL.

48–50 **my membris . . . Ynde**: *horrebant sacco membra deformia, squalida cutis situm Ethiopice carnis adduxerat* LgA, 'my disfigured limbs trembled under the sackcloth, my cracked skin took on the colour of an Ethiop's flesh.'.
For *man of Ynde*, P2 *ethiopien*, see note to 133.1–17.

52 **y leid my drie bones to the bare erthe**: *adonc se frotoient a peine mes os secs a la terre nue* P2, *nuda humo uix ossa herentia collidebam* LgA, 'I lay on the bare earth with the bones scarcely hanging together'.

53 **helde my pees**: *me tais* P2.
for: *cum etiam* LgA.

55 **and wilde bestes**: not in P2, *et ferarum* LgA; for LgD see next.

55–7 **and notwithstondyng . . . flesshe**: *et auec les caroles des pucelles bestes sauuaiges et les embrasemens des luxures croissoient en mon froit corps et en ma char* P2, *sepe choris interaram puellarum et in frigido corpore et carne premortua sola libidinum incendia pullulabant* LgA.

58 **with fasting . . . tyme**: *a la mesaise des sepmaines et joings souuent* P2.

59 **night**: add *et* P2.
that: *prius* (. . .) *quam* LgA.

61 **reuenging me of myself**: *yre et roide* P2, *mihi iratus et rigidus* LgA.

62 **that**: add *post multas lacrimas* LgA.

63–4 **al tho .iiij. yere**: *Per quadriennium igitur* LgA, beginning new sentence.

64 **and**: not in LgA.

65 **place**: *chastel* P2, *oppidum* LgA, see 2 above.

66–7 **closed bible that he had made with great studie**: *Bibliothecam autem suam quam summo studio sibi condiderat clausam* LgA; *MED bible*, sense 3, 'collection of books, library'.

67 **redde**: *relut* P2.

68–70 **for to laboure . . . ocupacion**: *Et ainsy laboura la en saint propos. et en la translation des escriptures .lv. ans et .v. moys* P2, *in sancto proposito et translatione scripturarum quinquaginta quinque annis et sex mensibus desudauit* LgA.

71 **his²**: *ceste* P2.

73 **Y . . . me**: *Je porte la virginite ou ciel* P2, *Virginitatem in celo prefero* LgA, 'I raise virginity to the sky'.

74 **y wondre . . . not**: *ie me merueille plus que ie ne lay* P2, *magis miror quod non habeo* LgA.

75 **he . . . werinesse**: *il fut lasse* P2.

79 **after Euesong tyme**: *quil auesproit* P2, 'towards evening'.

80 **an**: *la* P2.

81 **holtinge**: only E has *o*, all others *a*; *MED halten*, 'limp', records no *o* spellings, but one instance of *holt s.v. halt* adj. is noted as (?error); so this should have been emended.

82 **alle . . . arose and**: *et jerome* P2.

87–9 **and thanne . . . hole**: *Adhibita igitur diligenti cura leo conualuit et omni feritate deposita* LgA, last four words not in LgD.

90 **this . . . thought**: only GiL.

91 **of his goodnesse**: only GiL.

99 **certaine tymes atte**: *aux* P2.

100–1 **for to haue . . . ayen**: *ut se cibaret et asinus solitum perficeret opus* LgA.

104 **and ledde her forthe with hem**: *tantost* P2.

112 **asse**: add *qui test demouree* P2.

115 **partie . . . ani**: only GiL.

125 **in ferre contre**: *loing* P2.
an hors or: not in LgA.

129 **voys**: add *que il les fist tous fouir et il rongoit et feroit forment la terre de sa queue et horriblement* P2.

132–3 **make . . . fete**: *lauez les pies a voz* (*nostris* LgA) *hostes* LgD.

137–8 **and made . . . therwith**: *aussy comme en requerant pardon du pechie quil nauoit pas fait. Et ierome qui sauoit bien ce qui estoit a auenir dist aux freres. alez et appareilliez les neccessitez aux hostes qui viennent. Et sicomme il le disoit* P2.

143 **oyle**: add *pro benedictione* LgA.

146 **to that chirche**: *fratribus ipsis* LgA.

148–9 **whoso . . . lette**: *quiconques vouloit chantoit en leglise* P2, *in ecclesia* *unusquisque caneret quod uolebat* LgA, i.e. the singing of the Divine Office was unregulated.

151 **and devout**: only GiL.
and a Rule: only GiL.

154 **souerain**: *predictum* LgA.

154–5 **deuised**[1]: *deuisa* P2, *distinxit* LgA, **deuised**[2]: *establi* P2, *assignauit* LgA; *devisen* has a range of senses, none of which exactly matches *distinxit*. These instances are perhaps best translated 'divided up' and 'assigned'.

157 **psalme**: add *ut ait Sigebertus* LgA.

162 **one side of the creche**: *loraille de la cresche* P2, *ore spelunce* LgA.

163 **.iiij**^{xx}.: *nonaginta* LgA; his dates are usually given as *c.*341 or 342 to 420.

164 **slepte . . . and**: only GiL.

167 **frende**: *domino* LgA.

167–9 **right pure . . . charitee**: *tres net par honneur de garder charite et de la embracier* P2, *cultu sincerissimo caritatis obseruando atque amplectendo* LgA.

170–1 **and in . . . age**: *et es lettres saintes apeine a son derrenier aage* P2, *in locis sanctis atque in litteris sacris usque ad decrepitam uixit etatem* LgA.

171–2 **the nobilnesse . . . langage**: *cuius nobis eloquii* LgA, *cujus nobilitas eloquii* Graesse.

173 **of hym**: add *en ses croniques* P2.

176 **Ambigense**: *Albigensem* LgA; Benz (col. 236 and note col. 609) identifies this as error for a priest Abigaus, recipient of Epistola LXXVI, *PL* 22, 689.

178 **her**: *soy* P2, i.e. the 'proud head'.

179–80 **With al . . . resseiued**: *In monasterio hospitalitate ex corde intemdimus et* (. . .) *suscipimus* LgA.

181 **heretikes**: GiL omits a quotation from Isidore, Maggioni, 1009 (105–6), Dunn-Lardeau, 941–2 .

183–4 **the merite . . . vertu**: *douaire de merite de foy* P2, *fidei meritum dotemque uirtutum* LgA.

189 **unthriftely** *adj.* 'immoral'; *MED* gives no *-ly* forms for the adjective.

189–90 **of clerkes and other**: only GiL.

190–1 **and ioyed . . . of hym**: only GiL.

193 **day**: add *et ce dit seuer*, P2, add *Haec Seuerus* LgA.
continuelli ocupied: only GiL.

194 **as . . . hymselff**: *sicomme il appert par ces paroles et il le tesmongne souuent* P2.

197 **hate me**: add *et guesillent que je suis maleficie* P2, 'and they prattle that I am a malefactor'.

197–8 **y wote wel that men comithe to hevene bi defame and by good fame**: *scio ad regnum peruenire per infamiam et bonam famam* LgA, i.e. whether one is slandered or of good repute.

198 **nombre**: *uniuersa* (. . .) *turba* LgA.

199 **loue**: *doctrine* P2.

202 **blisse**: GiL omits one further similar sentence.

203 **.CCC.iiij^{xx}.xviij.**: *circa annos domini CCCC* LgA.

140 TRANSLATION OF ST REMY

Maggioni, ch. CXLIII, p. 1010; Dunn-Lardeau, ch. 142, p. 943.

2 **The quene . . . in tho dayes**: *le roy sy auoit femme* P2.

10–11 **that be . . . me**: *par quoy sa foy pouoit estre soubzhauciee* P2.

11–12 **the quene . . . for**: *elle dit* P2.

13 **and hope uerely**: only GiL.
acceptable and: only GiL.

18–19 **as sone as it was cristened**: *tantost* P2.

25 **in . . . might**: only GiL.

27 **that other fest**: i.e. 15 Saint Remy, vol. 1, pp. 89–91, which follows Paul the Hermit, Epiphany being chapter 13.

30 **the chirche**: add *Remensen* LgA, 'of Reims'.

31 **ouerride**: *auironneroit* P2.

32 **withinne the same ground**: *dedens ce que remy auoit enclos* P2, *intra fines* LgA.

33–4 **went . . . ground**: *aloit entour* P2.

35–6 **this mille . . . bothe**: *nous auons ce moulin ensemble* P2.

37 **one of the whelis**: *la roe* P2.

42 **knew**: add *par reuelacion de dieu* P2, not in LgA.

43 **togedre**: add *en vne ville* P2, add *in uilla* LgA, 'in a village'.

44 **hym and his wisdom**: *senis prudentiam* LgA.

46–7 **into declyning of his lyff**: only GiL.

47 **glad chere**: *lye cueur* P2, *tranquillo corde* LgA.

48 **and holsom**: only GiL.

49 **membres**: *genitaires* P2.

50 **gowtous**: *gutturose* LgA, 'goitred'. *MED* has only one citation, from Trevisa, for *goutisshe*, 'afflicted with gout', the D variant, in which *ou* is obscured by a blot but confirmed by the H2 spelling.
towne: *ville* P2, *uilla* LgA; see 43 above.

58 **thei constreined and**: *ilz contrains* P2, *coacti LgA*.

62 **encresed**: *se firent* P2.

63 **oritarie**: *cripta* LgA.

66 **thei went . . . midnight**: *ce* (*se* S) *mistrent celle nuyt a veiller en oroisons et sendormirent tous a mienuit* P2.

70 **more riche shrine**: *pulchriorem criptam. Floruit* LgA.

141 ST LEGER

Maggioni, ch. CXLIV, p. 1013; Dunn-Lardeau, ch. 143, p. 945.

1 **and**: not in LgA.

2 **of Aclus**: *de acluense* P2, *Eduensi* LgA, 'of Autun'.
of Fraunse: only GiL.

9 **he**: i.e. Ebronius.

10 **he²**: *le roy* P2.

12 **ayenst hym and**: only GiL.

14 **empeired**: *empirie* P2, *deprauatus* LgA, 'corrupted'; s.w. follows Vignay's imprecise translation.

19 **afore hym**: only GiL.

20 **had**: add *celle nuyt* P2.

28 **wepinge**: add *et precibus* LgA.

29 **citee**: *siege* P2.

33 **to hate**: *occidere* LgA.

34–5 **he wolde . . . malys and**: *eorum furori cedens* LgA, 'yielding himself to their rage'.

38–9 **in despite of Eubronien**: not in LgA.

40 **wisely**: add *et pacifice* LgA.

41 **night**: *die* LgA.

46 **the worde**: *usum loquendi* LgA.

59 **caste hymselff**: *proiectus* LgA, i.e. by the fiend.

62 **enlumyned and shined**: *illustrari* LgA, 'become famous'.

65 **Euel**: only GiL.

67 **worshipped**: *amplius commendauit* LgA.

70–1 **and in suche wise he**: *celluy felon* P2.

142 ST FRANCIS

Maggioni, ch. CXLV, p. 1016; Dunn-Lardeau, ch. 144, p. 948.

1 **of God**: only GiL.
the right: *tres hault* P2.

2–3 **was made marchaunt wel nigh .xxv. yere olde and wasted**: *negotiator effectus fere usque ad uicesimum etatis sue annum* (. . .) *consumpsit* LgA.

6 **Perses**: *perrusins* P2, 'Perugians'.

6–7 **alle hys felawes**: *les autres* P2.

7 **and²**: only GiL.

9 **y knowe wele**: only GiL.

13–14 **hastely (. . .) and gredely**: *gloutement* P2.

15 **of his knowleche**: *de ses congnoissans* P2.

16–17 **his purpos fro his gostly hele**: *de son propos de salu* P2.

17 **shewyd hym**: *cordi eius immittit* LgA.
disfigured: *bossue et contrefaicte* P2, *gibbosam* LgA, 'hunchbacked'.

18 **the**: *sa* P2.

20 **a voys that saide hym**: only GiL.

26 **of pore men and**: only GiL.
of sike men: *leprosorum* LgA.

31–2 **the passion of Ihesu Crist**: *crucifixi compassio* LgA.

34 **durst not**: *recusaret* LgA.

46 **gladly**: *alacriter* LgA.

35 **he**: Francis; **hym**: the priest.

56 **of God, for noble**: LgD and LgA end the thieves' speech after 'God', beginning the new sentence *moult de nobles*, which Maggioni rightly assigns to a new paragraph.

58–60 **the perfeccion . . . sympilnesse**: *euangelicam perfectionem implere, paupertatem apprehendere et per uiam sancte simplicitatis incedere* LgA.

62 **bretheren**: add *euz et a auoir* P2, i.e. present and future.

63 **shede**: add *les semences de* P2.

65 **And**: *Et si comme il estoit venu par dehors* **P2**, LgA as GiL.

outeward: not in P2, in LgA.

66 **perfeccion**: add *sed tamen admodum singularis* LgA.

69–71 **for y see . . . fende**: *ne ie ne loeray encores point que ce ne soit par faintise de dyable* P2, *nec mihi in eo dyabolica figmenta laudate* LgA.

71 **taught and charged**: *amonneste* P2.

72 **twies**: *semel uel bis* LgA.
by worde: not in LgA.

73 **foule**: *frauduleuse* P2.

77 **and wente oute of his ordre**: not in LgA.
cursidly: *en mauuais fais* P2.

79 **and**: not in LgA.
his bewpere: only GiL; Leonard was another friar and of noble birth, but not his *bewpere*, 'ecclesiastical superior or father confessor', which position was held by Leone di Assisi.
that folued hym afote: only GiL.

80 **as he walked**: only GiL.

87–8 **and she . . . brethe and**: *cuius lassitudinem et interclusos anhelitus miseratus* LgA.

94 **reson**: *equitatis* LgA, i.e. justice.

97 **a wode**: *quadam solitudine* LgA.

98–9 **for to comfort hym with**: only GiL.

101 **bi reuelacion of**: *instigante* LgA.

109 **of Greys**: *grecs* P2, *Grecii* LgA, i.e. the hermitage at Greccio, south-east of Terni.

110 **redi**: add *albis et* LgA.

112 **toke the array**: *mist en son chief le chapel* P2.

117–18 **upon the flore**: *en la pouldre* P2, *in cinere* LgA.

118 **drede**: *stupore* LgA.

125 **a pore woman**: *pauperculum* LgA; subsequent pronouns are ambiguous for gender in Latin, feminine in LgD and GiL.

126 **of this woman**: *huius* LgA.

127 **blamed**: *reprent* P2, i.e. present tense.
most: only GiL.

131 **a richer of his owne will**: *ditior uoluntate* LgA, 'plus riche en désir' (Roze).

138 **mortall**: *intestinum* LgA.

140 **upon the citee**: *sur la terre du bourc* P2, *de burgo super terram illam* LgA, i.e. from the outskirts he saw demons exulting above that place.

145–6 **And anone thei went oute**: not in LgA.

146 **anone**: *post modicum* LgA.

149–50 **in large brede**: *a lune et a lautre partie* P2.

154, 155 **synne, it**: *pecheur, le* P2.

155 **to his mercy**: only GiL.

158 **he laboured . . . laboure**: *il le vouloit alentir a bien faire* P2, *nisus fuerit eum ad teporem reducere* LgA.

159–60 **in no wise prevaile ayenst hym**: *riens faire ainsy* P2, *sic non preualuit* LgA.

161 **felt hymselff stered**: *le senty* P2.

163 **in this plite**: *ainsy* P2.
he sawe that: only GiL.

164 **hymself**: add *tout nu* P2.

165 **a vyne yerde . . . snowe**: *vne grant vigne toute plaine de noif* P2, *magnam niuem* LgA.

166 **and proposed . . . saide**: *quas sibi proponens cepit alloqui corpus* LgA, 'which he placed before him and began to speak to his body'.

171 **leue hem and serue oure Lorde perfitely**: *si serues curieusement a ung seul seigneur* P2.

174 **cardinal**: add *sancte crucis* LgA; Leo Brancaleone, titular cardinal of the Holy Cross in Jerusalem, d. *c*.1230 (Boureau, 1413 n. 25).

176 **iaillours**: *castaldi* LgA, 'agents'.

177 **and offences**: only GiL.

180 **thei . . . not**: *in me permisit irruere* LgA.

185 **he sawe**: *audiuit* LgA.

186 **assembled . . . hepe**: *assemblees* P2, *cateruas* LgA; s.w. took *assemblees* as the participle.

187 **trouble and**: only GiL.

189–90 **dessende downe and**: only GiL.

190 **to do in me**: only GiL.

191 **sustene**: add *tout* P2.

192 **enemy and**: only GiL.

193 **ye take veniaunce in my lyff**: *vous prendres de luy vengence en ma vie*

P2, *in ipso uice mea exercebitis ultionem* LgA, 'you exact vengeance on him instead of me'.

196–8 **in sperit . . . shininge**: *entre ces autres sieges du ciel vng tres digne siege et resplendissant de noble gloire. plus* P2.

199 **arraied and**: only GiL.

200 **a uoys that saide**: only GiL.
was: *fu a* S.

201 **bi his pride**: only GiL.
and kepte: only GiL.

203–4 **in youre owne conceit**: only GiL.

206 **what was**: *quia uera fuerit* LgA.

207 **pride**: add *en la vision de dieu* P2; LgA begins next paragraph *In uisione dei.*

208 **seraphin**: *cherubin* P2, *seraphin* LgA.

209 **he**: only GiL.

210 **he**: *et ipse* LgA.

212 **as longe . . . hem**: *diligenti studio ab omnium oculis* LgA.

215 **signes**: *stigmata* LgA, also at 227, 229, 245, 248.

216 **hem**: add *que post eius obitum contigerunt* LgA.

219 **a uision**: *illusion* P2.

226 **akinge and**: only GiL.

226–7 **sorw and peine**: *douleur* P2, *ardore et dolore* LgA.

233 **as for dede**: *comme demy mort* P2.

248 **of**: *ma gorge et mes plaies a* P2.

250–1 **thanne was pope**: *fut pappe apres* P2, i.e. Gregory IX.

251 **make ye**: *faisons nous* P2.
not: add *de* P2, i.e. some of.

256 **oure**: *mei* LgA.

258 **hope**: *specimen* LgA. Jacobus de Voragine, himself a Dominican, later became archbishop of Genoa, albeit reluctantly.

259 **Oure**: *mei* LgA.

260 **wolde not be called**: *fieri non presumant* LgA.

261 **right gret**: *Columbina* LgA.

262 **and humilite**: only GiL.

263–4 **he handelyd . . . planed hem**: *il les aplainoit* P2, *tanguntur ab ipso* LgA; *MED s.v. planen* v.1, 'plane, smooth' *etc.*; here 'stroked'.

265–6 **he comaunded . . . pees**: *elles se teurent tantost par son commandement* P2.

266–70 **bridde**: *cicada* LgA.

267 **before his selle**: *apud Portiunculam* LgA. This cell, the Portiuncula, survives within a sixteenth-century basilica near Assisi.
songe: add *souuent* P2.

272–3 **he wolde not defoule the fairenesse of his hondes**: *que il nenlaidisist la resplendeur de sa main* P2, *nolens sua manu deturpare fulgorem* LgA, 'not wishing to spoil its brightness with his hand'.

274 **hym that is saide a stone**: i.e. Peter.

276 **hony**: add *et optima uina* LgA.

285 **and bright**: only GiL.

287 **other**: add *per pectus* LgA.

287–8 **that hadde . . . sight**: *Quem cum nunquam uidisset, tali indicio recognoscens* LgA, i.e. he had never seen Francis before.
conuerted hym to God: *fut esmeu en cueur* P2, *compunctus* LgA.

297 **curable**: *curialis* LgA, 'courteous', which Vignay has mistranslated; *MED* gives only senses akin to 'remediable', rather than 'capable of curing' as required here. On adjectives in *-ble* with an active as well as a passive sense, see Burton, 'Drudgery, Bludgery and Fludgery', 23.

300 **eyelydde**: *sourcil* P2.

308 **matere**: *merite* P2.

311 **thus . . . will**; *ia soit ce quil se teust* P2, *licet inuitus* LgA.

311–12 **marchaunt . . . fole**: *mercenarium imperitum et inutilem* LgA, 'ignorant and useless lackey'.

313 **for thi trewe sayenge**: only GiL.

317 **to be General**: *generali officio* LgA.

321 **a frere hadd done anithinge**: *frater quidam* (. . .) *aliquid fecisset* LgA.

322 **alwey**: not in LgA.

323 **wolde comaunde**: *iussit* LgA.

324 **he**: *capucium* LgA.

325 **wolde comaunde**: *precepit* LgA.

330 **Houres**: add *canoniaux* P2.

338 **herborwed**: *deuotement conuie* P2.

342–3 **the knight**: only GiL.

344 **briddes**: add *et eas uelut rationis participes salutasset* LgA.

345 **and susteren**: not in P2, *volucres* LgA.

347–8 **withoute ani cure or besinesse**: *sans auoir nulle cure* P2, *sine uestra sollicitudine* LgA.

348 **turned her bek to hym**: *ceperunt uersus eum extendere colla* LgA.

349 **her hedes and**: only GiL.

353 **Maury**: *almaury* P2, *Aliuianum* LgA, variant *Almarium*, Alviano, small town south-east of Orvieto.

362 **hasted fast**: *uehementer instaret* LgA, 'insisted'.

367 **Money**: add *seruis dei* LgA.
a: add *dyabolus et* LgA.

373 **kepe it**: add *curieusement* P2.

377, 378 **cope, cote**: *chappe*, *cote* P2, *tunicam*, *tunicam* LgA.

379 **thou shalt reioyse**: *tu layes* P2.

380 **herborwed**: add *en alixandrie* P2, *Alexandriam* LgA, Alessandria.

383 **a good capon**: *vng chappon de sept ans* P2.

385 **mete**: *laumosne* P2.
name: *nom benoist* P2, *dei nomen* LgA.

387 **he**: *il le monstra et* P2; L clarifies, substituting *þis cursed man* for *he*.

390 **an hole capon**: *chappon* P2, *piscis* LgA.

392 **he that hadde mistake hym**: *cil qui ot mespris* P2, *preuaricator* LgA, 'the false accuser'.

395 **Virgine**: add *et filii eius* LgA.

399 **reuerence and dignite**: *dignite* P2, *reuerentiam* LgA.

405 **sone**: *uerbum* LgA.
passen: *poursient* P2, *possident* LgA.

407 **by**: add *moult de* P2.

408 **all syknesse**: *moult de malades* P2.

409 **man**: add *goutta et tantost* P2.
hele: add *et si fit plusieurs autres miracles* P2.

410 **greuous**: *longa* LgA.

411 **layde**: add *nudum* LgA.

412 **whan . . . present**: *et manus singulis imponens* LgA.

414–15 **and taught hem (. . .) for to praise her maker**: *Inuitabat* (. . .) *omnes creaturas ad laudem dei LgA.*

415–16 **he taught hem**: *hortabatur ad laudem* LgA, i.e. death itself was exhorted to praise.

416 **in his owne persone**: only GiL.

416–17 **he . . . hym**: *eique letus occurrens ad suum inuitabat hospitium* LgA.

421 **A frere**: add *qui auoit nom augustin* P2, *Minister fratrum* (. . .) *nomine Augustinus* LgA.

the londe of Laboure: *terre de labour* P2, *terra laboris* LgA. Terra Laboris was a region to the north-west of Naples, referred to by Pliny as *Leboria*; it was one of the early Franciscan provinces.

424 **ho that was**: *que cestoit* P2, *quid diceret* LgA.

427 **deied**: *uiam uniuerse carnis fuisset ingressa* LgA.

428 **do her seruice**: *celebrer les obseques dicelle* P2.

429 **sette her**: *se leua* P2.

432–3 **hathe gote me grace of lyff**: *jmpetra que ce peche reuele ie aye pardon* P2, *ad corpus mihi redire indultum est ut illo reuelato peccato ueniam merear* LgA.

434 **pees**: add *deuant vous* P2.

436 **Nice**: *Vitere* P2, *Nicera* LgA, variant *Nocera*, Nocera in Umbria.

borwed: *mutuo peterent* LgA.

442 **turmented hymselff**: *tournioit* P2, 'rolled about'.

444 **deuout synner**: *sancte, iam deuote precanti* LgA.

444–5 **blamyng the wickedly**: *impie blasphemanti* LgA, 'from the impious blasphemer'.

445 **and**: add *planctum prohibens* LgA.

458 **and**: not in LgA.

468 **it**: only GiL.

477 **a castell**: *in castro Pomarico* LgA, near Pisticci, south of Matera.

478 **so that she was dede**: *Cum* (. . .) *fuisset defuncta* LgA.

480 **and that of right gret sorugh**: only GiL.

487 **wyndowe**: add *du palais* P2.

488 **grounde**: add *et penitus expirasset* LgA.

493 **coughed**: *oscitauit* LgA, 'yawned'.

495 **vessell**: *nasselle* P2, 'skiff'.

496 **hasted**: *prepararet* LgA.

498 **for him**: *pro liberatione submersi* LgA.

499 **deuocion**: add *appelloit le saint en son aide* P2.

503 **him**: *sa cotte ne ne moulla riens de luy* P2, *ad tunicam* LgA.

143 ST PELAGIA

Maggioni, ch. CXLVI, p. 1033; Dunn-Lardeau, ch. 145, p. 963.

1 **þe worþiest**: *la premiere* P2, *prima feminarum* LgA.

2–3 **noble . . . bodi**: *habitu ambitiosa et uana, animo et corpore impudica* LgA.

3 **cloþing**: French *abit* and Latin *habitu* can mean either deportment or style of clothing; the former was doubtless intended in this case.

4 **quentises**: *ambitione maxima* LgA.

7 **swete**: *diuerses* P2.
bifore: add *elle et apres* P2.

8 **were**: add *aussy* P2.

10 Heliopolis and Damietta were, however, different cities in the Nile delta.

10–11 **passed bi þe cite and**: not in LgA.

12 **and besines**: only GiL.
he: *elle* P2, *ipse* LgA.

15 **cried on hie and seid: 'Lorde**: *disoit. tres hault sire* P2.

15–16 **þe grete cure . . . ouerpassed**: *laornement dune fole femme surmonte en vng seul iour la sagesce de toute ma vie* P2, *unius die meretricis ornatus totius uite mee industriam superauit* LgA.

20 **endeles**: not in P2, *immortali* LgA.

22 **with him**: *auec elle* P2, *secum* LgA.

23 **vs**: *vous* P2, *nos* LgA.

25 **forslouthe þe tyme**: *despisons* P2, *negligimus* LgA.

26 **many oþer**: *semblables* P2.

30–1 **of þe same bisshopp**: not in P2, *ab ipso episcopo* LgA.

35 **þrogh . . . God**: only GiL.

36 **lettres seying**: *lettres par vng message contenans ces paroles au* P2.

37 **þe seruant . . . and I**: *de ihesu crist* P2, *discipulo Christi* LgA.

38 **arte . . . verri**: *es vrai* S, *uere (. . .) comprobaris* LgA.

41 **dispise**: *temptes* LgA.
lownesse: add *ne ne lessaies pas* P2.

41–2 **thou desire to be savid**: *tu te veulx sauuer* P2, *saluari desideras* LgA.

44 **fell . . . his**: *le prist par les* P2.

45 **moder**: *mere* P2, *pelagus* LgA; SP1 as P2, though all three gave *mer* in the etymological preface to the chapter, which as usual s.w. omits. The play on her name is thus lost, as happens again with *Margarete*, 'pearl', at 49 below.

þe flode of synnes: *pelagus iniquitatis exundans fluctibus peccatorum* LgA.

46 **deuourer of soules**: *deluge et las a occire les ames* P2, *uorago et laqueus animarum* LgA.

46–7 **þe which . . . all**: *lesquelles choses toutes ie doubte* (*perhorrui* LgA) *maintenant* P2.

48 **For my birthe**: not in P2, *A natiuitate* LgA.

49 **pompe and pride**: *orgueil* P2, *pompam* LgA.

51 **þe lawe**: *lamour* P2, *timore* LgA.

52 **beyng . . . present**: *crioit* P2, *autem ibidem clamabat* LgA.

60 **forsake**: D *forsaine*, *MED forsaien*, renounce, with only two citations, from Ayenbite and Amis & Amiloun.

69 **of þe bisshopps**: *de celluy* (add *episcopi* LgA) P2.
þat had . . . hire: *supradicti* LgA.

74 **she . . . penaunce**: *pour la grant maigrete* P2.

75 **Ye haue**: *auez vous* P2.

75 **Ye²**: add *Dame* P2, add *domine* LgA; Vignay has missed the point of the story, but s.w. corrects.

77 **and**: add *mais quant il vint a la celle* P2.

78 **answhered**: *sibi aperuisset* LgA.

78–9 **went þan and**: only GiL.

79 **hire dede**: masculine in LgD, LgA.

81 **þe seruice**: *les obseques* P2.

85 **Octobre**: add *circa* LgA.
.CC.lxxxx.: *.CC.iiij*^{xx}*. et .ix.* P2, *CCLXC* LgA.

144 ST MARGARET PELAGIA

Maggioni, ch. CXLVII, p. 1036; Dunn-Lardeau, ch. 146, p. 966.

2 **freendis**: *parens* P2.

5 **desired**: *requise par mariage* P2.

11 **chambre**: add *iam paratum* LgA.

12 **and solempnite**: only GiL.
holi: only GiL.

14–15 **bigan to þenke (. . .) þe recompense**: *compensatione uibrauit* LgA, variant *liberauit*, *libravit* Graesse; Boureau (p. 1416 n. 2) rightly prefers the latter, translating as ‘fit la balance entre’.

16 **þat foloweth**: *des* P2.

17 **nought**: *ordure* P2.

20 **Pelagien**: *frere pelagien* P2.

23 **þe ruler and þe keper**: *prouisore* LgA.

23–4 **þat was þere fast by**: not in LgA.

24 **þe counseil of þe abbot**: add *et des anciens* P2, *seniorum consilio et abbatis imperio* LgA.

25 **þough . . . gretly**: *licet inuitus* LgA.

27 **gostli pastes of hevenli fode**: *les pastis des ames* P2.

28 **of þis grete vertu**: only GiL.

29 **put abak his goode name**: *occuper son bon cours* P2, *eius cursum* (. . .) *impediret* LgA.

29–30 **And . . . for**: *Sy que* P2.

30–1 **a virgine þat dwelled withoute þe yates**: she seems to have been some sort of extern sister, i.e. a member of a cloistered community authorized to attend to matters outside the cloister.

34 **wist . . . and**: not in LgA.

37 **iugement**: add *et sans condempnation* P2, add *et examinatione* LgA.
and he wist not whi: *cum ignominia* LgA.

42 **moost mekli . . . susteyned**: *et soustint tout paciemment* P2.

43 **the wronges**: only GiL.

44 **hertli loued and**: only GiL.
in his chastite: not in LgA.

49 **temptacions of þe worlde**: *pelagus temptationum* LgA, same wordplay as at 143 Pelagia 45 above.

49–51 **I am a man . . . vertu of man**: *Vir sum non pro deceptione mentita quod factis ostendi* LgA; *vertu of man*, 'qualities of a man', 51 *haue hadde vertu*, 'have gained virtue'.

51 **þat was put vppon me**: not in LgA.

55 **thei**: *les traitres* P2, *calumpniatores* LgA.

56 **þe abbot**: *ilz* P2.

60 **amonge þe virgines**: *en leglise des vierges* P2, *in monasterio uirginum* LgA.

145 ST THAIS

Maggioni, ch. CXLVIII, p.1038; Dunn-Lardeau, ch. 147, p. 969.

4 **and slough . . . tymes**: not in LgA.

5 **house**: *limina* LgA.

7–8 **So . . . went and**: *tant que vng saint homme pain par nom* P2, *Quod cum audisset abbas Pannutius* LgA.

10 **þat is to sey .xij.d.**: not in LgA.

16 **place**: *cubiculum* LgA.

17 **God**: add *Mais se tu doubtes dieu il nest nul lieu qui puisse estre mucie a sa diuinite* P2.
  Than: *Et quant le viellart oy ce* P2.

18–19 **and þat he seeth all þinges clerli**: only GiL.

19–20 **seeth . . . clerely**: *scay le regne du siecle auenir et les tourmens denfer pour les pechiez* P2.

20–4 **Than . . . beleue**: only GiL.

26 **thou . . . peyne**: *te conuendra rendre raison* P2, *redditura rationem dampnaberis* LgA.

27 **all . . . syn**: *ycelles* P2.

33 **and obeye**: only GiL.

34 **graunted her the terme and**: not in LgA.

40 **.vC.**: *quadrigentarum* LgA.

47 **abbot**: *senex* LgA.

48–9 **that the which comithe**: *aquam meam* LgA.

50–1 **praie to**: *aoreroit* P2.

55 **recordyng**: add: *souuent* P2.

56 **merci and**: only GiL.

57 **in this plite**: only GiL.

58 **remembrid . . . her**: *condoluit* LgA.

62 **of his mersy**: only GiL.
  declare: add *a aucun di ceulx* P2.
  declare the cause: i.e. make known the outcome.

66–7 **these: the first was**: only GiL.

67 **of the peynes in hell**: *de la peine* P2, *pene future* LgA.

68 **the secounde was**: only GiL.

69–70 **the thridde was**: *et* P2.

73 **Antony**: add *son pere* P2.

82 **synnes**: add *en vne somme* P2.

83 **from the mouthe and**: not in LgA.

84 **beholde hem and**: only GiL.

88 **in oure Lorde**: only GiL.

90–1 **drewe (. . .) foliously**: *attraisist* (. . .) *deshonnestement* P2, *impudenter illiceret* LgA; *MED* has two citations for *foliousli*, 'foolishly', from Knight of La Tour-Landry (?c1450) and Vegetius (a1460). Here the sense is 'lasciviously'; cf. *MED foli* adj. sense (c).

146 ST DIONYSIUS THE AREOPAGITE

Maggioni, ch. CIL, p. 1041; Dunn-Lardeau, ch. 148, p. 972.

1–2 **to . . . Paule**: *a la foy ihu crist de pol le benoist apostre* P2.

3 **strete**: *uico* LgA.

8 ***Pariopage***: so P2, *Ariopage* S, *Panopagum* LgA.

9 **gret**: *plus* P2.

11 **duelled the scolers**: *estoient lez escoles* S.

14 **in that tyme**: *la* S.

15 **the secte of**: only GiL.

17 **Stociens**: *stoici* LgA.
she: *i.e. the blessednesse*.
onli . . . soule: *en la seule vertu du corage* S, *in sola animi uirtute* LgA.

22 **of the sonne**: add *eclipsis uero fieri solet tantum in synodo solis et lune* LgA.
.xv.: L helpfully adds *daies olde*.

23 **there was an unperfite distaunce**: *in perfecta distantia* LgA, i.e. at its maximum distance.
in the sonne: *du soleil* P2.
and alweyes: *tum quia* LgA, 'also because'.

24–5 **and also**: *tum quia* LgA.

27–8 **for oure Lorde suffered peyne in alle his membris**: *ex eo quod uniuersitatis dominus patiebatur* LgA.

28 **in Ethiope, in Egipte**: *en eliopolim en egypte* S, *apud Elyopolim Egypti* LgA.

29–30 **in Grece**[2] **. . . Litell**; *Rome* LgA.

32 **and the**: *es* P2.

33 **right gret abundaunce of flodes**: *tres grans furondemens de pluies* P2, *maximarumque urbium plurime partes* LgA.

35 **and lost his light**: only GiL.
thorugh alle the parties of the world: *in totum* LgA.

36 **and in . . . Egipte**: *tetra nox subito obducta terris est adeo ut stellas tunc diurnis horis uel potius in illa horrenda nocte toto celo uisas fuisse referatur.' Hec Orosius. Fuit etiam et apud Egyptum* LgA; this last clause introduces the following reference to Denis's letter.

37 **in . . . Apolaphanes**: *et appolophanes disant en son epistre* P2, LgA as GiL.

39 **the onli**: *le seul* P2, *solis* LgA.
purged: add *regulam Philippi Aridei assumpsimus* LgA; for a fuller account with references see Boureau, 1420 n. 16.

40 **certeyne**: *notissimum* LgA.

40–1 **shulde . . . tristes**: i.e. no eclipse was due.

41 **tristes**: D *tristinesse* has only one citation in *MED* s.v. *tristines*, for ?c1450.

41–2 **ne we mowe not yet haue perceiued the misterie of this thing bi oure gret wisdom**: *aio ad te: 'Vaste peritie sanctuarium, adhuc nescius tante rei mysterium* LgA.

43 **shal y saie**: *ascribis* LgA.

43–5 **Y putte . . . saide**: *ie latribue a toy comme a bouche deuine. et non pas a parole humaine* P1, *Ad que tu mihi ore diuino et non humani sensus sermone* LgA; P2 and S have different misreadings for *a bouche deuine*; s.w. must have referred to LgA, though confusions in the rest of the passage show that no thorough revision was attempted.

45–50 **the chaunge . . . falshede**: *diuinarum permutationes sunt rerum.' Denique notatum ferie diem et annum annuntiationis quam Paulus noster auribus suspensis intonuit, signis acclamantibus recordari expertus dedi ueritati manus et falsitatis sum nexibus absolutus* LgA; '"there is some turmoil in the affairs of heaven." I made a careful note of the day and year of this event, and later, when I realized that all the signs corresponded with what Paul had repeatedly told us, as we hung upon his lips, then I surrendered to the truth, and was finally freed from the toils of delusion.' Stace's slightly paraphrased translation gives the clearest version of this passage. 48 *deif* GiL, *sourdes* P2, is for *suspensis* LgA, 'attentive'.

51–2 **and to Apoliphanes**: *de se et Apollophane* LgA.

51–116 For the long omission from E see note to 116 below.

53 **þe mone . . . disordenatli**: *inopinabiliter soli lunam incedentem* LgA, 'the moon going unexpectedly before the sun'. *MED* has *disordinat* in senses 'disorderly, immoderate', etc., but no adverb.

54–5 **And . . . here**: *Et de rechief. icelle de la ix*[e] *heure iusques au vespre au dyamettre du soleil sur tout naturel establissement. et nous veismes celle eclipse en orient commencant iusques au terme du soleil. et apres ce retournant de rechief et* *non pas purgiee de ce deffault. mais estoit fait au contraire* P2, add further *Hec Dionysius* LgA.

55 **into**: add *heliopolin en* P2.

55–6 **for to desire**: *pour desir* P2.

58 **Dictes of Euchiciens**: *dictiez des etheniciens* P2, *dictis ethnicorum* LgA, pagan writings; *MED s.v. dicte* offers senses 'saying, maxim, statement'.

60–1 **þe houre of none**: *hora sexta* LgA.

61–2 **also . . . derkenesse**: *ut stelle in celo uise sint* LgA.

64 **stories**: *hystoriis scholasticis* LgA.

65 **suffred dethe**: *patitur* LgA; also at 67.
or elles: *Alibi tamen legitur quod dixerunt* LgA.

67 **dethe**: not in LgA.

68 **derkenesse and**: only Gil.

68–9 **signifieth . . . come**: *quam nouam admiramur totius mundi ueram lucem aduenturam significat* LgA.

73 **sacrifise**: add *luy* P2.

76 **of sinners**: *pecorum* LgA, variant *peccatorum.*

78 **and stroof**: not in LgA.

84 **to here**: *aut discere aut audire* LgA.

88 **it is**: add *uerum deum* LgA.

89 **most . . . trouthes**: *ceteris magis doctum in diuinis* LgA.

91–2 **He . . . vnknowen**: *sed nobis est ignotus* LgA.

97 **mankinde**: *char humaine* P2.

100 **seist**: add *a cest aueugle* P2.
þi Lorde . . . sight: *ton roy et il voie* P2, *toi et il voie* S, *dei tui 'uide!' et uiderit* LgA.

102–3 **And Poule seid to him**: not in LgA; Vignay wrongly assumed an omission, but it was indeed Denis appointing the words.

104 **haue . . . þat**: only GiL.

106 **and from . . . worlde**: *uide* LgA.

112 **with**: *enseigne de* P2.

116 E's attempt to smooth its hiatus from 51 by substitution of *dredde* for *.iij.*, presumably in form *thridde*, shows that the omission must already have been in the exemplar.

128 **the good werkes**: *imitationes* LgA, 'emulations'.

129–30 **it . . . shewed**: *insinuare uidetur* LgA.

139 **diuerse**[1]: only GiL.

141 **debate**: add *ou peuple* P2.

142, 143 **and, where**: *et, ou* P2, *aut, aut* LgA, s.w. taking *ou* as 'where' instead of 'or'.

144 **and durst . . . abide hym**: only GiL.

146 **lordshipped and**: *multiplicatis fidelibus* LgA.

150 **of Rome**: *de rome* P2, i.e. 'from Rome'.

154–5 **was brought**: *amener* P2.

156 **he . . . anger and**: *il fut moult tristre. Et* P2, *ecce* LgA.

157 **gret**: *noble* P2.

158 **husbonde**: add *Lubium* LgA; LgD and GiL name him at 187 below.

159 **he**: *le mary* P2.
cruelly: *a tort* P2.

164 **the colis and upon**: only GiL.

165–6 **forciblement embraced**: *fort embrasee* P2, *Ignitum* (. . .) *uehementer* LgA; *MED* records *forcible*, but neither *forciblement* nor *forcibli.*

166–7 **sette betwene**: *erigitur et* (. . .) *proicitur* (. . .) *ad* LgA.

167 **two**: *tres* P2.

170 **a brennynge furneys of brennynge fire**: *vng fournel ardant* P2, *clibanum* LgA.

175–6 **gaue . . . bodi**: *luy bailla le pain* P2, *panem accipiens* LgA.

176 **resseiue me**: *tien* P2, *Accipe hoc* LgA.

182 **bi . . . aungeles**: *si comme les anges le menoient entre leurs bras* P2, *inter brachia angelo duce* LgA.

186 **prouost**: *preuost* P2, *prefati* LgA, 'aforesaid'; Graesse reads *praefecti*, but Maggioni records no such MS reading. He is referred to at 157 above merely as the husband of a *gret matrone*.

187 **beheded**: add *des felons* P2.

188 **Lybien**: *Nubius* LgA.

198–9 **.iiij^{xx}.x. in the .vj. yere of Domacien**: *XCVI sub Domitiano* LgA.

200 **.viijC.xxxij.**: *DCCCXV* LgA.

201 **kinge**: *roy de france* P2, not in LgA.

208–9 **he recorded . . . marteres**: *apostolorum nominibus in canone recitatis adiunxit: 'Et beatis martyribus tuis* LgA.

211 **lyued . . . ailed**: *vesquissent encores. et se commenca forment a esmerueillier comment il auoit ainsy dit ou canon* P2.

217 **.vjC.xxxiij.**: *DCXLIV* LgA.

220 **of**: add *clotaire* P2.

224 **the**[1]: *leurs* P2.

225 **of helle**: only GiL.

227–8 **by grace he was returned to lyff**: *par aduenture lame retourna au corps* P2.

231 **Ignacien**: *Hincmarus* LgA.

233 **Arroparexit**: *ariopagite* P2.

234–5 **witnessithe it not**: *ne le contredit point* P2.

147 ST CALLISTUS

Maggioni, ch. CL, p.1051; Dunn-Lardeau, ch. 149, p. 980.

2 **And . . . emperour**: *Cuius temporibus* LgA.

3–4 **with fire of vengeaunce**: *dembrasement diuin* P2.

8 **Thrusday**, 19 **Wednisday**, it is more obvious in French and Latin that these are the days of Jupiter and Mercury respectively.

9 **bi veineaunce**: *diuinement* P2.

10 **brent**: add *et sol obscuratus est ita* LgA.

12 **Palmachien**: add *consulte* P2.

13 **other**: *ses* P2.

14 **might be putte oute**: *delerentur* LgA.

15 **hadde**: add *receu* P2.

23 **verrei trouthe and liff**: *vray et vif* P2, *uerus et unus deus* LgA, variant *uiuus* for *unus*.

25 **the citee of Rauen**: *urbem Rauennatium* LgA, a part of the Trastevere area of Rome so called because crews from the Ravenna fleet had been lodged there.

29 **profitable**: *necessarius* LgA.

30 **and good werkes**: only GiL.

38–9 **in prison**: not in LgA.

39 **and .v. nightes**: only GiL.

40 **and . . . before**: not in LgA.

43 **his**: not in LgA.
the: *eius* LgA.

148 ST LEONARD

Maggioni, ch. CLI, p. 1053; Dunn-Lardeau, ch. 150, p. 982.

1 **was**: i.e. lived; L adds *borne.*

7 **name**: *sainctete* P2.

15 **there**: *ubique* LgA.

20–1 **with hym . . . quene**: *qui estoit la alee pour soy esbattre* P2.

23 **withoute comfort**: *pour le peril de la royne* P2.

39 **go about**: add *en vne nuyt* P2.

42 **felawes**: *monachis* LgA.

46 **and his helpe**: not in LgA.

47 **cheines**: add *ou ses fers* P2.

49–50 **leften the worlde**: *vendirent tout* P2.

52 **to vertues**: only GiL.

61 **was rested in**: *vouloit reposer* P2.
grene: *vvit* P2, 'empty'.

61–2 **there . . . made and**: not in LgA.

67 **fyched**: add *en vng tronc* P2, add *in cippo* LgA, 'to a beam'.

68 **bounde**: add *collo* LgA.

72–3 **he vowed hymselff (. . .) and besought hym**: *se voua* P2, *uoto* (. . .) *rogauit* LgA.

76 **y shall bere**: *deferas* LgA.

77 **arose**: add *et print la chaienne* P2.

80 **chirche**: add *que sanctus Leonardus sibi fecerat* LgA.

81 **horrible**: only GiL.

83 **that . . . worshipped**: *si habitoit a nobli* P2.

86 **in this wise . . . do for**: *en soy* P2.
for he: *qui* P2.

89 **wol deliuer hym**: add *se ie le peusse garder. ie le feisse raimbre de mil solz* P2; transferred to 94 below, with *peusse* translated as *shal* and *till* added.

94 **thus . . . shillinges**: see 89 above.

100 **deuout and true seruaunt**: *deuot sergent* P2, *fidelis* LgA.

101 **so moche**: only GiL.

107 **Almayne**: *Aluernia* LgA.
depe pitte: *vne fosse* P2, *cauea* LgA.

108 **to Seint . . . also**: *eos* LgA.

111 **pitously**: only GiL.

115 **dede nothinge**: *ne le voult en nulle maniere laisser aller* P2.

118 **all**: *pluribus* LgA.

119 **hippes**: *cuisses* P2.

121 **ofte**: only GiL.

123 **hougely**: only GiL.
into alle the hous: *in media domo* preceding 122 *apered* LgA.

126 **of one maner**: *eiusdem* LgA, i.e. also a monk.

128 **prelate in a chirche**: i.e. abbot.

129 **so that**: *mais si comme* P2, sentence continuing after 130 *goodnesse*.

130 **for his goodnesse**: *venoit a luy* P2, *ad eum confflueret* LgA.

133–4 **right cruel**: *nimis credulus* LgA.

139 **Seint Leonard**: add *si que a peine les* (add *detractores* LgA) *restabli le roy aux prieres du saint a leur estat arriere* P2.

148 **Whanne**: *Post hoc autem cum* LgA.

150 **and so he dede**: *circa annos domini DLXX* LgA.

149 ST LUKE

Maggioni, ch. CLII, p. 1059; Dunn-Lardeau, ch. 151, p. 987.

1 **of the nacion . . . phisik**: *Syrus natione Antiochenus arte medicus* LgA.

2 **disciples**: add *domini* LgA.
Seint: *sainement* P2, i.e. rightly.

6 **not**: not in P2, in LgA.

7 **yef**: *Ja soit ce que* P2.

8 **disposed and**: only GiL.

14–15 **foure square hede**: *le chief quarre comme vng fust* P2, i.e. a cube.

15 **quarter**: *carreure* P2, *superficie* LgA.

22 **the seintes**: i.e. the Church Fathers.

23 **yef it were**: *Ja soit ce que* P2.

24 **discriving**: i.e. in their writings.

25 **of Godhede**: only GiL.

32 **brething**: *cry* P2, *rugitu* LgA.

33 **to crie**: *le cry* P2, *rugitu* LgA.

35 **Crist**[2]: add *duquel il escript* P2, add *de quo scribunt* LgA; Graesse has *scribit*.

36 **bole**: *veel* P2, 'calf'.

38 **wel**[1]: only GiL.
Luke: add *sicut quilibet alius euangelista* LgA.

39 **and disposed**: only GiL.

45–6 **the ey . . . effecte**: *leul de son entalentement estoit aguisie a luy par pensee deffect* P2, *rostrum affectus ad Christum exacuitur per meditationem* LgA, 'the beak of his desire towards Christ was sharpened by meditation'. GiL follows Vignay's mistranslation, and what either meant by *thought of effecte* is obscure; perhaps 'consideration of its significance'.

46 **his age was putte out**: *sa viellesce estoit boutee hors* P2, *senectus effectus abicitur* LgA.

48 **is**: add *merueilleusement* P2.

49 **fishes**: *pisciculos* LgA.

49–51 **He hathe . . . eting**: *rostrum etiam nimis aduncatum ita ut impediatur in cibo capiendo petre allidit et sic usui cibandi habilem efficit* LgA, 'his beak being very crooked so that he might be hindered in taking his food, he grinds it on stone and thus makes it effective for the purpose of feeding'. Vignay, followed by s.w., turned the *ut* clause into a negative clause of purpose.

53–5 **and there . . . eyen**: *senectutem abicit, calore solis oculorum caliginem consumente et pennas alleuiante* LgA, 'casts off old age, taking away by the heat of the sun the blindness of his eyes and making his feathers light'.

57–8 **noblesse . . . conuersacion**: *generositatem per honestam morum conuersationem* LgA.

64 **oxe**: *uituli siue bouis* LgA.
was: add *recte* LgA.

65 **is wretin in**: *fu escrite en* S, *fut escripre* P2, *fuit scribere* LgA.

65–6 **morialli . . . moralite**: *morose* LgA, 'steadily'. E's spelling is not in other MSS, nor recorded in *MED*; but since it is repeated at 230 it has been retained.

66–7 **of the foregoer . . . natiuite**: not in P2, *precursoris et natiuitate* LgA.

70 **foryete or lefte behinde**: *laissie* LgA.

71–2 **taught in the maners**: *morigine. cest adire introduit* P2, *immoratus* LgA, i.e. he lingered over.

73 **moral**: *morosum* LgA, 'slow'.

75 **also . . . sacrifisable**: *immolaticium* LgA; *sacrifisable* is not recorded in MED.

82 **He went into Bethani**: *il alla* (. . .) *en bithinie* P2, *obiit in Bithynia* LgA.

83 **holy**: *mundam* LgA.

84 **soule**: *pensee* P2, *mente* LgA.
conscience: *pensee* P2, *cogitationis* LgA.

89 **Bi whiche**: *que* P2, not in LgA.

93 **seithe**: only GiL. LgD and LgA give what follows as a summary of Richard, not a direct quotation.

93–4 **shull haue**: *deuons* P2.

95 **and the ferthe . . . dedes**: *Et second y soit adiouste ce que nous pouons faire* P2, *ut quartum addatur nostrum agere* LgA.

97 **.iiij.**: not in P2, in LgA.

102–3 **as . . . Timothes**: *II Tim. IIII* LgA.

106 **And . . . Corinthes**: *Iterum II Cor. VIII* LgA.

108 **after**: *Secundo* LgA, 'second', but Vignay translated it as *selon* and added *Et* after *conseilz*, detaching this phrase from the following sentence, where it should begin the next paragraph. *furst* is at 99, *Thriddely* at 118, *Ferthely* at 122.

110 **to hem**: *au proffit de ses prochains* P2.

112 **Theophile**: *optime Theophile* LgA; Vignay transferred *optime* to the writing, 112–13 *right well.*

115 **to his neigheboures**: not in LgA.

118 **of his neigheboure**: not in LgA.

119–20 **as . . . Colecens**: *Colos. IV* LgA.

120–1 **he . . . you**: *eternam salutem exoptat* LgA.

126 **saien**: add *ut habetur in hystoriis scholasticis* LgA.

133 **compeynabli**: *MED compaignabli*, 'in a body, as equals', and also at 145, 147 below, has only one citation, dated *c.*1500(?a1475). Here 'sociably' is required.

137 **soueraignly good**: *souuerainement puissant. souuerainement sage. souuerainement bon* P2. E gives *soueraigly*; *MED* records *sovereigly* as an error.

143 **and chastite**: not in LgA.

144 **Also**: *Secundo* LgA.

147 **thei were**: *il dit* P2, *dicitur* LgA.

147–8 **.ij. disciples**: add *cest adire disciplines bien ordonnees en meurs* P2, '*duo*' *et in hoc quod dicitur 'discipuli', quasi disciplinati, id est bene morigerati* LgA.

150 **this . . . mekenesse**: *selon loppinion daucuns lucas par humilite tut son nom* P2.

152 **in his orison**: i.e. the prayer in the mass of the feast of St Luke.

153 **of . . . delites**: *de delices* P2, *Crucis* LgA.

156–7 **He was nigh . . . frende and**: *il fut sy prochain de dieu que il estoit tenu amy de tous. Et* P2, *adeo quippe fuit proximis fructuosus quod ab omnibus carissimus habebatur, unde Colos. IV* LgA.

158 **right[1]**: *tres cher* P2.

160 **a witte**: *sens debonnaire* P2.

162 **secounde**: *.iiij.[e]* P2.

163 **Thei . . . wounded**: *ilz sesbahissoient tous* P2, *stupebant* LgA.

164 **for . . . might**: *quia in potestate erat sermo eius* LgA.

171 **honeste**: *uenustate* LgA, 'elegance'.
gret: *multorum* LgA.
is[2] (. . .) ennobled, 176 **is made noble**, etc.: *fulcitur* LgA, 'is supported'.

172 **gret**: *moult de* P2.

177 **and bi that that**: *quia* LgA.
is made noble: *est enseignee* P2, *edocetur* LgA.

178 **shewithe Luke**: *Ostendit enim Lucas* LgA, beginning new sentence.
vertu: *ueritatem* LgA.

179–80 **bi the witnesse of his veritees**: only GiL.

181 **xxvij**: *XX* LgA.

183 **doctrine**: *iustitie* LgA.

185 **is**: *dicitur* LgA.

188 **saide**: add *X cap.* LgA.

189 **And . . . hym**: *Item XVIII: Interrogauit eum etc.* LgA.

191 **He hadd**: *Secundo* LgA.

192 **trouthe**: add *XI cap.* LgA.

193 **that prechen the dymes**: *qui decimatis', id est decimandam predicatis, 'mentam et rutam et omne olus* LgA, 'who tithe", that is you preach the need to pay tithes, "on mint and rue and every herb'.

194 **God**: add *item ibidem: 'Ve uobis legis peritis qui tulistis clauem scientie etc.'* LgA.

195 **saide**: add *XX cap.* LgA.

199 **.xiiij.**: *XIII* LgA.

202–3 **Poule . . . he**: *ille qui scripsit* LgA.

217 **pore**: add *Item VI cap: 'Ab eo qui aufert tibi uestimentum etc.'* LgA.

220 **mete**: *fermento* LgA, 'leaven'.

224–5 **in his gospel (. . .) and the storie**: *euangelii sui* (. . .) *hystoria* LgA, ending the sentence.

225 **saithe**: only GiL.
taught: add *la natiuite* P2, *naturalia* LgA.

226 **Wher**: *mais* P2, *Vnde et* LgA.

231 **these blessidnesses**: *ces beneurtez* P2, *ipsis beatitudinibus* LgA.

236, 237, 239 **honeste**: *uenustate*, *uenustus*, *uenustatem* LgA.

240, 241 **apere**: *pateat* LgA, i.e. be clear; this sense is not quite covered by *MED ap(p)eren* v. (1), nearest being sense 4 (a), 'become apparent or evident'.
stere or: only GiL.

241, 247 **gaily**: *aorneement* P2; *MED* records the adjective as referring to eloquence, literary style etc., sense 3 (c), but not the adverb.

242 **manere**: *triplicem modum* LgA.

249 **þat that**: add *cor ardens habuit* LgA.

250 **with**[1]: *dedens* P2.

251, 252 **seintes**: not in LgA.

251–2 **what meruaile was that**: *quippe* LgA.

252 ff. **she**: i.e. the gospel.

253 **wherof Seint Ierom saithe**: *Ier.* LgA, i.e. Jeremiah.

256 **not**: not in P2, in LgA.

259 **pleinli**: not in LgA.

260 **enforced**: *corroboratum* LgA.

266 **the apostle saithe**: *dicitur Apoc.* LgA.

268–9 **made of . . . Crist**: *ab eterno efficienter, id est a Christo qui est eternus, de eternis materialiter, ad eterna finaliter, in eternum perpetualiter* LgA.

269 **pronounced**: *prenuntiatum* LgA.

276–7 **the misterie of his godhede**: *le mistere de parfondete* P2, *profundi misterii* LgA.

278 **conteined**: add *et la resurrection de char* P2, add *carmen resurrectionis* LgA.

283 **of oure Lorde**: *de domino uel a domino* LgA.

286 **and clerely**: only GiL.

286–7 **to the . . . thinges**: *querentibus* LgA.

291 **of oure saueoure, anone of his messenger**: *maintenant du sauueur et maintenant de son message* P2.

297 **leuid**: add *specialiter* LgA.

301 **he**: *solus Lucas* LgA.

313 **of thinges**: *de uisis ponuntur extrema et alia duo que sunt de* LgA.

314 **hem . . . born up**: *de ces derrenieres qui sont plus certaines sy quilz en soient ennoblies* (*fulciantur* LgA) P2.

315 **In the .viij.**: *Huitiesmement* P2.
Paule: add *nam eius euangelium mirablíliter approbat* LgA.

316 **ledithe**: *adducebat* LgA, i.e. quoted.

320 **and saide**: *II Cor. VIII* LgA.

321 **preisynges**: *louenge est* P2.
chirche: *eglises* P2.

323 **there**: *multis flagitiis se dedissent* LgA.

323–4 **that dede . . . turmentes**: *fame ac miseria multiplici affligebantur* LgA.

324 **that**: *mais* P2.

326 **clothinge**: add *a vng homme qui veilloit* P2.

327 **thei**: *cil* P2.

330 **ayenst the Turkes**: not in LgA.

150 STS CHRYSANTHUS AND DARIA

Maggioni, ch. CLIII, p. 1071; Dunn-Lardeau, ch. 152, p. 999.

5 **withdrawe . . . wordes**: *earum seducatur blanditiis* LgA.

6–7 **with . . . bestes**: *a fera pessima carnali, scilicet concupiscentia* LgA.

9–10 **toke . . . ynow**: *le pristrent* P2.

11–12 **arraied . . . goddesse**: *ennobli de vesteure aussy comme se elle fut deesse* P2, *dee Veste dicata* LgA, 'consecrated to the goddess Vesta'.

12 **praied**: *rogatur* LgA.

18–19 **for thei had be . . . women**: *quos auctores ipsorum flagitiosos uiros et impudicas feminas affirmarent* LgA.

20 **felyn**: *sensisse* LgA, 'have conceived of'.

22 **and tilithe it**: only GiL.

28 **Claudian**: add *tribunum* LgA.

33 **Lamficiacre**: *lemphiceatre* P2, *amphiteatro* LgA; *MED* records one citation *s.v. amp(h)iteatre* from Trevisa; s.w. has taken it as a place-name.

42 **whanne thei come**: not in P2, *omnes a leone capiuntur et* LgA.

51 **stoned . . . erthe**: *accrauantez de terres et de pierres* P2.

52 **Crist**: add *tempore Cari Narbonensi episcopi qui cepit anno domini CCXXXV. Horum solempnitas hic crebrius recolitur* LgA.

151 ST URSULA AND THE 11,000 VIRGINS

Maggioni, ch. CLIV, p. 1073; Dunn-Lardeau, ch. 153, p. 1001.

For another prose version of this life up to l. 137, translated from LgA rather than LgD, in San Marino, Huntington, MS HM 140 and Southwell Minster MS 7, see Garmonsway and Raymo, 'A Middle-English Prose Life of St Ursula', and Görlach, 'A Second Version of the Huntington Prose Legend of St Ursula'.

6 **to submitte**: *et* (. . .) *subiugaret* LgA, 'and subjected'.

8 **his**: add *seul* P2.

9 **yonge lorde**: *iouuencel* P2, named as *Otherin* and *Etherin* (*Ethereus* LgA) at 103 ff. below.
her: *jcelle chose* P2.

12 **werned**: *uacui* LgA.

13 **of Bretaigne**: not in LgA.

22 **that**: add *comparatis XI trieribus* LgA.

25 **strengthe**: *difficultate* LgA.

26 **purpos**: add *Ou que ceste conuenablete il luy donnast et dediast les vierges* P2, add *aut hac opportunitate predictas uirgines secum deo dicaret* LgA.

27 **hasted his fader**: *apud patrem institit* LgA.

30–2 **and all . . . seruice** *uiros quorum solatio tam ipsa quam eius exercitus indigebat in comitatu suo haberet* LgA.

34 **companie**: *spectaculum* LgA.

34–5 **for to . . . pilgrimage**: *ut secum pergerent* LgA.

36 **of Luse**: *lusillence* P2, *Basiliensis* LgA.

41 **sent . . . thinges**: *signefie son secret par lettres* S.

46 **and fro thennis . . . Englond**: not in LgA.

50 **alle thinges**: *uirginibus, trieribus et sumptibus* LgA.

51–2 **knightes in her felawship**: *commilitonibus suis* LgA, i.e. the eleven thousand virgins.

53–5 **Thanne thei . . . purpos**: *Nam modo belli preludia inchoant, modo currunt, modo discurrunt, interdum bella plerumque fugam simulant omnique genere ludorum exercitate nihil quod animo occurrebat relinquebant intactum*

LgA, 'For now they began preparations for war, sometimes they ran, sometimes they practised manoeuvres, sometimes they pretended flight and every kind of war-game, and nothing that occurred to their spirit did they leave untried'.

71 **and his clerkes**: *cum omni clero* LgA.

77 **certaine**: *.xj.* P2.
after . . . pope: i.e. as nineteenth pope after Peter, but see 83–7.

78 **purposed . . . and**: *in conuentu omnium* LgA.

81 **his astate**: *leueschie* P2, *pontificatus* LgA.

83 **Methos**: *Anteros* LgA.

85–7 **that he . . . women**: *que il auoit eue de son temps celle saincte compaignie de femmes luy osta* P2, *quam sacer ille uirginum chorus in curia Romana habuerat, a tempore illo amisit* LgA.

88 **holi**: *magnam* LgA.

92 **Hynnorum**: *permas* P2, *Hunnorum* LgA.

93 **and that . . . Coleyne**: *cum uenirent Coloniam* LgA.

98 **of bisshop**: *archiepiscopatus* LgA.
had folued: *tunc tempore uisitasset* LgA.

99–100 **and made . . . hem**: *concitus rediit et itineris ac passionis se eis socium fecit* LgA.

100 **of Leuitane**: *Leuicane* LgA; this non-existent locality results from a misreading in an earlier version; see Boureau, 1431 n. 5.

104 **husbond**: *espoux* P2, *sponsus* LgA. They are in fact 'betrothed', as LgA; **spouce** at 109 below (*espouse* P2, *sponse* LgA) can mean either wife or betrothed.

108 **retorned**: add *cum predictis episcopis* LgA.

111–13 **made anone to baptise . . . came**: *fist baptizier sa mere et vint auec sa mere et florence sa petite suer qui estoit ia crestienne. Et auec leuesque clement et vindrent* P1, *matrem suam baptizari fecit et cum ipsa et sorore sua paruula Florentina iam christiana necnon et Clemente episcopo* (. . .) *obuians* LgA; S omitted *sa mere*[1], P2 omitted *et vint auec sa mere*. s.w. must have copied a version like P2 and tried to correct by giving plural *weren*, so that the clause comes to mean 'that thus became christian'; it seems that L attempted further correction by reference to LgA, inserting *with her and* and changing *and came* to *he came*, but leaving s.w.'s *weren*. It has seemed best in this instance to follow L.

115 **moder and**: *mere* P2, *neptis* LgA.

120 **her**: *predictis* LgA.

121 **beseged**: add *des huns* P2, add *ab Hunnis* LgA.

121–3 **and whanne . . . Hungry**: *Et quant ces huns les virent* P2, *Quas barbari uidentes* LgA; John of Trevisa similarly seems not to distinguish between Huns and Hungarians, translating *Hungari* as *Hungaries*, and *Hun*(*n*)*i* as *hungers* and *hungres* (see *MED s.v. Hungari*).

124 **whanne**: add *ces autres furent decoppees* (*iugulatis* LgA) *et* P2.

125–6 **her gret . . . meruaylous**: *sa beaute merueilleuse* P2.

128 **and**: add *il vit quelle* P2.

132 **she suffered dethe**: *morti se offerens* LgA.
with good will: *de son gre* P2.

140 **reawmes**: add *cum his fuisse dicatur cum uirginibus has reginas* LgA.

141 **whan Constantine was**: *post Constantinum* LgA.

142 **dedin . . . cristen**: *seuiebant tale* LgA.

143 **.CCCC.lix.**: *CCCCLII* LgA.

146 **riche**: *dargent* P2.

147 **his desire he**: only GiL.

148 **bisides**: *sur* P2.
And . . . ende: only GiL.

149 **weren atte**: *cantaret* LgA.
atte midnight: *vne nuyt* P2.

150 **arose from**: *descendy de dessus* P2.

157 **ayen**: *ou vng autre* P2.

161 **and a nobille**: not in LgA.

169–70 **woke hym**: *len enneulioit* P2, 'anointed him'.

172 **uirgines**: *vierge* P2.

152 STS SIMON AND JUDE

Maggioni, ch. CLV, p. 1079; Dunn-Lardeau, ch. 154, p. 1006.

1 **Thadee**: *qui et Thaddeus dicitur* LgA.

2 **that was sone**: *et filii* LgA.

12 **that thou . . . goddes**: *lun des deux* P2, 'one of two things'.

16 **y (. . .) be trauailed and laboured**: *iai* (. . .) *este trauaille* P2, *laboro* LgA.

17 **grochin and**: not in LgA.
ayens the: add *et te veulent espier* P2.

18 **citee**: add *mais elle est honneste* P2.

23 **sent me**: add *Cum ergo assumptus fuero* LgA.

25 **the stori aforsaid**: *lystoire ecclesiaste* P2.

26 **God**: *Christum* LgA.

27 **thridde**: *.iiij.^{e}* P2.

30 **might be comforted in**: *veit* P2.

32–3 **and hym thought . . . of hym**: *nec ipsam ut sibi iussum fuerat figurare* LgA.

34–5 **the print . . . therin**: *emprigny vne ymage dedens* P2.

36 **so gretli**: only GiL.
it was conteined: *legitur* LgA.
that stori: *eadem antiqua hystoria* (. . .) *sicut idem Iohannes Damascenus testatur* LgA.

37 **this uisage was discriued**: *celle ymage estoit figuree* P2, *ymaginis dominus fuerit* LgA.
She: i.e. the *uisage*, LgD *ymage*; in LgA the sentence is differently structured, with *dominus* as the subject.
wel eyed: *bien entre esueilliee* (*entreullie* P1) P2, *bene oculatus* LgA; French *entreoeil* 'the space between the eyes'.

38 **was**: *est* P2.

39 **is**: *esse dicitur* LgA.

40 **paynym**: *herese ne nul payen* P2.
come: *viure* P2.

42 **sette upon the yate**: *super portam stans* LgA.

50 **they were**: *il fut* P2.

53–5 **he saide . . . of God/And therwith . . . worshipped hym**: trs. and add after **God** *qui me dit. Je tenuoieray aucun de mes disciples qui te curera et donra vie* P2.

57–8 **wol y slee**: *octroie* P2, *occirroie* P1, *trucidarem* LgA.
haue: *auoie* P2.
power: add *et non pour tant que lauctorite de rome ne lempeschast* P2.

63 **streite**: *tout droit* P2, *touz .ij.* P1, *ambo* LgA.

65 **of Ynde**: *dethiope* P2; see 133.1–17.

67 **Iewes**: *Indos* LgA.

68–9 **in the citee**: *pres de la cite* P2 *proxime ciuitatis* LgA.

70 **thei**: *dii* LgA.

75 **hele**: *salutis uestre* LgA.

78–9 **and apese . . . rebelles**: *uel certe rebelles pacatissimos inuenire* LgA, 'or find the rebels eager for peace'.

81 **For . . . knowest**: *affin que tu congnoisses* P2.

83 **canne**: *ne sceuent* P2.

85 **the ydoles**: *ces fantosmes* P2.

89 **is betwene you**: *huc nobiscum intrauit* LgA.
mydday: *heure de tierce* P2.

90 **of Medis**: *Indorum* LgA.

93 **thou shuldest folily leue hem**: *incautus fueris* LgA.

95 **of all**: *cras* LgA.

104 **his**: *ses* P2, *leurs* P1, *illorum* LgA.

105 **y . . . that**: only GiL.

107 **hys**: *ces* P2, *predictis* LgA.

109 **purchasours of sotill malice**: *pourchassoient aucun malice subtillement* P2, *subtiliter cogitare* LgA. *MED purchasour* gives only senses relating to acquisition; here it means 'contrivers', after *MED purchasen* sense 4 (b).

110 **kinge**: *dux* LgA.
Dere frendes: *oserez vous* S, *Si audetis* LgA.

111 **how . . . haue**: *que ilz ne pourront parler* P2.

113–14 **lete . . . dispised**: *nos per omnia imperitos probabis* LgA.

119 **will suffre**: *ne les laisserons* P2, *permittemus* LgA.

125–6 **full foule and**: only GiL.

127 **ringes and precious stones**: *gemmarum monilia pretiosa composita. Quicumque ergo alicuius rei cupit esse possessor non magno opere gestatorium sed ipsum quod gestatur expectat* LgA.

138–9 **Meue you not**: *non moriemini* LgA.

139–40 **bi the rentinge and bitinge**: *lacerati* LgA.

141 **rentin and**: only GiL.

143 **might**: *les laissassent* P2.

159 **whanne . . . wost**: *a lenfanter* P2.

169 **child**: add *quis auctor huius sceleris fuisset* LgA.

185 **crie**: add *per energumenos* LgA, those possessed by devils.

185–6 **What will men with us and to you**: *que veult on a nous et a vous* P2, *Quid nobis et uobis* LgA, 'what is the issue between us and you'.

190–1 **We . . . here**: *Oranda est dei misericordia ut et istos conuertat* LgA.

191 **peyne**: *palmam* LgA.

195 **and horrible**: only GiL.

200 **thunder and lighteninge**: *fouldre* P2.

201 **thunder**: *fouldre* P2.

211 **that**: add *ante mortem suam* LgA.
men: add *Vnde cantatur de eo: 'Ter denos mortuos fluctibus mersos humane uite reddidit'* LgA.

212 **Ierusalem**: *ecclesiam Iherosolimitanum* LgA.
yere: add *et C et XX annum ageret* LgA.
into the tyme: *au temps* P2.

213 **vnto the tyme that**: *cum* LgA.
councellour was: *consulte estoit* P2, *consularis* (. . .) *haberetur* LgA.

214 **and**[2]: add *au derrenier* P2.

216–17 **but . . . another**: *Et aucuns vraiement dient que a la verite ce ne fut pas celuy* P2.

217 **crosse**: add *et qui episcopus Ihierosolimitanus fuit* LgA.

218 **And . . . verily that**: *mais* P2.

220 **Cronicle**: add *Idem dicunt Ysidorus et Beda in suis chronicis* LgA.

222 **felithe the same**: *qui se reprent auoir sentu ne touche de ceste chose* P2, *hoc sensisse redarguit* LgA, 'goes back on having thought this'.

153 ST QUENTIN

Maggioni, ch. CLVI, p. 1088; Dunn-Lardeau, ch. 155, p. 1014.

1 **of the citee of Rome**: *et ciuis Romanus* LgA.

2 **of Damyans**: *damiens* P2, *Ambianensem* LgA.

9 **right longe**: *tres longuement* P2, *durisssime* LgA.

11 **hote lime**: i.e. quicklime.
galle: *saneue* P2, 'mustard'.

16 **water**: *flumen* LgA.

27 **place**: Here GiL, LgD, and some LgA MSS omit two miracles, Maggioni, 1089 (10–20).

154 ST EUSTACE

Maggioni CLVII, p. 1090; Dunn-Lardeau, ch. 156, p. 1015.

1 **called**: add *antea* LgA.

3 **abondonid**: *MED abandonen* gives no spellings with *-bon-*.

7 **clered and lighted and brought to**: *esclarci a* P2.

10–11 **grettest desert of the forest**: *la plus deserte forest* P2, *in siluam uastiorem* LgA.

13–14 **as . . . he**: *Quem cum totis uiribus insequeretur, ceruus* LgA.

14–15 **neyghid . . . see**: *sy approprioit* P2, *appropians* (. . .) *animo sedulus reuoluebat* LgA.

17 **withinne**: not in LgA.

20 **bi the grace of the**: *tui gratia* LgA, 'for your sake'.

26–7 **light adowne**: *in terram decidit* LgA.

36 **of not**: *et conuertis les foloyans* P2, 'and bring back those who stray'.

38 **hide**: *nuntiem ut et ipsi pariter tecum mundentur* LgA.

52–3 **before the figure**: *in faciem suam* LgA, 'on his face'.

62 **beholde**: *respicias* LgA.

64 **the**: add *et in gloriam pristinam restituam te* LgA.

69 **the . . . kepe**: not in LgA.

75 **sum . . . felawshipp**: *Quidam autem scelestes eius depredationem uidentes* LgA.

77 D addition **his soonde**, 'his ordinance'.

78 **al . . . goodes**: *nudus* LgA.

110 **and ascried hym**: *sy crioient apres le loup* P2.

111 **fro hurtynge**: *de ses dens sans bleceure* P2.

112 **tyliers**: add *de uno uico fuerunt et* LgA.

115 **shined**: *pollebam* LgA, 'was strong'.

122 **sitte**: add *mihi autem nihil horum remansit* LgA.

124 **children**: add *Illi uxor est relicta* LgA.

125 **and yeue to another**: not in LgA.

126–7 **so . . . visage**: *ne declinet cor meum in uerba malitie et eiciar a facie tua* LgA.

128 **the**: *quendam* LgA.

128–9 **where . . . bretheren**: *Filii autem eius in altero uico educati sunt nec se esse fratres sciebant* LgA, but following 130 *towne*.

131–2 **straunge men**: *celluy estrange homme* P2.

132 **she . . . corrupcion**: *mais la garda sans atoucher et il mourut mauuaisement* P2, *potius eam intactam dimittens uitam finiuit* LgA.

138–9 **had be . . . viages**: *Placido ministrauerant* LgA.

139 **towne . . . strete**: *rue* P2, *uicum* LgA.

140 **sawe hem**: add *venir des champs* P2.
knewe hem: add *ex incessu* LgA, 'by their gait'.

142 **saide**: add *Sire. jay veu ceulx cy sans esperance de les veoir iamais. lesquelz ont este aucuneffoys auecques moy* P2.

145 **shalt resseiue**: *recouureras* P2.

164 **clothed him**: add *de nobles vestemens* P2.
emperoure: add *et errerent .xv. iours* P2.

166–7 **clipped . . . ioye**: *le baisa* P2.

168–9 **restabled . . . knighthode**: *restabli a la maistrise de cheualerie* P2.

173 **to hym**: only GiL.

178 **he wept**: *sy plora* P2, so changed to *si ly plurent* with *ly plu* in another hand over erasure S, *si li plurent* P1, *sibi* (. . .) *placuissent* LgA.

179 **the furst . . . bataile**: *inter primos conuiuas suos* LgA.

181 **his wiff duelled in an ostrie**: *sa femme demouroit pour hostelerie* (*poure hosteliere* P1) P2, *uxor sua pauper hospita manebat* LgA.

183 **what she was**: *que ce fut elle* P2, *quod mater sua esset* LgA.

188 **another**: add *mineur de moy* P2.

191 **moder**: add *nescio quomodo* LgA.

199 **Forsothe**: *par dieu* P2.

216 **corrupcion**: add *qui euz de moy .ii. filz agapit et theospic* P2.

218–19 **tho . . . tribulacion**: *les tourmentez* P2.

230–1 **clipped . . . ioye**: *les baisierent et accolerent forment* P2, *amplectentes eos super eorum collum plurimum fleuerunt et crebrius eos osculabantur* LgA.

231–2 **were . . . ioy**: *sesioy* P2.

235–6 LgD and LgA put the victory before the finding.

244 **a place**: *arena* LgA.

246 **fro hem**: add *humiliter* LgA.

246–7 **ordeine . . . fire**: *embraser .j. beuf de cuiure* P2.

252 **was atamid with the**: *ne toucha au* P2.
fire: add *ne le feu ne toucha oncques a nulle chose diceulx* P2.

255 La ends: *Here endith the lyfe of Eustas oþerwise called Placidas as hit is writt in Legenda Aurea.*

155 ALL SAINTS

Maggioni, ch. CLVIII, p. 1099; Dunn-Lardeau, ch. 157, p. 1023.

Four reasons for establishment of the feast are listed in 1–4, A for the dedication of a temple; B to compensate for omissions (to honour saints without individual feasts); C to expiate negligence; D to facilitate the granting of prayers:

A Building and later Christian consecration of the Pantheon and establishment of the feast 5–59.

B To honour saints:
- (i) to recognize saints without individual feast days 60–71;
- (ii) William d'Auxerre gives six (wrongly *.v.* in GiL) reasons to celebrate saints 72–4: (a) to worship God through the saints 74–7; (b) to help us in our weakness 77–84; (c) to increase our certainty of hope 84–9; (d) to give us examples to follow 89–92; (e) to exchange with them a place of celebration 92–6; (f) to obtain honour for ourselves 96–101;
- (iii) John Damascene gives reasons to honour saints and relics 102–6: (a) they are friends and sons of God and can lead us to him 106–12; (b) five reasons to value saints' relics, in that they comprise 113–15: (*i*) storehouses of God 116–17; (*ii*) Christ's temples in whom God dwells 117–27; (*iii*) jars of spiritual ointment 127–34; (*iv*) wells of divinity 135–9; (*v*) limbs of the Holy Ghost 139–48.

C We have neglected apostles, martyrs, confessors, virgins 149–65:
- (i) apostles: (a) pre-eminent in dignity 166–75; (b) supreme in power 175–80; (c) supreme in holiness 180–8; (d) the most profitable 188–93;
- (ii) martyrs: (a) bloodless martyrdom 194–208; (b) their profitability to us 209–44; (c) their constancy 244–52;
- (iii) confessors: (a) confession of heart is taken together with (b) confession by mouth 253–78, with subdivisions at 255, 264, 270, and 275; (c) confession by works 278–85;
- (iv) virgins: (a) spouses of God 286–91; (b) companions of angels 291–5; (c) nobler than other Christians 296–301; (d) have precedence over the married 301–23; (e) have many privileges 324–7.

D To facilitate the granting of prayers 328–39.

1 **was**: *fuisse uidetur* LgA.

2 **of a**: *cuiusdam* LgA, i.e. the Pantheon.
suplement of defauutes: *espier* (*souplier* P1) *les faultes* P2, *omissorum suppletionem* LgA, i.e. of other saints from the calendar.

5 **of a**: *cuiusdam* LgA.

6 **sawe that thei**: not in LgA.

7 **high**: *grant* P2.

9 **right in**: i.e. directly towards.

10 **ordeyned**: add *ut aiunt* LgA.

12 **warnyng**: *demonstrant* P2.

14–15 **turne hem**: *soustenoient* P2, *soumetoient* P1 *subiugabant* LgA.

18–19 **all the ydoles might not be in that temple**: *omnia ydola templum ibi habere non poterant* LgA, i.e. in Rome.

19 **right a grete**: *vng greigneur* P2, *mirabilius* LgA.

22 **goddes**: add *a pan, quod est totum, et theos, deus* LgA.

25–6 **all her enemyes**: *toutes gens* P2.

27 **was caste bi a spere**: *fut gette par lespere* P2, *sphericum iacitur* LgA. The sense here required for *bi* is 'in the form of', which is not, however, recorded by *MED*.

29 **multitude of the voydinge of the erthe withinne**: *la leeur de la vuidange dedens* P2, *latitudo testudinis* LgA, 'width of the vault-span'; the English appears to mean 'the large amount of the removal of the earth within'.

30 **not sustenable**: *non soustenable* P2, *insustentabilis* LgA; *MED* records *sustenable* only in the sense 'vegetable (as opposed to animal or mineral)', with two citations from *Lambeth SSecr* a1500 (?a1425). The DH2A1A2 variant *sustentable*, 'having ability to support something physically', is not recorded by *MED*, but the related noun *sustentacioun* is substantially attested.

30–1 **shewed a litell vpon the grounde**: *supra terram* (. . .) *aliquantulum processissent* LgA.

31 **the creues within the erthe**: *le creux de dedens de terre* P2, *totum intus terra* LgA; either *the*[2] is an early scribal error for *withe*, or s.w. visualized a hole in the ground beneath the building.

37 **a pyne tree**: *vng pin* P2, *pineam* LgA, 'pine cone'.
in an high place: *in summitate* LgA.

39–40 **in that pine tree**: *dedens ce pin* P2, *in hac* LgA.

42 **the place where it was**: *apertura* LgA.

45 **.vjC.**: *DCV* LgA.

49 **martires**: add *ac locum sancte Marie ad martyres appelauit* LgA.
she: i.e. the temple.
of the peple: *du temple* P2, a *populo* LgA.

55 **vendeged**: 'gathered (of grapes for wine)'; *MED* has only one citation for the verb, *s.v. vendengen*, for a1500.

60–1 **thinges . . . vndone**: *omissorum* LgA.

66 H1 *curtnes* is not in MED, and *court* adj. is rare.

67 **that is sette in**: *que* (. . .) *preponitur* LgA.

68 **founde**: *ascriptus* LgA.

70 **Ierome the pope**: *ecclesia rationabiliter* LgA.

71 **all togederes**: *generalment et ensemble* P2.

72 **.v.**: *sex* LgA.

74 **the Godhede**: *la diuine mageste* P2.

75 **a seint**: *aux sains* P2.

76 **he[2]**: *qui* P2.

81 **fourthe**: *III* LgA; 3 Kgs. 1: 30 in fact refers to Bathsheba and the promise to her son Solomon rather than the place-name Beersheba, meaning 'well of seven'.

83 **sone**: add *cest a dire leglise cheuauchant* P2, i.e. the Church Militant.

85 **to hem**: *nobis* LgA.

86 **sollempnite[2]**: *seurte* P2.

89 **ne may not be lessed ne**: only GiL.

89–90 **for . . . folowinge**: i.e. to give an example for us to follow.

92–3 **the dette of entrechaunginge of neighburhede**: *le deu dentre-changee voisinete* P2, *debitum mutue uicissitudinis* LgA, 'duty of mutual exchange'.

103 **in a chapitre**: *en vng chapitre* P2, *cap. VII* LgA.

107 **God[2]**: add *heredes dei et duces nostri. Et ponit istas auctoritates: de primo Ioh. XIII: 'Iam non dicam uos seruos, sed amicos etc.'; de secondo Ioh. I: 'Dedit eis potestatem filios dei fieri* LgA.

secounde: *tertio* LgA.

107–8 **secounde . . . Romaynes**: *tertio Rom. VIII* LgA.

110–11 **might . . . vndedlynesse**: *par mortalite te menra au roy* P2, *mortali te regi adduceret* LgA.

111–12 **That is . . . for the**: *Duces igitur humani totius generis qui ad deum pro nobis interpellationes faciunt nonne honorandum est? Vtique quidem honorandum templa erigentes deo et eorum memoriam uenerantes* LgA.

112 **of[1]**: *et* P2.

113 **bodies**: add *Et celluy iehan damacien met .iiij. raisons et vng autre* (*Augustinus* LgA) *adiouste la quinte par lesquelles il est manifeste la precieusete des corps sains ou de leurs reliques* P2.

114 **of Goddis**: *de dieu* P2; combination of 'of' with use of the genitive inflection is unusual in GiL.

115 **alabastre**: *alebastre* P2, *alabastrum* LgA, 'a box for unguents', also at 128 below. *MED s.v. alabastre* offers only the sense 'alabaster', a translucent form of gypsum, of which no doubt the boxes were generally made. *MED* also records *alabastrum*, with sense (b) 'an alabaster container for chrism or ointment', with only one citation.

spirituel: *precieux* P2, *spiritualis* LgA.

of lyff: *de vie* P2, *deuine* P1, *diuini* LgA.

membres: *organum* LgA, 'instrument', also at 139.

116 **For**: *Primo enim* LgA.

116–17 **bi whom . . . all the worlde**: *et purs aournemens* P2, *unde dicit: 'Hii enim promptuaria dei pura cenacula facti sunt'* LgA, 'These storehouses of God are made into pure dining-rooms'.

120 **you**: LgA develops the quotation (I Cor. 3 ff.), Maggioni, 1103 (61–2).

124–5 **it . . . grace**: *prestat uarietas uiuentium gratiarum* LgA, 'but it comes from the variety of graces of the living'.

126 **ferst**: add *pro tempore deicit et* LgA.

127 **understondithe euerlastinge edefienge**: *ediffie pardurable entendement* P2.

128 **it is saide**: i.e. by Damascenus.

128–30 **An oynement of swete sauour comithe of hymself, and this same yeuithe the reliques of seintes**: *Vnguentum boni odoris ex se manans sanctorum reliquie tribuentes et nullus hoc decredat* LgA, 'the relics themselves of saints exuding ointment giving off a sweet smell, no one can discredit this fact'.

136 **wellys of diuinite**: *fontes diuini* LgA.

137 **prescience**: *precieusete* P2, *pacience* S, *precience* P1, *presentia* LgA, 'presence'.

137–9 **and bene to us welles of heuene. Oure Lorde Ihesu Crist yeuithe to the reliques of his seintes benifices in mani maners** *et nous sont fontaines de salut nostre seigneur ihesu crist donna* (*donne* P1) *aux reliques de ses sains donner* (*arouser* P1) *benefices en moult de manieres* P2, *Fontes nobis salutares dominator Christus sanctorum suorum prebuit reliquias multiformia beneficia irrigantes* LgA, 'Our Lord Christ presented to us in the relics of his saints wells of salvation flowing with many benefits'.

139 **membres**: *organum* LgA, as 115 above.

143 **a membre of his owne**: *quibusdam organis* LgA.

143–4 **Ye seken**: *An* (. . .) *queritis* LgA.

147 **men . . . orgones**: *homme soit fait membre* P2, *homo* (. . .) *sit organum* LgA.

148 **bodies**: *corporalibus labiis* LgA.

151 **it**: add *sepe* LgA.
that we shulde do: only GiL.

153 **sympely and**: *aucune chose plus* P2, *sanctorum aliquid* LgA.
at the lest: *touteffois* P2, not in LgA.

154 **and amende . . . ourselff**: only GiL.

156 **he**: i.e. the sermon.

160 **of seintes**: add *in hac sancta obseruatione soluatur. Notandum autem quod quadruplex est differentia sanctorum* LgA.

163 **these**: add *secundum Rabanum* LgA.

168 **soueraynte**: *preeminentia* LgA.

169 **of Cristes peple**: *cheuauchant* P2.
accessours: *accesseurs* P2, *assessores* LgA; *MED s.v. assessour* n. 1 does not record this spelling, and the definition, 'an adviser of a ruler, lord or magistrate in matters of law', seems inappropriate to the context; perhaps 'assistant', or 'member of the court'.

174–5 **to the wey of trouthe**: *ad uiam et per uiam* (. . .) *que ducit ad ciuitatem* LgA.

175 **After**: *Secundo* LgA.

177 **aposteles**: add *super naturam ut eam curarent* LgA.

178 **meue**: *muer* P2.

185 **Crisostome**; add *sus mathieu* P2.

187 **bemys**: add *sicomme la rose est sentue en son oudeur. sicomme le feu est veu en ses estincelles* P2.

188–9 **is the bounte of moche profit**: *in efficacia utilitatis* LgA.

189 **Austin**: add *parlant des apostres* P2, add *ad Volusianum loquens de apostolis* LgA.

190 **porest**: *plus petis* P2, *paucissimis* LgA.

191 **right suete**: *cultissima* LgA, variant *dulcissima*.

192 **wisdom**: *peritias* LgA, 'skills'.

193 **be ioyned**: *sont soubzmis* P2.

194 **excellence**: *dignitas et excellentia* LgA.

195–6 **in mani maneres, profitabeli, stably, multiplyingly**: *en moult de manieres. proffitablement fermement multepliement* P2, *multipliciter, utiliter et constanter. Multipliciter* LgA. Vignay obscured the pattern by translating the first word as *en moult de manieres*, implying that it belonged to the previous clause. A section should start at 196 *Multiplyingli*, followed by 209 *profitable* and 244–5 *ferme and stable*.

197 **marterdomes**: add *sine sanguine* LgA.

199 **wisdom in pacience**: *saigesce en pourete* P2, *largitas in paupertate* LgA.

200 **and chastite yn youthe**: *et chaaste de veuue en sa ieunesse* S, *et uidua, castitas in iuuentute* LgA. For *Tobye* see Tob. 1: 19–20; the widow, omitted by s.w. following her misplacement by Vignay, must relate to 3 Kgs. 17 or Mark 12: 42–3.

201 **other**: only GiL.

202–8 In LgA these three martyrdoms are 202 *patientia aduersorum*, 204 *compassio afflictorum*, and *dilectio inimicorum* after 206 *mynde and*, the latter omitted by LgD and GiL. Vignay, followed by GiL, combined the first two by inserting *et auon*, GiL *and haue*, before *pitie/compassion*, making it part of the quotation, and omitted the third subheading.

204 **will**: *courage* P2, *animo* LgA, ending the *patientia* subsection.

204–5 **that be in sorw and tribulacion**: *des tormentez* P2, *afflictorum* LgA.

209 **Secoundely**: *Secondement* P2, *Secundo* LgA, referring to 195 **profitabeli** (*utiliter*); see note above.
marterdom is profitable: *cest profitablement* P2.
the[2]: *ceulx* P2.

230 **made**: add *la condition que tu prins* P2.

230–1 **wherto . . . upon the**: *a qui tu donna nom* P2, i.e. are enrolled.

232 **knighthode**: add *Hec Chrysostomus*.

233 **ye**: *ilz* P2.

241 **victories**: add *et triumphos* LgA.

242 **.vjC.**: *.vjC. mil* P2.

242–3 **praied for his enemyes**: *ueniam deprecatur* LgA.

244 **to us . . . defende**: *non* P2, not in LgA.

LgA adds: *Apostolus Paulus CCLXXVI sibi dicit in naui animas condonatas, et postquam resolutus cepit esse cum Christo, tunc ora clausurus est?*

244–5 **is . . . sufferinge**: *cest ferment* P2, *constanter* LgA; see note to 195.

246 **and rightwisnesse**: only GiL.

247 **braundisshinge . . . fightinge**: *brandy par* (add *la* P1) *vertu de dieu combatant* P2, *dei pugnantis uibrata uirtute, que* (i.e. the sword) *bella fecit* LgA.

251–2 **the toren . . . yrins**: *les crians vainquirent les ongles par leurs membres desrompues* P2, *laniantes ungulas laniata membra uicerunt* LgA.

256 **Crisostme**: add *super Matheum* LgA.

257–8 **faithe of . . . confession**: *foy. confession de cuer* S, LgA as GiL.

261 **the rote of**: not in LgA.

263 **of herte apere not in the mouthe**: *marcidata fuerit oris* LgA, 'is shrivelled in the mouth'.

264 **the confession**: *fides* LgA.

265 **it suffice**: *prodest* LgA.

266 **that . . . prest**: only GiL.

266–8 **thanne . . . mouthe**: so omitting *Crist* P2, *ergo et infideli in hypocrisi confiteri Christum prodest, etiamsi corde non credat* LgA.

269–70 **right . . . leuithe**: *il ne proffite point a toy qui le crois* P2.

271–2 **be not confessed**: *ne le confesses mie* P2.

273 **thou . . . God**: *tu* (add *ne* P1) *confesses ihesu crist deuant dieu* P2, *confessus non fuerit te coram deo* LgA.

279 **God²**: add *par euure* P2.

280 **Ierome**: add *in originali super illud: 'Confitentur se nosse deum'* LgA.

290–1 **hole . . . corrupcion**: *entiere sans corrupcion* P2, *innupta* LgA.

291–2 **felawshipped . . . and**: only GiL.

292 **aungeles**: add *Ambrosius:* LgA.

296 **other good cristen men**: *fidelibus uniuersis* LgA.

298 **ioy bounden**: *yoye lyee* P2, *leta indoles* LgA, 'of joyful disposition'.

300 **the holinesse**: *a la sainctete* P2.

303 **bi comparison multipliengly**: *par comparaison multipliable* P2, *ex multiplici comparatione* LgA.

304–5 **the mynde . . . Uirginite**: not in P2, in LgA.

305 **Uirginite chesithe more fairer that is rather**: *Virginite esleu plus noble* P2, *Generosius eligit* LgA.

306 **the nombre of dedli bodies**: *mortalite de char* P2, *numerum mortalium* LgA.

307 **Forsothe**: only GiL.

308 **with purete**: only GiL.

309 **peynefull**: only GiL.

gretnesse: *MED* gives only one citation for the sense 'pregnancy', for a1500(?c1450).

311–12 **but plenteuous . . . with children**: add *et celle du mary et de la dame remplist la terre* P2, *sed fecunda mater filiorum gaudiorum de marito te, domine.' Illa filiis replet terram, ista celum* LgA.

314 **labour and besinesse**: *curieusite* P2.

315 **rest and quietenesse**: *repoz* P2, *quietis* LgA.
Gilbert saithe: not in LgD, *Gilibertus* LgA; Boureau (p. 1441 n. 55) has identified this as an error for Hildebert of Lavardin.

320 **Continence in mariage**: *continence* P2, *Illa* LgA, referring to 319 *wedding*, LgA *nuptias*.

321 **Eustas**: *Eustochium* LgA.

322 **weddingis**: add *sed quia mihi uirgines generant* LgA.

323 **of the quarrei precious stones**: *de concauo margaritam* LgA.

325 **crowne that is called auriole**: *coronam aureolam* LgA, 'golden crown'. *MED* defines *aureole* as 'the crown or halo of a saint; esp. the reward of martyrs, virgins and preachers'. It is cited for *Hali Meiðhad* Titus MS *c.*1225, where it is regarded as a Latin word (*Auriole ihaten o latines ledene*), and then not till *c.*1450.

327 **whereuer he go**: *tousiours* P2.

328–9 **oure praiers**: *orationum nostrarum impetrationem* LgA.

329 **bi that that**: *pource que aussy comme* P2.

334 **of this day**: only GiL.

340 **for us to praie**: *a prier pour nous* P2.

341 **befell**: *contigisse narratur* LgA.

342 **clerke**: *custos* LgA.

344 **come**: *reuint* P2.

345–6 **sawe . . . thought**: *la vit vne vision. car il* P2, *extra se rapitur et ecce* LgA.

350 **hem, hem**: *Huic* LgA.

352–3 **auncien men (. . .) full worshipfulli**: *anciens hommes honnorables* S, *uenerabilium seniorum* LgA.

359 **this clerke**: *predictum custodem* LgA.

360 **in**^{1}: *qui luy exposa* P2.

371 **for her brede**: not in LgD, *auxilium* LgA.

373–4 **that were foryete . . . frendes**: *desquelz les amis ne tenoient compte* P2.

376 **that**: add *saltem* LgA.

377 **temperell**: not in LgA.

378 **speciall**: *espirituelz* P2, *specialia* LgA.

156 ALL SOULS

Maggioni, ch. CLIX, p. 1113; Dunn-Lardeau, ch. 158, p. 1036.

The structure of the chapter is outlined in 10–11 as A *purgacion* and B *suffrages*:

A *purgacion* has three parts 12–14:
- I Who are to be purged:
  - (i) those who died without fulfilling enjoined penance 16–26, incomplete in GiL because of a substantial lacuna;
  - (ii) those whose penance was inadequate through the priest's negligence 26–34, starting during the lacuna;
  - (iii) those punished according to their deserts 34–47;
- II by whom: the 'wicked' angels 48–66;
- III where: purgatory contains five 'places' 67–74:
  - (i) for lighter punishment 75–7;
  - (ii) for earlier deliverance 78–108;
  - (iii) for our instruction 109–31;
  - (iv) for sin committed in a particular place 132–45;
  - (v) in answer to a saint's prayer 146–8.

B *suffrages* deals with three questions 149–51:
- I varieties of suffrage 152–5:
  - (i) prayers 156–92;
  - (ii) almsgiving 193–226;
  - (iii) offering of mass 227–77;
  - (iv) fasting 278–304.

  Additional passage on value of indulgences 305–11.
- II for whom suffrages are made (misnumbered *thridde* in GiL) has four sections 312–16:
  - (i) who will profit? 317–22: (a) the good 323–56, (b) the bad 357–64, (c) the middling 365–71.

  Additional passage on periods allotted for suffrages 371–83.
  - (ii) how will they profit 384–5: (a) by unity with the Church 385–7, (b) by dignity 387–90, (c) by necessity 390–1;
  - (iii) will all profit equally? 392–7;
  - (iv) how will they know they are being prayed for 398–9, divided into four (but given in 399 as *.iij.* GiL, *tribus* LgA): (a) divine revelation 399–400, (b) revelation by angels 401–3, (c) revelation by newly arriving souls 403–5, (d) by experiencing reduction of punishment 406–8.
- III about those by whom suffrages are made 409–end.

3 **speciall**: *esperituel* P2, *specialia* LgA.

4 **in the yle of Vulcan**: *apud Vulcanum* LgA.

8–9 **all chirches**: *tous ses monstiers* P2, *suis monasteriis* LgA.

16 **do**: *completa* LgA.

17 **thei**: *silz* P2.

26 **ponisshed**: add *igne* LgA.
purgatorie: add *Se par aduenture aucuns de ses amis ne prennent a faire satisfation pour luy* P2, add *nisi forte eorum satisfactio ab aliquibus caris suis perficienda assumatur* LgA.
Here GiL omits Maggioni, 1114–15 (end of 11 to middle of 25), Dunn-Lardeau, 1036–7, skipping from *en purgatoire* to *en purgatoire*, the second of which is preceded by *Et se ceulx cy nont eu tres grant contriccion qui supplie a ce ilz acompliront* P2, *Hii enim nisi magnitudo contritionis suppleat totum* (. . .) *complebunt* LgA.
litell: *moins* P2.

28–9 **for . . . abide**: *que aucun pechie ne demeure* P2.

30 **enioined**: by the priest, as had been made clear in the omitted passage.

32 **ioy and glorie**: *gloire* P2.

33 **of synnes**: *totius culpe* LgA.

34 **might of the Godhede**: *diuine puissance* P2, *diuine iusticie* LgA.

GiL omits Maggioni, 1115 (31–4), Dunn-Lardeau, 1038.

The thridde: this relates to 16 *the furst*, the beginning of 'the second' having been omitted (see 26 above).

37 **to her richesses**: not in LgA.

38 **to her children**: only GiL.

39 **and tho be purged in purgatorie**: *illus tribus significantur* LgA, i.e. wood, hay, stubble.

40 **or shorte**: only GiL.

48 **turmented or ponisshed**: *purgiez* P2.

52 **good cristen sowles**: *bonos et* (. . .) *malos* LgA.

54 **counsaile hem and stere hem**: *les ammonestent* P2.

56 **thei knowe . . . glorie**: *ilz actendent certainement la gloire aduenir. car ilz ont certainete dauoir gloire* P2.

57 **in the cuntrei of ioye**: *ou pays* P2, *in patria* LgA.

58 **that lyuen**: *qui sont vifz* P2, *qui sunt in uia* LgA.
ioye: *pais de gloire* P2.

59 **withoute ani doute . . . lese it**: *sans actente et sans paour* (add *quia nec*

ipsam futuram expectant LgA) *car ilz lont presentement. sique ilz ne la doubtent jamais perdre* P2.

62 **and**: *cum* LgA.

62–3 **neuer . . . more**: *de cetero se peccare non posse cognoscunt* LgA; i.e. although confirmed in free will, they know they are incapable of sin.

64 **bothe almes and praiers**: *suffragia* LgA.

69 **mani**: *plurium* LgA.

70 **eyre**: add *ou* P2.
brennynge rounde place: *torrida zona* LgA.

72 **diuers**: add *ames* P2.

73 **hasti**: *celeriorem* LgA.

78 **after**: *secundo* LgA.
hasti: *celeriorem* LgA.

80–2 **how . . . comfort**: s.w. has reordered this passage, putting the description of St Thebaud's affliction first and expanding, e.g. adding 81–2 *that there might . . . medicines*.
Seint Thebaud: LgA gives the name in conjunction with the fishermen, *quidam piscatores beati Theobaldi*. Boureau and Maggioni take it as the name of an unidentified place, leaving the bishop anonymous. The story as given by Odo of Cheriton, fable 80, relates to *Dominus Theodosius, Sediensis episcopus*, and takes place *super ripam Rhodani*. In neither case has closer identification proved possible; he is perhaps St Theobald, bishop of Vienne (near Lyon) 970–1000.

97 **masse**: add *illa die* LgA.

100 **bi drede**: not in LgA.

101 **in the morw**: only GiL.

104–5 **for the chirche . . . ouer hym**: only GiL.

109 **instruccion**: *enfermete* P2, *instructionem* LgA.

110 **deth . . . bodi**: *ceste mortelle vie* P2, *uitam* LgA.
bodi: *sicomme* P2, *sicut* (. . .) *legitur* LgA.

110–11 **Hit . . . Parys**: *sicomme il aduint a paris* P2, *sicut Parisius contigisse legitur* LgA.

111 **the chaunter**: *cantor* LgA, i.e. Petrus Cantor.

111–12 **so as the chaunter . . . deie and the chauntour**: *Magister enim Silo, ut ait cantor Parisiensis, quendam suum scholarem socium egrotantem* LgA. *the chauntour* at 112, 116, 118, 130 should therefore have been LgA's *magister Silo*, for whose story Petrus Cantor is the source; but 123 and 126 *maister* have survived through Vignay. Maggioni (2007), 1687 n. 65 suggests that

Silo may be for Serlo of Wilton, d. 1181, on whom see Thomson, 'Serlo of Wilton'. A 12th-c. *logicus parisiensis magister Silo* is referred to in Paris MS BN lat. 3557.

115 **forwretin**: 'written over', not recorded by *MED*.

116 **chaunter**: *le saint* P2, *magistro* LgA.

119 **that y bere upon me**: only GiL.
melstone: *turrim* LgA.

121 **sophistiqes**: *MED sophistik*, 'deceitful', has only two entries, for a1500; *sophistical* and *sophisticalli* are recorded somewhat earlier.
that is . . . deceiuables: not in LgA.

121–2 **the skynne . . . bere**: *les peaux sont legieres* P2, *Porro flamma ignis qua cooperta est pelles sunt delicate et uarie quas ferebam* LgA , 'the flames of fire that cover them are the subtle and varying furs that I used to wear.'

123–4 **trowed . . . made of**: *tenoit celle peine assez legiere* P2.

130 **chaunter**: *magister* LgA.

131 **lefte**: *deliberauit deserere* LgA.
religion: add *unde mane scholaribus congregatis hos uersos composuit:*

Linguo choax ranis, cra coruis uanaque uanis.
Ad logicam pergo que mortis non timet ergo.

Et sic seculum deserens ad religionem confugit LgA.

132 **in places**: *ou lieu* P2.

135 **diuerse tymes**: *volentiers* P2, not in LgA.

139–40 **Y . . . holi**: *Iste panis sanctus est; ego autem manducare non possum* LgA.

141 **for to serue**: not in LgA.

144 **sacrifice**: add *pour luy* P2.

147 **purgatorie**: add *in terra* LgA.

148 **before in this place**: *par dessus en son lieu* P2, *post festum sancti Benedicti* LgA, i.e. 48 Patrick, pp. 223–7.

149 **thridde**: *secundum* LgA; this relates to the division at 10–11.

151 **to whom**: *pro quibus* LgA.
for whom: *par qui* P2.

154 **good folke**: *bons* P2, *fidelium* LgA.

154–5 **masses singinge**: *salutaris hostie immolatio* LgA.

155 **and fastinge**: not in LgD, *et ieiunorum obseruatio* LgA.

156 **And . . . þat**: *Quod primum genus suffragiorum, scilicet* LgA.
good men: *amis* P2.

163–5 **his bere . . . hole**: *vng demoniacle atoucha a sa domatique qui estoit dessus la biere il fut tantost gary* P2.

166 **of Campane**: *de capuenne* P2, *Capuanus* LgA.

169 **and so holy**: not in LgA.

175 **after**: *post paucos dies* LgA.

177 **and**: add *de ce* P2.

179 **to . . . feest**: *dune grant solemnite* P2 *in magna sollempnitate* (. . .) *ad matutinas* LgA.

180 **that**: add *ne nous donne nulle messe et sy* P2.

187 **for all cristen soules**: not in P2, *pro defunctis* LgA.

189 **for to haue be slaine**: not in LgA.

191 **that used to praie for hem**: *uiriliter* LgA.

192 **abasshed and full of fere**: *espouentez* P2.

195 **collacion**: since *MED* records *collage* only as an alternative spelling for *college*, the H2A1A2 variant *collage* is a previously unrecorded word with the same meaning as *MED collacion* sense 6, 'a collection of money or goods', which in turn has only two citations.

196 **.xij.**: add *mil* P2.

197 **dede**: add *etc.* P2, add *iuste et religiose de resurrectione cogitans* LgA.
auaile: add *aux trespassez* P2.

200–1 **that . . . sperit**: *ce qui en auoit este fait* P2.

202 **foule . . . stinke**: *puant et obscur* P2, *niger ac caliginosus et fetidus* LgA.

206 **brige . . . that**: *erat in predicto ponte probatio* LgA.
of the ministres: *iniustorum* LgA. L has corrected to *that were vnrightwis*, and for 207 *sum of that other* L reads *þe rightwis*.

207 **that horrible lake**: *ce noir fleuue puant* P2.
sum of that other: *iusti uero* LgA.

209 **sawe**: *se uidisse asseruit* LgA.
withoute the brigge: *deorsum positum* LgA.

215 **as**: *daussy grant auctorite comme* P2, 'as confidently as'.

217 **and so he hinge**: only GiL.

218–19 **ther . . . downe**: *aucuns tres noirs* (*teterrimis* LgA) *hommes qui se leuerent de fleuue le tirerent jus par les cuisses* P2.

219 **faire**: add *et tres blans* P2.

221 **awoke of his traunce**: *retourna a son corps* P2.

229 **his Dyaloges**: *.iiij.*[e] *liure de son dialogue* P2.

231 **ful sore**: only GiL.

237 **apered**: add *au* xxx^{e} *iour* P2.

239 **thanked be God**: only GiL.

250 **hym**: add *ou elle aloit* P2, *sui itineris causam* LgA.

253 **withinne the roche**: *dessoubz luy* P2.

258 **faire and**: only GiL.
ouer . . . is: only GiL.

263 **that he . . . defauute**: only GiL.

267–8 **And . . . Gramele**: in LgA this concludes the preceding narrative, and is followed by *Gregorius etiam refert . . .* LgA.

269 **was fallen**: add *par tourment* P2, add *naufragium perpessus* LgA.
praied for hym and: only GiL.

276 **sange**: *sacrifia* P2.

276–7 **that was to hym so gret comforte**: only GiL.

284 **clerke and**: not in LgA.

291–2 **in as moche as she might**: only GiL.

292 **the seruise of God**: *en leglise les oroisons* P2, *orantes in ecclesia* LgA.

294–5 **exorted her and**: only GiL.

296 **in no wise**: only GiL.

298 **laye sore**: *len hastoit en plorant* P2, 'tearfully urged her'.

299 **her sone sent**: *filium destinauit* LgA.

301 **so horribly that she deyed for fere**: *et elle mourust pour lorriblete deulx* P2, *quorum horrore ac timore mortua est* LgA.

303 **herde**: *uidit* LgA.

306 **noble man**: *strenuum militem* LgA.

307 **to the Abigeys**: *in terra Albiensi* LgA.

309 **al a lente**: *par vne quarantaine* P2, 'for forty days'.

312 **thridde**: *secundum* LgA.

319 **good**^{2}: add *aut mediocriter mali* LgA.

322 **clensynge**: *expiationes, pro mediocriter malis propitiationes* LgA.

323 **to heuene**: only GiL.

324 **peynes**: *feu* P2.

328–9 **and purged**: only GiL.

331–2 **make or do**: *feroit* P2.

332 **for**^{2}: add *sicut dicit Augustinus* LgA.

334 **be in purgatorie or none**: *ne soit vole en paradis* P2, *euolasset* LgA.

336 **after that that Dauid saithe**: *secundum illud* LgA.

338 **suche maner**: *Hiis tribus generibus* LgA.

342 **Luke**: add *IV* LgA, in fact 3: 21.

345 **withoute ani lettinge**: *tantost* P2.

346 **dedly**: add *et ueniali* LgA.

348 **Aposteles**: add *VIII* LgA.
I sawe: *Je voy* P2.

350 **hennes**: add *et si aliqua cremabilia habebant, omnia falce martyrii resecantur* LgA.

351 **Apocalipse**: *Apoc. IV* LgA.

354 **haue . . . veyne**: *nec uenialia admiserunt* LgA.

355–6 **to these .iij. maner of peple**: not in LgA.

357 **fire**: *baratrum* LgA, 'abyss'.

360 **a fende in helle**: *le dyable* P2.

362 **deliueraunce**: add *ut scilicet ad ipsis penis liberentur* LgA.

363 **grace**: *mitigationem, ut scilicet pena in eis mitigetur uel diminuatur, nec quantum ad suspensionem, ut scilicet ad tempus uel ad horam eorum dampnatio suspendatur, nec quantum ad fortificationem, ut scilicet ad tolerandum leuius roborentur, quantum enim ad aliquod horum* LgA.
as Iob saithe: not in LgA.

365 **good**: add *et mali dicuntur* LgA.

368 **of her frendes**: not in LgA.

370 **these be tho to whom onli**: i.e. only to these.

372 **.iij. dayes**: *triplicem numerum dierum maxime* LgA.
annuel: add *Et la raison de ces .iij. est assignee ou liure* (add *mitrali* LgA) *de loffice* P2, i.e. Sicardus of Cremona, *Mitrale*.

373 **hele**: *salu* P2, *sabbatum* LgA.

374 **by .vij. dayes**: *en leur vie quilz ont demenee par .vij. iours* P2, *in uita* (. . .), *que per septem dies ducitur* LgA.

375 **complexiones**: *humoribus, scilicet sanguis, melanconia, flemma et collera* LgA.

376 **uertues**: add *scilicet memoria, intellectus et sapientia siue uoluntas* LgA.

378 **Trinite**: add *et* LgA.

378–9 **it may . . . and**: only GiL.

384 **yef**: *pourquoy* P2.

386–7 **binethe laboringe**: *cheuauchant* P2, 'militant'.

397 **haue most nede**: *in equali uel in maiori necessitate existunt* LgA.

409–10 **wheþer . . . good:** *par lesquelz* (add *ces* P1) *suffrages sont fais* P2.

416 **so bisely**: only GiL.

419 **of me**: *daucune chose* P2, *de aliquo* LgA.

421 **violed**: *violay* P2; *MED* does not record this verb either under this spelling or the H1 spelling with initial *f*; H1 spells it with *v* below at 434.

422 **cope**[1]: add *laquelle est sur moy* P2.

435–6 **ne left . . . fall**: *uel aliquis eius amicus aliquibus etiam malis aliqua dispensanda reliquisset. Que tamen continuo dispensare debent ne sibi contingat* LgA, 'or some friend of his left some things to be dispensed by some bad people, who ought, however, to dispense them at once lest it should happen to them . . .'.

437 **archebisshop of Reynes**: not in LgA; a *Historia de vita Caroli Magni et Rolandi*, was formerly attributed to Turpin and is sometimes known as the *Pseudo-Turpin Chronicle*.

438 **Grete**: add *cum Mauris pugnaturus* LgA.

445 **nowe hast . . . me**: *tu nen es pas quicte* P2, *impune non feres* LgA.

157 FOUR CROWNED MARTYRS

Maggioni, ch. CLX, p. 1130; Dunn-Lardeau, ch. 159, p. 1051.

1 **Marters**: only GiL.

6, 12–13 **vnder the names**: *sub nominibus* LgA; i.e. in conjunction with.

6–7 **.v. . . . Simplicien**: it seems s.w. copied these five names correctly from LgD, but an early copyist having omitted *Castor*, the two GiL branches tried to correct it in different ways, the D branch by substituting *.iiij.*, H1 by dividing into two names, *Nicho strati*, though one might ask why in that case H1 gives a capital to the other four but not to *strati*. For a summary of the linking of these two groups see *ODS*, 155–6.

7 **Simplicien**: add *qui post duos annos a martyrio predictorum passi sunt* LgA.

10 **were put**: add *uiui* LgA.
tonnes: *tombeaux* P2, *loculos* LgA.

14 **or knowen**: only GiL.

16 **Marteres**: not in LgA.

158 ST THEODORE

Maggioni, ch. CLXI, p. 1131; Dunn-Lardeau, ch. 160, p. 1052.

2 **cite of Marme Vicanore**: *cite de marme nicanore* P2, *urbe Marmaritanorum* LgA; the Marmaritani were the inhabitants of a coastal region of Egypt and Libya, but Theodore is associated with Amasea, now Amasya in northern Turkey. Maggioni (2007, 1690 n. 1) has shown that the LgA sources refer to the legion rather than the city of the Marmaritani, thus explaining the geographical disparity.

3 **first knighthode**: *pristinam militiam* LgA, i.e. former military service.

4 **I ride to**: *Jay cheuauche a* P2, *Ego milito* LgA; *to* is *MED* sense 11 (a), 'on behalf of'.

8 **to sacrafice**: add *aux dieux* P2, *ut sacrificaret* LgA.

9 **Mars**: *martis* S, *matris deorum* LgA, i.e. Cybele.

13 **hope and**: only GiL.

159 ST MARTIN

Maggioni, ch. CLXII, p. 1133; Dunn-Lardeau, ch. 161, p. 1053.

2 **Ytaile**: add *a pauie* P2, 'at Pavia'.

2–4 **with his fader (. . .) And Martin rode under hem**: *cum patre suo* (. . .) *militauit* LgA.

3 **Constantine**: *constancien* P2, *Constantio* LgA.
Iulius Cesar: *Iuliano cesare* LgA; Constantius II, emperor 337–61, was succeeded by his cousin Julianus (the apostate), 361–3.

7 **nwe in the faithe**: *catechumenum* LgA.

11 **he wolde haue be but a**: *ne voult auoir que vng seul* P2.

15 **Martin**: add *hunc sibi seruatum intelligens* LgA.

16 **for he hadde not ellis to yeue**: not in LgA.

23 **was baptised**: *se fist baptizier* P2.

23–5 **behight . . . fulfelled**: *adhuc ad instantiam tribuni sui qui tempore sui tribunatus expleto se seculo abrenuntiaturum promittebat* LgA, 'at the instance of his tribune, who promised that at the end of his time as tribune he would renounce the world'.

25 **prouost**: *preuoste* P2, *tribunatus* LgA; *MED* records two instances of *provoste*, 'area under jurisdiction of a provost', from Proceedings of the Privy Council 1443; here it means rather the duration of tenure of the office;

provostrie is also recorded. A2 has *provestrie*, H1 *prouost`ri'*, recorded by *MED* from *c.*1380; all others are as E, lacking the final *e*.

28 **Iuliane**: *Julius* P2, *Iulianus* LgA; but at 32 P2 has *iulien*.

43 **fulli . . . knighthode**: *cheualerie* P2.

44 **colet**: 'acolyte', spelt *collet* H1, *Collette* H2; *MED s.v. colit(e* records no spelling with *ll*.

49 **hym**: add *parmi la teste* S.

49–50 **Martin . . . honde**: *ictum ferientis dextere sustinuit alter* LgA, 'another (of the thieves) skilfully restrained the blow of the striker'.

54–5 **tribulaciones and**: only GiL.

61 **y**: *le dyable* P2.
ayenst the and: only GiL.

62 **thou**: *homme* P2.

65 **encresed**: add *par tout le monde* P2.

71 *Eleborus* is the typical medieval Latin form for *Helleborus*. *MED* records forms such as *ellebor* beginning from the *Nun's Priest's Tale*, *c.*1390.

72 **and was . . . venym**: *et estoit en peril. il chaca la douleur et le peril* P2, *omne periculum et dolorem* (. . .) *fugauit* LgA.

72–3 **bi praier and**: only GiL.

79–80 **he kneled downe**: add *sus le corps* P2.

80–1 **praied . . . liff**: *par son oroison il le remist en vie* S.

82 **diuerse tymes after that**: *racomptoit souuent* P2.

82–3 **of dampnacion . . . upon hym**: *estoit donnee sus luy. que il fut mis en tres obscur lieu* P2.

84 **is plege**: *oraret* LgA.
he was conuerted ayen to the bodi: *il fu tenu quil fut ramene au corps* P2, *iussum est igitur ut per ipsos reduceretur* LgA; *conuerted* requires the sense 'restored', which is not recognized by *MED*.

89 **But . . . hym**: *Quidam autem ex episcopis qui conuenerant eo* (. . .) *resistebant* LgA.

89–90 **he used . . . visage**: *il estoit de lait habit et desprisable de voult* P2, *deformis esset habitu et uultu despicabilis* LgA, 'that he was sloppy in demeanour and contemptible in appearance'.

93 **hathe made perfit**: *tu as parfait* P2.

95 **defensour**: *et defensorem* LgA; it is not clear what this means. Vulgate gives *et ultorem*, Ps. 8: 3, but 'efforts to elucidate these difficult lines have not met with success' (*NJBC*, 528).

chased oute of towne: *chacie de tous* P2, *ab omnibus confutatus* LgA.

98 **disciples**: add *Nam ibi uinum nemo nouerat nisi quem infirmitas coegisset, mollior habitus ibi pro crimine erat* LgA.

100–1 **And . . . martir**: *Cum quidam sub nomine martyris coleretur* LgA.

102 **as . . . sepulcre**: *super sepulcrum stans* LgA.

104 **upon his right side**: *ad leuam* LgA.

108 **Sever**: Martin's disciple Sulpicius Severus, whose *Vita Martini* (*BHL* 5611–13) (edition with parallel French translation by Jacques Fontaine, *Sulpicius Severus, Vie de Saint Martin*) is the main source for his life.

Gall: see *Gallus: Dialogues sur les "vertus" de Saint Martin / Sulpice Sévère*, ed. Fontaine.

121 **behynde hym**: *a parte posteriori* LgA.

132–3 **of Crist . . . miracle**: only GiL.

134 **sensible thinges**: *les choses non sensibles vegetatiues et non raisonnables. les choses non sensibles* P2.

135 **he had . . . temple**: *in quodam fano ignem misisset* LgA.

140 **see**: add *ut in predicto dialogo legitur* LgA.

142 **the tempest . . . clere**: *ilz furent appaisiez et la mer serie* P2, *tranquillitas magna successit* LgA.

143 **lyuinge and growinge**: *vegetatiues* P2.

as trees: not in LgA.

144 **a right old tree**: *vng arbre* (*templum* LgA) *tres ancien. et larbre dun pin* P2.

fende: add *estoit illecques que il vouloit esrachier* P2.

145 **churles**: *les vilains et les poissons* (*paiens* P1) P2, *rusticis et gentilibus* LgA.

147 **wolt . . . downe**: *as fiance en ton dieu* P2.

149 **wel ynow**: only GiL.

157 **thei lefte anone**: *tantost ilz sarresterent et demourerent ainsy comme se ilz fussent vaincus* (add *in suis uestigiis fixi* LgA) P2.

serpent: *serpent deaue* P2, *serpens* LgA.

161 **into another riuer**: *a lautre riue* P2.

162–3 **understonde me ne here me**: *ne me veulent oyr* P2.

170 **clene**: add *Quant il estoit secretement ou reuestuaire. il nauoit nulle chaiere ne* P2.

172 **an olde cheiere . . . fete**: *vne selle de .iij. piez* P2, *sellula rusticana quam tripodes uocant* LgA.

173 **heir and felawe**: *per* P2, 'equal'.

174 **fire**: add *ad robur* LgA, 'to strengthen him'.

175–6 **as her disciple**: *tamquam comparem* LgA.

178 **Gall**: add *eius discipuli* LgA.

180 **hadde told**: *requisissent* LgA.

182–3 **not only . . . me**: *et confessa que ilz lauoient souuent visite et non pas vne fois seulement* P2.

184 **hym**: Here GiL omits a paragraph beginning *Multe iustitie*, belonging to the series 168 *gret humilite* and 185 *gret pacience*, 205 *gret continuaunce in praier, etc.*, Maggioni, 1144 (104–5), Dunn-Lardeau, 1059.

187–8 **thei dredde hym not**: *ne les doubtoit* (*deboutoit* P1) *il point* P2, *nec* (. . .) *eos* (. . .) *repellebat* LgA.

192 **of blew**: not in LgA.

196 **for anger**: only GiL.

197 **And he . . . hem**: *Ille autem mutus cedentibus terga prebebat* LgA.

199 **bete hym**: add *car il leur estoit aduis* P2.

200 **ouercome**: *arrestees a terre* P2.

200–1 **might . . . remeue**: *ne se mouuoient ne plus que vne roche* P2.

201 **ne for drawinge**: *ne pour ferir* P2, not in LgA.

203 **hadd do**: add *in eum* LgA.

and praied . . . leue: *et que il leur donnast congie* P2, *ille eis licentiam dedit* LgA.

204 **arose and**: only GiL.

206–7 **or redde or studied ne for none ocupacion that euer he releced his mynde from praier**: *ou a la leccon ne il ne laschast iamais que entre lire et aourer. Il ne cessoit de aourer en son couraige* P2, *Inter legendum tamen et operandum nunquam animum ab oratione laxabat* LgA. LgD MSS and Batallier all give forms indicating 'praise' rather than 'work' here. The error must have been scribal rather than Vignay's; s.w. apparently corrected loosely from the Latin.

210 **outwarde werke**: *autre chose* P2.

211 **inward**: only GiL.

212 **so harde and sharpe**: *de grant cruaulte* P2, *Multe austeritatis* LgA.

216 **a**: add *seul* P2.

217 **meued**: add *de courrour* P2, add *iniuria* LgA.

219 **on a light fire**: *ars de feu* P2, *igne accenditur* LgA; *light*, 'lighted, ignited', *MED lighten* v., sense 2 (c).

224 **wel smellynge**: *rorantes* LgA, 'like dew'.

225 **gretly meued**: *excitati* LgA, 'awakened'.

229 **offended hym**: *mesprenoient* P2, 'sinned'.

230 **conuerte hem**: *penitere* LgA.
euer: not in P2, *ad penitentiam* LgA.

232 **that . . . tyme**: *ceulx qui estoient encheuz vne fois* P2.

235 **in the . . . God**: *en nostre seigneur* P2.
y . . . the: *il tempetreroit misericorde* P2, *Christi misericordiam pollicerer* LgA.

237 **a pore man**: *pauper quidam nudus* LgA.

242 **hasted hym faste**: *lamonnestoit* P2.

244 **thei**: *il* P2, *Archidiaconus* LgA; 245 *thei sawe* and 246 *thei cared* are also singular in LgD, LgA.

246 **therfor thei . . . pore**: *pour ce ne le causoit il pas pour le poure* P2, *pauperem non adesse causatur* LgA.

247 **Whi . . . pore?**: *Mihi uestis deferatur et pauper non deerit uestiendus* LgA, 'Bring me a garment and a poor man in need of clothing will not be lacking'.

248 **ashamed and**: only GiL.

250 **cote**: add *et aussy comme nulle* P2, add *que dicitur penula, quasi pene nulla* LgA.

253 **was atte the masse**: *celebroit* P2, *missam celebraret* LgA.

255 **euen and felow**: *pareil* P2.

258 **slode**: add *arriere, car ses bras nestoient pas gros ne moult charnuz. et la cotte ne luy aduenoit que* P2.

260 **.ij. sleuis**: *vngs botiaulx* P2, *torques* LgA.

262 **shepe, These shepe**: *vne brebis, ceste* P2.

263 **sydes**: *cottes* P2.

268–9 **enforced her to confound moche peple**: *se forcenoit et confondoit moult de gens* S, *ubique seuiret et multos confoderet* LgA, 'raged everywhere and gored many'.

273–4 **Go . . . best of dethe**: *Discede, funeste de pecude* LgA.

279 **whereuer thei went**: *sub quacumque ymagine uiderentur* LgA.

280 **Iouis**: *jument* P2, *Iouis* LgA.

280–1 **or of sum . . . transfigure hem**: *aliquando Veneris uel Minerue transfiguratum se eius uultibus offerebat* LgA.

281 **knewe . . . and**: not in LgA.

282 **name**: add *Mercurium maxime patiebatur infestum, Iouem brutum atque hebetem esse dicebat* LgA.

286 **hym**: add *Martin, cognois celluy que tu aores. Je suis crist descendu en terre.*

et me vueil premierement manifester a toy. Et sicomme martin tout merueilleux se taisoit encores. le dyable dit P2.

296 **diosise**: Roze (p. 343) notes that the term as used by Sulpicius Severus refers to a parish distant from the cathedral church, but it was also sometimes used to mean parish in general. *MED diocise* offers only 'bishop's diocese'.

Dol: *Condatensem* LgA, Candes-St-Martin, near Saumur; it is hard to see how Vignay turned this into Dol.

297 **in a caue a manere of briddes**: *en vne eaue plungons* P2, *mergos in flumine* LgA; *plungons, mergos*, 'divers', i.e. birds of the family *Gaviidae*.

298 **This manere of fendes is for to aspie**: *Ceste* (*ce est* P1) *maniere de dyables. ilz espient* P2; s.w. followed P2S, the D branch made the obvious correction.

foles: *incautis* LgA.

299–300 **haue take**: add *saturarique nequeunt deuoratis* LgA, 'and cannot be satisfied with what they have devoured'.

305 **all**: add *flentes* LgA.

306–8 **Haue routhe . . . shepard**: only GiL.

327 **CCCC and xl**: *CCCC.xlviij* P2, *CCCXCVIII* LgA.

.iiij^{xx}.viij.: *iiij^{xx}. et .vij* P2, *iiij^{xx}. et vng* S, *LXXXI* LgA.

337 **Seuer**: *Seuerinus* LgA, i.e. not Sulpicius Severus.

348 **passinge**: add *qui eum retinere uoluerunt* LgA.

353 **Mateins**: add *si comme il le tesmoingne* (add *in quadam epistola* LgA) S.

354 **ful bright**: only GiL.

355 **honde**: add *dextera* LgA.

361 **slepte**: *sendormy* P2.

lesson and the: *leccon de la* P2, not in LgA.

364 **he saide**: *excitauerunt eum dicentes* LgA.

365 **abidithe and be anoyed**: *lassus expectat* LgA.

369 **thei assigned**: *ilz signerent* P2, *notantes* LgA; *MED assignen* does not record the necessary sense, 'note, record'.

377 **and in praiers**: only GiL.

381 **holi body**: *sepulchre* P2.

383 **disparbeled**: *se desapparut* P2, *nusquam comparuit* LgA; *MED disparplen* gives a range of meanings such as 'disperse', but none appropriate to this instance.

was made and done: *celebratur* LgA.

384 Here LgD and GiL omit: *Refert Odo abbas Cluniacensis quod tunc omnes*

campane in omnibus ecclesiis nullo tangente pulsabantur et omnes lampades diuinitus accendebantur LgA.

387–8 **trewant beggynge**: *truander* P2, 'begging'. GiL is tautologous. *MED* has only one citation for this adjectival form, *s.v. ?truaunt* adj., with the spelling *trowane*, from the Catholicon Anglicon. The noun *truandise* (391 below), A1 *trewandnes*, is, however, well attested, in such senses as 'knavery'; here some sense like 'wretched(ness)' is required.

389 **bi the presence of Seint Martine**: *quant le corps saint* (add *Martini* LgA) *fu porte a procession hors de leglise. sy se doubterent que le corps saint ne fut porte par delez leur maison et que par aduenture ilz ne feussent gariz* P2.

390 **but . . . miserie**: only GiL.

391–2 **thei went fro that place and went to another chirche**: *de illa contrata fugientes se ad aliam transferebant* LgA, i.e. from that *maison* to another; see note to 389 above.

394 **God . . . infinit and**: *pource que dieu* P2.

395 **heled**: *ilz furent* (. . .) *garis* P2.

398 **cursed errours**: *les temples de lerreur excommeniee* P2.
enforced: *efforca* P2, *erexit* LgA.

403 **the Lorde . . . clothed**: *mundi dominum induisset* LgA.

403–4 **that couered the diuinite**: *que la diuinite fist* P2.

404 **dividynge of clothinge**: *vesture au seigneur* P2, *clamidis* (. . .) *diuisio* LgA.

405 **inestimable yefte**: *doncques* (*don* P1) *que nul ne peut prisier* P2, *inextimable donum* LgA.

407–8 **thou puttest . . . Arryens**: *digne ei arianorum subiacuit feritas* LgA.

408–9 **of thi faithe**: only GiL.

410 **and sowle**: only GiL.

413 **comaundement**: *uisu* LgA, 'by sight of him'.

160 BRICE

Maggioni, ch. CLXIII, p. 1154; Dunn-Lardeau, ch. 162, p. 1067.

1 **to hym**: add *et luy disoit moult de laidures* P2.

2 **asked gode of**: *demandoit* P2, i.e. was looking for.

3 **wilt scorne**: *demandes* P2.
up to heuene warde as he dothe: *hault* P2, *eminus* LgA, 'further on'.

3–4 **for . . . upwarde**: *cest celuy qui regarde le ciel* P2.

7 **Haue y not herde it**: not in LgA.

8 **I telle the that**: *Amen dico tibi, quia* LgA.

9 **after me**: add *en leueschie* P2.

16–17 **there . . . for**: only GiL.

17 **a religious woman**: *vne femme qui estoit religieusement vestue* P2.

20 **suffered**: *dissimulauimus* LgA.
wreched vnclennesse: *luxure* P2.

25 **afore all this people**: not in P2, *coram omnibus* LgA.
be thi fader and: only GiL.

28–9 **to myn acuse**: *a moy excuser* P2, *ad me* LgA; *MED accus* n., 'accusation', gives only two citations, both from Lydgate (?1439).

30–1 **falsly (. . .) under colour of holinesse**: *faulcement soubz lombre de pasteur* P2, *falso pastoris nomine* LgA.

33 **Martine**: add *cunctis uidentibus* LgA.

35 **corrupcion**: *atouchement* P2.

36–7 **bete . . . iniurie**: *contumeliis et iniuriis afficiunt* LgA.

161 ST ELIZABETH OF HUNGARY

Maggioni, ch. CLXIV, p. 1156; Dunn-Lardeau, ch. 163, p. 1069.

6–7 **renounsed alle childisnes and putte her ful in the seruice of God**: *omnia puerilia aut omnino contempneret aut eadem in dei obsequium manciparet* LgA; *putte her*, LgD *se mettoit*, mistranslates *eadem manciparet*, which refers to *puerilia*.

7 **childisnes**: *childesnes* H1, *childenes* DH2, *childisshnes* LA2; not recorded in *MED*, first citation in *OED* for 1526 from Tyndale, 1 Cor. 13: 11.

9 **that**: *car* P2.

10 **custumes**: *studiis* LgA.

11 **for to profite**: *proficere* LgA.

15–17 **she . . . chirche**: *ancille uel coetanee obseruarent, aliquam de illis causa ludi uersus capellam insequi uidebatur ut ex hoc (. . .) opportunitatem captaret* LgA.

18 **and**: *ou* P2.

20 **before her**: add *en leglise* P2, *coram suis oculis* LgA.

22–4 **she was . . . occasion**: *cum puellis ad terram prostratam ludi specie mensurabat, ut sub tali occasione deo reuerentiam exhiberet* LgA.
of her astate: only GiL.

25–6 **her souerayne . . . hope**: *toute son esperance* P2.

29 **into the chirche**: not in LgA.

37 **Petre**: *Iohannis* LgA, *Petri* Graesse; Maggioni records no variant agreeing with Graesse.

38 **nothinge**: add *a ceulx* P2.

40 **propertees**: *prosperitez* P2.

41 **she toke plesaunce**: *il luy prenoit bien* P2, 'it was going well for her'.

42 **leue the remenaunt**: i.e. break it off.

43 **you**: not in LgA.
for: *propter* LgA.

43–4 **She . . . other**: *Ad choreas quoque a puellis ceteris aduocata, cum unum circuitum peregissent, dicebat: 'Sufficiat uobis unus circuitus, iam propter deum alios dimittamus.' Et sic per talem modum puellas a uanitatibus temperabat* LgA.

44 **as moche as she might**: only GiL.

45 **fresshe araye**: *jolis vestemens* P2, *Vestimentorum lasciuos* LgA.
she . . . honestly: *amoit tout vestement honneste* P2, *omnem in hiis honestatem dilexit* LgA.

49 **in her bedde**: *en veillant* P2.

50–1 **she wolde suffre nobodi to lase her sleuis**: *etiam manicas sibi consui nulla ratione pateretur* LgA, i.e. because they were regarded as an unseemly adornment. The original point of detachable sleeves was that they were more likely to get dirty than the rest of the garment, and so could be cleaned or substituted. But they tended to attract features of decoration, such as elaborate buttons.

52 **fulfelled**: GiL and LgD omit two sentences, Maggioni, 1158 (37–8), Dunn-Lardeau, 1071.

53–4 **the sacrement was lefte up**: *len faisoit le saint sacrement* P2, *sacra hostia conficeretur, manicas si forte consute essent solueret* LgA.

54 **broches of golde**: *monilia* LgA, 'necklaces'.
the cercle: *les aornemens* P2, *cetera* (. . .) *ornamenta* LgA.

55 **leye it on the grounde**: *les mettoit bas* P2, *deponeret* LgA.

57–8 **that . . . fruit of her**: *pour auoir fruit* P2, *fructum perceptura tricesimum, que fidem trinitatis seruauit cum decalogo preceptorum. Consensit igitur licet inuita in copulam coniugalem, non ut libidini deseruiret, sed ne patris preceptum contempneret et ut filios educandos ad dei seruitium procrearet. Quamuis enim fuerit legi tori coniugalis astricta, nulli tamen fuit culpande delectationi subiecta* LgA; for *fructum tricesimum* see Mark 4: 8, 20, parable of the sower.

60–1 **And thanne . . . confessour**: *Et dont voua es mains le* (*de maistre* P1) *conrat a quy elle fianca* P2, *Quod inde manifeste constat, quoniam in manibus magistri Conradi uotum emisit* LgA.

63 **Landegraue**: Vignay and s.w. take this title, LgA *lantgrauio*, as a name.

65 **God**: add *et enseignast les hommes rudes. ja soit elle muast estat, sy ne mua elle point la volente de sa pensee. Et elle fut de moult grant humilite et de grant deuocion a dieu et fut a soy de grant abstinence* (add *et fu as povres de grant largesce* P1) *et de grant misericorde* P2.

69 **to lye stille**: *que elle se reposast aucun pou* P2, *ut sibi parceret et quieti alicui corpus donaret* LgA.

71 **passed her hour**: not in P2, *non surgeret* LgA.

71–2 **that . . . awake her**: *la boutast du pie pour esueillier* P2, *eam pede tangens excitaret* LgA.

75 **let it passe**: *dissimulauit* LgA.

78 **ioyed with sorw**: not in P2, *de dolore gauderet et hoc quadam uultus letitia uenustaret* LgA.

79 **God**: add *uilia et abiecta non sperneret, sed hoc cum deuotione nimia exerceret* LgA.

84 **sitte**: add *comme poure* P2, *tamquam pauper et humilis* LgA.

85–6 **day of the Purificacion**: *purificatione post partum* LgA; Elizabeth had three children.

88 **it**: *ipsum ad altare* LgA, i.e. her son.

89 **the bobaunce and iapes**: *les mos et le boban* P2, *pompam* LgA.

90 **awey**: add *et pour soy confermer* (*conformer* P1) *auecques la vierge marie* P2, *et se illibate puerpere conformaret* LgA.

91 **that she . . . day**: *en quoy elle estoit alee a leglise* P2.

92 **bi . . . husbond**: *ipsa libertate precellens et dignitate sublimis* LgA.

93 **her**: add *saluo iure matrimonii et consentiente marito* LgA.

93–4 **a pore man . . . relygion**: *pauperis et mendici, sed tamen scientia et religione precipui* LgA.

96 **dethe**: add *imitaretur exemplum* LgA.

97 **called**: add *ab ipso* LgA, i.e. Conrad.

98 **Marquis of Losenge**: *marquise de messenne* P2, i.e. Meissen.

99 **her confessour helde hym not paied**: *ille egre ferens* LgA.

103–6 **She was . . . lene**: GiL broadly follows LgD, which omits most of a passage in LgA dealing with Elizabeth's personal privations, including having herself beaten by her maidservants, Maggioni, 1160 (62–5); Batallier restored it, Dunn-Lardeau, 1073.

105–6 **that she laye . . . lene**: *que elle amegrissoit* P2.

110 **metis**: add *Sepe tamen ad mensam sedens cibos manu contrectabat et diuidebat ut ex hoc comedere uideretur ne superstitionis notam incurreret, sed urbanitate tali cunctos conuiuias letificaret* LgA.

goinge: *longi itineris* LgA.

111 **that**: add *non credebantur* LgA.

111–12 **true conquest**: *bon conquest* P2, *iustis laboribus* LgA; *MED conquest* sense 3 (a), 'effort to obtain something' seems the nearest.

112 **refeccion**: add *cum suis ancillis* LgA.

112–13 **harde brede tempered with water**: *pain dur trempe en leaue* P2, *nigrum panem et durum in aqua calida madefactum* LgA.

113–14 **opposed her**: *luy assigna pencion* P2, *quosdam iustos redditus* (. . .) *sibi assignauerat* LgA, 'assigned her appropriate funds'. *MED* offers no sense for *oppose* or *appose* which fits this context, both carrying such meanings as confront, investigate, accuse. However, 'supplied her with funds' seems the only possible meaning in context here.

115 **purpos**: add *Sepe autem cibos curie respuit et aliquorum bonorum uirorum cibaria requisiuit* LgA.

117 **peple**: *gens* P2, *familie* LgA, 'household'.

120–1 **she . . . Crist was**: *Christo pauperi uicem rependeret* LgA, 'she might make amends to Christ for his poverty' (Stace).

123 **merily**: only GiL.

124 **state of a wedowe**: *vefuete* P2, *paupertatis* LgA.

126–7 **she . . . about her**: *elle ne souffroit que nul neust mesaise* P2, *nullum premi aliqua inedia pateretur* LgA.

127 **all**: add *ut omnes eam matrem pauperum acclamarent* LgA.

128 **.vij. werkes of merci**: *sex misericordie operibus* LgA, *septem* Re and Graesse. There were originally six corporal works of mercy, the seventh, burying the dead, being added later. LgD and GiL omit the rest of this sentence and the next two, Maggioni, 1161 (78–80), but Batallier restores them, Dunn-Lardeau, 1073–4.

136–8 **bi . . . other**: *ex hoc et bonorum laborum gloriosum fructum reciperet et exemplum uere humilitatis preberet et de propriis corporibus laboribus elemosinam deo daret* LgA.

139–45 LgA begins: *Ipsa esurientes pascebat*; these lines are a reordered and paraphrased version of LgA.

140 **emperor**: add *Friderici* LgA.

143 **cuntre**: add *Et quantumcumque alicui parum daret diuina tamen uirtute tota die illa sibi sufficiebat* LgA.

144 **arraye**: *aornemens* P2.

144–5 **but . . . hem**: *multa etiam sibi et ancillis suis consueuit subtrahere et pauperibus reseruare. Ipsa sitientes potabat. Quadam autem uice ceruisiam pauperibus distribuens, cum unicuique sufficienter dedisset, inuentum est quod uas nullam deminutionem pertulit, sed eandem quam prius mensuram seruauit* LgA.

146–52 LgA begins: *Ipsa hospitio peregrinos et pauperes suscipiebat*; LgD and GiL omit some words and clauses from these lines.

146 **the**: *son* P2.

147 **of pore folke**: *infirmorum* LgA.

150 **whanne . . . clothes**: *jasoit ce que les chamberieres ne le vouloient pas souffrir* P2.

152 **moder**: LgD and GiL omit Maggioni, 1163 (98–103).

153 **dede make**: *frequentabat* LgA.
whanne thei deyed: only GiL.

155–7 **mani tymes . . . therinne**: add *et estoit a leur mort moult deuotement* P2, *semel uelum suum magnum lineum in partes concideret et cuiusdam pauperis corpus inuolueret. Eorum etiam funera propriis manibus contrectabat et in ipsorum exequiis deuota manebat* LgA.

161 **inwarde thinges**: *ces choses* P2, *talibus* LgA.

163 **sowles**: *anime sue* LgA.

165–6 **leue . . . go and**: *conuertist sa force et sa puissance a* P2.

166–7 **meke and debonaire praiers**: *debonnaires admonnestemens* P2.

167–8 **And he . . . thedir**: *et il y ala* P2, not in LgA.

172 **weduhode**: add *ne uidualis continentie premio fraudaretur, sed fructum sexagesimum perciperet utpote que decalogum preceptorum cum sex misericordie operibus obseruaret* LgA.

173 **Frise**: *Turingiam* LgA; substitution of *Frise* by Vignay is unexplained.

174 **a fole and a wastour**: *dissipatrix et prodiga* LgA.
ungoodli: add *et totaliter* LgA.

174–5 **of the heritage**: not in LgA.

175 **And for that**: *ut ex hoc* LgA.
wisdom: *sapience* P2, *pascience* P1, *patientia* LgA.

176 **she went**: new sentence LgA.

177 **pore manys**: *dun tauernier* P2.

178 **with all her hert**: *moult* P2.

180 **tribulacion**: add *et 'Te deum laudamus' cantarent* LgA.

181 **she herself come**: *iussa est ingredi* LgA.
the place and: not in LgA.

182 **her**[1]: *un sien* P2.

183 **she sawe that**: not in LgA.

184 **and kissed**: only GiL.

185 **but y finde none**: *si beneficos inuenirem* LgA.

188–9 **foul . . . aboute**: *parfonde dessoubz* P2.

191 **but shoued her in the myre and**: *sy que* P2.

193 At this point P2S and GiL omit Maggioni, 1164–6 (119–49), Dunn-Lardeau, 1075–7, P1 ff. 306vb–307rb, but GiL inserts it, translating from the Latin, after 239 *Frere Menours*; see below.

196 **and whanne she come home ayen**: only GiL.

197 **apered**: LgD and GiL omit Maggioni, 1166–7 (151–2).

199 **thei . . . lowest**: *singulari tantum ad eam numero loquerentur, eo modo scilicet quo inferioribus loqui solemus* LgA.
in her hous: only GiL.

201 **wolde hide her**: *eas ad loca alia transmittebat* LgA.

203 **She chase . . . dede**: *Ceterum ut cum Maria partem optimam possideret sedule contemplationi uacabat. In qua quidem contemplatione* LgA, 'in order to possess the best part with Mary, she gave herself sedulously to contemplation, in which contemplation . . .' Luke 10: 42.

205 **God**: LgD and GiL omit Maggioni, 1167 (159–63).

207 **right . . . rauisshed**: *aussy comme se elle fut en la pensee diuine* P2, *ac si ibidem dei presentiam miraretur* LgA.

209–10 **and prophesied . . . in heuene**: not in LgA.

212 **hevenwarde**: add *per fenestram* LgA.

213 **endured . . . gladnesse**: *tam iucunda uisione letificata* LgA.

215 **she loked into heuene**: *oculos aperiens* LgA.

217 **uisiones**: *consolationibus* LgA.

219 **wilt . . . with the**: given as statement in LgA.

220–1 **whi . . . wepte**: *ut ad dei honorem et ipsarum edificationem quid uiderit indicaret* LgA.

222 **me**: add *uultumque ad me suum serenissimum ostendentem* LgA.

223 **and**[2]: add *Qui mei misertus iterum me sui uultus ostensione letificans* LgA.

224 **herde**: LgD and GiL omit Maggioni, 1168 (176–9).

225 **uertu**: *ardeur* P2.

226 **man**: add *seculariter indutum* LgA.

227 **lyff**: add *et tu deusses amer dieu* P2, add *cum deberes creatori tuo seruire* LgA.

228 **full gladly**: not in P2, *uehementer* LgA.
required her therof: *le vous requier* P2.

229 **the yonge man . . . hymself**: *iuuenem similiter pro se oratione incumbere monuisset* LgA.

232 **y begynne . . . brenne**: *ie deffail tout et suis tout ars* P2.

233–4 **and caste . . . mad man**: only GiL.

235–6 **and halpe . . . dispoile hym**: *ipsumque tenentes uestes eius pre nimio sudore madidas inuenirent* LgA.

237 **touche hym**: add *ipso clamante ac dicente: 'Totus ardeo et consumor'* LgA.

239 **and**: add *diuina gratia illustratus* LgA.
Menours: GiL and LgD omit Maggioni, 1169 (193–4).

240–313 Here GiL inserts the passage absent from P2S after 193 *lough*. It seems safe to assume that this is translated from the Latin rather than from another copy of LgD; notes to 240, 248, 249–50, 257–9 , 259, 282 *confusion*, and 284 show GiL following LgA where P1 diverges, and since in general s.w. was translating from LgD with occasional corrections by reference to a copy of LgA, use of a second LgD here seems unlikely, especially since in cases such as 248 and 259 s.w. would have no reason to want to change the French version if using it. In the notes to these lines the P1 reading is recorded only where it differs from LgA, to illustrate this point.

240 **an abbas that was of her kyn**: *abbatissa eius matertera* LgA, 'maternal aunt'.

241 **a bisshop**: *episcopum Bauenbergensem* LgA, Bamberg.

242 **resseiued . . . fully**: *honeste suscipiens caute retinuit, intendens* LgA.

243 **a gentill woman . . . herde**: *ancille* (. . .) *didicissent* LgA and likewise plural throughout the sentence.

245 **Trustithe**: *Confido* LgA.

246 **chastite**: *continentiam* LgA.

247 **purpos**: add *et omnem uiolentiam conteret* LgA.
mannys: i.e. *humanam* LgA.

248 **y shalle discent**: *ie descordera* P1, *dissentiam* LgA. GiL follows LgA closely, using a rare word to do so; *MED dissenten*, for which the EH1

spelling with *c* is not recorded, is first cited for Lydgate ?a1439. L substitutes *defende*.

249–50 **yef y see none other remedie**: *ie ne pouoie eschaper autrement* P1, *nullum aliud mihi euadendi superesset remedium* LgA.

257–9 **the bisshop and she resseiued these bones with solempne procession and grete deuocion and sheding of teres**: *les os furent receus de leuesque a grant honeur et dicele a grant deuocion et a lermes* P1, *ossa ab episcopo cum honorabili processione et ab ipsa cum multa deuotione et lacrimarum effusione suscepta sunt* LgA; s.w. has mistranslated, but *procession* shows use of LgA rather than LgD.

259 **she turned her to God and saide**: *dist a nostre seigneur* P1, *conuersa ad dominum dixit* LgA.

262 **yef y loued the**: *licet ipsum te amantem multum amauerim* LgA, 'although I loved him dearly as he loved you'.

270–1 **for . . . gospell**: not in P1, add *qui de sinistra miserie ad dexteram glorie transferuntur* LgA.

272–3 **the whiche . . . abiecte**: not in P1, *scilicet griseas humiles et abiectas* LgA.

274 **beclippinge**: *custodiens* LgA.
and: add *amplectens* LgA.
pouerte: add *Mendicando quoque ostiatim ire uoluit, sed magister Conradus non permisit* LgA.

274–7 **Her abit . . . clothe**: *Fuit autem eius habitus tam despectus ut deferret pallium griseum panno coloris alterius prolongatum, manicas etiam tunice ruptas alterius coloris panno habuit emendatas* LgA, 'her habit was so shabby that her gray mantel had to be lengthened with cloth of another colour, also the torn sleeves of her tunic had to be mended with cloth of another colour'.

279 **mischef and**: only GiL.

282 **shame and**: only GiL.
confusion: so LgA, *douleur* P1.
houge: only GiL.

284 **so vile an**: *tel* P1, *tam uili* LgA.
do . . . for to: only GiL.

287 **pouerte**: add *cum pauperibus* LgA.

287–8 **in all . . . worlde**: *cum diuitibus multis diuitiis* LgA.

288 **soule**: *voulente* P1, *animus* LgA.

289 *daielesse* in the addition in D means 'without effect', *MED s.v. dailes*, where, however, no etymology is offered; see too *OED dayless*.

291–2 **she might . . . afflixiones**: *contra omnes contumelias contemptum et constantiam largiretur* LgA.

293 **praiers**: add *audiuit dominum sibi dicentem: 'Exaudita est oratio tua.'* LgA.

295 **felthe and myre**: *stercora* LgA.

296 **no peyne**: only GiL.

299 **that**[1]: *quos* LgA, 'those that'.

299–300 **she would voide**: *separabat* LgA, i.e. with Conrad as subject.

300–1 **yonge men right good and true**: *ancillas fideles et predilectas* LgA.

301 **childehode**: add *ab ea remouerit* LgA.

302 **he**: *uir sanctus* LgA.

306 **gladde . . . pacient**: *uelox ad obedentiam et constans ad patientiam* LgA.

308 **ofte tymes**: *quoque* LgA.

314 **She was**: The text here returns to LgA, Maggioni, 1169 (196), preceded by *Et quant elle eust prins labit de religion* P2, *Ad summum uero cumulum perfectionis propter Marie contemplationis otium non deseruit Marthe officium laboriosum, sicut supra in sex operibus misericordie est ostensum. Nihilominus tamen, postquam habitum religiosum induit* LgA.

315 **.v. hundred marke**: *.ijC. marcs dargent* P2, *duo milia marcharum* LgA. **dower**: D *duree* appears to be *MED dure*, 'power of endurance'.

317 **hospitale**: add *in Marpurch* LgA, Marburg.

318 **and leude**: only GiL.

318–19 **she . . . tribulaciones**: *Et quia omnes iniurias nouerat gaudenter excipere* add *improperabant ei quod nimis cito memoriam uiri sui a corde suo abiecerat, que taliter exultabat* LgA.

321 **so humbely and so mekely**: *sy humblement* P2, *tam solliciter* LgA.

322–6 **that . . . hospitalite**: GiL follows LgD, which consists of a reduced and somewhat modified version of LgA, which ends its account of her nursing activities with the sentence *Ipsos autem infirmos ad confessionem et communicationem inducens uetulam quandam penitus renuentem uerbere castigatam induxit* LgA.

335 **Radegunde**: *Ildegundis* LgA, *Radegundis* Graesse.

338 **she shulde**: *on luy* P2.

342 **her here**: add *ne ne hantera aucunes vanitez* P2.

347 **religion**: add *et in hospitali cum beata Elizabeth degens laudabilem uitam duxit* LgA.

Here GiL and LgD omit a story about a couple abandoning their baby, Maggioni, 1170 (215–18); Batallier restored it, Dunn-Lardeau, 1080.

348 **God had ordeined**: *dominus dilectam suam de mundi ergastulo uocare disposuit* LgA.

350 **aungeles**: add *Christus sibi apparuit dicens: 'Veni dilecta mea, in preparata tibi intra tabernacula '* LgA, inserted in GiL after 361 *weddinge*, but not in LgD.

bedde: add *malade de fieures* P2.

351 **And tho . . . thanne**: *et ceulx qui la estoient et dont* P2, *a circumstantibus* LgA attached to the following clause.

356 **of**[1]: *ante* LgA.

357 **began to cry**: *dit* P2, *alta uoce* (. . .) *exclamauit* LgA.

359–60 **was bore**: *nasci uoluit et in presepio requieuit.' Appropinquante uero hora sui transitus ait* LgA.

360–1 **his weddinge**; *celestes nuptias* LgA.

361–2 **Thanne . . . God**: sentence misplaced; see 350 above.

363 **in this wise**: *Post paululum uero* LgA.

oure Lorde: *pace. Licet autem eius uenerabile corpus quatuor diebus inhumatum iacuerit, nullus tamen fetor ex eo prodibat, sed quidam odor aromaticus cunctos reficiens exhalabat* LgA.

364 **.Ml.CC.xxvj.**: *MCCXXXI* LgA.

364–7 **And thanne . . . of her**, 367–9 **And thanne . . . neighed her**: the sentences have been transposed in LgD and GiL, after which two sentences of LgA are omitted, Maggioni, 1171–2 (236–7).

365–6 **thei beganne . . . thenke it and**: *commancerent vng chant dessus leglise de tresgrant melodie aussy comme* P2, *tam suaui modulatione cantabant et tanta uarietate modos cantandi formabant ut cunctos in admirationem adducerent eo quod* LgA.

367 **seruice**: *obseques* P2.

370–1 **and thanne ther fell . . . dethe**: not in LgA.

Here LgD and GiL omit Maggioni, 1172–3 (239–56).

372 **diocise of Saxonie**: *saxonie ou dyocese discrenense* P2, *Saxonie monasterio quodam Hyldensis dyocesis* LgA, i.e. Hildesheim in Saxony.

monke: add *ordinis Cisterciensis* LgA.

373 **Hemer**: *Henricus* LgA.

373–4 **that he cried . . . aboute hym**: *ut omnes ad compassionem induceret et clamoribus inquietaret* LgA.

377–8 **bi . . . abbot**: *cum abbas et prior deessent de subprioris consilio* LgA.

379 **upon his shuldre**: *sur luy* P2.

380–1 **thei . . . meruaile**: *mirari quidem de sanitate ceperunt* LgA.

381 **and**: *sed* LgA.

uowe: add *cum nulli monacho liceat aliqua uota emittere nec se ad tala obligare* LgA.

383–4 **confessed of his auowe**: *que il confermast sa pensee non estable par confession* P2.

386 **toke hym**: add *et eisdem doloribus torqueri cepit* LgA.

386–7 **And . . . hole**: LgA gives more fully.

388–93 **A maide**: LgD and GiL greatly abbreviate this miracle, and omit the next, Maggioni, 1174–5 (278–87).

390 **she**: *lors commenca a crier et le ventre* P2.

394–400 LgD and GiL abbreviate this and omit the next two miracles, Maggioni, 1175 (294–7).

394 **of Tholose**: *Coloniensi* LgA.

401–13 LgD and GiL have three abbreviated miracles, followed by omission of nine, Maggioni, 1176–9 (309–51).

401 **one**: *vng homme* P2.

414–22 LgD and GiL give a shorter version of this final miracle in LgA.

416–17 **and . . . thedirward**: *et cum locus eius a tumulo tantum per decem miliaria distaret, uix in octo diebus potuit peruenire* LgA.

419 **angry**: add *contra socium* LgA.

420–1 **Y . . . wette the**: *Qui ait: 'Ego te non perfudi* LgA.

162 ST CECILIA 2

Maggioni, ch. CLXV, p. 1180; Dunn-Lardeau, ch. 164, p. 1083.

This is the correct LgA and calendar position of St Cecilia, but it also appears as chapter 124. Notes to both versions are given at pp. 339–45.

163 ST CLEMENT

Maggioni, ch. CLXVI, p. 1188; Dunn-Lardeau, ch. 165, p. 1091.

2, 3 In LgA the father is *Faustinianus* and the twins *Faustinus* and *Faustus*. GiL gives the twins as *Faustin* and *Faustinien*, and the father as 2 *Faustin* but from 198 on as *Faustinien*. L consistently gives *Faustin* for the father, presumably to bring it into line with line 2.

2, 4 **Melchiane, Machidiane**: *machidiane* P2, *Matidiana* LgA. L spells her *Matidiane*.

6–7 **turmented . . . entent**: *molestaret* LgA.

8–9 **but rather . . . trouble**: *a luy en nulle maniere* P2.

10 **malys**: only GiL.

12–13 **as for . . . best to her**: *par long temps* P2.

13–14 **foule and**: only GiL.

14 **that he hadd to her**: *car le regart de sa presence lenflamboit* P2.

16 **tonight**: only GiL.

22 **and goodes . . . with**: *affin quelle demourast la. et fist nourrir ses enfans* P2.

26 **by tempest**: only GiL.
she: *la mere* P2, *mater sine filiis* LgA.

27 **till . . . wawes**: only GiL.

28–9 **and sought . . . might**: *et se fut arriere gettee en la mer par grant douleur se ne feust que elle auoit esperance de trouuer les enfans* (*eorum cadauera* LgA) P2.

29–30 **And whanne she coude not finde hem quicke ne dede**: *que duos natos perisse considerans* LgA.

30 **as . . . herselff**: *forment et mordoit ses mains* P2.

32 **for to comfort her**: only GiL.
fortunes: *infortunia* LgA.

35 **husbonde**: add *qui estoit jeune homme* P2.

36 **comforted her**: add *et demoura auecques ycelle* P2.

37 **hondes**[2]: add *que elle auoit morses et desrompues* P2.

40–1 **to gete . . . begging**: *de querir son pain* P2, *mendicare* LgA.

41 **fonde**: add *luy et* P2.

44 **he**[1]: plural in LgA.

47 **in kepinge**: *sub tutoribus* LgA.

48 **and**[2]: *mais il* P2.

53 **studie**: *scholas* LgA.

56 **al confused**: *tristis* LgA.

59 **madde man**: add *sillogismorum tendiculas in eum tendere molientes. Ipse uero hec tamquam deliramenta ducens que proposuerat constanter prosequebatur* LgA; absent from some MSS and Graesse.

60 **scorned Barnabe**: add *et eius predicationem contempnebat* LgA.

61 **litell worme**: *vne petite barbelotte qui est nommee cuelex* P2, *culex animal* (. . .) *exiguum* LgA, i.e. a gnat; *worm* can carry a range of senses, here 'insect'.

64 **question**: H2 substitutes *question* for D *conquestion*, which is not in *MED* and must be an error.

68 **Clement**: add *phylozophe* P2.

69 **informed**: *entroduit* P2, *instructus* LgA.

70–1 **resseiued hym and**: only GiL.

82–3 **for pitee and compassion**: only GiL.

84 **into the yle**: *cum discipulis suis Antaradum et inde ad insulam per sex miliaria distantem* LgA.

85–6 **pelours of glas**: *columpne uitree* LgA; Boureau, 1463, notes that the ultimate source, *Recognitiones Clementinae* (*BHL* 6844–5), gives *uinee* for *uitree.* It is not clear what D *pereiles* means, unless it is for *appareil*, 'furnishings etc.' A1 substitutes *perles.*

88 **went so about and**: only GiL.

89 **y haue not only**: *Je nay tant seulement que* P2; s.w. retained *not* from the French idiom.

90 **bynome me**: *afoiblies par mes morsures* P2.

96 **one tyme**: *vne seule heure* P2.

99–100 **fader and his moder**: *matri et fratribus* LgA.

105 **abide**: *dissimula* LgA.

111–12 **sore . . . that**: *la reboutoit arriere aussy comme se* P2, *cum indignatione repellebat* (. . .) *tamquam* LgA.

112 **madde**: add *et estoit forment esmeu par yre contre pierre* P2.

113 **dredest thou not**: *ne doubtes tu pas* S, *ne deboute pas* P1, *noli repellere* LgA.

118 **how his fader deyed**: *de son pere* P2.

120 **sore wepinge**: only GiL.

122 **Aquile**: add *qui ny estoient mie* P2.

129 **Yef . . . mynde**: *Si non* (. . .) *nos insanimus* LgA.

132–3 **meruailed . . . thei were**: *leur dit que peut ce estre* P2.

138 **other shippemen**: *quidem pirate* LgA.

139 **woman**: *uidue* LgA.

140 **sette . . . scole**: *nous fist introduire es ars liberaux* P2.

144 **disciples**: not in P2, *fratribus* LgA.

147 **Frendes**: *Seigneurs* P2, *fratres* LgA.

haue pite of youreself: *misereor uestri* LgA.

148 **youre gret folye**: *que vous foles* P2, *uos grauiter errare* LgA.

149 **ne no worshippinge**: *ne son adourement nest nulle chose* P2, *neque cultus hic aliquid est* LgA.

whiche anythinge dothe: *ou monde* P2.

150 **engendrure**: 'birth', implying the astrological conditions at birth.

it: add *de* P2.

151 **in the see**: *manifeste* LgA.

wher y: *qui* P2.

mathesis: the only two *MED* citations are from Lydgate ?a1475(?a1430) in the more general sense 'scientific learning', but here it must refer to astrology; see Boureau, 1463–4 n. 34.

154 **his herte bare**: *le cueur luy disoit* P2, *animo pulsabatur* LgA; *MED beren* sense 5 (b), giving the passive as 'seem', is the closest to this usage (*in his herte it him bar*, Otuel), but cf. *MED herte* sense 3b, idiomatic expressions (c) *his herte bar him*, 'he was favourably disposed to'.

157–8 **euer . . . to hym**: *souuent* P2.

164 **laugh**: add *una cum sene et Petro* LgA.

167 **fader**: add *At ille negabat dicens: 'Vere nescio si eum patrem uocauerim'* LgA.

170 **wiff**: add *et ce que destinee et fortune a ordonne a chascun* (add *nostrum* LgA) P2.

176 **waters**: add *et ainsy est il fait et aduenu. car elle se enchey en lamour de son sergent et doubta le peril et le reproche. et sen fouy auecques luy et pery en la mer* P2.

180 **hadde . . . dreme**: *luy auoit faint le songe* P2.

184 **true and**: only GiL.

185 **anythinge**: *nulle chose* P2.

189–90 **in gret meruaile**: *resolutis membris* LgA.

194–5 **he herde . . . armes**: *elle crioit toute forsenee. le viellart la courut embracier et estraindre contre soy* P2.

196 **in this joye**: *ainsy* P2, not in LgA.

197–8 **this olde man**: only GiL.

207 **come**: *reuint* P2.

208 **hym in**: *en luy* P2.

211 **What ailithe you to**: *pourquoy* (. . .) *vous* P2.

212 **as ye . . . youre fader?**: *qui suis vostre pere* P2.

213 **in the**: add *Et symon auoit confit vng ongnement et len auoit oinct. et luy auoit empraint sa face par art magicque* P2.

214 **said**: add *quest il aduenu a moy maleureux* P2.

215 **children**: add *et sy ne puis estre lie auecques eulx. Et la femme et les filz ploroient forment et rompoient leurs cheueux* P2, *letari non potuerim cum eis. Vxor uero sparsis crinibus et filii plurimum flebant* LgA.

219 **to sle hym**: *carnes eius dentibus laniarent* LgA.

222 **persone**: GiL omits a passage in which Peter promises to restore Faustinien's appearance, and it is explained that Peter did not actually instruct him to lie, and that Clement's book is therefore not to be believed on such details, Maggioni, 1196 (151–7), Dunn-Lardeau, 1098.

226 **traitour ne deceiuour**: *traictre* P2, *seductor* LgA.

232 **to**: *en lamour de* P2.

239 **and now**: only GiL.

240 **with houge crie**: only GiL.

241 **oute of kinde**: only GiL.

242 **not**: add *nudius tertius* LgA, 'two days ago'.

242–3 **that**[2] **. . . hym**: not in LgA.

244 **dede . . . and**: *impetum in eum facientes* LgA.

248 **with**: *post* LgA.

250 **so that**: *ne* LgA.

251 **with hym**: *a soy* P2.

253 **will saie**: *veulent dire* P2, *asserunt* LgA.

254 **for**: only GiL.

259 **religion**: *regionum* LgA.

261 **an holy uirgine**: *vne damoiselle dun saint veel* P2, *Domitillam uirginem* (. . .) *sacro uelamine* LgA.

264–5 **hadde fere . . . wyff**: *zelo ductus* LgA.

265 **entred**: add *occulte* LgA.

268 **doume**: *sourt* P2.

272–3 **that thei went so aboute**: only GiL.

277 **my**: *uestrum* LgA.

283 **nere**: *pres de sa femme* P2, *iuxta coniugem suam stantem* LgA.

284 **deceiued**: add *par art magique* P2.

285 **and . . . faste**: only GiL.

286–8 **And thanne whanne . . . stones**: *et dont commanda que ilz loyassent clement et le trainassent et ilz lyerent fus* (*columpnas iacentes* LgA) *et roches et les traynerent et cuidoient* (add *sicut etiam Sisinio uidebatur* LgA) *trayner clement et ses clercs* P2.

291 **do**: *feray* P2.

291–2 **by cruel dethe**: only GiL.

292 **unhurte**: only GiL.

301 **emperoure**: add *Nerue* LgA.

303 **the erle of Sacrum**: *le conte des sacrifices* P2, *comes sacrorum* LgA, 'the director of the holy rites'.

304 **noyse and discorde**: *traison et discord* P2, *seditionem* LgA.

314–15 **into a desert . . . the citee**: *ou desert qui est oultre la pres de la cite* S, *trans Pontum mare in heremo quod adiacet ciuitati Tersone* LgA.

319 **the prouost fonde in that yle**: *Profectus autem in insulam inuenit* LgA.

320–1 **oute of roches**: not in LgA.

323 **crowne**: add *sed uestris meritis et orationibus* LgA.

326 **opin**: add *confessoribus suis* LgA.

327 **the stones**: *la pierre* P2.
Synay: add *et fluxerunt aque in abundantia* LgA.

334 **smite**: add *ou lieu ou laignel auoit este* P2.

335 **went oute**: add *et in fluuium creuit* LgA.

336 **of flodes**: *du fleuue* P2.

339 **distroied . . . yere**: *ydolorum templa destruentes per totam prouinciam intra unum annum* LgA.

342 **.lvj.**: *.C.* LgA, variant *CVI*, also in Graesse and P1. Trajan became emperor in 98.

343 **for the loue of God**: only GiL.

355 **.viij.**: *.vij.* P2.

363 **as a mad woman**: *ca et la plorant* P2.

364 **she might . . . wawes**: *le corps de son filz fut gette au riuage* P2.

365 **she coude . . . finde**: *il ny auoit nulle esperance* P2.
retorned: add *ad domum* LgA.

369 **auuter**: *tumulum* LgA.

375 **night**: add *moult souef* P2.

GiL omits Ambrose's comment on this miracle, Maggioni, 1201 (246–9), Dunn-Lardeau, 1103.

376 **One**: *Leon* P2.

378 **Philisophre**: add *et pour son grant gaaing il auoit este ainsy nomme des enfance* P2.

380 **wolde . . . but**: only GiL.

382–4 **in the tyme of Martin . . . barbaryns**: *ob incursum barbarorum tempore marini recessus uenientium templum destructum fuerat* LgA, 'the temple was destroyed through an attack by barbarians at a time when the sea was withdrawn'.

388 **place**: *insulam* LgA.

389–90 **and songyn ympnes and psalmes**: *cum hymnis et orationibus* LgA.

391 **bisydes hym**: *qui auoient este gettez en la mer auecques luy* P2.

394 **And**: *autem* LgA.

396 **Cerile bisshoppe of Moriane**: *Cyrillo Morauorum episcopo* LgA. For Cyril see *ODS s.n.* Cyril and Methodius; they were the originators of the Cyrillic alphabet; Cyril was buried in the church of San Clemente in Rome.

164 ST CHRYSOGONUS

Maggioni, ch. CLXVII, p. 1203; Dunn-Lardeau, ch. 116, p. 1104.

5–6 **cursed be the dedes of min husbond that y haue take**: *excommeniee par le fais du mary que elle print* P2, *Sacrilegi iugum mariti suscepi* LgA, 'I have taken on the yoke of an impious husband'.

6 **by the will of God**: *deo miserante* LgA.

7 **dissimulacion of siknesse**: *enfermete* P2, *mentita infirmitate* LgA.
folw and: only GiL.

8–9 **But this greuithe me sore that**: only GiL.

9 **wreched**: only GiL.
patrimonie: add *dont il est ennobli* P2.

13 **seruaunt to the spirit**: *amisso spiritu* LgA.

16–17 **Fare well . . . Lorde**: *dieu te gart* P2, *Vale* LgA.

18 **Doughter**: only GiL.

20–1 **in suffering . . . preued**: *tu ne puez estre deceue se tu es esprouuee* P2, *Non enim deciperis, sed probaris* LgA.

22 **this clowdi derkenesse**: *ces tenebres* P2, *noctis tenebras* LgA.

23 **lusti**: *seris* P2, 'calm'.

28 **I . . . that**: *anastaise* P2; see 5–6 above.

31 **whiche**: add *tu saras* P2.

37 **This is a see**: *Cest vne mer* P2, *Vnum mare est* LgA; here and at 39 GiL has lost the emphasis on singularity.

38 **of rowers**: *de notonnier* P2, *nautico* LgA; *rower*, *MED rouer(e*, can carry the general sense 'mariner'.

39 **the gouernaunce**: *le gouuerneur* P2, *uno* (. . .) *gubernatore* LgA.

42 **be . . . drowne**: *etiam in tranquillo uicinum morti conficiunt cursum* LgA. **the**: *toy* P2.

42–3 **haue . . . mynde**: *tota mente constringe* LgA.

46 **cristen peple**: *ces autres crestiens* P2, *ceteros christianos* LgA.

48 **prouoste**: add *et le consulte de ton lignage* P2, 'and the consulship to which your lineage entitles you'.

49–50 **thi goddes and thi dignite**: *tes dignitez* P2.

51 **beheded**: add *enuiron* P2.

52 **Seint Ely prest**: *saint zelin prestre* P2, *sanctus Zelus presbiter* LgA, i.e. the holy priest Zelus.

165 St Catherine

Maggioni, ch. CLXVIII, p. 1205; Dunn-Lardeau, ch. 167, p. 1105.

For this version of the life, substituted for that in LgA and LgD, see above, Introduction, pp. 39–41.

1–544 This section is from an unknown source (see Kurvinen, Thesis, 179–80) and corresponds to no identified surviving account of St Catherine. The remainder is from LgD, with no demonstrable reference to LgA, with the possible exception of the correction at 620.

1–2 **Here . . . Katerine**: this clause resembles the preliminary heading to the chapter in P1, *Ci commence la vie de la glorieuse vierge saincte katerine fille du roi costidien*, which is not found in P2S or LgA.

47–8 **Constantines sone**: this should have been emended to read *Constantine*, as H2T2K.

227 **elongacion**: *MED* has three instances of this word, two in technical senses relating to extension, and this one, for which is offered '?longing'.

429 **spirites**: *MED spirit* sense 3a (b) 'sense', the only citation for which is c1450 Alphabet of Tales, *He fell down in swownyng . . . when he come vnto his spyrittis agayn he went furth.*

545–9 **In this mene tyme . . . riche**: *Katherine fille du roy costidien* (*Costi* LgA) *fut introduite en tous les ars liberaux. Et si comme lempereur maxence ot* *assemble en alixaundre tous poures et riches* P2. This begins the chapter in LgD and LgA.

551 **to be cruelly tormented**: *occire* P2, *immolare* LgA.
This yonge quene: only GiL.

552 **duellinge**: add *seule* P2.

553–4 **as . . . spouce**: only GiL; the effect of this addition is deliberately to link this section to the earlier, non-LgD, part of the chapter.

554–5 **houge . . . instrumentis**: *la joie de ceulx qui chantoient* P2, *cantantium plausus* LgA.

555–70 **and wondered . . . chere**: *Et dont enuoya la vng message enquerir hastiuement que cestoit. Et quant elle le sceut elle print aucuns de ses gens de son palais et se garny du signe de la croix et ala la et trouua la moult de crestiens mener sacrifier pour paour de mort. dont elle fut moult greuee de douleur et se embati deuant lempereur tres hardiement* P2.

572 **were the creature**: *congneusses le createur* P2.
woldest call: *rappellasses* P2.

573 **goddes:** add *Et dont disputa de moult de choses auecques cesar deuant les portes du temple. et dont commenca elle a luy dire* P2, add *Stansque ante ianuam templi per uarias conclusiones sillogismorum allegorice et metanomice, diserte et mistice multa cum cesare disputauit. Deinde rediens ad commune colloquium dixit* LgA.

585–7 **only . . . creatoures**: *dieu des dieux. seigneur des seigneurs* P2.

593–4 **And . . . meruaile**: *Et se merueilloit moult* P2.

595 **before . . . lyued**: *a veoir a tous* P2.

595–9 **And so . . . faithe**: only GiL.

600 **emperoure**: *cesar* P2 and LgA; 612 **emperoure**: *cesar* P2, *rex* LgA; LgA uses an apparently random mixture of *imperator, cesar*, and *rex* (and once *tyrannus*), except that Catherine always addresses him as *imperator*; LgD usually, but not always, follows LgA; GiL always gives *emperoure*.

605–6 **That y . . . trouthe**: *Il est escript ne te blasme ne ne te loe. Car ce sont les folz que vaine gloire trauaille. Je te diray touteffois ma lignie non pas par amour de ventence. mais par humilite* P2.

607 **and norisshed**: only GiL.
taught: *introduite* P2, *non mediocriter instructa* LgA.

608 **yeue me frely**: *suy* P2, *suis fouiee* S, *sui fuie* P1, *confugi* LgA.

609 **most souerayne**: only GiL.
that . . . man: only GiL.

610–11 **be . . . profite**: *ne peuent aidier toy ne autre. O maleureux aoureur de telz dieux. quant ilz sont appellez au besoing ilz ne sont pas* P2.

618–19 **that so gret an encomberaunce of perturbacion be not in the corage of the that holdest thiselff so mighti**: *sy que cruel perturbation ne soit pas ou couraige de toy saige. que* (*Or le* P1) *poissant sy dit* P2, *in sapientis animo non stet turbatio dira. Sic namque poeta ait* LgA; it seems probable that Vignay correctly translated *poeta*, and that an early copyist misread *poete* as *poeste*, and substituted *poissant*; however, that is already the reading in P1. Boureau (p. 1468 n. 5) identifies the quotation as from the *Praeloquia* of Ratherius of Verona.

620 **thou wilt be gouerned**: *tu gouuernes* P2, *rexeris* LgA.
gode: not in LgA.

620–1 **ellys . . . thralle**: *se tu est gouuerne par corps tu seras sergent* P2. The complete Latin reads: *Tu si animo rexeris, rex es; si corpore, seruus.*

621 **thralle**: add *Et toy* P2, *Et roi* P1, *Et rex* LgA, introducing the emperor's reaction to Catherine's speech, 621–3 *Wherfor . . . philosopherres.* From 623 *Thei auaile* to 626 *kinge* is an addition by s.w. to what has become Catherine's speech.

627–8 **ansuere . . . wisdom**: *contrarier a sa sagesse* P2.

628 **parted . . . wonder and**: *secretement* P2.

632 **maistres**: add *de diuerses prouinces* P1, *de diuersis prouinciis* LgA, omitted by P2S.

635 **comynge**: add *de si lointaines parties* S.

636–7 **labourithe . . . lawes**: *confont tous les sages* P2.

639 **that . . . presumpcion**: *en ot despit et* P2, *indignatus stomachanti uoce* LgA.

642 **the symplest . . . haue**: *noz garcons* P2.

649–50 **her souerayne spouse . . . promesse**: only GiL.

651 **drede . . . faithe**: *que elle sy tenist fermement* P2.

651–2 **for . . . and**: *car elle ne seroit pas vaincue deulz mais les vaincroit et* P2, *sed insuper illa ipsos conuersos* LgA.

653–4 **Than . . . spouse**: only GiL.

655 **the emperour and**: only GiL.

657 **symple**: only GiL.

660–1 **and . . . guerdon**: only GiL.

663 **dethe**: only GiL.

664–5 **bi . . . shewed hem**: only GiL.

666 **Craton**: *platon* P2, *Plato* LgA.
had saide it: *astruit deum circumrotundum et decurtatum* LgA, 'describes a god spherical and with a segment cut off'.

668–9 **shewed . . . fals**: *eust sagement dispute auecques les maistres et que elle ot leurs dieux confunduz par appertes raisons* P2.

678 **prouable**: *probabiliorem* LgA, 'more convincing'.

686 **my dere bretheren**: only GiL.

687 **bapteme**: add *et corona* LgA.

688–9 **Blesse . . . heuene'. And whanne**: *Cum ergo signo crucis muniti* LgA.
with me: not in P2.

696 **O thou most fole**: only GiL.

697–8 **and y . . . do that**: only GiL.

699 **of my sowle**: not in P2, *et dilectio mea* LgA.

700–1 **from hym**: not in P2, *ab eius amore* LgA.

703 **streite**: *obscurum* LgA.

706 **had . . . uirgine wherfor**: *eprise par grant amour de la vierge* P2.

707 **her**: add *porphire* P2.

708 **wherinne . . . was**: not in P2, *uirginis* LgA.

709–10 **so gret . . . therto**: *la chartre replendissant par tres grant clarte* P2.

711 **glorious, benignely**: only GiL.

713 **with . . . that**: *et* P2.

714 **bade . . . for she**: *luy dit auant que elle* P2.

723–4 **Mi . . . wyff**: *fille* P2.

725 **laboure and**: only GiL.
bataile: add *soyes ferme car ie suis auecques toy* P2, which GiL incorporates in the following addition.

725–41 **And . . . thenke it**: only GiL.

728 **how shulde y not but yef y knewe you**: *not* appears to refer to 724 *knowest*, but how the following syntax fits this is obscure. Some of the non-GiL versions of the life made various attempts to clarify (Kurvinen, Thesis, 322), as have L and K (see apparatus). A2 *how shulde y not knowe you, that hast* is the most radical but effective solution offered.

745 **of her kepers**: only GiL.

748 **all this tyme**: only GiL.

749 **me**: add *par son ange* P2.

750 **faire virgine**: only GiL.

sadly: only GiL.

756–7 **foule . . . wrechidnesse**: *enferme mortel non noble et let* P2.

758 **in haste**: only GiL.

759 **greuous**: *diuers* P2, *exquisita* LgA.

761–2 **my souerein . . . herte**: *mon dieu mon amy* (*amor* LgA) *mon pasteur et mon seul espoux* P2.

763–4 **a cruell . . . taught hym**: *vng maistre amonnesta au roy soy forsenant* P2.

765 **nayles**: add *sy quil la fist horriblement trenchier en ce tourment affin quil espouentast les autres crestiens par lexemple de ce cruel tourment. Et dont fut ordonne que* P2.

765–6 **.ij. of . . . nether whelis**: *deux de ces roes courroient contre les .ij. autres* P2, *due uno ordine uoluerentur, due autem contrario impetu agerentur* LgA.

769–70 **so that . . . myracle**: *et pour conuertir le peuple qui la estoit* P2.

771–2 **was sent and**: only GiL.

774 **was . . . sorw and**: *sestoit celee jusques alors* P2.

775 **hem**: *lempereur* P2.

775–6 **hering this of her**: only GiL.

776–7 **and comaunded . . . sacrifice**: *pource que la royne ne vouloit sacrifier. il fist premierement* P2.

777–8 **with yren hokis**: only GiL.

782 **fayling**: *mortel* P2.

783 **endely**: *immortel* P2; for *endely*, 'ultimate', the non-GiL MSS of Catherine read *undedly*.

full . . . beauute: only GiL.

784 **foule . . . before**: *corrompable* P2, *mortali* LgA.

784–5 **this . . . faith**: *fut celle ferme* P2, *Tunc illa constans effecta* LgA.

789 **Whanne**: *Le iour ensuiuant que* P2, incorrectly ending the preceding sentence in EH1D. L and K have either corrected it or represent s.w.'s version.

792 **Crist**: add *et ay receu la foy de dieu* P2.

792–3 **beganne . . . tremble**: *commenca a fremir et a rungier* S, *rugitum terribilem emittens* LgA.

797 **Porphiri . . . and**: only GiL.

798 **for**[2] **. . . Crist**: not in LgA.

800 **smite of**: add *auecques porphire* P2.

802 **my wiff**: *la royne* P2.

803 **reawme . . . quene**: *palais* P2.

804 **and yef . . . anone**: *car tu sacrifieras au iourduy ou tu perdras le chief* P2.

805–6 **that thou . . . God**: only GiL.

810 H1 has a marginal insertion, *The peticion graunted by godde to Sceynt Katerine*, referring to the prayer which made her one of the 'Holy Helpers' (on whom see entry in *ODCC*).

815 **and be . . . askinge**: only GiL.

817 **my dere wyff**: *ma belle* P2, *speciosa mea* LgA.

819 **and . . . perisshe**: only GiL.

824–70 **But . . . hill**: After Maggioni, 1212 (135), Dunn-Lardeau, 1113, GiL inserts this passage, from an unidentified source (see Kurvinen, Thesis, 207–13) before returning briefly to LgD.

870–3 **plente . . . place**: *et huille decourt de ses os sans cesser qui garist tous malades* P2; GiL reverts to LgD in mid-sentence.

874 **Maxence**: *maximien* P2, *Maxentio siue Maximino* LgA; see 877 below.

875 **.CCC.ix:**: *.iij.^{C} et .x.* P2.
in²: add *lystoire de* P2.

875–7 For the death of Maxence see 61.116–24.

877 GiL ends, omitting Maggioni, 1212–5 (138–202), Dunn-Lardeau, 1113–16.

LgA concludes as follows (199–202): *Dubitationem autem habetur apud aliquos utrum a Maxentio uel a Maximino martyrizata sit. Tunc enim tres imperium tenebant, scilicet Constantinus, qui ex paterna successione imperium sumpsit, Maxentius Maximiani filius a pretorianis militibus Rome augustus appellatus et Maximinus in orientis partibus cesar effectus. Secundum autem chronicas Maxentius Rome, Maximinus uero in oriente contra christianos tyrannidem exercebat. Videtur ergo, ut aliquibus placet, quod uitio scriptoris factum sit ut pro Maximino Maxentius poneretur.*

166 ST SATURNINE

Maggioni, ch. CLXIX, p.1216; Dunn-Lardeau, ch. 168, p. 1116.

This short chapter deals with three saints of this name, the first of whom, of Toulouse, is generally known as St Sernin.

1 **ouer the**: *des* P2, *ab* LgA.

4–5 **thei shulde . . . ansuere**: *se ilz noccioient saturnin quilz nauroient nulles responces* P2.

6–8 **bonde . . . erthe**: *luy lierent* (add *a* P1) *vng thorel par les piez. et le trainerent en la haulte tour du capitole par les degrez. Et dont le tresbucherent a terre* P2, *ad pedes tauri ligauerunt eumque cum stimulis agitantes a summa arce per gradus capitoli precipitauerunt* LgA; they seem to have been driving the bull up the steps, though generally *praecipio* suggests downward motion; Graesse reads *ab* for *a*, as probably did Vignay's copy. *MED s.v. Capitol* gives only the Roman Capitol; but the Latin could also mean any citadel or a heathen temple, either of which may be intended here.

9 **marterdom**: LgD and LgA add a brief account of his burial and subsequent reburial.

11 **prison**: add *maceratum* LgA.

13–14 **and brenned . . . hanged**: only GiL.

14 **toke hym downe and**: not in LgA.

15 **.CC.iiij^{xx}.**: *CCLXXXVII* LgA.

17–18 **Saturnyne**: *Satir* P2, *Satyri* LgA.
Renouele: *Reuocato* LgA.
Felicite: add *sa seur* P2, *sorore dicti Reuocati* LgA.
Seint Perpetuel: *saint perpetuel* P2, *Perpetua* LgA; at 22 LgD corrects her gender, *saincte perpetuel*.

18 **his sustres that were**: only GiL.

19 **is done**: *recolitur* LgA, 'is celebrated'.

20–1 **sawe . . . ydoles**: add *leur dit quilz sacrifiassent aux ydoles. ilz le refuserent du tout en tout et* P2.

23 **doughter**: add *Quid fecisti?*

26 **fingeres**: add *et yssy hors* P2, add *et exclamans egressus est* LgA.

30 **one**: *unus et paruus* LgA.

30–1 **knives . . . alles**: *coutres et glaiues estoient fichez a destre et a senestre et* (om. *et* P1) *lymes agus* P2, *In dextera uero et leua erant fixi cultri et gladii ferrei limati et exacuti* LgA.

32–3 **on the right . . . nother**: only GiL.

34 **horrible**: *grant* P2, *teterrimus et ingentis* LgA.

35 **y saw a satire**: *sy vy vng satirel* P2, *Vidi etiam satyrum* LgA. The words *a satire* are here supplied on the assumption that they were in s.w.'s original, though in addition to those readings recorded in the apparatus L leaves a space, and H2A2 are as D. *MED* records several instances of *satire*, starting from Trevisa. It was probably given by s.w. but unfamiliar to an early copyist. However, at 14.33 GiL adopts the same word from LgD as *satirell*, so perhaps did the same here.

36 **us**: *vous* P2, *nos* LgA.

37 **suerly**: add *sy que vous puissiez estre auecques moy* P2.

41–2 **be parted . . . men**: *oster dauecques les femmes et mettre auecques les autres hommes* P2, *cum aliis uiris a mulieribus separari* LgA.

44 **thiself**: add *sy que tu viues mesmement* P2.
thou art quicke with childe: *tu as vng enfant ou ventre* P2.

47 **childe**: add *beate Perpetue* LgA.
sucking: *qui alaitoit encores* P2.

56 **her**: *leur* P2.

58 **was gret with childe**: *octo iam mensibus pregnans erat* LgA.

59 **childe**: *filium* LgA.

60 **knaues that kepte hem**: *garcons* P2, *custodibus* LgA.

64 **were dispoiled**: *ligatis post tergum manibus et nudis natibus* LgA.
places: *plateas* LgA; *MED* does not record the sense 'public streets' (for the nearest, see sense 2 (e)). See too note to 88.136.

167 ST JAMES INTERCISUS

Maggioni, ch. CLXX, p. 1219; Dunn-Lardeau, ch. 169, p. 1119.

2 **region**: *religion* P2, *regione* LgA.

3 **Elapene**: add *Hic ex christianissimis parentibus ortus est* LgA.

4 **was . . . princes**: not in LgA.

5 **one of the furst**: *le premier* P2, *inter optimates primus* LgA.

7 **were full of sorugh and**: only GiL.

8 **in this wise**: *tantost* P2.

16 **that is wedded to me**: only GiL.

25 **it is but**: *tamquam* LgA.

28 **Thanne Iames saide**: not in P2, *Cui Iacobus* LgA.

39 **membre**: *polce* P2.

41 **the ouergrowen braunches**: *le serment* P2, 'vine-shoots'.

49–50 **springe and bere the beter**: *gette* P2.

51 **sufferithe . . . Crist**: *Christo compactus est* LgA, 'is grafted into Christ'.

60 **was pronounced**: *pronuntiatus es* LgA.

61 **of Iuda**: *in Iuda benedicti* LgA.

66 **Ye know wele that**: only GiL.

70 **shulde not be glad**: *ne desdigneray pas* P2.

72 **yef thou be**: *si comme tu estoies* P2.

74 **boughtest**: *creas. et que tu rachetas* P2.
precious: *propre* P2.

75 Ps. 118: 164.

77 **day**: add *pour acomplir les commandemens de la loy* P2, add *et octauo die circumciditur Hebreus ut transeat ad legales cerimonias; et mens serui tui, domine, transeat ab hiis incircumcisis et coinquinatum habentibus preputium ut ueniam et conspiciam faciem tuam, domine* LgA.

82 **lawe**: add *et ioth prima littera nominis Ihesu Christi* LgA; yod is the tenth letter of the Hebrew alphabet.

84 **frende**: add *des jadis* P2.
confesse our goddes only: *confesse vng dieu* (. . .) *tant seulement* P2, *profitere tantum* LgA, 'only make a declaration', implying a false one.

87–8 **Goth . . . in me**: *Absit a me nefanda simulatio* LgA.

90 **too**: *pollicem* LgA, i.e. big toe.

93 **and what meruaile**: not in LgA.

94 **fully**: not in P2, *quippe* LgA.

97–8 **in the last dayes**: *ou derrenier iour* P2.

100 **hele and comfort of my chere**: *salu de mon voult et mon dieu* P2.

109–10 **Bi . . . vices**: *Tunsionibus firmatur incus* LgA, 'the anvil is hardened by repeated hammer-blows'.

111 **God**: add *de verite* P2.
in the: add *et in umbra alarum tuarum sperabo donec transeat iniquitas* LgA. GiL then further omits: *Et le quint fut couppe. Et il dit. Sire je suis .xx. fois sacrifie a toy.*

115 **enhaunce**: *exaudi* LgA; likewise at 130 and 134 below.

117–18 **Lorde . . . men**: *Tu es deus qui facis mirabilia* LgA.

122 **y shal . . . ayens hem**: *in nomine domini uindicabor in eis* LgA.

127 **youre hondes may not touche**: *voz plaies ne pourront toucher* (*conchier* P1) P2, *uestra uulnera maculare nequibunt* LgA, 'your wounds will not be able to defile'.

128 **And . . . rested hem**: *Et dont les bouchers defaillirent pource que des la premiere heure du iour* (add *ad nonam* LgA) *ilz auoient sue a le detrenchir. Et dont* P2.

132 **to ioyne**: *ut* (. . .) *extendam* LgA.

133 **fallen**: *casura* LgA, 'about to fall'.

135 **to the**: only GiL.

136 **the**: *lun des* P2.

168 ST PASTOR ABBOT

Maggioni, ch. CLXXI, p. 1224; Dunn-Lardeau, ch. 170, p. 1123.

3 **full gretly**: only GiL.

4 **yef . . . wise**: *sed non posset* LgA.

7 **after hem**: *contre luy* P2, *in faciem eius* LgA.

9 **vnderstode**: *entendy* P2.

11 **bare you and**: only GiL.

13 **another**: *lautre* P2.

14 **shal . . . elliswhere**: *vous verray ie la filz* P2.

15–16 **a litell . . . loue**: *sans doubte* P2.

16 **euer after**: only GiL.

17 **gladly**: not in P2, *gaudens*.

17–18 **Y wolde . . . foluinge ioye**: *Se ie vous doy veoir la sy vous vueil ie veoir cy* P2, *Si uos uisura sum illic, nolo uos uidere hic* LgA.

22 **pray**: *intercesserit* LgA.

23 **to his selle . . . sone**: *a luys du viellart* P2.

25 **with gret violence**: only GiL.

27 **myn**: add *seul* P2.

33–5 **It is not necessarie**: *il conuient* P2.
It is . . . lyff: *Custodire et se ipsum considerare et discretionem habere, operationes sunt anime*; *paupertas, tribulatio e discretio sunt operationes solitarie uite. Scriptum est enim* LgA.

35–8 Ezekiel 14:14.

38 **thurgh all the**: *de ce* P2.

39 **worlde**: add *Et querenti fratri que essent dixit.*
couetise: *repausatio* LgA, 'relaxation'.

42 **a**^{2}: *leur* P2.

43 **a solitarie man**: *un sien priue P2, cuiusdam solitarii* LgA.
awey: add *et si comme il veist que* P2, LgA as GiL.

43–5 **the whiche . . . benignely and**: *et sicomme il veist que cestuy ploroit aussy comme en soy desesperant. il le fist reuenir. et* P2, *Qui cum quasi flendo desperaret, abbas Pastor eum ad se adduci fecit, quem benigne consolans* LgA.

46 **Hering of the y desire to see the**: *Jay oy parler de toy et te desire a veoir* P2, *Audiens de te uidere to desidero* LgA.

48 **a dede bodi . . . owne**: *mors leurs sergens* P2, *mortuos suos* LgA.

50–1 **and vnderstode . . . wordes**: *il luy souffit ceste parolle* P2, *et intelligens in sermone eius compunctus est* LgA.

51 GiL omits two stories, Maggioni, 1225–6 (48–64), Dunn-Lardeau, 1124–5.

52–3 **That shall . . . cause**: *qui courroucera son frere sans cause etc.* P2, i.e. Matt. 5: 22.

55 **do**: add *autrement* P2.

64 **restithe well**: *bene quiescat* LgA, 'lives quietly'.
sike: add *et gratias agat* LgA.

67 **perisshed**: *periclitaretur* LgA.
the ayre: *le pur air* P2.

68 **take**: *apprehende* LgA.

70 **diuerse**: not in LgA.

71 **yef . . . with the**: only GiL.

GiL omits a further example from *Vitae Patrum*, Maggioni, 1227 (82–7), Dunn-Lardeau, 1226.

169 ST JOHN ABBOT

Maggioni, ch. CLXXII, p. 1228; Dunn-Lardeau, ch. 171, p. 1126.

1–2 **whan . . . asked**: *cum Episius per annos quadraginta in heremo habitasset, interrogauit* LgA, i.e. John asked.

4 **Episien**: *iehan* P2.
slepinge: *couchant* P2, *irascentem* LgA; P1 as P2, but Batallier substituted *courrossant*, which is no doubt what Vignay wrote.

7–8 **mete in ydelnesse**: *nulle chose oyseux* P2, *quicquam occisum* LgA; as Dunn-Lardeau observes, Vignay, or possibly his exemplar, has misread *occisum* as *otiosum*.

8–9 **y[2] . . . to me**: *Je ne laissay dormir nul qui me fut contraire* P2, *non dimisi aliquem dormire qui aliquid aduersum me haberet* LgA.

15 **forstungin**: 'badly stung'; *MED* records only one very uncertain example from this compound verb *s.v. forstong*.

25 **deied**: *mouroit* P2.

27 **Y dede . . . will**: i.e. I have never followed my own desires.

28 **dede[1]**: *monstrai P2, docui* LgA.
it: add *primus* LgA.
myselff: add *Hec in uitas patrum* LgA.

170 ST MOSES ABBOT

Maggioni, ch. CLXXIII, p. 1230; Dunn-Lardeau, ch. 172, p. 1127.

2 **he**: i.e. the cell.
that is nedefull: only GiL.

4 **wolde be greuous**: *ne greuast trop* P2.

5 **yef thou doest**: only GiL.

6 **wrothe**: *contristatus* LgA.

7 **thei sawe a uirgine that**: *vne vierge* P2.

9 **whanne . . . bore**: only GiL.

10 **Siche**: *Syti* (. . .) *coram multitudine fratrum* LgA.

11 **praied . . . saide**: *quant les autres ploroient il dit* P2.

12 **Wete ye well for certaine that**: only GiL.

20 **A brother . . . sent**: *Cum frater quidam pecasset, miserunt* LgA.

21 **upon his backe**: only GiL.

26 **an holy fader**: only GiL.
Prioure: *Pior* LgA; so *Vitae patrum*, but Graesse and many LgA MSS give *Prior*. Both a Pior and a Prior are recorded among the disciples of St Antony in Egypt.

29 **they asked . . . ment**: *interrogatus quid hoc esset dixit* LgA.

34 **allweye**: only GiL.

34–5 **to deface hem**: *pour eulx* P2.

GiL omits Maggioni, 1231 (27–34), Dunn-Lardeau, 1128.

171 ST ARSENIUS ABBOT

Maggioni, ch. CLXXIV, p. 1232; Dunn-Lardeau, ch. 173, p. 1128.

Rubric The MSS here run on from the previous chapter, omitting the usual rubric.

1–2 **Of . . . prince**: *Sicomme arsenien estoit encores maistre ou palais du prince* P2, *Arsenius cum adhuc in palatio consisteret* LgA.

2 **hertly**: only GiL.

5 **monkes clothinge**: *vie monial* P2.

7 **in the same place**: i.e. in *Vitas Patrum*.

9 **vnite and**: only GiL.

11 **to apese . . . debate**: *les contens des hommes* P2.

12 **werinesse and**: only GiL.

13 **all mate**: not in LgA.

20 **in the noyse of the worlde**: *ou milieu des hommes* P2.

21 **noyse**: *multitude* P2.

22 **and defauutes**: only GiL.

23 **hym**: *quendam in heremo* LgA.
herbes: *lerbe* P2.

26 **for wery**: only GiL.

27 **Whan**: *Quoniam* LgA.

31 **of Rome**: *ancienne* P2; LgD and LgA do not mention Rome till 39 below.

37 **shame and drede**: *honte et par vergongne* P2.

46 **the bisshop**: *larcheuesque* P2.

47 **Alas**: not in P2, *ecce* LgA.

49 **ouercome**: *impugnat* LgA.

49–50 **praied so**: *dist* (. . .) *ces parolles* P2.

57 GiL omits Maggioni, 1233–4 (48–50), Dunn-Lardeau, 1130: *Et vng autre frere. sicomme il deuoit porter sa mere qui estoit ancienne femme oultre le fleuue sy enuelopa ses mains de son manteau. Et elle luy dit. filz pourquoy muces tu ainsy tes mains. Et il luy dit. Le corps de femme est feu. Et pource se je atouche a toy le memoire des autres femmes me vendroit en courage* P2.

60–1 **and to praie**: only GiL.

61–2 **verrey . . . to slepe**: *il se vouloit dormir pource quil estoit lasse* P2, *propter nature lassitudinem dormire uellet* LgA.

62 **with heuinesse**: *au dormir* P2.

63 **sitting**: add *et se leuoit tantost* P2.

65 **continuel . . . vices**: *pugnator* LgA.

66 **was dede**: *uitam finiens et testamentum faciens* LgA.

67, 69 **Magistren**: *magistrianus* LgA, an official messenger.

70–1 **whanne he come home**: only GiL.

72 **sende . . . and**: only GiL.

77 **man of Ynde**: *ethiopien* P2.

80 **that clensed**: *qui espuisoit* P2, *haurientem aquam de* LgA.

82 **euer he laboured**: *il vouloit* P2.

85 **not**: add *pour le fust qui estoit de trauers* P2.

86 **birthen**: *iugum* LgA.

87 **hous**: *regne* P2.

93 **he left**: *il laissoit* P2, i.e. habitually.

94 **and kneled**: only GiL.

95 **come ayen before**: *luy leuoit* (. . .) *deuant* S, *illustrabat* LgA.

96 **all the night**: not in LgA.

172 ST AGATHON ABBOT

Maggioni, ch. CLXXV, p. 1236; Dunn-Lardeau, ch. 174, p. 1131.

Rubric **Arsenye**: the GiL MSS read **Moyses**, having run the previous two chapters together.

5 **table**: the DH2A2 variant *batelle* may be for *MED batel* n., 'a charge for provisions', 'a prebend', meaning that he was deprived of his right to these provisions.

17 **drede and**: only GiL.

17–18 **for . . . assuraunce**: *car souffrance nest pas pire que fiance* P2, *non est enim peior passio quam fiducia* LgA.

19 **And . . . wrathe for**: *Dixit iterum* LgA.

20 **God**: *dieu ne a autre* P2.

21 **all**: only GiL.

23–4 **and bare . . . the way**: *il versa a terre* P2.

27–8 **and of angir**:. only GiL.

31 **duelled**: *auoient conuerse* P2.

32 **wost . . . for**: only GiL.

36 **sacke**: *laterculum* LgA, 'small tile'.

43–4 **my brother**: *aucun* S.

50 **full of freelte**: only GiL.

51 **tho**: *tes* P2.

51–2 **that thou had do for God**: *qui sont deuant dieu* P2, *quia secundum deum sunt* LgA.

52–3 **to the iugement of God**: *deuant luy* P2.

57 **into the hondes . . . Lorde**: only GiL. LgA adds: *Videbant enim eum colligentem spiritum, quemadmodum si quis salutet amicos suos dilectos. Hec in uitis patrum.*

173 STS BARLAAM AND JOSAPHAT

Maggioni, ch. CLXXVI, p. 1238; Dunn-Lardeau, ch. 175, p. 1133.

5 **devout**: only GiL.

10 **all the desert**: *chascun desert* P2.

12 **and made all pale**: only GiL.

14–15 **of thi witte**: *et de pensee perdue* P2.

15 **made**: add *te* LgA.

16–17 **a praier**: *aucune raison* P2.

19 **and lette**: only GiL.

19–20 **ne herde**: only GiL.

20 **drawe . . . equite**: *assie sagesse et equite* S, 'let wisdom and justice be present'.

23 **take**: *aprendre* P2, i.e. understand.

24–6 **And he . . . not**: *Qui autem non gustauerit eorum que sunt dulcedinem non poterit eorum que non sunt addiscere ueritatem* LgA, 'He who has not tasted the sweetness of the things that exist will not be able to learn the truth about those which do not'.

33 **bi his wiff**; not in LgA.

34 **sone**: add *tresbel* P2.

45 **the citee withoute . . . paleis**: *au dehors de la cite vng tresnoble palais* P2, *in ciuitate seorsum palatium speciosissimum* LgA.

46 **for to duelle**: *habiter et demourer* P2, *ad habitandum* LgA.

46–7 **the fairest . . . chese**: *tresbeaux jouuenceaux* P2.

54 **were hardy to**: only GiL.

64 **y canne hele hym**: *congruam scio adhibere medelam* LgA.

67 **enuyous**: add *et malicieux* P2.

68 **knight**: *prince* P2.

70–1 **to that ende he hadde stered all his felawshippe for to do the same**: *et quil esmouuoit la compaignie et leur conseilloit quil fust* (*quilz feissent* P2) *ainsi* S, *turbam sollicitans et sibi concilians* LgA.

71 **And**: *Et ilz luy distrent. roy* P2.

73 **not and**: only GiL.

74 **worlde**: *regne* P2.

75 **so cruelly**: only GiL.

78 **for ioye**: only GiL.

purpos: add *et luy remembra la vanite du monde* P2.

86 **supposithe verrily that**: *doubte que* P2, *suspicatur ut propter hoc dixeris* LgA.

87–8 **Now dothe . . . counsaile**: only GiL.

88 **hede**: add *et ostes tes vestemens* P2.

89 **do on . . . monke**: not in LgA.

92–3 **it shall be lyghter to you**: *facilis mihi erit* LgA.

93 **me**: add *socium* LgA.

96 **and loued hym**: only GiL.

105–6 **and a fresshe . . . disporte hym**: *et faire yoieuses compaignies deuant luy que nulle chose deshonneste ne luy aduenist* P2, *et choros plaudentes ante eum mittens, ne quid sibi fedum occurreret diligenter prohibuit* LgA.

112 **by fortune**: *sans diffinition* P2.

115 **sight**: *chose* P2.

GiL omits *Et a vne autre foys il trouua vng homme moult viel qui auoit la chiere fronciee et les dans luy estoient cheoites* (*cadentibus dentibus balbutiendo loquentem* LgA). *puis fut esbahi et dit quil couuoitoit sauoir le miracle de celle vision* P2.

119 **and all that**: *Et apres ces ans* P2, *senectus inducitur, deinde* LgA.

121 **thought and**: only GiL.

124 **holy**: only GiL.

desert: add *de la terre de samar* P2, add *terre Sennaar* LgA; also at 318. Boureau, 1475–6 notes that Bartholomew of Trent places this in Egypt; a region so named south-east of Khartoum may be intended. *Barlam and Iosaphat*, ed. Hirsch, 185, note to l. 637, identifies the location in the original story as Sri Lanka.

128 **kinges yongest sone**: *chambellain du filz du roy* P2, *pedagogo filii regis* LgA.

that he had: *Ie suis marchant et ay* P2, continuing in direct speech.

stone: add *a vendre* P2.

129 **and sight**: only GiL.

131 **eldest**: only GiL.

132 **This yonge lorde**: *celluy* P2.

133–4 **and . . . stone and that**: *cum lapidum notitiam habeam, ipsum lapidem mihi ostendit et si* LgA.

134–5 **y wote well**: only GiL.

135 **and thanke**: only GiL.

136 **hathe**: add *encores* P2.

137 **chastite**: add *et il voit celle pierre* P2.

137–8 **lesithe . . . therof**: *pert la vertu de celle veue que il a* P2.

139 **clene**: *saine* P2.

140 **eldest**: only GiL.
hathe . . . hole: *est chaste et a tres beaux yeulx et sains* P2.

142 **but**: *et sy suis* P2.

142–4 **And he tolde . . . receiued hym**: *Et dont le chambellan* (*celi* S) *dit ceste chose au filz du roy et le mena bientost a luy. Et quant cil fut entre la et il eust receu* P2, *Nuntians igitur hoc filio regis ipsum ad eum quantocius introduxit. Cum ergo introductus fuisset et rex eum* (. . .) *suscepisset* LgA.

148 **totorn**: add *et macie attenuatis* LgA.

149 **dede . . . reuerence**: *se mist a leurs piez et les aoura et puis se leua* P2.

152 **gret**: *non digne* P2.

155–6 **that he was undertake**: not in LgA.

158 **full of . . . lyff**: *tout desespere de son sauuement* P2.

159 **In . . . testament**: *et fist son testament. Et au matin* P2.

162 **thou hast herde**: *timuisti* LgA.

165 **so greuously**: only GiL.

166 **miche more**: *plus clerement* P2.
atte thi yate: only GiL.

169 **with rotin dede bonis**: *dos des mors et de pourreture* P2, *ossibus mortuorum putridis* LgA.

175 **pris**: add *reliquas uero uilis pretii esse indicauerunt* LgA.
thei: *deauratas* LgA.

178 **stinke of synnes**: *dordure et de pechie* P2, *uero immunditia uitiorum pleni* LgA.

181 **so moche**: only GiL.

183 **take . . . that**: *ne prenez garde fors ad ce qui* P2.

192 **saide**: add *Quid tibi proderit, o homo, si me occideris?* LgA.

194 **wherewith**: *et se tu les gardoies diligemment* S.

195–6 **in hope . . . goo**: *promist quil le laisseroit aller se il luy disoit ces .iij. sens* P2.

198 **to leue**: add *garde ces .iij. choses et il te sera bien. Et dont celluy laissa aller loysel sicomme il auoit promis* P2.

202 **as gret as**: *qui passe de grandeur* P2.

203 **sori**: add *de ce quil lauoit laissie aller* P2.

208 **aspiest**: *essaies* P2.

209 **to take me**: add *cum nequeas meo itinere pergere* LgA.

213 **saie that . . . defendours**: *appellent ceulx que il gardent les gardes deulx* S.

214 **false delites**: *la falace et le delit* P2, *fallacem* (. . .) *delectationem* LgA.

216 **lyuen and**: only GiL.

217 **evyn cristen**: *ames* P2.

218 **for drede**: only GiL.

219–20 **caught a tre**: *se prist* P2, *arbustulam quandam apprehendit* LgA.

222 **that . . . atwo**: *la ou il estoit et estoit ia larbre pres de couppe* P2, *et iam prope erat ut ipsam absciderent* LgA.

223 **grete**: *horrible* P2.

228 **for a litell . . . atasted**: *et se donna tout a la doulceur de ce pou de miel* P2.
is: add *figure de* P2.

232 **and the myes signifien men**: *Et ces souris signifient les heures* P2, *quasi per murem album et nigrum* (. . .) *et incisioni appropinquat* LgA.
The slidinge place: *la puial* P2, 'the ledge'.

234–5 **elementis . . . bodies**: *elementis* (. . .) *quibus inordinatis corporis compago dissoluitur* LgA, 'elements which, if disordered, bring about the body's dissolution' (Stace, 349).

236–7 **The bowe . . . worlde**: *la doulceur du ram de larbre est delectacion du monde* P2, *dulcedo ramusculi delectatio fallax mundi* LgA, i.e. the drops of honey on the branch.

240 **as moche as**: *plus quam* LgA.

241 **a litell lasse thanne**: *tantum quantum* LgA.

242 **as litell or not**: *ainsy comme neant* P2, *minus quam se et quasi nihil* LgA.

243–4 **was in . . . drede and**: only GiL.

246 **what the eylithe**: *qui est cest homme* P2, *quis sis, o homo* LgA.

248 **a thinne clothe**: *deux flotaies* (for *flocaies*?) S, 'rough garments'.

250 **Holde . . . for**: only GiL.

253 **take of**: *entendre* P2; Horstmann, *Barlaam*, emended to *take hede of*.
nedis: *negoces* P2.

257 **to haue pite on me and**: not in P2, *et mihi ueniam prebeas* LgA.

260 **true**: *chier* S.
before the kinge: *deuant toy au roy* P2.

261 **the**[1]: add *ne in manibus inimicorum tradet te* LgA.

263 **he leuithe hym**: *il nen emporte* P2.
an olde clothe: *vilz robes et drapeaux* P2.

267 **almesdedes**: add *et ces autres biens* P2, add *et cetera bona opera* LgA.

268 **the kinge**: *dieu* P2.
for us: add *et sy nous peuent bien deliurer des dyables noz ennemis* P2.

269 **And yet . . . he**: *Et encore adiousta il et* P2.

270 **straunge**: add *et mescongneu* P2.

271 **all that yere**: only GiL.
wolde: add *et gouuernoit la terre sans nulle autre constitution* P2.

273 **atte the yeres ende**: only GiL.

274 **and dispoile . . . richesses**: only GiL.

285 **made**: *enuoyees* P2, i.e. having been given as alms.

287–8 **so that**: *et quil* P2.

289–90 **to whom . . . noblesse**: *a qui vng noble vouloit donner femme* P2, *cum quandam nobilem nollet desponsare uxorem* LgA.

291 **virgine**: add *cuiusdam senis pauperis filiam* LgA.

292 **What is that**: *Quest ce que tu fais* P2.

293 **thou labourest . . . yeue**: *touteffois rens* P2.

297 **gret**[1]: only GiL.

298 **oures**: add *Mais celles qui sont en nous sont nostres* P2.

299 **reson and**: only GiL.

300 **blisse**: add *et ma ya ouuerte la porte de son regne* P2.

300–1 **am y contynually bounde**: *me conuient il* P2.

304 **and my doughter**: only GiL.

305 **he praied effectualy**: *ce iouuencel luy prioit que il luy donnast* P2, *illo omnino instaret* LgA.

310–11 **her fader . . . dede**: *luy* P2.

318 **Sennar**: see note to 124 above.

322 **to God**: *in interiori homine* LgA.

328 **faithe**: add *eum osculatus est* LgA.

331 **dere**: only GiL.
kingges: add *qui auoit nom arachis* P2.

332–3 **olde felawe . . . thingges**: *viellart* (*senem heremitam* LgA) *qui ressemble balaan et est de nostre secte* P2.

334 **defende**: add *premierement* P2.

336 **you**: *nos* LgA.

343 **Thou . . . forsake**: *et reliquisti* LgA, combined with the preceding question.

345 **turned into lyght**: *couru a la lumiere* P2.

351 **norisshed**: *tenu* P2, *feci* LgA.

352 **kepte (. . .) so tenderly**: *ne tint plus* P2.

352–3 **thi pride and wicked will**: *la mauuaise volente de toy* P2, *prauitas tue voluntatis et contentio effrenata* LgA.

353–4 **With good right**: *Cest a bon droit*. P2, *Merito* LgA; the GiL MSS attach this phrase to the previous sentence.

358–9 **what ailithe . . . greuously**: *pourquoy te courrouces tu* P2, *Cur* (. . .) *tristaris* LgA.

359 **is it for**: *Car* P2, *quia* LgA.
prince: *particeps* LgA.

361 **y shal pursue the**: *te fuieray* P2.

367 **the worship of myn age**: *honnore ma viellesce* P2.

368 **drede**: *doubte* P2, *uerere* LgA, 'respect'.

370 **and . . . sori**: only GiL.

371–2 **It is tyme to loue**: *Il est temps damer* P2; *to me* for *tyme* is in all MSS. L tried to correct, but not by reference to LgA or LgD: *it is to me to love in tyme and to hate in tyme. in tyme of pees and tyme of batell*. The error must originate in an earlier copy of GiL, but not with s.w.

384 **furst**: add *simulare se* LgA.
faithe: add *des crestiens* P2.

385 **ouercome**: add *donc assemblerent ilz ensemble. Et donc* P2.

385–6 **that feyned hymselff to be Balaam**: not in LgA.

387 **lawe**: *foy* P2.

390 **the tunge of thin hede**: *cor tuum et linguam* LgA.

394 **hymselff**: add *et quil estoit pris a son las* P2.

396 **eschewinge**: add *le peril* P2.

397: **hym**: add *deuant tous* P2.
hardely: not in LgA.

398 **maistres**: *rethorum* LgA.

404 **creatures**: i.e. their own creations.

405 **saide**: *cuidierent* P2.

407 **Caldees**: so S, *egypciens* P2, *Greci* LgA.

409 **menbris**: add *dont il les engendra* P2, *uirilia* LgA.

413 **avoutrie**: add *Et dient que venus est vne deesse aduoustre* P2.
husbond: *mechum* LgA, 'adulterer'.

414 **bestis**: add *vne ouaille* P2.

416 **mankinde**: *char humaine* P2, *carnem* LgA.

416–17 **right mighteli**: *clerement* P2.

418 **other**: only GiL.
abasshed: *muti effecti* LgA.

427–8 **for . . . right**: *aut tuis mecum permissis accipe meum. Alioquin non iustitiam sed uiolentiam exercebis* LgA.

437 **hym**: *filium suum* LgA.
of his goddes: *de son pere* P2, *patrias* LgA.

444 **hym**: add *a luxure* P2.

446 **And thanne . . . ensaumple**: *Et dit encores* P2, not in LgA.
but: *apeine* P2, i.e. recently.

449 **was norisshed**: *il fist nourrir* P2, *manere fecit* LgA.
withinne . . . pitte: *in quadam petra spelunca excisa* LgA.

450 **and . . . oute**: only GiL.

453 **horses**: *uestibus splendidis, equis regalibus* LgA.

454 **and mani other thinges**: not in P2, *et omnium rerum generibus* LgA.

454–5 **and tolde . . . euerithinge**: *Et quant il eust demande les noms de chascune chose et les menistres luy eurent dit* P2.

456 **besily . . . were**: *les noms* P2.

456–7 **and for . . . anguisshe**: not in LgA.

458 **maister . . . king**: *spatharius regis* LgA, 'the king's swordbearer'.

462 **men**: add *In nullo enim sicut in hiis sic exarsit anima mea* LgA.
Sir kinge: only GiL.

462–4 **therfor . . . lycherie**: *ie ne cuide pas que autre chose surmonte ton filz fors femmes qui esmouuent tousiours a luxure* P2, *Non igitur aliter putes te filium tuum superare nisi hoc modo* LgA.

466–7 **shulde . . . plaie**: *lamonnestoient tousiours de juer et nauoit nul autre layens a qui il peust parler ne qui luy administrast* P2, *eum semper ad libidinem prouocabant nec habebat alium ad quem respiceret aut cum quo loqueretur uel cum quo uesceretur* LgA.

468–9 **for . . . inwarde**: *de lenchanteur contre le iouuencel. et vint laiens et enflamba vne grant chaleur. sy que il embrasa le iouuencel par dedens* P2, *a mago*

(. . .) *in iuuenem irruit et magnum intus caminum ignis accendit. Malignus igitur spiritus intus inflammabat* LgA.

470 **bataile**: *ardeur* P2.

472 **and all . . . awey**: *de toute la temptation* P2, *et omnis temptatio abscessit* LgA.

477 **mariage**[2]: add *sed laudant* LgA.

482 **me**[1]: *mon ame* P2.

483 **one**: *ceste* P2.
tomorw: add *au matin* P2, *summo diluculo* LgA.

484 **cristen**[2]: only GiL.

485 **penaunce**: add *grant guerredon est donc deu a celluy qui le conuertist* P2, add *auctori conuersionis nonne magna merces debetur* LgA.

487 **his soule . . . consciens**: *lame de luy. cest assauoir la conscience* P2, *anime illius* LgA.

489 **helpe her forthe**: *hurtons forment contre li* S.

491–2 **ouer laboured hym**: *lamonnestoit* P2, *incitabat* LgA; the MSS give *ouer laboured* as two words; it is of the type described by *MED s.v. over-* pref.

493 **sorw and**: only GiL.

499 **and siluer**: not in LgA.

508 **a place . . . was**: *tres horribles lieux plains de toute pueur* P2.

511 **careyne**: *ordure* P2.

512, 516 **Theodore**: *theodas* P2; see 435 above.

513–14 **We . . . sore**: *nous luy courusmes sus* P2, *super ipsum irruentes fortiter ipsum conturbauimus* LgA.

514 **as longe . . . crosse**: *auant quil fut signe du signe de la croix* P2.

516–17 **to haue peruerted hym**: *quod ei persuadere posset* LgA.

519 **pesible**: *loable* P2.

528–9 **warned ofte tyme the kinge Barachiell that he wolde flee into desert**: *ressembloit au roy barachiel et sen voult plusieurs foys fouir* P2, *Barachiam regem pronuntians pluries fugere uoluit* LgA, 'proclaiming Barachiel king, tried many times to flee'.

535–6 **renne . . . devoure hym**: *fremissoit contre luy et muyssoit durement* P2.

536 **mekely**: only GiL.

537 **thou**: *homme* P2.

539 **a pitte in the irthe**: *speluncam* LgA.

543 **with gret ioye**: *et ne sen pouoient saouler* P2.

545 **in gret pacience**: *en merueilleuse vertu* S, *in abstinentia mirabili* LgA.

552–3 **mani . . . Amen**: *moult de miracles furent fais au tombel de ces corps* P2.

174 ST PELAGIUS POPE

Maggioni, ch. CLXXVII, p. 1256; Dunn-Lardeau, ch. 176, p. 1150.

1–6 The popes referred to here are: Pelagius I (subject of the chapter) 556–61, John III 561–74, Benedict I 575–9, Pelagius II 579–90, Gregory I 'The Great' 590–604.

2 **oure Lorde**: *paix* P2.

3 **successoure**: *predecessor* LgA.

5 **Iohn**[1]: add *tertius* LgA.

6 **this**: add *primi* LgA.

9 **maister of the storie**: *hystorien* P2.
founde true: *exposee* P2.

11 **He saithe that**: only GiL.

12 **bi sailinge . . . Septemtrion**: *du riuage de la mer par deuers septentrion* P2, *de litoribus Oceani parte septentrionali egressa* LgA; in so far as capitals can be relied on, ME writers generally seem to treat *Septentrion* as a place-name for the northern region.

12–13 **yle of Shandynare**: *insula Scandinaria* LgA, referred to as an island from Pliny onwards.

15 **ordeined . . . sege**: *sedem sibi in ea perpetue habitationis instituit* LgA.

16 **Humiliens**: *Wynnuli* LgA; so too in Higden's *Polychronicon*.

18 **bisides a well**: *in piscinam* LgA.

18–19 **a misgouerned woman**: *une folieuse femme* P2, *meretrice* LgA.

19 **drowned**: add *lesquelz ceste folieuse femme auoit enfantez a vne foys* P2.

22–4 **he was . . . Lanceon**: *Quem rex uidens et stupens nutriri fecit et Lamissionem uocauit* LgA, i.e. in LgA he rescued only one of them.

24 **hoso . . . mighti**: *quil seroit moult puissant* P2.

25 **And . . . that**: *Et il fut de sy grant fierte que* P2, *Qui tante probitatis extitit quod* LgA.

26 **kinge**: the passage which follows here in the later phase of LgA (Maggioni, 1257 (11–15)), has been transferred to 320–32 below.

27 **.CCCC.iiij^{xx}.**: *CCCCLXXXX* LgA.

30 **with**: *ou* P2.

31 **that**: add *filium et* LgA.

32–3 **he . . . baptised**: *baptizandus ad ecclesiam confugit* LgA.

34 **Marke**: *Medardus* LgA. Whether Medard and Gildard were brothers is disputed.

35–6 The text should have been emended to: **born in one day [and made bisshoppes in one day] and in one day take of Ihesu Crist**; after **day**[2] LgA adds *uno die mortui.*

38 **.vC.lxviij.**: *.iiij.C et vij.* P2, *CCCCL* LgA.

Following this date, GiL has a long omission (Maggioni, 1257–9 (mid-19 to mid-34), Dunn-Lardeau, 1151–2), resuming at the LgA date *DLXVIII* with *they had of custume.* The missing passage includes the Lombard migration to Italy and Alboin killing in battle the king of the Gepidae, marrying his daughter Rosamund, and making a cup from the skull of her father, relevant to 64–5 ff. below.

39 **that whan**: *cum quadam uice* LgA.
discoverers: *descouureurs* P2; *MED discoverer* n. sense (b) 'a military scout or spy', gives only one citation, for c1440(?a1400).

42 **men**: *barbati homines* LgA.

44 **berdez**: add *barda enim in eorum lingua barbam sonabat* LgA.
thei: *Wynnuli* LgA.

45 **prophete**: this spelling is not recorded *s.v. MED prophecie.*

47 **atte**: *iuxta* LgA.

48 **wyndowe**: add *le matin* P2.
thei: *mulieres* (. . .) *de eiusdem consilio* LgA.

49 **in stede of a berde**: not in LgA.

50 **these longe berdes**: *ces lombars* P2, *isti Longobardi* LgA.

51 **praied hym**: *luy dit* P2, *adiunxit* LgA.

61 **was**[2]: add *aussy comme* P2.

63 **Cremone**: *Verone* LgA.

65 **yaue it**: *y fist boire* P2.

67 **her husbonde**: only GiL.

68 **misused**: *auoit charnellement a faire a* P2.

69 **she . . . and**: *absente rege quadam nocte* LgA.

71 **he . . . her**: *uenisset, regina predicto duci uice ancille se supposuit et postmodum* LgA.

72 **Ye . . . love**: *que cestoit telle samie* P2, *se esse talem amicam suam* LgA.

73 **the quene**: not in LgA.

79 **whanne . . . dede**: *quant celluy deust venir* P2, not in LgA.

80 **in his scauberk**: *laquelle estoit au cheuet de son lit* P2.

84 **longe**: *dune selette* P2, 'with a stool'.

86 **toke**: add *sicomme len dit* P2.

93 **And . . . kinge**: *Tandem rex quidam Longobardorum* LgA.

93, 95 **Adorolik, Cheudeku**: *Adoloath*, *Theodelina* LgA; Adaloald (*c*.626–*c*.636) was the son of Queen Theodelina.

96 **expouned**: *exposa* P2, *transmisit* LgA.

105 **was all**: *et conuersio amplius* (. . .) *fuit* LgA.

107 **an oratorie**: *predictum oratorium* LgA.

114 **had**: add *auant* P2.

117 **wrote hymself to be**: *se* (. . .) *scribebat* LgA; i.e. designated itself. **And**: *Huius Bonifacii tempore* LgA.

118 **Eracles regnid**: *et regnante Eraclio* LgA; in LgA this sentence is combined with the next and introduces the account of Mahomet which follows.

121 **and the**: *ou* P2.

123 **the court**: *Romana curia* LgA.

126 **god . . . peple**: *quil le vouloit faire dieu et seigneur de tout ce peuple* P2, *ei quod ipsum illi populo preficere uellet* LgA.

131 **the clerke**: not in P2, *Predictus uir* LgA.

131–3 **that he wolde make hym lorde and maister of all that the holy goste wolde shewe and vpon his shuldre he wolde alight in lyknesse of a dove**: *se illum sibi uelle preficere quem spiritus sanctus in specie columbe monstraret* LgA.

137 **for to denounce hem**: *et luy denoncast* P2.

140 **Alisaundre**: add *Et le dit on communement* P2.

141 **more levely credible**: *plus vraie* P2; *levely* 'credible', is not recorded in *MED*, though *levelike* is given with one citation.

142 **feyned propre lawes**: *proprias leges confingens* LgA, 'making his own laws'.

152–3 **Noes . . . drowned**: *le deluge du monde* P2.

164 **that . . . hym**: *semblable que il auoit fait* S, *hominem sibi similem hoc egisse uel passum esse docuit* LgA.

165 **Dygam**: *cadigam* P2, *Cadigan* LgA; she is *Cadycam* at 173 below.

166 **Crotayne**: *corataine* P2, *Corocania* LgA; this is perhaps for Quraysh, the name of the tribe to which Mohamet and Khadija belonged.

gouernour of the peple: *garde de compaignie* P2, *contubernio uallari* LgA, 'accepted in the company'.

167 **Sarisenes**: add *et de juifs* P2.

169 **was prince**: *obtinuit principatum* LgA.

170 **cristen men**: *Saracenos* LgA.

173 **by the passion of his foule euell**: *de passion* P2, *epilentica passione* LgA; *foule euell* is glossed by *MED s.v. ivel* n. sense 5. (b) as '? epilepsy'.

174 **wist**: *vit* P2.

174–5 **a persone . . . euell**: *vng tresort homme qui cheoit de ce mal* P2, *impurissimo homini et epilentico* LgA.

177 **of hym**: *uultus eius* LgA.

177–8 **but . . . tyme so that**: *Et donc ie deffail tout et aneantis* (*aduient* P2) *que* S, *in me deficio et tabesco* LgA.

anientised: the MSS appear to have *m* for *ni*. A2 substituted *amasid*.

178–9 **so . . . myself** : not in LgA.

179 **mani other**: *les autres* P2.

182 **for**: *et* P2.

an heretike Vastorien: *in errorem Nestorii* LgA.

185 **Iakobyn**: a follower of the 6th-c. Syrian monophysite bishop Jacob Baradaeus.

188 **beleued**: *croient* P2.

192 **the peple**: *uniuersa gente sua* LgA.

197 **Arabye**: add *cum Magumetho* LgA.

203 **only**: *mesmement* P2.

203–4 **his felawshippe**: *contribulibus* LgA, 'fellow tribesmen'.

204 **hadde . . . hym**: *auoient este tousiours greigneurs que luy* P2, *eo maiores fuerant* LgA, 'they were taller than him'.

204–5 **he made . . . holynesse**: *voult il faindre quil estoit prophete* P2.

205 **might submitte**: *actraist* P2.

206 **not**: add *soubzmettre a luy* P2.

207 **he toke for to byleue**: *adherebat* LgA.

209–10 **saide . . . hym**: *lappelloit gabriel* P2, *Gabrielum archangelum eum nominabat* LgA.

210 **feyned falsnesse of**: *faingnant estre* P2.

213 **that**: *ce que len dit* P2, *quod supra est dictum* LgA.

215 **gouernaunce**: *dabit* P2; s.w. took *habit* as 'customary practice' rather than 'clothing'.

217 **werche ordinatly**: *aourassent moult ordonnement* P2, i.e. pray at regular times. A2 corrects to *wurchip*.

219 **his secte**: *les siens* S.

222 **lerned**: *aprist* P2, *en prist* P1, *accepit* LgA.
wesshe: *lieuent* P2, *lauant* LgA.

223 **and praie**: only GiL.

224 **wasshe**: *lieuent* P2, add *uerenda sua, manus, brachia, faciem et os et* LgA.

228 **day**[2]: add *quilz peuent deuiser le blanc du noir* P2, *qua nigrum ab albo distinguere possunt* LgA.

229 **be with**: *toucher* P2, *commixtione fedare* LgA.

230 **the tyme**: *lendemain* P2.

232 **but**: only GiL; *Il* P2 and *Semel autem* LgA begin a new sentence.

233 **conisaunce**: *recongnoissance* P2, *recognitionis* LgA, 'formal acknowledgment'; *MED* records this sense for *reconisaunce* sense 2, but only for legal contexts, and not at all for *conisaunce.*
to: add *en la maison dieu au* P2.

235 **betwene her thies**: *per media foramina* LgA, variant *femora* for *foramina*.

239 **blody flesshe**: *char et sang ensanglante* P2, *sanguinem et morticinum* LgA, 'blood and carrion'.

240 **to hym**: *ensemble* P2.
refuse and take: *repudiare et rursus recipere* LgA.

241 **fourthe tyme they may not**: *quaternarium numerum non transcendant* LgA, 'they may not exceed four in number'.

242 **concubynes**: *ancelles achatees et enchetiuees* P2.
putte hem from hem: *les peuent vendre* P2.

246 **Whanne . . . another**: *Circa possessiones repetendas* LgA, 'Concerning asking for the return of possessions'.

247 **the asker . . . othe**: *obseruant ut actor testibus probet et reus iuramento se comprobet innocentem* LgA, 'the practice is that the asker must prove his claim by witnesses, and the accused that he is innocent by oath'.

253 **shulde not see**: *ne parlast a* P2.

259 **yet**: *usque hodie* LgA.

260 **lawe**: add *Le larron qui est batu et repris* (*repris est batu* P1) *la premiere foys et la seconde. et la tierce il a la main coppee. et a lautre* (*La quarte fois* P1) *il a le pie coppe* P2.

He: *il leur est* P2.

261 **oure Lorde**: *deus* LgA.

269 **shull come**: *deambulabunt* LgA.

270, 271 **he shall geve, he shall yeue**: *donront* P2.

274–5 **wyne . . . spices:** *tres bon vin a tres precieuses espices* P2, *uini optimi aromatici* LgA.

281 **saued**: add *sicomme ilz croient* P2, add *ut asserunt* LgA.

282 **prophete**: add *auoit esperit* P2.

283 **aungels**: *.x. anges* P2.

285 **God**: add *et nisi ipse Magumethus futurus fuisset nec celum nec terra nec paradisus fuisset* LgA.

287–8 **a lombe . . . in flesshe**: *Venenum insuper sibi in carne agnina oblatum fuisse* LgA.

293–4 **weren . . . empire**: *Romano imperio plurimum molesti erant* LgA.

295–6 **the grettest . . . Fraunce**: *princeps maior regie domus Francorum* LgA, i.e. the mayor of the palace.

296 **sone**: add *qui Cutides appellabatur* LgA, Charles Martel.

297 **dede mani batailes and**: not in LgA.

298 **Charles**[1]: *Karolum magnum* LgA; **Charles**[2]: *charles le grant* P2, *Karolus magnus* LgA; this son of Charles Martel was in fact called Carloman.

300 **worshipfully**: *proffitablement* P2, *strenue* LgA.

301 **not profitable but symple**: *inutilis et remissus* LgA.

303–4 **or . . . kinge**: *ou cil qui gouuernoit bien le royaume* P2, not in LgA.

312–13 **and came . . . Fraunce**: not in LgA.

314–15 **wanne hym and ouercome hym**: *le vainqui* P2, not in LgA.

316 **alle**: add *predia* LgA.

317 **wexe**: *tourmenteroit* P2, *inquietaret* LgA. H2L read *vexe*; *MED s.v. vexen* gives spellings with *w*.

320–32 **And . . . sodenly**: In the revised version of LgA as edited by Maggioni, this passage has been transferred to p. 1257 (11–15), following GiL 26 above.

321–4 **Phelip . . . Theoderik. And**: *et ariana heresi deprauatus esset et Boetius philosophus consularis patricius cum Symmacho patricio, cuius gener erat, rempublicam illustraret et auctoritatem Romani senatus contra Theodoricum defensaret, idem* LgA. The losses and confusion in this passage, including the appearance of *Phelippe*, are also in P1, and therefore attributable to Vignay.

322 **was gendered**: *estoit gendre* P2, *gener erat* LgA.

Chelderik; Childeric is not here mentioned in LgA, but appears erroneously in P1, P2, and S; and also randomly in some other places for Theodoric.

326 **and there he deyed. His wyff**: *Et touteffoys lestaint sa femme* P2, *et tandem eum exstinxit. Eius uxor* LgA. H2 shares the LgD punctuation, but with *heeded* for *lestaint*. The E version seems to be a subsequent attempt at correction but retaining the redundant *that*.

327 **whiche . . . ympne**: it appears, however, to have been written by Paulinus of Aquileia.

Paule: add *qui ce commence* P2.

328–31 **I . . . iuge**:

Elpes dicta fui, Sicule regionis alumpna,
Quam procul a patria coniugis egit amor;
Porticibus sacris iam nunc peregrina quiesco,
Iudicis eterni testificata thronum. LgA.

GiL follows LgD's prose translation, including *non pas* for *nunc*, but substitutes *place* for *portaux*.

332 **deied sodenly**: *subito defunctus a quodam sancto heremita uisus est a Iohanne papa et Symmacho, quos ipse occiderat, nudus et discalceatus in ollam Vulcani demergi, sicut ait Gregorius in dyalogo* LgA.

332–3 **about . . . one**: This begins the next paragraph in LgA; see note to 26.

vjC.iiij^{xx}: *DCXLIIII* LgA.

343 **praiers**: add *et eschappa des peines* P2.

348 **In that same time**: *Circa annum domini DCLXXXVII.*

a worshipfull . . . prest: *presbitre honnorable et moyne* P2, *uenerabilis presbiter et monachus* LgA. *MED*'s first record of English 'venerable' for Bede is in Purvey's *Determinacion*, c1405.

was a clerke: *claruit* LgA.

350, 358, 359 **worshipfull**: *honnorable* P2, *uenerabilis* LgA.

355 **peple**: add *qui attendoient tout quoiement* S, *qui* (. . .) *silenter et auide expectabant* LgA.

358–9 **And this . . . fader**: *pource est il ainsy appelle de leglise. Et si comme les autres dient les anges respondirent. tu as bien dit pere honnorable* (*uenerabilis* LgA) P2.

360 **devout clerke of his**: *vng clerc moult deuot a luy* P2.

to sette aboute: *quil fist entailler en* P2.

361 **Here stant the fossa**: *Cy sont en ceste fosse* P2, *Hac sunt in fossa* P2; *MED* does not record *fossa* with final *a* or with the sense 'grave'.

363 **and for . . . bedde**: *Et quant il ot assez pense et il ne pouoit trouuer fin assez couuenable toute vne nuyt* P2.

366–7 **And so . . . worshipfull**: *In die autem ascensionis cum morti appropinquaret ad altare portari se faciens antiphonam 'O rex glorie domine uirtutum' usque ad finem deuote dixit, qua finita in pace dormiuit tantusque odor omnes perfudit ut in paradiso se esse extimarent* LgA.

367 **Gonys**: *Ianuam* LgA; Bede's bones were transferred in 1020 from Jarrow to Durham Cathedral, where they remain. The Bede buried in Genoa is another monk of the same name.

369 **and . . . funtstone**: only GiL.

370 **withinne** : *ou lauatoire et en osta et retraist lautre* S, *in lauacro,* (. . .) *alterum retrahens* LgA.

371 **his predecessours . . . peple**: *ses grans predecesseurs* P2, *maiorum suorum* LgA.

375–6 **temperell . . . comparison**: *donner biens sans comparoison* P2, *quod tertia die abhinc imcomparabilia bona sibi daret* LgA.

378 **the champaine**: *Campania* LgA.
rye: *ble* P2, *legumina* LgA.

381 **to Florence**: *de Monte Cassino ad monasterium Floriacense* LgA.

382 **Charles**: *charles le grant* P2, *Karolus magnus* LgA, in fact Carloman, son of Charles Martel; see 298–9 above and note.

383 **body**: add *de saint benoist* P2.

384 **God**: add *et Francis resistentibus* LgA.

387–8 **all . . . withinne**: *cum muris et habitatoribus suis integre et salue* LgA.

388 **mo thanne .vjM^l^.**: *ultra sex miliaria ut dicitur* LgA; GiL follows LgD in taking this as the number of inhabitants rather than the distance travelled.

389 **Peter**: add *lapostre* P2.

389–90 **was brought thedir**: *fut transporte de la ou il estoit* P2, *transfertur* LgA; the presumed remains of Petronilla were translated from the catacomb of Domitilla to an old mausoleum near St Peter's in 757.

390 **it was wrete**: *fut trouue escript* P2, *ipsius Petri manu scriptu legebatur* LgA.
toumbe: add *de marbre* P2.

391 **doughter**: add *Et si comme sigibert dit. Ceulx de thir tourmenterent armenie* P2, *ut ait Sigebertus. Eo tempore Tyrii Armeniam infestant* LgA; LgA attributes the preceding paragraph to Sigebert.

393 **hedys**: *choses* P2, *capita* LgA.

394–5 **vse . . . yet**: *retindrent ceste maniere de tondre* P2.

396 **thanne**: *en la parfin* P2.

397 **the Grete**: add *son filz* S.

402 **came**: add *pars les mons* P2, add *per montem Cenisium* LgA.
gret[2]: *royal* P2.

404 **into Fraunce**: *en france* P2, *ad Gallias* LgA.

405 **Amys**: *amis* P2, *Amicus* LgA.

406 **Amylon**: *amilles* P2, *Amelius* LgA.

406–7 **in . . . Crist**: *en lost charles et estoient tresnobles cheualiers de ihesu crist* P2.

415 **to clothe**: *de vestir* P2, *inuestituram* LgA; *MED* does not record *clothen* in this formal sense.

416 **his**: *chascune* P2.

418 **of Gascoigne**: *daquitaine* P2.

419–20 **wolde . . . ouercome**: *de coniuratione contra patrem conuictus* LgA.

421 **.vijC.iiii^{xx}. and .iij.**: add *ou temps de* P2, *DCCLXXXII tempore scilicet* LgA.

422 **moder of**: *et de son fils* P2.

423 **walle**: add *Thracie* LgA.

427–8 **a noble man and**: only GiL.

429 **that he was enhaunsed**: *du son soubhaucement dicelluy* P2.

431 **ranne vpon hym and**: only GiL.

435 **Charles**: misplaced here in LgD and GiL, and should be at 436 **he;** it was the Romans who repudiated the empire of Constantinople.

437–8 **was made . . . augustien**: *cesarem et augustum appellant* LgA; see note to 81.52; *MED* does not record *augustien*.

438 **all**: GiL omits Maggioni, 1271 (217–23), Dunn-Lardeau, 1164–5, dealing further with the division of the empire, and including a hint that Charlemagne had been suspected by some of incest, from an account attributed to Alcuin but in fact by Einhardt.

440 **solempnely**: *forment* P, *sollempniter* LgA.

441 **auctorite**:add *de lempereur* P2.

443 **was awaited**: *insidiis urgeretur* LgA, was subject to attacks.

444 **he and his clerkes**: *luy et la gent catholique* P2, *cum plebe catholica* LgA.

445–6 **so that the peple shulde be made wery by synnes of that**

errour: *sy que le peuple ne salentist dannuy en lerreur* P2, *ne populus meroris tedio contabesceret* LgA, 'lest the people should fade away through the oppression of that grief'.

448–9 **as hym thought best**: only GiL.

451 **they had**: *la messe eust* P2.

452 **lessones**: *la leccon* P2, *lectione* LgA.

454–6 **in the begynninge . . . songe**: *introitum misse cum cantu ordinauit et quosdam uersos de illo psalmo qui totus cantabatur retinuit* LgA.
ye shull saie: *len chantast* P2.

456 **songen**: add *pseaumes* P2.
auuter: add *en maniere de coronne* P2, add *in modum corone circumstantes* LgA.

458 **Theodore**: Diodorus of Tarsus rather than his follower Theodore of Mopsuestia is named at this point by Honorius of Autun, the apparent source of the passage.

460 **verse**: add *Et le tindrent de Ignacien qui en fut enseigne diuinement* P2.

461 **night**: add *pour grant partie fors que le chant* P2.
Gelosyes and Gregorie: *ambroise gelause et gregoire* S, *Ambrosius, Gelasius et Gregorius* LgA.

462 **and the lessones**: *et lectionibus et euangeliis coaptauerunt* LgA.

463 **before the gospell**: *auant les euuangilles* P2, *ad missam cantari* LgA.
Pelusie and Gregorie: *ambroise gelause et gregoire* S.

464 **Hillarie**: add *uel secundum quosdam Symmachus papa uel Telesphorus papa* LgA.

465 **And**: add *Nocher* P2, i.e. Notker.

466 **with alleluya**: *des alleluies* S, *pro neumis ipsius alleluia* LgA; add further *Et le pape nichole octroya quilz feussent chantees a la messe* P2.

466, 470 **sequence(s)**: melodic extensions to the final syllable of the word Alleluia; for a fuller account see *ODCC*, 1494.

466–7 **Aryen the Contracte of Thewthonik**: *Hermannus Contractus Teutonicus* LgA; crippled from birth, Hermann spent most of his life at the monastery at Reichenau composing works of scholarship in various fields.

467 **made**: add *Rex omnipotens,* LgA.
gracia: add *Aue maria et les autres antiennes Alma redemptoris mater* P2.

467–8 ***Simond Bariona***: i.e. Simon Bar Iona, Peter the apostle; see Matt. 16: 17, the source of the antiphon.

470 **aforesaid**: only GiL.

471 **Turpin**: add *archiepiscopus* LgA; see note to 156.437.

472–3 **large pawme**: *MED* gives *paume* as 'a hand's breadth, usually 3 inches, sometimes longer'; and *large paume* as '? 4 inches or longer'. Lewis & Short give *palmus* as a measure of length of 'a span or twelve digits'. A span, according to *OED*, is about nine inches.

474 **a man**: *Militem armatum* LgA.
stroke: add *de son espee* P2.

475 **wolde breke**: *estendoit* P2, i.e. straightened.

476–7 **an armed man . . . hede**: *de terre a sa main .i. cheualier arme iusques a son chief tout droit* S, *Militem armatum rectum stantem super manum suam a terra usque ad caput suum sola manu uelociter eleuabat* LgA.

477 **and**[1,2]: *ou* P2.

479 **he passed neuer thries drinkinge**: *il ne beuuoit que .iij. foys* P2, *raro plus quam ter bibere solebat* LgA.

479–80 **He dede mani gret batailes**: *Cenobia multa construxit* LgA.

485 **disgises and arrayes**: *desguisees vestures* (. . .) *et autres cointz aournemens* P2, so and add *secularia* LgA.

491 **to the . . . anone**: *Et lempereur estoit la present et luy pleut tant que il* P2.

492 **dignite**: *siege* P2.

495–6 **of Aungeles**: not in LgA.

497 **twenty**: *XVIIII* LgA.

500 **bretheren**: *ses freres* P2.

500–1 **in a bataile**: only GiL.

505 **that is called Loreyne**: *quil nomma lorraine* P2, *ab ipso Lotharingia dicta est* LgA.
lefte: add *imperium* LgA.

506 **that . . . hym**: *qui depuis fut empereur* P2, not in LgA.

507 **Serge**: add *natione Romanus* LgA.

511 **hym**: *hiis* LgA.
to be apostle: *in apostolatum* LgA.

513 **to that perfeccion**: *a noble office* P2, *ad tam decorum officium* LgA.

515 **.viijC. and .vj.**: *.viijC. et .xvj.* P2, *DCCCLVI* LgA.

517–19 **spirites betin, spakin, thei**: all singular P2.

518 **spakin opinly in**: *manifeste loquendo et* LgA.

520 **Letanies**: add *et aquam benedictam spargentibus* LgA.

521 **And . . . lough**: *Et au derrenier se souffri* P2, *Tandem aliquando conquiescens* LgA.

523 **that was his . . . felawe**: *aussy comme de son familiaire* P2.

524 **emperours**: *procuratoris* LgA.

528 **wrechidly**: *jeunement* P2.

530 **toke hym**: add *effossisque oculis* LgA.
prison: add *Et puis il ordonna son autre filz le meneur en roy* P2.

532 **Itaile**: add *en la cite de brixe* S, i.e. Brescia.

533 **langustus right cruell**: *locuste innumerabiles* LgA; *MED* has only two citations for *languste*, 'locust', one for a1225 and one for a1500. A2 substitutes *locustus*; L calls them *a cruelle serpent*.
.ij.: *sex* LgA.

534 **and**[1]: add *duos* LgA.

535 **the cumpanye of armed men**: *castrorum acies* LgA.

535–6 **thei helde**: *extendentes* LgA.

536 **.v. or .vj. myle**: *iiij. lieues ou v.* S.

537 **see of Bretayne**: *mare Britannicum* LgA, English Channel.

540 **and stinke**: only GiL.

540–1 **so gret a pestilence**: *grant famine et grant mortalite* P2, *mortalitas maxima et fames perualida* LgA.

542 **furst**: add *en lan de nostre seigneur .ixC. xxxviij.* P2.

GiL omits Maggioni, 1275 (271–4), Dunn-Lardeau, 1168–9.

544 **of hem . . . Romaynes**: *Romam uenit et* LgA.

544–5 **a gret . . . comunes**: *vne feste commune a tous barons euesques et grans seigneurs* P2, add further *apud gradum ecclesie* LgA.

546 **alle**: add *latenter* LgA.

547 **compleint**: add *de uiolata pace* LgA.
named: *fit nommer* P2.
bi writyng: *in scriptis* LgA, 'from written documents'.

548–9 **grete feste and grete chere**: *fist* (. . .) *belle chere et les honnora moult* P2, *epulari satagebat* LgA.

551 **.ixC.iiij**^{xx}**. and .x.**: *DCCCCLXXXIIII* LgA.

552 **loued**: *voult estre aime a* P2, *se prostituere uoluit* LgA.

556 **innocent**: add *apres ce que il seroit mort* P2.

566 **after her will**: only GiL.

568 **and thanne of .iij.**: *et puis de .vij. et puis de .iij.* P2, *tertio septem quarto sex a uidua* LgA.

568–9 **til . . . knowen**: *Tunc imperator causa examinata et ueritate cognita* LgA.

569 **And . . . trouthe**: only GiL.

570 **for**: add *sa* P2.

572 **the termes of dayes**: *induciis dierum X, VIII, VII, VI* LgA.

573 **Harre**: *beatus Henricus LgA.*

574 **kinge**: add *Stephano* LgA.

575 **by grace . . . vertu**: only GiL.

577 **after**: only GiL.
so perfit and so holy: *si grant* P2.

578 **wrought for hym**: *lennobli par gloire de* P2.
Ragand: *Kunegundis* LgA; as at 110.257, the earliest LgA MSS give this correct version of the queen's name, but later ones give spellings in *R*-, as do LgD and Batallier.

579 **heuenly**: *celestiel* P2, *celibem* LgA.

581–2 **the whiche . . . sacrement**: this clause is an addition found in SZ, except that S reads *emprisonne* for Z *empoisonne*; it is not in P2, P1, or LgA, and the syntax of the French and English make it unclear whether the allegation of poisoning relates to *Henre* (the *Harre* of 573 and 578, Henry II), or his niece (Gisela of Swabia) or even *Conrade*. There seems to be no reason to suppose that any of these were poisoned.
Iacobyn: see note to 185 above. It is, however, hard to see why a monophysite assassin should be involved.

583 **beme**: *tref* P2, i.e. a wooden beam.

584 **sonne**: add *qui se tournoit ja au coucher* P2.

585 **bisshoppes**: add *de Ytalia* LgA.
and: add *quia Mediolanensis archiepiscopus de uinculis fugit* LgA.

587 **chirche**: add *secus urbem,* (. . .) *ad missam* LgA.

589 **masse**: add *et le secretaire de lempereur* P2, add further *cum aliis* LgA.

590 **secrete**: *sollempnia* LgA, i.e. the consecration.

596 **trauailed**: *pregnans uicinaque partui* LgA.

598 **ayre**: *gendre* P2.

600 **from the moder**: *a la mere a force* P2, *de manibus matris uiolenter* LgA.
sle: *le couppez parmy* P2, *per medium scindentes* LgA.

609 **it**: add *de uxore sua* LgA.
Harre: no such Harry reigned between Conrad and 651 *Harri the thridde*.

615 **slee**: add *Volens igitur esse securus* LgA.

616 **in this wise**: *contenant ces paroles* P2, *in hunc modum,* (*et*) *per eum uxori dirigit* LgA.

617–18 **the messengeres went**: *il aloit* P2.

622 **letter**: add *saluo sigillo* LgA, i.e. without breaking the seal.

624 **childe**: add *et mist* P2.

628 **Pays**: *Ais* P2, *Aquisgrani* LgA, Aix-la-Chapelle.

631 **that . . . childe**: not in LgA.

634 **gendre**: 'son-in-law', not recorded by *MED*.

638 **mynstrales**: *telz gens* P2, *hiis* LgA.

641 **the thother**: *illis* LgA.

644 **he passed . . . were well**: *faingnist toutes ces choses* P2.

645 **a sene**: the Council of Sutri, 1046.

645–6 **Gracian . . . downe**: *il conuainqui gracien de symonie* P2.

646 **Notwithstondinge**: *et touteffois est il dit* P2.

646–7 **in a lettre that he wrete**: *in libro* (. . .) *Bonizi, quem misit* LgA; Bonizo of Sutri, *c.*1045–90, was both author and sender of the book..

647 **emperise Mauude**: *lempereur maheust* P2, *comitissam Matildim* LgA.

647–8 **was to symple**: *estoit moult simple* P2, *simplicitate ductus* LgA.

649 **contraried to the discorde**: *schismati obuiaret* LgA.

655 **the songe**: *cantus* LgA, plural.

659 **of Betens**: *Betensis* LgA, i.e. of Bec, Vignay taking the adjectival form as the noun.

661 **fourthe**: add *lan mil .lvij.* P2.

667 **they songe**: *nondum* (. . .) *canteretur* LgA.

669 **Terentene**: *caritate* LgA, La Charité-sur-Loire (Boureau, 1485 n. 137).

670 **stori**: add *pource que celle hystoire nestoit encores pas commune* P2, not in LgA.

671 **hem**: add *Et dit que cestoit desordonnee chose de muer les anciennes coustumes en nouuelles* P2.

672–3 **of hym**: add *de ce nouuel chant. mais est mieulx a dire que chanconnettes soient chantees en mon eglise* P2, add *ut noua cantica immo ioculatoria quedam in mea ecclesia decantentur* LgA.

674 **saide**: add *aussy comme par tristesce* P2.
Mattins: *matines et vigilles* P2, *matutinarum uigilias* LgA; add further *Et quant tous furent couchiez en leurs lis* P2.

675 **of the dortour**: *et le frappoit au pauement du dortouer* P2, *a lecto* (*et*) *dormitorii pauimento collisit* LgA.

676 **singe**: add *antiphonam* LgA.

678 **melodiously**: *morose* LgA.

682 **abbot**: add *Roberto* LgA.

683 **desert**: *Cistercii solitudinem* LgA.

684 **hadde**: *establirent* P2.
ordre: add *ex ueteri* LgA.

686 **in Ordre of Menours**: *es mineurs ordres* P2, *in minoribus* LgA, i.e. in minor orders.

687, 689 **ouercome**: *conuainqui*, *conuaincu* P2, 'convicted'; s.w. mistranslates.

687 **merueilously**: add *a lyons* P2.

690 ***In nomine patris et filij***: *'Gloria patri et filio et spiritui sancto.' Ille 'gloria patri et filio' expedite dicebat* LgA.

694 **Brune**: *Bonizo* LgA; for Bonizo and *Mauude*, see 646 and 647 above.
Mauude the emperesse: *maheust empereur* P2, *comitissam Matildim* LgA.

695 **this Harre**: *Henrico quarto* LgA.
dede: add *len escript sur sa tombe ou si fu enterrez auec les autres roys. Cy gist Henry le filz Henry le pere Henry laiol et Henry le besaiol* S, add *Spire et cum aliis regibus sepulto, hunc uersum Henrici in epitaphio habent: 'Filius hic, pater hic, auus hic, proauus iacet istic.'* LgA. These burials are at Speyer, LgA *Spire*.

696 **.vj.**: *.vij.* P2, *VIII* LgA.
toke the cardinales: *prist pauie auecques les cardinaulx et les laissa en habis deuesques et dabbez. et prist le gouuernement de pasteur par lannel et par le baston* P2, *papam cum cardinalibus cepit et eos dimittens inuestituram episcoporum et abbatum per annulum et baculum pastoralem accepit* LgA, '. . . and in releasing them took over the investiture of bishops and abbots by the ring and pastoral staff'.

697 **toke the religion of Cisteaux**: *Cistercium ingreditur* LgA, i.e. joined the order at Cîteaux.

702 **other**: add *par les dos. et* P2.

703 **woman**: *canis* LgA.

708 **wel devoutely**: *cum multa instantia* LgA.

714 **hym**: *celluy quil ne pouoit prendre* P2.
and saide: *au ciel et aoura en ceste maniere* P2.

716 **disapered**: add *de la ou ilz le tenoient* P2, add *ibidem* LgA.

721 **the Patriarke**: *Porretanus* LgA, i.e. Gilbert de la Porrée.

728 **rightfully**: *canonice* LgA.
.iij. popis: *en papes* P2, *successiue in papam* LgA; the antipopes were

Octaviano Monticelli (Victor IV), Guido di Crema (Paschal III), and Giovanni di Struma (Calixtus III).

729 **Cremon**: *de cremonne qui estoit adonc de st calais* P2, *Cremensis tituli sancti Calixti* LgA, i.e. whose titular church was S. Calixtus.

729–30 **thei . . . emperoure**: *fauore imperatoris fulciuntur* LgA.
worshipped: *ennoblis* P2.

732 **of Rome**: only GiL.

732–3 **Mount Port**: the battle of Monte Porzio, or of Tusculum, took place in 1167.

739 **.xx.[ti] tymes .xM[l].xvjC. and an halff**: *.x. foys .M. et .x. et par .x. foys .xvjC. et demy* P2, *Mille decem decies et sex decies quoque seni* LgA.

741 **drowned**: add *et les autres dient que si comme il embatoit son cheual en leaue il chey la et morut* S.

742 **.M[l].C.iiij[xx].**: *MCXC* LgA.

744 **that neuer before had be sene no suche**: *que ilz nauoient onques este sy grans de memoire domme* P2, *quantas nulla meminit hominum antiquitas* LgA.

744–5 **heylestones . . . eye**: *pierres cheoient grandes et carrees aussy grosses comme oeufz* P2, *Lapides enim ad quantitatem ouorum quadranguli* LgA.

745–6 **bestes . . . trees**: *les vignes. les arbres et les blez. et occistrent moult dommes et de bestes* P2, so LgA without the beasts.

750 **Innocent**: add *tertius* LgA.
opposed: *sopposa* P2. *MED* records no verb corresponding to E *appased*, and D *appesid* is clearly inappropriate, but *s.v. opposen* offers a sense closer to that here required, 'opposed', which is given only for three instances of past participles.
sone: *frater* LgA.

751 **of the duke**: *Ottoni filio ducis* LgA.
that: *et* P2.

752 **to be**: *couronner* P2.

756 **messengeres**: *legatos* LgA.
to: add *phelippe* P2.

757 **Albiones**: *abigoys* P2, *Albigensium* LgA.

759 **Oton was crowned**: *couronna octon* P2.

760 **anone**: add *ipso die* LgA.

761 **dispoiled**: *fist despoiller et oster les rompetes* (*rommipetres* P1) S, *necnon et Romipetas expoliari fecit* LgA; *Romipetas*, 'pilgrims to Rome'.
he was acursed: *lescommenia il* P2, *papa eum excommunicauit* LgA.

762 **florisshed**: *fut* P2.

763 **Landegraue had wedded**: *fut femme* (add *de* P1) *landegraue* P2, *fuit uxor landgrauii* LgA.

764 **miracles**: add *ut scribitur* LgA.

765 **many . . . specially to**: only GiL.
blynde[2]: add *et encore dequeurt huille de son tombel au iourduy* S.

766 **his sone**: *filz de henry* P2.

771 **Gregori**: add *IX* LgA.

774 **.v.**[e]: *IV* LgA.

776 **And . . . voyde and**: *Et dont vacqua le siege et* P2, *Quo deposito et defuncto* LgA.
hedir: *usque hodie* LgA; Frederick died in 1250, and there was no emperor till 1312.

175 DEDICATION OF THE CHURCH

Maggioni, ch. CLXXVIII, p. 1283; Dunn-Lardeau, ch. 177, p. 1177.

1–4 The Church is divided into I Material, 5–408, and II Spiritual, 409–93.

5–7 dedication of the Material involves: A why 8–181; B how 182–355; C *per quos profanatur*, which GiL omits here but is covered in its correct place 356–408.

I A the altar (i) and the temple itself (ii) are to be consecrated (these words omitted by GiL):

(i) The altar is dedicated for three reasons: (a) to sacrifice to God 8–27, (b) to call on the name of the Lord 28–47, (c) for singing 48–74.

(ii) The temple or church is dedicated for five reasons 75–181: (a) to put out the fiend 75–91, (b) to protect the guilty 92–6, (c) as a place for prayer 97–112, (d) as a place to praise God 113–70, (e) as a place to administer sacraments 171–81.

I B How the church is dedicated 182–4: (i) the altar 185–266, (ii) the church 267–355.

(i) the altar: (a) four crosses 185–99, (b) the surroundings 200–14, (c) the sprinkling 215–30, (d) incense 231–42, (e) chrism 243–52, (f) white cloth 253–66.

(ii) the church 267–75: (a) bishop goes about three times 276–89, (b) bishop knocks at door 290–300, (c) sprinkling (*i*) to eject the fiend, (*ii*) to cleanse corruption, (*iii*) to put away cursing 301–22, (d) inscription of the alphabet 323–36, (e) (misnumbered *Thriddely* in GiL) painting of crosses 337–55.

I C By whom the church is profaned, 356–8:

(i) Jeroboam 358–81,

(ii) Nabuzardan 382–92,
(iii) Antiochus 393–402,
and on the contrary by whom dedicated: Moses, Solomon, and Judas Machabeus 402–8.

II The Spiritual temple, 409–end:

A The nature of the temple 410–419;

B The nature of the altar 419–30;

C Jesus in the person of the bishop:
(i) goes about three times 432–8,
(ii) knocks at door three times 439–49,
(iii) sprinkles with water three times 450–72,
(iv) writes the alphabet 473–81,
(v) paints the crosses 482–9.

2 **the double feste of the**: *il est double* P2.

3 **and**: not in LgA.

7 **sacred**: add *tiercement par lesquelz il est sacre* (*profanatur* LgA) *et pource que deux choses sont ou temple qui sont sacrees. Cest lautel et le temple. pour ce est il premierement a veoir comment* (*quare* LgA) *lautel est sacre et secondement pour quoy le temple est sacre* S.

8 **furst**: *autem* LgA.

8–9 **to sacrifie to God**: *a sacrifier aux dieux* P2, *ad sacramentum domini* LgA.

14 **recomaunded**: *recommanda* S, *commande* P2, *precepit* LgA; *MED recommaunden* does not record the sense 'command'.

15–16 **of oure Lorde**: *que nous auons par escript* P2.

16 **that other is**: *et lautre* P2, *scilicet* LgA; Vignay assumed this would be the second and had to adjust at 19–20 below.

16–17 **whanne . . . Crist**: *quant au voir. Car lymage de ihesucrist* P2, *quantum ad uisum*; *ipsa enim crucifixi ymago* LgA.

18–19 **to stere . . . peple**: *propter rememorationem excitandam, deuotionem et instructionem* LgA.

19–20 **and these two . . . one**[1]: not in LgA; added by Vignay to adjust erroneous *et lautre* at 15 above.

20 **but one**[2]: only GiL.

22 **transfigured**: *tam signanter expressa* LgA.

23 **is**: *continetur et nobis offertur* LgA.
soule: only GiL.

25 **embrasith the will**: *affectum nostrum accendit* LgA.

25–6 **and yef . . . hym**: *et celle qui est preschee embrase* P2, *et amplius predicata* LgA.

26 **this**: *ce sacrement* P2, *in hoc sacramento* LgA.

27 **signifiauntli**: all MSS have forms of *signifiethe*, but an adverb as in LgD and LgA is required. *MED* records no adverbial form of this word, but, given the similarity of *th* and *tli* in several of these hands, it is likely that s.w. gave that and was misread by an early scribe.

30 **called**: *inuocauit* LgA.

31 **vocacion or callynge**: *Inuocacion ou appel* P2, *inuocatio* LgA; *MED* gives two instances of *vocacioun*, the vocation of the apostles a1475(?a1430) and to an ecclesiastical office 1442. This instance is for *invocacioun*, which *MED* records first from *Hous of Fame*; Vulgate Gen. 12: 8 gives *aedificavit quoque ibi altare Domino, et invocavit nomen eius*.
called and: only GiL.

32 **to Timotheus**: *I ad Tim. II* LgA.
made: add *par adiuration* S.

34 **and for to kepe hem**: *aut per gratiarum actiones, que fiunt pro bonis habitis conseruandis* LgA.
The furst: *Inuocatio autem* LgA.

35 **for that Ihesu Crist is sent fro heuene**: *ex eo quod celestis missus, scilicet Christus*.

35–6 **And messe . . . Ihesu Crist**: not in LgA.

37 **she**: i.e. the host.

38 **he**: i.e. Christ.

41 **sethe**: *secundo* LgA.

41–2 **And . . . vs.**: *Et premierement il commenca a estre auec nous par saintifiement. et nous auecques luy par celle oblation qui prie pour nous.* P2, *Similiter in sacramento primo a patre nobis per sanctificationem qua nobiscum esse incipit, postea a nobis patri per oblationem qua pro nobis intercedit* LgA.

43 **Latin**: add *et est pour representer le tiltre qui fut mis sur la croix a sa glorieuse passion qui estoit escript en grec en hebrieu et en latin* P2.

44 **God**: add *que per hanc triplicem linguam intelligitur* LgA.

45 **gospeles**: add *et le chant* P2, add *orationes et cantus* LgA.

46 **come to**: add *societatem* LgA.

47 **Alleluya**: add *amen* LgA.

49 **Ho, hem**: *il, luy* P2.

50–1 **and made hem to be putte . . . to synge**: *et le fist oster denuiron lautel et fist chanter les chantres* P2, *et stare fecit contra altare cantores* LgA.

51, 52, 53 **melodie, melodyes, melodies**: *modulos* LgA, 'sorts of musical sound'.

52 **in wepinge**: *en plurier* P2, 'in the plural'.

54–5 **The touchinge and the smitynge**: *le bouter ou par ferir* P2, *pulsu* LgA.

60 **but in that**: *Et infra* LgA, i.e. this is also from Hugh of St-Victor.

62–3 **She brekithe . . . maners**: *Frangis uocem, frange et uoluntatem, seruas consonantiam uocum, serua concordiam morum* LgA.

64–5 **and bi . . . God** *per uoluntatem deo* LgA.

65–6 **this is (. . .) that**: *Hoc igitur* LgA.

66 **is reported**: *est rapportee* P2, *refertur* LgA, 'relates'; see note to 34.29.
difference: add *de loffice* P2.

67 **so as it . . . Chirche**: *ut dicitur in Mitrali de officio* LgA, by Sicardus of Cremona.

69 **The .v.**: *La premiere* P2.

70 **instrumentis**: add *et ad illud pertinet psalmodia: Ps.: 'Laudate eum in Psalterio et cythara.'* LgA.
is: add *le chant. sicomme de la* P2.

78 **blessed and halued**: *beneissoit* P2, *consecraretur* LgA.

79 **Seint Fabyan and of**: only GiL; the reason for the addition is unknown.

84 **And that night**: *Sequenti autem nocte* LgA.

91 **withholde**: add *Hec Gregorius* LgA.

93 **for socour . . . perile**: only GiL.
For: *donc aucunes eglises apres la dedication sont priuilegiees des princes que ceulx qui sont coulpables et senfuient a leglise soient sauuez. de quoy le canon dist* P2.

95–6 **toke the auuter**: *cornu altaris apprehendit* LgA, 3 Kgs. 2: 28.

98 **the boke of Kingges**: *III Reg.* LgA.

100 **thou . . . tabernacle**: *exaudies in loco habitaculi tui* LgA.

101 **and**: add *quant tu lauras exaulcie* P2, add *cum exaudieris* LgA.

102 **causes**: add *selon ce que daniel dit ou .iiij.*[e] *liure ou premier chapitre* P2, add *secundum Damascenum I. IV, cap. V* LgA.

105 **Daniel**: i.e. John Damascene; see 102 above.

105–6 **in the hous of the orient**: *in Edem secundum orientem* LgA.

108–9 **Before . . . chirche and**: *Antiquam igitur patriam exquirentes et ad ipsam aspicientes* LgA.

109 **orient**: add *Et nostre seigneur crucifie regardoit a occident. Et ainsy regardons nous et laourons deuers orient* (*ad ipsum respicientes* LgA) P2.

110 **hye**: add *ad orientem* LgA.

112 **cominge**: add *Hec Damascenus* LgA.

114 **Houres**: add *canoniaux* P2.

122 **in takinge (. . .) largely**: i.e. broadly speaking.

125–6 **that thinge . . . haue saide**: *traditionem apostolicam* LgA.

127 **of virgines**: only GiL.

129–30 **makin the fest the day**: *facent la feste le iour* P2, *festum agere diem* LgA, the Latin idiom carrying through to GiL.

132 **holy apostles**: *patrum* LgA, i.e. the Fathers in the harrowing of hell.
besyly and: only GiL.

137 **Egipciens**: add *et que nous rendons graces a dieu pour nostre creation et pour sa resurrection* P2.

139 **hym**: add *id est ad eum mane festinabat* LgA.

141 **apered**: add *premier* P2.

142 **therfor**: add *in hac hora* (. . .) *in ecclesia* LgA.

143 **hym**[1]: *ihesu crist et que nous rendons graces a icelluy resuscitant et apparant* P2.

150 **world**: add *sy que le soleil ploroit a la mort de son seigneur. et se couury de vestement noir quil* (add *ne* S) *donnast lumiere a ceulx qui crucifioient son seigneur* P2.

152 **Longius**: *le cheualier* P2.

157–8 **aposteles and**: not in LgA.

168–70 **ioynge . . . fre will**: *ioingnez le sens aux paroles et lentalentement au sens et lesleescement a lentalentement et meurte a lesleescement et humilite a la meurte et a lumilite franchise* P2.

172 **table**: *tauerne* S.

173 **be comuned**: *continentur* LgA.

175 **duellers as ordres**: *commorantibus et horum quidam sunt ministrantes, hiis datur ordo* LgA, i.e. these are ordained.

176 **sum falle**: *horum quidam pugne succumbunt* LgA.

183 **after**: *secundo* LgA.

186 **and**[1]: *secundo* LgA.
is avironed: *est auironnee* P2, *circuitur* LgA; *MED* does not record this verb, though *environen* sense 7 carries the same sense; cf. *environinge* at 201 below.

mani tymes: *sept foys* P2.

186–7 **with ysope springed**: *arrousee .vij. fois du guespillon* P2, *tertio aqua benedicta cum ysopo septies aspergitur* LgA.

187 **after**[1]: *quarto* LgA.
within the auter: *dessus lautel* P2, *in ipso* LgA.
after[2]: *quinto* LgA.

188 **and thanne**: *sexto* LgA.
blacke clothe: *draps noirs* (*neufz* S, *nez* P1) P2, *mundis pannis* LgA.

189 **that representithe hem**: *Hec representant ea que debent habere illi* LgA, *ea* = those qualities.

190 **maners**: add *per crucem acquisitam* LgA.

191 **hemselff**: add *in deum* LgA.

199 **continuel impression**: i.e. frequent making of the sign.

200 **thou shalt**: *ilz doiuent* P2.

202–3 **hem that . . . to hem**: *gregem suum* LgA.

204–5 **a foule thinge but moche more perilous:** *Ridiculosa an magis periculosa* LgA.

207 **ellis**: add *par les .vij. auironnemens de lautel sont signifiees* P2.

211 **kinrede**: *parens* P2, *parentibus* LgA; *MED kinrede* offers 'forebears' but not 'parents'.

211–12 **the power of his seruaunt**: *sub manu serui* LgA, i.e. the hand of a slave.

213–14 **as a debonair lambe**: *comme debonnaire* P2.

214 **praied**: add *piteusement* P2.
hym: in LgA and LgD this is followed by 224–30 **Or . . . heuene**, Maggioni, 1289 (123–4), Dunn-Lardeau, 1184–5.

216 **that betokenithe**[2]: *Septem enim aque aspersiones sunt* LgA.

218 **the seconde was in prayenge**: Luke 22: 44.

223 **the auuter is environed**: *ideo* (. . .) *aspergitur* LgA.

224–30 **Or . . . heuene**: these lines follow 214 **hym** in LgD, LgA.

225 **yeftes**: *auironnemens* P2.
comyngges : *uie* LgA.

229 **hell**[1,2]: *limbum, limbo* LgA.

231 **amerous**: not in LgA.

232 **upon the auuter**: only GiL.

233 **And than it**: *Thus enim* LgA.

234 **to comforte bi his qualite**: *consolidandi ex sua qualitate* LgA, 'of making whole by its nature'; GiL/LgD *comforte* has been caught from 235.
to ioyne bi that it glewithe: *conioindre parce quil glue* P2, *constringendi ex conglutinitate* LgA, 'of binding together through its stickiness'.

235 **that is to saie well smellynge**: not in LgA.

236 **to God bi true mynde**: *ou memoire de dieu* S, *in dei memoriam* LgA, 'into the memory of God'.

237 **gilt passid**: *coulpe passee* P2; GiL has retained the French order.

238 **come**: add *en impetrant* P2.
confermithe: *conferme* P2, *confortat* LgA.

239 **defence and kepinge**: *tutelam* LgA.

240 **orison**: add *est demonstree* P2.

240–1 **that she pertenithe that she stiethe to God**: *quia habet ad Deum ascendere* LgA, a clumsy translation by Vignay followed by s.w.

241 **Ecclesiast**: *Eccl. XXXV* LgA.

241–2 **Orison . . . enflawmed**: add *Et lappostre dit moult dencens luy sont donnez etc.* P2, *'Oratio humiliantis se nubes penetrat'; odorem deo reddere, Apoc. V: 'Habentes singuli citharas et phialas plenas odoramentorum etc.': ex corde inflammato procedere, Apoc. VIII: 'Data sunt illi incensa multa etc.' et infra: 'Et accepit angelus thuribulum et impleuit illud de igne altaris etc.'* LgA.

244 **oyle**: add *et de cresme* P2, add *et balsamo* LgA.

246–7 **and also . . . renome**: GiL incorporates this in the preceding quotation, which is from 2 Cor., but it should introduce the next: *Iterum bonam famam, unde I Tim. III.*

250 **soylour**: *conchieure* P2; L spells *solour. MED soilure*, 'pollution', has only one citation, from Gloucester Chronicle A, c1325(c1300).

251 **shulde be**: *sont* P2.

254 **white**: add *et netz* P2.

255 **coueringe and**: not in LgA.

257 **apostle**: *Apoc. III* LgA.

258 **nakednesse, confusion**: *trs.* P2.

261 **or enflawmithe**: *ou enflambent* P2, *en enflambant* P1, *inflammando* LgA.
wherof it is saide: *Iob XXXVII* LgA.
the: *tes* P2.

263 **lyff**: add *Bernardus:* LgA.

270 **crosse**: *baculo pastorali* LgA.

271 **blessed**: *arrousee* P2.

asshen: add *et sabulo* LgA.

273 **towarde**: *deuers* P2, *ex transuerso angulo* LgA.

275 **anointed with creme**: *enluminee de cresme et ointes* P2, *illuminantur et chrismate inunguntur* LgA.

276 **Now**: *Primum ergo* LgA.

280 **helle**: *limbum* LgA.
come and arose: *reuint denfer* (*limbo* LgA) *et il resuscita* P2.

283 **for to be sacred**: *a sauuer* P2.

286 **seintwarie**: add *signifie lordre des vierges. Le cueur signifie lordre des continentes. et le corps signifie lordre des mariees* (add *car le saintuaire* S) P2.

287 **herte, hert**: *cueur* P2, *chorus* LgA, 'choir'.
body: (i.e. of the church) add *quia pauciores sunt uirgines quam continentes et isti quam coniugati. Sanctior est etiam locus sanctuarii quam chorus et chorus quam corpus* LgA.

289 **maried**: add *Hec Richardus* LgA.

290 **he hurtithe**: *le hurter* P2, *trina percussio* LgA.

294–5 **y aught . . . thine**: *Je me doy du tout a toy* P2, *debeo amori tuo me ipsum totum, quia me redemisti debeo amori tuo me ipsum totum* LgA.

295–6 **all my loue aught to be thine**: *Je me doy du tout a ton amour* P2.

297–8 **to the**: *amori tuo* LgA.

300 **helle**: LgA adds a quotation for each of these, Maggioni, 1292 (169), which GiL, LgD and later versions of LgA omit.

301 **And that . . . sprenged**: *Tertio* (. . .) *aqua benedicta aspergitur* LgA.

303 **fendes**: *le dyable* P2.

304 **blessinge**: *exorcismo* LgA.

305 **blessed**: *exorcizata* LgA.

312 **she is dedyed**: not in LgA.

316 **she was sacred**: not in LgA.

318 **sum sayne**: *dit on* P2, not in LgA.

319 **it is not founde**: add *nommeement* P2, *non legitur* (. . .) *nominatim* LgA.

321 **lawe**: add *scilicet abstinendi aliquando a licitis et aliquando eadem comedendi* LgA.

322 **take awey**: add *et benedictio introducatur* LgA.

323 **in Latin and in Greke**: not in LgA.

327 **the table of**: not in LgA.

328 **the faithe . . . crosse**: *lassemblee de la foy faicte par ihesu crist en la croix* P2, *unionem in fide populi gentilis et Iudei per crucem Christi factam* LgA.

332 **And so**: *Secundo* LgA.

336 **whele**: in LgA and P1 343–8 **Thriddely . . . asshes** follows here.

337 **Thriddely**: *Quinto* LgA, following 323 *Ferthely*.

338 **the fende**: *demonum* LgA.

343 **Thriddely**: the number follows 332 *And so* for LgA *Secundo*; this sentence has been transferred from after 336 above.

346 **wicked**: *mauuaix* S, *noueueaux* P2, *neophyti* LgA.

in the faithe be taught: add *Et ceulx de lun et de lautre peuple* P2, *de utroque populo in ecclesia erudiuntur* LgA.

348 **Secundely**: relating to 337 *The furste*.

351 **dewly soget to God**: *diuinement* (*deument* S) *subgect a dieu* P2, *Christi dominio subiugatus* LgA.

GiL here omits reference to the raising of the imperial banner when a city surrenders and to Jacob raising up the stone he had laid under his head as a memorial, Maggioni, 1293 (201–2), Dunn-Lardeau, 1189.

352–3 **the crosse**: *la croix* P2.

354–5 **and anointed . . . lyff**: *Hee igitur cruces illuminantur et chrismate unguntur quoniam apostoli fide passionis Christi totum mundum illuminauerunt ad cognitionem, inflammauerunt ad amorem, unxerunt ad conscientie nitorem, quod per oleum, et ad bone uite odorem, quod per balsamum* LgA.

356 **And**: *De tertio, scilicet per quos profanatur* LgA; this is the third section on dedication of Material, which GiL omits at 7.

358 **the boke of Kinges**: *III Reg. XII* LgA.

359 **of golde**: not in LgA.

360 **Iudee**: *Dan* LgA.

361 **couetise**[1]: add *ne scilicet regnum ad Roboam rediret* LgA.

363 **Wherof Seint Ierom saithe**: *Ier. VIII* LgA.

365 **The whiche . . . prestis**: *Quem dabis mihi de numero prepositorum* LgA.

369 **after that is saide before**: only GiL.

373 **rapinesse of his vserie**: *rapines de son vsure* P2, *rapinis et usuris* LgA; as a result of Vignay's change, context here requires 'ill-gotten gains from usury', involving an extension to the meanings of *rapine* accepted by *MED*, 'robbery, plunder, rapine'. Earliest citations of the word are from Hoccleve, a1450(c1412).

374 **bisshop**: add *et les clers* P2, *cum suo clero* LgA.

377 **for thou hast not to do here**: only GiL.

381 **with . . . tempest**: only GiL.

382 **the .xxv . . . Kinges**: *IV Reg. XXV* LgA.

386 **shewithe**: add *in suo claustrali* LgA.

387 **God**: *dieux* P2.

389–90 **the wombe . . . temple**: *Deo siquidem uentri templum est coquina* LgA.

391 **sodin and rosted**: *cuites* P2.
encens: *fumus incensorum* LgA.

393–4 **that was . . . tyme**: only GiL.

395 **Machabeus**: *saint mathieu* P2, *I Mac. I* LgA.
pride: add *et la couuoitise* P2, add *et ambitio* LgA.
wallithe: *veille* S, *uiget* LgA.

396 **and the coueitise of hem**: only GiL.

396–7 **to sowlis**: only GiL.

397 **of goodes**: only GiL.

398 **pride and couetise**: *superba ambitione* LgA.

400–1 **thei go . . . abite**: *inde is quem cotidie uides meretricius nitor, histrionicus habitus, regius apparatus.*
golyardes: *goulardois* P2, *meretricius* LgA; *MED* has three citations for *goliardeis*, 'buffoon', from Chaucer, Mannyng, and Langland. Dunn-Lardeau glosses the French as 'libertin, débauché', which is more appropriate here, and in context is not impossible for any of the *MED* instances. H2 *a galondis* is perhaps an attempt at *galauntes*, 'men of fashion', the A2 reading.

402 **moche . . . men**: *plus calcaria quam altaria fulgent* LgA.
other men: *les autelz* P2.

407 **wysdom**: add *et discrecion* P2.

409 **After that**: *Secundo* LgA, referring back to the *spirituel*, 2–4 above.
the dedicacion: *consecratione siue dedicatione* LgA.

411 **Seint Petre saithe**: *I Pet. II* LgA.

413–14 **The iointures . . . polisshed**: *Tunsionibus pressuris expoliti lapides etc.* LgA, 'The stones are polished by the force of many hammer-blows', from the hymn *Urbs beata Jerusalem*; for references see Boureau, 1489 n. 38. Greimas glosses *jointure* as 'assemblage' (among other more obvious senses), but *MED* offers only senses more closely linked to 'joining'. This is simply a loose translation by Vignay.

414 **that is to saie**: *a .iiij. costez. cest a dire de pierres espirituelz qui ont .iiij. carres. Cest assauoir* P2, *quatuor enim latera lapidis spiritualis sunt* LgA.

416 **thou lyuest**: *tu croys* P2.

416–19 **As long . . . hem**: *Quantum credis, tantum speras, quantum credis et speras tantum diligis, quantum credis, speras et diligis, tantum operaris* LgA.

419 **the herte**: *cor nostrum* LgA.

421 **the apostle**: *Leui. VI* LgA.
fyre of loue: *Ignis, scilicet dilectionis* LgA.

422 **of the hert**: *scilicet cordis* LgA.

424 **Parlipomenon**, i.e. Paralipomenon, the OT books of Chronicles.
Fynees: *filii eius* LgA, a misreading by Vignay.
offered: *ardoient* P2.

425–6 **holocaustis . . . precious**: *holocaustomatis et thymiamatis* LgA.

427 **in**: *et in* LgA.

431 **is (. . .) of God**: *consecratur* LgA.

432 **bishop**: add *scilicet* LgA.

433 **of the temple**: *du cueur* P2, *cordis* LgA.

436 **saithe**: add *Ys. XXIII* LgA.

437–8 See Isa. 23: 16, the significance of which is itself subject to controversy among the commentators.

442–6 **To the wicked . . . scourgithe**: *quantum ad malos: 'Extendi manum meam etc.', hoc quantum ad collata beneficia; 'Despexistis omne consilium meum', hoc quantum ad inspirata consilia; 'Et increpationes meas etc.', hoc quantum ad illata flagella* LgA. Confusion on how this should be divided is already apparent in the LgD MSS.

446 **this . . . made**: *ter percutit* LgA.

447–8 **to resonable . . . hymselff**: *a raisonnable congnoissance de pechie et a douleur yreuse. et veniance de pechie et a blasme* P2, *rationalem* (. . .) *ad peccati cognitionem, concupiscibilem ad dolorem, irascibilem ad peccati uindictam et detestationem* LgA.

448–9 **by bitter . . . doinge**: only GiL.

450 **he sprengithe**: *intus et extra debet irrigari* LgA.

451 **manere of teres**: *lacrimarum interiorum uel aliquando exteriorum effusio* LgA.

452–3 **shulde be confused**: *afficitur* LgA.

454–6 **Where . . . glorie**: *Ou il fut dit en pechie ou sera en iugement ou il est en maleurete et la ou il nest mie cest en gloire* P2, *Vbi fuit, inquit, in peccato; ubi erit: in iudicio; ubi est; in miseria; ubi non est: in gloria* LgA.

457 **of the herte**: *interiores uel exteriores* LgA.

464 **water**[1]: add *Car auecques ces autres sacremens nous deuons auoir vin de leesce espirituel. Sel de meure sagesce ou vin a eaue* P2, add *quia cum hiis lacrimis debemus habere uinum spiritualis exultationis, sal mature discretionis et cineres profunde humiliationis* LgA; S is as GiL.

465 **in that he toke mankinde**: *quil eust en prenant char humaine. Le vin a eaue est parole humaine* P2.

466 **yeuithe suete savour**: *est saueur* P2.

468 **moist and wete**: *arrouser* P2.

470 **holy**: only GiL.

473 **gostly**: not in LgA.

474 **scripture**[2]: add *que ibi scribitur* LgA.

474–5 **the thinges of eueles done**: *dictamina faciendorum* LgA, i.e. 'the rules governing our actions' (Ryan).

476–7 **saithe . . . Romaynes**: *Rom. II* LgA.

477–9 **The men . . . her herte**: *Cum enim gentes que legem non habent naturaliter ea que legis sunt faciunt, huiusmodi legem non habentes ipsi sibi sunt lex qui ostendunt opus legis scriptum in cordibus suis* LgA; *gentes*, 'gentiles'.

479–80 **that is the furst . . . secounde**: *cest le premier. le second est le tesmoing de leur conscience* P2, *ecce primum testimonium; 'illis reddente conscientia ipsorum;'* LgA.

480–1 **He . . . acuse hym**: add *ou deffendre* P2, *inter se cogitationum accusantium uel etiam defendentium* LgA.

485 **but with good wille**: add *et par onccion* P2, *sed etiam libenter, quod per unctionem, et ardenter, quod per ignem* LgA.

486–7 **of Ihesu . . . crosse**: *crucem Christi portat* LgA.

487 **profiteth**: *proficit* LgA.

489 **youre, your**: *noz, noz* P2.

490–1 **shall be . . . God**: *templum ad honorem dei dedicatum erit* LgA; this belongs to and completes the preceding quotation from Bernard in LgA, followed by a new sentence *Dignus es . . .*

491 **God**: *Christus* LgA.
so that: add *tandem* LgA.

176 ADVENT

Maggioni, ch. I, p. 11; Dunn-Lardeau, ch. 1, p. 95.

Many of the categories have subdivisions, but only the longest of these are listed here.

Four weeks of Advent represent four comings, of which two will be treated, I in the flesh, II at the last judgement 1–17.

I Three aspects listed, timeliness, necessity, utility 18–19:
  (i) timeliness: (a) for man 20–33; (b) the fullness of time 34–41; (c) the universal sickness 42–54;
  (ii) necessity 55–80;
  (iii) utility 81–114.

II Last Judgement: what will precede and what accompany it: 115–17.
  (i) What will precede it 118–20: (a) fearful signs 120–89; (b) the deceit of Antichrist 190–208; (c) storm of fire 209–22;
  (ii) What will accompany it 223: (a) procedure of the judge 223–48; (b) separation of orders of those to be judged 249–70; (c) insignia of the passion, cross, nails, wounds 271–93; (d) severity of the judge 294–323; (e) accusers 324–54 (wrongly numbered *fourthe*; see note to 322); (f) infallible witnesses 355–67 (also wrongly numbered *fourthe*; see note to 355); (g) powerlessness of the sinner 368–77; (h) irrevocable sentence 378–98.

3 **dethe, thought**: transposed in LgA.

5 **that last Sonday**: *in ultimo aduentu* LgA.

8 **cominges**: add *Quis autem aut cui magis conueniat, prudens lector attendat* LgA.

11 **it is**: *patet* LgA.

16 **mercy**: add *et de exaulcement* P2.

17 **cruell iugement**: add *cest pleur* P2, *seuere iusticie et meroris* LgA.

21 **goodly**: *deuine* P2; *MED godli* adj. (1) records spellings with *-oo-*.

23 **to saye**: *clamare ac dicere* LgA.

25 **by non power**: *de non pouoir P2, de impotentia* LgA. At 31 *impotentia* gives *non poissance* P2, *vnmight* GiL.

25–6 **There is none . . . comaundithe**: *Il nest nul qui acomplisse mais qui commande* P2, *Non deest qui impleat sed qui iubeat* LgA.

28–9 **to saie . . . spekinge**: *nutare ac dicere* LgA, 'to waver and to say'.

35 **.vij.**: *IV* LgA.

45 **came**: add *de celo* LgA.

48 **multeplyeng**: *multiplicitatem* LgA.

49 **of medicine**: *du medicin* P2, *i.e.* of the physician.

51–2 **bounden . . . custume**: *mala peccati consuetudine uincti* LgA.

54 **outedrawer**: *soustraieur* P2, *eductore* LgA, 'guide'; Dunn-Lardeau glosses the French, apparently an unduly etymological translation of the

Latin, as 'celui qui soustrait', which GiL in turn translates literally. *MED* gives *outdrauen* in senses of withdrawing, and similarly *outdraught* n. and *outdrauinge* ger., but not this noun; what seems needed in each case is the sense 'one who leads out', i.e. from the condition described in 50–2.

enluminour: *illuminatore* LgA; *MED* does not record this spelling, but cf. *illuminere* and the verb *enluminen.*

55 **taught**: add *ab ipso* LgA.

58–65 **bought, beye, beyenge**: all from forms of *racheter* in LgD.

61 **the might . . . arme**: *ton bras estendu* P2.

62 **yef**: add *apres le rachet* P2.

67 **wolde**: add *Parum igitur prodesset si nos redemisset et liberasset, si tamen adhuc uinctos teneret* LgA.

69 **oute**: add *qui sommes liez* P2.

71 **derkenesse**: *carcere* LgA.
therfor: *et ne peuent veoir* P2.

76 **vnbounde**: *ab inimicis penitus liberati* LgA.

78 **men**: *gens* P2, i.e. nations.

80 **saue us**: add *In prima autem petimus salutem gentium, unde dicitur: 'O rex gentium etc.'. In secunda salutem Iudeorum quibus deus dederat legem unde dicitur: 'O Emanuel dux et legifer noster etc.'* LgA.

84 **Other**: *ou* P2, *Vbi* LgA.

85 **tho that were sike**: *contritorum* LgA, 'the afflicted'.

91 **he**: *mercator ille* LgA.
all marchaundises: *tout marchant* P2.

92 **gaue . . . had not**: all verbs in present, referring to practice of merchants P2.

96 **riot**: *riote* P2, *contumeliam* LgA, 'ill-treatment'. *MED* gives senses such as 'disorder'; s.w. follows Vignay's rather loose rendering, as with the next.

97 **to take pouerte**: *haurire ignominiam* LgA.

106 **mani soroughes and dissesis**: *moult de maulx* P2, *praua* LgA.

114 **freelte**: add *Hec Bernardus* LgA.

117 **after the**: *au* S, *concomitantia* LgA.

121 **sette**: add *quinque* LgA.

122 **and**[3]: add *en terre* S.

123 **men**: add *pre confusione sonitus maris et fluctuum* LgA.

125 **right as a gret**: *niger tamquam* LgA.

127–8 **the deyinge of men**: *patre familias, id est homine, moriente* LgA.

128 **gretter**: add *lumiere* P2.

129 **to speke by symilitude**: *ad metaphoricam locutionem* LgA.

130 **vengeaunce**: add *diuina* LgA.

131 **propre**: *misticam* LgA.

133 **Aeren**: 'of the air', not in *MED*, which has, however, *airi*.

134, 136 **Asuly, Ausli**: *asub* LgD/LgA, a rare astronomical term, ultimately from Arabic, for a shooting star; see Boureau, pp. xlix–l.

138 **that**[1]: *quia* LgA.

140 **put out flawmes of fire**: add *aussy comme crins* P2.

143 **greuaunce to men**: *pressura in terris* LgA; H2 follows LgD, L has *pressure in erthe*.

144 **Seinte Marke**: *Mt.* LgA.

149 **the Appostulle**: *Apoc.* LgA.

150 **it schalle be**: *ille sonitus erit* LgA.

151–2 **alle . . . worlde**: *les montaignes* P2.

152 **abasid**: *abaissiee* P2, *deprimetur* LgA; *abasid*, 'lowered', is adopted from LgD rather than representing a spelling from *MED abaishen*, which does not record this spelling or carry this sense; H2A2 *abatid* show substitution of a more familiar verb, with senses like 'knock down, diminish'.

154 **that neuer was hurde**: *inaudita* LgA, i.e. unheard of.

158 **bitwene**: *entreposeement* P2, *interpolatim* LgA, i.e. intermittent.

159 **the high hillis**: *la haultesce des montaignes* P2.
he shalle be: *stans* LgA, i.e. the sea.

161 **whales**: *beluez* P2, 'beasts of the sea'.

164 **the lande**: *leaue* P2.

166 **in a feelde**: *es champs* P2.

167 **bi hymselff**: *in ordine suo* LgA.
thei . . . noothinge: *non gustantia nec bibentia* LgA.

169 **tempestes**: *fouldres* P2, *flumina* LgA, variant *fulmina*, as also Graesse.
shulle brenne: *surgent* LgA.

170 **from the orient**: *ab occasu solis* LgA.

171 **occident**: *orient* P2.

172 **tothir**: add *et rompront* P2.

179 **speke**: *ne pourront parler* P2.

183 **that turne . . . stable**: *errantia et stationaria* LgA.

184 **fire**: *igneas comas* LgA.

than shalle . . . greued: *iterum tunc ualde generabuntur asub* LgA; for *Asub* see note to 134, 136 above.

185 **shulle assemble**: *vendront aux champs* P2.

186 **petuouslie . . . noothinge**: *non gustantia nec bibentia* LgA.

192 **malicious**: *callidam* LgA, 'artful'.

198 **discomforte**: *desolationem templi* LgA.

199–200 **be as in the time of oure Lorde**: *in templo dei sedebit* LgA.

200–1 **he shalle . . . puple**: *il sefforcera de deceuoir* P2, not in LgA.

202 **Danielle . . . chapiter**: *II Thes. XX* LgA.

204 **shewingis**: GiL omits a quotation from Apocalypse XIII with Gloss, Maggioni, 17 (101), Dunn-Lardeau, 101.

204–5 **The Apocalips seithe**: *Dan. XIII* LgA.

206 **to his plesaunce**: *a leur gre* P2, *gratuito* LgA; add further *Et la glose dit. Antecrist donra moult de choses aux deceuz et deuisera la terre a ses gens* P2. By omitting this GiL wrongly adds 206–8 *And thoo . . . tormentis* to the quotation from Daniel.

207 **to his errour by dreede**: *suo terrore* LgA.

208 **turmentis**: *auaritia* LgA; GiL omits the fourth subsection of this series, the imposition of torments, Maggioni, 18 (105–7), Dunn-Lardeau, 101.

211 **face**: *force* P2, *faciem* LgA.

216 **be**: add *lieu de* P2, i.e. instead of.

219 **of the fire**: *ou monde* P2.

224 **vnagreabulte**: *desagreablete* P2, *disceptatio* LgA, 'procedure'. This word (spelt *vnagreabilite* by LA2) is not in *MED*, which, however, records *vnagreable*, 'disagreeable, unpleasant', and *agreablete*, 'of favourable disposition', each with one citation from Chaucer's Boethius.

228 **vale**: add *quia hoc est puerile* LgA.

229 **be**[1]: add *ibi et* LgA.

230 **perauentur**: *si necesse fuerit* LgA.
the goode: *electi* LgA.

236 **waile and plaine**: *se plaindront* P2.

237 **deedelie**: *mort* P2.

238 **shulle be ouercome**: *se conuaincront* P2, *conuincentes se* LgA.

240 **veine**: *uariis* LgA.

243 **seruid and worshippid**: only GiL.

244 **Crist**: add *Et les hereges se plorerent qui distrent que ihesucrist estoit pur homme quant ilz le verront estre iuge que les Juifz escracherent* P2.
allemyghty God: only GiL.

246 **and to hide hem it is impossible**: only GiL.
flee: add *deuant lui* P2.

248 **that shalle plese hem**: *que pleur* P2.

249 **ordenaunce**: *ordinis* LgA, 'category'.

255 **forthewiþ**: *ja* P2.

257 **of þat chosyn**: *des bons* P2, not in LgA.

260–1 **but thei shulle accorde with the iuge**: *sed dicuntur iudicare id est iudicanti assistere* LgA.

262 **accordaunce**: *assistentia* LgA.

263 **to seintis**: only GiL.

264 **behotith**: *promist* P2.
aboue the seetis: *sur les sieges* P2.

267 **escriue**: *escriuent* P2, *subscribunt* LgA; *MED* records *inscriven* but not *escriven*.

269 **bi**: *ex* (. . .) *comparatione* LgA.

272 **that is**: add *crux* LgA.
of his hondis: only GiL.

287 **crucified**: add *ubi est tantarum iniuriarum mearum fructus?* LgA.

290 **for the redempcioune of your soulis**: only GiL.

292 **othir**: *voz* P2.

294 **cruelte**: *seueritas* LgA.

295 **powere**: *pouoir* P2S, *paour* P1, *timore* LgA.
allmyghti: add *Chrysostomus: 'Nec resistendi uirtus est contra eum'* LgA.

297 **proude**: *astuta* LgA.

301 **wille nat receiue the persoone of noo myght**: *nullius potentis personam accipit* LgA.

301–3 **of whom . . . nor siluer**: *du quel le palais nest ne dor ne dargent. ne nul euesque nul abbe nul prince ne le pourra corrompre par or ne par argent* P2, *cuius palatium auro argentoque nullus episcopus uel abbas uel comes corrumpere poterit* LgA.

303 **Nor bi hate**, 306 **Nor bi loue**: these refer back to 295 *noo powere* (for 'fear'), *nor bi noo yiftis*, and forward to 308 *Nor bi errour*.

308 **shal nat by**: *ne rachetera* P2.

309 **the sentence**: *scientia* LgA.

310–11 **right dredefulle and tremblinge biholdinge**: *tremblable regart* P2, *tremendus aspectus* LgA.

311 **to whom alle stabulle thingis ben litille**: *cui peruium est omne solidum* LgA, 'which can pass through every substance'.

313 **thoo that mowe nat speke**: *les taisibles* P2, *silentium* LgA.

317 **of maistris**: *oratorum* LgA.

318 **pride of fooles**: *astutie uersutorum* LgA, 'cleverness of the ingenious'.

319–20 **thoo without spekinge**: *ceulx sans langue et les muez* P2.

320 **than**: *et* LgD, *or* H2A2. L *than* correctly restores the sense of the Latin.

322 **philosophres**: add *quanti rustici oratoribus* LgA; in omitting this Vignay lost control of the numbering, and tried to rectify it by transferring the last, *quo ad quartum*, 324 *as to the fourthe*, to the larger series relating to 294 *fourthe*; he then read 324 *Quintum* as *Quantum*.

323 **argumentis of Seint Citerioun**: *argumens de cyterion* P2, *argutiis* (. . .) *Ciceronis* LgA, 'the subtleties of Cicero'.

324 **And as to the fourthe**: *Quintum* LgA; see 322 above.
accusacioun: *accusator* LgA.

325 **four**: *tres* LgA.

328 **and**: add *in quo loco et in* LgA.

329 **myght haue done**: *deuions adonc faire* P2.

333 **fulfillinge of my werkis**: *suasionem* LgA.

334 **pore**: *pannosam* LgA.

336 **and . . . me**: *Equissime iudex iudica illum meum esse et mecum dampnandum esse* LgA.

337 **in this plight**: *tel* P2.

338 **feende**: add *Hec Augustinus* LgA.

340 **thoo that haue doo hem**: *unumquemque* LgA.

340–1 **whereof the wise man seith**: *Sap. IV* LgA.

341–2 **that . . . wickidnessis of hem**: only GiL.

343 **The werkinges**: *leurs euures* P2.

344 **werkis**: add *non te deseremus, sed semper tecum erimus* LgA.

345 **and . . . myssedeedis**: *Multisque et multiplicibus criminibus eum accusabunt* LgA; the quotation from Bernard should end at *iugement*.

346 **the worlde**: *tout le monde* P2.

350 **erthe**: add *et eaue* P2.

354 **us**: add *fortiter* LgA.

355 **fourthe**: *.vj.^e* P2. This ordinal relates to 294 *fourthe* and incorrect 324 *fourthe* for *fifthe*, see note to 322 above; s.w. has erroneously attached it to the subseries of accusers at 325, 339, and 346.

vndesseiuable: *infallibilis* LgA; *MED undeceivable* has two citations, for *c.*1400 and ?a1425, with senses 'trustworthy' *etc.*

358 **Seint Ierome**: *Ier XXIX* LgA.

368 **that shal fellishipp the iuge**: not in LgA.

371 **dredefulle confusioun of helle**: *horrendum chaos* LgA.

373 **traueile and**: *traynans a* P2.

378 **nat ayenne callinge**: *non repellable* P2.

379 **be callid ayenne**: *reuocari nec ab illa poterit appellari* LgA.

381, 382 **repelle, repele**: *rappeller, rappeller* S, *appellari, appellari* LgA; the LgD substitution, followed by GiL *repelen*, carrying senses such as 'disavow, retract', for 'appeal' does not accurately reflect the context.

385 **prolongned**: *eslongniee* P2, *differendam* LgA, 'deferred'. L has *enloynyd*, for which *MED s.v. enlongen* has only two citations, one in this sense, 'delay', dated ?1440.

388 **kinge**: *juge* P2

392 **othere**: add *quia supra se nullum habet* LgA

393 **wickid synnes**: *meffais et pechiez* P2

395 **poyntis in a table**: *pains en vne table* P2, *tabula picta* LgA; Dunn-Lardeau (p. 1269, note 45) suggests that the French is for *paints*, 'painted'.

177 CONCEPTION OF THE VIRGIN

See pp. 41–2 above. LgD readings are recorded from Fb (Paris BN MS fr. 416).

1–3 There is no basis for the belief that Jerome wrote such an account. 1–93 derives fairly closely from the Gospel of Pseudo-Matthew, which begins by declaring itself to have been translated from Hebrew into Latin by Jerome.

12–13 **made a solempne vowe**: *vouerent* Fb.

14 **fulli**: only GiL.

16 **that**: add *en la feste* Fb.

18 **grete**: only GiL.

21 **it was nat**: *ce nestoit pas* Fb; *nat* is in neither of the running GiL MSS, but has been restored since its omission can scarcely be attributed to the translator.

22 **God**[1]: add *de faire offrance en la loy a dieu* Fb.
and: add *aussi que cellui qui* Fb.

24–5 **rebukid . . . turned**: *confus de honte quil ot ne retourna pas* Fb.

37 **meruouslie**: this H2 spelling, which occurs again at 47, is not recorded *s.v. MED merveillousli.*

42 **of God and**: only GiL.

45 For barrenness of mothers of Samson and Samuel see 1 Samuel 1 and Judges 13.

46 **bi**: *croy* Fb.

47 **but**: only GiL.

57 **hele and saluacioun**: *salut* Fb.

58 **to**: *en la cite de* Fb.

63–4 **And . . . for she**: *Anne pleuroit moult fort. Et ne* Fb.

75 **she**: *quelle* Fb.

76 **blessid**: only GiL.

78 **eselie**: only GiL.

86 **of**: *et* Fb.

88 **morowetide**: *Matin* Fb.

90 **an aungelle**: *les angres* Fb.

91 **thus**: *la* Fb.

96 **notable**: only GiL.

97 **Seinte Ancelme**: this promoter of the Conception was not in fact the archbishop, but his nephew, Abbot Anselm of Bury; see Thurston, 'Abbot Anselm of Bury and the Immaculate Conception', and Bishop, 'On the Origins of the Feast of the Conception of the Blessed Virgin Mary'.

99 **Denemark**, 100 **Denemarke**: *dacede* Fb, error for *Dace* in Munich, Bayerische Staatsbibliothek, MS Gall.3 and other manuscripts.

105–6 **for to saile . . . perissh**: *et tant que les nefs se desrompoient toutes entierement les cordes les voiles et toutes les autres ordonnances des dictes nefs. et tant que les mariniers nauoient point desperance de eschaper* Fb.

109 **semelie**: only GiL.
in pontificalibus: *pontificals* Fb; *MED* records *pontificals* from 1432, but it is apparently not recognized as an English term by s.w.

110 **hem, hem**: *lui, lui* Fb.

119 **the**: *sa* Fb.

121–2 **with . . . done**: *et tantost* Fb.

123–6 **and there . . . written**: *Et de la en auant il celebra et anonca partout la feste de la concepcion* Fb.

127–55 In this passage s.w. makes many additions to the original: 127 **notable**, 128 **foule**, 130 **sodeinliche**, 131 **wondir greuouslie**, 133–4 **wise . . . feendis**, 135 **we turmente . . . skilfullie**, 136 **and therein we toke hym**, 137 **blessid**, 138 **and is deede**, 138–9 **Matenes and**, 145 **ful deuouteli and mekeli**, 145 **O blessid Ladi** (for *Dame*), 146 **your high and worthy goodenes** (for *vous*), 147 **and benefete**, 147–8 **that yif . . . feendis**, 149 **blessid Virgine Marie**, 149–50 **and seide . . . preeste**, 150–1 **in the worshipp . . . of me**, 152 **to alle thi powere**, 155 **specialle**.

156–7 **alle thinge . . . dekenne**: *et en tant quil* Fb
alle thinge to leue, i.e. 'to leave everything'.

161 **blessid**: *doulce* Fb.

162 **to thi . . . plesaunce**: only GiL.

166–8 **and forsoke . . . monke**: *tout et deuint moine* Fb.

171 **clerk of devinite**: *dotteur en theologie* Fb.

172 **vniuersite**: *cite* Fb.

172–3 **in the rewme of**: *qui est en* Fb.

173 **euery daie**: *tous les ans* Fb.

176 **sholde haue redde**: *en lisoit* Fb.

178 ADAM AND EVE

See pp. 42–6 above. *Vita* = *Vita Adae et Evae*

35–41 Mabel Day, p. 112, gives the Latin and Greek for the four stars representing the compass points, and points out that 37 *southe* should be *west*.

101 Absence from EL of D's explanatory addition, *þereof to hide þerewith her preue membris*, suggests it is not attributable to s.w., so it has been excluded.

279–80 **My Lorde God liueth; to the is grauntid liffe and my life is grauntid to the**: *Viuit dominus meus, tibi concessa est uita* Vita. Only Do recognized Eve's use of *dominus* for Adam, and omitted *God* (but failed to omit *my*). H2, doubtless following D, made a different attempt at correction, and, mistaking the ambiguous spelling *leueth* for 'leaves', supplied *grace* as object.

281 **cursed**[1,2]: *preuaricatus, preuaricata* Vita; perhaps originally translated as 'accused', but it already appears as *cursed* in B, one of the sources from which this version was compiled (see above, p. 43).

351–2 **and felle with his chere**: *et concidit vultus eius* Vulgate, Gen. 4: 5; *with* is for 'therewith'.

354–7 **Shalt . . . hym**: *Nonne si bene egeris, recipies; sin autem male, statim in foribus peccatum aderit? Sed sub te erit appetitus eius, et tu dominaberis illius* Vulgate, Gen. 4: 7. *NJBC*, p. 13, col. 1, observes: 'Yahweh's response to the distressed Cain is extremely difficult to understand and may be corrupt; all translations are uncertain.'

366 **vagaunt**: 'wandering'. *MED s.v. vacaunt* notes that examples under senses I.(d) and (e), which include 'homeless, vagrant', may have been influenced by, or errors for, *vagaunt*, and cites this instance from H2. Hc has *vangaunt* (but first *a* is unlike his usual *a*, and may be meant as *e*), and spells it *vengeaunt* at 371, neither of which spellings is given in *MED*; in Do it looks like *dagaunt*.

379 **this Ennok**: *he* HbWhDoZ, i.e. Cain, which is correct; *Cognovit autem Cain uxorem suam, quae concepit et peperit Henoch; et aedificavit civitatem, vocavitque nomen eius ex nomine filii sui Henoch* Vulgate, Gen. 4: 17.

383 **he**: *Ada* Vulgate, Gen. 4: 20.

389–90 **I slough . . . wannesse**: *occidi virum in vulnus meum, et adulescentulum in livorem meum* Vulgate, Gen. 4: 23. For the problematical Lamech story, see *NJBC*, p. 13, col. 2. For *wannesse*, *MED* sense (c) gives 'mark of bruising, . . . bruise', citing both Wycliffite versions and Wh for this passage. H2L *warinesse* is hard to explain; the only *MED* citation not regarded as an error is from *Ancrene Wisse*, 'a malicious curse or act of cursing', and clearly irrelevant.

438–9 **cast me out of paradis in the visitaciouns fro the sight of God**: *eiecit me de medio paradisi uisitacionis et uisionis Dei* Vita; the sense of the Latin seems to be 'the paradise in which visitations and the sight of God might be experienced'. Other versions read *paradiso* for *de medio paradisi*, and omit *et uisionis* or substitute *et iussionis*.

584 **odoramenta**: *MED* gives *odorament* as a noun, citing only this passage from Wyclif Bible 1, *and of odoramentis*. Here *odoramenta* appears to be regarded as an adjective, 'sweet smelling'.

600 **yerde**: *ortum* Vita; as Day points out (p. 116, 95/36), '*Ortum* has been read as *hortum*'. In the Latin MSS, *ortum* is variously followed by *solis* or *orientalis*.

619 **besmes**: so L, *bismos* WhHbDo, *bysmes* Z; the word is not recorded by *MED*, which, however, records *s.v. bis* n. (1) this passage from the related passage in the version of *Adam & Eve* in the Vernon MS, *Twey cloþes, of sendel and of bijs*. Day (p. 117 n. 96/30) cites the passage from a Latin text in MS Harley 526, *tres pannos de sindone bissinos*, and suggests that *bismos* is a misreading of the Latin adjective. These forms derive ultimately from Greek *bussos*, gen. *bussinos*, 'fine linen'.

oone ouer Adam and anothir ouere his sone Abel: Day (p. 117 n. 96/

31) observes that the Wh addition *anoþir ouer Eue* is 'apparently due to the scribe's unwillingness to waste a cloth'. Vita solves the problem by giving two to Abel: *et alias sindones super Abel.*

621–2 On Adam's burial place see too 50.273–6 and note to 50.274.

633 **be**[2]: Day (p. 97, l. 19) supplies *ponyschid*, which is in none of the other MSS, from a marginal note in B, Oxford MS Bodley 596; Mozley's text gives *iudicabit*.

638–9 **melte . . . welle þat**: only GiL.

sokinge and drinkinge: 'soaking and absorbing'; L *dryvyng* may be the original GiL reading, for which see *MED driven* sense 7a (d) 'of waves: to surge', but since this is in an addition found only in the GiL MSS it is impossible to decide.

641 **wille**: Day supplies *the tablis of stone loose and* from B, lost by eyeskip by the compiler of our version or an early copyist. D *stone* is a misguided attempt at correction.

647 **Man**: *Men* D. A rubric in Wh suggests that Michael, having appeared to them all, speaks only to Seth; only D has changed the number to allow for the absence of this explanatory rubric.

664 **Archiliates**: *Achiliaces* L, *Achiliacos* HbWhDoHc; probably corruption of a Greek word meaning 'not made of matter, of heavenly origin'. See Day (pp. 117–18 n. 98/33).

179 FIVE WILES OF PHARAOH

See pp. 42–6 above.

The surviving leaf of this chapter in E is damaged and almost entirely illegible, so, as with the previous chapter, the text is based on D, and on L when D is defective.

111 **to see too**: perhaps 'visibly'.

154 **good livinge**: confronted no doubt by a spelling of 'living' with *e*, D has taken it as 'leaving' and supplied an object; cf. *good livinge* at 215 below, and see Vol. 1, p. xiii.

159 **shrewen**: other MSS have *v* or *u*, e.g. 81 above *shreven*, 172 below *shreuen*. *MED shriven* records some spellings with *w*.

173 The *Maistir of Sentence*, Peter Lombard, for whom the GiL scribes substituted the *Maistir of Stories*, Peter Comestor, frequently referred to throughout GiL.

176 **vppon Poulis epistelis,** *Commentarii in omnes Pauli epistolas.* HbDo give *epistel* in singular because the part concerned is only about Ephesians.

314 **lowing**: *lovyng* A2; *MED s.v. louen* v. (4), 'praise', observes that this is easy to confuse with *loven* v. (2), of similar sense, as perhaps indicated by the A2 spelling.

331 **outragiousnes**: *ouȝtragenes* Ya; *MED outrageousnes(se*, 'extravagance, licentiousness', etc., is first recorded for (1450) Scrope; *MED* records the Ya form as *outragenes(se*, 'excess, criminal conduct', with citations only from *Catholicon Anglicon* and two Chaucer MSS.

350 **he hathe the worke**: this appears to mean: 'he that has the profit of any work has had to do the labour'.

374 **do**: i.e. bring about.

383 **Ianuensis**, i.e. Jacobus de Voragine. 381–9 is based on his first sermon for the second Sunday after Pentecost: *Excusatio secundi pertinet ad auaros qui dixit iuga boum emi quinque. Per quinque iuga boum intelliguntur quinque sensus corporis: et dicuntur iuga quia sensuum combinantur. Duo enim sunt oculi due aures duo instrumenta gustus lingua cum palatum: due manus quibus fit maxime tactus.* This passage is in turn based on Augustine, *Sermo CXII*, *Caput III*, cols. 644–5, *PL* 38.

389 **distruccioun:** CbHb *discrecion* seems to be the original reading.

435 **Salamon**: CbHb correctly refer this to *ecclesiastes the thridde chapter*; it is Eccl. 3: 18.

541 **Anne**: Hannah; see 1 Kgs. 1, 2, esp. 2: 3.

544–52 The quotation from Ephes. 5: 3–4 ends at 547, but the passage continues as though all part of the same sentence.

GLOSSARY

The glossary is designed to include all obsolete words and any whose senses are not easily recognizable in modern English, but this policy has been rather generously applied. For words with a range of meanings, only those differing from modern English or likely to cause difficulty are recorded. References are usually given only to the first occurrence of a word in a particular sense within each chapter, and except in cases of likely difficulty, only two or three examples of each meaning are given. Cross-references are given only for words not easily referable to a headword. For citations of forms in passages where a manuscript other than E is being used as base, its sigil is given in brackets. Emended forms are indicated by an asterisk. Rare words are signalled by + before the headword, with information given in the appropriate note.

In the alphabetical arrangement, both *i* and *y* are treated as *i* when they represent a vowel and as *j* when they represent a consonant; *y* representing a semi-vowel is treated as *y*; *v* representing a vowel is treated as *u*, and *u* representing a consonant as *v*. In the forms supplied, *ow* and *aw* are not distinguished from *ou* and *au* unless the *w* is semi-vocalic; variations between endings *-s*, *-es*, *-is* in plurals, and *ed*, *-id*, *-ied* in past forms are also ignored.

Abbreviations: adj(ective), adv(erb), comp(arative), conj(unction), fig(urative), gen(itive), ger(und), imp(erative), impers(onal), inf(initive), interj(ection), intrans(itive), n(oun), neg(ative), num(eral), ord(inal), p(articiple), pa(st), pa. p. = past participle, pl(ural), poss(essive), ppl. = participial, pr(esent), prep(osition), pron(oun), refl(exive), sg. = singular, subj(unctive), superl(ative), trans(itive), v(erb).

A

abacke *adv.* behind, out of mind 47.196; backwards 123.95

abaied *v. pa.* 159.163; *pa. p.* barked 22.135, 163.309; **obeye** *inf.* 53.345

abandoned *ppl. adj.* unrestrained 28.115; **abondonid** devoted 154.3

abasshement *n.* dismay 84.225

aba(a)shin *v. imp. pl.* bend, bow the head 23.142; **abasshed** *ppl. adj.* upset 1.312, 4.177; amazed 35.7, 37.14, 53.167; embarrassed 8.142, 10.64, (G) 38.86, 48.9; **aba(i)sshid** frightened 4.36, 25.217, (G) 38.98; **abaished** amazed 13.188, 26.4, 52.14; **abassed** 149.163; **abasshinge** *ger.* astonishment 58.448

+abasid *ppl. adj.* lowered *176.152 *note*

abeggid *adv.* **go** ~ go begging *161.265

abhominacion *n.* loathing *20.128

abide *v. inf.* remain 5.105, 7.14, 26.238, 54.159; wait 11.49, 28.195, 36.321; await 80.150; 171.28; delay 90.114 *note*; **abideth(e** *pr. 3 sg.* awaits 1.194; **abidithe** 26.113, 85.12; **abide(n)** *pr. pl.* stay 22.45; await 79.523; **abide** *imp. sg.* wait 11.358, 16.41, 29.59; **abidethe** *imp. pl.* 90.152; **abydinge** *pr. p.* delaying 79.527; remaining 80.119; **abode** *pa.* remained (H2) 1.48, 5.57, 11.14, 15.53, 23.119; awaited 7.191, 9.113, 47.280, 53.212; waited 20.25, 24.56, 61.134; stopped (G) 38.150; **aboden** *pa. pl.* remained 6.23, 95.32; **abiden** (G) 3.11; **abidde** *pa. p.* awaited 29.178, 47.282, 86.50, 90.97; **abide(n** awaited 123.121, (H2) 176.300; **abydyn** 176.104; **abydde** remained 106.35; **abidden** still in existence 53.385 *note*

abydingge *ger.* delay 91.58; **abidinge** 123.132

abilite *n.* inherent possibility 65.205 *note*

abit(e *see* **habite**

abieccion *see* **obiecciones** *and note to* 45.507–8

abiecte *ppl. adj.* wretched 161.273

abondonid *see* **abandoned**

abound *v. inf.* abound, be plentiful 61.304; **habound(e** 53.163, 112.406; **aboundithe** *pr. 3 sg.* 47.94, 63.81,

176.89; **abounded** *pa.* 161.109; **habounded** prospered 45.275, 117.311, 155.372; *pa. p.* 11.6, 90.15; *pr. p.* **ouer aboundinge** exceeding its bounds 65.443
aboute *adv. as adj.* nearby 5.30; *prep.* in attendance upon 7.131; **abought** 139.21; **were aboute** performed 42.32–3
abregging *v. pr. p.* shortening 116.190
acceptest *v. pr. 2 sg.* show partiality towards 60.96
+**accessours** *n. pl.* 155.169 *note*
accompted *see* **acount** *v.*
acomplised *v. pa. p.* completed 7.74
ac(c)ord(e *n.* agreement 11.22, 20.114, 79.521, 93.107
acorde *v. inf.* consent 23.8, 106.111, 113.185, 173.307; conform 35.16, 47.47; **acordithe** *pr. 3 sg.* 61.141; **accorden** *pr. pl.* agree 83.442; **acorded** *pa.* 10.25, 11.33, 58.287; *pa. p.* 22.99; agreed 53.26, 79.408; **acording(e** *ppl. adj.* agreeing 65.25, 76.15; suitable 83.405, 138.178; **accordid** agreed (G) 43.115, (G) 44.45; **acorded** *ppl. adj.* united 112.680, reconciled 142.146
acordingly *adv.* harmoniously 174.457
acount *v. inf.* include 176.7; **acount** evaluate 175.346; **acounte** *pr.* count 30.30; consider *45.185; evaluate 161.294; **accountes** *2 sg.* 90.391; **acountithe** *3 sg.* 105.4; **acountith** *imp. pl.* recount 20.46; **acounted** *pa.* assessed 27.74, 84.439; counted as 28.98, 47.110, calculated 159.349, 173.320; attributed 92.52; **accompted** valued (H1) 144.17; **acounted** *pa. p.* counted as 65.389; included 174.349
acounte *n.* computation 146.235; **acountes** *pl.* financial records 133.159
acursed *v. pa. p.* excommunicated 56.21, 174.761
+**acuse** *n.* accusation 160.29 *note*
adayes *adv.* in the daytime 8.169
ademond(e *n.* extremely hard stone 84.370 *note*
admitte *v. inf.* recognize as authoritative 79.211
adoyng *ppl. adj.* happening 55.136
adowne *adv.* down 8.111
adradde *adj.* frightened 48.30, 128.29, 165.241
aduoutrie *see* **avouutrye**
+**Aeren** *adj.* of the air 176.133 *note*
afere *v. inf.* frighten 24.25; **aferd(e** *ppl. adj.* frightened 1.311, 2.255, 25.59
afere *adv.* on fire 2.113, 29.32, 47.217; **afire** 25.63
afer(re *adv.* far off 1.169, 25.148, 44.199
+**afface** *v. inf.* erase 117.240 *note*
affeccion *n.* emotion (G) 4.151, 49.88, 55.77, 74.11, 79.626
affermithe *v. pr. 3 sg.* asserts 13.13; **affermest** *2 sg.* 38.33; **affermed** *pa.* 87.22; **affermyngges** *ger. pl.* assertions 79.212
affinite *n.* kinship 26.172, 104.107
aforcith *v. pr. 3 sg.* compels 117.276
afore *adv.* previously 2.55, 20.122, 36.142; in front 149.16
afore *prep.* in front of (G) 1.74, (G) 4.24, 12.73; earlier in time 22.114, 104.68; superior to 65.326
afraye *n.* fear 84.173; commotion 112.431
afraye *v. inf.* frighten 45.432; **afraied** *pa.* 93.291; **affraied** *ppl. adj.* 84.178; **afrayed** 86.85, 88.75, 148.125
after *adv.* afterwards 2.4, 4.176, 5.30
after *prep.* after 2.8, 5.108, 8.2; according to 2.9, 5.2, 7.104; behind 2.264; in likeness of 4.204; **sende** ~ summon 11.78
age *n.* **last** ~ adulthood 36.129–30
aggreably *adv.* willingly 176.33
agreable *adj.* acceptable 1.162, 58.62; favourably disposed 133.240
aylethe *v. pr.* afflicts 54.54, 60.322; **ailithe** 163.211; **eylith(e** 173.246, (D) 178.231; **ayled** *pa.* 54.45, 58.266, 75.25, 94.36; suffered 165.348; **ayled** *pa. p.* afflicted 101.123
ayre *see* **eyre**[2]
aysell *see* **eisell**
aither *see* **either**
akeled *v. pa.* cooled 113.46
akinge *ger.* pain 84.365, 142.226
+**alabastre** *n.* container for unguents 155.115 *note*
alayed *v. ppl. adj.* reduced in strength 101.29
alder *gen. of* **al** *pron.* **her** ~ of all of them 8.146; **althir** of all (D) 178.259
alegeaunce *n.* relief 58.409
alegithe[1] *v. pr. 3 sg.* adduces 112.484;

aleged *pa.* pleaded 53.357; presented the case for 79.386
aleged[2] *v. pa.* alleviated (H1) 156.407, 159.400
alight *v. pa. p.* kindled 137.103
alleageaunce *n.* citation of authorities (H2) 176.315
allegate *adv.* nevertheless (D) 179.512
alles *n. pl.* awls 166.31
alliaunce *n.* agreement 23.41, 133.82
al(l)on(e *adv.* alone (G) 4.24; **alon** 134.15
almesfull *adj.* charitable 54.90
alon *see* **allone**
alonge *adv.* at length 79.422
alonly *adv.* solely 84.301, 112.156, 125.163; **aloonli** (H1) 146.95; **allonli** 155.325
alowe *adv.* below 66.234
als *adv.* also 18.27, 50.37, 102.49
also *conj.* ~ **sone as** as soon as 25.87, (H2) 178.99; just as easily 173.349
althir *see* **alder**
alway *adv.* nevertheless 117.386; **alwey** 154.149
ambassiatrie *n.* group of emissaries 151.10
amende *v. inf.* cure 110.280; reform 93.300, 106.148; **amendest** *pr. 2 sg.* improve 26.130; **amende** *imp.* 124.246; *pa.* **amended** *pa.* 58.404; **amendinge** *ger.* improving 149.205
amendement *n.* reform 112.701
amentised *see* **anientised**
amenused *v. pa. p.* reduced 74.48
ameuid *v. ppl. adj.* troubled 128.244
amyable *adj.* worthy of admiration 58.63, 87.15, 128.95
amynistre *v. pr. pl.* 112.658 *note*
aminiistresse *n.* female servant 112.306 *note*
amonestid *v. pa.* urged 142.262; **amonastinge** *ger.* persuasion 84.54; **amonestinge** *174.650; *see also* **monestid**
amountithe *v. pr. 3 sg.* signifies 173.91
an *num.* one 164.35; **a** 169.14; *see also* **o**
anciens *see* **aunciene**
and *conj.* if (G) 4.58, 7.12, 43.37, 44.25 *et passim*
anefelde *n.* anvil 159.209
aney *see* **annoye**
anentes *prep.* against 7.52; with respect to 79.198
anentisshed *see* **anientised**
angerly *adv.* sharply 163.112
angre *v. refl. imp.* become angry 168.54
anhungered *v. pa. p.* hungry 66.254
+**anientised** *v. ppl. adj.* brought to nothing *61.168; weakened *174.178; *pa.* **amentised** (*for* **anientised**) diminished 88.65 *note*; **anentisshed** *50.307
annoye *n.* uneasiness 171.12; **aney** weariness 97.12; **enoye** boredom 20.102
annuel *n.* anniversary 156.372
annunciacion *n.* announcement 146.47
anoye *v. inf.* harm 59.14, 112.442; **anoyed** *ppl. adj.* wearied 55.218, 117.39, 159.365; *see also* **noyed**
anone *adv., conj.* at once 2.106, 5.80, 6.36; **anoon** (G) 1.26; **anone as** as soon as 25.126, 26.177, 27.18
ansyen *see* **auncien**
Antiphoner *n.* service book containing antiphons 45.445
apaieng *v. pr. p.* pleasing 50.239; **apaied** *pa. p.* **euell** ~ displeased 173.150
aparacion *see* **apparicion**
aparayle *see* **apparaill**
apere *v. inf.* present oneself 5.262, 84.101; be revealed *or* seen 11.123, 13.154; *pr. subj. sg.* be clear 149.240 *note*; **apered** *pa.* were visible 161.197; **aperyng** *ppl. adj.* 27.3 *note*; **apperinge** *ppl. adj.* visible 50.203, (H2) 176.227; **apering** *ger.* apparition 138.1
aperseyued *v. pa.* understood 10.104
aperteyne *v. pr.* belong 60.27; **ap(p)erte(i)nithe** *pr. 3 sg.* 12.31; is relevant 44.170; is proper 11.197, 324, 28.116, 35.27; **apertenen** *pr. pl.* belong 53.298
apertely *adv.* clearly 149.241
apese *v. inf.* placate 8.114, 50.228; settle 53.24; soothe 54.8, 65.144; calm 63.66, 165.19; **appesith** *pr. 3 sg.* 12.66; **apesed** *pa.* 48.61, 58.294, 101.66, 104.172; placated 60.224, 106.165
apistell *see* **pistell**
apocrify *adj.* of doubtful authenticity (G) 44.3; **apocrifie** 60.290, 61.13; **apocriff** 50.354
apocrifum *n.* doubtful authenticity

44.79; **apocraphum** 60.168, 83.293; **apocrifom** 112.214; **apocrif** 112.216
aportenaunces *n. pl.* privileges 117.423
aposed *see* **apposed**
apostata *n.* apostate 29.138, 61.243, 112.529
apostoyle *n.* the papacy as successors to the apostle 16.38, 63.12
apostume *n.* morbid swelling 63.17
apparaill *n.* adornment 10.15, 128.81; preparations 133.175; **aparayle** apparel 47.185
apparaunt *adj.* visible 147.3
apparicion *n.* appearance 13.15; **aparacion** 13.20
appeled *v. pa.* accused 83.204
apperinge *see* **apere**
apposed *v. pa.* accused 112.482; **aposed** 174.341; **apposinge** *pr. p.* accusing (H2) 176.328
appropred *v. pa. p.* attributed 12.47
aproued *v. ppl. adj.* proved 128.137
araie(n) *see* **arraie(n)**
arbitrere *n.* judge 23.144
arblaste *n.* crossbow 142.222
arch(e *n.* coffin 78.57, 174.423; *see also* **arke**
arere *v. inf.* resurrect (G) 4.84, 8.80, 11.338; **arrere** (G) 43.41; raise 26.101, 36.53; **arerithe** *pr. 3 sg.* 60.191; **arere** *pr. subj.* raise up 8.24; *imp.* 99.54; **arered** *pa.* 83.12, 84.13, 91.73, 95.50; **areredest** *pa. 2 sg.* 99.53; *pa. p.* 8.93; **arerid** resuscitated 10.49, 47.162, 95.152
aresoned *v. pa.* addressed 2.101, 5.149, 13.80, 58.282, 124.18; called to account 10.54, 123.270; questioned 77.20; **aresond** requested 53.285; **aresonid** addressed 142.29; rebuked 2.239; *pa. p.* 79.765
arette *v. inf.* impute (D) *179.229; **aretted** *ppl. adj.* (D) *179.184
argue *v. inf.* assert 79.285; *pa.* **argued** reproached 80.140
argumentes *n. pl.* evidential signs 58.355
aryved *v. pa.* landed 90.224; **ariued** 93.93; *ppl. adj.* 24.104
arke *n.* ark (of the covenant) 13.225; (Noah's) 84.303; treasure chest 149.298; **arche** (of the covenant) 7.74, (Noah's) 84.301, 112.761; treasure chest 112.584
armee *n.* a military expedition *79.2
aromat *n. as adj.* aromatic 175.235; **aromatis** *pl.* spices 106.264
ar(r)ay(e *n.* clothing 6.24, 142.112, (H1) 143.16, 161.282; magnificence 25.26, 79.31, 110.25
a(r)raye *v. inf.* prepare 22.43, 28.58, 52.109; clothe 30.35, 175.256; **arayethe** *pr. 3 sg.* 23.26; **arraiethe** 175.259; prepares 149.204; **araie** *imp.* 64.360; **arayed** *pa.* *28.46; **arraied** *pa.* treated 59.6; adorned 61.261, 84.149; **arrayed** prepared 99.115; **araied** *pa. p.* adorned 1.172, 23.31, 50.202; **arraied** provided 65.410, 149.206; prepared 35.50, 37.112, 167.38; **arayid** (G) 4.102; *ppl. adj.* adorned (G) 3.13, (G) 4.45; **ar(r)ayed** prepared 11.47, 54.135; **arayeng** *ger.* displaying 163.257
arrere *see* **arere**
art *n.* cleverness 116.65; profession 149.1
article *n.* detail 90.222
arw(e *n.* arrow 122.44, 125.64; **harowe** 94.169; **arues** *pl.* 45.88; **arwes** 94.166, 119.44
asaute *see* **assaute**
ascape *v. inf.* escape 20.42; **askaped** *pa.* 10.119, 48.64; **ascaped** 120.20
ascried *v. pa.* shouted at 154.110
ascusid *v. pa.* excused *136.15
aseged *ppl. adj.* beset 58.229
askaped *see* **ascape**
aske *v. inf.* seek 64.160; **asketh** *pr. 3 sg.* requires 94.50; **asken** *pr. pl.* seek 4.132; **asked** *pa.* 109.62 *note*; requested 156.147; looked for 165.789; ~ **after** *pa.* 29.17; **askyng** *ger.* request 10.122
aspides *n. pl.* asps 92.82
aspie *v. inf.* find out 95.62; search out 159.298; spy on 174.40; **aspiest** *pr. 2 sg.* look for a means 173.208; **aspiethe** *3 sg.* entraps 117.273; **aspied** *pa.* laid a snare for 106.71; lay in wait for 159.297; **aspied** *pa. p.* detected 26.87, 37.57; trapped 66.66; **aspiynge** *pr. p.* laying traps for 20.9
aspies *n. pl.* traps 117.289
assaies *n. pl.* tests 48.50
assaie *v. inf.* attempt 4.163, 26.100, 54.142, 79.462; try out 17.28; **assaiethe** *3 sg. pr.* 26.154; **assaied** *pa.* tested 116.68; attempted 58.155, 163.307; *pa. p.* 53.101, 84.195; **assaienge** *ger.* test 47.291 *note*

assailingges *ger. pl.* attacks 113.69
as(s)aute *n.* attack 10.7, 20.18, 58.155; **assauutes** *pl.* 15.8
assemble *n.* assembly 36.304, 84.248, 154.8, 175.410; *pl.* collections 117.161
assemble *v. inf. trans.* gather 25.78, 93.168; *intrans.* 94.149; **assembeled** *pa. trans.* gathered 23.119; *intrans.* 95.94; **assembeled** *pa. p.* united 12.19, 66.15, 112.679; *trans.* gathered 112.516, 134.15; **assembelyng(e** *ger.* uniting 23.20, 112.288
asshen *n. pl.* asshes 29.142, 175.271; **asshin** 119.6
assiduell *adj.* assiduous 65.463
assiduelly *adv.* assiduously 58.52
+**assigne** *v. inf.* appoint 174.411; **assigned** *pa.* 106.255 *note*; 159.369 *note*
assoile *v. inf.* answer 1.306, 50.109; **assoyle** absolve 93.146; release 104.195; **assoileth** *pr. 3 sg.* absolves 65.216; **assoilithe** answers 64.158; **assoyling(e** *pr. p.* 44.176, 117.406; **assoil(l)ed** *pa. p.* absolved 45.356, 55.39, 78.91, 95.167; resolved 50.103, 116.144; released 79.448; *ppl. adj.* absolved 104.192; **assoillinge** *ger.* answering 50.104
assuraunce *n.* pledge of secrecy 80.246
astate *see* **estate**
astonyed *v. pa. p.* amazed 79.716, 124.83, 128.244
+**astrayeng** *v. pr. p.* wandering *7.180 *note*; *pa. p.* **astraied** astray 138.16
+**Asuly** *n.* shooting star 176.134 *note*; **Ausli** (H2) 176.136
asure *n.* azure 79.77
aswage *v. inf.* alleviate 113.24; grow calm 161.238; *pr.* 123.347; **assuageth** soothes 12.15; **asuaged** *pa.* 28.176
atamid *ppl. adj.* injured 154.252
atasted *v. pa.* tasted 173.228
athruste *adv.* thirsty 50.129; **athriste** 155.132
atte *prep.* ~ **all** completely 10.39
atteine *v. inf.* reach 154.103
at(t)emperaunce *n.* mildness 14.12; moderation 34.52, 117.254, 149.154
at(t)empre *adj.* temperate 4.199, 66.93; moderate 47.257
attempre *v. inf.* regulate 34.6; **attemperithe** *pr.* moderates 12.68, **attempereth** regulates *49.151; **attempre** *pr. subj.* moderate 142.298; *imp.* 84.87, 106.159; **attempred** *pa.* 117.314; **attempering** *ger.* regulation 176.38
atwayne *adv.* in two 110.203; **atweyne** 93.128; **atwo** 44.95, 55.163, 173.222
aube *n.* alb 159.258; **aubys** *pl.* 48.47
auctour *n.* creator 79.272, 161.5; **auutour** 49.160
auctorised *v. pa.* vouched for 62.18; *ppl. adj.* authenticated 149.171
auctorite *n.* authority 2.38, (G) 43.86, 102.51; authoritative statement 23.21; text 105.186; **auctoritees** *pl.* authoritative writings 53.386, 58.17, 84.41, 106.29, 117.61
audience *n.* legal hearing 174.555
auditour *n.* pupil 35.119
aught *pron.* anything 80.275, 165.390; **ought** 178.233
aught(test *v. see* **owe**
+**augustien** *n.* emperor of Rome 174.438 *note*
aumener(e *n.* almoner 8.227, 81.115; **awmonere** 26.8
auncien(e *adj. and as n.* old 1.313, 20.85, 38.77; **ansyen** 5.95; **aunsient** 115.3; **aunsien** 23.4; of former time 95.88; **anciens** *adj. as n. pl.* people of former times 13.210; **aunsiens** elders 50.197; **aunciens** 123.167; **auncyen** *sg. for pl.* 95.117
+**auriole** *n.* crown or halo of saint 155.325 *note*
au(u)ter(e *n.* altar 2.212, 5.170, 20.123; **awtere** 60.138 ; **autier** (H2) 177.17
auutour *see* **auctour**
auaile *n.* benefit 156.305
availe *v. pr.* bring benefit 11.56 **avaylith** *pr. 3 sg.* 4.154; **availeth** 9.48; **auaile** *pr. pl.* 156.197; **availed** *pa. sg.* 7.167, **auailled** 36.87; *pa. p.* 26.45
avauntages *n. pl.* monetary gains 133.212
avaunt(e *v. inf. refl.* boast 83.141, 113.293; **avaunted hym** *pa.* 135.95; **avauntyng** *ger.* boasting (of) 27.32 *note*, 127.97, 165.605
auenture *n.* occurrence 8.73, 66.207; chance 9.84, 37.11, (G) 46.7, 50.385, 52.5, 80.207; destiny 163.174; misfortune 44.74, 90.164; jeopardy 50.389; **at** ~ at random 161.35; **auentures** *pl.* events 78.71, 110.291,

161.39; destinies 173.113; **auenturis** vicissitudes (G) 4.146
+avironed *v. ppl. adj.* walked round 175.186 *note*
avys *n.* advice 79.136, 134.152, 165.107
avise *v. inf. refl.* think 5.165; **avised hym** considered 45.252, 123.241, 172.26, 173.395; *pa. p.* 113.291; **wel ~** sensible 79.34
avision *n.* instructive dream or vision 58.420, 106.176, 151.105; **auision** 142.206, 161.223, 165.342
avouterere *n.* adulterer 86.58; **auouuterere** 80.195; **auou(u)t(e)reres** *pl.* 79.996, 163.174; *see also* **vouuterere**
avou(u)trye *n.* adultery 53.358, 133.209, 173.413, 174.248; **avowtre** 149.191; **aduoutry** (H1) 144.31; **aduoutrie** (H2) 177.128
avowe *n.* vow 2.284, 15.26, 35.15, 49.24
auowe *v. inf. refl.* dedicate 161.376; **avowed** *pa. sg.* vowed 10.102, *58.336, 90.353, 123.90, 161.413; consecrated 58.358
awayte *n.* entrapment 53.72; trap 58.54; ambush 55.53, 142.231, 149.58; **awaytes** *pl.* traps 50.210, 58.51; **lye in ~** set a trap 139.33
awayted *v. pa. p.* observed 66.103; **awaited** lain in wait for 66.249; spied on 174.443
awne *adj.* own 53.165
axes *n.* attack of fever 58.363
ax(s)e *v. inf.* ask 1.285, 23.78, 95.121; **axse** *pr. 2 sg.* 25.18; **ax(s)ed** *pa.* 2.262, 23.72, 58.266
ayein *adv.* back again 5.37, 20.98; in return 2.213, 29.189; *44.74; **aȝen** back again (G) 1.15; **ayenne** 112.121 *note*; **ayenne callinge** revoking (H2) 176.378
aye(i)n *prep. see* **ayeinst**
ayeinbeying *ger.* redemption 30.83; **ayennebienge** (H2) 176.284
ayeinbyer *n.* redeemer 50.224, 52.20
ayeinsaie *v. inf.* deny 161.249; **ayeinsaiethe** *pr. 3 sg.* contradicts 61.84; **ayeinsaide** *pa.* contradicted 11.289, 79.905; spoke against 61.178, opposed 161.339; **ayeinsaiden** *pl.* 53.58; **ayensaienge** *ger.* denial 64.327
aye(i)n(st *prep.* towards 8.14, 10.71, 11.47, 35.35, 66.183, 78.15[2], 165.239; contrary to 2.97[2], 27.78; in the presence of 16.34, 26.18; opposite 60.283; **aȝens** towards (G) 1.98, (G) 4.91, (G) 43.113; **ayen** contrary to 117.206; against 173.214
ayeinstode *v. pa.* opposed 21.8
ayen *see* **ayeinst**
ayenne *see* **ayein**
ayensaiers *n. pl.* opponents 155.248
ayenwarde *adv.* once more (D) 178.444
azimes *n. pl.* unleavened bread or cakes 60.137 *note*

B

baylies *n. pl.* bailiffs 127.76
balaunce *n.* a pair of balanced weighing scales 26.36, 83.7 *note*, 110.272, 112.495
baleyne *n.* whale 112.989
bandon *n.* control (D) 179.54
banerer(e *n.* standard-bearer 134.74; *pl.* 134.71
bapteme *n.* baptism (G) 4.127, 16.19, 23.118; **baptime** 25.91, 61.82
barbaryn *n.* barbarian 129.54; **barbarins** *pl.* 61.62, 154.233, 159.27; **barbereyns** 129.84
barle *n.* barley 101.31; **barly** 101.111; **barli** (H1) 144.40
bataile *n.* army 154.179; line of battle 159.36
bathe *n.* bath house 8.163
bawme *n.* balsam 5.191, 58.210; **baume** 175.355
be *prep. see* **bi**
beclippe *v. inf.* embrace 79.930; **beclipped** *pa.* encircled 5.178; embraced *28.65; surrounded 30.69, 53.3; **beklippid** embraced *4.45; **byclipped** 79.674, 135.80; **biclypped** *pa. p.* surrounded 20.123, 23.30, 27.39; **beclipped** 141.49, 167.121,125; **beclippinge** *pr. p.* embracing 79.915, 161.274; *see also* **clippe**
bede *v. inf.* invite 8.215; **bede** *pa.* 29.2; **bade** 128.147; **boden** *pa. p.* 38.56; **bodin** 117.241, 128.148; **bode** 124.194, 128.150, 129.18
beden *see* **byde**
beestes *n. pl. see* **best**
before *prep.* in the presence of 5.33, 8.5, 83.94; **bifore** (G) 3.59, 22.4, (G) 41.7; **before** ahead of 13.150; **bifore**

superior to 29.143, 133.201; in front of 159.36
before *adv.* beforehand 16.29, 22.97, 83.11; in the lead 36.302
beforegoers *n. pl.* precursors 112.554
begile *v. inf.* deceive 79.383; **begilid** *pa.* (D) 178.114, (D) 179.161; **begylinge** *ppl. adj.* 79.976
begynne *v. inf.* begin 5.30, 48.64, 50.102; **bygynne** 24.32; **beganne** *pa.* 24.123, 63.45, 78.39; **bygunne** 95.44; **begannest** *pa. 2 sg.* 90.393; **bygannen** *pa. pl.* 54.209; **bygonnen** 22.38; **begonne** *ppl. adj.* begun 7.7; **begynnyng** *ger.* origin 23.9
behalue *n.* **in Goddes** ~ in God's name 10.75
beheste *n.* promise 54.151, 139.202; **byheste** 79.269, 125.4; **byhestes** *pl.* 38.14
behete *see* **behote**
beheueded *ppl. adj.* see **byheueded**
beholde *v. inf.* see 6.22; **biholde** watch 66.132; **beholdithe** *pr. 3 sg.* look at 8.184; **beholdethe** *imp.* look (at) 23.108, 85.11; **beholdyng** *pr. p.* looking 5.147, looking at 7.27, 28.62; **behelde** *pa.* looked 20.118, 155.9; looked at 95.96, 106.185; **bihilde** looked (G) 44.48; *pa. p.* **beholde** seen 48.25; **beholdyng(e** *ger.* appearance 23.22; **byholdinge** 74.61, (H2) 176.311; looking 81.41
behote *v. inf.* promise 58.87, 174.77; *pr. 1 sg.* 94.60; **behete** 2.83; **behotithe** *pr. 3 sg.* 127.83; **behote** *imp.* 58.89, 91.29; **behightest** *pa. 2 sg.* 47.282; **behight** *pa. 3 sg.* 2.275, 9.126, 23.7, 26.134; **bihiȝt** (G) 43.48; **behighten** *pa. pl.* 11.342; **behight** *pa. p.* 9.94; **bihote** (D) 178.179; **behightyng** *pr. p.* 38.14; **bihoting** 151.157; **made behight** promised 25.51
behouithe *v. impers. pr. sg.* is necessary 8.185, 20.68, 25.73; **behoued** *pa. sg.* was necessary 11.219, *36.85, *48.49
beiape *v. inf.* delude 79.383
beye *v. inf.* buy (G) 4.11, 8.30, 20.98; **bye** (G) 3.30, (G) 4.84, *93.320; **by** redeem *176.308; **beye aye(i)n** redeem 11.245, 161.267; *imp. sg.* 176.61; **beyethe** *imp. pl.* buy 8.58; **bought** *pa.* bought 26.189; redeemed 1.181, 50.343; *pa. p.* 17.48; ~ **ayein** 31.26, 36.66, 50.338; **beyenge** *ger.* redemption 176.62; **beyeng ayein** 36.76
beyer *n.* redeemer 50.324
beklippid *see* **beclippe**
beleue *n.* faith 28.67, 32.36, 58.22; **bileue** 2.73, (G) 3.16, 49.10
beme *n.*[1] beam of wood 139.76
bemes *n.*[2] *pl.* beams of light 50.308, 128.18
+bemyred *ppl. adj.* befouled 26.194 *note*
bendes *n. pl.* head-bands 66.76
bene *n. pl.* bees 53.3
benefice *n.* benefit (G) 43.83, 55.208, 59.16; **benifice** favour 73.3; **beneficis** *n. pl.* benefits (G) 3.81, 8.67, 23.24
benigly *adv.* (spelling of **benignely**) kindly 124.64, 165.381
benignite *n.* kindness 79.178
benison *n.* blessing 99.110
berdonis *see* **burdon**[2]
be(e)re *n.*[1] bier 8.23, 25.196, 88.126, 90.342; coffin 78.64
bere *n.*[2] bear 121.59
bere(n *v. inf.* carry 8.19, 25.193, 29.119; **bere** *pr.* 17.21; **berest** *2 sg.* 17.27; **berin** *pl.* 36.259; **beryng** *pr. p.* giving birth to 5.68; **bare herself** *pa. refl.* behaved (H1) 144.22; **bare** *pa. sg.* gave birth to 11.265; **bere** 15.43, **bare** carried 44.62, 61.257, 93.288; 163.154 *note*; **baren** *pa. pl.* 108.56; **barin** 111.55; **beren** 24.103, 54.213; expressed 79.155; **boren** *pa. p.* carried (G) 4.31; **born** 8.17, 36.176, 37.59; **bore** carried 20.48, 112.61; born 11.270; **borun** born 92.1; **bore** *ppl. adj.* carried 61.74; **bare upon** accused 93.179; **bere** carried 14.30, 18.13, 20.14; **bere hym on honde** accused him 80.144, 127.90; **beryng** *ger.* child-bearing 5.291, 28.27; demeanour 160.15
beriales *n.* grave 56.20; **beryels** 106.262
beryeng *ger.* burial 25.193
berker *n.* barking dog 117.175
besain *ppl. adj.* dressed 25.22; **biseyne** (G) 38.131
besechen *v. pr. pl.* entreat 112.354; **beseching** *pr. p.* 28.42; **besought** *pa. sg.* entreated 7.168, 20.8, 58.427; **bisouȝt** (G) 4.81
besecher *n.* suppliant 112.586
besemyng *p. ppl.* seeming (H1) 142.502

besette *v. pa.* surrounded 122.43; **besette** *ppl. adj.* 79.980, 134.85; filled 20.41; enclosed 86.117; **bysette** 137.87
besi *adj.* diligent 8.211, 123.309, 155.316; **busie** (D) 178.49
besieng sore *ppl. adj.* trying hard 165.270
besili *adv.* earnestly 8.143, 165.329; **bisily** 13.135, 74.56; constantly 47.32; **besely** 79.552; **besyly** 106.140; **besily** 173.456; **bisiliest** *superl.* most assiduously 28.212
besines(se *n.* activity 8.71, 84.356, 86.7; **don** ~ devote oneself to a task (D) 179.106
besmes *n.* fine linen(?) *178.619 *note*
besought *see* **besechen**
best(e *n.* animal 139.89, 159.273; **bestes** *pl.* 13.93, 19.5, 101.9; flock 155.301; cattle 86.75, 101.86; **beestes** animals 36.131; **bestis** cattle 5.55, 138.11; animals 18.36; **bestys** cattle (L) 179.370
bestadde *ppl. adj.* beset 79.646
bestaile *n.* cattle 11.346
betake *v. pr.* bestow 112.839; **betoke** *pa.* handed over 129.96; **betake** *pa. p.* 6.41
betenne *see* **bote**
bethenke *v. refl. imp.* think 115.20; **bethought** *pa.* 5.258, *7.42, 45.343; **byþouȝt** (G) 40.14
betoke *see* **betake**
betokenithe *v. pr. 3 sg.* signifies 32.17, 63.117, 175.201; **betokened** *pa. p.* 5.152; 12.62; **bytokened** 149.147
betrouthed *v. pa. p.* pledged marriage to 23.29
bewepe *v. inf.* mourn 54.30; **bywepithe** *imp.* 23.108; **bewepte** *pa. sg.* 28.30; **bywepte** 134.135
bewette *ppl. adj.* soaked 26.276, 79.310, 84.163
bewrapped *ppl. adj.* suffused 84.263; dressed up 113.188; surrounded 112.115
bi, be *prep.* from 9.73; with 29.181, 110.237; throughout *79.824; through 83.66; with reference to 61.243; during 79.145; by means of 29.153, 93.19; **bi ordre** in sequence 2.110; **bi cause that** so that 139.39
bible *n.* collection of books 139.66 *note*
byclipped *see* **beclippe**
bidde *v. inf.* command 25.69, 26.67, 28.164; invite 45.246, 129.17; **biddist** ask (G) 3.22; **biddest** *pr. 2 sg.* command 4.191; **biddithe** *3 sg.* 25.71; **bad** *pa.* (H2) 1.37, 7.165, 8.31, 16.65; **badde** *47.329; **bede** 16.69, 29.32, 58.282; **bode** 163.238; **bode(n** *pa. p.* 2.264; 16.67, 104.73; **bodin** 165.786; **boden** *ppl. adj.* (D) 179.82; **biddyng** *ger.* command (L) 179.324
byde *v. inf.* remain 47.326; **bode** *pa.* (G) 1.13, 165.740; **beden** *pa. p.* 64.50
bye *see* **beye**
bifore *see* **before**
bigge *v. inf.* build (D) 178.456
bygynne *see* **begynne**
byheueded *v. pa. p.* 49.225; **beheueded** *ppl. adj.* decapitated 79.469
byheste *see* **beheste**
biholde *see* **beholde**
bileue *see* **beleue**
bynde *v. inf.* bind (G) 42.60, (G) 43.96, 55.204; **bounde** *pa.* (G) 3.97, 79.367, 74.128; *ppl. adj.* (H2) 1.42, 2.127; **ibounde** 87.87; **bounden** 27.33, 87.9
binethe *adv.* below 25.179, 132.9, 156.386
bynome *v. pa. p.* paralysed 60.263, 163.90; deprived (D) 178.233
birthen *see* **burdon**²
biseyne *see* **besain**
bisshop *n.* high priest 44.169 *note*; **bisshoppes** *pl.* 152.91
bisily, bisiliest see **besili**
bisouȝt *see* **besechen**
bitymys *adv.* promptly (G) 3.70
blame *n.* blasphemy 7.52 *note*, 142.439; blame 142.307; *pl.* 7.43; **without** ~ respectfully (H1) 144.27; *pl.* blasphemies 7.102, 50.72
blame *v. inf.* reproach (G) 40.11, 139.32, 159.282; blaspheme 24.19, 125.101, 136.40; **blame** *pr.* censure 38.45; blame 117.283; **blamest(e** *2 sg.* blaspheme 54.145; blame 163.166, (D) 178.239; **blamithe** *3 sg.* blasphemes 29.200, (G) 42.56; **blamyng** *pr. p.* blaspheming 70.34, 142.444; **blamed** blasphemed *pa.* 11.102, 26.228, 94.179; reproached 1.314, 11.118, 19.1, 24.55; spoke slightingly of 58.220; blamed 76.25; *pa. p.* reproached 8.36, 13.116, 142.390; *ppl. adj.* 137.31; **blamyng** *ger.*

rebuking 175.445; blaspheming 7.105, 125.103
+**blandishe** *adj.* flattering 23.45 *note*
blandisshinge *v. pr. p. adj.* flattering 85.7
blaspheme *n.* blasphemy 7.45; **blasfeme** 79.214, 134.169; *pl.* 50.83
blenching *ger.* blinking 149.48
blessed hym *v. refl. pa.* crossed himself 61.297, 94.11, 95.70; ~ **her** 86.96
blewe *adj.* dark 64.198, 110.251
blowen *v. pr. pl.* inflate 45.187
bobaunce *n.* vain display 25.24, 161.89
bocher *n.* executioner, killer (*see note to* 9.84) 54.185, 83.101, 84.131; 55.60 *note*; **bochers** *pl.* 9.84 *note*, 22.16, *24.36; **bouchers** 38.66
bocherie *n.* 55.61 *note*
bode *see* **bidde, byde**
bofet(te *n.* blow with fist or palm of hand 26.129, 84.60, 110.262; **buffet** (G) 4.27; **boffetis** *pl.* 38.39; **bofetes** 50.153
boffeted *v. pa.* hit, 6.28, 96.52; **bofetid** 78.9
boystous *adj.* coarse 161.110
boldenesse *n.* encouragement 79.522
bole *n.* bull 60.139, 75.29; **boole** 11.321; **boles** *pl.* 93.122
+**bollen** *v. inf.* inflate 53.121; **bolwyng** *ger.* swelling 27.24 *note*
bolnithe *v. pr. 3 sg.* swells up 117.16; **bolnyd** *pa. p.* 110.35
bolnyng *ger.* swelling 12.66
bondes *n. pl.* bonds 47.240, 53.326, 64.184; **boundes** 5.277, 11.300
bone *n.* boon 173.482
bonte *see* **bounte**
boole *see* **bole**
bo(o)rde *n.* table 8.206, 15.18, 45.239, 60.283; side of a ship 2.283, plank *163.137; **bordes** *pl.* 84.304; tables 81.45, 106.197
borde *n.* **in** ~ , in jest 173.459
bordel(l *n.* brothel (G) 3.64; 23.50, 94.185, 150.32; **bordelles** *pl.* 26.102
bordone *see* **burdon**[1]
bote *v. pa.* bit 14.20, 17.61, (G) 38.142; **boote** (D) 178.542; **betenne** *pa. p.* (D) 178.586
bothom *n.* lowest part 8.221; **botum** 161.411
boucher *see* **bocher**
bought *see* **bey(e**
bounde *see* **bynde**
boundes *see* **bondes**
bounte *n.* goodness 12.45, 23.125, 36.177; generosity 60.348; **bonte** *26.253
bowe *n.*[1] bow 8.174
bowe *n.*[2] bough 13.113, *79.648, 83.295; **bowes** *pl.* 101.8, 155.259, 167.46
bowe *v. inf.* bend 1.196, change 10.69; **bouithe** *pr. 3 sg.* bends 65.334; **bowed** *pa. p.* swayed (H2) 176.299; **bowyng** *ppl. adj.* leaning 152.38; bending (L) 179.329; ~ **away fro** turn from 79.397; **bowinge asyde** turning away 79.1017
boxse *n.* jar 10.113 *note*
braste(n *v. trans. pa.* broke, shattered (G) 46.15, 47.18, 79.610, 148.124; *intrans.* burst open, broke 44.95, (G) 47.6, 93.321; **brosten** *intrans. pa. pl.* burst apart 55.226, 153.8; **brostin** *trans.* 116.149; **braste oute** burst into speech 80.38; **brosten** *ppl. adj.* burst apart *intrans.* 44.100
bray *v. inf.* roar 150.45; **brayd** *pa.* wailed 120.47; **braied** 163.30; **brayinge** *ppl. adj.* *90.143
brede *n.*[1] bread 14.40, 28.80, 161.105
brede *n.*[2] breadth 61.49, 102.74, 142.150
breke *v. inf. trans.* break 20.66, 22.87; **breke** break open *intrans.* 87.54; **brake** 83.341; **brekithe** *pr.* harms 65.61 *note*; terminates 65.224; **brekyng** *pr. p.* subduing (G) 43.74; **breke** *pa. trans.* broke 2.225, 22.93; *intrans.* 25.58; subdued 28.150; broke into 84.84; interrupted 10.84; broke into speech 79.283,934; **brake** *intrans.* broke 93.111; *trans.* 133.86; broke into 142.454; **broken** *pa. p.* damaged 33.2; destroyed 171.68
brenne *n.* bran 45.220
brenne *v. inf. trans.* burn (G) 4.71, 9.56; **brennyth** *pr. 3 sg. intrans.* *2.97; *trans.* *2.98; **brenneth** *intrans.* *8.187; **brennithe** *imp.* 102.51; **brenned** *pa. intrans.* 6.18; **brend** *trans.* 137.51; **brent(e** 23.90, (G) 38.146, 54.160; **brenden** *pa. pl.* 175.426; *pa. p.* 22.104, 24.58, 84.336; **brennyng** *ger.* fervour 20.27, 28.138, 33.69; *pr. p.* 12.74
breris *n. pl.* thorns (G) 39.7, (D) 178.128; **breres** 47.40, 79.615, 122.43

brethered *n.* brotherhood 78.93
brethinge *ger.* breath 65.86
brydde *n.* bird 8.171
brimstone *n.* sulphur 116.101
bringgers *n. pl.* bearers 20.136
broc(c)hes *n. pl.* sharp instruments 18.7; **broches** brooches or other ornaments 23.32, 131.72
broyle *v. inf.* burn (G) 45.571; *imp.* 65.309; **broyled** *pa. p.* consumed by fire *24.58, 87.85; **bruled** *ppl. adj.* 24.109; burned 52.7; **broyled** 110.251, 149.52, 156.42
broke *v. inf.* tolerate 138.82, 174.707
brond(e *n.* firebrand 36.209, (G) 45.571, 99.85; **brondes** *pl.* 54.112, 87.85
brosten *see* **brasten**
bruit *n.* commotion 112.696 *note*
bruled *see* **broyled**
buffet *see* **bofette**
bufones *n. pl.* toads 48.77 *note*
bulted *ppl. adj.* sifted 45.219
burdon *n.*[1] staff *93.275; **bordone** staff 48.3
burdon *n.*[2] weight 104.167; **burden** burden 171.78; **birthen** 171.86; **berdonis** *pl.* burdons 161.299
burgeys *n.* freeman or merchant 93.310, 95.51; *pl.* 79.488
burione *v. inf.* sprout *178.128
busie *see* **besi**
but *conj.* unless 25.212; **butte** 26.66; **but if** (G) 3.66; **but yef** 13.56, 31.7
buxome *adj.* humble (D) 179.227
buxomnesse *n.* humility (D) 179.285

C

caas, cace *see* **case**
caitiff *n.* wretch 125.67; **caytef** 87.79, 165.794
calamynt *n.* aromatic Eurasian plant *Calamintha* (D) 178.585
canelle *n.* cinnamon (D) 178.585
canker *n.* cancer 55.145; **cancre** *58.425, 83.419, 136.94
canne *v. pr.* know 1.307, 152.83; **canst** *pr. 2 sg.* 60.179, **konne** *inf.* (G) 43.55; **kon** know (H1) 146.102; **canne thanke** am grateful 79.65; *pr. pl.* **konnen** know (G) 4.3; **canne** 2.174; **cunne** are able 165.176; **coude** *pa.* was able 18.48, 22.81, 123.325; knew (H2) 1.36, 2.175, 106.89; **cowde** 53.34, (H2) 177.105; **couthe** knew 123.38; **kouthe** was able to (G) 43.18; **couth** (G) 43.41; *see also* **connyng(e, cunnyng**
capitlee *see* **chapitle**
capitaille *n.* the Capitoline hill in Rome 83.187; **capitoyle** citadel or heathen temple 166.7 *note*
careyne *n.* rotting flesh 173.511; **karions** *pl.* corpses 60.301; **carienes** 60.303; **careynes** 128.9
carnell *adj.* worldly 27.43, 156.37
caroles *n. pl. see* **karoll**
carte *n.* chariot 53.76
cas(e *n.* instance 29.93, (G) 46.7, 59.48; **cace** example 36.119; **by caas** by chance 53.123, 101.72; happening 165.295
cast(e *v. inf.* throw (G) 3.84, 7.106, 17.18; abort 68.10; add (D) 179.251; *pr.* 22.35; *imp.* 25.80; **caste** *pa.* threw (G) 1.33, 2.20, (G) 4.36, 20.136; **kist(e** 132.32, 142.453; **caste** *refl.* decided 128.191; **castin** *pa. pl.* 116.149; **casted** 128.35; **caste** *pa. p.* thrown 2.159, 8.213; defeated 112.490; vomited (D) 179.223; **castynge** *ger.* throwing 7.108; vomiting 138.82
castel(le *n.* castle, town (reflecting both *castrum* and *oppidum*) castle 29.88, 45.149, 49.244; town 60.212, 90.1, 92.99; citadel 80.225; **castellis** *pl.* castles 5.14; towns 99.4; *pl. for sg.* 7.106
casuelly *adv.* by chance 79.79
catel *n.* property 113.274
catheloge *n.* catalogue 10.91, *163.256; **cathologe** 58.233, 151.85
cause *n.* matter 5.225 *note*; 145.60; (legal) case 149.175; **causes** *pl.* matters 45.167; **causis** *pl.* ~ **of iugementis** judicial cases (H2) 176.379; **by cause** in order to prevent 83.71 *note*
caued *ppl. adj.* hollowed 47.93
cedre *n.* cedar 36.246
+**celebred** *v. pa. p.* performed, held 82.15 *note*
celers *see* **sellere**
celle *see* **selle**
cene *n.* synod 174.413; **sene** 174.412; **Sane** *63.157 *note*; **cene** the Lord's supper 107.26, 142.413
certayne *n.* certain person 13.71

certeficacion *n.* confirmation 13.143
certefie *v. inf.* instruct 35.17 *note*; **certefied** *pa. p.* 149.299
certis *adv.* truly 156.181, 175.294
cesar *n.* emperor 111.6
+**cesarien** *n.* heir to the empire 81.52 *note*, 174.437; **Cesariens** *pl.* 104.127
cese *v. inf.* cease (G) 3.57, 11.317; **sece** 18.38; **sese** *imp.* 87.58, 116.77; **cesed** 22.183; **sesid** 2.67; **sesed** 29.180; **secedin** *pa. pl.* 129.109; **seseden** 133.24
chayer *n.* throne 2.52, 53.53, 99.103; **chaier** 83.89; **cheyre** (G) 43.59; **cheier** 163.235; **chare** (G) 43.1; *also* **chare**
chayryng *ger.* enthronement 44.rubric
chamberers *see* **chaumbrere**
chamberleyns *n. pl.* household servants 68.2
chamel *n.* camel 155.352; **chameles** *pl.* 174.147
champaine *n.* open country *174.378 *note*
champion *n.* warrior 12.40, 54.169, 58.1
chanon *n.* canon 113.160; **chanones** *pl.* canons 93.168
chapelette *n.* coronet 50.161; **chapelettis** *pl.* 165.366
chapitle *n.* Chapter, formal meeting of members of religious community 58.233; chapter of a book 50.97, 64.63; **capitlee** 53.241
chapitre *n.* chapter house 5.241, 106.207; **chapitour** 5.251
chare *n.* chariot *64.250, 109.52, 127.41, 173.147, (H2) 178.402; **chayer(e** 11.49 *note*, 80.273, 104.9; **chayre** 111.60; **chare** wagon 93.119, 142.436; **chare man** charioteer 104.11; *see also* **chayer**
charge *n.* responsibility 1.201, 24.3, 65.378, 113.159; burden 25.11; load 36.145
chargeable *adj.* onerous 117.315
charged *v. pa.* instructed 7.158, 8.83, 14.32; loaded 90.129; *pa. p.* 90.348; *ppl. adj.* laden 2.77, 60.143, 66.176, 116.45; instructed 142.71
charite(e *n.* love 11.376, 90.313, 112.331; devotion 117.442; benefaction 120.7
charmes *n. pl.* magic spells 45.417, 113.25
chartre *n.* document 123.367, 142.373
chase *v. inf.* drive out 65.197; **chace** 65.199, 108.40; **chasithe** *pr. 3 sg.* hunts 22.58 *note*; **chased** *pa.* 122.9; **chasedist** *pa. 2 sg.* drove out 117.63; *pa. p.* **chasyd** driven out 117.343
chase, chasyn *v. pa. see* **chese**
chastelyn *n.* wife of castle-governor 29.83
chaufith *v. pr. 3 sg.* heats 33.68
cha(u)mbrere *n.* lady in waiting 6.6; serving woman *52.71, 90.45, 112.178, 117.276; **cha(u)mbrer(e)s** *pl.* 28.91, 45.201, 53.164, 68.19
chaundeler *n.* candlestick 112.648; **chaundelers** *pl.* *83.420
chauntour *n.* cantor 113.401; ~ **of chauntours** choir leader 112.104
cheyre *see* **chayer**
chemeney *n.* fireplace 37.76
cher(e *n.* facial expression 8.52, 45.303, 47.235, 54.149, 60.337; kindliness (G) 44.46 *note*; face (D) 178.129
cherete *n.* esteem 117.442
cherl(e *n.* peasant *47.222; **churle** 150.22; *as term of abuse* 142.56; **churles** *pl.* peasants 5.54, 140.44, 159.145
chersere *n.* favourer 25.27
chese *v. inf.* choose *21.2, 37.74, 60.235; *imp.* 1.268, 23.48, 61.198; **chase** *pa.* chose 28.58, 36.65, 56.14; **ches** (G) 1.125; **chese** *pa.* 7.16; **chosin** *pa. pl.* 106.121; **chasyn (L)** 179.420; **chose** *pa. p.* 21.4
chetyue *adj.* captive 66.272
chetivison *n.* captivity 30.47, 64.127, 66.264; **chetevison** 30.81; **chetifeson** 106.88
chetiuyte *n.* captivity 49.53, 66.266, *173.491; **chetevite** 30.58
cheualrie *n.* body of knights 154.1
cheueteynes *n. pl.* governors 81.60
cheuisaunce *n.* financial provision 113.264 *note*
chide *v. inf.* quarrel 44.58; **chiding** *pr. p.* 44.59; **chidden** *pa. pl.* 28.148; **chidde** *pa.* scolded 129.36; **chidde** *pa. p.* 2.138, 84.355, **chyd** 119.14; **chydyng(e** *ppl. adj.* quarrelling (G) 44.35; complaining 120.52; **chydyng** *ger.* quarrelling 9.17, rebuke 26.229; **chidyngges** *pl.* 25.33, 26.172
childe *n.* young man 141.5; **children** *pl.*

boys 117.79; **childers** *gen. pl.* children's 60.295
childid *v. pa.* gave birth (H2) 178.318; **childyng(e** *ger.* childbirth 5.36, 11.215, 112.187
+**childisnes** *n.* childishness 161.7 *note*
chine *n.* skin 47.267 *note*
chirche *n. frequently used for* monastery 10.37 *note*
chose, chosin *see* **chese**
churle *see* **cherl**
cirograff *see* **syrograff**
citronyen *n.* 139.17 *note*
cle(e *n.* hoof 149.74; **clees** *pl.* claws 52.107
clense *v. inf.* clean 147.15; **clensed** *pa.* 29.37, 106.148; healed 80.156
clepe *v. inf.* name (D) 178.73, summon (D) 178.152; **cleped** *pa.* summoned 8.33, 165.229, (D) 178.105; named 5.31, **clepid** (D) 178.24; *pa. p.* 116.264; **clepte** 117.151, 159.173; **cleping** *ger.* designation 45.182
cleped *see* **clepe** *and* **clippe**[1]
clere *adj.* bright 13.86, 60.134, 64.198; clear 51.84; resonant 84.140; excellent 11.19; lucid 117.405; illustrious 122.96, 139.174; certain 161.175
clere *adv.* brightly 61.71; **clerer** *comp.* 142.128
clered *v. pa.* made illustrious 161.4
clerenesse *n.* renown 64.289; brightness 94.142, 116.278; clarity *45.144, 112.148
clergie *n.* clerical status 81.79
clerith(e *v. pr.* brightens 65.290; reveals 55.25; **clered** *pa.* made illustrious 161.4; *pa. p.* enlightened 117.118; *ppl. adj.* 154.7; **cleringe** *ger.* shining 112.223
clerk(e *n.* writer (G) 43.138; cleric 71.30, 79.159; **clerkes** *pl.* 11.41, 25.9, 91.47, 117.202, 142.428, 146.139
cleue *v.*[1] *inf.* adhere 61.57, 79.499; **cleuyd** adhered 6.36, 80.263; **cleued** *pa.* was fastened 61.54
cleue *v.*[2] *inf.* cut in two 174.474; **clouen** *pa. p.* 146.33; **clouin** *ppl. adj.* 149.74
clippe *v.*[1] *inf.* embrace 50.315, 159.123, 173.366; **clipped** *pa.* 6.21, 14.38, 95.149; **cleped** 86.107 *note*; **klippid** (G) 43.23; **clipping(e** *ger.* embrace 31.33, 94.140; **clippyng(g)es** *pl.* 23.35, *25.65; *see also* **beclippe**
clipped *v.*[2] cut (hair) 174.393
clodist *v. pa. 2 sg.* clothed 26.61; **clodid** *pa.* 54.98; **cloded** *pa. p.* 72.12; **clodid** *ppl. adj.* 25.8
cloyster *n.* confined space 45.24, 79.279
close *n.* confinement 173.100
closith *v. imp. pl.* enclose 24.66; **closed** *pa.* 15.53, 60.207, 74.131, 86.104; **closid** (G) 42.17, 55.139, 116.247; **close(d** *ppl. adj.* closed 58.442, 95.37; confined 152.172; **clos** 79.247; closed 175.433
cloth(e *n.* garment (G) 4.88, 90.319, 137.53; clothing 26.49, (G) 45.557; 84.143, 86.128; **clothes** *pl.* cloths 7.146
clowt *n.* piece of cloth 2.20; **cloutes** 55.205; garments 13.188, 142.43; **clowtis** swaddling clothes 98.14
clowted *ppl. adj.* patched 161.276
clouen *see* **cleue**
cofre *n.* coffin 116.260, box 148.91; **cophre** 148.97; **cofer(e)s** *pl.* coffers 123.30 *note*, 152.125; **cophers** *n. pl.* 173.173
coyfe *n.* helmet 94.160
cokes *n. pl.* cooks 175.383
col(l)age *n.* community 47.45, 112.838
coldithe *v. pr. 3 sg.* cools *22.51
coler(e *n.* choler *34.32, 138.80 *note*
colere *n.* liquid eye salve *4.150
colet *n.* acolyte 159.44 *note*
collacion *n.* comparison 45.276; consultation 104.144, 173.425; discussion 142.394; collection of money or goods 156.195 *note*
colour(e *n.* pretext 148.133, 160.31
comaunde *v. pr. 2 sg.* commend 1.200; **comaunded** *pa.* 47.223, 58.164, 84.136, 93.13; *pa. p.* 90.168
comenaunt *n.* agreement 97.10, 149.255, 155.228
comfortable *adj.* comforting 6.12, 12.75, 65.433, 165.524
comforte *v. inf.* strengthen 175.234 *note*; **conforte** 7.27; **conforth** comfort (H2) 1.44; **comforted** *pa.* encouraged 11.87, 81.31; alleviated 163.120
comyn *see* **comune** *adj.*
cominitee *n.* community 12.29 *note*
commune *v. see* **comune** *v.*
+**communyalte** *n.* community (?) 45.414 *note*
communycacion *n.* communion 60.58

comon *see* **comune** *adj.*
comonli *adv.* universally 8.67, 146.38; **comonly** frequently 8.191; together 63.56
+**compeynabli** *adv.* sociably 149.133 *note*; **compainabli** 149.145
complaynte *n.* lament 55.134; **compleint** 65.94
compleyned *v. pa.* complained 95.35; lamented 142.236; *pa. refl.* 84.50, 131.18; **compleyninge** *ppl. adj.* 90.342, 112.831
complexcion *n.* constitution 83.410 *note*; **complecciones** *pl.* humours 33.25; **complexiones** 156.375
Complie *n.* Compline 142.231
compuncte *adj.* contrite 79.965; **conpunct** 168.51
comune *adj.* public 66.69 *note*, 81.94, 65.208; general 11.129; familiar 30.17; available to all 36.90, 117.227; universal 84.472; shared 112.729; ~ **woman** harlot 38.11, 132.25, 175.438; **comyn woman** (H1) 145.1; **comon** *adj.* public 5.50; general 44.128; ~ **peple** proletariat 32.14; **comune women** 23.50, 26.128; ~ **goodis** public goods (G) 41.13 *note*
comune *n.* nation 5.8, 104.119, 134.67, 147.29, 174.324; public 20.132; **comunes** *pl.* proletariat 165.130; **in** ~ publicly 123.157–8, 133.189 *note*, 163.260; **of comune** jointly owned 16.75
comune *v. inf.* receive holy communion 129.132; **commune** *pr.* have in common 112.916; **communed** *pa. p.* administered holy communion 21.9, 175.173 *note*
conable, conablete, conably *see* **couenable, couenablete, couenably**
concauete *n.* hollow 64.110
conceyued *v. pa.* experienced 9.103; understood 48.9, 101.139; **conceyuyng** *pr. p.* 9.19
conclude *v. pr.* include 124.236 *note*; **concludid** *pa.* refuted 117.384
conclused *v. pa.* ended 174.357
concordaunce *n.* agreement 149.173, harmony 175.56
concours *n.* crowd 1.166
condicion *n.* social or religious status 124.233, 139.15, 142.105, 155.229; stipulation 151.27; **condicyonis** *pl.* habits, attitudes (G) 44.46; **condicion(e)s** 44.160, 47.60; **condiciones** circumstances 52.28, 126.7
condit *n.* guidance 13.141, conduit 50.509; **condut** direction 32.48; **condyt** management 28.41; **condites** *pl.* water pipes 128.35; ~ **of nature** ducts which convey body fluids 145.49
condit *v. pa.* led 51.42
conditor *n.* guide 36.203
confeccion *n.* remedy 138.86
conferme *v. inf.* confirm 35.23; **confermithe** *pr. 3 sg.* makes secure 175.238; **confermed** *pa.* confirmed 18.44; strengthened 22.75, 32.51, 35.42, 81.68, 95.72; *pa. p.* 90.109; confirmed 84.25, 106.110
confessin *v. pr. pl.* reveal 35.11; **confessid** *pa.* acknowledged 13.102; **confessed** 149.160; 33.37 confessed; *pa. p.* avowed faith in 25.137 *note*
confession *n.* recognition 114.10
confessour *n.* saint who was not a martyr 18.8
conforte, conforth *v. see* **comforte**
confounded *v. pa.* put down 13.119, refuted 117.287
confused *v. pa. p.* humiliated 8.129, disgraced 26.266; *ppl. adj.* disconcerted 145.97, (H2) 177.24; mixed up 175.453
confusion *n.* disgrace (G) 4.56, 8.92; source of shame 26.269, humiliation 148.120
+**conisaunce** *n.* formal acknowledgement 174.233 *note*
coniuracions *n. pl.* invocations of spirits 58.377
coniure *v. pr.* implore 49.263, 52.27, 108.19; urge 83.194, 90.265; exorcise 58.373; **coniuringe** *pr. p.* imploring 77.58; **coniured** *pa.* 5.264, 61.321, 66.140; called up 53.100
coniurement *n.* exorcism 78.85; **coniurementes** *pl.* magic spells 29.160
connyng(e *ger.* learning 10.55, 13.228, 35.22; **cun(n)yng(e** 16.4, 84.256, 134.17, 165.90; knowledge 59.36; **cunninge** intelligence 124.132, 155.191; **conning(e** knowledge *65.288, 133.26; **konnyng(e** (G) 4.121; **kunnynge** 101.3; **kuninge** 113.431

conpact *adj.* solid 165.857
conquest *n.* acquisition by effort 161.112 *note*
conseit(e *n.* conception 146.45; opinion 165.127
consenta(u)nt *adj.* acquiescent 2.136, 102.11
conservaunt *n.* fellow servant 64.333
conserued *v. pa.* kept safe 65.220
considered *v. pa.* observed 150.45, 154.153
conspiraciones *n. pl.* conspiracies 79.18
constreininge *ger.* infliction 174.57
+**consult(e** *n.* consul 2.123 *note*, (G) 3.34, 29.154, 38.3, 57.1 *note*, 68.4, 83.403, 95.102, 127.10; 130.19, 174.321; **consultes** *n. pl. error* 7.132 *note*
contecte *n.* sedition 84.85; **contekt** dispute 104.172
continent *adj.* moderate 55.77
continentes *n. pl.* celibates 63.32 *note*, 155.350, 175.284
continua(u)nce *n.* perseverance 60.47, 159.205; constancy 165.136
continuel *adj.* frequent 90.299, 175.199
continuethe *v. pr. 3 sg.* perseveres with 32.40
contracte *n.* sufferer from paralysis 58.102, 84.13
contract(e *ppl. adj.* paralysed 29.36, 131.23
contrarie *adj.* opposed 22.102, 74.117, 113.364; opposite 142.41; adverse 138.89; **contrary** 74.19
contrarie *v. inf.* oppose 5.237, 168.70; **contrariethe** *pr. 3 sg.* 110.10; **contrarie(n** *pr. pl.* 7.83, 13.126, 33.48; resist 134.18, 175.177; **contraried** *pa.* 7.87, 156.225; **contrarieden** resisted 7.34
contrariewise *adv.* backwards 140.37
contre(y *n.* homeland 7.179; region 5.33, 29.79, 51.40; countryside 5.54; *pl.* regions 29.86; **cuntre** region (G) 46.13
contreued *v. pa. p.* devised 142.220
contricion *n.* harm 112.577
conuenient *adj.* appropriate 65.200, 152.77; **is conuenient** follows 112.934
conuersacion *n.* way of life 12.59, (G) 43.181, 50.51, 64.215, 149.46; behaviour 173.125; dwelling place 64.216, (H1) 146.95
conuersaunt *adj.* familiar (H2) 177.52
conuerted *v. pa.* transformed 8.54; *pa. p.* returned 159.84 *note*; *ppl. adj.* 156.337
cope *n.* cloak 58.112, 142.377, 156.114
cophers *see* **cofre**
coppe *n.* summit 79.636, 165.839; **coppis** *pl.* (H2) 176.177
corage *n.* spirit, disposition (G) 1.101, 23.5, 24.114; *pl.* 22.54 inclination 38.14
corde *n.* rope 139.76, 142.51; **cordis** *n. pl.* ropes 55.163; **cordes** 126.16; strings on musical instrument 84.268
corious(li) *see* **curious(li)**
cornes *n. pl.* cornfields 93.328
corone *n.* crown (G) 3.67, (G) 4.8, 30.79; tonsure (G) 43.150; **corownes** *pl.* crowns 155.241
corporat *adj.* incarnate 13.185 *note*
corrupte *v. ppl.* corrupt(ed) 2.123, (G) 3.66, 13.235, 16.31
corruptible *adj.* mortal 112.608
corse(s) *n. see* **curse**
corse *v. see* **curse**
corseint *n.* a saint's body 55.125, 117.419, 129.140; **corseintes** *pl.* 45.225
corumpe *v. inf.* become corrupt 74.88; **corrumped** *pa. p.* corrupted 25.55
corumpours *n. pl.* debauchers 69.17 *note*
corue *v. inf.* sculpt (H1) 157.8; **corven** *pa. p.* 122.84; **corue** 123.269, 155.38; **coruen** carved through 28.191; **kerving** *ger.* sculpting (H1) 157.8
cosin *n.* kinsman (G) 4.140, 9.124; *fig.* 30.18, 68.8; **cosenes** *pl.* kinsmen 110.5, 112.597; **cosynes** 128.147, 151.71
cosinage *n.* kinship 123.65
costes *n. pl.* sides 138.11
coude *see* **canne**
coule *n.* cowl 47.71; **covyll** 174.215
counceillour *n. error* 129.27 *note*; **councellour** 152.213 *note*
counsai(l)le *n.* secret 49.251, 95.89; counsel 5.85, 79.400, 106.286, 121.10, 123.169, 173.88; private matter 79.327; secrecy 10.34, 117.310, 142.101, 173.72; plan 106.89; secret *quasi adj.* 124.20; **counsell** secret plan 26.66, 151.51; secret 124.19; **counsel** advice (G) 4.142, 127.25; **councelle** 177.155; **counsaile** *error* 129.76 *note*, *error* 130.17 *note*; **counsailes** *pl.* secrets 117.182
counsaile *v. inf.* advise 106.288; **counceile** seek advice 123.170;

counsailed *pa.* advised 11.185; **councelled** 101.11; sought advice 81.57
couple *v. inf.* yoke together 86.40; join 133.90, 151.8; **coupeled** *pa. refl.* joined 150.25; *pa.* 44.73
courbe *adj.* bent 102.71
cours *n.*[1] race *84.258; stream 90.238
cours *n.*[2] *see* **curse**
couth *see* **canne**
coueite *v. inf.* desire 64.160, 113.55; **coueyte** *pr.* (G) 3.44, 45.218; **coveyten** *pr. pl.* 28.20, 116.49; **coveytinge** *pr. p.* desiring 79.340; **coueited** *pa.* 10.100, *36.220, 84.457, 122.20
coue(i)tise *n.* covetousness (G) 4.129, 11.306, 34.8; desire 5.254, 15.42, 36.242
coueytous *adj.* concupiscent 74.7 *note*; desirous 90.234
coueytously *adv.* avidly 139.8; rapaciously 146.230
couenable *adj.* appropriate 1.146, 5.276, 23.11, 49.3, 52.106, 55.235, 60.12; suitable 23.147, 93.104, 141.5, 148.8; licit 27.84, 58.53; qualified 44.162, 117.137; compatible 47.60; **couenabul** (G) 40.36, (G) 44.46; **conable** skilful 50.365; suitable 58.216, 64.258, 90.361, 93.89, (H1) 146.54
couenablete *n.* timeliness 176.19; **conablete** *n.* appropriateness 50.263
couenably *adv.* appropriately 117.75, 159.261; **couenablie** conveniently 141.16; **conably** *adv.* proportionately 5.281
covent *n.* monastery 112.535, 113.157, 148.12
couer *v. inf.* cure 5.266
couert(o)ure *n.* covering 22.166, 63.41; bedspread 26.189, (H1) 145.13
couetise *see* **coueitise**
covyll *see* **coule**
cowardise *n.* stupidity 79.54
cowde *see* **canne**
crach(e *n.* manger 5.55, 13.30, 64.120; cradle 106.291; **creche** 28.73, *61.153, 65.243, 139.66
craft(e *n.* art 2.176, 60.180; skill 55.105; trade (G) 1.15, (G) 4.3, 133.212
crafty *adj.* skilled (G) 4.10
creatoure *n.* creature 5.123, 116.106; **creature** creation 8.66, 64.152; created being 65.36, 102.21; **creatoures** *pl.* 79.628
creaunce *n.* belief 28.49 *note*
creche *see* **crache**
credence *n.* belief 26.124
cre(y)me *n.* oil of chrism 11.39, 15.31, 175.188
crestes *n. pl.* head-dresses 66.76
creueis *n.* hollow 83.348 *note*; **creues** 155.31 *note*, 156.245; *pl.* hollows **crevise** 18.21; fissures **creueys** 24.78 *note*; **trewens** 24.129 *note to* 24.78; **creueis** *156.414
crie *v. inf.* announce publicly (G) 4.17; speak aloud 24.12; shout 24.36, 29.68, 47.235, 84.85; make known 133.145; **cried** *pa.* shouted 50.66, 83.148, 90.146; called out 168.7; **cryeng** *ger.* screeching 24.97; **crieng** shouting 112.516
crye *n.* public announcement 54.152
crioure *n.* public crier 119.121, 173.156; **crier** 175.206; **crioures** *pl.* 116.239
crismatorie *n.* chrism vessel 99.114 *note*
crispe *adj.* curly 116.17
cristenly *adv.* in a Christian manner 6.2
crocum *n.* saffron *178.584
croked *ppl. adj.* misshapen (H1) 143.53
crossed *v. pa.* made the sign of the cross 25.141
crowne *n.* tonsure 142.281
cubites *n. pl.* measure of length (about 18 inches) 66.228, 90.295, 93.144
cuys *n.* 120.8 *note*
cunne *see* **canne**
cunnyng *n. see* **connyng**
cunnyng *adj.* knowledgeable 117.142; skilful 161.406; **konninge** able *92.86; *see also* **canne**
cuntre *see* **contrey**
curable *adj.* capable of healing 142.297 *note*
curacion *n.* healing 61.37
curatif *adj.* curative 149.207
cure *n.* care 20.138, 36.83, 54.88; responsibility 24.15, 82.36, 83.202, 88.89, 117.219, 122.62; cure (G) 38.83; liking 113.7 *note*; **cures** *pl.* responsibilities 155.316
curiosite *n.* diligence 13.62, (G) 43.32 *note*; inquisitiveness 33.35, sollicitude 84.474
curious(e *adj.* elaborate (G) 43.161; **corious** 112.682; concerned 155.240; inquisitive 174.620

curiously *adv.* diligently 1.180, 5.182, 25.73; solicitously 81.46, (H1) 144.2; **coriousli** 139.10; diligently 175.133; elaborately 142.110

curse *n.* curse 7.176, 10.76; **corse** 36.42; **cours** 49.67; **curs** 49.64; **corses** *pl.* 49.63

curse *v. inf.* lay a curse on 47.290; invoke evil upon 117.251; **corse** *pr.* curse 93.74; **cursed** *pa.* 7.175; *pa. p.* 93.76; *ppl. adj.* accursed 2.93, 6.19, 9.130

cussed *see* **kisse**

custume *v. inf. refl.* accustom oneself 161.10; **custumed** *pa.* was in habit of 83.27; *pa. p.* accustomed 13.212, 45.135, 47.124, *53.30, 93.213

custumable *adj.* customary 112.20; **customable** persistent (D) 179.215

D

dalue *v. pa.* dug 18.32

dampne *v. inf.* condemn 79.727, 117.284; **dampned** *ppl. adj.* condemned 50.6, 61.247, 79.137, 80.196, 102.25; damned 104.140

dar(e, darst *see* **dere**

daungere *n.* resistance 136.9

daunt(e *v. inf.* subdue 34.44, 50.385; **daunted** *pa.* subdued 66.39, 139.57; **dauntyng** *ger.* subduing (G) *1.205 *note*

debonayr(e *adj.* gracious 1.187, 25.89; gentle 20.139, 50.461, 54.68; clement 53.44, 60.348

debonayrli *adv.* calmly 11.345, 52.104, *57.32

debonairte *n.* gentleness 15.17, 58.63, 64.202, 65.376; graciousness 27.28, 112.981, 129.8; mercifulness 45.343

deceyuable *adj.* deceptive 124.245, 156.115, 173.237; **deceiuables** *pl.* 156.121

decerued *v. pa.* (*for* **deserued**) was worthy 105.53

dede *n.* written evidence of transaction 10.29; action 27.29; **dedis** *pl.* written evidence of lives 21.7, 22.174

ded(e)ly *adj.* mortal 5.160, 33.47, (G) 42.11, 45.221, 50.284; fatal 8.239, 45.463; **deedelie** (H2) 176.237

dedye(n *v. inf.* dedicate 79.61, 101.132, 138.182; **dedied** *pa.* 80.213, *83.464, 93.135, 124.277

dedly *adv.* fatally 58.151

dedlynesse *n.* mortality 112.594 *note*

deface *v. inf.* erase 170.35; **defasithe** *pr. 3 sg.* 149.61; **defaced** *pa. p.* 84.376

defail(l)e *v. inf.* weaken 22.6, 83.229; **defailethe** *pr.* 84.248; **defaile** *imp.* 154.62; **defaylinge** *ppl. adj.* 112.774

defame *n.* ill-repute 139.198; **diffame** disgrace 36.119

defame *v. inf.* reproach 26.119; **defamythe** *pr. 3 sg.* dishonours (G) 43.32; **defamed** *pa.* slandered 84.8, 86.127, 152.159; denounced 120.24; *pa. p.* dishonoured 175.263

defasithe *see* **deface**

defau(u)te *n.* sin 1.139, 10.104, 79.266; lack 55.231, 63.143, 156.263; *pl.* sins 2.251, 18.34, (L) 79.1054; omissions 155.2

defend(e *v. inf.* defend 103.22, 173.334; forbid 53.349; *pr. pl.* 11.56, 35.76; *subj.* 29.114; *imp. sg.* 84.111; *imp. pl.* 22.28; **defendithe** *pr. 3 sg.* 83.322; **defendethe** protects 12.51 *note*; **defended** *pa.* prevented 20.110, 97.15; forbade 26.226, (G) 38.75, 96.41; resisted 36.329; *pa. p.* forbidden 53.348, 103.3, 107.34; *ppl. adj.* protected 44.96

+defenderesse *n.* protectress (G) 3.94 *note*

defensour *n.* 159.95 *note*

deferre *v. imp.* delay 79.400; **deferred** *pa.* 79.517; *pa. p.* differentiated 59.43

defformyte *n.* ugliness (G) *43.162

deffowle *v. inf.* violate (G) 3.72; **defoule** 150.34; trample 65.424, defile 106.228, 132.34, 142.273; **defoulen** *pr.* 22.45 *note*, **deffoulen** (G) 38.104; **defouled** *pa.* defiled 20.129, 86.122, 152.167; trod 64.184; trampled 78.11, 128.158; raped 170.8; *pa. p.* trodden 64.177 *note*; raped 68.58, 152.160; **defouled** *pa. p.* trampled 38.64, 134.86, 142.275, 154.56; **defoilled** defiled 23.54; **defouled** *ppl. adj.* crushed *58.209; defiled 36.24, 44.97, 45.127, 50.142, 52.31, 64.167 *note*, 77.50, (H1) 143.28, 173.142; **defoulyd** 111.18; **diffoulid** (D) 179.113; **defoulyng(e** *ger.* defilement 16.58, 36.26, 124.68; abusing 142.310

defye *v. inf.* digest 45.28
degree *n.* step 60.81, (H2) 177.79; **degre** status 142.257, 161.94; **degreis** *pl.* stages (G) 4.116; **degrees** steps 22.144, 76.19, 117.163 *note*; honours 79.22
deie(n *v.*[1] *inf.* die 14.37, 28.122, 156.25; **deyen** *pr. pl.* 20.80; **deide** *pa.* 11.328, **deied** 140.8; **deyde** 63.18; **deiden** *pl.* 116.134
deyed *v.*[2] *pa. p.* dyed 11.281
delacion *see* **dilacion**
delectable *see* **delictable**
delectacio(u)n *n.* pleasure (G) 3.54, 117.269, (H2) 177.38; **delectaciones** *pl.* 65.251, 79.53, 133.180
delicat *adj.* fastidious 155.226
delices *n. pl.* luxuries 161.6; **delicis** pleasures (D) 178.269, (D) 179.503; delights 112.124
delicious *adj.* delicate 20.150
deliciously *adv.* luxuriously 58.49
delynge *ger.* behaviour *179.302
delite *n.*[1] pleasure 90.16, 113.11 *note*, 146.16; **delites** *pl.* 28.105, 133.181; delicacies 1.247, 47.21; luxuries 119.88
+**delite** *n.*[2] sin 112.100 *note*
deli(c)table *adj.* pleasant 14.12, 47.174, 156.208, 173.498; **delectable** (D) 12.75, 134.4, (D) 178.97
deliuer *v. inf.* release 23.87, (H2) 176.307; hand over 53.292, 54.24; **deliuereth** *pr. 3 sg.* *4.201; **deliuer** *imp. pl.* liberate 22.128; **deliuered** *pa.* gave 93.134; liberated 45.509, 96.40; **deliuerid** *pa. p.* rid of 6.9, released 6.13, 22.144, 58.449; liberated 23.85; **deliuered** freed from slavery 7.33, 30.59; freed from fiend's possession 81.108; rid 6.9
deliuer *adj.* strong 24.12
deliueraunce *n.* parturition 138.56
deluge *n.* dangerous sea 61.267 *note*
+**demaunde** *n.* interrogation 84.68 *note*; question 124.235; *pl.* 64.28, 128
deme *v. inf.* suppose 79.938, 112.943; *pr.* 44.145, 45.176; *pr. subj.* 86.93; **demed** *pa.* 117.199, 139.191; **demed** *pa. p.* condemned 116.185, (L) 176.259; supposed 129.9; **deminge** *pr. p.* considering 117.346; **demynge** *ger.* thinking 45.174
demened, demenid *v. pa.* treated 14.17, 79.798; persuaded 70.4; *pa. refl.* behaved 28.89, 113.76; *pa. p.* treated 83.238, 95.46,118; maltreated 105.184; *ppl. adj.* disposed 74.4
demoniacle *adj.* possessed by the devil 47.189; **demoniak** 161.391
demonyakle *n.* person possessed by the devil 53.93; **demoniak** 116.32
denyed *v. pa.* refused 79.99; **denienge** *pr. p.* (D) 179.293
denounce(n *v. inf.* announce 49.160, 91.70, 112.286; *pr.* (G) 3.92, 44.205; **denounsed** *pa.* 5.210; 45.430, 47.360
departe *v. inf.* share out 2.12; part company 79.350, scatter *80.203, separate (H2) 176.219; *pr.* depart (G) 4.30; **departen** *pr. pl.* separate 24.128; **departe** *imp.* set apart 74.36; **departed** *pa.* shared out 2.88, (G) 3.27, 50.17, 65.258; divided 23.90, 93.127, 104.108; dispersed 154.50; *pa. p.* separated 28.147, 84.139, 167.107; **departid** dispersed *1.30, 50.127; *ppl. adj.* **departed** dispersed 8.3, 106.133; 88.121 *note*; **departyng** *ger.* separation 35.55, 84.278; **departinge** dispersal 99.10; digression 117.325
departicion *n.* dispersal 60.124
+**departie** *n.* separation 74.81 *note*
depopulacion *n.* slaughter *79.115
depper *adj. comp.* deeper 17.46; **dipper** 24.130, 96.96; **deppest** *superl.* deepest 1.308, 105.114; **deppist** (G) 4.71; **dippest** 1.304
depressed *v. pa. p.* enfeebled 79.816
depriued *v. pa. p.* dismissed 91.58
deputed *ppl. adj.* sentenced 50.11
dere *v. inf.* dare 165.182; **dore** 173.391; **darst** *pr. 2 sg.* 54.102; **durst** 2.137, 9.32, 23.85; **derste** (G) 38.108; **durst** *3 sg.* 26.166; **dar** 45.364; **dare** need 138.150; **dur** *pr. pl.* dare 2.80; **dore** 152.113, 175.339; **durst(e** *pa.* 20.51, 29.72, 95.75, 161.59
derkith *v. pr. 3 sg.* dims 28.14; **derked** *pa. p.* 79.726, 146.38, 173.343; **derkyng** *ger.* dimming (G) 46.4
+**derogacion** *n.* disparagement 79.504 *note*
derthe *n.* famine 55.230, 122.22 *note*
descencion *n.* dispute 104.170
desclaundred *v. pa. p.* brought into disgrace 84.449 *note*; *see also* **disclaundre**

descripcion *n.* registration 5.19; **discripsion** 5.25
desert *n.*[1] wilderness 7.66, 13.32, 14.7
desert *n.*[2] deserved punishment, reward 11.42, 50.350, 64.289; merit 45.119, 49.133, 93.283; reputation 93.95
desese *see* **disese**
deseuered *see* **disseuered**
+**desiringly** *adv.* desirously 85.31 *note*
despice, despise *see* **dispise**
despit(e *see* **dispite**
despoile *see* **dispoile**
destende *v. inf.* reach out *175.193
destreyned *v. pa. p.* arrested 105.184; **distreined** oppressed 113.213
determyned *v. pa.* concluded 174.362
detracte *v. pa. p.* disparaged 58.321
detraccion *n.* slander 117.232
dette *n.* obligation 155.92
deue *n.* dew 60.355
deuiacion *n.* error 30.1
deuyde *v. inf.* distinguish 105.46 *note*
deuye *v. inf.* forbid *91.31, *168.69; **deuiethe** *pr. 3 sg.* *83.322; **deuiithe** 163.170; **deuied** *pa.* refused *2.34 *note*, 22.109, *52.36, *62.19, 64.330; **deuyed** forbade *91.19, 117.300; *pa. p.* forbidden *20.44; 27.83, 35.103, 117.236; refused 61.281, 174.384; **devyeng** *pr. p.* *53.354
devyne *n.* soothsayer 104.52
devined *v. pa. p.* predicted 11.295
devinours *n. pl.* soothsayers 127.43
deuyse *v. inf.* examine (G) 44.2; *pr. 3 sg.* **deuysith** 55.25; *imp.* decide 123.343; **deuysid** *pa. sg.* planned (G) 4.65; **deuised** divided 139.154 *note*; assigned 139.155 *note*; described 149.29, 173.21; *pa. p.* 133.122; **deuisinge** *ger.* reasoning 117.11
dewe *v.* wet 133.110; **dewithe** *pr. 3 sg.* *65.263; **dewed** *ppl. adj.* made wet 45.120
dewte *n.* obligation (G) 43.104; **duete** (G) 43.83, 50.233
diametre *n.* width 146.39
diesise *see* **diosise**
dyete *n.* diet 83.335
dieu(e *adj.* due 7.59, 50.389, 79.748
diffame *see* **defame**
difference *n.* dissimilarity 5.9; distinction 155.166
diffined *v. pa. p.* decided 9.59
diffinitif *adj.* conclusive 45.355
dight *v. pa.* clothed 80.57
dignite *n.* high reputation 5.8, 11.36, 64.221; high office 35.65, 52.87, 79.10
dilacion *n.* delay 25.216, 50.110, 110.121; **delacion** 104.31
dileccion *n.* spiritual love 7.127, 13.220, 35.26, 65.171
dyme *n.* tenth part 33.9; tithe 49.223; **dymes** *pl.* 11.109, 36.75, 149.193 *note*
diosise *n.* parish (?) 159.296 *note*; **diesise** diocese 93.271
dipnesse *n.* profundity 53.375
dirthe *n.* famine 47.252, 161.142
dys *n. pl.* dice 113.263, 142.457
disasent *v. inf.* dissent 79.25
disatemperaunce *n.* lack of moderation 34.47
disatempre *adj.* immoderate 8.63, 112.991
+**discent** *v. inf.* dissent 161.248 *note*
discipline *n.* chastisement 175.441
disclaundre *n.* malicious misrepresentation 26.101; shame 61.287; shameful conduct 79.935; *see also* **desclaundred** *and* **sclaunder**
discomfite *v.* defeat 134.26; *pa.* **discomfited** 149.331; **discomfit** *ppl. adj.* 137.29
discomfort(e *n.* distress 25.116, 173.121; desolation (H2) 176.198
discomforted *ppl. adj.* distressed 86.24, 90.95, 93.249; **discomfort** 159.306
discordinge *v. pr. p.* quarrelling 65.446
discover *v. inf.* reveal 26.106, 58.130, 61.190, 69.39; *imp.* 80.97; **discouered** *pa.* 83.69, 106.46, 156.295; uncovered 146.229, 174.345
+**discouerers** *n. pl.* military scouts *174.39 *note*
discrecion *n.* discernment 149.74
discrete *adj.* courteous 90.71; prudent 149.135, 165.21, 168.38
discriue *v. inf.* describe 165.175; **discreue** *pr.* 123.3; **discriven** *pr. pl.* 11.316; **discreuin** 123.3; **discriving** *pr. p.* writing 149.24; **discriued** *pa. p.* comprehended 61.56; described 149.10, 152.37, 165.315
discuted *v. pa.* investigated 111.84 *note*
disdeyne *n.* anger 29.181; distaste 105.41
disencresen *v. pr. pl.* diminish 23.18
disese *n.* discomfort 4.199, 5.113, 62.10;

harm 11.107, 48.121, 54.127; grief 53.332; **desese** harm *178.301; **dissesis** *pl.* (H2) 178.299; **disesis** *pl.* hardships 165.795

disese *v. inf.* harass 49.280; **dissese** (G) 1.76; *pr.* 20.59

disesi *adj.* troublesome 116.274

disgises *n. pl.* ostentatious styles of dress 174.485

disherited *v. pa. p.* disinherited 106.223

disobeisaunce *n.* disobedience 11.303

disordeyne *adj.* disorderly 58.154

+disordenatli *adv.* contrary to normality *146.53 *note*

disparbeled *v. pa.* disappeared (?) 159.383 *note*; **disperpled** *ppl. adj.* scattered 84.197; **disperplid** 129.89; **disparpled** 140.51; **disperbled** 90.56; **disparkelid** (G) 45.547; **disperpeled** separated (?) 64.282 *note*

disparkelid *see* **disparbeled**

dispende *v. inf.* spend 22.23, 28.128, disburse 137.72; **dispended** *pa.* spent 84.357; used 79.227; **dispendid** *pa. p.* spent (G) 3.48, 22.96; spent (the proceeds) 26.51, 107.18; (the time) 58.58; disbursed 95.36, 123.358; *ppl. adj.* 91.7

dispens *n.* expenditure 45.238

dispenser *n.* steward 26.142

disperbled, disperpled *see* **disparbeled**

dispeticiouns *see* **disputacion**

dispisable *adj.* contemptible 161.202; **despisable** 161.275

dispise *v. inf.* despise, scorn 8.30; **despise** 26.224; **despice** 60.7; **despisen** *pr. pl.* 22.34, 50.337; **dispised** disdained 136.24; *ppl. adj.* 11.232

dispite, despite *n.* contempt, scorn 2.134, 26.223, 35.88, (G) 43.153, 45.409; humiliation, disparagement 6.31, 129.110, (D) 179.288; hostility (G) 1.59; malice 9.57, 11.301, 16.40, 26.21; **despites** *pl.* insults 50.193, 79.238, 163.244

dispitfull *adj. as n.* wretchedness 50.1 *note*

dispitosons *see* **disputacion**

dispitous(e *adj.* harsh *28.136, 50.5, 90.390; insulting 50.151

dispitously *adv.* pitilessly 55.67

dispituson *see* **disputacion**

displesaunce *n.* source of displeasure 52.95

dispoile *v. inf.* rob 26.207, 137.98, 173.274; **despoile** 49.245; **dispoyle** undress 50.472, 161.236; *imp.* 142.133; **dispoi(l)led** *pa.* undressed 1.182, 6.35, 23.56; robbed 174.761; **despoiled** 104.118; emptied 175.121; **dispuled** divested 50.307; undressed 92.27, 99.48; **dispoiled** *pa. p.* robbed 6.69, 79.978, *146.224, 174.310; undressed 11.177, 51.56, 105.177; **deprived** 112.44; ~ **hym** *refl.* took off his clothes 26.49; **dispoillyng** *ger.* stripping off of clothing 11.185; **dispoiled** 64.196 *note*

disport *n.* pleasure 51.9

disporte *v. inf.* entertain 173.106[1]; *refl.* enjoy oneself (G) 44.22, 173.106[2]; **disportinge** *pr. p.* 98.7; *refl.* 127.16

+dispositiff *adj.* regulated, controlled 27.38 *note*

dispuled *see* **dispoile**

disputacion *n.* debate, discussion 7.21, 11.123, 79.175; **dispituson** 106.48; **disputison** 117.405; *pl.* **dispitosons** 83.64; **disputisons** 163.54; **dispeticiouns** (H2) 176.240

disputour *n.* debater 53.94

disseiuable *adj.* deceptive (D) 179.250

dissemblable *adj.* dissimilar *84.404

dissent *n.* ~ **of lyne** lineage 165.2

dissese *n.* death 10.8

dissessis *see* **disese**

disseuered *pa. p.* separated 66.275, 79.870, *83.154; **deseuered** *pa.* 83.382, 112.766

dissheuele *adj.* with hair in disorder *22.10

dissimulacion *n.* pretence 164.7, 167.87

dissimule *v. inf.* dissemble 66.184

dissolucion *n.* dissoluteness 139.32

dissolut *adj.* morally or religiously lax 28.152, *161.227

dissolutly *adv.* frivolously 112.534

distemperaunce *n.* inclemency 5.53, 148.69

distourbe *v. inf.* prevent 20.120; *imp.* 74.110

distreined *see* **destreyned**

diuersorie *n.* shelter 5.51

diuision *n.* distinction 11.174, 128.200 *note*; **diuisiones** *pl.* dimensions (?) 117.11 *note*

do *v. inf.* do, perform 1.235; cause 50.432, 52.70, 138.85; **done** *inflected inf.* do 2.29; **doone** (G) 4.133; ~ **awey** remove 94.195; ~ **dome** act in judgement 79.459; put on (clothing) (G) 4.88, 23.62; **doest** *pr. 2 sg.* do, perform, act 24.10, 79.209, 92.62; **doist** (G) 38.119, 86.77; **dest** 92.61; **doste** (G) 41.6; **doth** *3 sg.* 22.188; **dothe awey** gets rid of 173.295; **do** *pr. pl.* 11.136; **done** do 20.58, 84.394; **do** *imp. sg.* cause 88.44; ~ **on** continue 84.207; put on (clothing) 173.89; ~ **of** take off (clothing) 47.186; ~ **awaye** dismiss 173.17; **dothe** *imp. pl.* do 8.96; **dothe awaye** get rid of 22.127; **dede** *pa.* did, performed, practised 7.29, 8.98, 27.83; caused 9.6, 50.491, 148.43; **did** 9.104; **dide** did, performed 55.84 *note*; **dedest** *pa. 2 sg.* 86.99; **dedist** 172.16; **deden** *pa. pl.* 11.140; **dede of** *pa. sg.* took off (clothes) 7.107; **dide of** (G) 4.87; **dede on** put on (clothes) 119.6, 125.125; **dede awaye** gave up 30.47; got rid of 47.42, 95.144; **dede hym** placed himself 18.19; **done** *pa. p.* accomplished 5.1; put 26.271; given 49.15; ended 50.459; **done aweie** removed (D) 178.160; **do** performed 22.182, 65.204, 83.329; ended 79.625

doctour *n.* teacher 49.107, 58.181, 65.49, 84.228, 175.206; theologian 15.1, 25.1, 116.216, 117.1; **doctours** *pl.* learned men 11.122; teachers 74.9, 125.106

doctrine *n.* teaching 93.14, 112.751, 129.42

domatyk *n. for* **dalmatik** liturgical vestment 45.407 *note*

dome *n.* judgement 79.411; **domes** *pl.* (L) 79.1052

dominacions *n. pl.* the fourth order of angels 112.314

doole *n.* lamentation (D) 178.596

dore *see* **dere**

dortre *n.* monastic dormitory 5.240, 106.192; **dortour** 5.249, 174.675

dounwarde *adj.* below 14.31

doutable *adj.* doubtful 123.168

doute *n.* doubt 83.379; fear 94.78

doute *v. pr. pl.* fear *22.87; **douȝtist** *pr. 2 sg.* (D) 178.545; **doute** *pr. pl.* doubt 61.139; *imp. pl.* 124.38; **douteth** 2.111

dower *n.* dowry 161.315

doweri *n.* endowment 139.184

dowid *v. pa.* endowed 112.302

dowue *n.* dove 15.31, 43.185, 112.761; **douve** 21.3

dragma *n.* ancient Greek coin, drachma 31.20 *note*; **dragme** 31.26, 36.79; **dragmes** *pl.* 156.196

draue *v. inf.* persuade 26.211; **drawe** 94.138; pull 54.79, 80.276; attract 149.41, 165.541; associate (?) 128.187 *note*; **drawe** *pr.* pull 55.60; **drawyng(e** *pr. p.* pulling 24.125, 159.201; **drawinge** travelling on 79.348; **drowing** plucking 30.75; **drewe** *pa.* pulled 36.329, 58.344; dragged 79.367, 83.391; attracted 79.278; **drow hym** *refl.* betook himself 165.36; **drewȝ** dragged (G) 55.61; **drowe** attracted 58.65, 84.479; moved (of time) 79.323; **drowȝ** dragged (G) 1.51, (G) 55.66; **droue** 47.108; **drow(e** 25.160, 74.128; drew (sword) 29.100; ~ **in** drank 28.66; **drawen** *pa. pl.* dragged (G) 3.73; **drowen** 8.102, 74.124; **drue** 48.77; **drewe hem** *refl.* withdrew 79.324; **drawe(n** *pa. p.* dragged 24.6, 38.53; plucked (G) 55.190; withdrawn 28.61; **drowe to** came towards 26.136, 80.82; **drawe to hym** acquired 134.160

drede *v. inf.* fear 18.43, 20.11; doubt 49.7, 54.199, 64.54; *refl.* be in doubt 10.123; *refl. pr. 1 sg.* 84.341; **dredist** *pr. 2 sg.* (G) 45.569; **dredest** 51.23; **dradde** *pa.* 49.111, 80.16; **dred** 49.117; **dredde** 64.54, 112.226

drede *n.* fear 2.161, (G) 3.86; doubt 49.8, 90.205, 142.104, 159.41

dredfull *adj.* terrifying 20.109, 23.45, 24.12; menacing 165.297; frightened 22.87, 47.242, (H1) 144.33; awesome 112.38

dredfulli *adv.* fearfully 23.76, 48.125, 95.66

dresse *v. inf.* raise 83.248, 159.343; direct 161.303, 171.2; attend to 165.35; *imp.* raise 83.191; ~ **ayeinst** oppose 93.27, 173.402; **dressed** *pa.* directed 79.147; raised 84.134; ~ **hym** stood up 94.169; ~ **hym vpright**, stood up 2.5, 108.38; *pa. p.* raised up 13.234, 27.66, 166.29; directed 159.321; instructed 173.122; applied himself 142.49; **dressid** *ppl. adj.* erect 14.50

drewe *see* **draue**
driving forthe *v. pr. p.* whiling away 79.710
drowe *see* **draue**
drue *see* **draue**
ducherie *n.* lordship 81.38
duete *see* **dewte**
duke *n.* senior nobleman, often ruler of province, etc. 20.131, 45.293, 66.259; military leader 54.219, 81.4, 111.80, 112.230, 134.1; ruler 83.459; head of religious institution 106.1; guide 155.221
dur *see* **dere**
dure *v. inf.* last 5.86, 146.25; **durithe** *pr. 3 sg.* 32.1; **dured** *pa.* 60.42, 61.18, 66.201, 125.71; persisted 96.27; **duryng** *ppl. adj.* (L) 179.328
dures *n.* confinement 165.262
durst *see* **dere**

E

eake *n.* ache 117.127
ease *n.* relief 7.164, 79.601
ecule(e *n.* instrument of torture 24.23 *note*; 51.59, 54.109
edificacion *n.* spiritual improvement 20.143, 28.182, 149.136; building 155.121
edefie *v. inf.* build 29.44, 47.275, 95.3; **edifie** 11.108; **edifiethe** *pr. 3 sg.* 117.16; **edefiethe** *imp.* 93.120; **edified** *pa. sg.* erected 5.186; built 8.3, 64.32, 96.44; *pa. p.* 83.383; spiritually improved 113.229; **edefieng** *ppl. adj.* building 11.110; spiritually improving 113.248
eere *v. inf.* plough 29.36
effaced *v. pa. p.* erased 20.46, 25.181; **effased** 25.180, 26.279
effecte *n.* attainment 27.68, result 29.177
effectualy *adv.* earnestly 173.305
effectuel *adj.* diligent 165.843
efftsones *adv.* immediately afterwards (D) 179.168; **efftsoone** (D) 179.206
egal(l)(e *adj.* proportionate 28.157, 112.976; equal 64.307, 65.26, 83.449, 84.21, 156.30
egal(l)y *adv.* in the usual way (?) 112.20 *note*; equally 156.315
eghtely *ord. num. adv.* eighthly 53.282
eye *n.*[1] egg 173.202, 174.745; **eyren** *pl.* 28.134, *66.173, 99.44
ey(e *n.*[2] eye (G) 4.150, 78.85, 94.171; **ey** 149.44; **ye** 78.86; **yee** 64.311; **eyȝe** (D) 178.97; **eyen** *pl.* (G) 3.21, 7.148, 24.120; **eyghen** 2.127,10.106; **yen** 79.820; **eyȝen** (D) 178.95
eylithe *see* **aylethe**
eyre *n.*[1] air 5.139; 54.13, 55.235; **eyer** (H1) 143.7; **heir(e** 60.142, 84.144, 94.170, (H1) 156.447
eyre *n.*[2] heir 28.29, 36.8, 165.25, 174.480; **ayre** 174.598; **heyr(e** 28.23, 122.6
eyren see **eye** egg
eisell *n.* vinegar 1.145, 11.177, 50.130; **aysell** 50.133
either *conj.* or 11.282, 50.184, 58.59; **eythir** (G) 46.6; **ether** 49.170; **aither** 71.21
eleccion *n.* choice 27.61, 79.112
elongacion *n.* 165.227 *note*
ellumyninge *ger.* giving sight to 32.35
embraced, embrasithe *see* **enbrace**
embrasinge *see* **enbrasethe**
empeche *v. inf.* hinder 1.169; *pr.* 173.19
empeyred *ppl. adj.* harmed 58.257, 141.14 *note*; **empaired** 116.21
emplastre *n.* plaster-like salve (G) 4.152
emptes *n. pl.* ants 66.169
enbrace *v. inf.* ignite 92.78; **embrasithe** *pr. 3 sg.* inflames 175.25; **enbraced** *pa. p.* inflamed 84.448 *note*; **enbrased** *ppl. adj.* 84.471; **enbrasid** 116.282; **embraced** ignited 146.166; **enbrasinge** *ger.* kindling 65.126 *note*
enbrasethe *v. pr. 3 sg.* embraces 50.306; **enbrased** *pa.* 54.35, 105.100; enfolded 80.281; **embrasinge** *ger.* embracing 112.348
encence *n.* incense 88.47, 92.7; **ensence** 5.175
encense *v. inf.* offer incense to 70.27
enchaufe *v. inf.* kindle 65.29; **enchauf** enflame 65.228; **enchawfithe** 175.260, **enchaufid** *pa.* 117.99; **enchaufed** *pa. refl.* became heated 60.287; *pa. p.* 117.121; *ppl. adj.* 134.127
enchaunte *v. inf.* put under a spell 22.169
encheyned *v. pa. p.* chained *116.81
encheson *n.* cause 133.111
enclyne *v. inf.* persuade (to favour) 37.53, 54.107, 107.5; bend 60.245;

agree 79.525, 165.169; **enclinethe** *pr.* bends down 65.339; **enclined** *pa.* bent down 2.194, 47.336, 61.255, 93.266; **enclining** *ger.* bending down 65.338; **enclined** *ppl. adj.* bent 83.262

enclosed *v. pa.* confined 60.339, 101.19; *pa. p.* imprisoned 84.8, 87.46, 150.30; encompassed 11.316; covered 101.35

+**encortined** *ppl. adj.* enclosed with curtains (G) 47.369 *note*

endely *adj.* ultimate 165.783 *note*

endited *v. pa.* composed 53.142; dictated *53.188, 113.297; **enditinge** *ger.* composition 117.314

endure *v. inf.* continue 8.182, 25.98,112.460; **endured** *pa.* lasted 52.64; *pa. p.* continued 161.213; **enduryng** *ger.* duration 13.174

enfamynyd *ppl. adj.* starving *24.95

enflaume *v. inf.* start a fire 65.140; incite 135.47, 161.205, 173.444; *pr. 3 sg.* **enflawmithe** inspires 175.261; **enflaumed** *pa.* inflamed 47.36; *pa. p.* 15.41, 28.36; made to flame 22.53; **enflawmed** inspired 165.835, 175.242

enforce *v. inf.* compel *35.53: violate 127.81, 131.52; **enforsest** *refl.* strive 79.989; **enforce** *pr. pl.* exert force (G) 1.66, strengthen 22.54; **enforce(n** *refl. pr. pl.* strive 79.792, 173.23; **enforsinge** *pr. p.* striving 79.663; **enforsed** *refl. pa.* strove 7.81, 10.18, 25.158, 27.22, 53.73; **enforced** *refl. pa.* 38.4, 44.164, 47.145; **enforsid** (G) *pa.* 55.72; **enforced** grew strong 161.8; constrained 135.30; *ppl.* violated 127.70, 131.22; *ppl. adj.* strengthened 28.175, 74.17, 149.260; **enforsinge** *ger.* undertaking 27.31; effort 79.521

enfo(u)rme *v. inf.* teach 65.381, 165.93; **enfo(u)rmed** *pa.* taught 25.175; *pa. p.* 74.4, 175.471; informed 79.455

enformer *n.* instructor 165.84

engendre *v. inf.* beget 174.252; **engenderithe** *pr. 3 sg.* brings about 65.118; **engenderyng** *ppl. adj.* procreating 33.33,36; **engendered** *pa.* begot 168.28; *pa. p.* begotten 5.184, 11.242, 57.1, 64.84; **engendrid** (G) 4.54

engendrure *n.* birth 163.150 *note*

engine *n.* intelligence 28.165, 117.381, 134.6

engregged *v. pa.* became worse 47.363

engroged *v. pa.* oppressed 70.7 *note*

enhaunse *v. inf.* raise 11.302, 99.89 *note*; **enhaunce** promote 11.310; *imp.* raise 167.130; **enhaunsid** *pa.* (G) 43.64; **enhaunsed** *pa. p.* raised 28.18, 30.12; increased 26.253; advanced 45.185, 49.47 *note*, 56.29; *ppl. adj.* elevated to high rank 13.115, 60.254, 104.17; *see also* **haunsed**

enheriter *n.* heir 165.165

enioyne *v. inf.* command 28.164; **enioyned** *pa.* 47.138, 58.136, 138.20; **enioined** *pa. p.* 156.17; *ppl. adj.* (D) 179.4

enlased *ppl. adj.* put in bonds 35.47

enleueneth *ord. num.* eleventh (G) 4.133

enlumyne *v. imp.* enlighten (G) 41.21; **enlumynyth(e** *pr. 3 sg.* gives light to (G) 4.150; enlightens 65.306; **enlumyned** *pa.* gave sight to 44.166; enlightened 94.193; illuminated 106.9; *pa. p.* enlightened 27.61, 64.157, 74.7; illuminated 64.10, 141.62; *ppl. adj.* enlightened 133.119

+**enluminour** *n.* one who enlightens 176.54 *note*

+**enmured** *v. pa. p.* entombed 72.32 *note*

ennoblid *v. pa. p.* made great 55.27 *note*; **ennobled** *ppl. adj.* 29.5; refined, noble 26.282 *note*; **ennobled** illustrious 28.7

+**ennob(e)lisshed** *v. pa.* made noble 161.3; *ppl. adj.* 51.3 *note*, 84.340

enoye *see* **annoye**

enordinat *see* **inordinat**

enpechement *n.* hindrance *78.92

enpeyred *ppl. adj.* damaged 1.272

enpoison *v. inf.* poison 9.94; **enpoisoned** *pa.* 47.114

+**enponchementis** *n. pl.* punishments 117.112 *note*

enprentid *v. pa. p.* expressed 175.27

enquere *v. inf.* ask about 13.142, (G) 38.140; *pa. p.* 110.121

+**enquirable** *adj.* capable of investigation 65.64 *note*

+**enquisitour** *n.* inquisitor 58.134 *note*

ensampul *n.* example (G) 4.119; **ensaumple** 8.49, 11.152, 23.120; exemplar 74.61; **ensamples** *pl.* 4.184; **ensaumples** examples 117.99

ensele *v. inf.* seal 142.476; *imp.* 26.262; **enseled** *pa.* sealed 79.245;

authenticated 123.367; **enseallid** sealed (G) 45.541
ensence *n. see* **encence**
enspiring(e *ger.* breathing in (of life) 5.115, 112.967, (D) 178.29; **enspering** *36.50
ensure *v. inf.* promise 66.187; **ensured** *pa.* 93.154; *pa. p.* 91.32
entailed *v. pa. p.* carved 116.208; **entailled** *ppl. adj.* engraved 90.333
entamed *v. pa. p.* injured 58.120 *note*, 112.363 *note*
enteerid *see* **entered**
entencion *n.* devotion 38.25, 165.219; intention 149.80
entend(e *v. inf.* pay attention to 53.352, 112.180; *imp.* attend 99.84; **entended** *pa.* 1.276, 83.78, 84.23; planned 141.16; strove 141.46; desired (H1) 146.84; attended *90.10, 161.127, 169.12
entendement *n.* understanding 27.62
+**entendible** *adj.* intellectual 64.209 *note*; **intendibles** *pl.* understandable 65.300 *note*
entent *n.* understanding 27.43, 116.126; purpose 9.29, 13.138, 26.208, 54.107; opinion 156.162; **ententys** *pl.* aims 165.169
ententif(e *adj.* diligent 58.399, 83.355, 117.57; attentive 65.460, (H1) 146.89
ententif(f)ly *adv.* diligently *45.98, 47.11, 84.351, 117.37; attentively 61.317, 142.350, *154.185
enter *adj.* entire 112.1000; **entier** 58.228
entered *v. pa.* interred *23.95; **enteerid** (G) 39.14; **entryng** *ger.* burying (G) 38.157
enterly *adv.* entirely 112.999
entermeted *v. pa.* ~ **hym** set about 75.15; **entremetynge** *pr. p.* taking part (L) 179.341; *pa. p.* intervened 45.291
entier *see* **enter**
entisinge *ger.* instigation 110.257
entre *n.* beginning 45.26; entrance 88.105, 128.89
entrechaunginge *ger.* exchange 155.92
entredyt *n.* interdict *10.63; **entredit** 10.65
entredited *v. pa.* interdicted 113.351
entryng *see* **entered**
entune *v. inf.* sing 35.31
enuenemyd *ppl. adj.* poisonous 159.71
enuie *n.* hostility 93.60; **hadde** ~ was hostile 2.261
enuious *adj.* hostile 2.203
environe *v. inf.* surround 134.83; go round 175.208; **environde** *pa.* surrounded 1.220; **environyd** (G) 60.138, 112.715, 133.140; travelled through 84.292, 174.13; encompassed 84.305; **enviround** *pa. p.* 28.92; *ppl. adj.* surrounded 25.82, **environ(e)d** 50.500, 138.53, 154.116; **environde** 53.104; **environid** 112.242; **environinge** *ger.* encircling 175.201
episteles *see* **pistel(l**
er *conj.* or 31.21; **er . . . er** either . . . or 8.104–5
er *prep.* before 1.224, 8.21, 28.186, 61.285; **ere** 124.249, 173.503
erdely *adj.* earthly 13.119
ere *n.* ear 12.13, 83.125; handle of pot 110.275; **eere** ear 83.126
eresye *n.* heresy 53.272, 117.59
eritage *see* **heritage**
erith *v. pr. 3 sg.* ploughs 150.22; **ered** *pa.* 116.242; **ereden** *pa. pl.* 154.109; **ered** *pa. p.* 112.881
errest v. *pr. 2 sg.* make a mistake 121.7; **erren** *pr. pl.* 60.92, 125.171, 163.67; **erred** *pa.* 113.402; **erredest** *pa. 2 sg.* wandered 50.253; **erredyn** *pa. pl.* 121.53; made a mistake 173.404
erroure *n.* misguided belief 14.34
erst *adv.* before 165.647
eschaufith *v. pr. 3 sg.* warms up 167.47
eschewe *v. inf.* avoid 29.110, 45.415, 50.222; **eschue** (H1) 144.48; **eschewen** *pl.* (G) 4.133; **escheued** *pa.* 117.191; **eschued** 110.200; **escheued** *ppl. adj.* shunned 11.3; **eschewed** avoided 2.58, 112.654; *pa. p.* 26.269; **eschuyng** *ger.* avoidance 149.218; **eschewinge** 173.396
+**escriuans** *n. pl.* authors 53.383 *note*
+**escriue** *v. inf.* inscribe signature (H2) 176.267 *note*
ese *v. inf. refl.* relieve oneself 16.44, 161.323
esely *adv.* comfortably 79.810
espie *v. inf.* look upon (D) 178.120; **espied** *pa. p.* plotted against 79.329, 84.7
essence *n.* being (G) 4.117

estaffys *n. pl. for* **escaffys**, small boats, dinghies 28.192 *note*
estate *n.* condition 20.107, 30.76; status 53.162, condition 112.629; **astate** 22.137, 32.26, 113.182; status 151.81; **estates** *pl.* categories, ranks 49.43; **in al astates** in all circumstances 93.155
ether *see* **either**
euuangely *n.* reading from gospel during mass 99.109
euel(l *adj.* wicked 27.31; difficult 53.95; unpleasant 94.147
evell *n.* ill-repute 99.125 *note*; sickness 174.173 *note*
euen(e *adj.* level 26.42, (H2) 176.177; equal 5.282, 14.46, 80.190, 159.255; ~ **cristen** fellow Christian *106.20, 173.217
euenli *adv.* steadily 32.40; equally 113.105
euer *n.* jug 45.241
except(e *v. pa. pl.* excluded 112.911
exces *n.* ecstasy 106.252
excite *v. inf.* encourage (H2) 1.3
excusacion *n.* excuse 29.51, 60.129, 102.32; *pl.* 50.29
excused *v. pa. sg.* declared innocent 7.62
execucion *n.* punishment 79.490
exorte *v. inf.* exhort 45.101
experience *n.* proof 155.144
expositour *n.* commentator 36.151; one who explains or declares 112.634 *note*
expowne *v. inf.* explain 11.214; **expoune** 84.245; **expownithe** *pr. 3 sg.* 61.50, 64.159; **expowned** *pa.* told 5.44; interpreted 7.55; expounded 174.96; **expounid** 113.37, 171.85; **expouned** *pa. p.* told 9.70; explained 49.143, 50.492, 113.138, 155.82; **expouninge** *pr.p.* 117.407, 129.11

F

fader *n.* Father, honorific title for cleric 1.270, 106.1; honorific title for abbot 47.46; ancestor 13.68; **fadris** *gen. sg.* father's (G) 2.303
fayeres *n. pl.* markets 93.313
faile *v. inf.* grow feeble 161.232; come to an end 176.5; **faille** *pr.* are missing 49.257; **failest** *2 sg.* are in error 139.16; **failithe** *3 sg.* is missing 49.258, 117.389; is wrong 165.613; **faillen** *pr. pl.* are lacking 23.18; **faylen** grow feeble 92.29; **fayling** *ppl. adj.* weakening 165.782; **failled** *pa.* lacked 28.31, 49.272, 53.19; grew feeble 54.95; **fayled** were lacking 54.11; became used up 93.303; came to an end 128.190, **faylid** grew feeble (G) 43.9; **failid** *ppl. adj.* enfeebled (G) 43.23; lacking 84.227; **failed** ended 174.409; **were** ~ ceased to exist 123.33; **failnge** *ger.* becoming weak 113.123
fayn(e *adv.* gladly 1.203, 2.102, 11.296, 23.85
faint *adj.* weak-willed (D) 179.289
faitour *n.* imposter 165.262
fallace *n.* deceit 34.36
falle *v. inf.* happen 29.78; **fallithe** *pr.* 63.97; *pr. subj.* 29.63; **fel** *pa.* 5.37; **fell(e** 8.32, 20.117, 29.50; **fill(e** (G) 1.17, 2.245; **fall(e** *pa. p.* 15.14, 20.122, 25.133; **fell with his chere** was downcast (H2) 178.351
familyer *adj.* friendly 90.34, 104.8, 117.238, 174.523; **famulier** 144.35
famylier *n.* close friend 45.470; **familiers** *pl.* 84.455
familiarite *n.* fellowship 7.65, 79.453, 90.367
fantastik *adj.* imagined 12.103, 59.20, 117.18
fardeles *n. pl.* bundles 30.61
fare *n.* prosperity (D) 179.497
fare *v. imp.* behave 167.27; ~ **wel** prosper 26.6, 35.19, 37.51; **farithe** *pr. 3 sg.* happens 8.181, 20.67, 65.152; **ferde** *pa.* 173.217; ~ **withe herselff** behaved 88.104
fast(e *adv.* persistently 1.283; firmly 6.36, 23.130, 25.141
fastin *v.*[1] *imp.* fasten 113.176; **fasted** *pa. p.* fixed 24.24
faste *v.*[2] *inf.* abstain 11.96, 28.133; **fasten** *pr. pl.* 34.50; *pa.* **fast** 27.54; **fastyng** *ger.* period of abstinence 8.197
fatnes *n.* abundance *178.348
faune *n.* the young of a lion 66.249; **faunes** *pl.* 149.31; **fawnes** *pl.* offspring 36.131
feble *v. inf.* grow feeble 159.303; **febled** *pa. p.* enfeebled 31.8
feere *v. see* **fere** *v.*
feyne *v. inf.* invent 28.113; pretend (G) 43.54, 161.21, 173.333; **feynest** *pr. 2*

sg. refl. pretend 24.51; **feyned** *pa.* 6.4, 26.148, 29.139, 52.24, 117.441; *pa. refl.* pretended 29.139, (G) 44.28, 80.183, 81.56, 127.58; *pa. p.* invented 112.750; **feint** created 112.687 *note*; **feyning(e** *ger.* invention 112.225, 142.71

felable *adj.* palpable *65.63

felaw(e *n.* companion 24.133, 28.9, 29.66; **felow** 23.97; **felawes** *pl.* 2.45, 7.209, 23.75; social equals 142.81

felawship(pe *n.* companionship 6.5; company of adherents 7.207; group of companions 8.170; (hostile) crowd 83.232 *note*; **felaschip** social gathering (G) 4.35

felawshipped *see* **fellishippen**

fele *v. inf.* understand (G) 4.122, 79.174, 112.306; smell 50.123; **felest** *pr. 2 sg.* smell 124.90; **felithe** *3 sg.* feels 11.292; investigates 152.222 *note*; **felyn** *pr. pl.* know 150.20; **felt** *pa.* sensed 14.35, 28.165, 99.76, 113.48, 136.86; smelt 60.317, 61.209, 90.306; tasted 174.90; *pa. p.* smelt 105.66; **feling(e** *ger.* sensation 113.128; sense of smell 50.134

felenous *adj.* iniquitous 24.120

fell(e *v. inf.* fill 171.82; *imp.* (D) 178.10; **felled** *pa.* 148.43, 172.22; **fulled** supplied (D) 178.78; **felled** *ppl. adj.* 54.114

fell(e *see* **fall(e**

feller *adj. comp.* more cunning (D) 178.86

fellishippe(n *v. inf.* accompany (H2) 176.368; **feloushipped** *pa.* 64.136; **felaweshiped** *pa. p.* 106.254, **felawshipped** 112.864, 151.114; joined in membership 113.399; associated 155.293

felon *adj.* iniquitous 92.67, 151.87; impious 105.111, 112.442, 117.9

felon *n.* cruel person 37.104, 58.153, 90.96; **felon(e)s** *pl.* criminals 23.9, 84.5, 106.284; **felonis** 132.35

felonie *n.* crime 2.137, 9.89, 11.63, 20.120, 22.49; sin *28.45, 35.50, 104.30, 116.246; wickedness 91.43; 110.153 *note*

felonisly *adv.* wickedly 95.46

felow *see* **felawe**

feloushipped *see* **fellishippen**

fendely *adj.* fiendish 58.122

fenne *n.* dirt 124.222

ferde *see* **fare**

fere *n.*[1] fire 6.67, 12.67, 20.38, 65.268, 140.48

fere *n.*[2] frightening thing 117.179; fear 53.210, 66.206, 134.123; *pl.* fears *25.144

fere *v. inf.* frighten 27.47, 148.66, 175.338; **feere (H2)** 176.139; **ferithe** *pr. 3 sg.* 50.95, 63.160; **fered** *pa.* 7.25, 53.70; **ferde** *pa. p.* 165.295 *see also* **afere**

ferforthe *adv.* **so** ~ to such an extent (G) 1.108, 30.20, 45.25, 102.73

ferforthely *adv.* **so** ~ to such an extent 53.16, 54.15, 60.260–1, 94.77; **as** ~ **as** as much as 165.70–1

ferfull *adj.* frightening 47.234

fery(e *n.* feria, weekday on which no feast occurs 31.2, 50.266, 139.155; day *146.47; **feries** *pl.* 139.155

fer(re *adj.* distant 17.45, 29.79; **ferre** *comp.* 137.90; **ferrest** *superl.* 134.121, 139.2

ferre *adv.* widely 50.66, 165.195; **ferre** *comp.* further 112.423

ferthe *ord. num.* fourth 7.71, 8.68, 11.104

ferthely *ord. num. adv.* fourthly 5.73; **firthely** 64.5

fervens(e *n.* ardour 5.254, 149.249

feruent *adj.* ardent 14.2, 79.1013

feruent(e)ly *adv.* ardently 8.187; painfully 22.52; passionately 127.56

fesisyan *see* **fisicien**

fest(e *n.*[1] banquet (G) 4.19; religious festival 2.260, 7.202, 12.6; celebration (H1) 144.7; **festis** *pl.* banquets 117.250; religious festivals 123.92

festes *n.*[2] *pl.* fists 93.78

festful(l) *adj.* of religious celebration 55.144, 170.10

fetres *n. pl.* fetters *93.143; **fetheres** 104.95; **fethres** 104.97

fette *v. inf.* fetch (G) 4.32, 47.101, 154.98; **fette** *pa.* 174.713

feture *n.* created thing 112.364

fic(c)hed *v. pa.* fixed *50.329, *94.90, 117.158, 142.32; **fyched** *ppl. adj.* 148.67, 152.204, 166.31

fyers *adj.* fierce 11.321

fifte *ord.num.* ~ **day** Thursday 30.13

fiftely *ord. num. adv.* fifthly 64.5

figure *n.* representation 30.56, 61.106, 175.16; metaphor 44.129, 174.657, (L) 179.442; shape (G) 43.174; image

152.28; likeness 50.434, 163.203; appearance(?)/created structure 84.78
figured *ppl. adj.* figurative 36.114; represented 149.27
fylinge *ger.* filed particles 84.215
fill(e *see* **fall(e**
fillinge *ger.* satiety 117.272 *note*, 155.82
+**fynably** *adv.* finally 45.354 *note*
firthely *see* **ferthely**
fisicien *n.* doctor of medicine 133.226; **fesisyan** 173.138; **fesicianes** *n. pl.* 9.112, 138.80
flailes *n. pl.* scourges 126.10
flayne *v. pa. p.* flayed 76.22; **flaine** 116.131; **flein** 142.437
+**flaken** *n.* small flask 47.206 *note*
flambe *see* **flawme**
+**flaskons** *n. pl.* small flasks *47.199 *note*
flawme *n.* flame 26.95, 101.74, 119.37; **flambe** 84.502; **flawmes** *pl.* 47.146, 152.187; **flambis** *pl.* (G) 60.136
flee *n.* flea 17.61, *pl.* 84.439
fle(e *v.*[1] *inf.* flee 18.41, (G) 38.99, 88.52; shun (D) 179.302; *pr.* flee 84.111, 94.41; **fleith(e** *pr. 3 sg.* (G) 4.147; shuns 36.161; **fleen** *pr. pl.* 63.164; **fle(e** *imp.* 54.61, 90.297; **fleing(e** *pr. p.* 28.79, 30.79, 60.5; fleeting (G) 4.146; vacillating 175.266; shunning (D) 179.307; **fledde** *pa.* fled 18.41, 20.39, 138.58; **fledden** *pa. pl.* (G) 4.75, 18.10, 29.34; **fleyng** *ger.* shunning 28.18; escape 104.33
fle(e *v.*[2] *inf.* fly 11.340, 20.111, 63.82; **fleithe** *pr. 3 sg.* 8.183; **fle(en** *pr. pl.* 20.115, 138.126; **fleinge** *pr. p.* 83.192; **fleigh** *pa.* 84.467; **fly(e** 112.109, 116.91, (H1) 143.28; leapt 136.42; **fleye** flew 174.134; **fleghen** *pa. pl.* 20.111; **fleyen** 53.6
flees *n.* fleece 167.69
flein *see* **flayne**
fleith, fleyng *see* **flee**[1]
fles(s)(c)he *n.* meat 20.98, 60.44, 63.77, 66.189, 117.230; **flesse** human flesh 165.856
flesshely *adj.* carnal 112.262, 113.46, 150.27; worldly 134.76
flesshely *adv.* carnally *50.355
flete *v. inf.* float (G) 44.19; **fletyng(e** *pr. p.* 2.209; *ppl. adj.* travelling by water 112.585 *note*
fleumatik *adj.* phlegmatic 34.40
flewme *n.* phlegm 34.33
flies *n. pl.* biting insects 14.11, 17.64; flies 138.126, 142.293
flixe *n.* diarrhoea 16.45; **blody** ~ dysentery (G) 3.4, 90.41; **flux** 128.115
flode *n.* river 13.4, 29.117, (G) 38.143; **flood** (H2) 176.213; **flo(o)des** *pl.* currents 134.149, 138.58; floods 146.33; rivers 65.131, 174.273; **floodis** (D) 178.27
flom(e *see* **flume**
floter *v. inf.* float 163.364; **flotered** *pa.* 61.39
floure *v. inf.* thrive 13.227; **flourithe** *imp.* 8.59; **flouring** *pr. p.* 117.381; **floured** *pa.* blossomed 5.71, 13.225; flourished 16.73, 25.221, 53.217; **flowrid** (G) 40.46 **flouredin** *pa. pl.* prospered 117.331
flume *n.* river 52.3; **flom** 52.73, 60.211, 61.136; **flome** 64.121, (D) 178.188
flux *see* **flixe**
fnesed *v. pa.* sneezed 63.20; **fnesinge** *ger.* sneezing 63.21
foyson *n.* profusion 83.105, 91.34
fole *adj.* imprudent 172.18
foleye *v. pr. p.* act foolishly 60.94; **folyen** 60.99; **folied** *pa.* 60.109; **foled** *pa. p.* foolish 134.54
folily *adv.* foolishly 113.145, 134.18, 152.93
foliously *adv.* lasciviously 145.91 *note*
folisshe *adj.* lecherous 150.19; foolish 151.81
+**follissnesse** *n.* stupidity 50.287 *note*
fonde *see* **founde**[2]
font *see* **funte**
forbede *v. pa.* prohibited 29.29, 73.14; **forboden** *ppl. adj.* (D) 178.188
forbere *v. inf.* be patient 154.210, 163.110, 168.15
forbetin *ppl. adj.* badly bitten 17.64
+**forciblement** *adv.* strongly 146.165 *note*
forclosed *ppl. adj.* excluded 49.19, 84.457; **forclosid** 127.23
fordo *v. inf.* abolish 116.62; **fordede** *pa.* 53.274; **fordone** *ppl. adj.* erased (D) 179.167
foredrawe *ppl.* taken away *112.21 *note*
forgate *v. pa.* forgot 99.116, 101.15; **foryate** 128.250, (H2) 178.413; **foryete** *pa. p.* 37.20, 104.146, 112.554

forgoer *n.* precursor 80.89, *149.67; **forgoers** *pl.* 112.753
forgoo *v. inf.* relinquish 36.324
forgrowe *ppl. adj.* covered with long hair or beard 165.294
forlingne *adj.* 110.68 *note*
forloste *ppl. adj.* abandoned (G) 39.6
formable *adj.* 65.327 *note*
forme *n.* procedure *11.235; backless bench 119.35
forpined *ppl. adj.* tortured 173.276
forsaken *v. pr. pl.* renounce (D) 179.91
forscalded *ppl. adj.* severely scalded or burned 83.25, 139.49
forscorched *ppl. adj.* severely burned 139.46
fors(e *n.* force 10.70; **it is no fors** it doesn't matter 9.97
forslouthe *v. pr.* waste by laziness (H1) 143.25; *imp.* be slothful 64.353
+**forstungin** *ppl. adj.* badly stung 169.15 *note*
forsuere *v. inf.* repudiate 135.135
forthe *adv.* thenceforward 66.115
forthinkithe *impers. v. pr.* **it** ~ **me** I regret 163.91; **forthinkinge** *ger.* repentance 79.397; **forthenkinge** 79.983
forweried *ppl. adj.* tired out 29.122
forwounded *ppl. adj.* grievously wounded 2.246, 79.979
forwrapped *ppl. adj.* wrapped up 79.289, 83.341
+**forwretin** *v. pa. p.* written over 156.115 *note*
foryeue *pa. p.* forgiven 156.374; **foryoue** 156.376
+**fossa** *n.* grave 174.361 *note*
fouchesauf *see* **vouchesauf**
foule *adj.* unclean 5.270; of poor quality 26.187; lowly 26.77, 77.44, 161.284
foule *adv.* sorely 15.44, 60.352, 75.59; disgustingly 129.18
founde[1] *v. inf.* tempt (D) 179.43
founde[2] *v. pa.* provided for 45.236; **fonde** 163.41, 164.2; *pa. p.* **founde** 45.427
founde[3] *v. pa. p.* established 175.255
f(o)undement *n.* foundation 11.113, 28.180, 38.19; **fundament** 175.344
fount *see* **funte**
fourge *v. inf.* invent 165.196
fray *n.* uproar 78.81
fraitour *n.* refectory of a religious house 5.249; **froytour** 5.253, 64.21, 106.195
frankeleyne *n.* landowner 77.18
fraunchise *n.* independence 10.20, 99.132, 174.768; generosity 149.42
fre(e *adj.* exempt 26.175; of noble status 87.8; generous 149.42, 161.125; ~ **holde**, open arrest 84.32
fredom *n.* generosity 53.232, *60.349, 133.173
freel *adj.* feeble 1.205, (G) 4.145, 165.616; **frele** 165.640, 176.109
freelte *n.* weakness 8.181, 28.178, 176.114
freli *adv.* openly 18.5, 139.15; unhindered 20.112, 54.105, 79.384, 93.109, 117.356; without charge 29.52; generously 117.291
frendely *adv.* in a friendly way 7.66
frendes *n. pl.* kinsfolk 85.24 *note*
frendschip *n.* company (G) 41.3; **frenship** 111.23
frenetyk *adj.* frantic 135.60
frette *v. pa. pl.* gnawed at 9.110; **freting** *ger.* gnawing 58.113
frist *see* **furste**
froytour *see* **fraitour**
froyte *see* **fruit**
frore *v. pa. p.* frozen 113.44
frotithe *v. imp. pl.* rub 35.79; **froted** *ppl. adj.* rubbed 54.115, 61.290, 126.11
fruit *n.* progeny 83.347, 123.99; **froyte** fruit (L) 179.409
fulfell(e *v. inf.* feed us fully 11.297; perform 20.145; make up for 32.11; **fulfille** fill 135.67; **fulfill(e** *pr.* perform 25.84, 135.68; **fulfellest** *2 sg.* *22.187; **fulfellith** *3 sg.* fills 65.148; **fulfillid** *pa. sg.* (G) 1.94, (G) 2.309; *pa. p.* performed (G) 4.10; filled 28.136; **fulfilled** fulfilled 5.1, **fulfelled** filled 13.177, 87.77, 90.364; performed 79.235, 93.258, 112.335; **fulfilled** *ppl. adj.* filled 2.147; **fulfillid** (G) 3.83, 29.135; **ful(l)felled** *14.18; sorely afflicted 26.213; satisfied 87.43, 125.82; completed 26.185, 33.10; **fullfellyng** *ger.* supplementing 32.3
fulled *v. pa.* supplied (D) 178.78
fundement *see* **foundement**
funte *n.* font 128.69; **fount** 148.2; **funtston(e** 15.30, *106.8, 174.369; **font stone** 102.3

furst(e) *ord. num.* earliest 14.26, 123.66; foremost 22.134, 95.11, 167.5; **frist** earliest (H2) 176.148, (H2) 177.40, (D) 179.1

G

gadre *v. inf.* assemble *trans.* 4.169, 30.53; reap 83.47; collect 155.237; *pr.* 84.73; **gadered** *pa.* assembled *intrans.* 21.6; collected 7.214, 34.18; gathered up 50.255
+gaily *adv.* eloquently 149.241 *note*
gall(e *n.* bitter drink 1.145, 11.178, 50.130; gall bladder 36.163, 65.95
galpinge *ger.* yawning 63.23
game *n.* sport 24.126, 161.16, (D) 179.528; game animals 37.10; contest 8.103 *note*
gangefermour *n.* privy-cleaner 111.48
garnement *n.* garment 83.353 *note*
garner *n.* storehouse for grain 161.140; **gerner** 38.63; **garner(e)s** *pl.* 2.82, 140.45
garnison *n.* stronghold 60.49, 117.379
gate *n.* door 53.315, 84.51
gebet(te *n.* gibbet (G) 1.113, 44.152, 50.447, 134.108; **gibet(t** 61.176, 152.205; **iebett** (G) 1.111
gemel(le)s *n. pl.* twins 78.1, 163.17; **iemel** *adj.* twin 60.16
gendered *v. pa. p.* begotten 174.322
+gendre *n.* son-in-law 174.634 *note*
generacion *n.* origin 64.281–2; genealogy 123.3; **generaciones** *pl.* genealogies 123.29
General *n.* overall superior of religious order 142.317
genteles *n. pl.* non-Jews 7.3, 90.57; **gentiles** 12.73; **genteles** unbelievers 79.166
gerarchies *see* **ierarchie**
gerde *v. inf.* tie round the waist 142.51; **gert(e** *pa.* fastened 79.49, 80.81; *pa. p.* wearing a belt 88.3; **gurte** *ppl. adj.* 101.39; **gert** encircled 112.212
gerdon *see* **guerdon** *n.*
+gerdonable *adj.* deserving of reward 8.39 *note*; *see also* **guerdon**
gerdoner *see* **guerdonere**
gerdonyng *see* **guerdon** *v.*
gerner *see* **garner**
gert(e *see* **gerde**
gerthis *n. pl.* horse's saddle straps 174.475
gestes *n. pl.* historical tales 94.3
gete *v. inf.* obtain 5.48, 16.28, 25.187; *imp.* 25.183; **gate** *pa.* *8.159, 25.190, begot 123.16; **gete** caused 10.22; obtained (G) 41.25; **gote withe childe** impregnated 77.21; **gote(n** *pa. p.* obtained 24.137, 60.273, 93.4; begotten 15.45, 92.49, 117.145; **gete** 86.74; **gotin** obtained 140.33; **getyng** *ger.* acquiring 8.72, 26.210; engendering 8.74
geue *v. inf.* give 8.116, 26.142, 29.42; **geuest** *pr. 2 sg.* 47.193; **ȝaf** *pa.* (G) 4.27; **gove** *pa. p.* 106.82
gibett *see* **gebet(te**
gile *n.* **in** ~ deceitfully (G) 40.35
gilte *adj.* golden 84.461, 174.484
gilt(e *n.* guilt (G) 1.113, 2.248, 27.9; sin 30.71, 32.49, 175.237
gyse *n.* appearance 45.32, 174.216; **gise** custom 128.176
gladith(e *v. pr. 3 sg.* gladdens 65.443, 163.336; **gladed** *pa.* rejoiced 112.329; **gladid** *ppl. adj.* made joyful (G) 44.32
glas *n.* ice 48.106
glewe *n.* bitumen 84.307
glewithe *v. pr. 3 sg.* sticks together 175.234
+glorifiant *adj.* glorifying 7.60 *note*
glosed *v. pa.* used fair words 76.25; wrote an interpretation of 174.724
gloser *n.* commentator 64.159
gnast *v. pa. pl.* gnashed 7.92
gnew(e *v. pa.* gnawed 48.74, 173.222
gobet *n.* fragment, lump 20.37, 105.188, 156.84; **gobettes** *pl.* (H1) 157.3
godes *see* **good**
godhede *n.* divinity 11.284; deity 24.20, 146.12
+golyardes *n. pl.* libertines (?) 175.400 *note*
go(o *v. inf.* travel 13.88, (D) 178.117; walk 83.151, 90.193, 91.21, 125.91, (H1) 142.499, 152.119, 161.415; **gone** (H2) 177.78; **goest** *pr. 2 sg.* go 17.25; **goste** occupy yourself 104.67; **gothe** *3 sg.* departs 22.51; **gone** *pr. pl.* 22.42, 25.88; walk 80.155; **goynge** *ppl. adj.* walking (D) 178.102; **gothe** *imp. pl.* go 2.249, 8.58, 13.81; **goo(n** *pa. p.* departed (G) 4.42; travelled 93.172;

goyng(e *ger.* power of walking 12.79, 122.86, 152.120; walking 28.93, 142.78; travelling 161.110
good *n. pl.* possessions 8.39, 11.8, 26.46; **godes** 53.173; **goodes** virtues 84.401
goodli *adj.*[1] beautiful 10.101; convenient 134.47
goodly *adj.*[2] divine 176.21 *note*
goodly *adv.* fittingly 9.51; kindly 10.36, 26.205, 77.7; diligently 54.89, 90.357; joyfully 48.130, 146.134; virtuously 25.221, 90.76; blessedly 101.22
gospeles *n. pl.* passages from Gospels read during mass 139.158
gosteli *adj.* spiritual 20.67, 33.71, 80.50; **goostelie** (D) 178.228
gote *v. pa. p. see* **gete**
gowte *n.* gout 104.85 *note*
+**gowtous** *adj.* suffering from gout 140.50 *note*
gouernaile *n.* governance 93.93 *note*; rudder 93.104, 99.14; authority (D) 179.37
gouernaunce *n.* conduct 2.57, 13.40, 25.131, 26.108; 69.20, 52.30, 79.34, 104.113, 156.296; custody 5.39, protective keeping 8.138, 28.143, 117.223; guardianship 69.2; rules 79.51; government 88.88; means of steering ship *90.65
governe *v. inf.* govern 5.183, 11.377; **gouerned** *pa. refl.* behaved 29.80, 84.383, 174.528; **gouernid** *pa.* governed 117.155; **gouerned** *ppl. adj.* protected 109.40; **gouernynge** *ger.* steering 93.132
gouernour *n.* steersman 102.40, 116.258
grace *n.* sake 154.20 *note*
graiell *n.* gradual, service book containing gradual psalms 174.462
grasse *n.* cooking oil 113.131 *note*
grassope *n.* grasshopper 45.73
graunsere *n.* grandfather 61.169; **graundsire** 129.136; **grauntsyres** *pl.* ancestors 123.37
graunte *n.* permission 45.189; promise 80.184
graunted *v. pa.* agreed 45.479
gredill *n.* grill 24.57
gredyrne *n.* grill 24.116, 146.163; **grediren** 61.288, 110.182; **gredyrnes** *pl.* 126.13
greef *adj.* grievous 63.12
greef *n.* stylus or small sharp pointed tool 18.3 *note*; **greffys** *pl.* 18.7; **greves** 18.2
grees *n. pl.* steps 166.7, (H2) 177.81; *see also* **degree**
gres *n.* grass (D) 178.221, **gras** (D) 178.319
gret *adj.* coarse 161.275
+**gretnesse** *n.* pregnancy 155.309 *note*; size 154.95
grette *v. pr.* greet 49.269; *pa.* 121.54; **gret** *pa.* 161.184
greuaunce *n.* physical discomfort 49.84; annoyance 66.93, (D) 179.86; distress (H2) 176.143
greue *v. inf.* oppress 168.54; **greued** *pa.* worried 66.222; *pa. p.* afflicted 99.78; *ppl. adj.* oppressed 7.6, 31.41, 161.183, 167.124; afflicted 141.3
greves *see* **greef**
grevous *adj.* serious 25.178; severe 28.97; 29.124; burdensome 1.205, 30.21, 170.4
greuously *adv.* seriously 22.146, 84.267; heavily 94.75
grinte *v. inf.* gnash 165.793; **grynted** *pa.* *79.621; **gryntinge** *ger.* gnashing *79.994
groche *v. inf.* complain 7.4, 128.149; *pr. 2 sg.* 164.19; **grochin** *pr. pl.* 152.17; **groched** *pa.* 112.493; **gruched** 58.164; **grucchid** (D) 179.503; **grochinge** *ger.* grumbling 7.7; **gruchinge** 161.117
groueling(e *adj.* face downwards 125.116, (D) 178.229
growynge *ger.* vintage 107.27
gruched *see* **groche**
grucchers *n. pl.* grumblers (D) 178.672
g(u)erdon *n.* reward 2.270, (G) 3.25, 8.59, 26.210, 30.34; **gerdons** *pl.* 12.43
guerdon *v. inf.* reward 66.108, 115.9; *pa. p.* 45.270; **gerdonyng** *pr. p.* rewarding *12.43
g(u)erdoner(e *n.* giver of reward 1.213, 36.203
gurte *see* **gerde**

H

habirgones *n. pl.* coats of mail 37.73
habitacion *n.* settlement 5.29, dwelling place 20.90, (G) 46.21, 53.5
habitacle *n.* small dwelling 94.63, 163.351; **habitacles** *pl.* 45.441

habite *n.* clothing, characteristic attire 6.6, 26.117, 45.105; **abit(e** 1.248, 16.3, 25.23, 124.223 *note*
habound(e *see* **abound**
habundaunce *n.* plenty 27.70, 28.118, 47.259
habundaunt *adj.* plentiful 108.74, 134.6
hayre *n.* hair shirt, haircloth 10.12, 95.47, 101.36, 113.149; **haire** 132.11, 142.38, 173.89; **heyre** 101.33, 119.6, 124.9, 159.115; **heire** 28.98, (G) 40.6; **heires** *pl.* 63.41
hal(o)w(e *v. inf.* consecrate 11.210, 151.23, 79.919; celebrate 60.55; sanctify 138.175; **hallowe** celebrate (D) 177.164; **halwen** consecrate 101.130; **haluith** *pr. 3 sg.* celebrates 5.245; **halowith** (G) 43.68; **hal(o)wed** *pa.* sanctified 1.171, 11.172, 33.11, 65.445; celebrated 2.259, 23.110, *27.7, 102.8; **halwid** 55.58; **haludest** *pa. 2 sg.* consecrated 116.283; *pa. p.* **halowed** celebrated 11.27, sanctified 17.31, 88.135; *ppl. adj.* **hal(o)wed** consecrated 2.94, 22.181; celebrated 30.20, 112.332; **halued** sanctified 64.190, 138.172; **halowing** *ger.* consecration 11.174, 12.58, 112.949; **halwingges** *pl.* 49.79
halpe *see* **helpe**
halt(e *adj. as n.* lame 10.97, 44.167
halted *v. pa.* limped 60.82; **holtinge** *ppl. adj.* limping 139.81 *note*
handle *v. imp.* take action 113.301 *note*
hangged *see* **henge**
hapened *v. pa.* had the good fortune 29.88
happe *n.* chance 128.148
happed *v. pa.* happened 2.13, 90.203
happelie *adv.* by chance (D) 178.174
hard(e *adj.* having difficulty 4.233 *note*; deep (of sleep) 90.209; hard to bear 112.832; coarse 113.12; steadfast (D) 179.289
harded *v. pa.* hardened 26.123, 112.866; **hardied** strengthened 96.25; *pa. refl.* emboldened 149.331; **harded** *ppl. adj.* hardened 44.204
+hardefull *adj.* 84.372 *note*
hardeli *adv.* hardily 2.129; bravely 37.75, 54.62, 74.25, 106.70, 118.21; **hardely** certainly 79.532, 135.42; confidently 58.89, 165.269
hardest *superl.adj.* **at the** ~ at worst 20.147, 66.255
hardi *adj.* bold 9.61, 27.47, 29.214; **hardy** 2.166, 84.489, 102.55; foolhardy 66.232, 129.65; **hardyer** *comp.* bolder 106.36
hardied *see* **harded**
hardinesse *n.* audacity 27.40, *83.424; courage 54.226, 79.53; severity 28.158
harlotrie *n.* entertainment (D) 179.527; wantonness (D) 179.546
harme *n.* loss 44.89; penalty 45.369
harnettis *n. pl.* hornets 14.11
harowe *see* **arwe**
hasteli *adv.* quickly 2.157, 25.73, 44.56, 48.83; soon 5.185, 93.296; vehemently 45.471
hastest *v. pr. 2 sg.* hasten 26.274; **hast** *pr. pl.* 123.229; **hast(e** *imp.* 25.191, 125.41; **hasted** *pa.* urged 84.210, 86.4, 99.116, 142.362, 151.27 *note*; hastened 13.91, 25.132, 45.324; *pa.* **hast** 50.110; *pa. p.* 136.91; **hasting** *ger.* hastening 28.60
hasti *adj.* sudden 36.331; imminent 112.613
hastinesse *n.* speed 133.157
hatefull *adj.* full of hatred 34.37, 65.446
haunsed *v. pa. p.* elevated 29.154 *note*, (G) 43.2, 60.260, 74.94; raised up 64.283, 112.324; **haunsinge** *ger.* elevation 64.348; **haunsyngges** *pl.* 64.284
haunt *n.* place frequented 79.324
haunt *v. inf.* frequent 138.185; **haunted** *pa.* 2.8; 7.187; engaged in *58.52, 84.477, 90.384, 163.53; visited 81.111, 156.135, 163.265, 174.146; frequented 150.19; *pa. p.* visited 61.216, 112.273; frequented 133.201
haue *v. inf.* make 135.53; ~ **away** take away 93.329; **hast(e** *pr. 2 sg.* own 20.2; **had(d(e** *pa.* received 26.23, (H1) 144.51; owned 90.8; considered 36.63, 79.916, (H2) 176.290; ~ **vp** raised (G) 4.23; ~ **oute** brought out 61.207; ~ **leuer** would rather 9.106; **hadde** *pa. p.* captured 18.35; brought 112.244,265
hauers *n. pl.* possessors *178.116
hede *n.* notice (G) 1.67, 11.51, 26.121; care 90.124
hedid *v. pa. p.* beheaded (G) 42.54, 136.58

hedir *adv.* hither 1.306, 22.28, 54.73; **hidir** (G) 4.12
heelde *see* **holde**
heer *see* **here**
hegge *v. imp.* enclose (L) 179.450
height *v. pa. see* **hight**
heile *interj.* health, **al** ~ good health to you *2.101
heir(e see **eyre**[1,2], **hayre**
heyr(e *n.* heir 28.23, 122.6
he(e)le *n.* health 7.188, (G) 46.25, 55.206; healing 12.23, (G) 38.83, 79.177; welfare 22.135; salvation 30.73, 80.104
heled *v.*[1] *pa.* healed 29.2; *pa. p.* 22.80; **helynge** *ger.* 139.91
heled *v.*[2] *pa.* covered 63.40; **helid** *pa. p.* (G) 38.149; **helyd** concealed (L) 79.1050; **heling(e** *ger.*, roof 159.137, 175.85; *see also* **hille**
helme *n.* helmet 61.262
helpe *v. inf.* help 2.66; **holpe** *pa.* 156.389; **halpe** 109.6, 112.520; **holpe(n** *pa. p.* 31.39, 37.29; **holpin** 156.390
helthefull *adj.* curative 35.50
henge *v. pa. pl. intrans.* hang 79.959; **hangged** depended 2.39; **henge** hanged *trans.* 61.176; **hyng(e** 1.183, hung *intrans.* 17.25, 50.13
hennys *adv.* hence 2.182
hepe *n.* crowd 104.188
hepe *v. inf.* collect 58.313
herbe *n.* plant (D) 178.13; **herbes** *pl.* plants 34.14, 80.79, 90.239
herburgh *n.* lodging 29.8, 79.159, 128.191; **herborughe** 93.176
herburgh *v. inf.* take lodging 77.17; **herburith** *pr. 3 sg.* gives shelter to 4.224; **herborued** *pa. p.* lodged 15.19, 29.8, 54.214, 86.65, 93.202; **herboroughed** *ppl. adj.* 106.282; **herborwed** 99.96, 106.94, 119.98; **herbured** 119.97
here *v. inf.* hear 1.132, (G) 4.149; **hire** (D) 179.451; **heren** *pr. pl.* 63.94; **herithe** *imp. pl.* 79.862; **hire** (H2) 178.388; **herde** *pa.* heard 20.42; **herden** *pa. pl.* 26.175; **hurde** *pa. p.* (G) 4.156; **hiringe** *ger.* hearing (H2) 1.5; **heryng** 26.96
here *n.* hair 10.13, 23.57, 45.46; **heer** 10.11, 54.189, 176.125; **heres** *pl.* *116.100
hered *v. pa.* rented 53.75, 128.145; hired 58.330, 110.217
heritage *n.* inherited property 45.11, 53.236, 97.17; **eritage** 113.208; **heritages** *pl.* inheritances 8.31, 65.41, 69.3, 117.294; **heritagis** (G) 3.28
herke *v. inf.* listen 159.342
herkenithe *v. imp. pl.* listen to 13.203
hermitage *n.* desert 66.36; state of being a hermit 14.26 *note*
hert(e *n.* hart 29.75; **hertes** *pl.* 154.8
hert(e)li *adv.* fervently 7.186, 112.30, 148.108; **hertlyer** *comp.* 165.383
hertyng *ger.* injury 11.266
hestis *n. pl.* promises (G) 55.91; **heestis** (D) 178.454
hetithe *v. pr. 3 sg.* becomes hot 22.50
hette *v. ppl. adj.* inflamed 50.462, 113.79
heuely *see* **hevily**
heuene *n.* the heavenly bodies astrologically 13.72; the sky 101.98, (D) 178.4
heuy(e *adj.* heavy 1.201, 28.154, 47.150; sorrowful 8.52, 34.39, 66.185
heuied *v. pa. p.* saddened 88.98
hevily *adv.* sadly 52.50, 79.516, 134.136; **heuely** 79.322
hevinesse *n.* sorrow 65.224, 112.405, 113.384
hewith *v. pr. 3 sg.* cuts 11.291; **hew** *pa.* 159.150; **hewed** 171.77
hidously *adv.* violently 26.268
hye *v. refl. imp.* hasten 54.47, 79.667; **high** 54.52, 124.226, 165.274; **hyid** *pa.* (G) 55.148; **hied** 123.236; **highed** 79.352, 165.280
hygh *adj.* tall 20.51; **high** loud 126.4; serious 165.334; **hye** *adj. as n.* exalted 11.252; **an** ~ loudly 26.122
highe daies *n. pl.* church festivals 14.56
hyghnes(se *n.* excellence 5.102, *13.119, 25.12; highest status 101.5; **hynesse** nobility 12.81; height 45.114, 65.297, 134.17; sublimity 128.14; **hynes** 13.187 *note*
hight *v. inf.* be named 15.8, 83.311; *pr.* 15.7; *pa.* **hight** 2.43, 5.77, 6.2, 7.163, 25.200; **heiȝt** (G) 4.61; **height** (G) 44.3; **hightest** *pa. 2 sg.* promised 99.104; **height** *ppl.* promised (G) 43.49
hyght *n.* height 90.295; top 138.12; **higthe** 102.60; **highthe** height 93.144; **heith** (G) 55.177

hily *adv.* honourably 110.32; **hili** loudly 30.68
hille *v. inf.* clothe 26.48; **hile** *imp.* conceal (D) 178.505; *pa.* **hilled** covered 29.130; *ppl. adj.* roofed 5.51; **hillinge** *ger.* covering 90.374; *see also* **hele** *v.*[2]
hilt *v. pa. p.* flayed 116.142
hyndre *v. inf.* impair 11.261
hynes(se *see* **hyghnesse**
hyng(e *see* **henge**
hyre *n.* wage 37.87; payment 45.524; fare 52.39, 154.88
hire *v. see* **here**
hode *n.* cowl 142.323
holde *v. inf.* keep hold of (G) 4.147, conceal 24.42; continue 36.229; consider 79.533, (D) 179.498; remain unchanged 79.795; possess 80.141; **holdist** *pr. 2 sg.* consider 159.35; **holdith(e** *3 sg.* considers 18.8, holds captive 22.57; **holt** considers 61.134; **holde** perform (G) 4.130; **holde** *imp.* take hold 92.49; **holde the** stand 86.44; **holding** *pr. p.* having in mind 49.176; **he(e)lde** *pa.* considered 10.55; celebrated 45.527; possessed 80.138; **hilde** held (G) 2.301, (G) 4.20; **hilden** *pa. pl.* (G) 40.22; **helden** owned 90.4; **holden** *pa. p.* held captive (G) 1.114, 11.299, 79.266; maintained 24.17; **holde** kept to 55.172, considered (G) 45.543, 70.20; undertaken 81.79; held back 152.176; **helde her still** *pa. refl.* remained silent 28.205; **helde hym** considered himself 9.35, 86.51; stood 93.46; **holden** *ppl. adj.* considered 9.69; **holdynge** tenacious 45.461
hole *adj.* whole 8.42, 11.285, 22.98; healthy 5.82, 10.123, 11.363; **hool** whole 112.921
holely *adv.* holily (H1) 144.22
holme *n.* holly or holm-oak 113.117 *note*
holocaustis *n. pl.* burnt offerings 175.425
holpe(n *see* **helpe**
holt see **holde** *v.*
holtinge *see* **halted**
homly *adj.* unassuming 117.225
homly *adv.* impudently 165.301
honest *adj.* honourable 1.263, 117.2, 163.139; ordinary 10.14; of good quality 161.129
honeste *n.* goodness 149.57, 154.178, 175.259
honestly *adv.* virtuously 63.71; decorously 161.45
hore *adj.* white 45.254, 55.77, 116.18; white-haired 168.12
horne *n.* drinking vessel (G) 1.61
horshone *n. pl.* horseshoes 174.475
hosen *n. pl.* 78.45 *note*; **hosin** 128.85, 142.50
hoseled *v. pa.* gave holy communion 108.26, 111.2; **houseled** 82.3, 146.174; *ppl. adj.* 52.76, 112.506
hosyll *n.* holy communion 90.321, 156.240; **housill** 138.194
hoso whoever 106.305, 174.278
hospitaler *n.* hospitable person 84.356
hospitall *n.* hostel for travellers 29.119
hoste *see* **oste**[1,2]
hostiler *see* **ostiler**
houge *adj.* loud 105.143; **hugie** *adj.* huge (H2) 176.148
hougely *adv.* greatly 77.53, 117.107, 148.123
houre *n.* canonical hour 90.242; **houres** *pl.* 142.330
houseled *see* **hoseled**
housill *see* **hosyll**
hugie *see* **houge**
+humylinge *ger.* humbling 50.295 *note*
humoure *n.* moisture 34.6; one of the humours 45.388; **humour(e)s** *pl.* fluids (the four humours) 31.22; fluids 83.342
hurde *see* **here** *v.*
hurte *v. inf.* thrust 27.17; **hurtithe** *pr. 3 sg.* harms 36.165; knocks 175.269; *pr. pl.* **hurten** harm 45.187; **hurt** *pa. p.* 82.6 *note*; **hurte** *ppl. adj.* 1.278, 78.28; **hurtinge** *ger.* injury 62.12
hurtle *v. inf.* collide (H2) 176.172; **hurtelinge** *pr. p.* (H2) 176.173; **hurtlid** *pa.* (G) 55.103

I

yddes *n.* 127.21 *note*
idel(l *adj.* free for leisure 5.52; inactive 32.41, 84.486; lazy 90.37; trivial 26.233; **ydel** 112.525; **in idelle** worthlessly 179.455
ydeous *adj.* horrible 53.90
ydiotis *n. pl.* unlearned persons 155.190
idolatres *n. pl.* idolaters 54.166; **idolatris** 117.327

ierarchie *n.* hierarchy 112.85, 146.203; **gerarchies** *pl.* 146.117
ignoraunce *n.* **bi** ~ unknowingly 29.74; inadvertently 132.10; in error 142.232; ignorantly 110.282 *note*
ignorauntly *adv.* unknowingly 154.21
illuded *v. pa. p.* deluded 2.175; **illudid** (G) 1.108
illumined *v. pa.* illuminated 23.61
illusion *n.* mockery 50.2; **illusiones** *pl.* 50.151
ymagine *v. inf.* plot 141.11; devise 165.806; **ymagened** *pa.* plotted 2.145; *ppl. adj.* pictured in the mind *175.16
ymolte *see* **meltithe**
imperial(l) *adj.* empyrean 1.300 *note*, *64.249
ymped *v. ppl. adj.* grafted 65.206; **ympinge** *ger.* 116.244
ympne *n.* hymn (H2) 1.91, 13.23, 63.105
importune *adj.* persistent 25.186
imposicion *n.* imposition 12.3; ~ **of honde** laying on of hands for ordination 82.44
impression *n.* imprint 28.175; *175.199 *note*
iniurie *n.* insult 38.40, (G) 40.28, 53.69, 79.772; injury 79.446, 112.537, 160.37
inobedience *n.* disobedience 47.325, 170.12
inordinat *adj.* immoderate 25.39, 44.139, 79.53; **enordinat** 5.162
inow *adv.* enough 6.70, 9.117, 11.72; **ynowȝ** (G) 45.575
inperfit *adj.* incomplete 133.159
inportunite *n.* insistence 79.819
instaunce *n.* insistence 45.65, 77.43, 90.392
instrument *n.* document 112.458; implement 156.190; **instrumentes** *pl.* musical instruments 124.11
intendibles *see* **entendible**
intendynge *ppl. adj.* listening 79.764
inuencion *n.* discovery 7.202, 105.87, 165.865
irchon *n.* hedgehog 22.142
iren *n.* iron 22.34, 84.470; **yrne** 119.32; **irne** iron part 47.97; **irnes** *pl.* fetters 90.380, 91.41, 93.141; iron blades 110.264; **yrins** hooks 155.252
yreux *adj.* angry 22.47; **irouse** 34.26; **irous** irascible 74.7 *note*
yseyne *see* **see**
ysope *n.* hyssop (aromatic herb) 175.186
issewe *n.* children (G) 40.13; **issue** way out 108.53
istrengthid *see* **strengthe** *v.*

J

iaillours *n. pl.* jailers 142.176
iangle *v. inf.* chatter 112.534, 106.206; *imp.* 38.40; **iangelyd** *pa.* 106.202; **iangeled** 112.525; **iangelinge** *ger.* chattering 50.174, 110.201, 156.293
iangeler *n.* idle talker 168.60
iape *n.* joke 93.299; **iapes** *pl.* 11.295, 38.19; **iapes** frivolous pastimes 161.89
iape *v. inf.* trifle 173.467 *note*
iaper *n.* trifler 113.259 *note*
iapinge *ger.* trifling 94.140
iebett *see* **gebette**
iemel *adj. see* **gemel(le)s**
iocounde *adj.* joyful (D) 179.523
iogelo(u)r jester (G) 40.26; entertainer 94.9; **iogelour(e)s** *pl.* entertainers 68.53; jesters 174.637
ioie *n.* heavenly joy 1.266 *note*, 5.212, 7.54; (earthly) joy (G) 2.294, 9.114, 12.13
ioye *v. inf.* rejoice 49.204; **ioyeth** *pr. 3 sg.* 49.55; **ioyen** *pr. pl.* 22.44; **ioye** *imp. pl.* 23.109, 35.19; **ioyed** *pa.* 47.137, 79.259, 80.31, 84.483, 139.190; **ioieden** *pa. pl.* 5.5, 79.925; **ioyed** *ppl. adj.* 163.328; **ioyeng** *pr. p.* 155.327
iointours *n. pl.* joints 164.41; **iointures** 175.413 *note*
+ioyouste *n.* enjoyment 117.276 *note*
iorney(e *n.* journey 58.402, 90.165, 113.380, 123.236; **iourne** day's march 174.535; *pl.* **iorneyes** 45.71; **iourney(e)s** 58.412, 165.822; **iorneis** days' travel 29.174
iuelys *n. pl.* treasures 2.184; **iuelles** 79.126
iuge *n.* official invested with judicial powers (representing *iudex*, *preses*, *tribunus*, *proconsul*, *prefectus*) (G) 1.99, 24.13, 38.41
iuge *v. inf.* condemn 112.444, 129.143; judge 56.10, 83.140, 117.283; arbitrate 25.38; **iuged** *pa. p.* condemned 2.157, 22.8, 79.505; judged *137.27
iugement *n.* law court 1.155, 2.132, 7.44;

trial 2.216, 93.182; Last Judgement 25.93

iuys *n.* drink 20.149

+Iulit *n.* July 28.160 *note*

iuste *v. inf.* joust 79.66

iustes *n. pl.* jousts 79.62

iustified *v. pa. p.* made righteous 11.168; **iustefied** 11.169

K

karfoke *n.* crossroads 2.224 *note*; **karfont** 2.265

karions *see* **careyne**

karoll *n.* 112.92 *note*; **karolles** *n. pl.* round dances accompanied by singing 50.166, 161.44; religious songs 112.92,

kele *v. inf.* cool 156.81

kembithe *v. pr. sg.* combs 9.97

kepe *n.* heed *13.71, 59.8, 93.279

kepe *v. inf.* guard 2.46, 35.48, 79.245; preserve 112.986, 124.5; control 47.287; look after 2.220, (G) 4.58, 5.40, 8.142; restrain 90.39; perform 113.415; remain in 17.60; imprison 133.53; *pr. 1 sg. refl.* ~ **me** preserve myself 23.37; **kepithe** *pr. 3 sg.* preserves 13.235, 87.43; **kepen** *pr. pl.* look after 8.86; *imp.* perform 20.75; **kept(e** *pa.* looked after 7.109, 81.46, 87.4; guarded 22.61, 45.104, 100.15; remained in 28.212; preserved 105.20; **kept not** did not wish 101.81; **kept(e** *pa. p.* observed 11.25, (G) 45.530, 69.42; preserved 24.93, 37.65; guarded 53.43, 79.421, 175.163; looked after 90.192, 93.328; kept secret 113.417; **kepte** *ppl. adj.* observed 8.195, preserved 159.36; **kepyng** *ger.* care, guardianship 19.5; **keping(e** 5.203, 29.145, 91.55; custody (G) 41.20, 83.201; custodianship 53.306; protection 24.93, 112.743, 136.81, 175.239; restraint 154.126; preserving 149.205

keper(e *n.* protector (G) 4.7, 23.55, 28.9; guardian 8.147, 79.421, 88.100; governor 79.95; attendant 133.53; **kepers** *pl.* guards 9.126, 24.78, 79.245, 104.76; protectors 79.91

kerch(i)ef(f) *n.* handkerchief 83.19; woman's headcloth 84.129, **kercheff** 84.137, **kercheef** 84.153; **kerchefes** *pl.* 161.150

kerving *ger.* sculpting (H1) 157.8; *see also* **corve**

kesse *see* **kisse**

kynde *n.* nature 2.97, 5.110, 8.184, 23.145, 30.11, 55.196, 79.178, 83.330; lineage 28.5, (D) 178.632; physical condition 31.7; kindred *125.66

kindely *adj.* according to nature 49.117; by nature 87.69

kindely *adv.* naturally 65.448

kyne *n. pl.* cattle 121.44

kynrede *n.* family 1.248, 2.2, 5.35, *84.17; relatives 8.17; nation 22.1, 74.1, 110.1; forebears 175.211 *note*

kisse *v. inf.* kiss 154.202; **kesse** 26.170; **cusse** 104.99, 106.174; **cusse** *imp.* 112.186; **kessed** *pa.* 8.157, 22.108; **cussed** 80.61, 88.113; **custe** 154.159; **kist** 124.110; **kisten** *pl.* 118.18

kist(e *v. pa. see* **caste**

klippid *see* **clippe**

knaues *n. pl.* young men 166.60

knette *v. pa.* knotted 2.19, 47.13; *pa. p.* joined 165.465; paired (L) 179.386

knewe *see* **knowe**

knighthode *n.* military status 126.3; military service (H1) 158.3

knotte *n.* knot in wood of tree 167.46

knowe *v. inf.* know 1.133; specify 2.120, 11.373; be known 36.126, (G) 43.151; *pa.* had carnal knowledge of 23.16, 79.188, (H2) 178.337; **kneugh** (H2) 178.378; **knewe** acknowledged 79.271; recognized 79.1021, 163.114; **knowin** *pa. p.* recognized 139.128

knowing(e *ger.* acquaintance 142.288 *note*; knowledge 149.94, 161.19

knowlache *n.* knowledge 5.152, 32.30; **knoulage** 104.80; **knowlage** close friends 84.367

knowlache *v. inf.* acknowledge 5.22; **knowlage** 79.298, 123.376; **knowleche** 155.278; **knoulage** confess 48.16; **knowlage** *pr. 1 sg.* acknowledge 51.52; **knolage** 123.290; **knowlegest** *pr. 2 sg.* 51.51; **knowlache** *pr. 2 sg. subj.* 112.704; **knowlegithe** *3 sg.* 95.76; **knowlage** *imp.* reveal 61.167; **knowlaged** *pa.* confessed 18.33; acknowledged 20.7, 22.187; **knowlechid** revealed (G) 42.31; acknowledged (G) 55.123; **knowleched** confessed 123.327

koy *adj.* quiet 102.81
kon, konnen, kouthe *see* **canne**
konninge *see* **connynge**
kowghed *v. pa.* coughed 9.111
kunnynge *see* **connynge**

L

laboure *n.* trouble 29.105; task 55.84; weariness 78.52
laboured *v. pa.* afflicted 29.31, 45.375, 113.336, 173.491–2 *note*
ladde *see* **lede**
laie *adj.* secular 142.57
laye *v. pa.* ~ **sore upon** strongly urged 156.298
langoure *v. inf.* be ill 106.218
langoure *n.* infirmity 45.519, 90.261; **langoures** *pl.* 7.142, *45.375
+**langustus** *n. pl.* locusts(?) 174.533 *note*
lappe *n.* loose part of garment 168.68
lapped *v. pa.* wrapped 84.154; *pa. p.* 28.124; *ppl. adj.* 13.129
large *n.* **at** ~ at liberty 72.16, 124.137
large *adj.* generous 45.232, 124.224, 133.174; wide 79.558, 142.150; big in amount or extent 9.79, 79.233, 116.262, 165.519
largely *adv.* generously (G) 3.26, 50.316, 90.325; copiously 5.142, *28.155, 64.180, 79.244; in a broad sense 175.122; widely 36.241
largenesse *n.* size 138.38
largesse *n.* breadth 64.258, 117.15; generosity 49.51, 53.136, 65.230, 159.403
lassed *pa. p.* reduced 44.108, 79.575
late *v. see* **lete**
lauatorie *n.* cleansing 61.299
laugh(e *v. inf.* laugh 8.87, 45.397, 47.288; **lawgh** (G) 45.560; **laughest** *pr. 2 sg.* 53.125; **laghe** *pr. pl.* 124.173; **lough** *pa.* 5.43, 20.135, 24.129; **lowgh** 20.63; **lawghyng** *ger.* laughter 28.106
lazar *n.* leper 8.64, 99.11 *note*
leche *n.* medical doctor 38.75, 50.415, 57.6, 60.180; **leches** *pl.* 55.202, 94.152, 122.53
lecherie *n.* self-indulgence 139.54; lechery 139.56; **lycherie** 173.464
lecherous *n. pl.* fornicators (G) 3.72
lecto(u)r *n.* cleric in first of four minor orders 81.57, 159.91
lecture *n.* book-learning 53.15
lede *v. inf.* lead 95.85, 139.94; **ledith** *pr. 3 sg.* drags 111.63 *note*; **ledde** *pa. p.* led 11.16, 107.6; brought about 30.27; **ladde** led 10.49; **ledinge** *ger.* guidance 99.16
lederin *adj.* of leather 80.81; **letheren** (D) 178.135
ledyr *n.* leather 47.227, 60.307
left(e *v. pr. 1 sg.* raise 11.345; **leftithe** *pr. 3 sg.* 65.119; **lefte** *pa.* 9.123, 10.30, 49.207; **lefft** *pa. p.* 11.158; **lefte** 20.43, 29.19; exalted 142.308; **lyffte** *ppl. adj.* 44.163; **loftyng** *pr. p.* raising 2.127 *note*; **lefftyng** *ger.* raising 27.80; **lefting(e** 60.257, 65.339
lefte *see* **leue** *v.*[1] and *v.*[3]
lefull *adj.* suitable 60.290, 79.256, 113.194 *note*; **liefull** lawful 80.141; **leefulle** (D) 179.304
legacion *n.* mission 129.97
legat *n.* emissary 156.306, 174.687; **leget** 113.353
leyser(e *n.* leisure 165.87; opportunity (H2) 176.246
leme *n.* flame 45.110; **lemes** *pl.* 24.60, 48.81
lene *v.*[1] *inf.* lend 142.438; *pr.* 93.255; **lent** *pa. p.* 93.255; *ger.* **lenynge** 125.35
lened *v.*[2] *pa.* leaned 94.64; **lenid** rested 173.225
lengthinge *ger.* lengthening 117.305
lente *n.* period of forty days fasting 156.309
lepes *n. pl.* baskets 174.735
leper *n.* leprosy 11.81; **lepore** 61.130
lepre *n.* leper 29.131, 90.21; **lepres** *pl.* 44.167, 80.155, 91.63
lepre *adj.* suffering from leprosy 152.59
lered *v. pa.* learned 27.64, 28.186
lerninge *ppl. adj.* teaching (D) 179.309
lese *v.*[1] *inf.* lose 1.254, (G) 3.65, 8.148; *pr. 1 sg.* 22.13, 106.210; **lesest** *2 sg.* 54.32; **lesithe** *3 sg.* 173.137; **lesithe** *imp. pl.* waste 163.152; **les** *pa.* destroyed (H2) *178.274; **loste** *pa. p.* lost the use of 83.390; wasted 109.13; **lorne** *ppl. adj.* lost (D) 178.428; **lesyng** *ger.* loss 8.73, 29.46
lese *v.*[2] *inf.* release 53.336
lesing(e *ger.* untruth 29.72, 119.107, 124.253; **lesyngges** *pl.* 127.88, 155.282
lesion *n.* injury 11.278

lesse *v. inf.* diminish 79.885; **lessid** *pa. p.* 2.84; **lessed** 155.89

lesson *n.* reading 47.245, 117.231, 139.192; **lessones** *pl.* 117.432

lesse *pr.* lessen *24.53; **lessid** *ppl. adj.* 2.84; **lessed** 112.978, 161.145

lest(e *v. pr. 3 sg.* wishes 26.119, 152.154; *see also* **liste** *and* **luste**

lete *v. inf.* cause to (G) 4.17, 26.182; **lat(e** *imp.* 1.285, 7.11; allow 1.199, 2.31, 7.204; **lete** permit to depart 36.183; allow 159.320; *pa.* caused to *2.279, 5.162, 8.212, 9.114, (G) 43.8

letheren *see* **lederin**

lette *n.* hindrance 52.47

lette *v. inf.* hinder, prevent 1.218, 8.200, 9.123, 13.123, 35.45; **lette** *pa.* 9.124, 45.73, 113.74; **lete** 66.175; **lettid** 152.101; **lette** *pa. p.* 7.110, 104.33, 117.192; delayed 45.500; **lette** *ppl. adj.* kept away 1.216; hindered 79.1024, 112.179; **lettyng** hesitating *44.177; *ger.* impediment 24.3, 49.247, 52.58

lettrez *n. pl.* documents 29.45; **letteres** writings 139.4; epistles 167.8; **litteres** 167.15

lett(e)rid *ppl. adj.* literate (H2) 1.4, 49.230, 132.2

letterure *n.* book-learning 117.404

letuse *n.* lettuce 33.73, 128.249

leude *adj.* ignorant 58.83, 124.236, 161.318; wicked 112.373; 113.60

lewdely *adv.* discourteously 113.222; foolishly 122.44

leudenes *n.* foolishness 113.407

leue *v.*[1] *inf.* abandon 7.91, 8.8, 29.114; let go 104.169; bequeath 28.123; cease *63.113; leave aside 149.71; **leuithe** *pr. 3 sg.* abandons 28.19; omits 128.229; remains 33.54; **leue** *pr. 3 sg. subj.* 32.42; **leve** *pr. pl.* abandon 7.9, 22.33; **leuen** cease 63.99; **leve** *imp.* 20.133; **lef(f)te** *pa.* 10.42, 28.27, (G) 44.38; abandoned 45.13, 79.194, 11.117, 174.440; survived 54.162; *pa. p.* (G) 43.13; omitted 36.37; **levynge** *ppl. adj.* leaving 106.11

leve *v.*[2] *inf.* believe 5.240, 15.10; **leue** 8.108, 13.64; **liue** 64.310; **levest** *pr. 2 sg.* 80.18; **lyuest** 175.416; *pr. subj. sg.* (G) 3.10, 8.115, 11.334; **leuithe** 90.277, 95.126; (L) **levith** 176.255; **leue** *pr. pl.* (G) 3.7, (G) 4.167, 60.107; **leven** 1.148, 12.34, 23.93, 31.24; **leuyn** 4.175; **leue** *imp.* (G) 3.8, (G) 4.94, 26.166, 84.170[1]; **levinge** *pr. p.* 66.20; **leued** *pa.* 5.80, 8.47, 11.230; **leuyd** (G) 55.120; **leuedyn** *pa. pl.* 13.63, 124.199; **leuedin** 119.24; **leueden** 91.18; **leued** *pa. p.* 11.156, 23.144; **lyued** 80.42

leve *v.*[3] *inf.* live 4.225, 84.94; **leue** 87.39; **lyue** 65.439; *pr.* 25.210, 29.192, 84.170[2]; **leuithe** *pr. 3 sg.* 26.63; **leue** *pr. pl.* (G) 3.24, 22.113; **liven** live 64.224; **leuyd** *pa.* 7.159; **leued** 163.92; **lyued** 88.28; **leved** *pa. p.* 95.98; **leued** 63.13; **levinge** *ger.* means of living 79.162; **lyvinge** 81.46

+levely *adj.* credible 174.141 *note*

+leuer *n.* believer 27.59 *note*; **lyuers** *pl.* believers 79.327 *note*

leuer *comp. adv.* **had(de** ~ would rather 1.254, 9.106, 24.118

libardes *n. pl.* leopards 166.66

libertynes *n. pl.* freedmen 7.32

licence *n.* permission 30.50, 79.700

liche *adj.* similar (G) 4.44, (L) 179.373

lyche *prep.* like 113.198

lycherie *see* **lecherie**

lyc(k)ly *see* **lik(e)ly**

licour(e *n.* liquid (derived from plants, animals, etc.) 5.191 58.210; oil 5.141, 116.172; **licoures** *pl.* sauces 28.133 *note*

liefull *see* **lefull**

liegemen *n. pl.* vassals (D) 179.532

lyffte *see* **lefte**

lyflode *see* **lyuelode**

lifte *adj.* left (hand side) 175.331

lygingges *ger.* ~ **in awaite** ambushes 149.58

light *v.*[1] *pa.* lit 29.127, 101.133; *ppl. adj.* 36.194, 159.219 *note*; **lighted** enlightened 154.7

light *v.*[2] *imp.* mount 86.132, 93.165; *pa.* mounted 20.139; ~ **downe** dismounted 45.335, 82.23, 112.447; came down 51.36, 80.112

lyght *adj.* easy 5.263, (G) 43.52, 176.108; little 13.114; lightly regarded 28.153; gentle 58.62; gentle 65.136; **lyghter** *comp.* easier 173.93

lyghtly *adj.* easy 65.144

light(e)ly *adv.* easily 13.92, 20.75, 47.258, 53.77, 58.130; **liȝtly** (G) 1.56, **lyghtli** 11.64; **lyghtly** gently 25.47; casually

45.221; easily 104.140; **lightlier** *comp.* more quickly 156.128
lightenith *v. pr. 3 sg.* gives sight to 65.288; **lightened** *pa. p.* illuminated 75.49; **lyghtned** enlightened 106.148
lightloker *comp.adv.* the more easily 155.331
liȝtne *v. inf.* flash with lightning (G) 55.72
lyghtnesse *n.* levity 34.47; weakness 33.33; mildness 65.145
like *adj.* similar 23.107, 29.93; *see also* **liche**
like *adv.* likely (G) 1.55, 8.113, 165.196; **lyk** 53.197
lyke *v. inf.* please 102.76; **likith(e** *pr. 3 sg. impers.* pleases (G) 3.37, 11.288, 79.395; **liked** *pa. sg.* pleased 1.203, 2.278, 7.15, 25.43; **likinge** *pr. p.* pleasing (D) 179.520
lik(e)ly *adj.* similar 5.290, 7.177, (G) 44.45, 64.281, 81.122; **lycly** 112.226; **lyckly** 112.830, **lykly** 106.47, 169.5
lymes *n. pl.* organs of the body 90.258
lynage *n.* lineage 9.25, 16.39, 120.1; tribe 44.158; descendants 53.164; **linages** *pl.* tribes 36.128
lyne *n.* line of descendants 165.116
lyngnye *n.* lineage *44.31; **lingne** 90.2; **lyne** 123.22
lisse *v.* relieve 117.132; 156.86; **lissed** *ppl. adj.* (D) 178.537
liste *v. pr. 2 sg.* wish (G) 4.5; **list** *pr. subj. 2 sg.* 133.108; **liste** *pa.* 55.141; *see also* **leste** *and* **luste**
liue *v. see* **leve** *v.*[2,3]
lyuelode *n.* property 45.341, 113.103; necessities of life 66.39, 95.19; **lyflode** 163.37; **lijfloode** (L) 179.370; **lyuelode** food 68.40, 155.52
lyueray *n.* provision of food or clothing to servants 14.42; membership of household 165.489
livers[1] *n. pl.* dwellers (D) 178.86
lyuers[2] believers *see* **leuer** *n.*
liuynge *ger.* way of life (H2) 1.1; **lyving** 26.130; *see also* **leve** *v.*[3]
loftyng *see* **lefte** *v.*
loke *v. inf.* find 106.118; *imp.* take care 47.191; **lokyng(e** *ger.* appearance 11.19; looking 16.15, 47.240; facial expression 174.472; **loke what** whatever 124.72
longithe *v. pr. 3 sg.* pertains 2.243, 11.276, 13.216; **longethe** 52.15, 57.29; belongs 23.146; **longith** 53.302; **longen** *pr. pl.* 25.53, 79.197; **longithe** 29.84; **longid** *pa.* (G) 44.50; **longed** 53.173, 79.59, (H1) 144.7
lords(c)hipped *v. pa.* ruled 5.6, 146.146
lorne *see* **lese** *v.*[1]
lose *v. inf.* dissolve (D) 178.638; **losithe** *pr. 3 sg.* loosens 148.87; **losed** *pa.* released 83.169; loosened 47.240, 79.822, 148.47; **losid** 117.237
loste *see* **lese** *v.*[1]
lothe *adj.* reluctant 112.564
lotte *n.* decision or allocation made by opening book at random, drawing straw, etc. 11.186, 66.112, 86.31
louringe *ppl. adj.* frowning (D) 178.147
loues *n. pl.* friends 58.331 *note*
lough *see* **laughe**
louithe *v. refl. pr. 3 sg.* humbles 56.28; **loued** *pa.* humbled 134.165
lowe *v. inf.* cry out (of animals) (H2) 176.185
low(e)ness(e *n.* humility (H1) 143.41, (D) 179.285
lowing *ppl. adj.* praising (L) 179.314 *note*
lucree *n.* profit 2.17
lust(e *n.* pleasure 106.79, 135.26, (D) 179.323; **lustis** desires *pl.* (D) 179.23
luste *v. pr.* wish 1.268, 82.21, 83.434; *pr. subj.* 35.103 ; *pa.* wished 29.190, 79.891; **lust(e** *impers. pr.* pleases 35.66, 94.113; **lust(e** *pa.* 1.319; 2.192, 10.95, 29.190, 35.103, 45.89, 60.227, 82.24, 90.91; *impers. pa.* pleased 8.170, 9.60, 13.92; 26.231; *see also* **leste** *and* **liste**
lustely *adv.* vigorously 45.338
lusti(e *adj.* enjoyable 164.23, (D) 179.497; joyful (D) 179.539
luxvrie *n.* lechery (G) 4.54, 106.157, 113.337
luxurious *adj.* lecherous 34.35, 36.141
luxuriously *adv.* lecherously 163.178

M

mache *n.* wick 36.262
+maculaciones *n. pl.* defilements 50.501 *note*
maddyng *pr. p.* going mad 112.695; **maddyd** *pa. p.* gone mad 95.80
made *v. pa.* ~ **hym** pretended to be 26.118

mageste *n.* magnificence (D) 178.453; 84.82 *note*
may *see* **mowe**
mayde *n.* virgin 5.89; **made** 87.25
mayne *see* **meyne**
maister *n.* principal 7.17, 16.8, 165.673; ruler 8.41; teacher 49.231, 148.28, 174.419; **maistres** *pl.* learned men 11.121, 165.632; high officials 13.58, 81.1; teachers 113.135, 165.7
maistrie *n.* pre-eminence 23.149
make *n.* mate 36.160
makinge *ger.* creation (D) 178.612
makithe weye *v. pr. 3 sg.* makes a path 138.54
male *n.* baggage 93.177
malecoly *n.* melancholy 34.33
malefice *n.* act of sorcery 45.424; **maleficis** *pl.* 3.79, 54.174
malicolyous *adj.* melancholic 34.38
+**malignancion** *n.* hatred (G) 43.67 *note*
malis *n. pl.* males 36.88
malisoune *n.* curse (D) 178.165
manas(s)e *v. inf.* threaten 24.29, 29.20; **manace** 128.150; **manasest** *pr. 2 sg.* 53.248; **manast** 2.169 *note*; **manassheth** *3 sg.* 20.134; **manace** *pr. subj.* 2.184; **manas(s)ed** *pa.* 7.20, 10.24, 11.7, 23.45, *45.444, **manaced** 90.86, 106.68; **manasing** *ger.* 23.48
maner(e *n.* nature 23.12; category 22.15, 23.146; custom 117.254; way (of doing something) 26.178, 28.146; **maners** ways (of doing something) 5.69, 12.92, 47.48; customs 10.16, 81.15; behaviour 11.59, 84.86, 113.168; **good maneres** moral principles 127.11
manere *n.* manor (G) 2.297; **maners** *pl.* houses 156.38
manhede *n.* humanity 12.19
mankinde *n.* human nature 12.102, 175.465
manly *adv.* boldly 61.75
manna *n.* miraculous food from heaven (Exod. 16) 1.227, 8.219, (D) 179.502
mansleer *n.* murderer 124.187, 133.217, 163.218; *pl.* 79.805
mantell *n.* cloak 23.31, 52.12; (*fig.*) status 22.5; **mantellis** *pl.* 8.52; **manteles** carpets 47.369; coverings 138.193
marber *n.* marble 26.180; **marbre** 44.154, 155.124, 163.320
marchaunt *n.* hireling 142.311 *note*
margarete *n.* pearl 87.16; **margarites** *pl.* 116.267
+**mariage** married couple (G) 4.40 *note*
marie *n.* bone marrow (G) 42.46
mary(e *v. inf.* arrange marriage for 66.24, 135.88; *refl.* ~ **hym** get married 23.124; **maried** *pa.* arranged marriage for 2.23
marked *v. pa. sg.* designated 16.17
martir *n.* martyrdom 23.146; **marteres** *pl.* 7.215
martirdomes *n. pl.* torments 125.111
mased *v. pa. p.* bewildered 95.100
masedly *adv.* confusedly *163.271
massage *n.* messenger 5.34, 47.157, 65.18, 79.181; message 80.172, 94.106; **message** messenger 80.191, 173.162; **messages** *pl.* messengers 146.201; **go in a** ~, **do a** ~ perform an errand 165.246, 258
massangeres *n. pl.* messengers 87.7; **messengeres** legates 174.756
mate *adj.* defeated 171.13
mater *n.* material 13.176, 65.206; **materes** *pl.* 84.464
+**mathesis** *n.* astrology 163.151 *note*
maugre *prep.* despite 16.76, 60.219, 70.35
maunde *n.* Last Supper (G) 1.125
meche *see* **moche**
mede *n.*[1] meadow 48.115
mede *n.*[2] reward 30.78, 53.183, 79.555, 112.580; payment 131.71, 154.86; *pl.* *30.73, 84.445
medicinables *adj. pl.* medicinal 116.245
+**medicine** *n.* physician 116.256, 133.235 *note*; remedy 175.237; **medicynes** *pl.* medication 142.294
medle *v. inf.* be concerned 25.36, 45.294, 159.29; mingle 79.865; *refl.* associated 74.23; involved 133.210; *imp.* mix 94.172; *pa.* **medled** 47.54, 54.124, *65.60; *pa. p.* 123.71; **medeled** *ppl. adj.* 20.113, 28.79, 44.189; **medlid** 60.144, 155.31
medue *n.* meadow 47.173, 162.261; **medwe** 156.203
meyne *n.* household, retinue 10.41, 25.205, 53.171, 55.51, 101.50; nation 149.255, 176.60; family (L) 179.333; **meyni** retinue 22.110, 28.58, 45.317, 49.253, 70.37, 147.26; **meny** 2.168; **meni** 161.67; **meiny** company 155.359;

mayne company 2.114, 48.124; **meyne** (G) 38.132; household 67.8; army 81.5
meke *v. inf.* make humble 5.274, 155.154, 171.86; **mekithe** *pr. 3 sg.* 134.164; **meked** *pa. p.* 50.296, 134.166
mele *n.* meal, ground grain 47.261
+**mellyngly** *adv.* in a mixed manner 113.139 *note*
meltithe *v. pr. 3 sg.* melts 148.87; **ymolte** *ppl. adj.* 147.5; **molte** 156.107; **moltin** 37.72; **multen** (G) 42.16; **moltyd** 142.31
membre *n.* part of the body 79.609; limb (fig.) 90.91; **membres** *pl.* *1.179, 7.178, 13.215; genitalia 33.33, 93.223, 140.49; **menbris** 173.409
memorie *n.* commemoration 155.62
mende *n. see* **mynde**
mene *v. pr.* say 25.213; mean 26.13; **menith** *pr. 3 sg.* 135.66; **ment** *pa.* said 53.13; spoke 88.48; ~ **by** said about 61.243
mene *n.* intermediary 2.274, (G) 43.168, 64.157, 80.192; mediator 112.632; intermediate state 156.61; **menis** *pl.* mediators 63.149; means of attaining an end 165.221
mene *adj.* middling 28.146
meneli *adv.* middlingly 156.319
meny *see* **meyne**
menisid *pa. p.* reduced 155.89
mercer *n.* merchant 174.147
mercerye *n.* goods 26.69
merciable *adj.* merciful (D) 178.612
meroure *n.* story (H2) 1.1
meruailithe *v. refl. pr. 3 sg.* wonders at 84.395; **meruailen** *pr. pl.* 23.17; **mervailed** *pa.* 94.12, 95.69; **meruailedin** *pl.* 95.82, 112.68
mervaylous *adj.* to be wondered at 5.94, 156.129
merveylable *adj.* admirable 12.84
+**meruouslie** marvellously (H2) 177.37 *note*
mesell *adj.* leprous 11.43
mesill *n.* leper 133.147; **mesell** 142.23
message *see* **massage**
messengeres *see* **massangeres**
messis *n. pl.* dishes 161.104
mesure *n.* **ouer** ~ excessively 6.30, 20.67; **without** ~ 25.132; **aboue** ~ 165.295
mete *adj.* suitable 61.23
mete *n.*[1] food 1.141, 2.75, (G) 4.153; **meete** (H2) 176.253; **mete** bait 50.321; **metes** *pl.* foodstuffs 20.95, 27.84, 90.241, 161.107; provisions 25.35
metes *n.*[2] *pl.* limits 117.278 *note*
meteles *adj.* without food 71.23
mette *v. pa. p.* joined (G) 44.45
meu(e)able *adj.* changeable 11.241; mobile 65.138
meue *v. pr.* waver *79.437; speak 165.211; **meued** *pa.* stirred up, incited 8.101, 23.81; stirred (emotionally) 27.42; changed 8.236, 27.18, 36.226; stirred (physically) 50.487; *pa. p.* stirred (emotionally) 2.96, 44.55, 45.335; changed 35.18; **meving** *ger.* motion 29.175; motivation 117.282; **mevyngges** *pl.* impulses 20.94, 33.70, 36.248
miche *see* **moche**
midday *n.* south 138.191, 155.164, 174.219, 175.194
myde *v. pa.* probed (?) 5.78 *note*
myȝt *n.* power (G) 4.89; **myght** 23.22, 24.35; **myghtes** *pl.* 28.16, 34.26; the sixth order of angels (*potestates*) 112.315
myghtly *adv.* strongly 28.172
+**militacion** *n.* military service (G) 43.66 *note*
mylnstone *n.* millstone 24.101; **melstone** 156.119
milwarde *n.* miller 140.34
mynde *n.* memory *26.53, 31.23, 99.125, 124.132; remembrance 32.34, 45.472, 65.116, 87.95, 90.272[1,2], 156.1, 164.17, 175.13; mind 32.39; memorial 138.2, 68; **mende** *n.* memory (G) 4.120, (G) 55.6
ministre *n.* servant 95.22, 110.66, 142.421; **mynistres** *pl.* 59.6; **mynystris** officers (G) 3.96, 24.64, 125.85; servants 79.366
ministring *ger.* supplying *26.250
mynstre *n.* church 165.354
myre *n.* mud *124.222, 161.188, 164.50; **myrre** 162.220
misauenture *n.* misfortune 2.136
mysbeleue *n.* false belief 8.129, 22.94, 45.400; lack of faith 64.26, 163.296
mysbileued *ppl. adj.* unbelieving 7.151, 99.15, 112.262, 127.18
mysbileuers *n. pl.* pagans (G) 3.88, 13.147, 22.89, 23.90

mische(e)f *n.* misfortune 2.27, 161.279; **mischiefs** *pl.* 50.518
mysdo *v. inf.* harm 48.125, 150.49; **misdede** *pa.* 84.15, 101.63; **mysdone** *pa. p.* done wrong 34.58
misdoer *n.* wrongdoer 168.21
mise *n. pl.* mice 173.221; **myes** 173.232
misericorde *n.* mercy 44.162
misgouernaunce *n.* sinful behaviour 2.16; **mysgouernaunce** 5.258
misgouerned *ppl. adj.* wicked 174.18
misknewe *v. pa.* was ignorant of 61.154
mislyked *v. impers. pa.* displeased 120.38
missay(e *v. inf.* speak ill (of) 53.226, 58.220, 117.235, (H1) 156.417; **missaied** *pa.* 142.456; **missayd(e** *pa. p.* 53.228, 148.137
mistake *v. pa. p.* wronged 142.392, 160.40
misterye *n.*[1] office 44.124; ministry 49.12, 90.286, 123.70
misterie *n.*[2] mystery 49.40
mo *comp. adj.* greater or additional number 2.149, 58.206, 66.22; larger 16.17; **moo** (G) 3.82
mo *n.* greater number 22.90, 44.191, 45.469; **moo** (G) 38.130, (G) 43.121, 55.43
moche *adj.* large 83.385
moch(e *adv.* much 1.158; **mich(e** 1.202; **meche** 128.187
moist *v. inf.* moisten 175.468
moyster *n.* moisture, bodily fluid 24.61; **moistour** 34.39
moltyd *see* **meltithe**
monestid *v. pa. refl.* exhorted 117.78; **monisshed** *pa. p.* 79.495; **monestynge** *ger.* persuasion 174.562
monicion(e)s *n. pl.* admonitions 79.464
monisshed *see* **monestid**
mooste *adj.* moist (D) 178.71
morcel *n.* fragment (G) 1.125; **mossel** morsel 11.14; **morsell** 58.221; **mussell** 58.224
more *n.* marshland 142.327
more *comp. adj.* bigger 9.80, 64.45
morialli *adv.* 149.65 *note*, 230
morsell *see* **morcel**
mortays *n.* mortise 61.46
morted *see* **morutide**
mortefied *pa.* subdued by abstinence 84.290; *ppl. adj.* made as though dead 34.20
mortherer *n.* murderer 142.234
morutide *n.* next morning 26.105; dawn 45.494; **morwtyde** morning 29.97, 54.215, 84.177; dawn 123.154; **morted** *n. as adj.* morning 112.48 *note*
mor(o)w *n.* next morning, next day 1.154, 2.21, 7.155, 11.9; **moru** 120.48
mossel *see* **morcel**
most(e *superl. adj.* greatest 17.38, 29.108; **moost** (H1) 143.55; uppermost 50.203
moste *v. see* **mot**
mot *v. pr.* may 112.536, 161.389, 172.39; **most(e** *pr.* must 1.239, 2.53, 11.32
motes *n. pl.* specks of dust 138.129
moton *n.* mutton 29.30; sheep 83.103
mouyng *pr. p.* motivating 49.138
mowed *v. pa.* grimaced 44.199; **mowing** *ppl. adj.* 113.328
mow(e *v. inf.* be able 24.35, 29.196, 50.95; **may(e** *pr. sg.* may, can (G) 1.113, 2.103, 4.201; **maist** *2 sg.* 2.169, 17.8; **mow(e(n** *pr. pl.* (G) 3.23, 7.13, 8.59; **myght** *pa.* 1.195, 2.12, 5.48; **movinge** *pr. p.* being able to 79.818 *note*
mulerye *adj.* legitimate 50.363
multen *see* **meltithe**
+multiplyingli *adv.* in many ways 5.65 *note*, 155.196; **multipliengly** 155.303
mured *v. pa.* imprisoned 60.339
murmure *v. inf.* complain 7.3; **murmerin** *pr. pl.* 152.17; **murmure** *imp.* mumble 24.12
mussell *see* **morcel**

N

namely especially 45.207, (G) 46.5, 58.392; **namelie** (H2) 176.230
nayles *n. pl.* claws 20.19; spits or skewers 153.13
nard(e *n.* spikenard 128.22; **nardum** (D) 178.584
nas *v. pa. neg.* was not 58.92, 125.17
nauill *n.* navel 12.112
neded *v. impers. pa.* was necessary 11.206, 58.438, 110.78
nedes *adv.* necessarily 11.288, 48.105, 68.12; **nedis** 2.53, 90.141, 165.1684
neygh(e *v. inf.* approach 33.39, 44.200, 53.103, 79.201; **neghe** 53.102; **neyȝ** (D) 178.499; **neigheth** *pr. 3 sg.* *142.376; **neighed** *pa.* approached

2.101, 5.42, 11.375; **neghed** (H1) 144.46
nemene *v. inf.* pronounce 22.122; **nempne** 145.51
ner *v. pr. subj. neg.* were it not 76.30, 161.116
ner *conj.* nor 149.107, 233, 152.104
nerehond *adv.* in the vicinity 54.12
ner(r)e *comp. adv.* nearer (G) 45.558, 49.262, 79.810
nete *n.* cattle 84.290, 138.10; **neete** (L) 179.362
nether *adj.* lower 165.766; ~ **cloth** under garment (G) 45.558; ~ **clothis** *pl.* 10.13
newynge *ger.* renewal 107.29
ny(e *adj.* near 8.227, 13.66, 26.65; **nyȝ** (G) 1.72; **nigh(e** 13.28, 47.286, 49.173; **nyȝe occasiouns** immediate temptations (D) 179.29–30
nye *adv.* almost 45.29, 47.102, 48.100; **nigh** 15.3, 29.126; **nigh honde** almost 174.53; **wel ney** very nearly 45.25
nyest *superl. adj.* nearest 35.9
nigh(e *see* **nye**
nygromancye *n.* witchcraft 58.327 *note*
nis *v. pr. 3 sg. neg.* is not 11.137, 79.593, 133.220; **nys** 12.11, 23.140, 48.97
nobilnesse *n.* majesty 1.178; nobility of status 23.12, 50.83, 165.110; **nobelnesse** 79.195
nobles(se *n.* nobility 38.34, 50.74, 53.380, 129.19; noble status (G) 44.32
noye *n.* weariness 90.313
noy(e *v. inf.* offend 49.280, 93.54; harm 79.201, 116.90, 123.300, 138.145, 152.40; **noye** *pr.* 94.16; **noiethe** *pr. 3 sg.* 120.12, 159.274; **noyed** *pa.* offended *47.53; harmed 59.15; **noying(e** *ppl. adj.* harmful 34.6, *104.34
noyfull *adj.* annoying 45.388
noyous *adj.* distressing 142.415
noyse *n.* disturbance 163.304
none *n.* ninth hour (about 3 p.m.) 61.222, 88.7, (H1) 146.61
nonri *n.* nunnery 144.23
norice *n.* nurse (G) 3.29, (G) 47.3, 75.55; **norise** 47.9, 87.2; **norse** 9.83; **norice** foster-mother 86.140
noris(s)(h)(e *v. inf.* look after 23.134, 83.348; **norishest** *pr. 2 sg.* feed 29.193; **norissithe** *3 sg.* cherishes 65.108; **norisched** *pa. sg.* brought up 9.100; **norisshed** 113.5, 126.6; suckled 88.106, 113.8; **norshed** nourished 8.20; *pa. p.* brought up 79.423, 84.405, 154.197, 161.301, 174.329; fed 83.347; educated 163.142; **norsched** *ppl. adj.* brought up 1.247; **norsching** *ger.* supporting 1.205 *note*; nourishment 23.9; **norisching** *pr. p.* looking after 28.75
nor(i)sher *n.* supporter 25.35; feeder 64.14; foster-parent 83.397
not *adv.* not at all 17.30, 173.242
not *n.* nothing 20.60, 24.40, 28.153
notarie *n.* secretary 53.189, 61.302
note *v. pr.* do not know (*for* **ne wote**) 79.383, 94.53, 95.78, 154.190, (D) 178.159
nother *conj.* neither 5.220, 11.14, 29.207; nor 14.15
noumbrarie *n.* numeration (H2) 1.7
nouthe *adv.* now 119.47
nouelte *n.* new thing 49.164; strange occurrence 79.181, 494; new beginning 106.26; newness 155.223
nwe *adj.* new 5.97, 9.24, 11.96
nwe *adv.* recently 22.159; **nwly** 79.382

O

o *num.* one 12.33, 26.229, 45.290, 124.130, 155.241; **O** 50.91; **oo** 11.30, 25.55, 34.59, *84.486; **on** 20.47, 79.297, 113.81, 124.54, 152.95; *see also* **an**
obeyed *v.*[1] *refl. pa.* ~ **hem** submitted themselves 79.801
obeye *v.*[2] *inf.* bark 53.345 *note*; *see also* **abaied**
obeysinge *ger.* obeying 105.191 *note*
obiecciones *n. pl.* accusations *44.169; objections 106.30; **abieccion** accusation 45.508; *pl.* accusations 45.507 *note*
obiecte *n.* objection 112.494
oblacion *n.* offering 49.194, 156.281, 175.42 *note*; *pl.* 36.74, 47.295
obliged *v. pa.* committed 94.30; *pa. p.* bound up 115.13 *note*
occasion *n.* cause 45.126, 90.362; occurrence 101.11; opportunity 161.17; **occasiones** *pl.* causes 149.218; **nyȝe occasiouns** immediate temptations (D) 179.29–30; **bi any occasyen** 22.88 *note*
ocupied hym *v. refl. pa.* concerned

himself 79.461; **ocupied** *ppl. adj.* busy 29.52

+odoramenta *adj.* sweet-smelling *178.584 *note*

oeptas *see* **vtas**

offys *n.* function 13.172; **office** 13.175, 49.205, 74.36, 106.167; church service 113.29; liturgy 139.151; Offis 139.158; office for the dead 99.106; **offices** *pl.* functions 50.17; domestic departments 5.239

ofter *comp. adv.* more often 120.37

oynement *n.* anointing 12.23; ointment 44.85

oynt *ppl. adj.* anointed 12.39

oynter *n.* act of anointing 12.38

olyfaunt *n.* elephant 163.62

omely(e *n.* sermon 81.110, 85.20, 129.33

onys *adv.* once (G) 1.308, 68.20; **ones** 65.255

on *see* **o**

onli *adv.* only, alone 11.245, 36.178; **oonli** 20.150, 54.74

oo *see* **o**

oost *see* oste *n.*[3]

open *adj.* uncovered 50.168

open(e *v. inf.* reveal 49.177, 107.35, 112.261; **openithe** *imp.* open 125.77; **opened** *pa.* revealed 151.51; **openid** *pa. p.* 149.280; **iopened** (H2) 178.299

opposed *v. pa.* (?) 161.113 *note*; ~ **ayens** argued against 174.750 *note*

or *prep.* before (G) 3.21, (G) 4.30, 45.77, (G) 60.150, 69.27

or *conj.* either 37.103; **or . . . or** either . . . or 152.189

ordeine *v. inf.* invest with holy orders 7.13; **ordeyne** command 9.36; provide 83.405; **ordeyne** *pr. 1 sg.* command 24.15; **ordeynest** *2 sg.* are preparing 47.20; **ordeyne** *imp.* give orders 2.167; **ordeyned** *pa.* prepared 2.97; commissioned 2.232; provided 11.24, 23.86, 27.37; invested with holy orders 15.38; established 11.25, 45.440, 53.81, 63.8; commanded 45.211, 95.57, 174.444; appointed 47.275; composed 113.422 *note*; *pa. p.* 7.205, 13.117, 31.3; provided for 112.749; required 26.182; provided 22.22; disposed 149.8; **ordeynyd** appointed (G) 4.58; **ordeined** prepared 79.885; **ordeyned** 11.46; well disposed 74.31; appointed 13.117; **ordeynyd** appointed (G) 4.102

ordinat *adj.* well-ordered 65.344, 74.6, 149.98

ordinatly *adv.* correctly 49.47; in an orderly way 154.204, 161.331, 175.256; regularly 174.217

ordinaunce n. ruling 2.54, (G) 46.9; establishment (G) 43.3; arrangement 50.314, series 123.5; **ordenaunce** decree 11.53, 54.22, 129.43; guidance 90.189, arrangement 64.49; control 96.49, 106.102; category (H2) 176.249; decrees *pl.* **ordynauncis** (G) 3.35; **ordenaunces** dispositions 149.10; **ordenauncis** equipment (H2) 177.106

ordyner *n.* ruler 27.36

ordre *n.* religious order 82.16; rank 117.339; **bi** ~, in sequence 2.110, 11.90, 93.242; control 96.50; **ordres** *pl.* ordinations 175.175; categories (H2) 176.250

orgones *n. pl.* tools (*fig.*) 155.147

oriso(u)n *n.* prayer 1.198, 7.14, 12.93; *pl.* **orisonis** 1.318

orphanyn *n.* orphan 84.237, 163.49; **orphelyn** 173.474, 174.190; **orphenyne** 69.1; **orphanies** *pl.* 84.240; **orphanins** 112.607; **orphanions** 112.825; **orphelyens** 106.223; **orphelyns** 11.23, 174.558; **orphelions** 84.227; **orphenyns** 88.6

ostage *n.* **in** ~ as hostage 50.371

oste *n.*[1] guest 79.224, 99.9; host 79.196, 93.176, 99.104, 113.314; **hoste** 161.183

oste *n.*[2] army 29.212, 61.65, 63.88; **hoste** 29.212, 81.21, 138.96

oste *n.*[3] bread for eucharist 175.37, 174.709; **oost** 45.396

ostesse *n.* hostess 90.34, 99.1, 106.278

ostiler *n.* inn-keeper 61.151; **hostiler** 61.149; **osteler** inn-keeper's servant 93.177 *note*

ostrie *n.* small inn 86.65, 154.181

other either 174.74; **other . . . other** either . . . . or 152.42–3

ought *see* **aught**

ought *v. see* **owe**

ouneth *v. pr.* unifies 65.336 *note*

oure *n.* hour 5.202, 64.61, 78.63; **Oures** *pl.* office of Little Hours 123.340

oure *possessive. pron.* ours 5.273

ourned *v. pa. p.* adorned 65.382

ournement *n.* ornament 65.380
+outedrawer *n.* one who leads out 176.54 *note*
outetake *prep.* except 165.273; **outake** 165.497; **owtake** (L) 179.425
outrage *adj.* excessive 28.111
outrage *n.* wrongdoing 66.125, 124.145
+outragiousnes *n.* unruliness (L) 179.331 *note*
ouer *adj.* upper 142.149, 165.765
ouer *adv., prep.* in addition 20.79, 23.29
ouer *prep.* throughout 8.100; in addition to 79.497, 83.116; beyond 163.187
ouer alle everywhere 177.115,152
ouercharged *ppl. adj.* weighed down 148.90
ouercome *v. pa.* convinced 108.64; convicted 174.687 *note*
ouerdrawe *v. imp.* pull over 24.127
ouergilte *adj.* gilded 142.148, 155.37
ouerleyd *v. pa. p.* covered 156.210
ouerlyue *v. inf.* outlive 161.62; **ouerlyued** *pa.* 112.15; **ouerleued** *pa. p.* continued to live 112.256
ouerpasse *v. inf.* disregard 79.394; **ouerpassed** went beyond 66.228; *pa. p.* worked through 127.20; omitted 155.61; exceeded 143.16
ouerplus *n.* surplus 88.28
ouerpressed *ppl. adj.* weighed down 150.51
+ouerride *v. inf.* ride over 140.31 *note*
ouertake *v. pa. p.* captivated 102.4
ouerthrawe *v. pa. p.* destroyed 79.142, 152.86
ouerthwart *adj.* crossways 61.46; across 159.158; **ouertwarte** 171.84
owe *v. pr. 1 sg.* owe 175.297; **ought (to)** should *pr. 1, 3 sg.* 64.91, 66.2, 83.247; **oght** 123.255; **aught** 8.216, 18.43, 32.4; **aughttest** *2 sg.* 112.146; **owith** *3 sg.* (D) 178.431; **owe** *pr. pl.* owe 115.10, 134.79; **owen (to)** should 49.19, 156.387, 175.420; possess 125.37; **aughten (to)** should 31.7; **ought** *pa.* 112.726, (D) 179.215
owher elsewhere 148.57

P

paces *see* **pase**
pacient *n.* one who undergoes an experience 27.15
paes *see* **pase**
paied *ppl. adj.* satisfied 161.99
payne *see* **peyne**
paynim(e *n.* pagan, non-Christian 4.225, 6.2; **panyme** 17.43; **panymes** *pl.* 2.94; **payneims** 115.25; **paynemes** 166.4; **peinymes** 79.373
paynym(e *adj.* pagan, non-Christian 15.23; **painime** 87.2
+pais *n. pl.* coins of specific weight and great value 22.97 *note*
pal(l)asie *n.* paralysis 10.131, 93.67, 163.39; **palsy** 96.98; **palsei** 128.102; **palesey** 130.10; **pallesie** 147.32
palme *n.* palm branch (G) 4.42, 112.25, 165.848; **palmes** *pl.* palm leaves 14.55
palmer *n.* palm tree 57.18, 128.13; *pl.* 14.30
pament *see* **pauement**
panier *n.* basket 86.97, 110.219; **panyers** *pl.* 105.48
paper *n.* document 11.24
paraffe *n.* paragraph (D) 179.124
paraile *see* **pareille**
parchemyn *n.* parchment 25.178, 88.71, 142.372
pare *v. inf.* peel 9.121, 29.195; **pared** *pa.* 9.133
pareil(l)(e *adj.* equal 65.26, 112.975; **paraile** 84.295
parfit *see* **perfite**
parfourme *v. inf.* act upon (D) 179.22
part *n.* fate 1.159
part(e *v. inf.* divide 14.44; share 113.265; depart 14.37; **partest** *pr. 2 sg.* depart 54.39; separate 83.222; **partith** *3 sg.* (G) 1.106; **parte** *imp. sg.* depart 20.74; **partithe** *imp. pl.* separate 124.203; **parted** *pa.* distributed 54.97; departed 2.11, 16.72, 18.23, 20.69; *pa. p.* departed 8.219, (G) 45.536; divided 8.103 *note*, 16.77; shared 29.115; **parting** *ger.* distributing 26.250
parteriche *n.* partridge 8.169
+participans *n. pl.* followers 12.39 *note*
part(i)e *n.* part 2.113, 61.256; direction 155.40; side 25.42; division 14.46, 113.105; faction 25.74, 134.15; **party** part 28.197, 65.219, 90.6; **partyes** *pl.* parts 23.90, fragments 8.44, regions 4.235, 5.32, 134.13; sides (of battle) 152.86
partinere *n.* participant 7.110

pas(e *n.* pace 58.424; footprint *43.120, 138.188; **a gret** ~ quickly 23.151, 66.210, 159.204; **pas** *pl.* units of linear measurement (about 5 feet) 61.218; **paes** paces 110.259; **paces** 119.62
paschall *adj.* relating to Passover 175.320
Paske *n.* Passover 34.22; **Pasch** 50.107
passe *v. inf.* go past 48.49; convey 94.57; **passithe** *pr. 3 sg.* disobeys 50.120; leaves out 128.200; **passin** *pr. pl.* neglect 149.193; **passinge** *pr. p.* disobeying 50.292; **passed** *pa.* transcended 45.24, exceeded 9.79, 117.278, 174.479; died 101.127; disobeyed 175.106, **passid** (D) 178.631; *pa. p.* disobeyed 36.102; **passed** dead 113.435; **passed** conveyed 9.55; *ppl. adj.* dead 49.241; **passinge** *ppl. adj.* exceptional 165.594; *ger.* death 99.78, 146.131; disobeying 50.292
+**passer** *n.* transgressor 137.67 *note*
passio(u)n(e *n.* suffering (H2) 1.2, 22.50, 23.2; pain 18.36; sickness 174.173; **passiones** *pl.* sufferings 35.80, 57.8, 79.698, 116.245, 173.109
pastes *n. pl.* meals (H1) 144.27
pastoure *n.* nourishment 84.501; **pasture** 122.58
patene *n.* dish for bread at Eucharist 113.358
+**patricyen** *n.* high official 26.155 *note*; **patrice** 26.161; **patricien** *45.116, 91.24, 174.322
paued *error* 37.6 *note*
pauement *n.* paved or tiled floor 18.51, 47.332, 175.272; **pament** 10.80, 69.28, 83.104
pawme *n.* hand-span(?) 174.473 *note*; **paumes** *pl.* palms of hands *85.15 *note*; 131.21
peces *n. pl.* fragments 24.72; **peses** 26.179; **armed at all** ~ fully armed 174.476
pecunie *n.* money 156.234
peerce, peersed *see* **perse**
pees *n.* peace 18.26; **pes** 35.34; **pees** silence 152.192; pax at mass 18.51; **holde p**~ be silent 133.9; **helde** ~ 11.210, 95.91, 161.218; **in** ~ silent 133.80
peyne *n.* pain 24.7; punishment 7.177, 8.83, 11.158, 30.71, 45.25, 65.218, 116.185; difficulty 94.79; **payne** pain 87.88, punishment 156.28; difficulty 88.140; **peynes** *pl.* punishments 27.73, 156.28; torments 87.88, 95.6; **peynys** (G) 3.71; **paynes** 37.46; **upon the** ~ **of** on penalty of 10.76; **in paine of** 29.46
peyne *v. inf.* hurt 79.609
peinymes *see* **paynim(e**
peyntyng *v. pr. p.* applying cosmetics (H1) 143.24; **peinted** *pa. p.* 28.104; portrayed in paint 23.127, 78.53; **peinted** colourful 45.181
peinture *n.* painting 4.205, 69.16
peyse *n.* weight 125.131
peise *v. inf.* weigh 140.56; **peysed** *pa.* *110.274
pelotes *n. pl.* 110.150 *note*
pencion *n.* tax 26.175
penitensere *n.* confessor 1.241
peny *n.* money 8.69, 30.78, 65.175; **pens** *pl.* coins 156.231; *33.18 *note*
penne *n.* wing 149.21; **pennes** *pl.* 64.271; **pennys** 63.80, 142.346
pensef *adj.* anxious 113.388, 173.114
peple *n.* family 28.57; household 161.117; **pople** inhabitants 99.17; **puple** mankind (H2) 176.192
perced *see* **perse**
perche *n.* rod 60.117; pole 94.63
perdicion *n.* damnation 27.60; **perdision** 156.234
perdurable *adj.* everlasting 65.171, 96.114, 133.110, 149.268
perdurabilite *n.* everlastingness 64.257, 65.316, 155.28; **perdurablete** 128.19
+**perduringe** *ppl. adj.* persistent 60.63 *note*, 152.156
perfides *n.* 9.47 *note*
perfit(e *adj.* perfect 8.40, 30.64, 32.33; complete (H1) 146.62; **parfit** perfect 11.237; **made perfit** fully formed 36.22; **perfite age** adulthood 87.3, 88.13, 123.147; **parfite age** (H2) 177.81
perfitely *adv.* perfectly 12.26, 30.35; completely 26.185
perfo(u)rme *v. inf.* complete 37.94, 83.193, 90.336; **perfo(u)rmed** *pa.* 58.405, 112.154
perisshe *v. inf.* die 90.123; **perishe** kill 22.27; **perische** *pr.* die 29.124; **perisshed** *pa.* destroyed (H1) 145.25; died 168.67 *note*; **pershid** 2.79;

pershed 16.44; **perissed** was rotting spiritually 113.180 *note*; **perished** *pa. p.* wasted 24.7; killed *79.842, 163.28; **perisshed** *ppl. adj.* killed 79.625, 90.356; **pershinge** *ger.* death 84.457; *see also* **perse**
perpetuel *adj.* immortal 83.43
perschid *see* **perse**
perse *v. inf.* pierce 113.84; **peerce** enter 47.349; **perced** *pa. sg.* penetrated 4.235, **peersed** 36.244; **persid** 116.199; **perschid** pierced (G) 46.2, (G) 55.80; **perisshed** 112.915; **persid** *pa. p.* 4.236 pierced; **persed** 22.131, 48.5, 50.316; **pershed** 50.163; **perced** *ppl. adj.* 14.10; **persed** 171.81; **persinge** *pr. p.* penetrating 64.266
perseueraunt *adj.* constant 60.57, 65.404, 112.898
perseuerauntly *adv.* with constancy 61.57, 74.19
perseuerithe *v. pr. 3 sg.* endures 65.450
persh~ *see* **perisshe, perse**
perteynen *v.* belong 87.15; **perteynyd** *pa.* (G) 44.37
pes *see* **pees**
pesed *v. pa.* placated 174.175
peses *see* **peces**
pesibilte *n.* tranquillity 139.59
pesible *adj.* peaceful 1.187, 28.208, 64.64
pesibly *adv.* tranquilly 16.47, 47.59, *88.15
pestilence *n.* plague 22.175, 138.66; wickedness 134.123
phisik *n.* medical science 136.3, 138.89, 149.1
piche *v. imp.* thrust 94.87; **pight** *pa.* threw 84.189
picois *n.* mattock 11.112, 163.334
pight *see* **piche**
pigones *n. pl.* young doves or pigeons 36.137
pilyon *n.* felt cap 79.20
pinche *n.* sharp instrument 18.2 *note*
pyne appell tree *n.* pine tree 101.7
piscin(e *n.* pool 11.79, 61.35
pistel(l *n.* letter 4.226, 53.244; **pistle** 123.152, 139.195; **pistille** 177.97; **apistell** 32.34; reading from epistles during mass 45.116; **pistel(l** 30.73, 32.32; *pl.* **pistoles** 175.45; **episteles** 139.157; **pistel(l)es** letters 74.52, 84.141, 104.196; **apisteles** 35.121
pitee *n.* piety 111.85, 159.398, 160.20, 163.148; compassion 2.18, 11.53, 24.47; **pete** (D) 179.286
pit(e)ous *adj.* sorrowful 2.267, 6.11, 37.26; merciful 27.28, 88.4, *95.48; **piteuous** (G) 42.42
pit(e)ously *adv.* pitiably 29.123, 93.189, 121.30; mercifully 64.174, 90.363
pit(te *n.* grave (G) 1.70, 14.53, 52.106, 93.229; cave 14.3, 37.3, 80.243; lair 11.350, (G) 40.4; hole in ground 8.212, 47.12, 48.45, 53.93; well 155.82
place *n.* public square 58.312, 88.136 *note*, 124.224; house 132.28; monastic house 133.140; **places** *pl.* public streets 166.64 *note*; **gaue** ~ yielded 101.17
plaie *n.* game 151.56; **pleie** 161.23; **play** 173.16; **playes** *pl.* 75.17, 110.25, 161.10; **pleies** 151.53
plaine *see* **pleine** *v.*
planed *v. pa.* stroked 142.264 *note*
platte *adj.* flat 63.126
pleg(g)e *n.* surety 2.213, 45.513, 50.331; **pleges** *pl.* 125.85
pleine *adj.*[1] complete 30.56, 117.424; full 142.379
pleine *adj.*[2] level 64.105
plein(e *v. inf.* complain 6.26; **pleyne** 9.21, lament 65.96, 66.123; **plaine** (H2) 176.236; grieve for 87.37; **pleyned** *pa.* complained 26.122, 50.506, 93.237; **playninge** *ger.* complaining 96.113
pleinly *adv.* fully 20.96, 28.195, 49.27; clearly 23.53, 79.536, 131.48
pleintes *n. pl.* laments 65.99
plenier *adj.* complete 28.48
plente(e *n.* abundance 20.95, 36.123, 49.52; entirety 112.864; fulness 176.39
plentevous *adj.* fertile 28.82, 58.208, 155.311; copious 58.210, 134.4
plenteuously *adv.* copiously 64.262, 79.309, 87.34
plenteuosnesse *n.* fecundity 49.71
plesaunce *n.* pleasure 59.27, 80.179, 135.27
+**ply** *v. imp.* close (books) 84.244; **plied** *pa.* folded 84.154 *note*
pliaunt *adj.* flexible (D) 178.141
plight *n.* situation 35.70, 173.273; **plite** 75.5, 142.163, 145.57
plites *n. pl.* pleats 11.153
plometis *n. pl.* pieces of lead at end of

whip 70.18; **plommes** 71.28; **plummes** 130.6
poeste *see* **pouste**
+**pointerie** *n.* pricking *45.411 *note*
pointes *n. pl.* spots on dice 142.459; **poyntis** (H2) 176.395 *note*
pointles *n. pl.* styluses 18.7
pollicion *n.* impurity (G) 4.55
pople *see* **peple**
porpre *see* **purpure**
port *n.* gate 59.36
porter(e *n.* door-keeper (G) 4.82, 150.33; **portour** 2.150
possede *v. inf.* possess 106.226, 161.307; **possedithe** *pr. 3 sg.* 37.87, 84.469; **possedid** *pa.* 99.4, 125.33; **posseded** 84.284, 117.295; *ppl. adj.* ~ **withe** owner of 112.345; *pr. pl.* **possedinge** 112.947
postil *n.* apostle (H2) 1.78
postume *n.* swelling 142.474
potage *n.* meals 25.37 *note*; vegetables 45.40, 101.26; **potages** *pl.* 117.229
potagre *n.* gout 45.379
pou(u)der *n.* dust 12.22, 22.20, 45.127, 92.76; **pouudre** 96.72
poudry *adj.* dusty 79.636
pouer(e *n.* authority 1.241, 23.74; **power(e** ability 2.10, 29.121; a military force 60.196
pounce *n.* pulse 25.203 *note*
pourchasours *n. pl.* contrivers 152.109 *note*
pourpre *see* **purpure**
pouste *n.* dominion 13.218, (H2) 176.390; **poeste** authority *91.78
pouert *n.* need 110.209, 112.394
praie *n.* prey 60.314 *note*, booty 63.116, 64.124, 134.96
praihers *n. pl.* prayers 58.413; **preiours** 123.265
praisable *adj* praiseworthy 79.735
prece *see* **pres**
preciouste *n.* value 84.465, 117.225, 128.11; **preciosite** 155.105
+**precognicion** *n.* foreknowledge 64.162 *note*
predicacion *n.* preaching (G) 4.68, 7.15, 12.59; **predicasion** 4.236
prees *see* **pres**
prefe *n. see* **profe**
preisable *adj.* praiseworthy 160.52
preisers *n. pl.* worshippers 28.11
preiudice *n.* unfair judgment 25.165
prerogatyf(f *n.* pre-eminence 36.250, 60.29, 112.946, 116.194
pres *n.* crowd 79.563; **prees** 58.180, 108.27; **prece** *165.566
prescience *n.* 155.137 *note*
presentli *adv.* in person 152.26
pressure *n.* press (for wine, oil, *etc.*) 64.167
presumed *v. pa.* ventured 79.567
presumpcion *n.* impertinence 124.238, 165.639
presumptuouse *adj.* audacious 79.776
pretendist *v. pr. 2 sg.* profess (G) 1.98
preuaricacion *n.* transgression 49.6
preue *v. inf.* prove 11.318, 104.73, 134.140; try out 47.205; discover 79.781, 90.117; approve (H2) 176.267; **proue** experience 1.130, test 1.298, 35.114, 106.37, 121.42; prove 11.179, 29.149; find out 47.183; **preue** *pr.* prove 2.111; **preuithe** *pr. 3 sg.* 79.416, 112.281; **prouithe** demonstrates 11.65, 112.287; **proue** *imp.* demonstrate 2.63; **preue** test 110.68; **preued** *pa. p.* demonstrated (D) 178.559; *pa. p.* approved 106.118; discovered 110.68; tested 164.21; **proued** tested 5.80, 137.35, 173.311; **proued** *ppl. adj.* proved 8.117, 10.90, 11.129; **prouide** proved 87.16
preu(e)y *n.* privy 22.152 *note*, 71.26; **priuey** 111.45
preueli *adv.* secretly 1.253; **preuili** 7.154; **priuely** 9.19, 13.134, 22.94; **priuily** 2.20, 26.151
preuy *adj.* private 1.242, 165.301; **preue** secluded 136.84; **pryve** intimate (H1) 156.417; **priue** *adj.* 50.417; tame 131.84; secret 45.108, 88.15, 107.34; personal 47.336
preuis *see* **profe**
price *see* **prise**
pricke *n.* spur 27.17; **prik** sting 64.357; *pl.* spikes 48.78
prikkinge *ger.* piercing (L) 179.451
+**prince** *n.* chief 7.50, 8.140, 27.31; governor (G) 41.22; **prinse** chief 165.707; **princes** *pl.* principalities, the seventh order of angels 112.315 *note*
principalite *n.* primacy 83.465
printed *v. pa.* imprinted 142.209
pris(e *n.* price 8.42, 65.39, 106.15; value

17.49, 117.228, 173.175; victory 123.239; **price** value 8.47; pre-eminence 79.76
priue *adj. see* **preuy**
priue *n.* courtier 132.27
priuely *adv. see* **preueli**
priuey *see* **preuey**
priuyd *ppl. adj.* excluded (G) 44.26 *note*
priuetees *n. pl.* secrets 49.114, (D) 178.447
probacion *n.* testing 61.35 *note*
proceded *pa. sg.* advanced 16.2
proctour *n.* finance manager 44.83; **procutour** 45.38
procuracion *n.* procurement 53.77, 123.370, 155.97
procuresse *n.* female provider 90.35
procutour *see* **proctour**
profe *n.* proof 5.74, **prefe** (H1) 156.406; **proef** 104.70; **preuis** *pl.* proofs 123.32; **preues** 165.668
profession *n.* declaration 5.20; affirmation of faith 25.92, (H2) 176.327
profitable *adj.* beneficial 2.59, 124.65; effective 174.301
prolongned *ppl. adj.* delayed (H2) 176.385
promission *n.* **londe of** ~ promised land 50.270
promte *adj.* liable, disposed 33.43
pronounce *v. inf.* recite 117.93; *pa.* announced 149.269, 167.60
+**pronouncer** *n.* propounder 117.139 *note*
pronounsynge *ger.* announcing 47.291
properte *n.* characteristic feature 28.188; **propirte** (D) 178.74
prophecie *n.* the prophetic books of the Old Testament 159.362
prophete *n.* prophesy 174.45 *note*
propre *adj.* (its, one's, etc.) own 5.22, 13.161, 17.63; **propur** (G) 1.22; **propre** goodly 45.252
+**prouable** *adj.* probable 61.183 *note*, 112.14; capable of proof 165.678
proue *see* **preue**
prouoked *ppl. adj.* encouraged 79.789
prouost *n. indiscriminately used for prefects, proconsuls, and other high officials*; *also*: head of a monastery 127.48, 144.35
+**prouoste** *n.* area under jurisdiction of provost 127.4, *164.48; office of provost 104.67 *note*; **prouostie** 127.110; **prouost** duration of term as provost 159.25 *note*
+**prunelles** *n. pl.* pupils of the eye 84.222 *note*
publican *n.* tax collector 33.37, 133.187
publyshed *v. pa.* made known 52.113; **publisshed** 58.259, 84.36, 93.152, 113.63; **puplisshid** *pa. p.* 38.138; diffused 174.440
puissaunce *n.* power 175.299
puple *see* **peple**
+**purchasours** *n. pl.* contrivers 152.109 *note*
purpoos *v. inf.* propose 1.288; **purpose** *pr. 1 sg.* intend 49.109
purposest *2 sg.* propose 79.419; **purposen** *pr. pl.* are plotting 83.84, assert 137.13; **purposyng** *pr. p.* intending 20.45; **purposed** *pa.* decided 2.25, 17.56, 29.97; intended 88.52; **purposid** 1.237, (G) 4.71, 6.9, 60.177; stated as a proposition 28.115, 53.16, 112.490; cited 106.29; **purposed** *pa. p.* proposed *32.31; stated 32.33; put forward 155.85
purpure *n.* purple robe 53.365, 68.5, 80.281, 165.378; **po(u)rpre** 11.153, 279; **purpre** 159.283; purple 11.280
pursue *v. inf.* persecute 27.22; **pursuest** *pr. 2 sg.* 113.362, 173.42; **pursued** *pa.* 62.33, 133.207; pursued 174.530; persecuted *pa. p.* 173.75
pursuer *n.* persecutor 53.98, 66.136, 133.216; **pursuers** *pl.* 18.19, 50.89; **pursuours** 159.408
purueaunce *n.* prudence 58.34; providence 82.10, 146.184; **purveiaunce** 20.51, 106.85; contrivance 2.47; **puruiaunce** provisions 36.149; provision 49.41; **purueiaunce** 139.132
purvei(e *v. inf.* provide (for) 2.37, 28.118, 49.28, 53.20; **purueyed** *pa.* 106.86; contrived 135.21; *pa. p.* provided 113.225, 122.26; **purueide** *ppl. adj.* far-sighted 44.177; **purueied** 163.250; furnished 60.268
puttithe *v. pr.* puts aside 64.271; **putte** *pa.* pushed 25.47, 58.346, 113.366, 123.95; gave 173.189; ~ **hym** *refl.* placed himself 25.94; ~ **fro** removed 79.1072; ~ **awey** *pa.* cured 136.3; ~ **vpon** attacked 23.52; imposed 2.217; ~

to informed 26.151; proposed to 30.72; added 174.461; ~ **hym up** arraigned 44.179

Q

qualite *n. error for* **equalite** 64.241 *note*
quarell *n.* bolt 142.221
quartayn, quarteyne, *n., adj.* **quarteyn(e** quartan fever, a type of malaria 58.176, 127.52, 149.63; **quartayn** 58.360
queint *see* **quenche**
queynte *adj.* elaborate 43.166
queken *see* **quicken**
quenche *v. inf.* extinguish 141.69; **quenched** *pa.* 4.196, 25.108, 58.252; *pa. p.* destroyed 5.225, 134.169; extinguished 101.133; **queint** 84.223; **quenchid** *pa. intrans.* extinguished itself (G) 1.62, 48.70
quentises *n. pl.* finery 143.4
quere *n.* choir (part of church) 53.363 *note*, 90.293, 106.191
queresters *n. pl.* choristers 36.308
quicken *v. inf.* bring to life 65.436, come to life 11.192; **quik(k)en** 23.19, 152.24; **queken** bring to life *179.237; **quikenithe** *pr.* brings to life 65.156; **quekeneth** (D) 179.239; *pa.* **quykened** came to life 45.498
quik *adj.* flowing 4.192, 8.222, 12.61; alive 4.219, 9.119, 11.361; **quycke** 28.129, 44.205, 84.102; **quyk** 93.102; **quicke** pregnant 166.44
quite *adj.* free 2.223, 65.181, 66.250
quite *v. pa. p.* repaid (H1) 156.445

R

race *v. inf.* pluck (out) 175.305; **raced** *pa.* 76.17, 116.245; **rasid** *ppl. adj.* (G) 46.14
radde *see* **rede**
rage *n.* amorous longing 66.16
+**rapinesse** *n.* ill-gotten gains 175.373 *note*
rasid *see* **race**
rather *comp. adv.* more greatly 11.269; sooner 125.132; instead 25.110, (D) 179.264; **neuer the** ~ none the more 45.461–2
raught *see* **recke**
raunson *n.* ransom 128.96
raueyn *n.* **foules of** ~ birds of prey 79.910
rauische *v. inf.* take possession of 47.221; **rauisshed** *pa.* 74.132, 78.36, 110.195; **rauis(c)hed** *pa. p.* possessed (by fiend) 1.224, 26.135; **raueschid** (G) 40.26, (G) 44.12; **rauisshed** 104.159; **rauished** enraptured 20.40; taken away 31.13; **rauished** raped 26.240; **rauisshed** seized 36.220, 53.79, 63.154, 79.582, 84.340, 112.65, 139.14; possessed (by fiend) 53.89; enraptured 25.4, 26.35, 53.376; **raueschid** (G) 55.139
ravon *n.* carrion crow 24.95; **ravin** 84.310; **ravonis** *pl.* 174.746
real(l *adj.* royal 11.109, 47.184, 90.2; **rial(l** 1.247, 13.54, 112.740; fit for a king 26.47; **reals** *pl.* 161.6; *pl. adj. as n.* **reaws** 53.293 *note*
really *adv.* regally 161.104
reaume *n.* realm 2.185, 54.20, 141.12; **reawme** 10.43; **rewme** 9.27, (G) 40.12, (G) 44.27; **rewmes** *pl.* 13.127
reaws *see* **reall**
reboundethe *v. pr. sg.* abounds 58.209, 112.352
receyt *n.* refuge 121.53
rechelesly *adv.* recklessly 45.338, (G) 47.6
re(c)k(e *v. pr.* ~ **of** care about 161.296, 166.43; **raught** *pa.* cared 84.27, 117.207; **roght** 117.312 *note*; **roughtest** *pa. 2 sg.* 93.318 **rought** *pa. p.* 87.64
+**reclusage** *n.* hermit-like seclusion 15.15 *note*
reclused *pa. p.* confined 144.38
recomaunde *v. pr.* commend 10.77, 50.149, 58.165; **recom(m)aunded** *pa.* 10.37, 11.86, 47.244; commanded 175.14 *note*; *ppl. adj.* recommended 148.112; **recomaunding** *ger.* 124.14
recomforted *v. pa. p.* reinvigorated 156.274
reconsiled *pa. p.* reinstalled 2.205
recorde *v.* remember 1.204, 66.164, 79.614; repeat (G) 4.26, recount 50.503; **recordest** *pr. 2 sg.* remember 131.16; repeat 12.50; **recordithe** *3 sg.* recounts 112.896, 123.82; **recording(e** *pr. p.* remembering 117.383; repeating 145.55, (H2) 176.327; **recorded** *pa.* recounted (G) 4.36, 93.198, 117.302; remembered

95.55, 101.138; repeated 28.208, 60.160; *pa. p.* 123.6; *ppl. adj.* 133.203, 155.90
recoueren *n.* recuperation 11.68 *note*
recouered *v. pa.* restored 123.22; **recoueringe** *ger.* restoration 49.16
recours *n.* return 64.244
rede *v. inf.* read aloud 44.79, **reden** *pr. pl.* read 35.2; **redde** *pa.* 20.135; taught 117.51; **radde** read (H1) 146.58; **redde** *pa. p.* 20.1
redely *adv.* easily 10.61; quickly 95.62
redempcion *n.* ransom 174.571
redemptor *n.* redeemer 12.60, 36.203, 65.43
redressed *v. pa.* straightened 84.13; ~ **hym up** raised himself again 137.38
refeccio(u)n *n.* nourishment (G) 43.105, 47.17, 95.27, 101.30
reformed *v. pa. sg.* restored 8.237; **refourmed** *pa. p.* 78.67
ref(f)reyne *v.* restrain 16.43, 113.127; **refreine hym** *refl.* restrain himself 142.291; **refreineth** *pr.* *12.65; **refreined** *pa.* 26.243; *ppl. adj.* 129.59, (L) 179.408; **refre(y)nyng(e** *ger.* 1.206, 129.11, 138.136
refres(s)he *v.* relieve 29.33, 49.162, 65.128, 90.87; **refressheth** *pr.* restores 65.130; **refres(s)hinge** *ger.* comfort 28.116, 65.118, 110.185
refusen *v. pr. pl.* reject 13.111, 22.35
refute *n.* refuge 1.256, 11.107, 32.48, 121.47
+**register** *n.* recorder (?) 21.3 *note*
regular *adj.* belonging to an order (i.e. Augustinian) 113.160
reherce *v. inf.* instruct 28.149; repeat 79.880, 146.211, (D) 179.284; recount 154.227; **rehersin** *pr. pl.* 104.197; **reherse** *imp.* repeat 154.28; **rehersed** *pa.* repeated 45.204, 133.80; told 173.245; **rehersid** recounted *pa. p.* (H2) 1.6, 133.220; **rehercid** (D) 179.250; **rehersed** 63.132; *ppl. adj.* recounted 58.107, 163.97
reyne *n.*[1] reins 61.273
reynes *n.*[2] *pl.* kidneys 65.309, 99.129
reioyse *v. inf.* enjoy possession of 13.123, 142.379; **reioysen** *pr. pl. refl.* rejoice 5.46; **reioysethe** *pr. 3 sg.* rejoices in 112.351
reke *see* **recke**
relacion *n.* story 53.45; report 116.211
relece *v. inf.* release 161.100; **relesith** *pr. 3 sg.* commutes 65.218; **relessyng** *ger.* relieving (G) 43.103
releue *v. inf. trans.* resuscitate 133.50; **releuen** *pr. pl.* alleviate 65.435 *note*; **releued** *pa. intrans.* recovered 56.7; revived 93.230; *trans.* resuscitated 84.49, 133.55; *pa. p. trans.* 16.19 *note*, 23.78, 83.150, 91.30
religion *n.* religious community 60.34, 113.77, 123.304, 141.10, 156.131; *pl.* 60.33
religious *adj.* in religious orders 45.111, god-fearing 60.324, 113.3; ~ **woman** nun 2.99, 128.186; *adj. as pl. n.* members of a religious order *12.34, 26.127, 28.154
remenaunt *n.* remainder 5.196, 25.191, 84.23
remeve *v. inf.* move (G) 3.77, 90.337, 102.72; **rem(e)we** (G) 3.76, 45.77, 159.320; **remowe** depart 93.209; **remeue** change *75.16, 134.125; **remeued** *pa.* moved 13.83, 29.67, 142.331; departed 66.195; **remeuyng** *ger.* power of moving (G) 3.82
remission *n.* pardon 30.4
remorded *v. pa. p.* afflicted with remorse 79.385
rende *v. inf.* tear 154.104; **rent** *imp.* 35.68; **rent(e** *pa.* 2.151, 8.147; **rent** *pa. p.* 79.229, 159.145; **rent** *ppl. adj.* 37.54, 165.777; **rendyng** *pr. p.* 22.10; **rentynge** *ppl. adj.* 155.252; **rentyng** *ger.* 17.24, *35.56 ; **rentinge** destruction 60.313 *note*; laceration 152.139
renewethe *see* **renue**
renye *v. inf.* renounce 22.84, 61.242, 110.63; **reneye** 24.18; **renye** forsake 58.272, 86.61; disbelieve 87.21; **renye** *pr.* 22.36; **reniethe** *pr. 3 sg.* denies 155.179; *imp.* 25.85, 38.57, 61.292; **renied** *pa.* 95.7, 125.58; **reneyed** refused to acknowledge 123.366; **renyed** *pa. p.* renounced 25.91, (G) 43.108, 79.512, 83.23; **renyeng** *ger.* renunciation 25.138; **renyinges** *pl.* 24.19
renne *v. inf.* run 4.201; **rennithe** *pr.* continues 28.192; **rennynge** *pr. p.* flowing 2.204; **ron(ne** *pa.* ran 22.108, (H1) 143.79, 146.168; **ranne** flowed

24.60; **ronnen** *pa. pl.* moved 24.60; **bene ronne** *pa. p.* fallen into 8.84; **rennynge** *ppl. adj.* (of money) current 44.88; **rennyng** *ger.* sailing 28.192
renner *n.* runner 30.79
renogate *n.* apostate 125.70; **renegat** 125.80
renomed *adj.* famous 58.203, 110.27, 167.4; **renoumed** *174.123
renome(s *n.* reputation 1.272, 15.15, 47.44; rumour 13.114, 28.113, (G) 44.30; fame 81.42, 106.15, 141.69; *error* 80.187 *note*; **renoun** fame (G) 3.2, 9.2, 117.189
renouacion *n.* renewal 30.3
renoueled *v. pa. p.* renewed 128.101
renoun *see* **renomes**
rent(e, rentynge *see* **rende**
renue *v. inf.* renew 45.117, (H2) 176.211; **renewethe** *pr. 3 sg.* begins again 22.52; **renued** *pa.* renewed 128.158; *ppl. adj.* (D) 179.188
repaire *v. inf.* return 13.237; **repairest** *pr. 2 sg.* abides 116.285; **repayred** *subj.* returned 66.143; **repayringe** *pr. p.* returning 66.161
reparaile *v. inf.* restore 128.105
repele *v. inf.* call back 45.70 *note*; retract 173.335; **repel(l)e** appeal (H2) 176.381, 382 *note*; *pr.* call back 60.92; *pa.* **repeled** 45.352, 50.515, 97.9 *note*; *pa. p.* repealed 8.12, 112.489
repentaunt *adj.* penitent 122.73, 143.40
reperacion *n.* restoration 49.5, 64.358 *note*
replenisshed *v. pa. p.* filled 142.278, 161.208, 173.4
+**reported** *v. pa. p.* related, connected 34.29 *note*, 64.60, 175.66
reproef(f *n.* shame, dishonour 49.64, 50.511, 112.290, 123.85; **repre(e)f** 80.29, 112.929, 125.71, 142.310, 161.296; **repreue** (H2) 177.6; **reproue** 143.60; **reproues** *pl.* 64.198, 113.205
reprouable *adj.* wicked 79.998
reproue *v. inf.* reproach 65.23; **reprouithe** *pr. 3 sg.* 50.31; **repreuithe** denounces 133.162; **reproued** *pa. p.* reproached 5.47, 8.34, 22.145, 23.99, denounced 90.80; **repreued** blamed 17.62; condemned 35.25; *ppl. adj.* (H2) 176.251, **reprouid** (H2) 176.283; **reproued** refuted 127.88
repugned *v. pa.* resisted (D) 177.174
require *v. inf.* request 2.154, 78.20; **requere** *pr. 1 sg.* 1.213; **requerest** *2 sg.* 23.47; **requerith** 31.38; **requerithe** *imp.* 45.220; **required** *pa.* 15.30, 16.28, 20.142, 29.42, 44.183; **requered** 45.32, 54.204; **required** *ppl. adj.* sought after 53.46, 127.9
rere raise 95.165; *pa.* 83.6, 133.153; **rered** *ppl. adj.* raised 59.11
resolued *ppl. adj.* decomposed 112.905
resonable *adj.* rational 13.158, 74.7, 113.120; with power of reason 90.266; ~ **age** the age of reason 2.277
resonabli *adv.* according to reason 11.268, 139.157
resorted *v. pa.* sprang up again 102.83
respire *v. inf.* breathe 65.136; **respired** *pa.* 90.208; **respeired** *ppl. adj.* breathed again 33.4
+**ressoude** *v. inf.* repair by soldering 110.229 *note*
+**restable** *v. inf.* restore 11.82, 83.393; **restab(e)led** *pa.* 15.65, 82.11, *91.74, 94.192; **restablissed** 120.30; **restabled** *pa. p.* 10.28 *note*, 16.19, 123.370, 154.168
+**restresse** *v. inf.* restrain 20.69 *note*
restreyne *v. inf.* withhold (G) 3.87; **restreyned** *pa. pl. refl.* refrained from 5.63; **restreined** *pa. p.* staunched 49.221
resuscite *pa. p.* resuscitated 95.155; **resussytynge** *ger.* resuscitation (G) 43.50
rethour *n.* orator 117.5
rethoriens *n. pl.* orators 165.629
reuested hym *v. pa. refl.* 133.127; **reuest** *ppl. adj.* ceremonially dressed 48.47; **reuestid** *177.109
revigured *v. pa.* revived 20.15
revished *ppl. adj.* wearing ceremonial vestments 36.309
reuoke *v. inf.* call back 79.444; **reuoketh** *pr. 3 sg.* retracts *179.177
rewme *see* **reaume**
rewthe *see* **routhe**
rial(l *see* **reall**
ribauude *n.* dissolute person 104.111, 113.259; **ribau(u)dis** *pl.* (G) 3.72, 45.489
ribaudrie *n.* immoral behaviour (G) 3.48
richesse *n.* wealth 2.12, (G) 4.104, 7.58

ride *v. inf.* ride in battle 117.249 *note*, 156.307, 159.9; *pr.* 158.4; *imp.* 93.295; **rode** 159.3; jousted 123.244
rie *adj.* made of rye grain 26.39
ryght *adv.* very 9.130, 11.129, 27.34; directly (towards) 125.172, 139.126, 155.9; ~ **as** just like 84.397, 93.99
right *n.*[1] entitlement 142.379
rightes *n.*[2] *pl.* rites 79.434
rightfull *adj.* just 53.352, 79.1049, 106.279, 135.22
ryghtwys *adj.* just 11.1, 123.84; **rightwi(s)se** 50.23, 60.47, (H2) 177.6
rightwisnesse *n.* justice 65.209, 69.30, 112.481
riot *n.* ill-treatment 176.96 *note*
risshes *n. pl.* rushes 50.179
riuage *n.* shore 28.42, (G) 44.22, 45.132, 90.194; river bank 52.79
ryuere *n.* shore (G) 1.24; 8.54, 159.161 *note*; river bank 148.13; river 66.89, 93.111, 94.57
roche *n.* stone 68.43; rock 47.327, 90.161, 94.154, 154.14; cliff 156.243; rocky area 144.38; **rochis** *pl.* stones (G) 39.146; cliffs 47.81, 163.321
roght *see* **recke**
ronne *see* **renne**
rosen *n.* resin 51.82
roser *n.* rosebush 17.50 *note*
rotenesse n. rottenness 84.349; **rotones** *84.364, 112.289
rought, roughtest *see* **recke**
routed *v. pa. sg.* snored 6.38
routhe *n.* pity 159.307; **rewthe** *179.305
rubbid *v. pa. p.* robbed (G) 3.98
rude *adj.* common *79.8; coarse 161.272; foolish 163.65; ignorant 175.345
russet *n.* rough woollen cloth 161.275

S

Sabot *n.* sabbath, i.e. Saturday 11.27
sacke *n.* sackcloth 95.144, 101.36; **sackes** *pl.* lengths of sackcloth 63.41
sacre *v. inf.* consecrate 2.44, 25.62, 124.273; **sacren** *pr. pl.* 107.23; **sacrid** *pa.* 101.20; **sacred** 47.142, 80.213, 102.11; *pa. p.* 10.81 19.3, 23.92; **sacrid** (G) 4.61
sacrifie *v. inf.* make a sacrifice 29.20, 51.56, 94.133; **sacrefye** 90.78; *imp.* *35.63; **sacrified** *pa.* 60.51, 78.17; **sacrifiden** *pa. pl.* 36.213; **sacrified** *pa. p.* 20.130, 32.27, 53.291; **sacrifienge** *ger.* 81.82
+**sacrifisable** *adj.* which can be sacrificed 149.75 *note*
+**sacrilege** *n.* committer of sacrilege 58.162 *note*
sad(de *adj.* firm 48.48, 53.379, 58.43; steadfast 85.11, 87.106, 161.306, 179.287; steady 113.282; mature 34.52; seriously engaged 165.287; **sadder** *comp.* more firm 38.16; **saddest** *superl.* steadiest 113.284
sadde *adv.* steadfastly 65.360
sadly *adv.* firmly 53.153, 165.678; steadfastly 74.19, 79.297, 91.81, 106.65
sadnesse *n.* maturity 34.49, 152.38; constancy 53.151, 65.363, *66.153, 79.873; firmness 84.387, 124.250, 125.73, 131.4, 173.375
sagh *see* **see** *v.*
saie *see* **see** *v.*
sai(e *v. inf.* tell 7.203, 9.6, 29.132; signify *18.3; declare 29.54; **sai** (H1) say 146.104; **sei** (H1) declare 146.64; **seie** *pr.* 27.65; **saiest(e** *2 sg.* 38.42, speak 86.14; **say(e)(n** *pr. pl.* declare 5.53, 12.110, 18.3; 11.135; **sayne** declare 29.1; **seine** 1.226, 5.190; **saie** designate 11.145; **saieth(e)** *imp. pl.* declare 18.37; name 20.47; **saide** *pa.* told, informed 20.56, 83.10; recited 58.408; called, named 142.274; **saied** said 15.11; **seyden** *pa. pl.* declared 11.157; **seyne** declared 53.221; **saiden** declared 18.38; said 20.46; **saide** *pa. p.* named 4.222, described as 7.57, named 13.24, 18.1; told about 13.77; told, informed 45.481; **sayed** described as 12.55; **seide** named (G) 43.71; **seid** spoken (H1) 146.104
saigh *see* **see** *v.*
sailed *v. pa.* attacked 174.732
sakering *ger.* consecration 175.184; *see also* **sacre**
salue *v. inf.* greet 84.236; **sal(o)we** 112.382, 165.571; **salue** *pr.* *116.278; **saluithe** *pr. 2 sg.* 49.271; **saluid** *pa.* greeted 1.170; **salued** 18.33, 35.121, 37.38; **sal(o)wed** 11.89, 112.22, 117.164
Sane *see* **cene**
+**satirell** *n.* satyr 14.33 *note*; **satire** 166.35 *note*

satisfaccion *n.* reparation as part of penance 48.16, 142.179, 156.16
sawdid *see* **sowde**
saw(en *see* **see** *v.*
sauf *prep.* except 7.138, 16.32, 17.31
sauf(f *adj.* safe 12.12, 20.75, 36.188
sauf(ly *adv.* safely 2.131, 60.280
Saughter *see* **sauuter**
sauh *see* **see** *v.*
sau(u)te *n.* assault 7.103, 83.132, 92.87
sauuter *n.* psalter 58.408; **Saughter** 139.155
sawter *n.* heraldic saltire 79.77; **sawtier** saltire cross 118.9
sawtry *n.* psaltery 84.267, 175.70
sauir *v. inf.* add flavour to 101.27
sauour(e *n.* odour 1.228, 13.230, 23.18; taste 65.254; **sauoures** *pl.* 143.7
sawer *n.* sower 80.192
+**scabbes** *adj.* mangy 45.170 *note*
scape *v. inf.* escape 134.84; **skape** (G) 55.73; **scaped** *pa.* 112.519, 159.220; **skaped** 47.219
scars *adj.* scant 172.42
scauberk *n.* scabbard 174.80
sch- *for words beginning with* **sch-** *see under* **sh-** *below*
science *n.* knowledge 49.166, 60.6, 64.160; **sciences** *pl.* studies 127.8; branches of learning 165.82, 174.706
sclaunder *v. inf.* offend 26.117; **sclaundre** bring into disrepute 135.95; **sklaundre** 113.417; **sclaundred** *pa. p.* spoken ill of 53.392, 80.157; *see also* **desclaundred**
sclaundre *n.* abuse 84.368
sclauein, sclavyne *see* **slaven**
scle *v. see* **slee**
sclewe *see* **slee**
sclow *see* **slee**
scorne *v. inf.* delude 135.95; **scorned** *pa.* 13.41, 101.54; **scorned** *ppl. adj.* deceived 9.35, 54.151, 96.66
scornere *n.* mocker *10.109, 13.39
scrache *v. inf.* scratch 25.124; **scratte** *pa.* 76.14
screueners *n. pl.* writers 149.293
scripture *n.* inscription 95.112, 175.326; written text 175.325; **scriptures** *pl.* writings 45.167; scriptural authorities 123.207
scrowe *n.* scroll 18.47, 25.59, 26.267, 88.91, 90.374; **scrowes** *pl.* pieces of parchment 161.33
sece, seced, secedin *see* **cese**
seche *v. inf.* seek (D) 178.34; **secheth** *pr. 3 sg.* (H1) 146.76; **sechithe** *imp. pl.* 79.526
secte *n.* system of religious belief and practice 79.984, 129.70
seculer *adj.* lay non-religious 16.3, 83.416, 139.23; temporal 50.18; ~ **chanon** canon not in a religious order 106.16; ~ **preste** 142.147
seculers *n. pl.* lay people 20.81, 58.124
sede *n.* descendants 5.45; seed 159.70; (*fig.*) 124.45, 155.297
see *n.*[1] sea (G) 4.25, 83.5; ~ **side** shore 138.58
see *n.*[2] seat 94.118
se(e *v. inf.* see 1.221, 2.32, 6.36; **see** *inf. for passive* (D) 179.111; **seest** *pr. 2 sg.* 25.6; **seyst** 83.18; **seithe** *pr. 3 sg.* 86.13; **sethe** *imp. pl.* see 13.202, 145.38; **sagh** *pa. sg.* (H2) 1.42, (H1) 143.11; **sauh** (H2) 1.77; **sawȝ** (G) 4.26; **sawe** 1.169, 2.232; **segh** 1.196; **seghe** 49.114; **seigh** 2.194, 5.42; **seye** 7.95; **saigh** 63.110; **sawe** *pa. 2 sg.* 113.323; **sawest** 113.322, 152.20; **sayn** *pa. pl.* 23.75; **saien** 4.215; **saye** 47.285; **sayen** 53.221, 84.492; **sawen** 84.189; **see** 84.178; **seen** 5.147, 7.6; **seien** 7.77; **seye** 47.315, 136.11; **seyen** 84.491; **sein** 4.217, 124.70; **seine** 5.190; **sene** 13.177, 50.70; **saien** *pa. p.* seen 11.99; **saie** 171.40, 176.18; **sayn(e** 8.220, 23.84, 79.394; **sain(e** 13.99, 22.102, 28.90; **sayen** 58.245; **saye** 61.215; **seyn** 18.8; **sene** 2.284; **yseyne** 149.311; **seinge** *pr. p.* being aware of 84.495; observant 159.278
sege *n.* abode 13.184, 50.184; seat 94.161, 106.242; ecclesiastical see 2.203, 16.38, 45.447, 56.1, 63.12; throne 10.50, 11.190, 53.28, 93.205, 174.264; headquarters 174.15; *pl.* thrones 23.110; abodes 33.32
seged *v. pa.* besieged 174.402; *pa. p.* 149.323
segh(e, seigh *see* **see** *v.*
sei(ne *see* **saie, see** *v.*
seithe *see* **sithe** *adv.*, **see** *v.*
seke *adj.* sick (G) 4.108, 84.358
seke(n *v. inf.* look for (G) 4.3, 29.87,

70.7; **sekithe** *imp.* 165.187; **soutest** *pa. 2 sg.* 116.48
seker(ly *see* **siker(ly**
selden *adv.* infrequently 66.95; **selde** 83.17, 101.39
sely *adj.* blessed 55.221, 77.33
sell(e *n.* monastic cell 17.56, 20.82, 66.45; small room 121.13; **celle** monastic cell 20.80; monastery 139.131; **sellis** *pl.* 66.182
sel(l)er(e *n.* cellar 15.22; 117.264; **selers** *pl.* storerooms 155.114; **celers** 155.116
sellerere *n.* cellarer 47.321
seluer *n.* silver 20.32; **siluer** money 142.449
sembeled *v. pa.* assembled 25.154
semblable *adj.* comparable *4.232; **sembelable** *adj.* co-equal 64.281
semblably *adv.* comparably 116.236
semblaunce *n.* appearance 163.233, (H2) 178.404; **semblaunt** 116.25, 161.77, (H2) 178.408; **sembelauntes** *pl.* 60.17
semely *adj.* handsome 54.218, 134.5; **semelie** worthy (H2) 177.109; **semeliest** *superl.* most handsome 165.449
semelyhede *n.* seemliness 79.88, 127.55
semethe *v. impers. pr.* ~ **you** appear to you 79.539; **semithe** seems 149.112; **semyn** *pr. pl.* think 156.70
senacle *n.* cenacle, upper chamber where apostles used to meet 65.400
sendelle *n.* fine linen (D) 178.618
sene *see* **cene** *n.*, **see** *v.*
senescal *n.* chief administrator 79.152
sengil *adj.* single 152.95
sensible *adj.* able to be felt 45.368; *error* 159.134 *note*; **sensiblis** *pl.* susceptible to reason (G) 4.118
sensualite *n.* 28.172 *note*
sent *v. pr. refl.* **y me** ~ I assent 149.112
sentence *n.* decision 8.109, 45.476, 79.795, 93.182; opinion 9.69; judgement 11.130, 25.57, 149.175; saying 11.254, 53.378; teaching 165.678
sentuari *n.* the Church 163.252
Septemtrion the northern region 174.12 *note*; north 175.194
sepulture *n.* burial 11.29; 13.217, 22.23; tomb 17.1, *29.185, 47.350
sequence *n.* melodic extension of word Alleluia 174.470; *pl.* 174.466 *note*
sermones *n. pl.* discourses 79.764, 931
seruage *n.* enslavement (G) 2.299, 7.33, 32.22, 66.82; *pl.* 65.183
seruaunt *n.* slave 6.23 *note*, 25.65, 26.74, 36.66; **servauntes** *pl.* 32.19, 53.333, 65.182
seruen *v. pr. pl.* minister 23.17; **serued to** *pa.* worshipped 2.91; **seruid** ministered to 102.9
seruice *n.* religious ceremony 21.10; **seruyse** servitude 19.6
sese, sesed, seseden *see* **cese**
sethe *adv., conj. see* **sithe**
sethenes *see* **sithen**
sette *v. inf.* attribute 2.72 *note*; **settist so littell by** *pr. 2 sg.* regard as of little value 124.157; **setten litul** *pr. pl.* *4.90; **settithe** *imp. pl.* prepare 60.69; **sette** *pa.* put 2.99, 58.407; ~ **not by** put no value on 173.65; **sette** *pa. p.* positioned 13.101; imputed 7.116, attributed 112.94, 149.26; esteemed 22.134; changed 128.12; brought (to judgement) 26.35; appointed 79.493; ~ **to** *pa. p.* added 32.11
seude *see* **sowed**
seuerte, seurete *see* **surete**
sewe *v. inf.* follow (D) 179.33; **sewen** *pr. pl.* (L) 179.320; **sewynge** *ppl. adj.* (H2) 1.6; **sewinge** *ger.* (D) 179.22
sewrely *see* **surely**
sewte *n.* matching clothes 124.66
sextayne *n.* sexton 99.115, 112.388; **sexstayne** 99.119
sexte *ord. num.* sixth (G) 4.129
sextry *n.* sacristy 58.372; **sextrie** 159.240
schadde *see* **shede**
shad(o)we *v. inf.* overshadow 13.167, 49.143, 133.108; **shadu** 79.190; **shaduithe** *pr. 3 sg.* puts into the shade 28.15; **shadued** *pa.* overshadowed 65.82; *pr. p.* **shadowynge** shady 99.37
shadue *n.* shadow 28.19; **shadowe** darkness 156.77; **schadowis** *pl.* (G) 43.138
shaken *v. pr. pl.* brandish 25.144
shamefast *adj.* humble 173.255
shamefastnesse *n.* modesty 49.41
shamfully *adv.* ignominiously 135.115
share *n.* cutting edge 29.37
sharpe *adj.* harsh 90.235, 94.34; rough 159.192; incisive 117.406;
sharpithe *v. pr.* sharpens 149.50; **sharped** sharpened 83.361

sharpely *adv.* keenly 51.55; painfully 79.467

sharpenesse *n.* roughness 28.107

shede *v. inf.* pour out 12.90, 113.9; spread 65.137, 142.63; **shedithe** *pr. 3 sg.* pours out 133.235; **shedde** *pa.* 110.106, spilled 172.23; **schadde** *pa.* poured out 2.225; spread (G) 45.550; **shedde** *pa. p.* poured out 10.80, 76.19; dispersed 65.269; **sheding** *ger.* outpouring 165.687

shelinges *n. pl.* shillings 124.225

shelle *n.* potsherd 84.350

scherdis (G) *n. pl.* fragments of pottery (G) 39.112

shere *v. inf.* shave 62.8; *imp.* 173.88; **shering** *ger.* hair-cutting 174.395

Sher Thoursday day before Good Friday 15.55; **Sheresthorsday** 52.72

shert(e n. upper body undergarment 10.13, 93.332, 128.86

shete *v. inf.* shoot 8.180, 20.65, 136.54; *pr. pl.* 8.175; **shette** *pa. p.* shot 119.44

shette *v. inf.* shut 25.41, 159.113; **schette** *imp.* (G) 3.21; **shet(te** *pa.* shut 14.36; ~ **vp** imprisoned 6.8; confined 15.63, 25.141; *pa. p.* 37.44; shut 15.58, 51.74; **schette** *pa. p.adj.* 2.133, (G) 4.50

shewe *v. inf.* tell 66.259, 79.295, 90.84; reveal 95.132, 110.63; *pr. 1 sg.* demonstrate 26.243; **shewithe** *pr. 3 sg.* is seen 74.20, 139.165; **schewed** *pa.* revealed 2.45; showed 2.207; **sheued** revealed 5.168, 13.205; **shewed** *65.83, 76.39, 79.181; demonstrated 44.165; **schewed** *pa. p.* revealed 2.46, 5.65; **schewid** (G) 43.101; **sheued** 12.83, 65.75, 90.331; declared 84.20; **shewing(e** *ger.* proof 64.36, 113.145, 139.115; revelation 112.236, 113.16, 144.54; indication 106.174; **shewyng** manifestation 7.141, 138.25; **shewingges** *pl.* manifestations 60.164, 174.169

shynyng(e *ppl. adj.* being eminent 20.40; *ger.* brightness 117.64; **shininge** sunlight (D) 178.103

shipman *n.* mariner 125.169; **shipmen** *pl.* 24.103, 90.146, 105.108; **shippemen** 163.138; **schipmen** 2.61, (G) 55.99

shoft *v. pa. p.* pushed 79.564; **shoued** 161.191; gouged 166.26

schone *n. pl.* shoes (G) 55.40; **shone** 60.307, 79.231, 101.39

shortid *v. pa.* grew short (D) 178.484

shoued *see* **shoft**

schouen *v. pa. pl.* shaved (G) 43.153

shrewe *n. error* 93.327 *note*; rascal 121.61

shrew(e)dnesse *n.* wickedness (D) 178.464, (D) 179.198

shrifft *n.* ~ **of mouthe** oral confession (D) 179.4

shriue *v. inf. refl.* to be formally absolved of sin by a priest 122.73, 142.71; **shriue** *pr.* (D) 179.155; **shriuithe hym** *pr. 3 sg.* 155.269; **shriue(n** *pa. p.* 26.261, 53.259, 93.220, 142.75; **shreue(n** *ppl. adj.* 142.430, (D) 179.81; **shreuin** 155.265; **shrewen** (D) 179.159 *note*

sicles *n. pl.* shekels 36.125

sydoyne *n.* shroud 112.712 *note*; **sidoine** 112.731; **sidoigne** 112.747

sidre *n.* strong drink 60.43; **syder** 80.14

sigh *n.* breath 45.496

sigh *v. inf.* sigh (G) 2.304, 52.50; **sighed** *pa.* breathed out 27.30, 29.216; **sighyng** *pr. p.* 27.43; *ger.* panting 9.111

signacle *n.* seal 65.50

signe *n.* (false) appearance 65.208; insignia 79.159 *note*; battle-standard 138.115; **signes** *pl.* miracles 7.19

signed *v. refl. pa.* ~ **her** crossed herself 28.174

signettes *n. pl.* seals 25.42

signifiauntli *adv.* symbolically *175.27 *note*

siker *adj.* certain (D) 179.117; **sekir** (D) 179.65; **siker** *as adv.* 45.168, 49.266; **seker** 90.108

sikerly *adv.* certainly 2.215, 10.34, 84.61; **sekirly** 86.15, 93.295; **sekerly** 125.54; **sikirlie** (D) 179.10

similitude *n.* similarity 36.60, 45.167; representation 84.232; comparison 105.47, 176.129; likeness 176.134

sympely *adv.* inadequately 155.153

symple *adj.* ordinary *1.3, 10.53, 84.477, 165.309; lowly 155.189; innocent 58.154; slow-witted 10.55, 123.324, 174.301; worthless 140.10; **symplest** *superl.* slowest witted 165.642

synamom *n.* cinnamon (D) 178.585

singuler *adj.* exceptional 50.81, 58.217, *128.235; specific 149.26
singulery(e *adv.* uniquely 49.140, 80.105; separately 63.86,130, 149.26
synow *n.* sinew, tendon 138.142; **synues** *pl.* 60.262, 76.9, 153.9, 166.13; **synwes** 125.11
syrograf(f) *n.* formal document 50.329, 102.52; **cirograff** 102.54
+**sisterne** *n.* cavern 60.218 *note*
sithe *n.* scythe 17.11, 47.100, *83.48; **syth** 47.97
sith(e *adv.* afterwards (G) 1.22, 2.3, 5.61, 10.37, 71.25; **sethe** 35.79, 58.203, 71.24; **seithe** 7.38
sithe *conj.* inasmuch as (G) 1.114, 4.188, 5.111; **sethe** 13.51, 29.115, 90.82; **sithe** since the time when 11.349, **sethe** 4.225, 20.47; 26.60
sithe *prep.* after 28.93; **sethe** 81.8
sithen *adv.* subsequently 15.35, 58.204, 68.63; **sethenes** 152.44
sithen *conj.* inasmuch as 148.73
sythes *n. pl.* times (D) 178.668
sit(te *v. pr. 3 sg.* is fitting 25.33, 142.82, 152.170; **sittithe** 25.36, 44.126; **sittyng(e** *ppl. adj.* fitting, (G) 1.98, 5.110, 33.61, 44.97, 49.14
sittyng *n.* location 13.163
syve *n.* sieve (G) 47.5
skape *see* **scape**
skilfullie *adv.* fittingly (H2) 177.135
skille *n.* reason (D) 179.123
sklaundre *see* **sclaunder** *v.*
skrippe *n.* bag 80.240
slaven *n.* cloak 79.345; **sclavyne** 79.509; **sclauein** 165.294
sle(e *v. inf.* kill 9.29, 29.77, 47.125; **scle** (G) 4.76, (G) 40.34; **slee** *pr.1sg* 17.22; **sleith(e** *pr. 3 sg.* 9.107, 17.22, 36.246; **sleyng(e** *pr. p.* 28.78, 81.28; **slow(e** *pa.* killed 2.224, 6.68, 7.64; **slough** 23.74, (H1) 145.4, (H2) 178.334; **slewe** 7.86; **sclewe** (G) 38.117, (G) 44.41; **slowgh** destroyed (D) 179.225; **sclowȝ** *pa. pl.* killed (G) 1.73; **slowen** 60.189; **slain(e** *pa. p.* 8.11, 9.106; *ppl. adj.* 7.135, 22.30
sleer *n.* slayer 90.140
sleight *n.* trick (D) 179.47
sleper *adj.* slippery 48.106
slinge *n.* hand-held weapon for throwing stones *50.362
slode *v. pa.* slipped 156.217, 159.258
slowe *adj.* lazy 34.41, 66.181, (D) 178.48
slowgh *n.* muddy place (D) 179.224
smal *adj.* little in quantity 28.162; **smalle** delicate (G) 45.556
smellyng(e *ppl. adj.* scented 34.15, 62.48, 124.103; *ger.* sense of smell (G) 4.126, 50.123
smerte *n.* pain 48.121
smyte *v. inf.* kill 9.123, strike 20.147, cut 61.21; *pr.* strike 20.144; **smite** *imp. sg.* 156.254; **smitithe** *imp. pl.* 156.257; **smote** *pa. sg.* (G) 4.110, 6.27, 8.151; **smite** *pa. p.* smitten 7.177, 122.7; **smyten** struck (G) 3.102, (G) 4.30, 17.11; **smetin** 21.13; **smete** 11.54, 37.101, 61.300; **smytyng** *ger.* **hede** ~ **of** decapitation (G) 3.101
smocke *n.* woman's undergarment 161.101
smokyng *ppl. for adj.* smoke-blackened 13.187 *note*
sobernesse *n.* moderation 5.254
socour *v. imp. pl.* rescue 83.370
sode(y)n *ppl. adj.* cooked *60.317, 139.54; **sodin** 175.391
sodued *v. pa.* subjugated 165.39
soget *n.* subject 142.316
soget(t)(e *adj.* subject (G) 4.146, 5.23, 45.207, 60.175, (D) 178.11; **soget(t)is** *pl.* 13.181, 49.63, 173.406
soyled *v. pa. p.* defiled 175.357
+**soylour** *n.* pollution 175.250 *note*
soked *see* **soukedest**
sol(l)empnyte *n.* festival day (G) 2.309, (G) 3.5, 78.67, 83.462; ceremony 88.72, 102.8; religious celebration 103.13, 155.98
soler(e *n.* upper chamber 47.132, 84.41, 93.256
solitarie *adj.* alone (as a hermit) 168.43, 169.3
+**solucion** *n.* payment to discharge an obligation 36.116 *note*
someres *n. pl.* pack-horses 96.19
sommed *v. pa. p.* assembled (?) 54.38 *note*
sonde *n.*[1] sending 15.33
sonde *n.*[2] sand 175.272; **sondes** *pl.* 79.613
sone *adv.* immediately 33.58, (G) 42.9, 72.4; **sonner** *comp.* sooner 13.57, 20.68, 24.104; **sonnest** *superl.* 79.877
sool *n.* plough 29.37

+sophistiqes *adj. pl.* sophistical 156.121 *note*

sore *adv.* sorrowfully (G) 2.304; grievously 17.54, 22.124; *comp.* **sorer** 45.37

sorep *n.* syrup (G) 4.151

sori *adj.* sad 26.51; of poor quality 159.249

sorier *comp.adv.* the more severely *22.54

sorifull *adj.* lamentable 20.118, 22.18, 29.110

sorte *n.* choice made by casting lots 44.131, 54.16, *60.229, 80.6; **sortes** *pl.* 44.127

sorugh *n.* sadness 2.285, 17.38, 20.29; pain 18.38, 49.84, 96.60; **sorw(e** sadness 7.179, 28.196, 29.116; pain 5.113, 142.226, 149.324; **sorwes** *pl.* sorrows 79.848, 84.409, 117.344; pains 152.151, 167.86

sorugh *v. inf.* grieve 9.117, 87.65; **sorued** *pa.* 20.115, 163.214; **sorughed** 35.107; suffered 50.167; **sorueden** *pa. pl.* grieved 121.56, 154.81

sostened *v. pa. p.* sustained 28.139

sote *see* **suete**

sotel *see* **sotille**

sothe *n.* truth 2.112, 73.20, 94.86

sothe *adj.* true 2.63; proper (D) 179.133

sothe-saier *n.* speaker of truth 152.97; **sothesaiers** *pl.* 79.1037

sothely *adv.* truly 58.50, 79.198, 81.49; **sothli** 158.5

sotill(e *adj.* clever 55.22, 117.407; cunning 152.109; **sotel(l** clever 128.35, 134.6, 149.61, 174.208; **subtile** 28.165

sotilly *adv.* cleverly (G) 3.30, 55.128; **sotelly** 47.279; circumspectly 95.41; cunningly 101.19, 174.623; **suttelli** subtly 10.14

sotilte *n.* cleverness 149.58, 159.278; **sotelteys** *pl.* 165.622

sowdan *n.* sultan (G) 2.312

sowde *v. inf.* join 110.29; **sawdid** *pa.* healed (of wound) 142.245

sowke *n.* **yeue** ~ suckle 15.12; **yeuing it souke** 60.311

soukedest *v. pa. 2 sg.* suckled 38.71; **soked** *pa. p.* suckled 83.366

sowkers *n. pl.* sucklings 159.94

sowne *n.* sound, noise 2.29, 14.13, 20.34; **soun(e** 64.100, 65.233, 112.120; **sownes** *pl.* 63.51

soune *v. inf.* sound 11.322; **sowne** 173.157; **sounithe** *pr. 3 sg.* 133.45; **sownithe** 65.59; **souned** *pa.* 45.179, 84.266; **sownyd** 112.104; **sowned** pronounced 28.187, 79.441; **sowninge** sounding 84.230

sowter *n.* cobbler 55.40

souerein *adj.* excellent, supreme 1.256, 38.34, 65.341; **souereyne** (G) 2.317, (G) 43.17; **souera(y)n(e** 19.1, 33.70, 65.339; uppermost 138.118; ~ **preste** high priest 44.132; **s~ bisshop** pope 82.8; ~ **prestes** *pl.* 80.4, 112.666; ~ **bisshoppes** popes 163.254, 174.639

souer(r)eynli *adv.* above all 11.2, 49.70; **souerainly** 165.417

sou(u)erai(g)ne *n.* master 112.665, 178.4; lord 116.207; mistress 133.67

sowed *v. pa. p.* sewn 10.60, 174.234; **seude** 10.57

sower *n.* one who sows 146.79, 124.44

spake *see* **speke**

spare *v. inf.* avoid 24.48; **sparithe** *pr.* leaves unhurt 9.107; **spared** *pa.* avoided 142.272; **sparinge** *ger.* frugality 155.199

sparhauke *n.* sparrowhawk 10.117

sparkle *n.* spark (G) 45.573; **sparkeles** *pl.* 116.101, 155.187

spede *n.* success 12.75

spede *v. inf.* succeed 81.24; **spedde** *pa.* 8.106; *pa. p.* 17.30

spedefull *adj.* beneficial 71.6, 165.141

spedie *adj.* quick (D) 179.301

speke *v. pa.* spoke 25.21; **spake** 7.39; **speken** *pa. pl.* 37.67; **speking** *ger.* power of speech 12.79, 26.96

spended *v. pa.* disbursed 95.16

spere *n.*[1] spear (G) 46.3, 23.91, 60.135; **speres** *pl.* stings 14.10

spere *n.*[2] sphere 155.27

spille *v. inf.* destroy (D) 178.274

spired *v. pa.* breathed (D) 178.20

+spirites *n. pl.* senses 165.429 *note*

spite *n.* humiliation (G) 42.41

spotil(le *n.* spittle 55.44, 83

spouce *n.* spouse 23.24, 112.647, 151.109

spowen *pa. p.* vomited (D) 179.223

sprengithe *v. pr. 3 sg.* sprinkles 175.450; **sprengid** *pa.* (G) 1.62; **sprenged** 159.115, 161.419; **springed** sprinkled 18.15; **springed** *pa. p.* 175.187; **sprynginge** *ger.* sprinkling 175.216

springe *v. inf.* spring up 5.144, 8.221; sprout 167.42; **springgith** *pr. 3 sg.* springs up 8.220; **springgen** *pr. pl.* 8.221; *pa.* **sprong** 5.142, 15.21; *see too* **sprengithe**
springes *n. pl.* sprouting shoots 167.48; **spryngges** streams 12.61
sputinge *ppl. adj.* arguing 79.659
stabilnesse *n.* stability 22.187, 32.48; **stabelnesse** 53.151
stable *adj.* steadfast 1.161, 8.211, 22.75
stabled *v. pa.* made steadfast 165.683; **stab(e)led** *pa. p.* 16.24; **stablid** (H2) 1.5; *ppl. adj.* steadfast 27.69
stably *adv.* steadfastly 23.115, 74.28, 79.960; **stabilly** 135.155; **stabely** 134.125
stacion *n.* special mass held at station church in Rome 12.112, 45.322
staffe *n.* staff, walking stick 2.217; support 22.24, (D) 179.283; rod 22.178, 63.108; **staues** *pl.* *22.151, 37.44, 75.7
stanke *n.* lake (G) 1.17; **stange** 54.3
stappes *see* **steppes**
states *n. pl.* authorities 165.97
staunch(e *v. inf.* stop 7.8, 53.250, 156.96; **staunched** *pa.* 165.22
staues *see* **staffe**
steyed *see* **stie**
stele *v. inf.* ~ **away** creep away 66.185; **stalyst** *pa. 2 sg.* stole 10.110; **stale** *pa.* 18.31, 44.84; 79.1039, 93.91; **stole** (G) 55.74; **stele** 98.10; **stale awey** crept away (G) 44.42; **stole** *pa. p.* stolen 25.108, 29.28, 44.86; **stolen** abducted 53.77
stened *v. pa. p.* stoned 53.310, 84.4
stent *see* **stint**
steppes *n. pl.* footsteps 50.146; **stappes** 113.196
stere *v. inf.* persuade (H2) 1.3, 26.15, 90.87, 151.105; waken 29.69; provoke 173.467; move (from location) 47.339, 66.247; **stirre** provoke 26.101; **sterith(e** *pr. 3 sg.* exhorts (G) 42.23, 49.34; **stere** *imp.* goad on 29.69; **stered** *pa.* made it move 66.196; exhorted 28.166, 44.76, 45.77, 112.164, 122.60, 173.71; provoked 47.287, 53.72, 92.87; persuaded 133.75; **stered** *pa. p.* (sexually) aroused 22.161; *ppl. adj.* 142.161; **stering** *pr. p.* motivating 49.138; **stering)e** *ger.* wakening by disturbance 6.39; urging 74.89, 79.756, 112.869; **stiringe** movement 84.345; **sterynges** *pl.* sexual arousals *14.19, *63.69
sterte *v. pa.* jumped 78.80, 79.657
stie *v. inf.* ascend 33.15, 54.225, 123.145; **stiȝe** 178.576; **stieth(e** *pr. 3 sg.* *47.375, 58.418, 112.124; **styen** *pr. pl.* 88.46; **stied** *pa.* ascended 1.173, 7.130, 11.201, 29.131, 138.12; **steyed** 11.37; **steie** 64.77; **stiedest** *pa. 2 sg.* 112.785; **styeden** *pa. pl.* 112.121; **stiedin** 166.32; **stienge** *pr. p.* 63.117; **steyenge** 64.315
+stiers *n. pl.* those who ascend 112.586 *note*
stiked *v. pa.* planted 17.50, 79.953; thrust 142.234
stikill *adj.* steep 165.862
still(e *adj.* silent 11.133, 28.206, 50.171
still(e *adv.* continuously (G) 1.27, 77.29, 80.119; even so 95.86
stint *v. inf.* cease 45.478; **stynte** 55.105, 84.267; **stinte** *pr.* 44.120, 88.118; **stintithe** *pr. 3 sg.* 79.624; **stent** *pr. pl.* (D) 178.167; **stynt(e** *pa.* 2.204, 79.832, 123.155, 139.4; **stintinge** *ger.* 79.252
stirre *see* **stere**
stocke *n.* trunk of tree 167.45; block of wood 112.871
stody *n., v. see* **study**
stole *n.* robe 30.33; **stoole** (H2) 176.334; **stole** ecclesiastical vestment 15.51, 58.373; *pl.* 26.276
stonding(e *n.* situation 64.254
stont *v. pr. 3 sg.* stands 137.63
stoppe *v. inf.* obstruct the flow of 4.193, 84.328
strayles *n. pl.* bedclothes 28.98
strangeler *n.* killer 84.95 *note*
strangle *v. inf.* kill 49.270, 98.10; **strangelithe** *pr. 3 sg.* 22.58; **strangeled** *pa.* suffocated 35.100, 70.35; **strangled** *pa. p.* killed (H2) 1.80; **strangelid** choked 11.15; killed 66.233; **strangeled** 23.71, 83.171; choked 37.24, 60.360
straught *see* **streche**
straunge *adj.* unfamiliar 1.248, 17.6; foreign 11.57, *15.27; 26.67, 28.124; estranged 167.13; not related to the family 112.988; ~ **for** remote from 112.110; **strange** *45.486 *note*

straunger *n.* foreigner 13.111, 83.225, 119.108; *pl.* 11.56; *error* 28.219 *note*; **strauniour of** *n.* stranger to 123.4
strawed *v. pa. p.* sprinkled 22.20
streche *v. inf.* stretch 20.67, 50.450, 102.71; **stroght** *for inf.* (?) stretch 1.142 *note*; **streched** *pa.* spread 24.77, 90.303, 110.182; extended 36.240; **streight** stretched 134.59; *pa. p.* 1.141, 24.22; **straught** 8.214, 50.166, 142.285; **streight** *ppl. adj.* 50.315; prostrate 53.123; constricted 176.230; **streite** stretched 90.295; prostrate 99.51; **streched** extended 20.109, 50.317; prostrate 27.81
streight *see* **streche**
streyne *v. pr.* clench 26.194; **streinithe** *pr. 3 sg.* constricts 64.182; **streyned** *pa.* gripped 93.284, 110.238; hugged 163.195; *pa. p.* gripped 23.34; **strened** 116.10; **streined** *ppl. adj.* made tight 123.298
streites *n. pl.* narrow tracks 66.74
streit(e *adj.* strict 2.57, 45.505, 142.66, 161.125; frugal 52.2; cramped 72.26, 91.45, 161.182; troublesome 79.135; narrow 48.105, 137.57, 145.44, 166.30, (H2) 176.370; **streyte** narrow 5.251; **streiter** *comp.* narrower 175.286
streitely *adv.* in close confinement 6.8; strictly 47.49, 174.683; tightly 47.228, 79.266
strened *see* **streyne**
strengid *v. pa.* pressed 117.443 *note*
strength(e *n.* force 2.133, (G) 3.67, 10.68; violence 90.137; army 112.355, 129.94; effort 117.13 *note*
strengthe *v. inf.* strengthen 175.177; **strengthed** *pa. p.* 24.83; **istrengthid** (H2) 1.6
stryf(f) *n.* dispute 14.43, 79.789, 106.54; struggle 20.25, 23.148; **striff** 24.121
striken *ppl. adj.* afflicted 29.30
striue *v. inf.* argue 44.58; **strofe** *pa.* 11.34, 156.223; **stroof** (H1) 146.78; **stroue** 90.124; **striuen** *pa. p.* 93.235; **striuynge** *ppl. adj.* 120.51
stroght *see* **streche**
stronge *adj.* difficult *65.348 *note*
study *n.* zeal 129.54, 139.27; **stody** 28.59; **studie** 117.297; **studyes** *pl.* efforts 79.1057; **stodies** 22.188
study *v. inf.* strive 79.1057; **stody** *imp.* 78.23; **studye** consider 112.498; **stodied** *pa.* 112.359; **studied** studied 127.8; strove 129.28
stuffed *ppl. adj.* suffocated 79.620
suayre *n.* linen cloth used to wrap head of corpse before burial 28.124 *note*
subieccion *n.* governing control 5.158, 60.226, 79.14
submitte *v. inf.* subjugate 110.29, 174.205; **submitted** *pa.* 61.63; *pa. p.* 29.194
subscripcion *n.* inscription 174.328
substaunce *n.* material wealth 25.118, 106.14
subtile *see* **sotille**
successours *n. pl.* descendants 13.67
suerly *see* **surely**
suerte *see* **surete**
sufferable *adj.* bearable 50.41; long-suffering 84.352; capable of suffering 149.62
sufferably *adv.* patiently 54.144, 134.128
sufferaunce *n.* permission 79.95, 135.83, 138.125; tolerance 149.59
suffisaunt *adj.* sufficient 28.10, 84.283; **sufficiaunt** 99.8
suffrage *n.* intercessory prayer 10.89; **suffrages** *pl.* 156.11
suffre *v. inf.* tolerate 16.12, 18.42, 79.514; allow 22.101, (G) 38.90, 60.345, 95.163; endure 27.70; **sufferist** *pr. 2 sg.* 90.93; **sufferithe** undergoes 79.725; *imp. sg.* suffer 20.146; allow 55.118, 125.124; **sufferith** *imp. pl.* 26.227; **suffredist** *pa. 2 sg.* suffered (G) 38.82; **suff(e)red** *pa.* allowed 9.89; 21.9; endured 16.47; *pa. p.* allowed 8.148, 52.45, 90.279
suithe *v. pr.* follows *28.20
sumtyme *adv.* on one occasion 113.128
superflue *adj.* extravagant 79.407
+**supersubstancial** *adj.* above the material world 64.209 *note*
suplement *n.* supplying 155.2
sure *adj.* safe 24.132, 58.54; untroubled 112.567; certain 117.32
surely *adv.* safely 48.114, 60.199; **suerly** 54.225, 84.28, 136.82; certainly 45.6, 47.122, 54.106; confidently 11.356, 83.305, 90.256; **sewrely** (G) 4.6
surete *n.* guarantee 81.15; **suerte** *4.54; **seurete** security 64.318; **seuerte** 155.85; **suerte** 90.329

surmounted *v. pa. sg.* subjugated 100.2; excelled 84.406
suspecious *adj.* untrusted 9.92
suste(i)ne *v. inf.* support 2.219, 60.263; withstand 75.26; undergo 79.301; **susteyned** *pa.* underwent 20.4; provided for 45.235, 93.192; supported 123.295, 156.161; held back 159.49; **sustenid** suffered 123.214; **susteyned** *ppl. adj.* supported 58.437, 90.389; **susteynynge** *ger.* undergoing 36.48
+sustenable *adj.* supportable 155.30 *note*
sustinaunce *n.* subsistence 6.7, 18.24; support 22.24
suttelli *see* **sotilly**
suall(e *see* **suelle**
sualw *v. inf.* swallow 112.813; **swalued** 54.179; **sualued** *pa.* 87.53; **swolued** 11.13, 140.40
suelle *v. inf.* increase 90.133; **suall(e** *pa.* swelled 47.267, 161.390; **suolle** 9.109; **swolle** 83.334; **suolle(n** *ppl. adj.* 58.434, 63.125; **swellinge** *ppl. adj.* 139.177; **suellynge** *ger.* 58.435
suere *v. inf.* take an oath, vow 45.485; *pr.* 135.121; *imp.* 136.81; **suore** *pa.* 29.208, 45.484, 79.865; **swore** 1.186, 28.71, 136.83; **suore** *pa. p.* 135.134; **sueringges** *ger. pl.* oaths 136.9
suete *adj.* sweet 1.209; **swete** 12.76; **swote** (G) 55.96; **sote** 105.67
swete *n.* sweat 28.185; **suete** 92.85, 156.127; **swotes** *pl.* 112.826
suetnesse *n.* fragrance 112.716
suette *v. pa.* sweated 12.93, 50.256, 175.162; **swette** 161.233; **suetinge** *ger.* 84.382, 142.45; **suetingges** labours 116.227
suolle, swolle *see* **suelle**
swolued *see* **sualw**
swore *see* **suere**
swote *see* **suete**

T

tabernacle *n.* portable sanctuary of the Israelites 7.46; dwelling place 112.168, 161.362, (D) 178.146; **tabernacles** *pl.* dwellings 28.83, 116.185
tabul *n.* tablet (G) 38.134; **table** 58.262, 61.46, 175.327; **tables** *pl.* 13.227; **tablis** (D) 178.634
tabur *n.* small drum (G) 4.20; **tabre** (G) 4.36
take *v. inf.* capture 9.114, 26.86, 66.79; seize (G) 42.24; take in marriage 38.4; give 37.105; **taketh** *pr. 3 sg.* receives 79.212; **taken** *pr. pl.* take 66.3; take *imp. sg.* give 84.128, 112.574; **take aȝen** *imp.* regain (G) 43.24; **takithe** *imp. pl.* seize 87.8; **tokest** *pa. 2 sg.* gave 112.688; ~ **upon the** decided 93.215; **toke** *pa.* gave 2.220, (G) 4.65, 7.165; handed over 102.58; received 9.10; sent 21.6; seized 29.55, 79.275; welcomed 74.24; grasped 175.95; **toke hym** *pa. refl.* committed himself 173.526; **token** *pa. pl.* seized 59.28; gave 74.29; accepted 78.90, 138.98 *note*; **take(n** *pa. p.* given 1.215, 18.5, 28.143, 79.744; captured (G) 2.299, 14.8, (G) 46.12; received 25.170, 47.237, 79.322; seized 83.219; asserted (G) 43.111; derived 112.548; taken up 174.36; **takin** understood as 60.59 *note*; **takyn** captured 18.4; **takyng(e** *pr. p.* partaking 28.135; *ger.* capture (G) 2.302, 79.447, 175.131; taking in marriage 38.5; **takinge ayen** repetition 110.296
takelyng *ger.* rigging 2.67
takked *v. pa. p.* secured with nails 24.58
tamed *v. pa.* injured 165.691
tapit *n.* decorative carpet 58.238
tarie(n *v. pr. pl.* stay 20.79; delay 66.232, 124.181; **taryest** *pr. 2 sg.* (G) 3.70, 29.69; **tarie** *imp.* 165.760; **tarying** *pr. p.* staying 20.80; **taried** *pa.* delayed 53.362, 112.387, 125.82; stayed 64.50; **tarienge** *ger.* delay 45.90, 79.820, 117.107, 165.254; **tariengges** *ger. pl.* periods of staying 64.54
+tariengly *adv.* slowly 65.139 *note*
taste *v. inf.* ~ **his pounce** feel his pulse 25.203
taste *n.* odour 58.236; **to the** ~ for tasting 17.27
taverner *n.* tavern-keeper 26.164
taxed *v. pa.* prescribed 45.359
teche *v. inf.* teach, direct (G) 4.116, 7.158; **techinge** *pr. p.* instructing 111.23; **taught** *pa.* showed 125.175; commanded 23.66; advised 47.201; instructed 25.155; *pa. p.* 13.236, 22.17,

93.204; suggested 112.539; **techinge** *ger.* instruction 138.47
tedius *adj.* bored (D) 179.526
teye *v. inf.* tether 5.55; **teyed** *pa.* 99.32
teler *see* **tiliere**
tell *v. inf.* narrate 20.47; proclaim 66.1; **tellithe** *pr. 3 sg.* teaches 116.232; **tolde** *pa.* counted 45.250, 154.170
temperalteis *n. pl.* worldly things (G) 43.172
temperaunce *n.* forbearance 49.88
tempered *ppl. adj.* mixed 161.113 *note*
temperel(l *adj.* secular 55.182, 74.68; earthly (G) 43.102, 65.218, 174.375; **temporall** 106.228; 54.170; **temperell** (prayers) of the general rather than sanctoral cycle 155.377
tempre *adj.* temperate (G) 42.51, 79.630
temptaciones *n. pl.* trials 154.63
tende *v. inf.* pay attention 1.219, 88.137, 117.355, 165.603; **tenden** *pr. pl.* 175.366; **tended** *pa.* *24.4; **tendid** (G) *42.33; **tended** given itself to 28.105
tendre *v. inf.* soften 22.38
ter(r)estre *adj.* earthly 61.4, 133.41
terme *n.* end (G) 3.86 *note*, 30.32; time limit 64.45, 83.432, 142.451, 145.32, 151.22, 174.567; for the duration 79.503; stipulation (H1) 158.8
termined *v. pa. p.* ended 31.2
+**tesmonage** *n.* testimony 7.74 *note*
thanke *n.* reward 8.232
thankyngges *n. pl.* thanks 7.199, 8.215
thau *n.* tau, letter t in Hebrew and Greek alphabets 138.148
thedir *adv.* thither 2.78, 6.65, 25.81; **thidir** (G) 4.144
thennes *adv.* thence 11.203, 14.37, 22.184; **thennis** 18.23, 28.70
theolegens *n. pl.* theologians 112.665 *note*
therfore *conj.* because 106.285, 117.16
thinkithe *v. impers. pr.* it seems 22.118, 51.18–19; **thought** *pa.* it seemed 6.32, 17.56, 79.889
thraldom(e *n.* servitude 32.20, 106.93, (D) 179.38
thralle *n.* slave 165.621
thrawe *v. inf.* throw 48.67, 58.249, 79.1031; **þrouithe** *pr. 3 sg.* 50.85; **threwe** *pa.* 26.31, 48.83, 50.499; **threuȝ** (D) 178.140; **thrawe(n** *pa. p.* 2.287, 54.138, 93.138; **thrauen** 126.17; **throwe** 2.288, *20.140; **throuen** 116.128
threst *n.* thirst 18.12, *90.84; **thruste** 11.298, 12.68, 53.250
thrested *v. pa.* thirsted 79.641; **thristid** was thirsty (H2) 176.253
thretyng *pr. p.* threatening 35.37; *ppl. adj.* 79.376; **thretinge** *ger.* threat 85.7; **thretyngges** *pl.* 69.15, 79.364
threwe *see* **thrawe**
þridde *ord. num.* third (G) 4.125; **thridde** 5.72, 17.29
thries *adv.* three times 11.80, 13.29, 142.152
thristid *see* **thrested**
throwe *see* **thrawe**
thruste *see* **threst**
thuart *adj.* crossways 37.24
tierce *n.* **houre of** ~ third canonical hour, 9 a.m 5.177, 99.101
tiers *n. pl.* tears 117.42
tyle *n.* brick 104.122
tilie *v. inf.* cultivate (H2) 178.323; **tilithe** *pr. 3 sg.* 150.22, *167.42; **tilled** *pa.* cultivated 18.31
tiliere *n.* cultivator of soil (H2) 178.332; **teler** 116.231; **tyliers** *pl.* 154.112
tilthe *n.* cultivation 116.231
tyme *n.* season 5.53; *pl.* 33.24
tiraunt *adj.* tyrannous 116.210
tiraunt *n.* tyrant 4.225, 38.69, 53.350; torturer 165.763; **tyrauntes** *pl.* tyrants 61.115, 84.390; persecutors 10.67; torturers 54.99, 84.438; **tyrauntis** *pl.* (G) 55.188 *note*
tyrauntrie *n.* tyranny 11.42
tissu *n.* rich fabric 23.31; **tyssue** 104.40
title *n.* inscription 5.90, 146.70
titled *v. pa. p.* inscribed 116.98
to *adv.* too 5.251, 11.55
tobete *ppl. adj.* beaten 75.6
tobreke *v. inf.* break 4.214, 116.126; violate 20.126; **tobrekithe** *pr. 3 sg.* 155.237; *imp. pl.* destroy 59.9; **tobreke** *pa.* broke apart *22.106; **tobrake** 96.57; **tobracke** 163.26; **tobroke** *pa. p.* 96.69, 116.104; **tobrokin** *ppl. adj.* 116.128; **tobroke** worn out 101.35
tobreste *v. inf.* burst apart 18.30; **tobrast(e** *pa.* 54.137, 93.141, 118.5; **tobreste** *pa. p.* destroyed 20.129; **tobroste(n** *pa. p.* torn asunder 24.25; beaten 68.43; broken (G) 42.46, 47.162,

79.686, 102.62; **tobrostin** *ppl. adj.* 125.91, 148.119
tocutte *v. pa.* cut to pieces 108.65
todrawe *v. inf.* pull apart 93.123; **todrewe** *pa.* lacerated *24.44, 53.159; pulled out 88.96; **todrawe(n** *pa. p.* lacerated 37.81; pulled apart 94.155
tofor(e *prep.* earlier than 5.198, 12.93, 93.29; in presence of 5.262; in front of 8.32, 92.39
tohewe *v. pa.* cut to pieces 134.103, 152.198; **tohewen** *pa. p.* 106.78; **tohewin** 134.86
toke(n *see* **take**
tolde *see* **tell**
+tomang(e)led *ppl. adj.* mutilated 60.156 *note*, 131.8
to(o)n(e *num.* **the toon** etc. that one 5.42, 13.189, 14.8, 16.75; **too** (H2) 177.8, (H2) 178.382
tong(g)e *n.* speech 24.3; language 28.182, 84.135; tongue 24.49; **tvnge** speech (G) 43.36; **tunge** language 94.95; speech 119.107; **tong(g)es** *pl.* tongues (anat.) 28.3, 65.89, 175.145; languages 133.25; flames 48.73, 65.271; **tunges** tongues (anat.) 65.89
tonne *n.* large barrel 8.5, 15.20, 45.107; **tonnes** *pl.* 157.10
torende *v. inf.* tear to pieces 113.165, 131.33, 165.766; **torent(e** *imp. pl.* 35.78; *pa.* (G) 4.33, 10.129, 20.19; lacerated (G) 46.18; tore up 25.173, 116.129; **torent(e** *pa. p.* torn 2.248, 55.37, 73.7, 92.47; **torent** *ppl. adj.* 6.23, 17.24, torn apart 24.26, (G) 38.88, 48.73, 54.110
torment *n.* torture 7.22; **turment** 87.40; **turnement** 113.124, 116.146, 128.159; instrument of torture 118.9; **torment** 24.23, 54.110; **turment** 87.35, 125.93, 165.771; **torment** tempest 60.175; **turment** (G) 55.109, 101.66; **tormentes** *pl.* tortures 54.120, 91.72; **turmentes** 96.112; instruments of torture 125.96; tempests 128.213; **tormentis** 54.118; **turmentis** (H2) 177.104; **turnementes** tortures 119.33; **turnementis** 165.735
torned *see* **turne**
toswolle *v. pa. p.* swollen 58.435
totor(e)n *ppl. adj.* torn 20.100, 87.37, 173.148
touche *v. inf.* refer to 61.47; **touched** *pa.* pertained to 10.26
tough *see* **towe**
tourbe *n.* crowd 64.191, 79.430, 80.160; **tourbes** *pl.* 112.345
towasted *v. pa. p.* consumed 92.71
towe *n.* tow, unworked flax 156.42; **tough** 84.482
+towounded *v. pa. p.* wounded 47.41 *note*
trace *n.* scar 137.49; ~ **of his fete** footstep 149.61; *pl.* 64.33; **traces** scars 161.197; **trases** 139.25
tracte *n.* treatise 90.311; chant sung during mass from Septuagesima until Easter 30.40, 174.463
traied *v. pa. p.* betrayed 11.177
traytourly *adv.* seditiously 79.96
translacion *n.* removal and reinterment 80.290, 105.91, 159.383
translated *pa. p.* disinterred and removed 12.109, 126.21
trases *see* **trace**
trauaile *n.* labour 30.40, 45.26, 66.38; suffering 83.324, 113.81; **traueile** labour (D) 178.127; **trauaile** child-bearing 90.137
trauayle *v. inf.* labour 152.15, 176.90; afflict 135.58; suffer 71.11; give birth 90.136, 148.21, 166.59; *pr.* suffer 35.91, 50.165; labour 86.47, 105.144; *imp.* 61.6, 173.346; **travailinge** *pr. p.* 66.7; **travelinge** *ppl. adj.* 63.90 *note*, giving birth 84.374; **trauelled** *pa.* troubled 36.44; **trauailed** laboured in childbirth 174.596; laboured 171.11; **travail(l)ed** *pa. p.* wearied 1.203, troubled 17.55, laboured 25.9, afflicted 91.71; **travelled** 5.268; **trauailed** *ppl. adj.* 36.46, 159.400; wearied 161.110; **traueiled** afflicted (H2) 178.291; **trauelinge of child** *ger.* childbirth 87.97, 90.211; **travayleng** *pr. p.* travelling 20.34; **traueling** 29.7
traueilous *adj.* difficult 165.725
trauers *adj.* **in** ~, crosswise 24.24, 175.272; **a** ~ upside down 83.459
trauers *n.* cross-piece 61.51
tre(e *n.* cross 1.136; wood 1.142, (G) 4.124, (G) 43.18, 47.98 *note*, 58.103, 110.214, 115.28, 128.4,42, 148.91, 164.42; beam 37.54, 61.45, (H1) 158.21,

171.84; plank 55.179; **trees** *pl.* types of wood 48.12, 61.42; beams 61.47
treede *v. inf.* trample upon (D) 178.119; **trode** *ppl. adj.* 79.895
tremble *v. pr.* cause to tremble 86.60 *note*
trentale *n.* set of thirty masses for the dead 156.376
treson *n.* betrayal 11.184, 84.297
trespace *n.* transgression 47.182; **trespas** 124.145, 156.232
trespasour *n.* transgressor 161.337
trete *n.* treatise 113.140, 117.432; **tretys** *pl.* 113.36
trete *v. inf.* discuss 58.141; **treten** *pr. pl.* 83.442; **treted** *pa.* discussed 9.19, 53.205
+**trewant, truandise** *adj., n.,* wretched, wretchedness 159.387 *note*, 159.391
trewe *adj. see* **true**
trewe *n.* tribute (G) 44.43; **true** 50.371
trewens *see* **creueis**
tribute *n.* tax 79.99; **tribuct** 165.18; **under** ~ under obligation to pay tax 79.5
trifeles *see* **trufulles**
trippest *v. pr. 2 sg.* dance 50.164; **tripped** *pa.* 113.51
tristes(se *n.* sadness 34.38, *84.371, 84.447, 146.41
+**trivmphancion** *n.* (G) 43.67 *note*
trode *see* **treede**
trompe *see* **trumpe**
tromped *v. pa.* sounded trumpets (D) 178.611
trone *n.* throne 13.195, 29.199, 58.415; **trones** *pl.* the third order of angels 112.314
trouble *n.* turbulence 45.142, 90.135, 133.48; **trowbul** distress (G) 3.90
trouthe *n.* oath 125.48; trustworthiness 129.99
trowe *v. inf.* believe (D) 179.110; *pr. 1 sg.* believe 24.99, 95.77, 172.10; **trouest** *2 sg.* 4.188, 29.184, 135.25; **trowist** (G) 42.11; **trowest** 54.191; **trowithe** *3 sg.* 63.145; **trowe** *pr. pl.* 61.164, 66.235; **trowed** *pa.* 79.838, 156.123; **trowyd** *28.44; **trowidden** *pa. pl.* (G) 43.136; **trowed** *pa. p.* 101.42
truage *n.* payment of tribute 13.216, 50.34,374, 53.301; dues 26.175; liability to pay tribute 81.30
truandise *see* **trewant**
true *adj.* genuine 2.188, 8.56; christian 7.153, 36.85, 75.1; faithful 10.33, *11.311, 13.146, 61.302; correct 9.69, 11.123; **trewe** genuine 25.30; christian (G) 3.87; faithful 129.139, 156.1; correct 11.231
true *n. see* **trewe**
trufulles *n. pl.* trifles 11.316; **trifeles** trivialities 117.20
truys *n.* truce 138.98
trumpe *n.* trumpet 173.155, 175.74; **trompe** 173.166; **trompes** *pl.* 63.89, 64.99
trustely *adv.* uncompromisingly 129.37
tuelfe *ord. num.* twelfth, ~ **day** feast of Epiphany 25.7
tunge *see* **tong(g)e**
turment *see* **torment**
turne *v. inf.* change 10.18, 53.349; be reconciled 10.68, 25.135; change direction 13.126; roll (G) 38.114, (of eyes) 49.261; revert 112.909; ~ **ayen** go back 30.50, 48.123; **turned (ayein)** *pa.* went back 9.30, 11.74; **turned** became 10.123; turned over 174.21; turned round 29.76; **torned** directed 28.158; went back 49.29; *pa. p.* restored 10.97; twisted 11.288; gone back 13.237; persuaded 102.43; changed 142.95; **torned** changed 24.73, 28.3; **turnid aboute** *ppl. adj.* encircled 112.348; ~ **aȝeyne** *ppl. adj.* come round again (of year) (G) 38.144; **turnyng** *ger.* ~ **ayein** going back 17.54; coming round 30.27
turneye *v. inf.* joust 79.66; **turneid** *pa.* *123.238
turnement *see* **torment**
turtull *n.* turtledove 36.158; **turtelys** *pl.* 36.97
twey(n)(e *num.* two **tweye** 1.295; **twey** 24.24; **tweyne** 37.74, 44.118; **twayne** 9.19; **a tweyne** in two 35.115

U

vmbeli *adv.* humbly 146.75
vnagreable *adj.* unpleasant 129.79 *note*
+**vnagreabulte** *n.* disagreeable nature (H2) 176.224 *note*
+**vnap(p)ered** *v. pa.* disappeared 112.238 *note*, 113.434, 143.30

+**vnbeysaunce** *n.* disobedience 49.6 *note*
vnbodely *adj.* incorporeal *49.148
unccion *n.* anointing 12.25, 65.145
vnchast *adj.* lecherous 14.17, 143.3
vnchasteli *adv.* lasciviously 14.17
vnclene *adj.* impure 4.187, 5.261
vnclennesse *n.* lechery 33.69, 47.129, 63.15
+**vncondempnithe** *v. pr. 3 sg.* approves 11.259 *note*
vnconninge *ger.* ignorance 86.99
+**vncorded** *v. pa.* disagreed 44.132 *note*
vncouthe *adj.* unfamiliar 79.223
vncouenable *adj.* unsuitable 123.178; illicit 58.53
vncun(n)ynge *ppl. adj.* ignorant 65.306 *note*, 92.18, 159.299; **vnkunnynge** (H2) 176.323
vncustumable *adj.* extraordinary 79.714; unfamiliar 173.114
+**vncustumed** *v. pa. p.* unaccustomed 47.53 *note*
vndedly *adj.* immortal 5.161, (G) 42.12, 63.152, 79.848
vndedlynesse *n.* immortality 11.308, 155.111, 163.52
+**vndefaillynge** *adj.* unfailing, 1.219 *note*
vndefouled *ppl. adj.* undefiled 1.142, 124.13, 125.159
vnderstonde *v. inf.* receive (H2) 178.315; *inf. for passive* **to** ~ to be understood 32.35; **understondithe** signifies 155.127; **vndirstondyng** *ger.* intelligence (L) 179.399–400
vndertake *v. inf.* undertake 125.60; **vndirtoke** *pa.* rebuked (G) 1.121; **vndertoke** 28.115, 45.463, 47.329, 56.9, 64.25, 90.29, 101.10, 106.23; **vndertake** *pa. p.* made a commitment to 22.73, 37.94; **rebuked** 82.26, 173.156
+**vndesesed** *ppl. adj.* unharmed 79.344 *note*
+**vndesseiuable** *adj.* (H2) trustworthy 176.355 *note*
vndiscrete *adj.* injudicious 64.28
vnduely *adv.* uncanonically 16.60; **vndewly** improperly 146.229
vngilty *adj.* guiltless 79.773
vngoodly *adv.* wrongly 36.320, 161.174
vnhilled *v. pa.* uncovered 60.319; **vnheled** 110.282
vnhonest(e)ly *adv.* irreverently (G) 40.9; improperly 105.11
vnkinde *adj.* unnatural (D) 179.222
vnkindenesse *n.* unnaturalness (D) 179.230
vnknette *ppl. adj.* undone 7.170
vnknowe *v. pr.* are ignorant of 163.66; *pa.* refused to recognize 28.45; **vnknewe** lacked knowledge of 13.205, 117.390; **vnknowen** *ppl.* not knowing 112.763 *note*; **vnknowe** unrecognized 88.56; **vnknowynge** *ppl. adj.* unknown 49.174; it being unknown 50.398, 77.14
vnkunnynge *see* **vncunnynge**
vnlefull *adj.* illicit 135.47; sinful 137.104
unliklyhede *n.* dissimilarity 117.66
vnlowse *v. inf.* undo 11.301; **vnlosed** *pa.* 79.675
vnmevable *adj.* immobile 24.62; unmoveable 38.10; immutable 64.257, 65.25
vnmight *n.* impotence 176.31
vnmyghti *adj.* powerless 50.88, 106.199
vnnethe(s *adv.* with difficulty 11.326, 22.175, 23.95; scarcely 28.131, 45.28, 113.289
vnnoble *adj.* of low rank 38.5
+**vnobediensers** *n. pl.* persons who defy church teachings 135.69 *note*
vnordeyned *ppl. adj.* detached (?) 112.829 *note*; disordered 173.235
vnordinat(e *adj.* unrestrained 33.69, 63.69; inappropriate 124.24, 135.31; disorderly 175.204
vnordenatly *adv.* unrestrainedly 1.141, 113.56; **vnordinatly** 79.564, 120.11, 163.5; improperly 167.27
vnouercome *adj.* undefeated 24.120
vnperfit(e *adj.* unfinished 26.183; imperfect 63.143
vnpitous *adj.* merciless 7.85
vnpossible *adj.* impossible 5.89, 155.331
+**vnpouruoiedly** *adv.* unexpectedly (G) 60.145 *note*
+**vnremuables** *adj. pl.* immutable 116.284 *note*
vnresonable *adj.* irrational 13.158; without power of reason 116.242 *note*, 124.110, 163.311, 167.69, (D) *178.5; improper 22.49
vnsaueri *adj.* lacking in taste 65.125
+**vnsent** *ppl. adj.* ~ **for** uninvited 16.33 *note*

vnshamefull *adj.* shameless 14.21
vnshette *v. inf.* unlock 54.200
vnsittinge *adj.* inappropriate 120.13
vnspekeable *adj.* ineffable 112.350
vntamed *ppl. adj.* uninjured 68.66 *note*; untouched 79.331 *note*
+**unthriftely** *adj* immoral 139.189 *note*
vntrouth *n.* infidelity 34.10
vntrue *adj.* infidel 58.187, 142.384; lacking faith 155.266; **vntrewe** 79.1061; lying 173.96; ~ **beleuers** pagans 22.111; ~ **lyuers** 79.327
+**vnuincyble** *adj.* invincible 135.145 *note*
vnvisibly *adv.* invisibly *65.53
vnware *adj.* incautious (G) 55.177; unexpected 79.356
vnweting(e *adj.* unknowing 58.306, 79.656, 146.212, 159.393; (H1) **vnwyting** 143.64
vnwetingly *adv.* unknowingly 29.10
vnworship(p *n.* dishonour 116.249, 128.13, 165.559
vnworship *v. inf.* dishonour 79.9; **vnworshipped** *pa. p.* 166.23, 173.342
vp(p)londis(s)he *adj.* rustic 113.279, 136.64
upright *adv.* supine 159.319
vpsodoune *adj.* upsidedown 38.59, 110.233, 118.13, 148.97
vsage *n.* custom 5.120, 83.17, 157.15, 175.255; use 50.508
use *n.* **in** ~ customarily 26.212
vse *v. inf.* make use of 28.162, 35.51; enjoy 137.12; practise 31.30; **vsest** *pr. 2 sg.* 79.205; **usithe** *3 sg.* is accustomed 165.284; **vsed** *pa.* practised 2.93, 14.52, 23.121; enjoyed 24.74; treated 66.117; *ppl. adj.* current 9.69; **vsyng** *ger.* use (L) 179.333
vssher *n.* doorkeeper 112.178
usure *n.* interest on money or goods loaned 50.331
vtas *n.* ecclesiastical octave, the eight days after a church festival 12.2, 110.293, 123.217; **oeptas** 110.294; **vtauuce** 123.209
vtter *v. inf.* reveal 2.35; **vttred** *pa. p.* *127.69
vtterest *adj.* utmost 129.117
vtterly *adv.* completely 37.105; amiss 124.246
vtwarde *adj.* external *83.413

V

uailable *adj.* valuable 156.24
vagaunt *adj.* wandering *178.366 *note*
vayne *adj.* useless 135.69; **veyn(e** 8.37; meaningless 38.46, 79.788, 113.78, *129.11; foolish 87.25; proud 143.3; **in** ~ useless 8.37; **in** ~ *adv.* uselessly 25.9
vantinge *ppl. adj.* boastful 45.179
variable *adj.* capricious 143.3
variaunt *adj.* changeable 110.129
vaunted *v. pa.* boasted 23.43
Veer *n.* Spring 33.68, 34.4, 107.33; **Ver** 36.159
veyne *see* **vayne**
+**veynquor** *n.* conqueror 50.391 *note*
velayn *n.* peasant 47.232
velanie *n.* degradation 173.15; **velanye** shame (H2) 177.34; **vyleni** churlishness 142.310
+**vendeged** *ppl. adj.* gathered (of grapes for wine) 155.55 *note*
venemous *adj.* poisonous 48.11, 52.31
venge *v. inf.* avenge 4.216, 45.327, 161.409; **vengest** *pr. 2 sg.* 24.38; **venge** *pr. pl.* 91.59; **vengid** *pa.* 60.121; **venged** *pa. p.* 98.23
venge(ou)r *n.* punisher 82.5, 113.44
veniall *adj.* minor 156.328
vermyn *n.* parasitic infections 9.110, 13.216
verray *adj.* real, genuine 4.204, 6.55, 8.117, 9.26 *note*; indisputable 5.73; complete 45.487, 57.15, 93.121; **verrey** real (G) 3.39, 37.108, 90.27; complete 29.99; **verri** real (H1) 146.90
verray *adv.* truly 8.56, 11.274, *64.151; totally 10.104, 57.22, 79.290
verre *n.* drinking glass 47.56; **verres** *pl.* *142.110
verr(e)ily *adv.* exactly 1.295; truly 26.85; completely 13.97; **verili** 8.127; **verrily** correctly 29.9; **verrayly** truly 45.480
vertu(e *n.* power 4.229, 20.6, 37.108; moral goodness (H2) 1.4, 1.260, 8.160, 12.53, 18.42, 66.154, 144.51 *note*, 146.17; inherent quality or condition 49.96, 58.128, 65.206, 112.86, 144.50 *note*, 173.136; **vertuis** *pl.* good moral qualities(G) 4.51; **vertues** 2.56, 87.69, 133.27, 134.76, 155.317; virtuous acts 179.536; inherent qualities 31.22, 156.376; powers 86.60, 135.124, (H2)

177.37; the fifth order of angels (H2) 178.310; **vertuous** powers (G) 43.25; good moral qualities 173.183

vertuous *adj.* morally good 2.55, 53.46, 58.65; **vertues** 58.64, (H1) 145.22

vestement *n.* garment 47.184, 60.38, 80.234; religious garb 25.8; **vestementis** *pl.* 10.98, 84.161; **vestimentis** clothes 26.47, 173.182; **vestementes** 72.12, 112.748; clerical garments 53.61; **vestimentes** 165.492

vexed afflicted, tormented 6.24, 22.79, 26.108, 45.376; molested 135.8; **wexe** *inf.* trouble 174.317

viage *n.* journey 2.280, 27.34, 47.167; **viages** *pl.* 154.139

vicarie *n.* deputy 23.86; **viker(y** 96.45, 109.56, 123.356; **vyker** governor, deputy 96.45

+**victoriaunce** *n.* triumph (G) 43.78 *note*

+**vigorosite** *n.* vigour 65.297 *note*

vyker *see* **vicarie**

vikership *n.* position of deputy 123.360

vile *adj.* of low quality 26.73, 45.14, 64.196, 88.25

vyleni *see* **velanie**

+**vynge** *n.* vineyard 117.268 *note*

viol(l)e *n.* phial 15.32, 17.25; **violes** *pl.* 128.166

+**violed** *v. pa.* desecrated *156.421 *note*, 434

virgine *adj.* virginal 5.67, 91.34; pure, unsullied 11.216, 50.285

virgynel(l *adj.* virginal 7.213, 58.6; **virgynial** 11.269

visage *n.* face 1.277, 2.137, 7.25

vision *n.* prophetic dream 2.45, 5.169, 7.73, 121.15; delusion 142.219; *see also* **auision**

visitacion *n.* episcopal visit for instruction 15.40; arrival of missionaries 79.1068; visiting of relics 112.273; **visitaciouns** (D) 178.439 *note*

visytours *n. pl.* ecclesiastical inspectors 58.121

vocacion *n.* invocation 175.31 *note*

voide *adj.* empty 10.50, 13.211, 26.259, 45.459; worthless 87.25

voide *v. inf.* expel 128.246, 161.300, 165.206; depart 165.514; empty 175.366; **uoide** expel 116.14; **voide** *pr.* depart (H1) 143.29; **voideth** *pr. 3 sg.* 36.113; **voided** *pa.* emptied 155.36; **voydinge** *ger.* process of emptying 155.29 *note*

volatiles *n. pl.* birds (D) 178.4

vouchesauf *v. inf.* grant 45.269, 79.919, 117.38; **fouchesauf** 161.260, 165.188; **vouchithe** *pr.* attests to 36.159; **vouched sauf** *pa.* 79.645

vowed *v. pa.* pledged 93.330, 148.72, 151.117

vouterer(e *n.* adulterer 124.187, 133.217, 144.55; **vouutereres** *pl.* 24.41; *see too* **avouterere**

W

wached *see* **wake**

way(e *n.* road, path 20.32, 45.66, 47.369, 124.33; distance 25.161; **weye** 138.54; **weyis** *pl.* paths (G) 3.87, 119.113; **in the waye** on the way 156.60

waye *v. inf.* weigh 94.75; **weye** 94.77; **weie** *imp.* (D) 179.452; **wayed** *pa.* 83.384; **weyed** 94.81; **wayed** *pa. p.* 112.496; **weied** 138.44

wayle *v. inf.* lament 79.1054; **weille** 84.224; **waylithe** *pr.* 36.159

waytes *n. pl.* watchmen 175.202

wake *v. inf.* stay awake 2.25, 5.207; keep vigil 94.52, 99.77, 112.599; keep watch 175.200; **wakyng** *pr. p.* staying awake 2.57; **woken** *pa.* 5.203; **woke** kept vigil 23.104, (G) 40.7, 45.105; kept watch 135.103; **wached** stayed awake 129.94; **wokyn** kept a funeral vigil 110.198; **waken** *pa. p.* kept awake 101.47; **waked** stirred up 112.120; **wakingges** *ger. pl.* vigils 88.66, 113.214, 159.377

wallithe *pr. 3 sg.* abounds 175.395

wamelynge *v. pr. p.* rolling around 106.78 *note*

wamentacion *n.* lamentation 2.267, 26.193

wannesse *n.* (H2) *178.390 *note*

wantith *v. pr.* lacks (D) 179.455

warde, in ~ **to** *n.* in charge of 77.43

ware *adj.* mindful 79.768, (D) 179.243

warnes *n.* awareness 175.238

wasshe *v. inf.* wash 112.133, 139.85; *pr. pl.* 174.224; **woschen** 61.36; **wesshe** 174.222; **wos(s)he** *pa.* washed 10.16, 90.23; **wissh(e** (G) 40.29, 90.46, 121.55 **wosshen** *pa. pl.* 77.69; **waschin** *pa. p.*

10.98; **wesshe** 139.181; **wasshe** soaked 76.23; made clean 110.104
wast(e *adj.* desolate (G) 39.6, *66.96, 139.45
waste *v. inf.* consume (G) 43.136; **wastithe** *pr. 3 sg.* destroys 65.225, 84.482; **wasted** *pa.* devastated *82.19, 108.14; consumed 84.372; destroyed 84.482, 104.121; **wasted** *pa. p.* devastated 15.3, 101.59, 117.344; consumed 24.102, 159.228; ~ **awaye** eaten up 54.17; **wastid** *ppl. adj.* wasted away (G) 43.22, 52.68; **wasted** destroyed 156.328; **wastinge** *ger.* diminishing 112.777; **wasting(e** *pr. p.* consuming 36.268, 117.163
water *n.* river 153.16, 154.192
wawis *n. pl.* waves (G) 44.19, 55.164; **wawes** 50.487, 58.278, 90.135, 138.57, (H2) 177.109; **waues** 44.70
wawithe *v. pr.* waves 80.161
wax(s)e *see* **wexen**
wedde *v. inf.* betroth 80.109; **weddid** *pa.* gave in marriage 29.82, 123.49, 174.574; **weddid** *pa.* married 123.188 *note*; **wedded** *pa. p.* married 80.105; betrothed (G) 42.1 *note*, 151.116; **wedded** *ppl. adj.* pledged 90.358; **wedding(e** *ger.* wedding ceremony 90.359; state of marriage 155.319; **weddingges** *pl.* marriages 112.819 *note*, 155.322
weddes *n. pl.* pledges 105.158
wede *n.* garment 1.322
wedyr *n.* weather 29.122
wedu(e *n.* widow 8.238, 108.59, 123.262, 174.558; **wedowe** 88.121, 161.124; **widue** bereaved parent 9.91; **wedues** *pl.* 49.44, 88.6; **wedwes** 174.558; **widwes** 7.7; **wydues** bereaved parents 9.90; **wedowes** deprived institutions 117.343 *note*
weye *n. see* **waye**
weye *v. see* **waye**
weille *see* **wayle**
wele *n.* wealth 2.144, prosperity 50.382; well-being 79.536, 87.72
welked *v. pa. pl.* withered 84.437
well(e *n.* spring 2.200, 4.186, 5.140; **welles** *pl.* 8.222; **wellys** 11.254, 65.412
welled *v. pa.* poured forth 161.370, 165.870
welthes *n. pl.* good things 112.791
wemme *n.* defilement 165.322
wende *v. inf.* travel (H2) 178.285; **went** *pa.* travelled 142.320; walked 83.5, 96.78; (of money) passed as current 95.113 *note*; **wentist** *pa. 2 sg.* travelled 136.90; **wentin** *pa. pl.* moved 156.257; **wente** *pa. p.* set off 55.160
wene *v. inf.* think, believe, expect 44.139; *pr.* 152.11; 90.119; **wenest** *2 sg.* 11.256, 24.31, 27.46; **wenyth** *3 sg.* (G) 4.147, 22.56; **wene(n** *pr. pl.* 28.135, 58.83, 84.180; **wenyn** 165.513, 173.407; **wenyng** *pr. p.* 5.137, 6.28; 7.104; **wentist** *pa. 2 sg.* 136.90, **wendest** 163.134; **wende** *pa.* 4.172, 6.24, 9.75, 11.6, 18.22; **wenyd** (G) 4.85; **went** 6.20, 83.93, 113.78, 133.5, 164.26; **wenden** *pl.* 36.232; **wendin** 151.80; **wende** *pa. p.* 28.100; **went** 52.25
went *see* **wende, wene**
wenw *v. inf.* winnow 80.205
werche *v. inf.* cultivate (D) 178.139; **worche** labour (D) 178.323; **werke** behave 23.115; work 29.168; **werchist** *pr. 2 sg.* cultivate (D) 178.366; **worchith** *3 sg.* (D) 179.149; **wrought** *pa.* peformed 1.292, 8.198; worked 20.104, 64.261; *pa. p.* performed 49.209, 58.26, 79.717; worked 123.242, 156.190; **werchinge** *pr. p.* bringing about 80.103; *ger.* work 79.130; **wirchinge** (D) 179.49
were *v. pr.* (?) 30.51 *note*
wery *n.* weariness 171.26
werke *n.* labour 29.49, 88.23; manner of building (G) 4.14; **werkis** *pl.* deeds (G) 4.167; **in werke** into effect 2.9
werne *v. inf.* refuse 8.224, 53.235, 106.146; **wernithe** *pr.* 129.69; **werne(d** *pa.* 47.47, 106.141, 161.38; **werned** *pa. p.* refused 129.72, 159.114; *ppl. adj.* 151.12
werrei *v. inf.* wage war against 139.188
wesshe *see* **wasshe**
wete *v.*[1] *inf.* know 2.26, 5.13, 8.55; be known 4.185, 5.64; specify 13.221, 27.53; **wite** know (H2) 178.296; **wote** *pr. 1 sg.* (H2) 1.82, 2.102, 11.318; 30.31; **wotist** *2 sg.* (G) 4.89, (D) 178.241; **woste** 25.206; **whost** 93.211; **wote** *pr. pl.* 84.196; **wete** *imp. sg.* 2.170, 11.202, 25.122; **wite (G)** 38.94; **wetithe** *imp. pl.* 11.330, 13.140, 26.93;

wiste *pa. 1 sg.* (G) 3.50, (G) 4.142; *pa. 3 sg.* (G) 4.22; **wist** 121.60; **wyst** 84.174; **wost(e** 2.125, 7.160, 9.127, 93.261, 121.60; **wost** *pa. p.* 26.149; **wetinge** *ger.* knowledge 117.43; **wetyng** *pr. p.* 37.92

wete *v.*[2] *inf.* moisten 138.87, 175.468; **wetynge** *ger.* wetting 113.302; **wetynges** *pl.* 175.451

wetyngly *adv.* knowingly 48.6

wex(e *n.* wax 36.259, 93.98, 117.131; **wexse**(G) 4.215, 94.163

wexen *v.*[1] *inf.* become 34.13; **wexe** *pr. subj.* 22.48; **wexe** *imp.* (D) 178.557; **wax(s)e** *pa.* became 2.113, 6.19, (G) 42.51; **wexe(n** 28.198, 58.265; **woxen** *pa. pl.* 139.191; *pa. p.* 79.898, (D) 178.504; **woxe** 25.111, 171.53; **wexing(e** *ger.* growing 34.51, (H2) 178.390 *note*

wexe *v.*[2] *see* **vexed**

whedir *conj.* if, whether 6.45, 79.528, 139.113

whedir *interrog. adv.* whither 17.25, 60.177, 86.135; **wheder** 112.605, 154.190

whennes *adv.* whence 20.32, 95.87

wher *conj.* whether 113.111; 151.161, 163.128, 174.302

whereto *interrog.* why 79.422; **wharto** 169.23

wherfor(e *interrog.* why (G) 3.14; *conj.* for which reason 17.16; for which purpose 22.96, 24.16

whightes *see* **wight**

whost *see* **wete** *v.*[1]

wiche *n.* witch 23.82; **whiche** idolater 58.167

widue *see* **wedue**

wight *n.* weight 2.280, 36.126, 64.116; **whightes** *pl.* 75.48

wiȝt *n.* person (G) 38.105

wikkidly *adv.* cruelly (G) 42.21

wilde *adj.* uncultivated 8.236; wanton 112.372

wilfull *adj.* willing 45.274, 79.42, 106.226, 161.274

will(e *pr. 1 sg.* wish, desire 8.118, 24.52; **wol** 136.40; **wilt** *2 sg.* 8.114, 11.12, 20.52, 25.68; **wolt** 159.147, 161.260, (D) 178.498; **will(e** *3 sg.* 7.205, 20.90, (G) 60.128; **wol** 112.280, 148.89, (H1) 143.22; **will** *pr. pl.* 106.146; **wol** 112.708; **wolde** *pr. subj.* 20.103; **wil** *imp. pl.* 20.147; **willethe** 22.40; **wold(e** *pa.* 5.13, 14.37, 37.75

willed *adj.* willing 66.109

wilne *v. inf.* desire 112.442

wynde *n.* air 66.195

wynne *v. inf.* gain 22.56; profit 26.209; *pr.* gain 106.210; **wan** *pa.* 161.26; **wanne** fought 174.314; **wonne** *pa. p.* gained 106.215, 113.273; **wynnynge** *ger.* financial success 58.313, 133.211; profit 115.15; **wynningges** *pl.* 133.218

wynter *n. pl.* years 83.280; years old 117.143, 125.115

wirchinge *see* **werche**

wysely discreetly 95.103

wissh *see* **wasshe**

wiste *see* **wete** *v.*[1]

wite *see* **wete** *v.*[1]

withedrawe *v. inf.* remove 8.63; restrain 90.72, 113.268 *note*, 116.254; distract 150.5; take away 53.283; **withedrawest** *pr. 2 sg.* 84.72; **withdrow** *pa.* removed 116.276; *pa. p.* **withdrawe** released 117.284

witheoute *adv.* outside 6.23, (G) 43.181, 54.136, 77.29, 83.110, 88.43

with(e)oute *prep.* outside (G) 1.72, *7.105, 51.34, 83.77, 84.158; **witheouten** 5.185; **with(e)oute** apart from (G) 4.136, 84.428, 155.196

withesaie deny 146.235; refuse 112.420, 161.59; **withesai(e)d(e** *pa.* denied 7.92, 10.30, 79.272; repudiated 10.39; refused 74.117; contradicted 112.493; spoke against 151.79; prevented 159.118; **withsaieng** *ger.* denial 137.84

with(h)olde *v. inf.* hold back 20.116; **withholde** remember 149.292; **withholdith** retains 65.242 *note*; **withelde** *pa.* 49.234; **withhelde** 53.138, 149.284; **with(h)olde** *pa. p.* 119.101, 154.88; occupied 175.91; **witheholde** *ppl. adj.* held back 45.9; restrained 58.397; **withholdyng** *pr. p.* preserving 131.80

+**withholders** *n. pl.* those who withhold 79.141 *note*

withsittyng *ppl. adj.* resisting (L) 179.331

wiþstondyng *ppl. adj.* resisting (L) 179.325

witles *adj.* senseless 179.430

witte *n.* intelligence 2.165, 10.6, 27.46, (G) 38.105; disposition 149.132; *pl.* mental powers 38.72, 79.1057, 165.271; senses 50.64; **wittis** (D) feelings 179.22

witty *adj.* wise 149.161, 165.291

wode *adj.* insane 37.64, 45.421, 54.70; raging 75.52; angry 79.934, 113.168, 136.55; **wood** angry 83.251; insane 57.22, (H2) 176.179

wodely *adv.* madly 127.80

wodenesse *n.* anger 9.58, 23.68, 27.72; madness 28.78, 29.99, 45.423; **woodnesse** anger 54.9, 124.122

woke *n.* week 30.23, 31.9, 80.7; **all a** ~ one whole week 169.14; **wokis** *pl.* 139.58

woke(n, wokyn *see* **wake**

wolde *see* **will**

wol(le)warde *adj.* dressed in wool as penance 161.83, (D) 179.86

wombe *n.* belly 65.132, 83.7, 90.93

wonderly *adv.* miraculously 47.242

woned *v. pa.* dwelt (D) 178.153; **woninge** *ppl. adj.* (H2) 178.288

wont(e *v. pa. p.* accustomed 2.29, 6.31, 10.60

wood *see* **wode, woodnesse** *see* **wodenesse**

wordeli *adj.* worldly 159.43

wordi *adj.* worthy 139.196

worldes *n. pl.* **in** ~ for all centuries 84.58 *note*

worme *n.* insect 163.61 *note*; serpent (D) 178.555

wors(c)hip *n.* honour 2.144, 6.32, 43.61; **worschippes** *pl.* 1.265, 54.148, 94.131

wors(c)hip *v. inf.* honour 4.169, 5.11, 9.29; conduct religious service 174.219; **worshipithe** *pr. 3 sg.* honours 112.276; **worshipen** *pr. pl.* glorify 11.269; **worshipped** *pa.* honoured 58.75, 141.67; worshipped 146.7, 174.48; **worshepeden** *pa. pl.* 146.5; honoured *pa. p.* 61.113, 129.80; glorified 13.1

wortes *n. pl.* vegetables 18.31, 83.17, 117.229

woschen, wosshe *see* **wasshe**

wost(e, wote, wotist *see* **wete** *v.*[1]

woxe *see* **wexen**

wrappe *v. inf.* envelope 53.170; **wrappid** *ppl. adj.* 55.110; **wrapped** 79.391, 90.94, 138.58, 174.281; enclosed 79.510; combined 119.17

wrathe *v. inf.* anger (G) 3.45, (G) 4.18, 23.124, 26.166; be angry with 168.52; **wrethe** anger 79.770; **wrathe** *refl.* become angry 173.358; **wratthist** *refl. pr. 2 sg.* 168.55; **wrathe** *pr. pl.* 20.60 *note*; *imp.* 168.56; **wrethed** *pa.* grieved 28.26; angered 44.102, 45.68; **wrethid** *pa. p.* grieved 6.46, angered 7.175, 83.182; **wrathed** 121.3

wrenchis *n. pl.* strategems (D) 179.54

wreth(e *n.* wrath 10.22, 54.101, 74.17

wrethe(d) *see* **wrathe**

wrete, wretin *see* **write**

wryed *v. pa.* turned 80.60

write *v. inf.* write 8.196, 25.59; **wrote** *pa.* 11.120, 14.1; inscribed 5.90; decreed 174.117; **wretin** *pa. p.* inscribed 5.19; written 7.56, 18.47; **wrete** 124.53; *ppl. adj.* 112.895

writte *n.* scripture 9.1, 20.74, 117.136; written statement 113.332

wrote *see* **write**

wroth(e *adj.* angry 4.194, 9.18, 13.118, *159.119

wrought *see* **werche**

Y

yaldithe *see* **yelde**

yane *v. inf.* yawn 63.24, **yaned** *pa.* *63.23

yate *n.* gate 62.9, 113.270, 160.19; **yates** 54.200, 134.9; doors 122.87; **yatis** (H2) 178.355; gates (H2) 178.499

ye *interj.* yes 20.87, 26.59, 168.15[1]

yede *v. pa.* went (D) 178.154; **yoode** *pl.* (D) 178.540

yee *see* **eye** *n.*[2]

yeft(e *n.* 36.200, 44.142, 50.215; **yeftes** *pl.* gifts 2.146, 9.126, 13.108

yelde *v. inf.* give 2.81, 5.21, 8.153; *pr.* 8.215, 26.252; **yaldithe** *pr. 3 sg.* 167.96; *pr. subj.* 22.151; **yelde** *imp.* 1.180; ~ **the** *imp. refl.* acknowledge yourself to be 142.133; **ȝeldyng** *pr. p.* giving (G) 4.85; **yald(e** *pa.* 2.256, 50.256, 75.62; **yelde** 24.86, 25.221, 26.280; **yelded** 23.70; **yeldid** 2.197; **ȝeldid** (G) 55.68; **ȝolde** (G) 3.104, **yolde** 25.48, 90.290; **yildid** gave back

(H2) 1.91; **yolde(n** *pa. p.* given 11.70, 22.107, 25.49
yeman *n.* manservant 142.169
yen *see* **eyen**
yender *adj.* yonder 26.84, 37.59, 54.50
yerde *n.*[1] rod 5.71, 13.225, 49.26; **yerdes** *pl.* 8.53, 45.444, 84.3
yerde *n.*[2] garden *178.600
yestereven *n.* yesterday evening 95.58
yesternyght *n.* last night 95.129
yet ouer (that) *adv. phrase* furthermore 11.261
yeue *v. inf.* give 5.10, 8.103, 17.26; **yif** 156.439; **yeuithe** *pr. 3 sg.* 7.70, 23.24; **ȝeuyth** (G) 4.153; **yeue** *imp.* 20.3; **ȝaf** *pa.* gave (G) 4.27; **ȝouen** *pa. p.* (G) 3.92; **youe** 90.181, 145.39, 156.444; **yeue(n** 18.50, 25.31, 120.4
yever *n.* giver 7.55
yocke *n.* yoke 53.281, 165.16; **ȝokkis** *pl.* (L) 179.383
yolde *see* **yelde**
yollinge *v. pr. p.* howling 116.108
yoode *see* **yede**
yote *v. pa. p.* poured 73.23

Z

zeme *n.* seam 50.457

INDEX OF PROPER NAMES

Where it may help identification, the Latin name is given in italics and the modern in Roman. Conventions for alphabetical arrangement are the same as for the glossary (see p. 511 above). If a name occurs with the same spelling more than once in a passage, only the first line number is cited. Instances of the names of saints within the chapters devoted to their own lives are not recorded, nor, except in cases of possible difficulty, are the names of books used as sources and their authors. For a detailed bibliography of these sources see Maggioni, pp. xxxviii–lxvi. Dates where supplied are given in brackets. Names in chapter 162 *Cecilia*, which duplicates 124, are not included. Abbreviations used are: adj(ective), ap(ostle), *c*(*irca*), d(ied), ev(angelist), pl(ural), VM = Virgin Mary.

A

B

D

E

F

G

K

L

M

P

Q

R

S

U

V

W

Z

CORRIGENDA FOR VOLUMES 1 AND 2

p. 16 apparatus: *for* 133 *read* 132

p. 20, l. 249: *for* thinges *read* thingges

p. 23, l. 52: *for* ȝe *read* [ȝe]

p. 27, l. 64: *for* After *read* Aftir

p. 63 apparatus 69: *after* obeye G *add* the[1]] þre G

p. 65, l. 13: *for* God *read* god

l. 21 *for* [cite], whanne he *read* [cite, whanne he]

p. 74 apparatus 310, 311, 312: *in every case for* EM *substitute* EH1M

p. 115 apparatus 102: *for* be] *read* be[2]]

p. 142 40: *delete* of

p. 150 11: *for* for[1] *read* of

apparatus 11: *substitute* of[2]] for E

p. 153 apparatus 18: *delete* L

pp. 161–8 apparatus 3, 7, 30, 65, 128, 130, 167, 168, 199, 251: *add* T2 *after* EH1G *or* H1G

p. 164, l. 87: *for* the[2] *read* thei

p. 179 running head: *for* 40 *read* 39

p. 194, l. 145: *add* ; *after* deme

p. 218, l. 194: *for* kepe read *kep*[*t*]*e*

apparatus: *after* 194 *add* kepte] kepe E, kepe *changed to* kept H1

p. 236, l. 9: *delete* ’

11: *for* servaunt? *read* servaunt?’

p. 245, l. 327: *after* blode *add* ,

p. 255, ll. 42 and 59: *begin paragraphs* ‘And

p. 265 apparatus 308: *after* L, *insert om.*

p. 274, l. 197: *for* comdampned *read* condampned

p. 296, l. 423: *for* Magalomun *read* Magaloun

p. 303, l. 156: *for* tomangled *read* tomanglid

p. 312, l. 117: *for* kitle *read* kitte

p. 318, l. 16: *for* apostell *read* apostell[es]

p. 330, l. 205: *for* heuene. *read* heuene.'

p. 335, l. 33: *for* Hoy *read* Holy

l. 50: *for* hele. *read* hele.'

p. 343, l. 301: *new paragraph should begin at* The *and not at* 303 And

p. 360, l. 30: *for* [hem] *read* hym

apparatus: *delete entry for* 30

p. 376 apparatus: *for* 1 subdued *read* 2 subdued

p. 396 apparatus 634: *for* welle] . . . H1 *read* see note in vol. 3, p. 222

p. 408, l. 1050: *for* [hidde] *read* [hidde

p. 431 apparatus: *before* 319 *add* 317 deyed] dide G

p. 442 apparatus 159: *for* than H2A2 *read* than DH2A2

p. 448, l. 317: *for* kindrede *read* kynrede

p. 468, l. 132: *for* some *read* sone

p. 478, l. 309 *for* afore *read* af[ter]

apparatus: *add* 309 after] afore E

p. 499 apparatus: *add* T1 *after* H1 *in list of MSS running*

p. 504, l. 195: *for* siknesse. *read* siknesse.'

p. 524, l. 35: *for* [.xxx.^{ti}] *read* [.xxix.^{ti}]

p. 555, l. 128: *for* heuene. *read* heuene.'

p. 600, l. 235: *for* lake. And *read* lake, and

p. 607 apparatus: *add* T1 *after* H1 *in list of MSS running*

p. 619, l. 105: *for* [w]lepte *read* [w]epte

p. 625, l. 302: *for* recorden *read* recorde[d]

apparatus: *add* 302 recorded] recorden EH1

p. 648, l. 259: *for tumit read tumuit*

p. 663, l. 102: *after* turmentid, *add* for blamyng of hem

l. 103: *delete* for blamyng of hem

apparatus: *for* 102 *read* 103

p. 696, l. 17: *for* thanne, ye *read* thanne ye,

p. 725, l. 16: *for* sone. *read* sone.'

p. 727, l. 32: *for* af[or]de *read* af[or]e

p. 741, l. 421: *for* laboure *read* Laboure

p. 748, l. 55: *for* vouterer. *read* vouterer.'

p. 749 apparatus 9: *delete* that

p. 753 apparatus 52: *after* Heliopalin] *add* L,

p. 760, l. 3: *for* Re[m]es *read* Reynes

apparatus 3: *delete entry*

p. 767, l. 82: *for* Luke. *read* Luke:

apparatus: *delete* 89 to serue] EH1H2

p. 772, l. 250: *new paragraph should begin at* Fertheli

l. 258: *for* for *read* "For

l. 259 *for* hem.' *read* hem."

p. 787, l. 189: *delete first comma*

p. 800 apparatus first variant: *for* 36 *read* 35 *and for* gret] *om.* H2 *read* gret[1]] *om.* DH2

p. 801, l. 68: *delete comma*

apparatus 80: *for* may H2 *read* may DH2

p. 803 apparatus 113: *after* DH2 *insert* 113–14

p. 819, l. 199: *for* dede without, *read* dede, without

p. 820, l. 234: *for* donghill ,saieng *read* donghill, saieng

p. 825, l. 414: *for* hin *read* him

p. 826, l. 14: *for* known *read* knowen

p. 827, l. 20: *for* men *read* me

p. 830, l. 60: *for* wolde. *read* wolde.'

p. 831, l. apparatus: *for* 112 *read* 113

p. 878, ll. 47–8: *for* Constantines sone *read* Constantine apparatus 47–8: *for entry substitute* Constantine] Constantines sone EH1

p. 911, l. 119: *for* lord *read* Lord

p. 912, l. 9: *for* thou, here *read* thou here,

p. 916, l. 3: *delete* he *before* hele *and insert after modulus*

p. 922, l. 44: *after* make *add* in

p. 934, l. 491: *for* ch[etiu]ite *read* ch[etiv]ite

p. 938, l. 35: *delete* and in one day *and insert before* 36 take

p. 941 apparatus 141: *delete* A2

p. 946, l. 317 and apparatus: *for* wexce *read* wexe

p. 949 apparatus 429: *for* chaufed E *read* chansed EL

p. 960, l. 21: *for* passinge *read* passi[on]

apparatus: *for* 22 *read* 21 *and insert* 22 *before* transfigured

p. 966, l. 248: *delete* forthe

l. 262: *for* warme. *read* warme?

p. 982 apparatus 308: *for* E *read* H2

p. 985 apparatus 385: *for* enloyned *read* enloynyd

p. 990, l. 166: *for* heuen. *read* heuen.'

p. 991 apparatus: *list of MSS running should begin* DH2E

Vol. 2, p. vi, 151: *for* 11,776 *read* 11,000